THE
FINANCIAL
MANAGER

The Financial Manager

Jerome B. Cohen

Professor of Finance and Dean (Emeritus)
Bernard M. Baruch College
The City University of New York

Sidney Robbins

Chase Manhattan Professor Emeritus
of Financial Institutions
Columbia University

James F. Bender Distinguished
Visiting Professor of Finance
Adelphi University

Visiting Professor of Finance
University of Hawaii

Allan Young

Professor of Finance
Syracuse University

Publishing Horizons, Inc.

Columbus, Ohio

©Copyright 1986, Jerome B. Cohen, Sidney M. Robbins, and Allan E. Young
Distributed by Publishing Horizons, Inc.
2950 North High Street
P.O. Box 02190
Columbus, Ohio 43202

Printed in the United States.

1   2   3   4   🔺   7   6   5   4

Library of Congress Cataloging in Publication Data

Cohen, Jerome Bernard, 1915-
  The financial manager.

  Includes bibliographies and index.
  1. Corporations—Finance. I. Robbins, Sidney M.
II. Young, Allan E. III. Title.
HG4026.C534   1986   658.1'5   86-9298
ISBN 0-942280-31-8

CONTENTS

PART II TECHNIQUES OF FINANCIAL ANALYSIS

PART III   MANAGEMENT OF WORKING CAPITAL

7   Working Capital Policy

8   Cash Management

9   Credit Management and Policy

10   Inventory Management

25   Financial Aspects of Employee Pension Programs and Other Forms of Extra Compensation

FOCUS

This text consists of six parts, each of which focuses on a particular area of financial management. Such a categorization is in some ways artificial, because, as will be seen throughout the book, the various functions of the financial manager tend to overlap and interface with one another. Yet, we feel that the clarity of exposition and understanding of material are enhanced through the sectional breakdown. Moreover, this approach facilitates a sequential presentation that takes advantage of the logical flow underlying the activities of the financial manager.

Our book has an applied bias. Its thrust is to gain an understanding of the typical problems encountered by the financial manager and how they may be resolved. Nevertheless, the basis of effective application lies in theory. This tie-in is reflected in Part I of the text, entitled Perspectives of Finance: The Interrelationship Between Theory and Practice. The section begins with an overview of the functions and organization of financial management (What Financial Managers Do). The theoretical underpinning is reflected in the immediately following discussion of the evolution and present status of financial theory (The Origins and Development of Financial Theory and Some of Its Tests, Limitations and Applications).

Building upon an awareness of what is done in the field and how theory has evolved to support these functions, Part II introduces the area of implementation under the caption Techniques of Financial Analysis. In this vein, chapters are devoted to the disclosure of company operating results (External Financial Reporting); the tools available to analyze these operating results (Techniques of Financial Statement Analysis); the relevance of dividing costs into their fixed and variable elements (Volume-Cost-Profit Analysis); and the administration of the interrelated elements in order to achieve optimum performance (Financial Planning and Control through Budgeting).

In the next section, Management of Working Capital, attention is shifted to the role of the short-term circulation of cash and credit in reaching targeted financial outcomes. Reference is made to the theory and techniques of financial analysis, presented earlier, to help understand the management of a firm's current assets and current liabilities. Five chapters are included (Working Capital Policy, Cash Management, Credit Management and Policy, Inventory Management, and Short-Term Sources of Funds).

Part IV, the Management of Intermediate and Long-Term Sources of Funds, is concerned with the raising of investment capital. As a background, we initially take a look at the centers where the providers and users of funds meet (Financial Markets). Thereafter, attention is given, in turn, to the raising of money outside the firm (Financing in the Primary Market) and within the firm (Internal Funds and Dividend Policy). We conclude by integrating the various elements into a unified financing structure for the firm (Long-Term Financing).

Continuing in the same path but veering direction, Part V is addressed to controlling the uses of the funds that have been raised—Capital Budgeting. The starting point is a consideration of the administrative aspects of capital budgeting decisions (Forecasting and the Capital Budgeting Process). With this base established, the key decision variables and criteria are oulined (Rate of Return on Investment). Intertwined with the issue of return is the risk involved, an aspect that is introduced into the decision framework (Risk Analysis in Capital Budgeting). The final step in the capital budgeting path is an analysis of the effects of alternative investments on the firm's capital structure (The Cost of Capital).

The book ends with Part VI, Special Financial Problems and Basic Corporate Changes, where we take up six major contemporary issues that are treated independently, either because they fall outside the mainstream of the ongoing business process or because the nature of their operations uniquely affect the business process. (Mergers and Acquisitions, Repurchasing and Other Capital Structure Rearrangements and Reorganizations, Leasing, Financial Aspects of Multinational Operations, Corporate Tax Planning and Management, and Financial Aspects of Employee Pension Programs and Other Forms of Extra Compensation).

In recognition of our goal to explain the complicated role of the financial manager in clear and explicit terms, we hold to a minimum mathematical notation which both students and persons of affair often find mystifying. The numbered paragraph style has been employed not only because it facilitates cross referencing but also because it mirrors the continuity in a firm's development.

Following most chapters are appendices containing information which throws further light on material presented in the chapters but are outside the logical flow of the presentation. Included are such items as operating forms, glossaries, and distinctive techniques.

Parts I through V constitute the core of the book, representing a basic text in financial management. As has been stated, the emphasis is on providing a realistic portrayal of the field, with theory introduced to support and explain practice. Both Part VI and the appendices are additions directed to the specialized interests of the practitioner and to selective use by the instructor.

ACKNOWLEDGEMENTS

We are grateful to the many people who helped in the preparation of this book. We feel, however, that formal acknowledgements should be held to a minimum. Accordingly, mention is made in footnote form within the text itself of a number of people whose contribution to a particular segment of the book was invaluable. Nevertheless, it is clear that some provided such a significant contribution to our overall effort as to require their specific credit here.

Professor Lewis Freitas of the University of Hawaii not only is co-author of the teachers' manual, but also aided materially in the preparation of Chapter 17, Rate of Return on Investment, and provided helpful suggestions throughout the text. Professor Geoffrey Booth of Louisiana State University and Moon Kim, William Foote and Peter Koveos of Syracuse University were of considerable assistance in formulating some of the theoretical perspectives. Professor Lawrence Goldberg of the University of Miami provided a number of very useful overall thoughts. Professor Walter Holman of Loyola University of Baltimore helped in developing the outline and organizational structure of the book. As a student at the Graduate School of Business of Columbia University, Nicholas De Monica wrote the initial draft of the chapter entitled Financial Aspects of Multinational Operations, which thereafter experienced numerous revisions.

Adelphi University, Syracuse University, and the University of Hawaii, with which the different authors are associated, were generous in providing administrative and research assistance. Ms. Sheryl Sumner was particularly helpful as a research assistant when she was a student at the University of Hawaii.

PART I
PERSPECTIVES OF FINANCE: THE INTER-RELATIONSHIP BETWEEN THEORY AND PRACTICE

Our book is concerned with financial management. In Chapter 1 we start with a discussion of what financial managers actually do. Our second concern is financial theory, a concern shared by the academic community. Ours, however, is not a purely academic interest. We wish to assess the extent to which theory has already impinged upon and may further influence practice. Accordingly, following the discussion of Chapter 1, we describe, in Chapter 2, the origins and development of financial theory. We seek to strike a balance between the limitations and practical applications of theory.

WHAT FINANCIAL MANAGERS DO

1.1 INTRODUCTION

A *Fortune* article entitled "The New Power of Financial Executives" described the rise of financial executives in the corporate hierarchy by saying, "Top financial officers now have a hand in everything from mergers and budgets to personnel and marketing. They also woo bankers and stock analysts. Because they usually know more about the company than anyone else they often move, finally, right into the driver's seat."

The arrival of the computer, operations research, and new financial techniques, the rise in corporate mergers and acquisitions, the increasing need for capital, the magnitude and complexity of tax problems, the expanded use of stock options and other forms of employee compensation, the emphasis on rate of return on investment, the growing need for financial evaluation and control of decentralized operations in large companies—all have combined to produce a more complex business environment and broadened responsibilities for financial officers.

Financial responsibilities now include not only financing and controlling a company's funds, but also analyzing and interpreting the economic situation, appraising managerial performance, negotiating mergers and acquisitions, maintaining credit lines with banks, holding the good option of security analysts and the investing public, and, in fact, helping to set almost any of the policies that determine the company's future.

At least in large corporations, where operations and control are separated, management perspectives normally extend well beyond those of shareholders. For these firms there is also concern with such areas as employee relations; community, regional and national interests; political and governmental policies at the local, national and even international levels; and customer and supplier relations. Moreover, at times, the direct self-interest of management, may even come into conflict with the singular objective of maximizing shareholder wealth. This broadened view of the corporation is reflected in the responsibility of financial management which embraces the concept of "repositioning" the corporation to bring its varied facets into clear and positive focus in the community.

[1] EVOLVING IMPORTANCE OF FINANCIAL DECISION-MAKING

Financial decision-making has become the central focus of those in finance. Emphasis has shifted from making detailed analyses regarding the acquisition, custody and disbursement of funds to formulating decisions on the optimal use and allocation of funds. In more advanced companies financial decision-making has become fully integrated in the creation of corporate policy. Financial managers in these companies set up capital budgets, evaluate long-range investment opportunities, and establish measurable standards of financial performance for many corporate activities.

Financial managers are being asked a host of questions. How should the cost of funds be measured? How should proposals for capital-using projects be evaluated? How does financing influence the cost of capital? Should corporate funds be committed to certain purposes? How are expected returns on projects measured? How can performance be improved? What financial standards may be established to measure performance?

Financial planning, dealing with both sources and uses of funds, has now assumed a large role in top managerial decision-making. New measurement techniques, utilizing computers, have facilitated the capital budgeting process and have made it possible to test basic capital allocation procedures. The traditional approach which focused on sources of funds was too often largely concerned with specific procedural details. The newer, broader approach aims at formulating rational policies for the optimal use, procurement, and allocation of funds.

[2] TOTAL FINANCIAL PLANNING—MAJOR FUNCTIONS OF THE FINANCIAL MANAGER

Regardless of his or her title, someone in every firm is responsible for pulling together, reviewing, analyzing, interpreting, and planning the financial requirements and consequences of operations. Total financial planning has been defined as the advance programming of all financial management and the coordination of these strategies with the firm's operating plans. It involves essentially three significant kinds of corporate decisions:

- the investment decision;
- the financing decision; and
- the dividend decision.

Because these three kinds of decisions define the major functions of the financial manager, they are discussed below.

(a) The Investment Decision[1]

The capital investment decision determines the level of investment or volume of total assets held by the firm, whether these assets are current or fixed, and the allocation of investment funds among competing projects. In the allocation of current assets, the objective is to maintain adequate liquidity without sacrificing profitability. In the allocation of fixed assets, the firm makes investment decisions that offer benefits in the future. Since future returns are uncertain, risk must be considered. Also, since capital is limited and investment opportunities are numerous, an acceptance criteria for investment alternatives must be developed.

(b) The Financing Decision[2]

The financing decision is important because a firm may be able to change its total valuation in the marketplace (e.g., market value of common stock) by varying its capital structure. The financial manager therefore seeks the financial mix which maximizes or, at least increases, the total value of the firm. (As discussed in Chapter 19, there is some academic disagreement about the ability of a firm to alter its market valuation by changing its financial mix.) Moreover, the attractiveness or profitability of an investment proposal depends, in part, on the cost of financing which may be influenced by the financing mix (e.g., debt versus equity).

(c) The Dividend Decision

The firm's decision to pay out a certain amount of current earnings as cash takes into account opposing elements. It measures the value of a cash dividend to shareholders against the cost of retained earnings lost as the result of the dividend. In effect, therefore, the dividend decision must be co-ordinated with the investment and the financing decisions.[3]

[3] THE SCOPE OF FINANCIAL MANAGEMENT ACTIVITIES

To perform the investment, financing, and dividend functions effectively, the chief financial officer (CFO) of a company must be familiar not only with financial matters, but also with company activities and policies in such areas of operations as production, marketing, purchasing, labor, personnel relations, and general management problems. The broadened scope of modern financial management is outlined in Figure 1-1.

FIGURE 1.1   *Scope of financial management activities*

1. Planning
   a. Operations
   b. Growth
   c. Adjustments and readjustments

2. Coordinating and controlling
   a. Accounting
   b. Budgeting
   c. Reporting

3. Financing
   a. Ensuring the availability of funds
   b. Allocating funds to alternate uses
   c. Managing funds
   d. Investing funds
   e. Raising funds
   f. Hedging funds

4. Costing
   a. Measuring the cost of capital
   b. Measuring company costs
   c. Controlling the cost of capital
   d. Controlling company costs

5. Pricing
   a. Profit requirements in pricing for profitability
   b. Impact of pricing

6. Forecasting
   a. Overall economic trends
   b. Industry trends
   c. Firm's operations
   d. Financial requirements
   e. Profit planning
   f. Estimating the rate of return on investment

7. Miscellaneous
   a. Credit and collections
   b. Fixed asset and inventory management
   c. Insurance
   d. Pensions and welfare
   e. Tax management
   f. Computer operations
   g. Decisions on common stock repurchasing
   h. Mergers and acquisitions
   i. Lease-versus-purchase decisions
   j. Managing foreign exchange and other multinational
      financial management problems

From this overview of the scope of the financial management function, it is apparent why the financial vice president of a firm so often moves up the corporate hierarchy to become the chief executive officer (CEO). Financial management is essential to effective corporate management.

1.2 ORGANIZATION FOR FINANCIAL MANAGEMENT

As would be expected, the organizational structure necessary to achieve the objectives of financial management has evolved considerably. The outcome is a roster of reasonably standard practices overlaying differences that reflect the operating characteristics and historic ties of individual corporations. These similarities and differences may be observed in Figures 1.2 and 1.3 that depict the organization of the finance function at two major corporations.

In both cases, the line of command runs directly to the board of directors. In both cases, too, because of the importance attached to the finance function, an executive vice-president is represented as the top financial officer. In the General Motors plan, under the executive vice president is a vice president to whom both the treasurer and controller, as well as a vice president for economic development and a director of internal auditing, report. The Mobil plan specifies that the executive vice president "also has functional responsibility for finance activities throughout the Mobil organization." The treasurer and controller (who holds the title of vice president as well) report directly to the executive vice president. Reflecting the specialized aspects of the finance function, there is, in the Mobil plan, a general manager of the tax department/general tax counsel, who reports directly to the

FIGURE 1.2 *Organization of the finance function at General Motors Corporation*

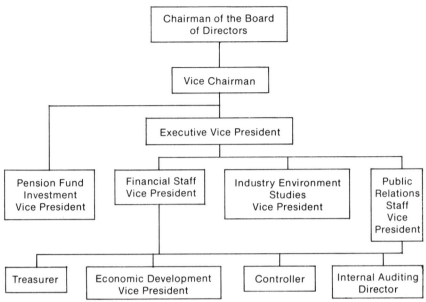

executive vice president. Indicative of the breadth of the finance function, within this category are also included a general manager of purchasing and general services, and a general manager of real estate and land development.

In general, it is clear that the finance function emanates from the board of directors, where top authority rests. Administrative responsibility is centered in a senior vice president, who may be an executive vice president, but is often designated as the vice president-finance. There is usually both a treasurer and a controller reporting to him, as well as other senior officers responsible for the specialized areas that may be grouped under finance, such as purchasing and real estate. The number and type of areas covered vary with the nature and size of the corporation, as well as the background and interests of the senior management officials. In older firms with less modern management techniques, the treasurer or controller may be the chief financial officer. Smaller companies often have a treasurer but no controller, or the president may also serve as treasurer.

In the following sections we address the likely major actors on the finance scene—the board of directors, the vice president—finance, the treasurer and the controller.

[1] BOARD OF DIRECTORS

In this section we address the board's major functions, developmental trends, selection of members, and their responsibilities and potential liabilities.

(a) Functions

The typical board of directors is ultimately responsible for the finance functions within the firm. The board handles its responsibilities in various

FIGURE 1.3 *Organization of the finance function at Mobil Oil Corporation*

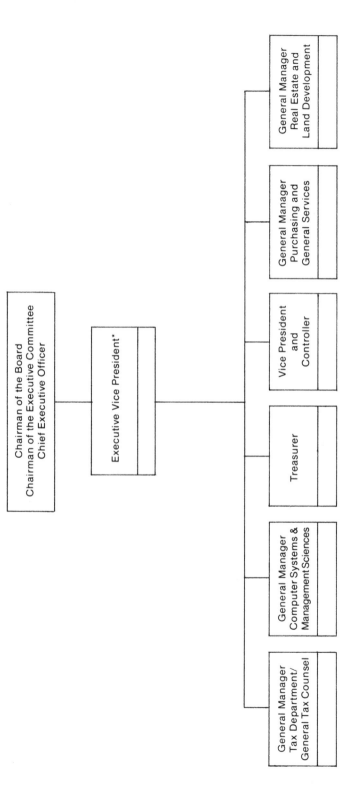

Chairman of the Board
Chairman of the Executive Committee
Chief Executive Officer

Executive Vice President*

General Manager
Tax Department/
General Tax Counsel

General Manager
Computer Systems &
Management Sciences

Treasurer

Vice President
and
Controller

General Manager
Purchasing and
General Services

General Manager
Real Estate and
Land Development

*Also has functional responsibility for Finance activities throughout the Mobil organization ways. In some firms, the board may delegate both routine functions and policy decisions of a prefunctory nature, merely ratifying what is brought before it. In other cases, routine functions are delegated, but the board insists on making basic financial policy decisions. In such cases, the board is likely to organize itself to handle this function by establishing a finance committee consisting of three or four directors.

Using finance committees to coordinate and determine financial policy has been gaining wider acceptance as firms grow, diversify, and decentralize. Finance committees strengthen corporate communication and control as well as bring the special skills and experience of seasoned executives to bear on major financial problems.

(b) Trends

The impetus to more responsible corporate boards came when the New York Stock Exchange required all its listed firms to form audit committees of outside directors. These committees analyze and make recommendations on a firm's financial strategies and accounting practices. In addition, the boards of large corporations now have executive committees, dominated by outside directors, that monitor the performance of managers and advise on management succession. Corporations are also favoring nominating committees of outside directors, a policy intended to further the independence of the directors.

The addition of outside directors is only part of the change in composition that contemporary boards have been undergoing. In board rooms these days one is likely to see more women, more minority members, fewer lawyers and commercial bankers, more former government officials and educators than ever before.

One is also likely to see smaller boards and rising compensation for directors. Current directors tend to be older with an average age of 53 plus, because the number of retirees serving have risen. Increasingly, there are more "professional" directors—those who spend more than 50% of their time serving as outside directors and who are often retired executives. More boards have varied their geographic representations. Still unchanged is the fact that a very small number of companies have consumer group or employee representation.

Because of the heavier workload, the complexity of the issues, and the growing liabilities involved, fewer people are seeking seats on boards. Some firms are requiring that board members make a minimum commitment of, say 30 days a year, forcing them to limit the number of boards on which they serve. The pool of outside directors is further reduced by the Securities and Exchange Commission (SEC) ruling that CPA's cannot serve on boards of companies that they audit. Accountants are reluctant to serve on boards of other companies if it means eliminating them as future clients. CEO's have also become reluctant to serve on outside boards, further limiting the traditional supply of outside directors, just at the time the demand for such directors has increased.

(c) Choosing Directors

The increased popularity of the board of directors' nominating committee can be expected to change the composition the board and result in more independent directors. Following the adoption by General Motors of the first widely publicized nominating committee, the number of major corporations that took a similar step grew rapidly. Some nominating committees include the CEO, but most corporations adopt the composition recommended by the SEC and the American Bar Association—outside directors only.

Today's boards look for more than prestige. They contribute expertise and active participation. The still favored choice is the CEO or the next lower ranking officer of another firm, partly because he or she speaks the same language and is already coping with similar problems. There is also a desire to balance expertise, for example, to have directors with specialized knowledge in some areas as energy, technology, and international affairs.

Although public discussions, search committees and publicity have led to boards that are more independent of management than previously, substantial interrelationships still exist. Often, outside directors are previously known by the chairman of the selecting company and may have had professional connections with the company. As a result, they may be hesitant to criticize the firm or challenge the chairman.

Because of these difficulties with outside directors, some companies prefer inside boards.[4] They feel that strong internal representation can provide more useful detail about company operations, better convey the news of the board back to the company, and avoid bickering. The prevailing trend, however, is to the outside board.

(d) Director Responsibility and Liability

The corporate board is increasingly expected to exercise general supervision over chief executives and officers, set policy, and monitor corporate activities. As a fiduciary body, it must act in the shareholders' interests. Laws, regulations, SEC enforcement action, and court decisions that protect public shareholders have stimulated a much higher sense of legal accountability in the corporate boardroom and the development of more activist boards.[5]

When a fraud does occur, if the board can demonstrate self-policing and can prove itself ignorant of the illegality, the SEC and the courts tend not to hold it liable. Individual liability may depend on the degree to which the director was acquainted with the major issues involved, the information he was provided, possible conflicts of interest, negligence, what the director did when he became aware of suspicious circumstances, and on the use of business judgement. It is not uncommon for attorneys to bring suits against directors for whatever reason that can be found on the possibility of extracting a financial settlement. As a result, directors now worry over charges of misconduct and want liability insurance as well as their own counsel. As a further protection, corporations usually indemnify their directors to the fullest extent allowed by law.

[2] VICE PRESIDENT—FINANCE

The integrated operating characteristics of large firms unify the whole financial operation. As indicated above, a vice president—finance generally presides over it, who is himself a policy making officer and the link between top management and corporate financial activities. Often, he has few or no operating responsibilities. Although he may supervise and coordinate the work of the controller and the treasurer, his main concerns are planning and determining overall financial policy. A survey of the relative importance of financial activities in large firms reveals the following as significant:

 1. Participating in long-range firm planning
 2. Carrying out accounting operations
 3. Advising the board of directors
 4. Maintaining contacts with bankers and other suppliers of short-term funds
 5. Reviewing the long-term budget
 6. Advising on expenditures for capital assets
 7. Preparing and reviewing cash budgets
 8. Handling credits and collections
 9. Revising and approving terms of contracts for capital acquisitions
10. Maintaining contacts with investment bankers
11. Planning security issues, and
12. Advising on dividend policy.

Of these functions, seven involve planning ahead (1, 3, 5, 6, 7, 11, and 12), and it is with strategic planning rather than supervision of routine operations that the vice president—finance is primarily concerned. The traditional preoccupation with asset administration and with securing financing has been left to the treasurer. The profit planning function, however, had tended to lodge ultimately in the office of the financial vice president because a great deal more than interpreting accounting results is involved. In fact, one can relate the growth of the controller's role to his willingness to assume interpretive functions arising out of his data collecting activities. Interpreting data to others easily leads to participation in the formulation of policies growing out of the facts. Thus, vice presidents of finance are often created.

Normally companies distinguish between line and staff organization, and finance is customarily a staff function. To load the financial vice president down with operating functions, such as purchasing and traffic may be a mistake, because they cut into the time and energy he can devote to financial decision-making. Ideally, financial policy formulation is centered in one top level officer, the vice president—finance, who reports to the president and to the finance committee of the board of directors. This person should have a good working knowledge of accounting and finance, but should be freed from operational problems in those fields. Ordinarily, operations are better handled by a controller and treasurer, who concentrate on such matters and report to the vice president—finance. Many companies already follow this practice; others are moving in this direction.

[3] TREASURER

Since the treasurer is the oldest of the three financial officers, its functions are fairly well defined, though even here there will be variations from company to company. In small firms the functions of the treasurer and controller are not usually separated, and the corporate by-laws provide only for a treasurer who performs all accounting and financial functions. As firms grow, the accounting function tends to be separated from the financing function and the controller's office is split off from the treasurer's. In large companies this is almost invariably the case. Apart from its necessity because of the volume of work and the growing differentiation of function, this separation is also a result of the acceptance of the internal auditing principle that the power to authorize the disbursement of funds and the actual disbursements should not be assigned to the same officer.

In general, the main functions of the treasurer are:

1. Keeping custody of funds
2. Maintaining relations with banks
3. Managing cash flow
4. Forecasting financial needs and requirements
5. Making corporate investments
6. Procuring additional needed funds, short or long term
7. Handling corporate securities
8. Managing the corporate debt
9. Managing foreign exchange problems
10. Supervising credits and collections
11. Handling insurance matters, and
12. Overseeing cashier and payroll activities.

These functions vary somewhat from company to company, but they are generally the treasurer's responsibilities. Of increasing importance are items 3 and 5 above. Through more effective cash management, modern corporations have often found themselves with excess funds which they can temporarily invest. Moreover, the growth of welfare and pension funds has created large long-term investment responsibilities. As a result of these developments the treasurer has in many cases been forced to become a close student of the money and capital markets. Indeed, when a corporation engages in much borrowing, handling and investing cash may become a major preoccupation of the treasurer, perhaps in part to fill the functional gap created by the shift of the data recording and interpreting function to the controller. The handling of cash includes bank selection, which in a large decentralized firm can be of major importance.

What was once regarded as an exotic activity, but has become an accepted financial function, is the international management and transfer of funds. This area has created a new range of decision-making issues and opportunities. For example, in order to reduce exposure to exchange fluctuations, it is desirable to match currency inflows and outflows. When this cannot be done adequately, the financial manager must decide whether to hedge, and, if undertaken, how best to do it. Also, in carrying out a long-term financing probram, he must determine whether to sell new securities in the domestic or international markets. If the international market is chosen, the cost of capital could be significantly affected by the currency in which the security is denominated. As a result, success or failure in judging the foreign exchange market can often make or break a corporate treasurer. In a growing number of corporations, international activities have become sufficiently important to place their administration in a separate organizational area.

[4] CONTROLLER

While the controller is the chief accounting officer of the corporation, his functions now extend well beyond the mere maintenance of accounts and records. In most companies, these functions generally include the following:

1. Designing and operating the accounting system
2. Preparing financial statements and reports
3. Establishing and maintaining systems and procedures
4. Designing and maintaining internal auditing procedures
5. Supervising electronic computer applications
6. Overseeing department cost controls
7. Preparing budgets
8. Making forecasts and analyses
9. Reporting financial information to top management, and
10. Handling tax matters

The term *controller* is, in a sense, a misnomer. As a staff, not a line, officer, the controller neither makes nor enforces management decisions. He essentially performs a staff function by marshalling, analyzing, and interpreting significant data so as to enable line management to make intelligent decisions and then take responsible action. To the extent that the controller transcends his data and their interpretation, demonstrating their significance to management, he becomes increasingly important in the corporate hierarchy. He does not, however, exercise management authority over line operations. In that sense he does not control.

The effectiveness of the financial reporting system the controller establishes and maintains, the completeness of his cost and expense control system, and the reliability of his budgeting procedures have a good deal to do with the overall capacity of management. Effective financial control facilitates financial planning and is absolutely essential for "management by exception." This practice, widespread among large, decentralized corporations, allows each major division to operate as a relatively independent enterprise as long as it moves ahead, earning its expected rate of return on investment and maintaining or expanding its share of the market. Thus, these divisions need only routine supervision, so that top management can devote its energies elsewhere— to the exception, to the area or division which is not doing well, which is not meeting goals. Using his data, the controller spots those trouble areas, calls top management's attention to them, and therefore saves the time and energy of top officials. These time and energy savings are inherent in "management by exception."

1.3 THE CARE, FEEDING, AND FUNCTIONS OF THE CHIEF FINANCIAL OFFICER (CFO)

A significant percentage of the CEO's in American Industry have come up through the financial ranks. Former CFO's who have made it to the top insist that there is nothing magical about their backgrounds or their skills, but today's CFO must have far more than a generalized understanding of finance to function effectively.

Today's CFO's are highly educated professionals who have gone through a broad range of experience to get where they are. They are expected to lend their financial point of view to top level management decision-making. Reflecting this fact, the great bulk of financial executives have a college degree and a large percentage have taken further professional training. In general, their reading preferences are for broad-range financial journals, rather than technical periodicals.

With respect to compensation, there tends to be a hierarchy. The compensation of the chief operating officer usually is second in line, standing in 1980, at about 74 percent that of the CEO. Next was the compensation of the top international executive, reflecting the growing importance of that activity as an independent operation; these payments were about 50 percent of those made to the CEO. The compensation of the CFO followed closely behind, running about 46 percent that of the CEO. These ratios tended to be higher in small companies. Within senior financial management, top financial relations executives tend to be the highest paid, followed by the top tax executive. (The top credit and collection position was lowest.)

A significant compensation trend, noted in the recent executive compensation studies conducted by the Financial Executives Institute, was for salaries to constitute a decreasing portion of total executive compensation, and for a greater portion to be derived from variable components which are performance based. Moreover, for companies with bonus plans, there tends to be an increasingly consistent relationship between bonus payments and corporate performance.[6] It has also been suggested that in order to give financial executives more planning freedom, these incentives should be tied to longer term objectives.[7]

The CFO's primary functions include the responsibility for long-range planning as well as his traditional and continuing obligation to oversee the return on capital and to safeguard the assets producing it. Furthermore, as corporations have grown and diversified, the central financial operation increasingly takes on the role of a bank—directing the flow of money from one subsidiary to another. This has radically changed the demands on the CFO; the resultant new responsibilities can be grouped into five major areas:

1. Seeking new and specialized funding instruments
2. Managing a network of financial intermediaries
3. Working with different suppliers of capital
4. Improving the timing of financial decisions, and
5. Integrating financial planning with the corporate planning process.

Financial executives also find their job responsibilities include interpreting and implementing pronouncements and rules of the SEC and the Financial Accounting Standards Board, as well as those of other regulatory agencies. Added to this function is the need to keep abreast of developments in such areas as international finance and the money and capital markets. Moreover, pension fund assets are growing at such a rapid rate that in many corporations they may soon equal or surpass operating assets. The effective handling of these fields, therefore, represents both a new challenge and an opportunity for the CFO.

1.4 CHAPTER SUMMARY

In this chapter we have discussed the primary function of the corporate financial manager. We saw that the broad scope of financial management activities are directed toward the answering of three strategic questions: (1) how much capital to invest and how to allocate it amongst competing proposals; (2) how to finance the accepted capital investment alternatives; and (3) what cash dividend policy to implement. The chapter also focused on the organizational evolution which has followed the expanding role of financial management in business. In the next chapter, we examine the financial theory which the financial manager may use as a guide in answering the three strategic questions above and in pursuing the many activities which constitute the job of modern financial management.

FOOTNOTES

1. Chapters 16, 17, and 18 discuss the capital investment decision in detail.
2. Chapter 19 focuses on the financing decision and specifically addresses the relationship between the financing mix and firm value.
3. Chapter 14 addresses corporate dividend policy.
4. Johnson & Johnson, and Dow Chemical are two prominent companies that are known for their inside boards. In 1980, the former had 11 insiders and 9 outsiders, while the latter had 3 insiders and 4 outsiders. W.M. Wrigley Company, which in 1982 had a board of directors of 5 insiders and 6 outsiders, and W.R. Grace Co., whose board had 9 insiders and 22 outsiders, have had a policy of rotating insider seats on their boards.
5. The SEC has adopted rules that give shareholders more information about the board of directors. A company is required to report how often the board of directors has met and identify any director who has missed 75% of board meetings. It must also disclose when a board member resigns because of a disagreement with management. If a director resigns, his views can be published if he wishes. Companies are still required to provide detailed information about any business or professional relationship between board members and management. The Commission, however, dropped its controversial proposal to require that companies tag their board members with labels to disclose the extent of their independence from management.
6. See Edwin S. Murk and James A. Giardina, "Executive Compensation During 1980: Ninth Biennial Study," *Financial Executive*, November, 1981, pp. 46-52; "Executive Compensation, Tenth Edition Study," pp. 49-55; and "Executive Compensation, Eleventh Edition Study," October, 1983, pp. 42-48.
7. Gordon E. Pilcher, "Free the Financial Executive," *Financial Executive*, May, 1983, p. 53.

SUGGESTED READINGS

Abdelsamad, M.H., "How to Think Like a Financial Manager," *Management World*, March, 1981.

Andrews, Kenneth R., "Directors' Responsibility for Corporate Strategy," *Harvard Business Review*, November-December, 1980.

Baruch, Hurd, "Audit Committee: A Guide for Directors," *Institutional Investor*, September, 1980.

Brown, Arnold, "Eroding Power of the CEO," *Business Horizons*, April, 1980.

Casler, Darwin J. and Frederick L. Neumann, "Attracting Outside Directors," *Financial Executive*, July, 1980.

Collis, Roger, "The New Role of the Chief Executive," *International Management*, July, 1980.

Donnelly, Robert M., "The Changing Role of the Controller," *Financial Executive*, April, 1982.

———, "The Controller's Role in Corporate Planning," *Management Accounting*, September, 1981.

Golden, Edward W., "The Changing Role of the Financial Executive," *Financial Executive*, October, 1981.

16

Grant, Edward B., "The Financial Executive's Role in External Reporting," *Financial Executive,* February, 1981.

Hartman, Bart, et. al., "Mission Control Starts in the Controller's Department," *Management Accounting,* September, 1981.

Miller, Leland B., "The Buck Starts Here: The Role of the Financial Officer in Corporate Expansion Planning", *Industrial Development,* July-August, 1980.

Pilcher, Gordon E., "Free the Financial Executive," *Financial Executive,* May, 1983.

Sathe, Vijay, "Controller Involvement in Management," *Financial Executive,* June, 1981.

APPENDIX A:
EXAMPLE OF A CORPORATE FINANCIAL MODEL

A corporation conducts numerous interrelated activities that bear upon significant areas of revenues, costs, profits, and assets. It is clearly important that top management visualize beforehand how its plans affect this scheme, so that management can introduce modification to obtain optimum results.

A financial model provides the structure to obtain this objective. In this appendix, we provide a succinct outline of the major elements entering into the construction of such a model. These include an explanation of how the model functions, the variables used, the reports generated, and the center of responsibility.

Actual construction of the model, of course, is a complex operation that will entail the cooperation of various finance and computer specialists. The summary presented here simply illustrates the form employed by a major corporation. It is intended to provide an introduction of the scope and flexibility of such a model.

CORPORATE MODEL

A. Description

The Corporate Model is used to forecast monthly and yearly financial data through the use of a number of computer programs. The model essentially consists of two modules, the control logic, and the projection logic. Each of these contain numerous programs.

The control logic is the Generalized Executive for Modeling or GEM. GEM controls all input/output to the projection logic and formulates the reports produced by the Model. In addition, GEM is the framework of the Model, in that it controls the data validation and verification, file maintenance, and study runs. As a generalized execution program, GEM can be adapted to other uses and has built in logic for producing various reports and, through specific requests, can produce comparative reports.

The projection logic is the distillation of an extensive analysis of prior years' financial results to define the relationships that exist between external events and the financial results of operations. Thus, the Model is responsive to those changes in electric rates, tax rates, wages, customer growth, inflation, etc., that have an impact on the company. The results of these thousands of calculations are summarized into monthly or annual financial statements. There is no restriction on the projection period, although data has been gathered and is available for only 20 years. The most useful time frame is most likely 10 years, since this is the common planning horizon for generation and transmission requirements.

B. Responsibility

The Corporate Model information consists of three separate areas of data on one file.

1. The Report Data—This section of the data file contains all the report type layout information as well as the specific data to be combined for the standard and special reports produced in a Corporate Model study run.

2. The Array Data—This data is used to calculate and project financial conditions of the Company. The following are some of the variables in the array data:

- Actual Operating Expenses;
- Electric Rates;
- Wage Rates;
- Tax Rates;
- Fuel Consumption and Inventories;
- Debt and Stock Issues;
- Residential and Commercial Sales; and
- Construction Budgets.

3. The Dated Changes—This final section is used to temporarily change assumptions made on data and dates. For example, anticipation of stock sales two years in the future would be controlled in the data change section of the data file.

C. System Reports

The results of a study are summarized into monthly or annual financial and supporting statements or reports. The basic statements are:

1. Income Statement—This report contains the actual and projected operating revenues and expenses. In addition, debt interest, stock dividends, and common stock earnings are reported on this statement.

2. Balance Sheet—This report contains the actual and projected assets and liabilities of the company.

3. Cash Flow—This report summarizes the income and outflow of the Company's cash.

4. Financial Ratios—This report contains summaries of capital amounts of stocks and bonds, stock-bond ratios, and other data pertaining to the financial picture of the Company.

5. Construction Expenditures—This summary shows the current and projected capital outlay that must be made to cover construction expenditures.

6. Sales by Revenue Class—This statement gives a breakdown of revenues by various classes of customers such as residential, commercial, etc.

In addition to the above standard reports, many special reports are readily available to supplement the calculated results.

THE ORIGINS AND DEVELOPMENT OF FINANCIAL THEORY AND SOME OF ITS TESTS, LIMITATIONS, AND APPLICATIONS

2.1 INTRODUCTION

This Chapter introduces us to the world of financial theory. Here, it is easy to become bogged down in a morass of equations. To avoid this difficulty, we make a conscious effort to employ prose rather than mathematical notations. Nor do we seek to catalogue the entire range of theoretical developments; rather we highlight the significant directions that theory has taken, as well as indicating the limits of its practical applications.

2.2 BASIC CONCEPTS UNDERLYING MODERN FINANCIAL THEORY[1]

The first concerns with the fabric of what has come to be known as modern financial theory, or variously as the Capital Asset Pricing Model (CAPM) or Portfolio Theory (all offshoots of the same gendre), go back as far as the eighteenth century.

[1] THE SAINT PETERSBURG PARADOX

In 1738, the Swiss mathematician, Daniel Bernoulli, published his classical "Specimen Theoriae Novae de Mensura Sortis" ("Exposition of a New Theory on the Measurement of Risk") in which he posed an investment idea in the form of a gaming problem which has come to be known as the Saint Petersburg Paradox. The essence of this paradox is a probability problem or game concerned with the measurement of risk and the determination of the value of a participant's expectation. In this problem, the conclusion derived from the principles of mathematics is unacceptable to the common sense person, hence the paradox. The outline of this game is shown in Figure 2.1.

In the game, player A tosses an unbiased coin and player B pays, as shown in Figure 2.1, an amount based upon the first toss which produces a head. Then the game stops. Thus, at the outset, there is a 50 percent chance that

FIGURE 2.1 *The Saint Petersburg paradox.*

Sequence of Tosses by Player A	Probability (P_j)	Payment by Player B (R_j)	Expected Value ($P_j \times R_j$)
H	50.000%	$ 1	$.50
TH	25.000%	$ 2	$.50
TTH	12.500%	$ 4	$.50
TTTH	6.250%	$ 8	$.50
TTTTH etc.	3.125%	$16	$.50

player A will toss a head and if he does, player B pays one dollar. There is a 25 percent chance that player A will first get a tail and then a head, and if that sequence occurs, player B pays two dollars. Thereafter, the probability of A deferring the toss of a head continues to decrease and this condition is reflected in the proportionately greater payment made by player B. Therefore, the expected value of each outcome continues at $.50. Such a game might continue through an infinite number of tosses, because conceivably, the head would never turn up. Therefore, the total expected value of the game is the sum of an infinite number of individual expected values of $.50 each. Such a sum is infinite, but the paradox results from the fact that while the total expected value of such a game is infinite, no one would pay an infinitely high price to enter the game.

Bernoulli's solution to the paradox centered on the assumption that the marginal utility of money is inversely proportional to the amount held, and in each case an individual's present resources are the determining factor in what price he would pay to enter the game. That is, each dollar of each successively higher payoff has a declining marginal utility. What was unique and revolutionary about this contribution was that the notion of utility was introduced in an economic setting. Bernoulli presented the idea that the satisfaction of investors or businessmen is determined by the maximization of their expected utility as opposed to the maximization of their investment expectations or returns, as had before been accepted.[2]

[2] INVESTMENT RETURN

In order to understand the difference between investment return and utility, these two concepts need to be defined. Investment return represents a monetary outcome which may be measured by the change in investment value between two periods, given as a percent of the starting value. Thus, the return, R_j, on an initial investment of V_0 at the beginning of a period, which has a value of V_1 at the end of the period, and which has resulted in a payment (for example of interest or dividends) of D_1 during that period, may be expressed as follows:

$$[1] \qquad R_j = \frac{V_1 - V_0 + D_1}{V_0}.$$

When there is uncertainty about the change in investment, probabilities may be assigned to the different outcomes. Let us assume that an individual has the opportunity of investing in a Broadway Show which, if successful, will increase his $100,000 initial investment to $150,000 in one year's time, when his interest in the show will be terminated. There is a 50 percent chance of this successful outcome. On the other hand, there is a 50 percent chance that the show will be a failure and close with the terminal value of his investment falling to $80,000. To compute the mathematical expectation or expected value, the following expression may be applied, where P_j represents the probability of one of the events occurring and R_j the return from that event:

$$[2] \qquad E(R_p) = \sum_{j=1}^{n} P_j R_j.$$

Based upon this expression, Figure 2.2 shows the expected value from investing in the Broadway Show:

FIGURE 2.2   *The expected value from the Broadway Show*

Possible Outcomes	Terminal Investment Value	Probability	Expected Value (Terminal Investment Value x Probability)
Success	$150,000	.50	$ 75,000
Failure	$ 80,000	.50	$ 40,000
	Total Expected Value		$115,000

The expected change in value is $15,000 ($115,000-$100,000); the initial investment was $100,000; and, therefore, the expected investment return is 15 percent ($15,000/$100,000).

[3] UTILITY

Utility is the physical and psychological satisfaction one derives from buying, owning, or doing something. It is not as easily expressed in equation form as is investment return. Utility is perhaps best understood in terms of the concept of *marginal utility* and the idea of *diminishing marginal utility for wealth*. Suppose a destitute individual were to receive an initial grant of $1,000. He would, no doubt, first satisfy his most pressing needs with this sum. If an additional $1,000 were received, however, additional, less immediate desires, would then be taken care of. Further $1,000 increments would result in the satisfaction of successively less pressing needs until the point is reached (at least theoretically) when additional $1,000 increments would add little, if any, toward the satisfaction of the monetarily-based needs of the individual. Therefore, as each successive increment in wealth results in the satisfaction of increasingly lesser needs, we can say that the *marginal utility* of money, or wealth, diminishes as additional funds are received. The rate at which this

22

decline takes place depends upon both the physical and psychological circumstances of the individual. For most individuals, however, additional wealth
does seem to have declining marginal utility as pictured in Figure 2.3 in terms
of units of utility often called utils.

FIGURE 2.3 *The declining marginal utility of most individuals*

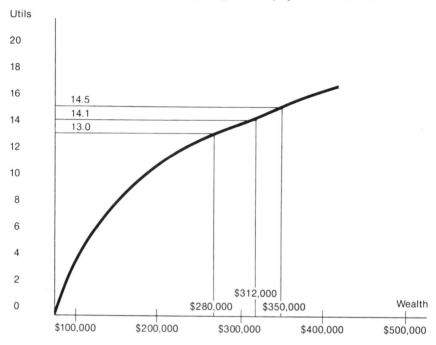

Such an individual may be said to be *risk averse*[3] in that at any point on his
utility-wealth curve, the decline in his utility from a loss of a given amount of
his wealth is greater than the increase in his utility which results from an equal
increase in his wealth. This individual would therefore probably not accept a
monetary wager in which the chance of his winning or losing a given
sum was 50:50.[4]

On the other hand, some individuals appear to enjoy taking monetary risks
(such individuals often frequent gaming casinos or betting parlors). They are
said to be *risk takers* and may therefore be thought of as having an *increasing
marginal utility for wealth.*[5] For them, the increase in utility from a given
dollar gain is greater than the decrease in utility from a same dollar loss and a
wager with less than 50 percent probability of winning could still be desirable.
The utility-wealth curve for such an individual is pictured in Figure 2.4.

Relatively few individuals are indifferent to risk, but if they were they
would display the curve shown in Figure 2.5.

The individual whose utility-wealth curve is shown in Figure 2.5 will value
each dollar of extra return just as highly as each dollar of lost return and be
indifferent to a bet with a 50:50 probability of winning or losing a given sum.

FIGURE 2.4   *The increasing marginal utility of most gamblers*

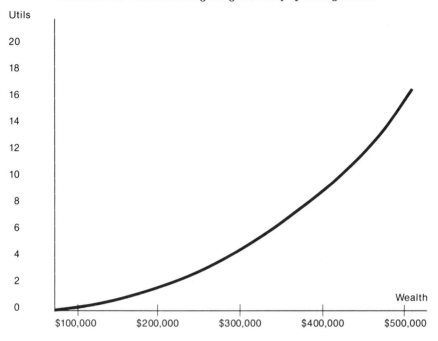

FIGURE 2.5   *The constant marginal utility of those indifferent to risk*

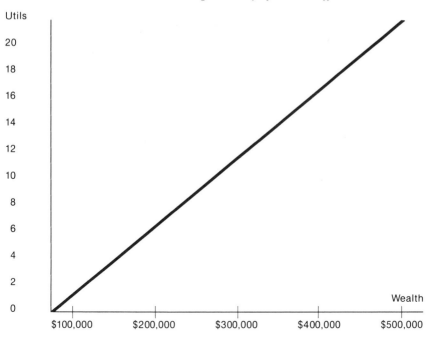

[4] COMPARING INVESTMENT RETURN AND UTILITY

The development of utility theory was considerably enhanced and refined by the contributions of Von Neumann and Morgenstern towards the evolution of the utility theory of investment for an individual. The basic propositions of this theory are that investors in capital assets usually have diminishing marginal utility of wealth and return on their investments and that they should undertake investment commitments on this basis. This normally can be done by a blending, which is appropriate for the individual decision-maker, of two opposite aspects of any financial commitment: (1) the expected return (which is positive—the greater the better) and (2) a risk factor which is associated with this expectation (which is negative—the greater the less desirable).

Suppose a risk-averse individual whose utility-wealth curve is shown in Figure 2.3 has $300,000 in wealth and also has an opportunity of investing $100,000 in government bonds which will mature in one year and pay a coupon of 10 percent. Since the interest and principal payments are certain, the expected return need not be adjusted for the probability of receiving them. The expected return can be calculated as follows:

$$\frac{\$100,000 - \$100,000 + \$10,000}{\$100,000} = 10\%.$$

Assume that this same individual could also invest in the Broadway Show described earlier, with an expected investment return of 15 percent, which is substantially greater than the 10 percent return from the investment in government bonds. According to modern theory, before reaching a decision he should also measure the utility he would derive from each of his investment opportunities.

In the case of government bonds, the investment return is presumed to be certain and the investor's terminal wealth, therefore, is $310,000. Referring to Figure 2.3, which measures the investor's utility-wealth predilections, we find that at a lower level of wealth of $310,000 his expected utility is 14.1.

As described in 2.2.[2], if the investor makes a commitment in the Broadway Show, there is a 50 percent chance that his investment value would rise to $150,000, which would result in a terminal wealth of $350,000; there is also a 50 percent chance that the value of the investment would fall to $80,000, which would produce a terminal wealth of $280,000. Based upon the investor's utility of 14.5 utilies for $350,000 of wealth and a utility of 13 for $280,000 of total terminal wealth, and a probability of 50 percent for each occurrence, we can compute the total expected utility as 13.75. These relationships are summarized in Figure 2.6.

When expected return alone is considered, the 15 percent return from the Broadway Show is clearly superior to the 10 percent return from government bonds. The investor, however, is risk averse, which is typical. When his utility-wealth curve is considered, therefore, the relative attractiveness of the two investments are reversed. The investor's expected utility from government bonds is 14.1 (based on Figure 2.3) compared with the 13.75 from the Broadway Show investment. Accordingly, this time, the government bonds investment is superior.

FIGURE 2.6   *Expected utility of wealth from the Broadway Show*

Possible Outcomes	Terminal Investment Value	Total Terminal Wealth	Utility	Probability	Expected Utility (Utility x Probability)
Success	$150,000	$350,000	14.5	.50	7.25
Failure	$ 80,000	$280,000	13.0	.50	6.50
			Total Expected Utility		13.75

Problems in defining the utility-wealth curve for corporations have limited its practical applications in the corporate setting. Nevertheless, in evaluating investment decisions, it is necessary for the financial manager to recognize these two elements of an investment—return and risk. His concern with maximizing returns cannot overlook the likely corresponding increase in risk. We have previously defined investment return (2.2[2]), but have only indirectly referred to risk in our discussions. We now consider various types and measurements of risk.

[5] INVESTMENT RISK

It is sometimes said that there are four kinds of risks inherent in any business investment. We outline them briefly as follows:
• **Price Level Risk:** This is the risk that when one liquidates his investment, the price level will have risen above what it was when the investment was undertaken, thereby causing a diminution in the real (inflation adjusted) return the investor earns or possibly causing a loss in real terms;
• **Money Rate Risk:** This is the risk of loss (particuluarly in the case of securities promising a fixed return) which can result from an increase in the interest rate;
• **Marketability Risk:** This is the risk of loss when one attempts to liquidate his investment when market conditions are temporarily depressed. Such a loss can occur, for example, from the market being inefficient or simply unable to absorb a temporary increase in supply;
• **Business Risk:** This is the type of risk most commonly referred to. It represents the risk of loss from deteriorating business circumstances.

Underlying the above listing of the kinds of risks is the notion of loss, which is probably the major concern of the businessman. In this context, however, risk can only be measured by individual expectations. As a result, a measure calculated on this basis is likely to be both vague and inconsistent. To avoid these difficulties, the most common (and useful) definition of risk employed in financial theory is the probability that actual future returns will differ from expected returns. In this sense, risk is the dispersion or variability of future price changes. This is typically calculated on the basis of historic data. An investment in which the price changes are more volatile than another investment (or more precisely—expected to be more volatile) is said to be more risky. In financial theory, therefore, risk is normally measured by the variance, standard deviation, or coefficient of variation of expected returns, or by the beta coefficient, which will be defined in 2.3[5].

The variance of the expected return on an investment is the weighted sum of the squared deviations from the expected returns.[6] That is, in computing this measure of risk, we first calculate the expected return, $E(R_p)$, as defined in 2.2[2]. Then we determine the variance σ_p^2, by summing and squaring the deviations of the probability weighted individual returns, R_j, from the expected return, $E(R_p)$. The expression for this measure is as follows:

[3]
$$\sigma_p^2 = \sum_{j=1}^{n} P_j (R_j - E(R_j))^2$$

In Figure 2.7, we calculate the variance of the Broadway Show investment discussed in 2.2[2]. Recall that the expected return $E(R_p)$, was computed at 15 percent.

The standard deviation of expected returns, σ_p, which is another measure of investment risk is simply the square root of the variance.[7] The coefficient of variance, $\sigma_p/E(R_p)$, incorporates the additional step of adjusting the standard deviation for the size of the expected value. Finally, another measure of risk, which will be defined in 2.3[5], is the beta coefficient, β. In general, the larger the variance, standard deviation, coefficient of variation, or beta coefficient, the greater the possible dispersion of future returns around the expected return and the greater the investor's uncertainty or degree of risk.

FIGURE 2.7 *Variance of investing in the Broadway Show*

Possible Outcomes	Return $R_j = V_1 - V_0 + D_1$ / V_0	Probability P_j	Expected Return $E(R_p)$	Deviations $R_j - E(R_p))$	Squared Deviations $(R_j - E(R_p))^2$	Probability Adjusted Squared Deviations $P_j(R_j-E(R_p))^2$
Success	50%	.5	15%	35%	.1225	.06125
Failure	-20%	.5	15%	-35%	.1225	.06125

$$\Sigma\,\sigma_p^2 = .1225 = 12.25\%$$

2.3 THE DEVELOPMENT OF MODERN FINANCIAL THEORY

The contribution of Von Neuman and Morgenstern endowed financial theory with the concepts of return, risk, and the nature of their respective utilities. Still, it was recognized that the positive aspect (return) is inseparable from the negative aspect (the risk of attaining this return). And thus historically, a coherent analysis of the decision-making framework was dependent upon the development of an analytical model by which returns and risks could be played off against each other in such a manner as to optimally satisfy the trade-off between the two that the decision-maker wishes to attain. But the financial decision-maker is normally faced with a multiplicity of financial investments. Therefore, a practical solution to the problem posed by financial theory required the consideration of all the relevant returns and risks and the optimum blending of these individual investments. This is the portfolio selection problem.

The process by which these notions could be put to practical use could proceed no further until an analytical model could be developed which effectively accounted for the trade-off between the respective utilities on all available investments. Such a model had to deal with the development of portfolios or combinations of various investments, which in concert, maximize utility relative to all other combinations that might be made. In terms of a historical perspective, the first effective attempts at a solution to these problems came with the work of Harry Markowitz, who developed the initial principles of portfolio theory.

[1] THE INITIAL PRINCIPLES OF PORTFOLIO THEORY

In 1952, Harry Markowitz published a paper in which he treated the problem of portfolio selection as one of the utility maximization under conditions of uncertainty.[8] Markowitz employed the Von Neuman and Morgenstern utility theory in which the investor preferences were assumed to be defined by the mean and variance (return and risk) of the probability distribution of single-period portfolios. He then developed a model by which decision-makers were able to select a combination of assets which, given their individual trade-offs of returns and risks, was "efficient". What Markowitz meant by the word "efficient" was that, on a before-the-fact basis (ex-ante), assuming one knows the relevant returns and risks for all of the available investments, his model would provide an allocation scheme such that the expected return is maximized for the level of risk the decision-maker is willing to tolerate, or the risk is minimized for the target level of return the decision-maker desires.

Markowitz' model was almost entirely normative in the sense that it provided the user with a norm to which to adhere. Risks were reduced through diversification, which could be accomplished as long as returns were not perfectly and positively correlated. Thus, diversification was the keynote to the Markowitz model. Yet a realistic method of determining the appropriate amount of diversification in an environment with a potentially vast array of financial investments was dependent upon a method of determining the relationship or correlation between the volatility of the returns on all other investments. This task fell to those who sought to refine and operationalize Markowitz' theory.

[2] THE ASSUMPTIONS OF MODERN FINANCIAL THEORY

In "The Foundations and Current State of Capital Market Theory"[9], Michael Jensen notes two major directions in which the normative Markowitz model were taken on the positive plane (or in terms of attempts to explain reality). One path was originally followed by James Tobin who utilized the underpinnings of the Markowitz approach to draw implications with respect to the demand for cash holdings or liquidity.[10] The more important trail for our consideration here was taken by the early portfolio theory pioneers, particularly William Sharpe, who extended the Markowitz contributions toward the development of a positive general equilibrium model of asset prices.[11]

This work[12] (to be described in greater depth below) simplified the Markowitz portfolio selection process so that it could be applied to problems in which many financial investments could be considered. Yet these early simplifications required a set of assumptions which may, in certain situations, be of questionable validity. We must understand these assumptions since the appropriateness of any theory rises or falls with the validity of its assumptions. Those underlying modern financial theory must be understood before one can appreciate the theory. These assumptions may be catalogued as follows:[13]

- Financial decision-makers are one-period expected utility of terminal wealth maximizers;
- The totality of the choice of financial decision-makers among alternate portfolios of financial commitments is on the basis of their utility function which is risk averse and solely dependent on the expected mean return and standard deviation (or variance) of returns on the available commitments;[14]
- All financial decision-makers can borrow or lend an unlimited amount of funds at the risk-free lending rate;[15]
- All financial commitments are perfectly divisible and perfectly liquid. That is, they can be added to or disposed of without affecting the market price;
- There are no transaction costs attendant to making or disposing of a financial commitment;
- There are no taxes;
- Financial decision-makers are price takers; and
- The quantities of all financial commitments are given and known to all financial decision-makers.

In addition to the above assumptions, a major linchpin interconnecting modern financial theory is that there exists a linear relationship between the rate of return on any particular financial investment and a common underlying factor for all such investments. This means that it is no longer necessary to measure each investment's covariance with those of all other available investments. As will be expressed more explicitly below, modern theory indicates that the rates of return on the available financial investments are explained by a systematic factor related to the market for all financial investments and a nonsystematic factor which is unique to the particular investment being considered. Moreover, the theory assumes that the unique factor for a particular financial investment is uncorrelated with the unsystematic response of any other financial investment.

While the above assumptions may appear restrictive and perhaps in some cases unrealistic, their contribution toward formulating the original Markowitz model in such a manner that it might have some practical applications (as will be discussed later in this chapter) are indeed considerable. For these assumptions not only reduced the computational procedures of the original model, but also required far less data. But even the most enthusiastic supporters of the modern theory recognize that some of its assumptions are of questionable validity, particularly as they relate to the problems of the financial manager.[16] Nevertheless, most academicians as well as some business decision-makers, have come to accept some form of this model.

[3] THE EQUILIBRIUM EXPECTED RETURN ON A FINANCIAL ASSET

Thus far in our discussion we have developed several principles which may be summarized for clarity before moving ahead. These include:

- Any individual investment must be considered in the light of its contribution to a portfolio of financial assets;
- The return on a portfolio of financial assets consists of the weighted average return of each of the assets in the portfolio;
- The average risk of a portfolio of financial assets is dependent on the correlation or covariance between the volatility of the returns on each asset with the volatility of the returns on all other assets; and
- In lieu of determining each such separate correlation, the covariance of returns on each financial asset could be measured against a systematic factor related to the market for all financial assets.

In the light of these principles and the foregoing assumptions, (2.3[2]), the equilibrium expected return on any financial asset has been expressed as:

[4] $E(\overline{R}_j) = R_F + \lambda$ covariance $(\overline{R}_j, \overline{R}_m)$;

where $E(\overline{R}_j)$ = the equilibrium expected return on a financial asset j;

R_F = the riskless rate of interest;

[5] $\lambda = [E(\overline{R}_m) - R_F] / \sigma^2 (\overline{R}_m)$;
which is the market risk premium per unit of risk;

$E(\overline{R}_m)$ = the expected return on a portfolio of all available financial assets which consists of an investment in every financial asset in proportion to the relation of its value to the value of all assets;

$\sigma^2 (\overline{R}_m)$ = the variance of the return on the portfolio of all available financial assets; and

Covariance $(\overline{R}_j, \overline{R}_m)$ = the covariance of the return on financial asset j and the return on the portfolio of all available financial assets.

(The ‾ (bar) above each of the R's except R_F indicates that all other R's are random variables.[18] This notation will be used from here until the end of this section and then dropped for simplicity.)

The economic meaning of the above expression is that, according to modern financial theory, the equilibrium expected return on any financial asset, say investment j, is equal to the riskless rate of interest plus a risk premium per unit of risk (λ), and the relative risk of this investment (as measured by covariance $(\overline{R}_j, \overline{R}_m)$).

The financial manager has no control over the riskless rate of interest or the market return. He can, however, influence the riskiness of the portfolio of financial assets his firm holds and its correlation with the market average, and therefore, its expected return. This can be done by diversification and selection of financial assets whose rates of return do not move in a parallel fashion.

[4] REDUCING RISK THROUGH DIVERSIFICATION AND THE SELECTION OF FINANCIAL ASSETS

Financial decision-makers may believe that the variance of investment returns, $(\sigma^2(\overline{R}_j))$ is the appropriate measure of risk to use. As mentioned in 2.3[3], however, the appropriate measure of risk of any individual investment is its contribution to the riskiness of the portfolio, determined by its co variance with the portfolio of all available investments (Cov. $\overline{R}_j$, $\overline{R}_m$).[19] The reason for this condition is that diversification may be able to eliminate most of the effects of a financial asset's own variance on the variance of the portfolio, but diversification cannot eliminate the effects of a financial asset's covariance with all other financial assets in the portfolio.

Thus, not all of an investment's total variability need be borne by its holder.[20] For when the investment is combined in a portfolio with other investments, some of its variability will be offset by the variability of the other investments. That is, as long as the returns on two investments are not perfectly and positively correlated,[21] combining them into a portfolio will reduce the variability of the returns from what it would have been had either investment been held in isolation. And in general, the lower the positive (or the higher the negative) degree of correlation among the returns on various investments, the greater the chance to reduce the total variability of a portfolio through diversification.

To achieve this effect, however, does not require a large number of securities. Studies have shown that the reduction in risk is normally slight beyond ten securities,[22] although a considerable reduction in risk tends to occur when the first few additional securities are taken on.

Since some variability can be reduced through diversification, not all of an investment's total variability of returns or risk is relevant in determining its likely return. That portion which cannot be eliminated through diversification, referred to as systematic or non-diversifiable risk, will be compensated for and be in alignment with return. On the other hand, the diversifiable or unsystematic portion which can be eliminated through diversification, will not be compensated.

In effect, therefore, increasing diversification gradually tends to reduce the unsystematic or market related risk. The gains from this diversification, however, tend to decline as the number of additional securities taken on increases. But no matter how many securities are held, total elimination of all risk is unlikely. Once the number of securities in a portfolio gets large, the portfolio begins to take on the characteristics of the security market as a whole, and a holder is exposed to general market risk. This pattern is illustrated in Figure 2.8.

Since total security risk can be divided into systematic and unsystematic components,[23] and since risks and returns are related, we would expect to be able to divide total security returns into systematic and unsystematic segments. Thus:

Total Security Return = Systematic Return + Unsystematic Return.

Systematic returns on a security are perfectly correlated with, and dependent upon, general market returns. However, unsystematic returns on a security are independent from and uncorrelated with general market returns.

FIGURE 2.8 *Systematic and unsystematic risk*

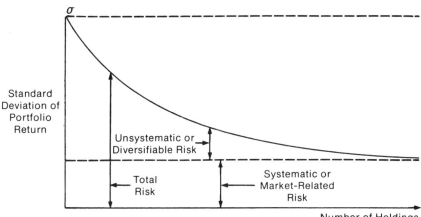

[5] BETA β AS A MEASURE OF RISK

Understanding systematic returns allows us to develop one of the most widely used concepts of contemporary financial theory—beta (β). Beta is a market sensitivity factor which designates the degree of relationship between the returns on a particular security and the returns on the general market. In effect, beta represents the systematic risk of a security (and as we shall shortly see in 2.3[9], of a portfolio as well) relative to the risk of the market in general. Thus, beta is a concept which is useful as a relative measure of risk.

The beta of a security represents the expected increase (or decrease) in the security's return for a given increase (or decrease) in the general market return.[24] For example, if a security has a beta of 2.0[25] (a rather high beta) a 5 percent return on a holding of the general market for a given period would be expected to generate a systematic return for that security of 10 percent. And the total return on that security for that period would be 10 percent plus the unsystematic return on the security. On the other hand, if the security has a beta of 0.5 (a rather low beta) a 5 percent return on a holding of the general market would be expected to generate a systematic return for the security of 2.5 percent. In this case, the total return on the security for the period would be 2.5 percent plus the unsystematic return.[26]

[6] THE MEANING OF ALPHA (α)

In order to understand the factors bearing upon the total return on a security, we must further explore the notion of unsystematic return, which we have defined as that portion of the total return which is independent of market returns. The unsystematic return is often represented by a factor epsilon (e[1]) and it depends on factors unique to the company, such as its market share, labor, community, stockholder and employee relations, and

32

cost relationships.[27] Thus, where market returns are $\overline{R}_m$, security returns, $\overline{R}$, may be expressed as:

$$\overline{R} = \overline{R}_m + e^{'}.$$

The above expression is often altered by introducing a term alpha (A) which represents the average value of the unsystematic returns over time. Any difference between e^{1} and α is denoted as a residual term e, that is:

$$e^{'} = \alpha + e.$$

Then substituting into the prior expression,

$$\overline{R} = \alpha + \overline{R}_m + e$$

where the average e over time is expected to be equal to zero.[28] The above equation for the determination of security returns is often called the "market model". This model can be shown as a linear least-squares regression line fitted to a plot of security returns on one axis and the rates of return on the market as a whole on the other axis. Figure 2.9 depicts this line which is also called the characteristic line.

FIGURE 2.9 *The market model for security returns*

(the characteristic line)

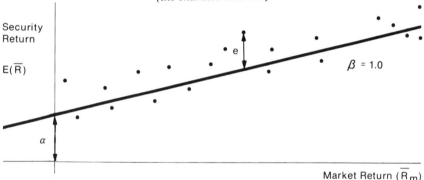

Beta (β) = The market sensitivity index (the slope of the line)

Alpha (α) = The average of the return residuals (the intercept of the line on the security return axis)

Epsilon (e) = The return residuals (the perpendicular distances of the points from the line).

Source: Franco Modigliani and Gerald A. Pogue, "An Introduction to Risk and Return, Concepts and Evidence I," *Financial Analysts Journal,* March-April 1974, p. 77.

[7] THE CHARACTERISTIC LINE

The slope of the characteristic line measures systematic risk or beta, (see Figure 2.9). As the market return increases, the security return also increases. The security return would depend entirely on the market return and beta, if all the observations ($\overline{R}, \overline{R}_m$) fell on the characteristic line. At any one time, however, these observations are represented by the perpendicular distances (e) between each observation and the characteristic line. Presumably, they are caused by the special circumstances peculiar to the security and represent unsystematic risk. Presumably, also, all other things being equal, a higher alpha signifies better performance.

The standard deviation (σ) of the return component may also be used to measure systematic and unsystematic risk.

Systematic Risk = σ_m

where σ_m is the standard deviation of the market return. And

Unsystematic Risk = σ_e

where σ_e is the standard deviation of the residual return factor.

[8] THE CAPITAL ASSET PRICING MODEL

It will be remembered that the equilibrium expected return of a security was expressed in equation [4]. By substituting equation [5] into equation [4], we can also write

[6] $E(\overline{R}_j) = R_F + [E(\overline{R}_m) - R_F]/\sigma^2(\overline{R}_m)$ covariance $(\overline{R}_j, \overline{R}_m)$

Rearranging the terms, we can see that

[7] $E(\overline{R}_j) = R_F + [E(\overline{R}_m) - R_F]$ covariance $(\overline{R}_j, \overline{R}_m)/\sigma^2(\overline{R}_m)$

Equation [7] shows that the expected return on security j equals the risk free return plus the risk premium on the market multiplied by the ratio of the risk of security j to the risk of the market. This latter ratio, covariance $(\overline{R}_j, \overline{R}_m)/\sigma^2(\overline{R}_m)$, is beta ($\beta$). It can be shown that the beta derived from the characteristic line, as described previously, approximates this beta, based on expected values, as shown above. Equation [7], therefore may be rewritten as

[8] $E(\overline{R}_j) = R_F + \beta [E(\overline{R}_m) - R_F]$

Equation [8] has become known as the Capital Asset Pricing Model (CAPM)

[9] THE THEORY APPLIED TO PORTFOLIOS

The concepts and principles applicable to individual investments may readily be extended to portfolios. The beta value of a portfolio, β_p, is equal to the averge of the individual security betas which make up the portfolio, each weighted by the respective proportion that each individual security bears to the portfolio as a whole. Thus,

$$\beta_p = \sum_{j=1}^{n} X_j \beta_j$$

where

X_j = the proportion of portfolio market value represented by security j, and

n = the number of securities in the portfolio.

The systematic risk of a portfolio, paralleling the derivation for individual securities, is equal to the beta value of the portfolio, β_p, multiplied by the risk of the market as a whole, σ_m. Thus:

Portfolio Systematic Risk = $\beta_p \sigma_m$.

Since the systematic risk of individual securities equals β, in order to determine the systematic risk of a portfolio we merely compute a weighted average of the systematic risk of the individual securities which comprise the portfolio. Similarly, the unsystematic risk of a portfolio is determined by the unsystematic risks of the individual securities which make up the portfolio. This risk can largely be eliminated by efficient diversification. Thus for portfolios, as well as for individual securities, rates of return[29] over long periods of time should be related to the systematic risk rather than the total risk. The market will not provide a risk premium for bearing unsystematic risk since such risk, at least in theory, can be eliminated.

In this context, therefore, prices of securities or assets in the capital market will adjust until equivalent risk assets have identical expected returns. Thus, an investor who places all his funds in a riskless asset (β equals 0.0) should expect to earn no more than the return given by such riskless assets as treasury bills. One who holds a portfolio of stocks with a risk equal to that of the market as a whole (a β of 1.0) should expect to earn a return equal to that of the market as a whole. But what should be the return to an investor who holds some portion of his wealth in riskless assets and some portion in assets with a risk equal to that of the market as a whole? In order to answer this question we first need to determine the risk of such a portfolio. Since the β of a portfolio is a weighted average of the βs of the component securities (with the weights determined by the proportion of each security in the portfolio) the β of the above portfolio, β_p, is determined as follows:

$$\beta_p = (1 - X) \cdot 0 + X \cdot 1$$
$$= X$$

where X is the proportion of funds placed in risky assets and $(1-X)$ the proportion in riskless assets. Thus the β of the portfolio is equal to the proportion of funds placed in risky assets.[30]

Remembering that the expected rate of return of a portfolio is equal to the expected weighted rates of return of the component parts, we can compute the expected rate of return, $E(\overline{R}_p)$ on a portfolio of capital assets as follows:

$$E(\overline{R}_p) = R_F + \overline{R}_p [E(\overline{R}_m) - R_F].$$

As in the case of individual securities, this formula indicates that the expected return on a portfolio is equal to the risk free rate plus the product of the β of the portfolio and the risk premium on the market. The formula represents the expected rate of return of a security $E(\overline{R}_j)$ when R_F is the risk free rate and $E(\overline{R})$ the return on the market as a whole. Expressed differently, the CAPM indicates that the expected return on an investment should exceed the riskless rate of return by an amount which is proportional to β.[31]

[10] THE SECURITY MARKET LINE

For investments with a β equal to zero, the holder should expect to earn the risk free rate, while for risky investments, the rate of return should be proportional to its β. A graph showing this relationship, which is often called the "security market line"[32] or the CAPM theoretical line is presented in Figure 2.10.[33] In this Figure, each plotted point represents a stock's realized return versus the stock's β. The vertical distances of the points from the line represent residual returns as defined previously.[34]

FIGURE 2.10   *Capital asset pricing model theoretical line (security market line)*

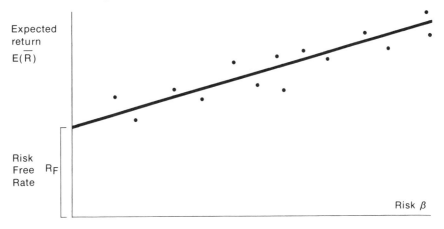

The slope of the security market line indicates the degree of risk aversion on the part of investors. For highly risk-averse average investors, the slope will be quite steep. In effect, as risk aversion increases the risk premium increases as well, causing the slope of the security market line to rise. Alternatively, a lesser degree of risk aversion results in a decline in the slope of the security market line. At the extreme, with no risk aversion at all, there is no risk premium and the security market line is therefore horizontal.

[11] CAPITAL MARKET LINE

An extension of the security market line, which usually deals with the pricing of individual securities, is the capital market line. This line, however, is concerned primarily with the pricing of portfolios. If investors have homogeneous beliefs as to security risks and returns, and equilibrium conditions persist, they will all have the same linear efficient set of securities (portfolios), called the capital market line. This is shown in Figure 2.11.

In this figure, the vertical axis, $E(\overline{R}_p)$, represents the expected return on a portfolio of securities. The horizontal axis, σ_p, represents the risk of the portfolio. The point $E(\overline{R})$ is the expected return for the market in general, with σ_m, the risk of such a holding. Since the intercept is the risk free rate, R_F, and the slope of the line is $\dfrac{[E(\overline{R}_m) - R_F]}{\sigma_m}$ [35] the equation for the capital market line is

$$E(\overline{R}_p) = R_F + \frac{E(\overline{R}_m) - R_F}{\sigma_m}\, \sigma_p.$$

This equation tells us that the expected return on any portfolio is equal to the riskless rate plus a risk premium equal to $E(\overline{R}_m) - R_F / \sigma_m$ times the portfolio's standard deviation.

36

FIGURE 2.11 *Capital market line*

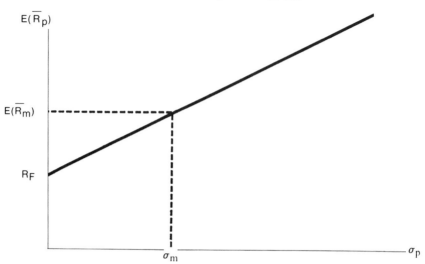

The capital market line shows a linear relationship between expected return and risk for portfolios of assets. If it is assumed that investors can borrow or lend any amount they choose at the risk free rate, the capital market line reveals the various risk-return positions an investor can take. By appropriately borrowing or lending at the risk free rate, R_F, (lending is equivalent to buying risk free securities) the investor can move anyplace he chooses along the capital market line. Thus, individual stocks and imperfectly diversified portfolios will all fall below (have an inferior risk-return relationship) the capital market line. This is a further demonstration that the market does not compensate for unnecessary risk, i.e., for diversifiable or unsystematic risk. Portfolios whose risk consists of systematic risk only and which will therefore lie on the capital market line are called "perfectly diversified portfolios" or "efficient" portfolios.

[12] EFFICIENT PORTFOLIOS

The concept of an efficient portfolio is associated with the principles of diversification. To help understand this concept, refer to Figure 2.12. The shaded area shows the set of all feasible portfolios that reflect the subjective probability beliefs of an individual investor. The left-most boundary of this area, represented by line EE, is the efficient frontier. It is given this designation because it depicts efficient portfolios. These have the smallest variances of return among all feasible portfolios with the same expected return or the largest expected return among all feasible portfolios with the same variances of return.

Consider portfolio X. It provides the same expected return as portfolio Y but embodies more risk; therefore, it is not efficient. On the other hand, portfolio Y has less risk than any other portfolio affording the same rate of return; therefore, it is efficient. All portfolios falling on the efficient frontier are efficient; either they provide a higher rate of return at a given level of risk, or less risk at a given level of return. Presumably, investors will be interested only in portfolios on the efficient frontier because of their superior characteristics.

FIGURE 2.12   *The efficient frontier*

Expected
Returns
$E(\overline{R}_p)$

Y   X   E

All Feasible Portfolios

E

0   Risk
σ_p

[13] OPTIMAL PORTFOLIOS

Of the portfolios on the efficient frontier, one will give a particular investor the most satisfaction; in other words, have a greater utility to him than any other. To find the efficient portfolio whose expected utility exceeds that of any other efficient portfolio, we return to the concept of utility originally developed in 2.2[3]. Keeping in mind that most individuals have declining marginal utility, as defined in 2.2[3], reference can be made to indifference curves, as portrayed in Figure 2.13. In this case, these show the combinations of expected return (on the vertical axis) and risk (on the horizontal axis) that yield the investor the same utility.

FIGURE 2.13   *Utility function of a risk-averse investor,*
represented by a family of indifference curves (u)

Expected Returns

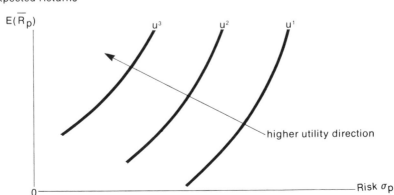

$E(\overline{R}_p)$

u^3 u^2 u^1

higher utility direction

0   Risk σ_p

As stated above, the CAPM assumes investors to be generally risk-averse. This means they seek higher returns, but also prefer to avoid risk as far as possible. Accordingly, they are prepared to have some trade-off between return and risk in their search for maximizing expected utility. A risk-averse investor would require greater proportional increases in expected returns as risk increases and therefore, the risk-return trade-offs of such an investor take the shape shown in Figure 2.13.

When the indifference map of an individual investor is ascertained and the efficient frontier is known, he can determine the portfolio which will maximize his utility. Such a portfolio will be at the point of tangency between the efficient frontier and the highest indifference curve. In Figure 2.14 this will be portfolio A; it is efficient because it falls on the efficient frontier, EE; it is optimal because it maximizes the investor's utility.

FIGURE 2.14 *An optimal portfolio*

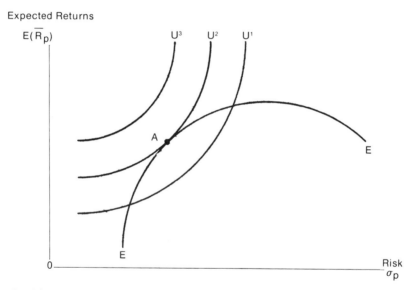

In this way, a rational investor could choose an optimal portfolio. He then would gauge the risk of particular securities in terms of their contribution to this basic, reference portfolio.

2.4 TESTS OF THE VALIDITY OF THE CAPM[36]

In the prior section we presented the CAPM. In this section we look at some of the tests of its validity.

The CAPM would predict that realized returns and risk would generally have a positive and significant relationship. However, this relationship was found to be somewhat weaker than that predicted by the model.[37]

More specifically, β was found to have a positive significant relationship to individual security returns.[38] Similar tests were undertaken, comparing portfolio betas to portfolio returns and again a strong positive association was found.[39] While a linear relationship between portfolio risks and returns seems to hold generally, the extent of this relationship may not be as pronounced as that predicted by the CAPM (the slope of the regression line of risk and return is less than expected by the model).[40] Modigliani and Pogue, upon reviewing the evidence analyzing the validity of the CAPM conclude, "Obviously, we cannot claim that the model is absolutely right. On the other hand, the empirical tests do support the view that beta is a useful risk measure and that high beta stocks tend to be priced so as to yield correspondingly high rates of return."[41]

One of the noteworthy departures from the model which has been observed is that stocks and portfolios with systematic risk (beta) lower than that of the market in general seem to have had greater returns than that predicted by the CAPM, whereas stocks and portfolios with betas higher than that of the general market exhibit lower than expected returns. In effect, high-risk stocks and portfolios have not been compensated to the full extent expected by the theory, while low-risk stocks and portfolios have been overcompensated according to the model. Furthermore, the higher the beta, the greater the undercompensation and vice-versa.[42] Still, although analyzed by many empirical investigators, the model appears to work reasonably well and it has achieved widespread academic acceptance.

The major results of the general tests of the CAPM can be summarized as follows:

(a) the relationship between systematic risk and expected return is significant, positive and generally linear as predicted by the theory;

(b) the slope of this relationship is somewhat less than expected by the model; and

(c) to the extent there are departures from theory, higher β stocks and portfolios have not been fully compensated for the risk taken and vice-versa for lower β stocks and portfolios.

2.5   THE EFFICIENT MARKET HYPOTHESIS[43]

One of the major implications of the CAPM is the efficient markets hypothesis (EMH). Before looking at efficient markets, we should indicate the conditions of the more extreme perfect market. In such a market: (1) all relevant new information is immediately and costlessly available to all present and potential investors; (2) all market participants agree on the significance of all information for the current price and distributions of future prices of each security; and (3) the cost of action (transaction costs, taxes, etc.) is zero. While it is clear that the assumptions of perfect markets are not prevalent in reality, the CAPM has been used to determine the extent to which the capital markets are efficient, a more limited condition. That is, the CAPM has been employed to test the EMH.

The EMH, in effect, states that in an efficient market each common stock is, at any moment, priced fairly with respect to its value (that is, each stock is in equilibrium).[44] In such a market, all information available at any given moment is immediately discounted into the current market price. As a result, this price is equal to the discounted mean value of the distribution of prices in the next period as determined by the present state of knowledge. Thus, in an efficient market, no investor can consistently expect to earn (either through inside information or security analysis) an abnormal return, defined as one in excess of that paid for risk-taking. In order for this to occur, systematic risk and return need to be related, as provided in CAPM theory.

Should the EMH hold, price changes, immediately and fully reacting to new information,[45] would move according to a pattern known as a "martingale." In such a system, all information about future prices is already impounded in the present price which, therefore, is an unbiased estimate of tomorrow's price.[46] A special case of a martingale, in which price changes from one period to the next are assumed to come from independent distributions, is known as the theory of random walks (to be defined below in footnote 48). This theory conforms to the EMH which asserts that, at any given moment, the next period's price change is random with respect to the state of knowledge at this moment.

[1] TESTS OF THE EFFICIENT MARKET HYPOTHESIS (EMH)

Tests of the EMH have been classified as weak, semi-strong, and strong, depending upon the type of information which the designed tests are to analyze.[47] Thus, weak form tests predominantly revolve around the historical price of securities and often deal with the question of the validity of the theory of random walks.[48]

Semi-strong form tests largely look at the security markets' reaction to significant public announcements, such as stock splits or stock dividends, earnings changes, new mandated Securities and Exchange Commission (SEC) requirements, or revisions in a company's principles of financial reporting.[49] In these tests, risk-adjusted returns of securities generally are observed over periods just prior and subsequent to the news development in question.[50]

Tests of the strong form of market efficiency seek to assess the importance of so-called "inside information." Accordingly, they are directed towards measuring the risk-adjusted investment performance of investment companies, corporate insiders, and stock exchange specialists.[51]

In general, these tests of the EMH have found the security markets to be reasonably efficient in the weak form sense. Relatively little, if any, hard evidence has been collected which contradicts the theory of random walks. Similarly, the market seems efficient in the semi-strong form. Most empirical studies have shown that publicly available information tends to be instantaneously impounded in security prices upon its disclosure. It was also found that the accounting convention used to report information to stockholders makes little difference as long as the information is reported in a consistent manner.[52] Questions have been raised, however, about inefficiencies which may result from returns in excess of the risks being taken by certain classifications of investors. Thus, corporate insiders and stock exchange specialists generally were found to earn returns that were greater than the risks they were taking in relation to the market average. On the other hand, the risk-adjusted performance of investment companies, in the main, was only about equal to and, indeed, often below that of the market average.[53]

2.6 ANALYZING AND RELAXING THE ASSUMPTIONS OF THE CAPM

As mentioned in 2.3[2], eyebrows have been raised about the assumptions that underly the CAPM. In response, theoreticians have undertaken many studies, some of which are cited below, to allay this skepticism. Thus, it has been found that the assumption regarding financial decision-makers as being one-period expected wealth maximizers could be extended to cover many periods without causing any major change in the basic underlying model.[54]

Similarly, as long as the distribution of expected returns is symmetric (actual returns have been found to be symmetric) and stable, investors can use measures of dispersion other than the standard deviation or variance in valuing financial commitments and the basic principles of portfolio choice would still hold.[55] Moreover, should a third parameter, such as the chance of loss, be deemed important, the security market line concept developed above, (2.3[10]), could be changed to a three-dimensional concept and converted to a Market Plane. In this case all assets above the Market Plane would be desirable and vice-versa.[56]

It is true that the assumption of homogeneous expectations among all market participants as to the means, standard deviations, and covariances of returns of all available financial commitments, is based on the unlikely expectation that all market participants assign the same probability distribution to all future returns. Nevertheless, theoretical work has found that the basic conditions of the CAPM still hold (albeit the formulation of the model is far more complex) even if heterogeneous expectations exist among market participants.[57] In this case, expected returns and covariances are expressed as complex weighted averages of investor expectations.

Perhaps the most practically unrealistic assumption of the CAPM is the invariable ability of all market participants to borrow and lend at the same risk-free rate. On the contrary, generally large institutional investors ordinarily borrow at lower rates than small individual investors; the rate at which an investor can lend money is less than the rate which he will pay in order to borrow it; and the ability to achieve unlimited borrowing or lending is unrealistic. Nevertheless, even when this assumption is relaxed, the expected return on an asset still appears to increase linearly with increases in systematic risk.[58]

Finally, there is the assumption of perfect capital markets. To the extent that transaction costs exist (as, of course, they do), they may prevent prices from fully adjusting to equilibrium levels. It is generally believed, however, as our discussion of the EMH suggested, that such relatively minor imperfections do not detract significantly from the implications of the CAPM.

When all the evidence is put together, a logical basis for the model still exists and the major implications still hold even when most of the basic assumptions are relaxed. Both theory and empirical studies tend to justify this conclusion.

2.7   APPLICATIONS OF THE CAPM

In this section we outline some of the applications of the CAPM which have been suggested to meet practical business problems. In the chapters of the text where the relevant subject matter is treated, we develop in greater depth the applications most useful to the financial manager. But first, we look at the limits to practical applicability of the CAPM.

[1] LIMITS TO THE PRACTICAL APPLICABILITY OF THE CAPM

As indicated above, we have no quarrel with the essential tenets of the CAPM. Quite the contrary, we believe that the debate has gone far beyond the point of no return. It will be remembered that the CAPM was largely developed with respect to the U.S. securities markets. The mechanism of these markets permits prices to be arranged through the active bids and offers of many participants; a combination of legislation, SEC supervision, and the action of professional accounting bodies has made available to the participants a reasonably reliable body of contemporaneous information; institutions which dominate the markets are able to attract security analysts and money managers who have received good training in academic institutions. For these reasons, one might expect security prices to move towards equilibrium. However, while the model was developed predominantly with respect to financial assets, the financial manager is more directly involved with making decisions concerning the selection and control of physical assets such as inventory and equipment. Product markets are likely to be far from perfect, and may not even be as efficient or competitive as security markets.

As noted in 2.3, a central concept of the CAPM is the relationship or covariance between the returns on a given security and those on the market portfolio. An analogous relationship in applying the CAPM to the area of capital budgeting is the covariance of the returns on a particular capital budgeting proposal to the returns on all of a firm's assets. Needless to say, such a relationship is not as easily determined for physical assets as for securities.[59] Moreover, a CAPM which is unstable for individual securities, is likely to be even more unstable for individual physical assets. Thus, efforts to apply the CAPM to the non-securities activities of the financial manager encounter serious methodological difficulties.

[2] CAPM AS A CAPITAL BUDGETING TECHNIQUE

Perhaps the most popular effort at applying the CAPM to the corporate setting in which the financial manager operates is in the area of capital budgeting. For this purpose, available financial commitments are regarded as encompassing not just the pool of financial assets for which the model originally was intended, but also the arena of operating assets. An early and classical formulation of this sort was offered by J. Fred Weston.[60] Weston employs as a starting point the basic CAPM equation that was developed in 2.3.

$$E(R_j) = R_F + [E(R_m) - R_F] \beta_j.$$

To apply this relationship to capital budgeting decisions, Weston replaces the variables for the securities of an individual firm, $E(R_j)$ and β_j, with variables for the capital project under consideration (the market constants, R_F and $E(R_m)$ remain unchanged). He states that the risk premium on a capital asset is "equal to the market risk premium weighted by the index of the systematic risk of the...real investment."[61] For the project to be acceptable, its expected return over the risk free rate must exceed the market risk premium weighted by the measure of the individual project's systematic risk.[62] Using the terminology developed earlier in this chapter, we would accept all projects whose expected rate of return, $E(R_j)$, as plotted on the vertical axis, is above the security market line (Figure 2.10), when the project risk, β_j, is plotted on the horizontal axis. This can be seen in Figure 2.15.

Project j′ is the only acceptable one, although it promises the lowest expected return $E(R_{j'})$. It is acceptable because its expected return exceeds its equilibrium expected return, $E(R_{E'})$. Project j″ is unacceptable although it offers the highest expected return $E(R_{j''})$, because this is below its equilibrium expected return, $E(R_{E''})$. Project j‴ is marginal since its expected return $E(R_{j'''})$ equals its equilibrium expected return $E(R_{E'''})$.

When acceptable projects using the above criteria are added to the firm's operations, the expected returns on the firm's common stock will be higher than required by the security market line. These "excess returns" will induce a rise in price for the firm's common stock until equilibrium is restored at a higher level. Thus the security market line represents a capital budgeting criteria in the sense that it portrays the opportunity cost of invested capital, the cost of new capital, and the equilibrium level toward which risks and returns move.

FIGURE 2.15 *Security market line as applied to three capital budgeting projects j′, j″ and j‴*

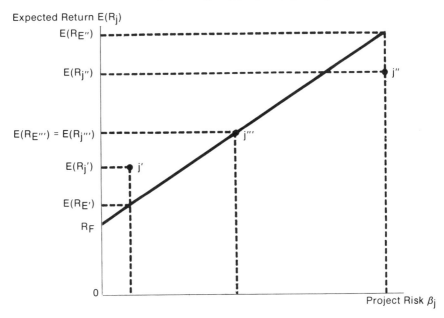

In more recent work, efforts have been made to refine and extend the application of the CAPM to more complex capital budgeting problems. Issues created by capital structure variations as the result of differing use of debt[63] and the introduction of taxes[64] have been treated. An extension to a multiperiod context has been developed.[65] Also, complexities caused by multiple cash flows and growth in the cash flow stream have been considered,[66] as well as the case of uncertainty in the timing of the cash flows.[67] These and other studies have led to a rather extensive number of capital budgeting models derived from the CAPM, although at least one analyst contends that they are all essentially equivalent.[68] Despite the interest in this area, the appropriateness of applying an investments theory to the capital budgeting problems of the firm is by no means clear.

[3] USING CAPM TO FIND THE COST OF CAPITAL

If capital markets are efficient and if the CAPM is an appropriate valuation construct, then in equilibrium, every risky asset must be priced so that it falls on the security market line. Therefore, if we know an asset's risk (or more appropriately the average risk of the corporate portfolio of assets), we can estimate its required rate of return (or the firm's required average rate of return). This notion can be used to gauge the cost of capital for firm j, with a given degree of business risk and financial leverage. For this purpose, we compute the firms beta, B_j, as the covariance between the return on the firm's common stock and the market index. We can then determine the cost of equity capital as equal to the expected return on the firm's common stock, $E(R_j)$, if we know the expected market return, $E(R_m)$, and the risk-free rate, R_F. (This is further developed in chapter 19).

[4] THE CAPM IN CAPITAL STRUCTURE DECISIONS

A major purpose of the CAPM is in exploring risk and risk relationships. As shall be discussed in Chapter 19, the capital structure (debt-equity relationship) of a firm contributes to the riskiness of its stock. Therefore, the CAPM can be employed as a guide in determining the firm's capital structure in the light of its influence on the riskiness of the stock. By observing the effects of a changing capital structure upon a firm's beta value, the financial manager gains some insight into the relationship between capital structure and risk for the firm.

[5] THE CAPM AS A TESTING MODEL

The CAPM has also been applied to test alternative financial strategies or to determine the viability of a particular financial strategy. For example, it has been employed in assessing the appropriateness of option buying, option writing, option hedging or similar operations utilizing warrants and other forms of convertible securities.[69]

The use of financial theory varies somewhat in each of these areas. However, in most cases the risk-adjusted return, as given by the model, on a particular strategy or investment plan, is compared to the return on the market average or on a buy-hold strategy. The CAPM thus becomes the criterion through which the value of various investment strategies or plans can be tested. In a slight variant of this approach the model is used in order to test for excess returns on a particular strategy.

[6] THE CAPM AS A GUIDE TO INVESTMENT OR PORTFOLIO COMPOSITION DECISIONS

The CAPM helps an investor select the security with the highest return among securities with the same risk. It also can be used to select the security with the lowest risk from among securities with the same return. Further, in choosing a portfolio of securities, some portion of the risk on securities individually can be removed (nonsystematic risk) through diversification. By this means, the financial manager can develop a portfolio of financial commitments that provides the highest return at the degree of risk he is willing to tolerate or the lowest risk at the return level he seeks. The financial manager may serve as trustee of his firm's pension and other employee benefit plans or may supervise the activities of an outside trustee and as the result find the CAPM a useful guide for investing in financial assets.

[7] OTHER CAPM APPLICATIONS

A popular use of the CAPM is to clarify the operations of the capital markets. For this purpose, the systematic character of capital assets is employed to help explain some of the characteristics of the markets on which these assets are traded.[70] Such characteristics include, among other things, the nature of the risk-return relationships, equilibrium conditions, and market efficiency, the testing of which was discussed earlier.

Additional applications of financial theory (some of which overlap the applications mentioned earlier) are valuation theory, governmental cost-benefit analysis, and the term structure of interest rates. The concern of the academic community with such issues has been largely to explain economic relationships. The effort to seek practical applications is a logical, but sometimes uncertain, outcome of these theoretical formulations.

2.8   AN ALTERNATE CONCEPT OF FINANCIAL THEORY— THE ARBITRAGE PRICING THEORY (APT)

While the CAPM is still the most widely accepted approach to explaining the relationship between risks and returns on capital assets (or at least securities), this model has recently come under increasing academic criticism. This criticism has gone beyond the admittedly unrealistic assumptions of the model and questions of its empirical validation. Current criticism of the CAPM centers largely on three areas:

1. Questions of the validity of the theoretical extension of the model into such areas as multiple holding periods, the impact of inflation on returns, taxation, non-marketable assets and international investments.

2. The theoretical testability of the CAPM because of the difficulty of determining a suitable market portfolio to use as a benchmark. The market portfolio contains all risky assets and thus cannot be readily measured.

3. The development of an alternate model for the explanation of the relationship between risks and returns on securities—the APT.

Fundamental to the APT is the notion that investors undertake arbitrage activity between both securities and portfolios of securities. Security returns are then determined by a number of economic "factors" and the sensitivity coefficients of these factors. If this model holds for all securities and if the coefficients of each security remain constant with respect to the economic factors, then by simply using a proper weighting mechanism, a portfolio can be created whose return is zero, or else arbitrage will take place. This arbitrage process will continue until an equilibrium is reached in which a zero portfolio is created.

APT, in essence, eliminates the market portfolio of the CAPM via weaker assumptions as to the return generating process. This model, however, by no means obliviates the need for assumptions, for it requires a finite number of common market factors and their coefficients.[71]

2.9 THE USE OF FINANCIAL THEORY BY THE FINANCIAL MANAGER[72]

The evidence based on surveys and questionnaires suggests that the CAPM has not penetrated to any significant degree into the programs of the financial manager. From a series of personal interviews dealing with corporate practice in the capital budgeting area, James Mao concluded some years ago, that while financial managers may accept the notion that risk is related to the variability of returns, in a technical sense, they were largely concerned with the chance of negative deviations from a particular point on a probability distribution (usually the chance of loss).[73] Rex Brown offers an explanation for the slowness of financial managers to apply financial theory and other quantitative financial techniques. His reasons include a lack of trained personnel, the skepticism of management with respect to the potential benefits, corporate organizational structures not conducive to staff-management interaction, and ineffective relations with outside consultants.[74] Finally, C. Jackson Grayson sees some additional reasons for this remoteness of theory from practice: the time, money and personnel necessary to gather the data needed to apply financial theory, the resistance to change on the part of some financial managers, and the simplifying assumptions of financial theory which often frustrate the financial manager's efforts to relate financial theory to his actual problems.[75]

From a rather detailed questionnaire survey by J. William Petty and Oswald Bowlin of the use of quantitative decision models by businesses, some relevant evidence was collected as to the degree of use of financial theory by financial managers. They found that only 2.2 percent of the responding firms applied the CAPM as a means of estimating common stock values, but 16.1 percent used it for portfolio selection purposes. Of the firms applying financial theory as a means of portfolio selection, most used it for security and portfolio analysis and other purposes. In addition, 10.1 percent of the responding firms indicated that they applied risk-return indifference curves and 3.7 percent said they used utility theory—in both cases the problems being dealt with were capital investment, financial leverage and working capital management decisions. Petty and Bowlin conclude that "....three basic limitations of quantitative methods become apparent: (1) inadequate education on the part of the managerial participants, (2) data problems, and (3) the general applicability of the techniques within the firm striving to apply such tools."[76]

Recent in-depth interviews by one of the authors of this text tended to confirm this lack of acceptance of financial theory on the part of financial managers. Only four of the more than twenty-five financial managers of both large and medium-sized corporations queried on this point could cite specific applications of financial theory that they or their predecessors had instituted. The other managers stated that either they made no use of such theory in their work, or had never heard of the CAPM. Among firms which indicated that they applied financial theory, its use in the capital budgeting area was the one most frequently mentioned.

At present, the CAPM is generally accepted among academicians. Its offshoot, the EMH has hooked together theory and practice in the securities field, where, as mentioned previously, some portfolio managers seek to duplicate the return of an overall index on the grounds that no better performance can be achieved in an efficient market. Beta, which traces the relationship between the price movements of a particular stock and the general market, is a widely used measure of risk.

In general, the CAPM has not made a similar penetration outside the securities field. As discussed in this chapter and amplified in later relevant sections of the text, the model has found some application in such areas as capital budgeting, cost of capital, capital structure, and in the testing of financial strategies. Even in these areas, however, the efforts to use the CAPM in a practical way have thus far been largely limited and probing.

Efforts have made some headway which seek to bridge the gap between financial and physical assets by means of financial models which take as their goal the maximization of either the firm's common stock price or shareholder wealth. Perhaps the next step is for the financial manager to take into account the appropriate risk-return relationship for his firm. As financial theory becomes more relevant to him, the financial manager eventually may accept as an objective maximizing the price of his firm's common stock (or maximizing the returns to stockholders), given the beta value (or risk) his firm will accept.[77]

2.10   CHAPTER SUMMARY

In this chapter we began with some basic building blocks relevant to the development of financial theory, which we then presented in a historical setting. The CAPM was presented along with its assumptions, implications, tests of its validation, and applications. The APT was then briefly reviewed as an alternative to the CAPM. Finally, we discussed the extent to which financial theory is currently being used by the financial manager.

FOOTNOTES

1. Some of the ideas in this section were taken from George M. Frankfurter, "Index Funds: Fad or Foe?" *Journal of Accounting, Auditing, and Finance,* Winter 1978, pp. 116-123, and George M. Frankfurter and Allan Young, "Financial Theory: Its Message to the Accountant," *Journal of Accounting, Auditing, and Finance,* Summer 1983. Also, it should be noted that while the current chapter focuses almost exclusively on the Capital Asset Pricing Model and related concepts, other components of financial theory, where useful, are presented throughout the text in the relevant chapters.

2. For more on this see the classical article, David Durand, "Growth Stocks and the Petersburg Paradox," *Journal of Finance,* September 1957, pp. 348-363.

3. The concept of risk will be defined more precisely in 2.2[5].

4. Another reason most individuals are said to be risk averse comes from a phenomenon known as "gambler's ruin." This refers to a particularly unfortunate

outcome of an investment under which one loses all his funds and is thus excluded from further participation as an investor. Thus, there is no possibility of recovering from such a loss.

5. The needs satisfied here may very well be more psychological than physical.

6. By squaring the deviations from the expected value we allow both deviations above and below the expected value to contribute equally to the determination of the measure of variability regardless of sign. In this way, deviations of opposite sign do not cancel each other out.

7. In the case of normal distributions, approximately two-thirds of the possible returns can be expected to lie within one standard deviation on either side of the expected value, 95 percent can be expected to fall within two standard deviations, and 99 percent within three standard deviations.

8. Harry Markowitz, "Portfolio Selection," *Journal of Finance*, March 1952, pp. 77-91.

9. Michael C. Jenson, "The Foundations and Current State of Capital Market Theory," in *Studies in the Theory of Capital Markets*, New York, Praeger Publishers, 1972, pp. 4-7.

10. James Tobin, "Liquidity Preference as Behavior Towards Risk," *Review of Economic Studies*, February 1958, pp. 65-85.

11. An equilibrium occurs when there is no systematic tendency for prices to change. Thus a security is said to be in equilibrium when there is no pressure for its price to change. In this sense, a general equilibrium model of asset prices is one which attempts to include the relationships necessary to describe the level toward which asset prices tend.

12. For example see, Jack L. Treynor, "Toward a Theory of Market Value of Risky Assets," unpublished manuscript, 1961; John Lintner, "The Valuation of Risky Assets and the Selection of Risky Investments in Stock Portfolios and Capital Budgets," *Review of Economics and Statistics*, February 1965, pp. 13-37; John Lintner, "Security Prices, Risk and Maximal Gains from Diversification," *Journal of Finance*, December 1965, pp. 587-616; Eugene F. Fama, "Risk, Return and Equilibrium: Some Clarifying Comments," *Journal of Finance*, March 1968, pp. 29-40; and Jan Mossin, "Security Pricing and Investment Criteria in Competitive Markets," *American Economic Review*, December 1969, pp. 749-756. See, also, particularly William F. Sharpe, "Capital Asset Prices: A Theory of Market Equilibrium Under Conditions of Risk," *Journal of Finance*, September 1964, pp. 425-442, and *Portfolio Theory and Capital Markets*, New York, MacGraw-Hill, 1970.

13. This listing was developed from Jensen, *op. cit.*, p. 5.

14. The covariance between two variables a and b is equal to their coefficient of correlation, r_{ab}, multiplied by the standard deviation of each variable. Thus, covariance $_{ab} = r_{ab}\,\sigma_a\,\sigma_b$. A positive covariance means that the variables move in the same direction (which is typically the case for most common stocks); a negative covariance means that the two variables move in opposite directions.

15. The rate at which money can be lent when there is assumed to be no chance of loss from business risk.

16. Some of the problems of the financial manager in applying financial theory relate to the lack of anything close to perfect markets for many types of capital equipment and other products.

17. This expression can be found in many sources and is now commonplace in the academic literature of finance. It is developed and discussed in a form quite similar to that shown in Jensen, *op. cit.*, p. 5.

18. That is, they can fluctuate in an unbiased fashion and take on any value.

19. As noted in the prior subsection, this was a major simplification introduced by those who sought to refine, extend, and operationalize, the original Markowitz model.

20. Much of the remainder of this section is drawn from Franco Modigliani and Gerald A. Pogue, "An Introduction to Risk and Return Concepts and Evidence I and II," *Financial Analysts Journal*, March-April and May-June 1974, pp. 68-80 and 69-86.

21. Two investments are said to be perfectly and positively correlated when their return patterns have a coefficient of correlation of 1.0. Perfect negative correlation results in a correlation coefficient of -1.0, while totally uncorrelated return patterns will result in a coefficient of correlation of 0.0.

22. See, Wayne Wagner and Sheila Lau, "The Effect of Diversification on Risk," *Financial Analyst's Journal*, November-December 1971, pp. 48-53. The theory underlying the Capital Asset Pricing Model was largely developed with respect to the securities markets, but the basic principles are applicable to financial assets generally.

23. It has been found that unsystematic risk typically accounts for about 70% of total risk (systematic risk thus accounts for about 30% of total risk) for the market as a whole. (Modigliani and Pogue, *op. cit.*, p. 80.)

24. Most studies have found that β coefficients vary very little over time. This is especially true for large portfolios, less so for small portfolios, and not generally true for individual securities whose betas have often been found to vary somewhat over time. For example, see Robert A. Levy, "On the Short-Term Stationarity of Beta Coefficients," *Financial Analysts Journal*, November-December 1971, pp. 55-62.

25. The market-weighted average β for all stocks (or the β of the market in general) is 1.0 by definition. The β of any security is found by regressing its returns on the returns for the market in general.

26. We might note that much controversy surrounds β analysis and attempts to employ it in practical situations. The theory is therefore not quite as straight-forward as this discussion might make it appear. Nevertheless, it has been shown that the σ of a security j, depends upon (1) its own standard deviation of returns, σ_j; (2) its correlation with the market average, r_{jm}; and (3) the volatility of the market average, σ_m. Thus,

$$\beta_j = \frac{\sigma_j \, r_{jm}}{\sigma_m}$$

27. On the other hand, the systematic component of total return depends on such factors as inflation, recessions and interest rates, which affect all firms simultaneously and thus cannot be altered by diversification.

28. e is also assumed to be independent from one period to the next. Further, e's for any two capital assets are also assumed to be independent of each other and independent of the movement of the market as a whole.

29. The rate of return of a portfolio is equal to the rates of return on the individual securities of the portfolio each weighted by the proportion which it bears to the total portfolio value.

30. A portfolio beta greater than 1.0 can occur if the investor borrows at the risk-free rate and invests the proceeds in the risky portfolio.

31. In effect, risk and return should have a linear relationship.

32. The security market line normally refers to individual securities rather than portfolios.

33. Such a graph has also been referred to as the "opportunity line."

34. For well diversified or efficient portfolios (those in which all opportunities to reduce risk through diversification are taken so that the highest return is earned for the degree of risk undergone or the degree of risk is minimized for the return earned) this line is called the market portfolio or reference portfolio. Such a portfolio is often thought of as an index of the risk-return performance of the market as a whole. For studies dealing with security pricing, the market portfolio

is usually approximated by one of the most common market averages, such as the Dow Jones Industrial Average, the Standard and Poor's 425 Stock Average or the New York Stock Exchange Index.

35. The slope of the capital market line is the market price of risk. It reflects the attitudes of investors in the aggregate toward risk.

36. Empirical tests of the CAPM are fraught with difficult econometric problems. For an excellent discussion of this see, Merton Miller and Myron Scholes, "Rates of Return in Relation to Risk: A Reexamination of Recent Findings," in *Studies in the Theory of Capital Markets, op. cit.*, pp. 47-78. Furthermore, Roll maintains that the CAPM is an untestable theory. See, Richard Roll, "A Critique of an Asset Pricing Theory's Tests," *Journal of Financial Economics*, March 1977, pp. 129-176.

37. Nancy Jacob, "The Measurement of Systematic Risk for Securities and Portfolios: Some Empirical Results," *Journal of Financial and Quantitative Analysis*, March 1974, pp. 815-834.

38. Miller and Scholes, *op cit.*

39. Irwin Friend and Marshall Blume, "Risk and the Long-Run Rate of Return on NYSE Common Stocks," Working Paper No. 18-72, Wharton School of Commerce and Finance, Rodney L. White Center for Financial Research.

40. Marshall Blume and Irwin Friend, "A New Look at the Capital Asset Pricing Model," *Journal of Finance*, March 1973, pp. 19-33 and Fisher Black, Michael Jensen and Myron Scholes, "The Capital Asset Pricing Model: Some Empirical Tests," in *Studies in the Theory of Capital Markets*, ed., Michael Jensen, New York: Praeger, 1972, pp. 79-121.

41. Franco Modigliani and Gerald Pogue, "An Introduction to Risk and Return: Concepts and Evidence II," *Financial Analysts Journal*, May-June 1974, p. 182.

42. Black, Jensen and Scholes, *op. cit.*

43. The tests of market efficiency to which we refer in this section comprehend market efficiency in the operational, as opposed to the allocational, sense. While an operationally efficient capital market will assist allocational efficiency, the existence of allocational efficiency does not necessarily insure operational efficiency. By operational efficiency we refer to the pricing mechanism of the secondary securities markets. Allocational efficiency deals with the distribution of new capital among competing users.

44. In these circumstances, one should not waste time trying to "beat the market" or pay for investment counsel which makes such promises. This conclusion is important for the financial manager in the administration of corporate marketable securities and trust funds. Instead of trying to analyze stocks for such portfolios or paying others to do so, financial managers should merely decide how risky a portfolio they wish to hold, and then pick a diversified list of securities with the appropriate coefficients. While for some time financial managers behaved as if they did not believe in the EMH, in 1976 and 1977, a number of companies, including AT&T, began to manage security portfolios under their administration by designating the desired β value. Moreover, so-called index funds have as their objective equaling the returns of the general market, measured by some index.

45. The logic of this is manifest. If the market were not efficient in reacting to new information and did so slowly, an investor might attempt to earn extraordinary profits (profits in excess of that granted for risk-taking) by quickly purchasing a security upon the announcement of good news and quickly selling it whenever bad news occurs. However, implementation of this strategy would lead to its own downfall. By quickly reacting to favorable and unfavorable news, the investor would increase the pace at which the market responds. As others reacted in a like manner, the market would begin to instantaneously impound new information in security prices.

46. Strictly speaking a martingale is a type of "fair game." A fair game means that, on average, over a large number of samples, the expected return equals the actual return. The CAPM is a fair game model. Games of chance in a casino are examples of fair games. Because of the house percentage, the expected loss (return) of the average player, say 8 percent, is what, across a large number of players, people actually lose. A fair game does not necessarily imply either a positive or a neutral return but only that expectations are not biased.

A martingale is a fair game in which tomorrow's price is expected to be the same as today's price. A submartingale is a fair game in which tomorrow's price is expected to be greater than today's price, that is, in which expected returns are positive.

47. This classification was originally devised by Eugene Fama, see "Efficient Capital Markets: A Review of Theory and Empirical Work," *Journal of Finance,* May 1970, pp. 383-417.

48. Briefly stated, this theory maintains that security prices move randomly from one level to the next without any discernible pattern or influence from prior price movements. For some of the evidence related to the testing of this theory see Sidney S. Alexander, "Price Movements in Speculative Markets: Trends or Random Walks," *Industrial Management Review,* May 1961, pp. 7-26, and "Price Movements in Speculative Markets: Trends or Random Walks No. 2," *Industrial Management Review,* Spring 1964, pp. 338-372; *The Random Character of Stock Market Prices,* ed., Paul H. Cootner, Cambridge, Mass., M.I.T. Press, 1964; Paul A. Samuelson, "Proof That Properly Adjusted Prices Fluctuate Randomly," *Industrial Management Review,* Spring 1965, pp. 41-49; Bendit Mandelbrot, "Forecasts of Future Prices, Unbiased Markets and Martingale Models," *Journal of Business,* Special Supplement, January 1966, pp. 242-255; M.F.M. Osborne, "Brownian Motion in the Stock Market," *Operations Research,* March-April 1959, pp. 145-173; Michael C. Jensen and George Bennington, "Random Walks and Technical Theories: Some Additional Evidence," *Journal of Finance,* May 1970, pp. 469-482. And for a treatment of this as well as other issues related to financial theory but written in a style more akin to the layman's understanding, see Burton G. Malkiel, *A Random Walk Down Wall Street,* New York, W.W. Norton and Co., Inc., 1973.

49. Just a few of the many studies conducted along these lines are Ray Ball and Phillip Brown, "An Empirical Evaluation of Accounting and Income Numbers," *Journal of Accounting Research,* Autumn 1968, pp. 159-178; Nicholas Gonedes, "Capital Market Equilibrium and Annual Accounting Numbers: Empirical Evidence," *Journal of Accounting Research,* Spring 1974, pp. 26-62; Nicholas Gonedes, "Risk, Information and the Effects of Special Accounting Items on Capital Market Equilibrium," *Journal of Accounting Research,* Autumn 1975; Shyam Sunder, "Relationship Between Accounting Changes and Stock Prices: Problems of Measurement and Some Empirical Evidence," *Empirical Research in Accounting: Selected Studies,* 1973, pp. 1-45; Shyam Sunder, "Stock Price and Risk Related to Accounting Changes in Inventory Valuation," *Accounting Review,* April 1975, pp. 305-315; Thomas E. Copeland, "Efficient Capital Markets, Evidence and Implications for Financial Reporting," *Journal of Accounting, Auditing, and Finance,* Fall 1978, pp. 33-48; Robert S. Kaplan and Richard Roll, "Investor Evaluation of Accounting Information: Some Empirical Evidence," *Journal of Business,* April 1972, pp. 225-257; Hai Hong, Robert S. Kaplan, and Gershon Mandelker, "Pooling vs. Purchase: The Effects of Accounting for Mergers on Stock Prices," *Accounting Review,* January 1978, pp. 31-47; D. Collins, "SEC Product Line Reporting and Market Efficiency," *Journal of Financial Economics,* June 1975, pp. 125-164; Bertrand Horwitz and Richard Kolodny, "Line of Business Reporting and Security Prices: An Analysis of an SEC Disclosure Rule," *Bell Journal of Economics,* Spring 1977, pp. 234-249;

Sherman Chottiner and Allan Young, "A Test of the AICPA Differentiation Between Stock Dividends and Stock Splits," *Journal of Accounting Research,* Autumn 1971, pp. 367-374.

50. For the development of the original model see, Eugene Fama, Lawrence Fisher, Michael Jensen, and Richard Roll, "The Adjustment of Stock Prices to New Information," *International Economic Review,* February 1969, pp. 1-26.

51. Jeffrey F. Jaffe, "Special Information and Insider Trading," *Journal of Business,* July 1974, pp. 410-428; Victor Niederhoffer and M.F.M. Osborne, "Market Making and Reversal on the Stock Exchange," *Journal of the American Statistical Association,* December 1966, pp. 897-916; William F. Sharpe, "Mutual Fund Performance," *Journal of Business,* Special Supplement, January 1966, pp. 119-138, William F. Sharpe, "Risk Aversion in the Stock Market," *Journal of Finance,* September 1965, pp. 416-422; Jack L. Treynor, "How to Rate Management of Investment Funds," *Harvard Business Review,* January-February 1965, pp. 63-75; Michael Jensen, "The Performance of Mutual Funds in the Period 1945-64," *Journal of Finance,* May 1968, pp. 389-416; Michael Jensen, "Risk, the Pricing of Capital Assets and the Evaluation of Investment Portfolios," *Journal of Business,* April 1969, pp. 167-247.

52. This observation flies in the face of financial managers' great concern with the reporting of earnings per share and their desire to use accounting conventions to influence their reported earning figures, as discussed in Chapter 3.

53. Some evidence is also being developed which shows excess returns to some institutional investors and a "small firm" effect, in which small firms outperform their larger counterparts.

54. In this connection, see Eugene F. Fama, "Multiperiod Consumption-Investment Decisions," *American Economic Review,* March 1970, pp. 163-174.

55. Eugene F. Fama, "Portfolio Analysis in a Stable Paretian Market," *Management Science,* January 1965, pp. 404-419.

56. Robert Higgins, *Financial Management: Theory and Applications,* Chicago, Science Research Associates, Inc., 1977, p. 86.

57. John Lintner, "The Aggregation of Investors' Judgements and Preferences in Purely Competitive Security Markets," *Journal of Financial and Quantitative Analysis,* December 1969, pp. 347-400.

58. Fisher Black, "Capital Market Equilibrium with Restricted Borrowing," *Journal of Business,* July 1972, pp. 444-455 and M.J. Brennen, "Capital Market Equilibrium with Divergent Borrowing and Lending Rates," *Journal of Financial and Quantitative Analysis,* December 1971, pp. 1197-1208.

59. Thomas J. Frecka, "Capital Asset Pricing Model and Traditional Risk Measures for Capital Budgeting: A Comment," *Financial Review,* Fall 1977, pp. 97-99 and Herbert E. Phillips, "Capital Asset Pricing Model and Traditional Risk Measures for Capital Budgeting: A Comment," *Financial Review,* Fall 1977, pp. 91-97.

60. J. Fred Weston, "Investment Decisions Using the Capital Asset Pricing Model," *Financial Management,* Spring 1973, pp. 25-33.

61. *Ibid.* p. 25.

62. This is analogous to using the cost of capital as the decision criterion.

63. Mark E. Rubenstein, "A Mean-Variance Synthesis of Corporate Financial Theory," *Journal of Finance,* March 1973, pp. 167-181.

64. Thomas E. Copeland and J. Fred Weston, *Financial Theory and Corporate Policy,* Reading, Mass., Addison-Wesley Publishing Co., 1979, Chap. 11.

65. M. Bogue and R. Roll, "Capital Budgeting for Risky Projects With Imperfect Markets for Physical Capital," *Journal of Finance,* May 1974, pp. 601-613, and Haim Ben Shahar and Frank M. Werner, "Multiperiod Capital Budgeting Under Uncertainty: A Suggested Application," *Journal of Financial and Quantitative Analysis,* December 1977, pp. 859-877.

66. Stewart C. Meyers and Stuart M. Turnbull, "Capital Budgeting and Capital

Asset Pricing Model: Good News and Bad News," *Journal of Finance*, May 1977, pp. 321-332.

67. Sylianos Perrakis, "Capital Budgeting and Timing Uncertainty Within the Capital Asset Pricing Model," *Financial Management*, Autumn 1979, pp. 32-40.

68. Lemma W. Senbet and Howard E. Thompson, "The Equivalence of Alternate Mean-Variance Capital Budgeting Models," *Journal of Finance*, May 1978, pp. 359-401.

69. For some examples of these applications see, Fisher Black and Myron Scholes, "The Pricing of Options and Corporate Liabilities," *Journal of Political Economy*, 1973, pp. 637-659; George M. Frankfurter, Richard Stevenson and Allan Young, "Option Spreading: Theory and an Illustration," *Journal of Portfolio Management*, Summer 1979, pp. 59-63; Clifford W. Smith, "Option Pricing: A Review," *Journal of Financial Economics*, January 1976, pp. 3-51; Dan Galai and Ronald Masulis, "The Option Pricing Model and the Risk Factor of Stock," *Journal of Financial Economics*, January 1976, pp. 53-81; Jimmy E. Hilliard and Robert A. Leitch, "Analysis of the Warrant Hedge in a Stable Paretism Market," *Journal of Financial and Quantitative Analysis*, March 1977, pp. 85-103; Dick A. Leabo and Richard J. Rogalski, "Trading in Warrants by Mechanical Systems," *Journal of Finance*, March 1977, pp. 87-101.

70. William F. Sharpe, "Capital Asset Prices: A Theory of Market Equilibrium Under Conditions of Risk," *Journal of Finance*, September 1964, pp. 425-442 and William F. Sharpe, *Portfolio Theory and Capital Markets*, New York, McGraw-Hill, 1970; *Studies in the Theory of Capital Markets, op. cit.*

71. For some of the recent criticism of the CAPM and the development of the APT see, Richard Roll, "A Critique of the Asset Pricing Theory's Tests," *Journal of Financial Economics*, March 1977; Stephen Ross, "The Arbitrage Theory of Capital Asset Pricing," *Journal of Economic Theory*, 1976, pp. 341-360 and Stephen Ross, "The Current Status of the Capital Asset Pricing Model (CAPM)," *The Journal of Finance*, June 1978, pp. 885-901.

72. An interesting aspect of the interplay of the actions of management itself upon the development of financial theory is that given by agency costs theory. Agency costs result from the conflict of interest between shareholders and bondholders. The shareholder wishes to lever his investment to the maximum, while the bondholder desires to eliminate all fixed claims after he becomes a creditor of the firm. Since all decision-making power is in the hands of stockholders, however, a transfer of wealth from the bondholders to the stockholders may occur. In order to accomplish this transfer, shareholders hire managers as their agents. By doing so, shareholders may find the solution to one area of conflict, but more certainly, they create a new conflict: that between the agent (manager) and themselves. The risk that is taken by the manager in the case of corporate bankruptcy is normally greater than that taken by the shareholder, since the former normally has a larger share of his own financial health tied up with the well-being of the firm. Thus, the manager should side more with bondholders than with stockholders and make capital structure decisions which are suboptimal from the point of view of stockholders. The real cost of this suboptimality must be borne by some or all of the participants. These costs are known as "agency costs". The optimum capital structure of the firm, according to this agency cost theory, is that which minimizes the costs of agents. For more on agency costs theory see, R. Haugen and L. Senbet, "Resolving the Agency Problems of External Capital Through Stock Options," *Journal of Finance*, June 1981 and M.C. Jensen and W.H. Meckling, "Theory of the Firm: Managerial Behavior, Agency Costs and Ownership Structure," *Journal of Financial Economics*, October 1976.

73. James C.T. Mao, "Survey of Capital Budgeting: Theory and Practice," *Journal of Finance*, May 1970.

54

74. Rex A. Brown, "Do Managers Find Decision Theory Useful?" *Harvard Business Review*, May-June 1970, pp. 78-89.
75. C. Jackson Grayson, Jr., "Management Science 2nd Business Practice," *Harvard Business Review*, July-August 1973, p. 41.
76. J. William Petty and Oswald D. Bowlin, "The Financial Manager and Quantitative Decision Models," *Financial Management*, Winter 1976, pp. 32-41.
77. An area which has come into both theoretical and practical prominence recently, but which seemed to experience a rather extended period of relative obscurity is that of duration and immunization. Immunization refers to the prevention of fixed income portfolios from failing to meet their liability needs as the result of interest rate changes. Duration represents a procedure by which immunization can be achieved. For more on this see, Martin L. Liebowitz, "How Financial Theory Evolves Into the Real World—or Not: The Case of Duration and Immunization," *Financial Review*, November 1983, pp. 271-280 and G.D. Bierwag, George G. Kaufman and Arden Toevs, "Duration: Its Development and Use in Bond Portfolio Management," *Financial Analysts Journal*, July-August 1983, pp. 15-35.

APPENDIX A: SUGGESTED READINGS ON FINANCIAL THEORY CLASSIFIED BY MAJOR SUB-AREAS

Theory is a mixed bag. In some cases it paves the way for the introduction of a new approach to some phase of financial analysis, planning, or control. In other instances, the efforts expended do not produce useful end-results and fall by the wayside.

This chapter is devoted to theory and different aspects are discussed as they appear important to an explanation of a procedure in vogue. Moreover, throughout the book, we indicate the major areas where theory has materialized into practical applications.

In a book which focuses primarily on financial management, however, restraint must be exercised in the presentation of theory in order not to overstep the boundaries that separate polemics from actual issues. The aim in this area is to have sufficient discussion to provide an understanding of the current status and role of theory in the development of useful financial management principles.

Still, there may be some financial managers who are interested in the fine points of theory, the details of the disagreements that exist, or in phases whose applications are so far distant that they do not warrant discussion in the book at this stage. For those who do want to probe further, therefore, we have developed a bibliography (classified by major sub-areas) that is much more detailed than that shown in other chapters of the text.

A. SOME OF THE MAJOR CONTRIBUTIONS IN THE DEVELOPMENT OF CAPITAL MARKET THEORY

Black, Fisher, "Capital Market Equilibrium with Restricted Borrowing," *Journal of Business*, July 1972.
Blume, Marshall, E., "On the Assessment of Risk," *Journal of Finance*, March 1971.
———, and Irwin Friend, "A New Look at the Capital Asset Pricing Model," *Journal of Finance*, March 1973.
Fama, Eugene F., "The Behavior of Stock Market Prices," *Journal of Business*, January 1965.
———, "Portfolio Analysis in a Stable Paretian Market," *Management Science*, January 1965.

Lintner, John, "The Aggregation of Investors' Diverse Judgement and Preferences in Perfectly Competitive Security Markets," *Journal of Financial and Quantitative Analysis,* December 1969.

———, "The Valuation of Risk Assets and the Selection of Risky Investments in Stock Portfolios and Capital Budgets," *Review of Economics and Statistics,* February 1965.

Markowitz, Harry M., "Portfolio Selection," *Journal of Finance,* March 1952.

———, *Portfolio Selection: Efficient Diversification of Investments,* New York, John Wiley and Sons, 1959.

Merton, Robert, "An Intertemporal Capital Asset Pricing Model," *Econometrica,* September 1973.

Roll, Richard, "A Critique of the Asset Pricing Theory's Tests," *Journal of Financial Economics,* March 1972.

——— and Stephen A. Ross, "An Empirical Investigation of the Arbitrage Pricing Theory," *Journal of Finance,* December 1980.

Ross, Stephen, "The Arbitrage Theory of Capital Asset Pricing," *Journal of Economic Theory,* 1976.

———, "The Current Status of the Capital Asset Pricing Model (CAPM)," *Journal of Finance,* June 1978.

Sharpe, William F., "A Simplified Model for Portfolio Analysis," *Management Science,* January 1963.

———, "Capital Asset Prices: A Theory of Market Equilibrium Under Conditions of Risk," *Journal of Finance,* September 1964.

Von Neuman, J., and Oscar Morgenstern, *Theory of Games and Economic Behavior,* Princeton, N.J., Princeton University Press, 1947.

B. TESTS OF CAPITAL MARKET THEORY

Black, Fisher, Michael C. Jensen, and Myron S. Scholes, "The Capital Asset Pricing Model: Some Empirical Tests," published in *Studies in the Theory of Capital Markets,* ed. Michael Jensen, New York, Praeger, 1972.

Blume, Marshall E., "Betas and Their Regression Tendencies," *Journal of Finance,* June 1975.

——— and Irwin Friend, "Risk, Investment Strategy, and Long-Run Rates of Return," *Review of Economics and Statistics,* August 1974.

Blume Marshall E., "The Relative Efficiency of Various Portfolios: Some Further Evidence," *Journal of Finance,* May 1980.

Brennen, M.J., "Capital Market Equilibrium with Divergent Borrowing and Lending Rates," *Journal of Financial and Quantitative Analysis,* December 1971.

Fama, Eugene F., and James D. MacBeth, "Risk, Return and Equilibrium: Empirical Tests," *Journal of Political Economy,* May-June 1973.

Friend, Irwin, and Marshall E. Blume, "Measurement of Portfolio Performance Under Uncertainty," *American Economic Review,* September 1970.

Graver, Robert R. and Nils H. Hakansson, "Higher Return, Lower Risk: Historical Returns on Long-Run, Actively Managed Portfolios of Stocks, Bonds, and Bills, 1936-1978," *Financial Analyst's Journal,* March-April 1982.

Jacob, Nancy, "The Measurement of Systematic Risk for Securities and Portfolios: Some Empirical Results," *Journal of Financial and Quantitative Analysis,* March 1971.

Jensen, Michael C., "Capital Markets: Theory and Evidence," *The Bell Journal of Economic and Management Science,* Autumn 1972.

King, Benjamin F., "Market and Industry Factors in Stock Price Behavior," *Journal of Business,* January 1966.

Klemkosky, Robert C., and John D. Martin, "The Effect of Market Risk on Portfolio Diversification," *Journal of Finance,* March 1975.

Levy, Haim, "A Test of the CAPM via a Confidence Level Approach, *Journal of Portfolio Management,* Fall 1982.

Lorie, James H., and Lawrence Fisher, "Some Studies of Variability of Returns on Investment in Common Stocks," *Journal of Business,* April 1970.

Modigliani, Franco, and Gerald A. Pogue, "An Introduction to Risk and Return: Concepts and Evidence I and II," *Financial Analyst's Journal,* March-April and May-June 1974.

Roll, Richard, "A Critique of the Asset Pricing Theory's Test—Part I: On Past and Potential Testability of the Theory," *Journal of Financial Economics,* March 1977.

Sharpe, William F., "Risk-Aversion in the Stock Market: Some Empirical Evidence," *Journal of Finance,* September 1965.

———, "Risk, Market Sensitivity and Diversification," *Financial Analyst's Journal,* January-February 1972.

Sunder, Shyam, "Stationarity of Market Risk: Random Coefficients Tests for Individual Stocks," *Journal of Finance,* September 1980.

C. SOME OF THE SIGNIFICANT TESTS OF THE EFFICIENT MARKET HYPOTHESIS

A. Weak Form Tests

Alexander, Sidney S., "Price Movements in Speculative Markets: Trends or Random Walks," *Industrial Management Review,* May 1961.

———, "Price Movements in Speculative Markets: Trends or Random Walks No. 2," *Industrial Management Review,* Spring 1964.

Fama, Eugene, and Marshall Blume, "Filter Rules and Stock Market Trading Profits," *Journal of Finance,* May 1970.

Mandelbrot, Bendit, "Forecasts of Future Prices, Unbiased Markets and Martingale Models," *Journal of Business,* Special Supplement, January 1966.

Osborne, M.F.M., "Brownian Motion in the Stock Market," *Operations Research,* March-April 1959.

Rosenberg, Barr and Andrew Rudd, "Factor-Related and Specific Returns of Common Stocks; Serial Correlation and Market Inefficiency," *Journal of Finance,* May 1982.

Samuelson, Paul A., "Proof that Properly Adjusted Prices Fluctuate Randomly," *Industrial Management Review,* Spring 1965.

B. Semi-Strong Form Tests

Ball, Ray, and Phillip Brown, "An Empirical Evaluation of Accounting Income Numbers," *Journal of Accounting Research,* Autumn 1968.

Black, Fisher, and Myron Scholes, "The Effects of the Dividend Yield and Dividend Policy on Common Stock Prices and Returns," *Journal of Financial Economics,* May 1974.

Chottiner, Sherman, and Allan Young, "A Test of the AICPA Differentiation Between Stock Dividends and Stock Splits," *Journal of Accounting Research,* Autumn 1971.

Fama, Eugene, Lawrence Fisher, Michael Jensen, and Richard Roll, "The Adjustment of Stock Prices to New Information," *International Economic Review,* February 1969.

Figlewski, Stephen, "Information Diversity and Market Behavior," *Journal of Finance,* March 1982.

Gonedes, Nicholas, "Capital Market Equilibrium and Annual Accounting Numbers: Empirical Evidence," *Journal of Accounting Research,* Spring 1974.

Grossman, Sanford J. and Joseph E. Stiglitz, "On the Impossibility of Informationally Efficient Markets," *American Economic Review,* June 1980.

Hong, Hai, Robert S. Kaplan, and Gershon Mandelker, "Pooling vs. Purchase, The Effects of Accounting for Mergers on Stock Prices," *Accounting Review,* January 1978.

Horowitz, Bertrand, and Richard Kolodny, "Line of Business Reporting and Security Prices: An Analysis of an SEC Disclosure Rule," *Bell Journal of Economics,* Spring 1977.

———, and Allan Young, "An Empirical Study of Accounting Policy and Tender Offers," *Journal of Accounting Research,* Spring 1972.

Kaplan, Robert S., and Richard Roll, "Investor Evaluation of Accounting Information: Some Empirical Evidence," *Journal of Business,* April 1972.

Morse, Dale, "Wall Street Journal Announcements and the Securities Markets," *Financial Analyst's Journal,* March-April 1982.

Patton, J.M., "Ratio Analysis and Efficient Markets in Introductory Financial Accounting," *Accounting Review,* July 1982.

Sunder, Shyam, "Relationship Between Accounting Changes and Stock Prices: Problems of Measurement and Some Empirical Evidence," *Empirical Research in Accounting: Selected Studies,* 1973.

———, "Stock Price and Risk Related to Accounting Changes in Inventory Valuation," *Accounting Review,* April 1975.

C. Strong Form Tests

Cooley, Phillip L., "The Impact and Efficiency of Institutional Net Trading Imbalances," *Journal of Finance,* March 1977.

Finnerty, Joseph E., "Insiders and Market Efficiency," *Journal of Finance,* September 1976.

Jensen, Michael C., "The Performance of Mutual Funds in the Period 1945-64," *Journal of Finance,* May 1968.

———, "Risk, the Pricing of Capital Assets, and the Evaluation of Investment Portfolios," *Journal of Business,* April 1969.

Nierderhoffer, Victor, and M.F.M. Osborne, "Market Making and Reversal on the Stock Exchange," *Journal of the American Statistical Association,* December 1966.

Sharpe, William F., "Mutual Fund Performance," *Journal of Business,* Special Supplement, January 1966.

D. General or Survey Treatments

Baumol, William J., *The Stock Market and Economic Efficiency,* New York, Fordham University Press, 1965.

Blanchard, O.J., "Output, the Stock Market, and Interest Rates," *American Economic Review,* March 1981.

Cootner, Paul H., *The Random Character of Stock Market Prices,* Cambridge, Mass., M.I.T. Press, 1964.

Copeland, Thomas E., "Efficient Capital Markets: Evidence and Implications for Financial Reporting," *Journal of Accounting, Auditing and Finance,* Fall 1978.

Dyckman, Thomas R., David H. Downes, and Robert P. Magee, *Efficient Capital Markets and Accounting: A Critical Analysis,* Englewood Cliffs, N.J., Prentice-Hall, 1975.

Elton, Edwin J., *Modern Portfolio Theory and Investment Analysis,* New York, John Wiley and Sons, 1981.

58

Fama, Eugene, "Efficient Capital Markets: A Review of Theory and Empirical Work," *Journal of Finance,* May 1970.

Frankfurter, George M., "Index Funds: Fad or Foe?" *Journal of Accounting, Auditing and Finance,* Winter 1978.

— — —, and Allan Young, "Financial Theory: Its Message to the Accountant," *Journal of Accounting, Auditing and Finance,* Summer 1983.

Ibbotson, Robert G., and Rex A. Sinquefield, "Stocks, Bonds, Bills, and Inflation: Year-by-Year Historical Returns (1926-1974)," *Journal of Business,* January 1976.

Jensen, Michael C., "The Foundations and Current State of Capital Market Theory," in *Studies in the Theory of Capital Markets,* ed., Michael C. Jensen, New York, Praeger Publishers, 1972.

Malkiel, Burton G., *A Random Walk Down Wall Street,* New York, W.W. Norton and Co., Inc., 1973.

E. Tests of Securities Other Than Common Stocks

Black, Fisher, and Myron Scholes, "The Pricing of Options and Corporate Liabilities," *Journal of Political Economy,* 1973.

Brennan, Michael J. and Eduardo S. Schwartz, "Bond Pricing and Market Efficiency," *Financial Analyst's Journal,* September-October 1982.

Frankfurter, George M., Richard Stevenson, and Allan Young, "Option Spreading: Theory and an Illustration," *Journal of Portfolio Management,* Summer 1979.

Gultekin, N.B., et. al., "Option Pricing Model Estimates: Some Empirical Results," *Financial Management,* Spring 1982.

Hilliard, Jimmy E., and Robert A. Leitch, "Analysis of the Warrant Hedge in a Stable Paretian Market," *Journal of Financial and Quantitative Analysis,* March 1977.

Kose, John, "Efficient Funds in a Financial Market with Options: A New Irrevelance Proposition," *Journal of Finance,* June 1981.

Leabo, Dick A., and Richard J. Rogalski, "Warrant Price Movements and the Efficient Market Hypothesis," *Journal of Finance,* March 1975.

Manaster, Steven and Richard J. Rendleman, Jr., "Option Prices as Predictors of Equilibrium Stock Prices," *Journal of Finance,* September 1982.

Merton, Robert C., et. al., "The Returns and Risks of Alternative Put Option Portfolio Investment Strategies," *Journal of Business,* January 1982.

Rogalski, Richard J., "Trading in Warrants by Mechanical Systems," *Journal of Finance,* March 1977.

D. SOME APPLICATIONS OF CAPITAL MARKET THEORY

Ben-Shahar, Haim, and Frank M. Werner, "Multiperiod Capital Budgeting Under Uncertainty: A Suggested Application," *Journal of Financial and Quantitative Analysis,* December 1977.

Blume, Marshall E., "Portfolio Theory: A Step Toward its Practical Application," *Journal of Business,* April 1970.

Bogue, M., and R. Roll, "Capital Budgeting for Risky Projects With 'Imperfect' Markets for Physical Capital," *Journal of Finance,* May 1974.

Brigham, Eugene F., and Roy L. Crum, "On the Use of the CAPM in Public Utility Rate Cases," *Financial Management,* Summer 1977.

Gahlon, J.M. and J.A. Gentry, "On the Relationship Between Systematic Risk and the Degrees of Operating and Financial Leverage," *Financial Management,* Summer 1982.

Grinyer, John R., "The Cost of Equity, The CAPM and Management Objectives Under Uncertainty," *Journal of Business, Finance & Accounting,* Winter 1976.

Hamada, Robert, "Portfolio Analysis, Market Equilibrium and Corporation Finance," *Journal of Finance*, March 1969.

————, "The Effect of the Firm's Capital Structure on the Systematic Risk of Common Stocks," *Journal of Finance*, May 1972.

Haugen, R. and L. Senbet, "Resolving the Agency Problems of External Capital Through Stock Options," *Journal of Finance*, June 1981.

Jensen, M.C., and W.H. Meckling, "Theory of the Firm: Managerial Behavior, Agency Costs and Ownership Structure," *Journal of Financial Economics*, October 1976.

Litzenberger, Robert, Krishna Ramaswamy and Howard Sosin, "On the CAPM Approach to the Estimation of a Public Utility's Cost of Equity Capital," *Journal of Finance*, May 1980.

Myers, S.C., "The Application of Finance Theory to Public Utility Rate Cases," *Bell Journal of Economics and Management Science*, Spring 1972.

————, and S.W. Turnbull, "Capital Budgeting and the Capital Asset Pricing Model: Good News and Bad News," *Journal of Finance*, May 1977.

Roll, Richard, "Investment Diversification and Bond Maturity," *Journal of Finance*, March 1971.

Rubenstein, Mark E., "A Mean-Variance Synthesis of Corporate Financial Theory," *Journal of Finance*, March 1973.

Rudd, Andrew and Barr Rosenberger, "The Market Model in Investment Management," *Journal of Finance*, May 1980.

Senbet, Lemma W., and Howard E. Thompson, "The Equivalence of Alternate Mean-Variance Capital Budgeting Models," *Journal of Finance*, May 1978.

Sharpe, William F., and Guy M. Cooper, "Risk Classes of New York Stock Exchange Stocks, 1931-1967," *Financial Analyst's Journal*, March-April 1972.

Tobin, James, "Liquidity Preference as Behavior Towards Risk," *Review of Economic Studies*, February 1958.

Weston, J. Fred, "Investment Decisions Using the Capital Asset Pricing Model," *Financial Management*, Spring 1973.

PART II
TECHNIQUES OF
FINANCIAL
ANALYSIS

After demonstrating the relationship between the theory and practice of financial management, we now look at some techniques of financial analysis. Each of the following four chapters represents differing modes of financial analysis and each is applied from the perspective of the financial manager.

3

EXTERNAL FINANCIAL REPORTING: PROFIT AND FUNDS MEASUREMENT AND THEIR USE

3.1 INTRODUCTION

The economist has long been concerned with profits and has fashioned theories to explain both their meaning and distribution. He has associated profits with such notions as underlying property, innovation, social class and monopoly conditions. These ideas cover a wide range and often intertwine and interact. In general, however, there has been a tendency to give more emphasis to the future and to the uncertainties that interfere with the realization of expectations. Three measures of profit which economists frequently discuss are relevant here:

- distributable profits;
- realized profits; and
- economic profits.

Distributable profits, sometimes referred to as sustainable profits, are the amounts that can be distributed to the owners without normally impairing the firm's capacity to maintain operations at current levels.

Realized profits, ordinarily referred to as historical profits, are distributable profits plus (or minus) any realized holding gains (or losses) of the period.

Economic profits, are distributable profits plus (or minus) *all* holding gains (or losses) of the period whether realized or not.[1]

The theorizing of the economist has brought about a better understanding of the term profits and has helped the accountant to develop methods of quantifying it. For the accountant has the responsibility of formulating in actual dollars the net result of all the transactions of a business during a stated period of time and of reporting these results to stockholders, creditors, tax authorities, stock exchanges, the Securities and Exchange Commission (SEC), and other regulatory agencies. Financial management, in turn, not only employs these quantified results in various ways to measure the performance of the whole business and its major segments, but along with the accountant is responsible for the accuracy of the reported information. Consequently, it is essential for financial management to know something about how the accountant obtains his figures.

In small firms, where personnel is limited, the bridge between accounting and finance is easily crossed by having the chief accountant serve as the financial officer. In larger companies, accounting has become so technical that its supervision requires the attention of a specialist, probably reporting to a financial officer, who may not be a professional accountant. It is even possible for the chief financial officer of a division or company to come from an entirely different field, such as sales or engineering, and to *acquire* his understanding of the company's accounting operations through experience. The relationship between the bundle of characteristics and attitudes expected of a firm's top financial officer and his knowledge of accounting is much like that between the skills of the bartender and the art of the brewmaster. The bartender must have some awareness of the flavor and alcoholic content of the ale he stocks in order to provide the brands that best suit his customer's tastes. To run a successful establishment, however, he does not have to understand the technology of preparing mash and adding hop to the liquid wort or the chemistry of breeding yeast strains. These responsibilities fall upon the brewmaster, who has the training and skills to carry them out.

It is important, however, for the financial officer to be reasonably knowledgeable in accounting. This means that he should be familiar with the principles underlying accounting procedures, the type of information that can be obtained, the usefulness and limitations of the data, and the meaning of major financial statements. It is not necessary that he understand the details of accounting technique or be capable of developing and implementing independent systems. These are the responsibilities of the professional accountant. An understanding of accounting concepts is, however, indispensable. And perhaps the most basic of these is the notion of profits.

3.2 THE ACCOUNTING CONCEPT OF PROFITS AND ITS RELATIONSHIP TO FUNDS

In order to measure the results of a company's operations in terms of dollars, the accountant must ascertain both revenues and costs. Revenues represent the inflow of assets, usually charges to customers, resulting from the sale of goods or the rendering of services during a specified period of time, called the accounting period. Costs are measured by the acquisition prices paid for the goods sold or the services rendered, and include not only the costs in the current period but also allocations of outlays in prior periods plus accruals for outlays to be made in future periods.

This represents income determination through historical cost. In recent years, with the rapid pace of inflation casting increasing doubt upon the meaningfulness of profit figures based on historical cost, the accounting authorities in this and other countries have begun requiring supplementary profit reports which account for the effects of price level changes. These developments will be considered at some length later in this chapter.

The net income or profits of any period are arrived at by matching costs against revenues recognized in the period. For this purpose a determination must be made of the revenues that should be allocated to a specific period, as in the case of a long-term contract extending over several periods. The matching process then requires an allocation of costs between the revenues of the current period and the expected revenues of the future period. For the specified accounting period, therefore, the profits reported depend upon the portions of the total flows of revenues recognized during the period and the related costs included in the period's financial statement. The difference, called income or profits, reverts to the benefit of the proprietors and is reflected in the change that takes place in their ownership interests, after allowing for any amounts withdrawn.

Qualitative factors of judgment are so important in profit determination that the same accounting methods may not be appropriate for measuring and reporting in different cases. Results shown, however, may be strikingly different in each case.

Thus, behind the very concrete facade of profits expressed in specific dollars-and-cents terms is a flexible structure of accounting conventions resting upon the opinions of the accountant and the aims of management. Within the framework of accounting consistency, therefore, there are many opportunities for the decisions of the accountant to influence the reported income.

It seems to us that two principal reactions stem from the fact that profits are not only the inevitable outcome of decisions to use limited resources in certain ways, but depend as well upon recording and interpretive *judgments*. The first is the acceptance of reported profits as a tool of operating policy so that for purposes of external reporting they may be varied, within legal and accounting limits, to conform with immediate objectives. The second is the quest to standardize the profit concept as much as possible so that for analytical purposes profits may be employed as a measure of performance.

These two reactions seem poles apart because one exploits variability while the other seeks stability. Yet, more deeply, they both arise from the tenuous nature of profits, a characteristic that enables management to use profits according to its own needs—which means deliberately creating variability in certain instances, and trying to minimize it at other times. In both cases, the criteria are management's awareness of the extent to which reported profits may be controlled and its willingness to do so.

Of the profit related figures a firm produces, clearly the most widely used item is earnings per share. In its simplest sense earnings per share represent income (revenues less expenses) divided by the number of shares outstanding. And for many years companies computed their earnings per share in this manner. Considerable confusion arose, however, when companies began financing their external equity needs and paying executives with securities which were convertible into common stock (such as convertible preferred stock, convertible bonds, warrants, stock options, and rights) rather than with common stock itself. Such securities, when issued in lieu of common stock, often represented common stock in the eyes of their holders and were traded as such. Under these circumstances, firms issuing such convertible securities could avoid an increase in shares outstanding and thus a reduction in earnings per share, while firms issuing common stock would reflect a decrease in earnings per share as the result. In trying to ameliorate this inequitable situation, the Accounting Principles Board (APB) (then the rulemaking body in the accounting profession) issued a mandate (APB Opinion #15) which called for convertible securities which were essentially common stock issues to be reflected as such in the computation of earnings per share. As a result, companies with outstanding securities which are convertible into common stock with a potential diluting effect on the computation of earnings per share of 3 percent or more are required to report two earnings per share—primary (using only common shares and common share equivalents outstanding) and fully diluted (assuming the conversion into common shares of all securities with conversion rights).[2]

[1] PROFITS AS A TOOL OF POLICY

In the early days of corporate development that stockholders who owned the business also ran it. As the enterprise grew, an increasing number of shareholders found it necessary to entrust the operations to a small number of talented individuals. And gradually there emerged a new group of professional corporate managers.

The gap between ownership and control has continued to widen. On the one hand, the typical large corporation now has so many stockholders that it is difficult to conceive of any suitable administrative technique that would permit them as a group to assume serious operational responsibilities. In the future the large institutional investors may become focal spots around which more authority may be centered, but even the institutions have thus far avoided assuming this responsibility. On the other hand, the increasing difficulty of administering such complex organisms has continued to strengthen the role of the managerial class in our corporate society.

Control of the corporation today, therefore, rests largely with its management, represented by its officers. True, the officers are appointed by directors, who in turn are elected by the stockholders. In fact, the officers initially designate the directors, who select them—and the stockholders, in the ordinary course of events, simply approve the directors chosen by the officers. Occasional proxy fights ripple the smooth waters of this arrangement and lead to major organizational changes. But these are passing storms, and the administration of the modern corporation is substantially in the hands of its professional managers in their role as virtually self-perpetuating trustees. This disenfranchisement of stockholders is further exacerbated by the system through which external auditors are chosen. External auditors are assumed to be independent of and watchdogs of managerial actions. Yet since the auditors are proposed by management and rarely ever challenged effectively in the proxy system, an anomalous situation results in which management chooses its own watchdog. This has called into question the degree of independence of external auditors, which has been highlighted by huge bribes to foreigners and others by corporate officials and by impending insolvencies which have gone undiscovered by the external audit. Further, the degree of managerial choice inherent in accounting principles additionally serves to enhance managerial discretion over reported profits.

The action which results from this situation depends largely upon the primary objective of management, which, many business students contend, is to maximize profits. Perhaps it is true that all management's decisions, even those that appear to be guided by social aims, are actually drawn by the profit magnet, so that corporate expenditures of funds to eliminate community inconveniences like excessive noise are designed to cultivate community goodwill in order to obtain profitable franchises; expenditures to improve the lot of employees are intended to minimize turnover and reduce costs; gifts to universities are motivated by a desire to develop a future source of professional employees; and subcontracting jobs are awarded to small suppliers with an eye to Congressional reactions to corporate bigness. Certainly, the history of pricing policies and conflict-of-interest situations in some of the country's best known firms has at least tarnished the notion of a public-interest objective.

Nevertheless, there are appraisers of the business scene who feel that the objectives of the modern firm go beyond the profit drive. They contend that management recognizes its broader responsibilities to labor, suppliers, customers, the communities where its plants operate, and the public in general. To meet these varied objectives, management may deliberately incur expenditures that cut profits but serve some social end. In the words of one writer, this view appears to urge the executive to assume an infinitely broad-gauge burden of responsibilities to all of the various 'publics' with whom he deals.[3]

Even the professional economist has wondered about the truth of his traditional theory of profits maximization, outside the hypothetical realm of pure competition. The fact may be that in the real and uncertain world the profit motivation has been so obscured by offsetting circumstances that it can no longer be recognized as the single, all-inclusive drive. Authors of finance textbooks generally presume that management is seeking, as its primary goal (or at least should seek as its primary goal), the maximization of shareholder wealth. The complex nature of our business environment, and indeed our society, makes the validity of such a simplistic notion highly dubious. Thus, although for analytical purposes it may be convenient to assume that management's prime objective is the maximization of shareholder wealth (in order to more easily present managerial techniques) the reality may be quite different.

In the light of these conflicting issues, it seems reasonable to assume that even if corporate managers have profits in mind, they must make money decisions, based upon more immediate objectives, which are less than optimal from the standpoint of profits alone. During the conduct of their year-to-year activities, some managements undoubtedly will find it desirable to report conservative profits for different reasons: to reduce current tax payments, to ward off efforts at absorption by larger firms, to discourage the entry of new competitors in the field, to ease pressure for higher dividend and wage payments and to decrease the likelihood of government intervention and increased regulation. Similarly, they may prefer reporting liberal profits to facilitate financing, to take advantage of large losses by other divisions in the same organization, to raise bonus payments, to gain shareholder support, to enhance the value of stock options, and so on.

We do not think it necessary to attempt to resolve these issues now. Whatever its immediate or long-term objectives, the important thing is that management and the public generally must be provided with facts. And the facts in this case are that in any one year profits may be oriented, within certain bounds, to conform with immediate objectives, which may differ from one period to another. The financial officer has the responsibility of establishing these limits of possible variation, of keeping attuned to the shifting requirements of management, and of attempting to bring reported profits in line with these aims.

[2] FUNDS AND THEIR RELATION TO PROFITS

Before moving further with our analysis of external profit reporting techniques, it is appropriate in delineating the gossamer nature of reported profits to discuss their relationship to corporate funds. And before this can be done, a description of corporate funds is needed.

In Part III of this text, we analyze in some detail the problems associated with short-term sources and uses of funds. In Parts IV and V, we extend this analysis to the intermediate and long-term areas. At present, though, we are only concerned with explaining the various funds concepts commonly used and those additional fund concepts which have been proposed.

We will begin with the most narrowly based and easily defined fund concept and then move to successively broader and more complex notions of corporate funds. Throughout it is necessary to keep in mind that any of the foregoing funds concepts can be, and in some cases have been, used as the pivot around which is developed the Statement of Source and Application of Funds. (These statements are often called Statements of Changes in Financial Position, and are discussed below.) Moreover, while many fund concepts are possible, the one which is best for a particular firm depends upon the nature of its short-term asset and liability accounts. For example, if a firm's non-cash current assets can be readily converted into cash, a rather broad fund concept is perhaps called for to appropriately comprehend the firm's fund position. If some or all of a firm's non-cash current assets are somewhat illiquid, however, a narrower funds concept would be appropriate in order to retain like items within the funds sphere.

The various funds concepts are listed below:

(a) *Cash.* This is the narrowest funds concept.[4] As indicated, this concept is appropriate when there are potential liquidity problems with other current assets. Perhaps there is some question as to the speed with which receivables will be collected or the amount which will be realized. Alternatively, inventories may be substantially raw materials or work-in-progress, in which case the realization of cash may be some time away. In these cases cash alone would probably be the appropriate funds concept to avoid confounding the funds pool with both liquid and illiquid items. When cash is used as the funds concept, the Statement of Source and Application of Funds is similar to the cash budget analyzed in Chapter 8. The primary difference is that a cash budget is future oriented, or pro forma, whereas the Statement of Source and Application of Funds is historical.

(b) *Quick Assets.* When a firm's cash, marketable securities and accounts receivable are similar in liquidity, but its inventories are rather far removed down the liquidity scale, the quick assets might be grouped to form the funds concept.

(c) *Net Quick Assets.* A slight variation is the net quick assets concept, which would be appropriate when the bulk of the current liabilities are due in a short period of time and thus represent virtually an immediate cash drain. Net quick assets are quick assets less the current liabilities.

(d) *Current Assets.* When the liquidity of all current assets is assured,[5] they may be treated as a whole, so far as the funds concept is concerned. In this case we are assuming that cash runs freely and rapidly from inventory to accounts receivable to cash and back to inventory.

(e) *Net Current Assets or Net Working Capital.* By far the most common funds concept in use is net current assets or working capital (current assets less current liabilities). Under this concept all working capital items are assumed to be similar in terms of liquidity. The working capital accounts are then grouped together in preparing the Statement of Source and Application of Funds so that only the net change in the working capital total need be shown; changes in the individual accounts which make up the working capital pool need not be discussed.

(f) *All Resources.* The all resources concept is both the most difficult to explain and the most complex to present in statement form. In preparing Statements of Source and Application of Funds using the other fund concepts we are only trying to present those transactions which gave rise to either a source or application (use) of funds. For this to occur, in effect, both a fund account and a non-fund account must be involved in the transaction. For example, the sale of common stock for cash reflects a change in both a fund account—cash, and a non-fund account—common stock. However, if the stock was sold for land, buildings or some other non-fund asset, only non-fund accounts would be involved and the transaction would be excluded from the Statement of Source and Application of Funds under all fund concepts other than the all resource concept. Using the all resource concept, even transactions affecting only non-fund accounts are included in the Statement of Source and Application of Funds, in this regard a more complete, though at times a more complex, statement is produced. Because more forms of financing and fund utilization are included in the all resource funds concept it is often considered by authoritative opinion to be the superior funds concept for purposes of maximum disclosure of financial information.

We should note that the APB, in its Opinion No. 19, mandated the preparation of a Statement of Changes in Financial Position (to be included in the annual report) which, in effect, is a Funds Statement or Statement of Source and Application of Funds. This statement is to be prepared for external reporting purposes using either net working capital or cash as the funds concept. These concepts are to be expanded, however, to the all resources level and should include any exchanges between non-fund accounts.

Now that we have reviewed the various fund concepts, let us look at the relationship of funds to profits. Perhaps the best way to begin is to show how one adjusts, in a typical Statement of Source and Application of Funds, the profits figure to reach the funds obtained through operations. In doing this we must keep in mind that there frequently is a difference between the theoretically optimum disclosure which could be made (in terms of presenting the information in its most meaningful form) and the actual disclosure made in practice.

Regardless of the fund concept used, there are often a number of transactions (and almost always at least one transaction) which, while affecting the corporate profits figure, does not affect the firm's fund position. (That is, there are certain transactions which either serve to increase or decrease corporate net income but which do not result in either an increase or decrease in corporate funds.) By far the most common of these transactions is the annual recording of depreciation. The typical entry to accomplish this is:

Depreciation	XXX
Allowance for depreciation (To record annual depreciation)	XXX

The Allowance for Depreciation is a valuation account and serves to reduce the original cost of the fixed asset by the amount of depreciation charged (or written-off) to date. The difference between the original cost of the fixed asset and the Allowance for Depreciation represents the so-called book value of the fixed asset, which is the amount of depreciation to be charged to subsequent periods. Further, the depreciation account will appear in the income statement as a deduction from profits. While profits are reduced by the above transaction, no outflow of funds has occurred. Thus profits after depreciation do not correctly represent the amount of funds that operations generated. Because of this, it is necessary to add back depreciation, to profits after depreciation, in order to reach the amount of funds generated by operations. This is accomplished as follows:

Profits or Net Income	XXX
Plus Depreciation	XXX
Total Funds Generated by Operations	XXX

This form of disclosure gives us a very clear answer to the sometimes confusing issue of—"Is depreciation a source of funds and if so, in what sense?" It should be clear that, in and of itself, depreciation provides no funds and is *not* a source of funds. The annual recording of depreciation is merely an accounting allocation of a portion of the original cost of a fixed asset to the current period in the form of a deduction from profits. And since this deduction from profits does not require an outflow of funds, it needs to be added back to profits in order to compute funds generated by operations. In itself, however, depreciation is not a source of funds. In order to see this more clearly and also to understand the only sense in which depreciation may be thought of as a source of funds, we might ask the question—"Would we have more funds if for some reason, we had more depreciation?" The answer to this question is yes, but only on an after-tax basis. On a before-tax basis if we have more depreciation we have lower net income and the same amount of funds generated by operations. Since depreciation is a tax deductible item, however, on an after-tax basis more depreciation will mean less taxes to pay and therefore more funds retained by the firm. Therefore, in itself, depreciation is not a source of funds.[6]

There are other items, like depreciation, which must be added back to net income to determine funds generated by operations. Some of these items are tax deductible, but some are not. Some examples of non-fund deductions from net income which are tax deductible are depletion, losses on sales of fixed assets, casualty losses or expropriations of assets, and ammortization of certain items other than goodwill. Goodwill is amortized or written off by charges to net income which do not require an outflow of funds. Thus amortized goodwill is added back to net income in computing funds generated by operations. However, in no sense can the amortization of goodwill be considered a source of funds as the procedure does not result in a tax deductible item.

In addition, there are other transactions which give rise to additions to net income which do not add to the corporation's funds pool. And just as non-fund deductions from net income must be added back to reach funds generated by operations, non-fund additions must be subtracted. Some examples of such items are amortization of premiums on initial issuance of a bond; the capitalization of certain interest payments during construction which results in cash outflows for the interest payments without corresponding deductions from net income; and increases in net income which result from non-consolidated subsidiaries carried as investments on the equity basis which have earnings in excess of the dividends they pay.[7] (In effect, the parent company's income is increased by an amount greater than the cash it receives from its subsidiaries as dividends.)

Finally, in terms of the relation of funds to profits, funds are far more definite and determined with less choice of measurement techniques (as will be shown below, for cash there is *no* choice of measurement technique), whereas, reported profits are substantially under managerial discretion. In addition, profits may not be at management's disposal to use for the enterprise (especially if wide latitude has been used in profit reporting techniques), while funds (especially if they are in the form of cash) can be used to pursue the goals of the firm. Thus both the external analyst and the financial manager must look at the firm's fund position and any change in it, as depicted in the Statement of Source and Application of Funds, just as carefully as they look at a firm's reported profit figures; further, they can probably have more confidence in the funds analysis.

[3]   THE STATEMENT OF SOURCE AND APPLICATION OF FUNDS AND AN ACCOUNTING SYSTEM BASED UPON CASH FLOWS

We now expand our discussion of funds generated by operations to an analysis of an entire Statement of Source and Application of Funds. We will not be constructing such a statement, for that is purely an accounting job. We will, however, focus on those transactions which give rise to an increase in the funds pool (source of funds) and those which constitute uses of this pool (applications of funds).

We first present the typically major components of additions to and uses of corporate funds. It is rather easy to do this in a systematic manner because for each source of funds there is a corresponding and frequently related use of funds. Moreover, the difference between sources and uses of funds during any time period must, by definition,[8] be precisely equal to the change in the funds pool. If sources exceed uses, an increase in the funds pool equal to the difference will have occurred. If uses exceed sources, a decrease in the funds pool equal to this difference will result.

There are four major sources of corporate funds and we list them in what is at the present time their order of importance for U.S. corporations in the aggregate.

1. *Funds Generated by Operations.* As noted above, this is net income plus non-fund deductions from net income less non-funds additions to net income.

2. *Issuance of Debt.* This represents the incurrence of non-fund debt. If cash—or any concept which does not include current liabilities—is the funds concept used, the incurrence of any debt would be viewed as a source of funds. On the other hand, if net working capital is the funds concept, only long-term debt would constitute a source of funds.

3. *Sale of Corporate Stock.* When the corporation sells its common or preferred stock this is another source of funds if the consideration received is an asset which is part of the funds pool or the elimination of a liability which is included within the funds concept.

4. *Sale of Assets.* If assets are sold, this represents a source of funds if the consideration received is an asset which is part of the funds pool or the elimination of a liability which is within the funds concept.

As noted above, there is a corresponding and often associated use of funds for each of the above sources. Therefore, our listing of uses is meant to relate to the above ordering of sources.

1. *Cash Dividends on Common or Preferred Stock.* Stock dividends or stock splits are not uses, only cash dividends, which are frequently compared to net income to produce the payout ratio—cash dividends per share on common stock divided by net income per share to common stockholders (see chapter 14).

2. *Repayment of Debt.* This represents sinking fund or other repayment of debt with fund assets.

3. *Repurchasing of Corporate Stock.* A relatively recent phenomenon in its large scale occurrence is the corporate repurchase of its own stock. If cash or other fund assets is the consideration given up by the repurchasing corporation, this constitutes a use of funds (see chapter 21).

4. *Purchase of Assets.* If non-fund assets are purchased with fund assets or if fund liabilities are incurred, a use of funds results. Acquiring fixed assets is the largest single use of funds by U.S. corporations in the aggregate.

Schematically, the above may be presented as follows:

Sources of Funds	Uses of Funds
Funds Generated by Operations	Cash Dividends
Issuance of Debt	Repayment of Debt
Sale of Corporate Stock	Repurchase of Corporate Stock
Sale of Assets	Purchase of Assets

Difference Represents Change in Funds Pool

It has been argued that the funds statement was an underutilized accounting tool that has recently come into its own. Its value to the financial manager both for planning and controlling the flow of funds and for strategic planning purposes is now becoming increasingly recognized.

But even beyond recognizing the value of the funds statement, some accounting theorists have begun to advocate using a fund or cash-flow based accounting system to substitute for the now accepted cost-based accrual accounting system. This makes for something of a cycle in the development of accounting thought in that the conceptual framework of that discipline began with cash-basis accounting, has moved to the present state of cost-based accrual accounting, and will probably in the future move to the utilization of some concepts of value accounting among which cash-flow concepts are being proposed.[9] [10] The value of cash-flow accounting, its advocates maintain, goes beyond the difficulties created by the considerable managerial choice inherent in the present state of cost-based accrual accounting. The major benefits of cash-flow accounting lie in their greater congruence to one of the basic objectives of business, which is to make a cash return, and the primary means of evaluating investment decisions, which is through analysis of projected cash flows.

"A firm may hold various types of assets, but the reason that the firm holds such assets is always attributable to a cash-flow objective, i.e., to recover more than was invested."[11] The AICPA recognized this in terms of financial statements by stating in 1973 that "An objective of financial statements is to provide useful information to investors and creditors for predicting, comparing, and evaluating potential cash flows to them in terms of amount, timing and related uncertainty. If cash flows are the central issue, then well-classified data on the past cash flows of the firm seems to be more directly relevant to this objective than data on the assets and liabilities of the firm"[12] as presented in traditional cost-based accrual accounting. Moreover, capital budgeting decisions are largely determined on the basis of forecasted cash flows, yet performance evaluation is largely based on profit reports that employ cost-based accrual accounting. This is confusing since an investment can look good on one basis and poor on another. "To avoid the discrepancy in the two bases, we have to either base investment decisions on profit flows, or base performance evaluation on cash flows."[13] Relevant to the above, it has been noted that, it is impossible to argue against the applicability of discounted cash flow concepts for decision making. Thus, we must convert performance evaluation from accrual accounting to cash flow accounting. Otherwise, we will put managers in the intolerable position of making decisions one way and having their performance evaluated another way. At present, however, cost-basis accrual accounting remains the basic framework in use.

In light of the above, a system of cash flow accounting has been proposed which is similar to, but has important differences from, the old cash basis of accounting. Under this system some related cash receipts and disbursements are netted (residual cash flows) and some cash flows unaccompanied by cash receipts or disbursements are still recognized (constructive cash flows). With these changes, the old cash basis of accounting is converted to a system which is akin to the cash-flow concept used in capital budgeting. By employing the premise that "cash flows are the fundamental blood circulation in business life and that accounting should be geared to focus upon them," this system of accounting represents a rather drastic departure from traditional cost-based accrual accounting.[14]

Of course, the present practice of classifying assets into the various asset accounts normally shown on the balance sheet makes some sense from a cash-flow standpoint in that these accounts are listed in order of their respective liquidity and thus the ordering is somewhat indicative of the amount and the risk of the cash that is expected to be received upon liquidation. If the objective of accounting is to generate better forecasts of future cash flows, however, a classification system by types of investment projects—perhaps by industry and related business segments—is far more appropriate than the present one based on the types of goods and services acquired. This is particularly the case for a firm engaging in different types of business with differing business risks.

We have looked at funds statements, the difference between cash flow and profits, and a proposal for an accounting system based on fund-flows as opposed to the profit concept of cost-based accrual accounting currently in use. It is now appropriate for us to analyze the present system of accounting for profits.

3.3   ACCOUNTING FOR PROFITS

[1]   AN HISTORICAL PERSPECTIVE

We begin our analysis of accounting for profits with a historical overview of the development of the concept as perceived by accountants and economists. An understanding of the evolution of profits is useful in attempting to grasp the meaning of the efforts of the accounting profession to come to grips with this concept in the contemporary environment. Moreover, the current accounting issues developed later in the chapter will come more clearly into focus with such a historical perspective.

The methods and concepts employed by the accounting profession to determine business profits have changed over time paralleling, but lagging behind, the development of economic theory in this area. Perhaps the first great and unifying economic theorist, and almost certainly the first to treat the question of the determination of business income within a consistent and comprehensive framework of the economic behavior of society, was Adam Smith. Yet although the theory of double entry bookkeeping had been developed almost three centuries before *The Wealth of Nations* was written (1776), (and it is generally believed that this system of recording and classifying business transactions was in operation for an even longer time) during this entire period there was no generally accepted method of computing the income of an enterprise on a conscious and consistent basis over regular time intervals; nor were there any noteworthy theoretical expositions on this subject. Even in the latter part of this period, when the greatest progress was made, the principal accounting treaties dealt mainly with the treatment of types of ledger accounts and different types of transactions. Some authors dealt with the closing of individual accounts, and others advanced a little further by considering the appropriate procedure for the formal closing of the ledger from time to time. But the subjects which preoccupy the accountants of our era, primarily the valuation of assets and the calculation of profit, took up very little space in the accounting treatises of that day and generally were touched upon only in passing in connection with the closing of the accounts.

Even when, in a few rare instances, methods of stating asset values were dealt with in some slight detail, the effect of the method on the calculation of profit was not considered.[15]

Moreover, the practice of accounting for profits was certainly not in advance of the theoretical expositions. Frequently, books were kept in such a manner that there was no attempt to separate the capital account of the proprietor or partners from the profit and loss accounts. It was common to find that not all of the assets or liabilities of a firm were included in the ledger. Hence, the account books of a business were frequently imperfect documents for establishing its wealth. Yet in those days, the needs of business usually did not require the determination of profit. Business ventures were small and outside equity capital was rarely used. And until the theory of an appropriate method of income determination could be developed, the practice of accounting, which normally lags behind theory anyway, spent little time calculating profit. Therefore, both in England and America, practicing accountants did not begin to attempt to determine income on a consistent basis until well into the nineteenth century.

However, in *The Wealth of Nations,* Adam Smith defined income as what can be consumed or is available for consumption by an individual or an economic entity without encroaching upon its capital. An accountant could work with this definition in computing a firm's income for a period in the following fashion: He would determine the difference in the value of the net wealth as of two points in time and then add back a consumption allowance. Equipped with this basic definition of income, accountants had a direct procedural device for computing it. This is the so-called net worth method.

The translation of Smith's definition of income into accounting theory and the creation of the net worth method of income determination are marked by what has come to be known as the balance sheet approach. In this approach, the balance sheet is thought of as the crystallization of the financial position of a business and its primary financial statement. The chief emphasis of the accounting procedures are placed upon obtaining a balance sheet which will adequately reflect a firm's assets, liabilities, and ownership equity as of a specific date. Therefore, transactions are analyzed in terms of their effect upon the assets and liabilities of the firm, and profit can be computed by comparing the difference between these two quantities as of specific dates.

In 1818, F.W. Cronhelm enunciated the net worth method in a form close to the one used until well into the modern era. In *Double Entry by Single,* published in London, he tells us that:

the purpose of bookkeeping as a record of property is to show the owner at all times the value of his whole capital, and of every part of it. The component parts of property in trade, are in a state of continual transformation and change; but, whatever variations they undergo, and whether the whole capital increase, diminish, or remain stationary, it is evident that it must constantly be equal to the sum of all its parts. This equality is the great essential principle of bookkeeping.[16]

From here it is but a short jump to applying Smith's definition of income to the accounting records. For once Cronhelm laid down the principle that assets and liabilities are opposite in nature and mutually destroy each other so that the net worth or capital must always be equal to the difference between them,[17] the idea of computing income as the difference between the respective net worths at two points in time could not be far off. Thus, Cronhelm was able to conceive of measuring profits and losses as increases and decreases in capital.

However, perhaps reflecting the low order of importance which was given to income figures at that time, the theoretical accounting foundation for the net worth method of computing income was not completed and made operational until a full 42 years after Adam Smith had laid down the basis for this method by defining income. Moreover, there was a much greater time lag until this method became the generally accepted accounting procedure for computing income. A guide to the beginning of general acceptance of the net worth method in Great Britain is the Companies Clauses Consolidation Act of 1845. Sections 115-119 of this act, among other things, regulate the accounting procedure of the nation's railroads,

> ...a bookkeeper was to be appointed to 'enter the accounts in books', and accounts were to be kept and books balanced at prescribed periods. 'On the books being so balanced an exact balance sheet shall be made up, which shall exhibit a true statement of the capital stock, credits, and property of every description belonging to the company, and the debts due by the company at the date of making such balance sheet, and a distinct view of the profit or loss which shall have arisen on the transactions of the company in the course of the preceeding half-year.'[18]

While this statute did not prescribe that the net worth method be used to determine profit and loss, it clearly requires a company to take a balance sheet approach to their accounts and, therefore, makes this method the most feasible one for them to use. Eventually, almost all other enterprises followed the railroads, and accounting practice began to utilize the balance sheet approach. Once this approach was adopted, the net worth method of income determination was the natural counterpart. This occurred by the 1850's, more than three-quarters of a century after *The Wealth of Nations*. General acceptance of the net worth method in the United States came somewhat later than in Great Britain. In the nineteenth century, Great Britain was more industrially developed than the United States and so probably had an earlier need for profit figures. But eventually, the net worth method also gained ascendancy here, as our business system became more complex and the need for balance sheet figures in the normal conduct of business became widespread.

There were many great economic theorists in the decades immediately following Adam Smith, but from the viewpoint of the development of accounting theory none had as much influence in laying the groundwork for the emergence of the cost-revenue matching theory of income determination as did Alfred Marshall, whose *Principles of Economics* first appeared in 1890. Marshall maintained that the net income of a business should be computed by deducting from its revenue the expenditures incurred in the production of this revenue. "If a person is engaged in business, he is sure to have to incur certain outgoings for raw material, the hire of labor, etc. And, in that case, his true or net income is found by deducting from his gross income the outgoings that belong to its production."[19]

Yet although Marshall's work had gone through eight very popular editions by the late 1920's, a review of accounting literature at that time suggests that the matching concept, the equivalent of which he had laid down as his definition of income, was not generally accepted either in accounting theory or practice. The leading authorities at that time, both in Great Britain and in the United States, seemed to agree that the "increase in net worth" concept of income was acceptable in principle.[20]

For the purpose of dating the general acceptance of the matching concept, September 22, 1932, is of great significance. On that day, the American Institute of Certified Public Accountants (AICPA) officially commenced the drive to attain general acceptance of this concept. A committee of the AICPA, which was to work with the New York Stock Exchange to adopt more effective methods of income determination, sent a letter to the Exchange. In this letter, the Committee rejected the "increase in net worth" concept and accepted the position that the matching concept was preferable since it emphasized the cardinal importance of income determination. However, again we find a large time lag between the derivation of the definition of income by an economist and general acceptance of this definition for accounting purposes.

After the matching concept was adopted there was a shift in emphasis from the balance sheet to the income statement. Yet much criticism was leveled at the accounting profession from within for, among other things, failure to take the now burgeoning cash flow approach which was discussed earlier. But economists had been voicing this criticism for many years before accounting theorists had begun to take account of these concerns.

Perhaps the most noteworthy economist critic of the accounting profession during the early twentieth century was Thorstein Veblen. Of his criticisms of the profession none were more penetrating nor perhaps more apropos than his rebuke for their use of the stable monetary unit assumption. (This assumption is largely still in use—though techniques which result from it are now popular—and will be discussed below.)

But once again a considerable time lag is evident between the relevant writings of Veblen (*The Instinct of Workmanship* in 1914 and *Absentee Ownership and Business Enterprise in Recent Times* in 1923) and the first serious attempts by accounting theorists to face the patent fallacy of the assumption that in income determination related costs and revenues are matched although their incurrence may have taken place during times of widely differing price levels. Henry Sweeney's *Stabilized Accounting* in 1936 was the first serious attempt to adjust financial statements to take account of price level changes. But Sweeney's techniques have never been adopted.

The Study Group on Business Income in 1952 was one of the first groups of eminent accountants to really give serious consideration to the questions first raised by Veblen almost forty years before. And, as shown below, it hasn't been until recently that the SEC and the accounting profession have begun to issue specific proposals for providing alternate reported profit statements which take account of changing price levels. Recent pronouncements of the FASB, as well as those by accounting theoreticians, have further attempted to infuse current accounting practice with the thinking of economic theorists some years ago. The relationship between the proposals with respect to cash flow accounting discussed earlier and the views of Milton Friedman and other monetarists is another case in point and makes highly tenable the expectation that in the not-too-distant future, accounting concepts for reporting profits will be primarily based on cash flow.

Yet accountants and economists have divergent goals and perspectives and thus the lags noted above should be expected. The financial manager must look beyond these divergent views of accountants and economists with respect to income determination and the lag before the practice of the former begins to catch up with the theories of the latter can be highlighted by the following dilemma, noted in an era when the matching concept is well accepted by most practicing accountants: "If earnings is the difference between the worth of the firm at the beginning and at the end of the accounting period, then analysis of a firm's worth logically precedes measurement of earnings, rather than the other way around."[21]

[2]   THE FASB, THE SEC AND THE ACCOUNTING PROFESSION[22]

We now briefly review the rulemaking bodies in the accounting profession and their interrelationship. Basically, with the exception of various governmental regulatory agencies which have accounting jurisdiction over the industries they regulate (i.e., the Interstate Commerce Commission with respect to the railroads), the rulemaking bodies in the accounting profession are the SEC and the FASB.

Since 1973, the FASB has been the designated organization in the private sector for establishing standards of financial accounting and reporting.[23] Those standards are, in effect, rules governing the preparation of financial reports. FASB standards are officially recognized as authoritative by the SEC (Accounting Series Release 150, December 1973) and the AICPA (Rules of Conduct, as amended May 1973).

The SEC has statutory authority to establish accounting and reporting standards under the Securities Act of 1934. Throughout its history, however, the Commission's policy has been to rely on the private sector for this function so long as this sector fulfills its responsibilities in the public interest.

The seven FASB members have diverse backgrounds, but they must possess knowledge of accounting, finance, and business and a concern for the public interest in matters of financial accounting and reporting. They serve full time, are compensated, and are required to sever all previous business or professional connections before joining the Board. They are aided by a staff of forty technical specialists plus administrative and other support personnel.

The FASB is the operating part of a tripartite structure that is independent of all other business and professional organizations. The other two parts of this structure are the Financial Accounting Foundation (FAF) which is responsible for organizing, funding, and exercising general oversight over the FASB, and the Financial Accounting Standards Advisory Council, the activities of which will be described below. Funds are obtained through contributions and sales of publications.

Contributions are received by the FAF, which is incorporated to operate exclusively for charitable, educational, scientific, and literary purposes within the meaning of Section 501(c)(3) of the Internal Revenue Code.

Approximately half the funding is provided by industry and the financial community, and approximately half by the public accounting profession. No single contribution of more than $50,000 (less than 1 percent of the budget) can be accepted under the FAF's By-Laws.

The FAF is responsible for selecting the members of the FASB and its Advisory Council and for exercising general oversight (except with regard to the FASB's resolution of technical issues). The FAF has a salaried executive director.

The FAF has no other functions; it is separate from all other organizations. Its Board of Trustees, however, is made up of nominees from six sponsoring organizations whose members have special knowledge of, and interest in, financial reporting. The sponsoring organizations are:

1. American Accounting Association (academic);
2. American Institute of Certified Public Accountants (public accounting);
3. Financial Analysts Federation (investors and investment advisors);
4. Financial Executives Institute (corporate executives);
5. National Association of Accountants (primarily management account-ants); and
6. Securities Industry Association (investment bankers, brokers).

The Financial Accounting Standards Advisory Council has responsibility for consulting with the Standards Board as to major technical issues, the Board's agenda and the assigning of priorities to projects. They also consult with the FASB on matters likely to require the attention of the FASB, selection and organization of task forces, and such other matters as may be requested by its chairman or the FASB chairman. The Council has 35 members who are broadly representative of relevant constituencies including government, law, academe, large and small businesses, large and small accounting firms, investors, credit grantors and other users of financial information. The Council has a chairman and an executive director, both salaried.

The FASB issues statements of financial Accounting Standards (and Concepts) and Interpretations. Statements establish new standards or amend those previously issued. Interpretations clarify, explain, or elaborate on existing standards. Before it issues a Statement, the FASB is required by its rules to follow extensive "due process" procedures.

The FASB has sought to expand its role and rule on all technical accounting issues for the private sector. But pressure from some members of Congress and public interest groups for standard-setting to be taken away from practicing accountants and placed in the public sector has constantly followed the efforts of the FASB. Such groups assert that it is questionable whether CPA's are independent of business interests which hire their services. Thus, the FASB's ability to act in the public interest, they assert, is also questionable.[24] The attitude of the SEC toward the FASB has generally been favorable. SEC reports to Congress on the accounting profession show that they feel accountants have taken significant strides in regulating themselves but warn that much more needs to be done. The accounting profession, at the prodding of the SEC and some members of Congress, has also sought to strengthen the degree of independence of external auditors. Its success in this regard, however, has been questioned. The Commission has expressed concern that the growing array of non-audit services offered by independent public accountants and the importance of revenues generated by such services to the profits and competitive position of such accountants may have an adverse effect on the independent objectivity and professionalism of auditors.

A special category of SEC practicing accounting firms for those auditing publicly held corporations has been set up. In addition, the system of peer reviews, (extensive checking by outside auditors of the internal procedures, controls, and performance of an auditing firm) has been strengthened— though perhaps not to the extent demanded by many public interest groups and the critics of the accounting profession—and even has been extended to foreign affiliates of American companies.

[3] KEY AREAS IN ASSET DISCLOSURE AND PROFIT REPORTING

It has been often stated that all accounts in the balance sheet, except cash, present management with the opportunity to choose among a variety of accounting principles, each of which is said by the profession to be generally accepted. Moreover, balance sheet assets are unexpired costs which, when removed from the balance sheet, appear as deductions from revenue in the income statement. Therefore, choices with respect to accounting principles for balance sheet assets inevitably affect the reported profits of the firm. In this subsection we look at some of the areas of choice for recording and disclosing balance sheet assets. We are not attempting to provide a complete compendium of all of the choices or all of the accounts which are subject to choice. Nor are we attempting to delve into all of the currently debated issues of accounting choice. We will, in this subsection, merely present some of the more important asset areas in which significant accounting choices are available.[25] In the next two subsections some additional areas of accounting choice which affect reported profits are presented.

(a) Accounting for Accounts Receivable

Practices may differ with respect to modifying the carrying value of accounts receivable through bad debt allowances to take varying business conditions into account. The allowance will presumably be based upon experience, but there is considerable latitude in reaching the final decisions. This latitude, in turn, has its influence on reported profits through the recognition of bad debt expense.

Where receivables are large, as in the case of commercial banks, hidden reserves may be established by writing down outstanding accounts. In other instances no reserves are established, and receivables may be written-off as they become worthless. If no allowances are provided, the amount reported in the balance sheet may be overstated.

(b) Accounting for Inventories[26]

Aside from some of the more unusual methods of costing out inventory[27] as products are sold, the three predominant inventory costing assumptions are FIFO (first-in-first-out), LIFO (last-in-first-out), and Average (moving or weighted). Companies are free to choose from among these methods although they can differ considerably in reported profits and inventory carrying values. Figure 3.1 relates these differences to changing price levels. The extent of the difference in reported profits between one inventory costing method and another depends upon the extent of the price change for a firm and the level of its cost of goods sold.

FIGURE 3.1 *Profits and ending inventory carrying value of various inventory methods in relation to price level movements*

	PROFITS		INVENTORY CARRYING VALUE	
	Prices Rising	Prices Falling	Prices Rising	Prices Falling
FIFO	Highest Profits	Lowest Profits	Highest Ending Inventory Value	Lowest Ending Inventory Value
LIFO*	Lowest Profits	Highest Profits	Lowest Ending Inventory Value	Highest Ending Inventory Value
Average	Middle Profits	Middle Profits	Middle Ending Inventory Value	Middle Ending Inventory Value

*However, an invasion of the LIFO base can seriously distort earnings as holding gains can then come into play.

In addition to differences in reported profits in any year, the various inventory costing methods result in differences in the stability of year-to-year reported profits when both increases and decreases in prices occur. Contrary to popular belief (which often has it that the average, being in the middle for both rising and falling price levels, would have the greatest stability in year-to-year reported profits), LIFO gives the greatest stability in year-to-year reported profits with FIFO the least stable. LIFO gives the closest temporal matching of costs and revenues, minimizes realized holding period gains or losses, and so results in the most stable year-to-year reported profits. FIFO, on the other hand, maximizes realized holding period gains or losses and so results in the least stable year-to-year reported profit figures. However, it should be remembered that we are not speaking of real economic differences in profits, but only differences in accounting reported profits. Thus, the appearance of stable reported profits for a LIFO firm or volatile reported profits for a FIFO firm may be spurious and purely the result of the inventory costing convention each firm chooses to use.[28]

Finally, as to inventories, there is a basic inconsistency in accounting theory with respect to the "lower of cost or market rule". This rule states that inventories should be carried at their original cost only if this amount is lower than their market value. When the market value of inventories falls below their original cost a write-down of inventories and a reduction in profits is to take place in the period the decline in market value occurs. The purpose of this is to place the accounting recognition of the loss in the period of decline in economic value rather than in the period of sale. No complementary entry, however, is to be made as the result of inventory market values rising above their original cost. Thus, according to the lower of cost or market rule, unrealized losses are to be recognized in a firm's financial statements, but unrealized gains are not accorded a similar treatment. This result grows largely out of a philosophy of conservatism on the part of accountants, but is at variance with objectivity. Consistency is thus sacrificed for conservatism. But more serious is the consideration that in practice, market values of inventories are not always objectively determinable and considerable estimation is normally required. Thus, with discretion over write-downs (especially as to timing), the lower of cost or market rule often gives management another area of accounting choice and one which is potentially amenable to manipulation.

(c) Accounting for Non-Consolidated Subsidiaries or Investments

A common cause of income variation is the treatment of the activities of subsidiaries. To provide a complete view of earnings, companies may prepare a consolidated statement on the theory that the undistributed earnings of a subsidiary eventually revert to the benefit of the parent firm. Within the framework of regulations prescribed by both the SEC and the Internal Revenue Code, therefore, they prepare financial statements that aggregate the revenues and costs of the parent and subsidiaries in a combined statement reflecting their net overall operations. Conversely, when a company does not consolidate the statements of controlled subsidiaries, it may be able to influence its own reported earnings by changing the flow of dividends received from units within the system.

In order to take advantage of broadening world markets, American corporations have established many wholly or partially owned subsidiaries abroad. The extent to which the profits from such subsidiaries should be counted creates interesting problems. If the foreign country imposes restrictions against the transfer of funds, it would seem reasonable not to count such profits. Even if restrictions do not appear at the moment, unsettled international conditions and experiences with once stable countries like Cuba or Iran suggest that such profits cannot be treated on the same basis as those from domestic operations. To resolve this uncertainty, some United States companies show earnings from foreign operations in their own accounts only to the extent that funds have been transferred to the United States. (For accounting for international operations generally, see Chapter 23.) This is the so-called "cost or market whichever is lowest," or more simply the "cost basis," mentioned above. The other method of interest in this area is the "equity basis."

Generally speaking, under the cost basis, only dividends paid by a subsidiary to a parent are counted in determining the earnings of the parent. Also, in using the cost basis, a parent company retains the carrying value of its investment in the non-consolidated subsidiary at its original cost so that all of the profit or loss on a subsequent sale of this investment will be allocated to the year of sale. On the other hand, under the equity method, a ratable share of the yearly profits or loss of the subsidiary are considered profits or loss to the parent. Further, the carrying value of the non-consolidated subsidiary is changed under the equity method to conform ratably to changes in the equity accounts of the subsidiary. Thus the profit or loss on subsequent sale of the subsidiary will be different under the equity basis than under the cost basis. Also, to the extent that dividends and earnings are not equal, a parent company's profit will vary depending upon the method used.

The above can best be illustrated by means of an example. Let us assume that on 1/1/x1 investor company I buys a 20% interest in investee company I' and accounts for this investment on a non-consolidated basis due to the modest percentage of ownership. We illustrate accounting for this investment on both the cost and equity basis in Figure 3.2. Let us assume that I paid

$1,000,000 for its investment in I', that during each of the years x1, x2, and x3, I' had total net income of $100,000 and paid total dividends of $50,000. Finally, on 1/1/x4 I sells its interest in I' for $1,300,000.

FIGURE 3.2 *Cost vs. equity basis for non-consolidated subsidiaries*

	Cost Basis		Equity Basis*	
Original Purchase of I' (1/1/x1)	Investment in I'	1,000,000	Investment in I'	1,000,000
	Cash	1,000,000	Cash	1,000,000
Dividend Payments (12/13/x1, 12/31/x2, 12/31/x3) ($50,000 x 3 x .2)	Cash	30,000	Cash	30,000
	Profits from I'	30,000	Investment in I'	30,000
Net Income of I' (12/13/x1, 12/31/x2, 12/31/x3) ($100,000 x 3 x .2)	No transaction recorded		Investment in I'	60,000
			Profits from I'	60,000
Sale of I' (1/1/x4)	Cash	1,300,000	Cash	1,300,000
	Investment in I'	1,000,000	Investment in I'	1,030,000
	Gain on Sale of I'		Gain on Sale of I'	
		300,000		270,000

*In addition to the treatment shown here, the equity basis also calls for a reduction of both the investment account and retained earnings by the investor firm for the amortization of goodwill on the investment should it be recognized. (A discussion of goodwill appears later in this chapter.) This reduction of the investment account is considered an expense of the investor associated with its share in the earnings of the investee. Of course, where the excess of purchase price over net assets can be allocated with specific assets, such an allocation should be made. In this case no goodwill is recognized.

Note that by using the cost basis the investment's total profits for x1, x2, and x3 would be lower by $30,000. However, in x4 I would have a $30,000 larger gain on the sale of I' under the cost basis than under the equity basis.

Which of these methods a financial manager might use depends largely upon the ownership percentage of the investee company by the investor and the individual circumstances of this relationship. Ownership of less than 20 percent of the voting control of a firm is considered insufficient by accounting authorities to justify any special treatment beyond recognition of the investment as a holding of marketable securities which calls for the cost or market whichever is lower basis described above. Further, when the degree of ownership of one corporation by another reaches the 20 percent level, there is presumed to be a relationship in which the investor firm exerts a significant influence over the affairs of the investee company. When one corporation exerts such a considerable influence upon another, accounting authorities now maintain that it is appropriate to account for this investment on the equity basis. Finally, in cases where the degree of ownership exceeds 50 percent and thus a majority interest exists, the relationship is normally considered to be that of a "parent and a subsidiary." In such cases consolidation of financial statements is normally deemed to be appropriate (except where reason dictates that the entities should not be combined, as for example, in the case of legal or governmental restrictions or when the firms are not economically compatible, such as a bank and a manufacturing firm). The current required accounting treatment of intercorporate stock ownership as a function of the degree of voting control is illustrated in Figure 3.3.

FIGURE 3.3 *Intercorporate stock ownership and accounting treatments*

Degree of Voting Control	Accounting Treatment
Less than 20%*	Lower of Cost or Market Basis
20% - 50%**	Equity Basis
In excess of 50%	Consolidation (except where consolidation is unreasonable)

*The equity basis can be used in this case if the investor firm can demonstrate a significant influence over the affairs of the investee firm.
**The cost basis can be used if it can be demonstrated that a significant influence does not exist.

Presumably, however, a firm owning 39 percent of the outstanding common shares in another firm and wishing to use the cost basis to account for its investment, might transfer half of its holdings to a 100 percent owned subsidiary, whereupon cost treatment would be allowed both for the parent and the 100 percent owned subsidiary. (Throughout the past few decades some rather "creative" accounting has been employed to account for nonconsolidated subsidiaries.)

The policies of IBM in this area represent a classic illustration of a corporation that has gone through three accounting stages. Through 1960, the company reported in its income statement the dividends received from its wholly owned World Trade Corporation (cost basis). Effective January 1, 1961, the firm changed its policy and included in its earnings the net earnings of IBM World Trade Corporation, instead of only the cash dividends received by IBM from that corporation. The net earnings of IBM World Trade Corporation, in turn, were defined to represent cash dividends, royalties, and income received by it in the United States, less expenses and foreign income taxes (modified equity basis). Thus the undistributed net earnings of IBM World Trade's foreign subsidiaries continued to be excluded.

Finally, starting with the statement for the first quarter of 1964, IBM changed its policy again and reported its financial results on a worldwide fully consolidated basis (effectively on a full equity basis.)

By and large, corporations which are against consolidating the earnings of foreign subsidiaries claim that such a practice would be misleading because it would place in retained earnings funds not necessarily available for dividends. The SEC simply requires that a registrant not consolidate any subsidiary which is not majority-owned. At the same time, the company must make appropriate disclosure of its consolidation policy.

(d) Accounting for Fixed Assets

Current values arise from economic conditions which, in turn, reflect numerous business, monetary, technological, psychological, and political forces. This combination of circumstances may cause sweeping changes in values and, if incorporated into financial statements, will affect reported earnings. Adjustments in plant valuations, as an illustration, correspondingly modify depreciation charges, which are an accepted earnings deduction.

Accountants favor the cost theory of reporting fixed assets for income purposes, but some insist that accepting current values is more realistic for other purposes. Because of the importance of this decision, it may be decided on grounds of financial policy. As a result, many companies which express depreciation on the basis of the acquisition prices of assets in their published financial statements, restate it for planning purposes in their internal cost accounts using specific price indices.

The management of many firms still have a dual attitude toward depreciation: on the one hand, they feel that this procedure leads to inadequate depreciation charges and an overstatement of reported income and thus use current replacement cost for internal purposes. Another factor that may affect the periodic depreciation charge is the amount of salvage ascribed to obtain the net value of the assets to which the depreciation is applied. In general, therefore, the higher the salvage value the lower the periodic depreciation charge. But it is not always easy to establish the amount that will be recovered through salvage, and variations in this estimate will affect reported profits.

A company acquires its buildings, equipment, and other fixed assets because they are believed essential to carry on the firm's activities. It is logical, therefore, to prorate the costs of these assets over the time that they contribute to production or sales. This writing-off process takes place through periodic allocations called depreciation or depletion, depending upon the type of asset involved. The amount of these charges is determined according to accounting convention, income tax regulations, market conditions and personal judgments. Not only may the decisions reached cause sharp variations in the earnings of particular years, but their long-run influence may be significant. The importance of the depreciation charge may be gauged by the fact that it is one of the major variables affecting reported profits.

In addition to the straight line procedure, the tax code permits firms to use various methods which accelerate the depreciation of the fixed assets.[29] By using one of the faster write-off procedures, a company is able to keep more funds during the early years of an asset's life when its productivity is highest and its use greatest. Once a method is chosen, it must generally be applied consistently for tax purposes, although changes are permissible for good reasons. These elections give management considerable leeway in determining the annual depreciation charge to income.

It is not uncommon for a corporation to report depreciation on one basis for tax purposes and on another basis for financial reporting purposes. When the amount of the depreciation charged in the accounts is materially less than that deducted for income tax purposes, long-standing generally accepted accounting policy stipulates that a charge be included in the income statement to recognize that future tax will be paid on the amount by which the tax depreciation exceeds the book allowance. The implications of the difference between the two depreciation rates may be seen in the fact that the deferred income tax established as a result of this procedure may actually exceed the amount currently reported.

(e) Accounting for Intangibles

An old problem that has been given renewed life with the growing importance of business combinations and research is how to account for the intangible assets of goodwill, patents, trademarks, trade names, copyrights and other such items.

Their inclusion in balance sheets appears justifiable because they represent an outlay which will contribute to earnings, but this factor is extremely difficult to gauge. In addition, assuming these intangible assets are counted, the question arises of the appropriate amortization period. Theories on this problem range from legal life to usable life to the indefinite retention of value. Once more, these issues may be resolved by the financial manager on the basis of policy rather than accounting principles. And again, management has a good deal of choice in these matters.

The merger movement of recent years has put the spotlight on the accounting for merger and acquisition transactions. When two companies combine, the acquisition may be recorded as a purchase or a pooling of interests. Assume Company A, through issuing its own stock with a market value of $2.5 million, buys the net assets of Company B, carried on B's books at $2 million. If the transaction is treated as a purchase, the $500,000 differential will be recorded as an intangible asset like goodwill and will probably be amortized over time; if the transaction is treated as a pooling of interests, Company A will record the acquisition at the carrying values on the books of the acquired company, or at a net asset value of $2 million, recognizing no goodwill.

The above indicates a significant difference between purchase and pooling of interests accounting. But the differences between these two methods and the reasons why acquiring firms normally much prefer the pooling procedure go far deeper.

First, contrary to the sound of the term, acquiring firms do not like to have goodwill recorded on their books. Among the reasons for this are the effects of recording goodwill on the calculation of the return on total assets of the firm. With goodwill placed on the books of the firm, total assets are greater and the return on total assets lower. In addition, once goodwill is recorded, it is normally amortized or written off (usually over the expected life of the assets which are acquired) by charges against net income. This results in a lower reported income subsequent to the purchase transaction than would have been the case if pooling of interests accounting had been used and no goodwill initially recorded. This disadvantage of purchase accounting is increased by the fact that amortization of goodwill does not result in a tax deductible item. Therefore, while the incurrence of a tax deductible expense of $1.00 results in an after-tax reduction of net income of $.50 (assuming a 50% tax rate), the amortization of $1.00 of goodwill results in a $1.00 reduction of net income.

But the advantages in the mind of the financial manager of the acquiring firm of pooling of interests accounting over purchase accounting are often greater than that shown above. In the case of purchase accounting no earnings on the acquired assets are assumed to have accrued to the acquiring firm until the acquisition occurs. Only from the acquisition date forward can purchase accounting result in earnings to the acquiring firm. In the case of pooling of interests, however, the recording makes it appear as though the acquired and acquiring firms had always operated as a single combined entity. Therefore, all retained earnings of the acquired firm are added to the retained earnings of the acquiring firm. Moreover, and perhaps more importantly, all earnings of the acquired firm during the year of acquisition are added to the earnings of the acquiring firm. This is so not only for earnings on the acquired assets subsequent to the acquisition date, but also with respect to earnings for the year which occurred prior to the acquisition date. Thus, even though a pooling of interests acquisition may occur on the last business day of the year, the entire yearly earnings of the acquired firm will be added to the yearly earnings of the acquiring firm. Undoubtedly, many acquisitions which were accounted for by the pooling of interests method were undertaken in order to increase the net income of the acquiring firm in the year of acquisition.

There are even more advantages of pooling of interests over purchase accounting to the acquiring financial manager. Let us take the case of the acquiring firm A mentioned above, which issued its own stock with a market value of $2.5 million to buy the net assets of Company B which are valued on B's books at $2.0 million (assume total assets of $3 million and total liabilities of $1 million). Further, assume this transaction takes place on 12/31/x1. If this transaction is accounted for as a purchase it would be recorded on A's books as follows:

Purchase

12/31/x1	Assets	3,000,000	
	Goodwill	500,000	
	Liabilities		1,000,000
	Shareholders' Equity		2,500,000

On the other hand, if the transaction is accounted for as a pooling of interests it would be recorded on A's book as follows:

Pooling

12/31/x1	Assets	3,000,000	
	Liabilities		1,000,000
	Shareholders' Equity		2,000,000

Note that the pooling treatment not only employs the fiction noted above that the two firms always operated as one, but, in effect, also compounds this fiction by valuing the consideration given up by Company A at $2,000,000, when the market value of this consideration was $2,500,000. And this seeming Alice in Wonderland game of calling a transaction something one knows it is not can go on still further under the pooling method. Let us assume that two years later Company A sells Company B for $2,250,000. All reasonable businessmen would understand this as a loss of $250,000 (Purchase for $2,500,000 worth of stock and sell for $2,250,000 in cash.) And, in fact, purchase accounting gives this result:

Purchase

12/31/x3	Cash	2,250,000	
	Liabilities	1,000,000	
	Loss on sale of		
	Company B	160,000	
	Assets		3,000,000
	Goodwill		410,000*

*Assume goodwill is written off over a 20 year period. Thus $90,000 of the original goodwill has been written off, leaving a balance of $410,000.

In the fiction-ladened world of pooling of interests accounting, however, the sale of Company B for $2,250,000 would result in a gain of $250,000 as follows:

Pooling

12/31/x3	Cash	2,250,000	
	Liabilities	1,000,000	
	Assets		3,000,000
	Gain on sale of		
	Company B		250,000

It is not surprising from the above that pooling of interests accounting is much favored by acquisition minded firms. It should also be obvious from the above, however, that not only is pooling of interests accounting theoretically deficient, but also that the method has been much maligned by security analysts and the investing public generally. Yet there have been cases of mergers and acquisitions not being consummated solely because the auditor of the acquiring firm would not allow the pooling treatment. This seems odd in that the advantages of pooling over purchase accounting are all in the accounting cosmetics of the transaction rather than in any real economic superiority.

The disaffection of security analysts and the investing public with the pooling approach grew to such an extent that the accounting rule-makers finally had to limit the application of this procedure. This resulted in the regulation that pooling could only be applied to a business combination which lasts at least two years and holdings in the newly formed company between the former separate entities is no greater than 9:1.[30] In other words, if Company A and Company B pool their separate interests to form Company C, the stockholders of the smaller, formerly separate entities must be given an ownership interest in the newly formed company of at least 10%. The idea was to prevent a large company from acquiring a far smaller firm and calling the transaction a pooling of interests when the former owners of the smaller acquired firm retained a relatively insignificant proportion of the ownership of the newly formed firm. Yet this rule is presumably easily subverted (in a manner similar to that discussed above for accounting for non-consolidated subsidiaries on the equity basis) by using a dummy corporation to engage in the acquisition. For example, assume Company A is worth 20 and wishes to acquire Company B, worth 1, and still account for the transaction as a pooling of interests. Seemingly, all Company A need do is transfer 9 of its value to a newly formed firm, say, Company C.

Finally, in terms of intangibles, a brief note is in order as to the sense in which accountants ascribe the state of intangibility to the assets which fall in this category. Contrary to popular belief, intangibility is not in the sense of a lack of knowledge or agreement upon the appropriate valuation for the items in this category. In the illustration above, once purchase is agreed upon, the appropriate valuation for goodwill is readily determined once the terms of the acquisition are ascertained. Thus, intangibility is not in terms of an uncertain valuation. The sense in which accountants apply the term "intangible" is in terms of the corporal or physical state of the item not being readily observable. For, while the amount of goodwill at the time of an acquisition is easily determined, its physical presence cannot be observed. One can observe cash, marketable securities, inventories, fixed assets, etc., but one cannot observe goodwill.

(f) Asset Items Not on the Balance Sheet

Finally, before leaving the asset area and moving on to some additional areas of accounting choice, a concluding note is in order as to what are and what are not the kinds of assets found on the balance sheet. In order for an item to appear as an asset on the balance sheet, it must stem from an external exchange and there must be a related identifiable service potential and future benefit stream (i.e., the timing of future benefits must be known). This satisfies the accountant's requirement of a systematic matcing of costs and revenues. In this sense, assets are unexpired costs and once their expiration occurs, a write-down is indicated and a charge in the income statement results. (This is the sense in which the income statement and the balance sheet tie into one another.) Thus the acquisition of plant and equipment results in an exchange and a service potential, which leads to charges to income as the service potential declines and as the original cost is allocated to the period of use. Frequently, however, some of a company's most valued service potentials do not appear as assets on its balance sheet.[31] This often occurs when no direct exchange has taken place in order for the firm to have developed the service potential. For example, the quality of the research people at Corning Glass Works does not appear anywhere on that company's balance sheet. Yet it may represent the company's most valuable service potential. The new uses for glass developed by the Corning research staff has been of incalculable value to the firm in the past and may be of similar value in the future. Yet lacking a direct and measurable relationship between the service potential of its research staff and an observable exchange, Corning cannot place the quality of its research staff on its balance sheet. Similar statements can be made about the value of the *espirit d'corp* and general employee relations at IBM. Yet here, too, the service potential does not appear on the balance sheet. Thus, one needs to remember that the balance sheet is not meant to be the repository for all of a firm's service potentials.

[4] SOME ADDITIONAL ISSUES AND AREAS OF ACCOUNTING CHOICE

There are a number of further accounting choices available to the financial manager, some of which we will now develop.

(a) Influencing the Flow of Reported Earnings

Management has some leeway in determining the period in which it elects to recognize revenues in its financial statement, in allocating certain credits to income, and in deflecting revenues directly to retained earnings rather than first moving them through current income. We consider each of these areas in turn.

[i] TIMING THE REPORTING OF REVENUES: In theory, revenues are recognized in the period when they become reliably measurable, provided that a substantial portion of the revenue-related costs have been incurred and any remaining costs can be estimated with reasonable accuracy. In practice, accountants have generally relied upon the occurrence of a market transaction to signal revenue recognition, which in turn has led to the common point-of-sale timing policy. In manufacturing, construction, or service contracts, this is normally when the goods have been delivered and accepted, the facilities completed and accepted, or the services satisfactorily rendered. Under certain types of contracts, however, particularly where performance extends over a substantial period of time and where total profit may be estimated with some degree of confidence, there is precedent for prorata recognition of profit as the work progresses. To make this determination, estimates may be based on deliveries, expenditures, or percentage of completion.

The timing of the recognition of revenues thus becomes a problem whenever a company is engaged in contracts involving long-term construction, deliveries in installments, or the performance of services over a period of time. In such cases, management has a degree of freedom in stretching out or shortening the delivery or performance schedules to complete the job. These decisions, in turn, affect the amount of profits reported from period to period.

A good illustration of timed recognition of profits on long-term contracts is seen in shipbuilding. Here it is common practice for a company to prorate estimated earnings by applying the percentages of completion in each year to the estimated total earnings for its contracts. Thus, profits will be recorded prior to the completion of all matters relating to a contract, and estimates of final results may be revised as work progresses. Consequently, the amount of profit recorded in a particular period could include a portion applicable to work performed in prior periods. Recording profits on a percentage of completion basis, however, can avoid the reported earnings distortions which can result from following the more conservative completed contract method.

[ii] ACCOUNTING FOR CREDITS TO INCOME: The investment tax credit (ITC) offers an interesting illustration of accounting problems that arise in coping with a legislative enactment and the differing effect on income of available choices. Following the adoption of the original measure, there was considerable discussion about the most appropriate means of accounting for the ITC. Various methods were suggested. Reflecting these diverse attitudes, the statement of the APB on the subject indicated some internal disagreement. Essentially, it was generally accepted that the taxes payable should be reduced by the amount of the ITC in the year during which the eligible equipment was acquired; the disagreement arose with respect to the accounting periods during which the ITC should be reflected in income.

The APB suggested two basic concepts regarding the substance of the ITC. According to one, (the so-called "deferral method") the ITC reflected a reduction in the cost of property, with benefits to income arising from the subsequent reductions of depreciation; the APB indicated that this method "may be preferable in many cases." The other approach considered the ITC a reduction in reported income tax expense, with the prevalent view favoring the recognition of the benefit in net income over the productive life of the acquired property rather than having it "flow through" the income statement in the year of acquisition.[32]

In effect, therefore, two basic methods of accounting for the ITC are permissible, with differing influences on income. To illustrate their effects, let us assume that at the beginning of the taxable year a company acquires property at a cost of $10,000 with a depreciable life of 10 years, employs a straight line basis of depreciation, has a net income each year of $11,000 prior to depreciation, and a federal income tax rate of 50 percent. The company's ITC is $1,000 ($10,000 x 10 percent).[33] Under the deferral, by which the carrying value of the asset is reduced by the amount of the ITC, the entries might appear as shown below. Within the framework of this method, the same result could be obtained by originally offsetting the debit entry of $1,000 of taxes payable against a deferred income account, and subsequently eliminating this account over a 10-year period by annual credits of $100 to net income or tax expense. Whichever approach is used, in this method the cash benefits of the ITC are obtained immediately but the profit effect is spread over the life of the asset. Thus, net income after taxes would be $5,100[34] each year (assuming the same conditions), and after 10 years the full $1,000 of ITC would be recovered. The accounting entries appear as follows.

Property	$10,000	
Cash		$10,000
(To record the acquisition of the property for cash.)		
Tax expense	$ 5,000	
Taxes payable		$ 5,000
(To record the original tax expense, which is		
50 percent x [$11,000 - ($10,000/10)])		
Taxes payable	$ 1,000	
Property		$ 1,000
(To reduce taxes payable and write down the		
carrying value of the asset by the amount		
of the ITC.)		
Depreciation	$ 900	
Allowance for depreciation		$ 900
(To record the annual depreciation charge		
on the acquisition cost of the property		
less the amount of the ITC.)		

Under the flow through method, the total income effect is fully reflected in the year of asset acquisition. The entries appear as follows:

Property	$10,000	
Cash		$10,000
(To record the acquisition of the property for cash.)		
Tax expense	$ 5,000	
Taxes payable		$ 5,000
(To record the original tax expense.)		
Taxes payable	$ 1,000	
Tax expense		$ 1,000
(To reduce taxes payable by the ITC and include this amount in the income of the period.)		
Depreciation	$ 1,000	
Allowance for depreciation		$ 1,000
(To record the annual depreciation charge on the acquisition cost of the property.)		

In this method, income is benefited immediately and there is no effect on the results of subsequent periods. Thus, in the year of property acquisition, net income would be $6,000[35] and in each subsequent year would be $5,000 until the property is written off (assuming the same conditions). With two basic methods permissible for handling the ITC, corporations clearly would be inclined to select the one most suitable for their own purposes.

[iii] DEFLECTING REVENUES TO RETAINED EARNINGS: Ordinarily, revenues can result in profits that are either distributed to the owners or kept within the business. When a company has diverse activities, reporting problems may ensue; and it may show income as gains from nonrecurring transactions,[36] or conversely, it may direct certain income items directly to retained earnings. With respect to costs, too, a company may also make certain nonrecurring charges to income or directly to retained earnings. Accountants have tended to favor the so-called clean surplus rule, under which all the gains and losses of a period are reflected in that period's net income. Nevertheless, a contrary viewpoint exists, and disagreement may occur with respect to both the inclusion of unusual and nonrecurring items in the calculation of net income and the disclosure of such items; accordingly, management has some discretion in determining the extent to which such items may affect net income.[37]

(b) Influencing the Amount of Costs Reported

In most instances, management probably has more control over the extent to which costs are taken up in the income statement than it has over the inclusion of revenues. The decisions affecting costs, in turn, may revolve about what specific charges should be created, and what allocation methods to use.

[i] COSTS CREATED THROUGH SPECIAL CHARGES TO EARNINGS: By appropriating some retained earnings for a specified purpose, management limits dividends and provides a buffer against future contingencies. But management has at times elected to extend this practice by charging *the current* year's earnings to create special reserves that suit its own ends.[38] This technique has been employed to give an appearance of stability to profits that otherwise would fluctuate widely and has come to be known as income smoothing.

[ii]   ALLOCATING COSTS TO REVENUES[39]: In the course of operating its business, a firm experiences many different kinds of costs. Some are clear-cut and easy to record. Others are difficult both to gauge and to account for; their treatment depends upon personal judgments which could materially affect earnings. The areas discussed below provide some indication of this elasticity—of how differing opinions on the recording of costs could influence reported profits.

(A)   Product Costs vs. Period Costs: Products costs are included in the inventory value of an item and are therefore taken into account as an expense when the product is sold; period costs are expensed on a time consumption basis regardless of the number of products sold. A firm's policy may range from full costing, which includes in the value of inventory all costs associated with making the final product salable, to direct costing, which includes in inventory only those costs that vary with output.[40] But whatever policy is adopted, the problem remains of decomposing the two kinds of costs into those applicable to the product and those applicable to the period. Accordingly, reported earnings may vary because of both accounting policy and the cost-differentiating techniques employed within a given area.

(B)   Joint-Product and Joint-Facility Costs: Joint-product costs refer to those incurred in producing a raw material which is converted into different end items, as in petroleum refining. Here the problem is to work out a method of distributing the basic production costs among the various processed goods. Joint-facility costs occur when one plant makes different items. An example is the heat and light used in a multi-product building, where it is necessary to work out a method of allocating the joint costs to the different end products. While these decisions affect the distribution of costs rather than the total amounts involved, they may influence prices charged customers, taxes paid, inventory values, and, as a result, overall profits.

(C)   Capitalized Costs: The decision involved in handling cost outlays is whether to write them off during the period they are incurred or to consider them as capitalized items to be amortized over several years.

The question typically arises in connection with large expenses for plant maintenance, as for repainting a factory. In this case the choice is between adding the costs to the value of the building to be written off through depreciation charged over time, or including them with the expenses of the current year. Theoretically, the answer depends upon whether or not the outlay increases the service life of the plant, either by augmenting its rate of production or by extending its economic life. If this occurs then capitalization is appropriate. But often this distinction is not easy. To resolve the problem, some firms simply establish materiality guideposts based on designated amounts of expenditures; costs greater than a minimum level are capitalized, while those below are expensed.

In the technologically competitive aircraft industry, costs to develop new programs run into large sums. Once more, the question arises of how these expenditures should be treated. The policies of the companies have varied with respect to when charge-offs should occur. These policies, in return, have exerted a considerable influence on reported earnings and have even affected financial decisions.

Squarely within this area is the question of what disposition a company should make of its research and development outlays. Expenditures of this nature, while made in one period, may very well result in either cost reductions or increased revenues in a subsequent period. The question then arises as to whether research and development expenditures should be charged against revenue in the period such outlays are incurred or capitalized and charged against revenue in subsequent periods.

FASB Statement No. 2 "Accounting for Research and Development Costs" largely decided this issue in the direction of deducting virtually all internal research and development costs in the period they are incurred. FASB Statement No. 2 maintains that in order for an asset to be created from an expenditure (as opposed to a currently deductible expense) an economic resource must result with future measurable benefits. Thus, since rarely could research and development expenditures be expected to lead to economic resources with future benefits which are measurable at the time the expenditure is made, such outlays would, in virtually all cases, be deducted as an expense in the period they are incurred rather than capitalized and deducted in subsequent periods. In providing a rationale for their treatment of research and development costs, the FASB noted that in order for an outlay to result in a capitalized item which is to be written off over subsequent periods, measurable future benefits must result so that a systematic and rational procedure can be developed for allocating these benefits to future periods as expenses.

Another relevant area in the continuing accounting controversy over which costs should be capitalized and which expensed, is how to treat interest expense incurred in the acquisition of assets. As the result of FASB No. 34, interest costs incurred on borrowings which are obtained in order to finance construction of assets are required to be capitalized and added to the depreciable cost of the asset. Requiring such treatment are assets such as facilities under construction for a company's own use as well as assets intended for sale or lease. On the other hand, inventory which is routinely manufactured or produced in large quantities on a repetitive basis does not qualify as an interest capitalizable asset. The capitalization period is the period required for construction. The interest rates used in determining the amount of interest to capitalize are to be based on the average rates on a company's outstanding debt. If debt is issued specifically for an asset's construction, however, a firm may apply that rate in capitalizing interest. By capitalizing interest, a firm does not charge this item against revenues until the relevant asset begins to produce revenues. Imputed interest on equity capital (other than by rate-regulated public utilities) is not to be capitalized. Similarly, interest cost which is unrelated to the development of an asset for its intended use, but which simply represents a "carrying cost," is not to be capitalized. For example, interest cost related to the holding (but not developing) of land for eventual resale is not capitalizable.

The question of interest capitalization was first raised by accountants over sixty years ago. Until recently, however, the issue has never been fully resolved by an authoritative accounting body. Thus, divergent practices were prevalent, with some companies charging all interest on debt to expense when the interest payment was made, and other firms capitalizing interest on debt under varying circumstances and in varying amounts. The FASB acted to standardize practice in this area because of the increased use of borrowed money and the sharp rise in interest rates.[41]

[5] SOME OTHER CONTEMPORARY ACCOUNTING ISSUES

(a) Earnings Forecasts

Although for many years the SEC had discouraged companies from predicting their earnings, sales, dividends and other important financial data because of the unreliability of such forecasts, the Commission eventually changed its position because of the potential usefulness to investors of such information. In June 1979, the SEC approved a rule intended to encourage companies to make earnings forecasts by protecting them against fraud charges in the event that their forecasts did not prove to be accurate.[42] In effect, the Commission provided companies with a so-called "safe harbor" against liability if their projections had a "reasonable basis" and were made "in good faith." Under this rule, in order for either the Commission or private parties to successfully launch a legal attack on management over the inaccuracy of their SEC filed forecasts, the plaintiffs would have to prove that management had knowingly misled investors through these projections. In addition to earnings forecasts, the "safe harbor" rule also applies to capital expenditures, dividends, management objectives and plans, and future economic performance. At present, disclosing projections is voluntary.

(b) Segment Reporting[43]

At the prodding of the SEC, the FASB issued Statement No. 14, "Financial Reporting for Segments of a Business Enterprise." Under this ruling annual reports are to breakdown sales, profits, assets and depreciation by divisions. Companies doing business in more than one industry are expected to disclose the above information for each significant industry segment. Foreign operations, export sales, and dependence on major customers (if any) must also be disclosed under FASB Statement No. 14. While the procedure by which industry segments are determined is left to management, disclosure is required for any segment whose revenue, operating profit or loss, or identifiable assets comprise 10% or more of the corporate total. Moreover, a sufficient number of segments have to be reported to total at least 75% of the entire corporate amount. No segmented data need be reported if a company has one segment whose revenues, profits and assets exceed 90% of the entire corporate amount.

The three types of information to be disclosed are as follows:

(A) *Revenues.* To be disclosed for each segment with intersegment sales shown separately.

(B) *Operating Profit or Loss.* To be computed after all expenses traceable to a segment's operations have been deducted and an allocation of those expenses which are not directly traceable to a particular segment has been made. Excluded from operating profit or loss are revenues earned and expenses incurred at the corporate level and therefore not attributable to a particular industry segment. Items in this category include interest and dividends, general corporate expenses, corporate interest expense, domestic and foreign income taxes and the equity in the income of unconsolidated subsidiaries.

(C) *Identifiable Assets.* These are assets used by by one or more industry segments and can be allocated. Assets beneficial to general corporate purposes such as the corporate portfolio of marketable securities are not to be allocated to industry segments.

The SEC has also taken an active role in this burgeoning accounting area, particularly through its Accounting Series Release No. 244, which goes a long way toward defining segments in various industries. As a practical matter, however, companies frequently consult in advance on such matters with the SEC. For example, forest product companies felt that they had such a high degree of product interdependence that they should be allowed to disclose their operations in terms of one industry segment. The SEC, however, strongly suggested that they use at least three industry segments as follows:

1. Paper and paper products,
2. Building materials; and
3. Container and packaging products.

While Accounting Series Release No. 244 gives the impression that companies are giving, or are being required to give, careful consideration to the definition of an industry segment, it is apparent that management has great flexibility in selecting industry segments and in allocating revenues, costs, and assets to each segment. In practice, any systematic and rational method of allocation is permitted by both the SEC and the FASB. All that is required is that the allocation method chosen be applied consistently. Finally, while separate disclosure is required for foreign revenues, profits and identifiable assets, no single method for grouping by geographic area is stipulated.[44]

(c) Accounting for Price Level Change

As mentioned above, during periods of inflation, the stable monetary unit assumption has been a difficult burden for the accounting profession to handle. The weakness of this assumption was particularly apparent when inflation persisted throughout the world, but the accounting profession was loath to deal with this issue in a definitive manner.

Following World War II, on several occasions, the existing U.S. rule-making body indicated support for the use of supplementary financial schedules to explain the impact of inflation on a company's financial statements. Many companies began voluntarily to apply an FASB exposure draft, that affirmed this principle. In effect, accounting interest in price-level adjustments parallelled that of businessmen generally. It waxed and waned with the vagaries of price movements and finally, in the virulent inflationary spiral of the late 1970's, resulted in FASB Statement No. 33, "Financial Reporting and Changing Prices," issued in September 1979 on an experimental basis.

This regulation required major companies to disclose the effects of changing prices as supplementary information in their published annual reports. Two methods were employed to reflect the effects of changing prices: (1) "constant dollar accounting," in which price level adjustments were made to all items by means of a designated consumer price index and (2) "current cost accounting", whereby various types of information, including specific price indices, may be used to adjust each of the relevant items. The FASB also refers to recoverable costs which are to be used when they are lower than current costs. Recoverable costs refer to the present worth of the amount of cash expected to be obtained from the use or sale of an asset. In late 1984, the FASB issued Statement No. 82 that deleted the requirement to disclose data on an historical cost/constant dollar basis.

In general, the supplementary information required of companies that meet prescribed tests cover the current fiscal year and each of the five most recent fiscal years.

With respect to the current fiscal year, a company must now disclose:

1. Income from continuing operations on a current cost/constant dollar basis;

2. The purchasing power gain or loss on net monetary items for the current fiscal year (not to be included in income from continuing operations);

3. The current cost of inventory and property, plant and equipment at the close of the year; and

4. Increases or decreases in the current cost of inventory and property, plant and equipment, net of inflation (not to be included in income from continuing operations).

With respect to each of the five most recent fiscal years, a company must now disclose:

1. Net sales and other operating revenues;

2. Income from continuing operations on a current cost basis;

3. Income per common share on a current cost basis;

4. Net assets at the fiscal year-end on a current cost basis;

5. Increases or decreases in the current cost of inventory and property, plant, and equipment, net of inflation;

6. Purchasing power gain or loss on net monetary items;

7. Cash dividends per common share; and

8. Market price per common share at the fiscal year-end.

Recognizing the conceptual difficulties in reporting financial information that reflects the implications of rapidly changing prices, the FASB established an inflation data bank at the Accounting Research Center of Columbia University and conducted various surveys leading to the conclusion to drop the reporting of constant dollar information.

The present status of inflation accounting is complex and introduces new principles. In order to help understand them, we illustrate the application of both current cost and historical cost/constant dollar standards (even though the latter basis has been dropped) to an extremely simple company that manufactures and sells toasters. The following operations are assumed for the company during a two-year period:

1. Acquires one toaster on October 1, 19x0 @ $25;

2. Acquires one toaster on December 31, 19x0 @ $30;

3. Acquires one toaster on June 30, 19x0 @ $35;

4. Sells one toaster on December 31, 19x1 @ $50;

5. Current cost of the toaster, December 31, 19x1, $40;

6. Inflation rate for years 19x0 and 19x1 = 10%;
7. Net monetary liabilities = $100, December 31, 19x0; $150, December 31, 19x1;
8. Property valued at $100 acquired on December 31, 19x0; property valued at $120 acquired December 31, 19x1;
9. Depreciation rate 10%; and
10. Inventories valued on FIFO basis.

If an enterprise presents the minimum required data, it must use the year's averages in providing current cost/constant dollar information; if it presents comprehensive statements, it may use either average or year-end data. Both comprehensive statements and year-end data are rare in practice. Nevertheless, for convenience of presentation, we use year-end data.

Paragraph 216 of the FASB Statement No. 33 calls for 7 steps to get the desired information. We follow them based on the simple example shown above:

Step 1: Analyze inventory and cost of goods sold. Little analysis is required here since we know the precise acquisition dates of each item of inventory (the toasters).

Step 2: Restate historical cost of inventory and cost of goods sold into historical cost/constant dollar and current cost dollars:

Inventory	Historical Cost Nominal Dollars	Inflation Rate	Historical Cost Constant Dollars	Current Cost
Bought Dec. 31, 19x0	$30	1.10%	$33	
Bought June 30, 19x1	$35	1.0476%*	$36.67	$80**

Cost of Goods Sold (FIFO Basis)

Inventory bought at $25 on October 1, 19x0 is sold one and one quarter years later.	$25	1.1282%***	$28.205	$40

*Represents the price index at the end of the year 19x1 (1.10) divided by the index as of June 30, 19x1 (1.05).

**Two toasters @ $40 each.

***Represents the price index at the end of the year 19x1 (1.10) divided by the index as of October 1, 19x0 (.975).

In applying these figures, comparison should be made with recoverable cost to see if it is lower. The market value of the toaster at the year-end is $50, which even after allowing for costs of disposal would probably exceed the recoverable cost. This figure also is above both the current cost and the historic cost in constant dollars. So, no writedown is necessary.

Step 3: Analyze property, plant and equipment and depreciation. Property valued at $100 was acquired December 31, 19x0. Property valued at $120 was acquired on December 31, 19x1. The annual rate of depreciation is 10%.

Step 4: Restate property, plant and equipment and depreciation into constant dollars and current cost:

Property, Plant & Equipment	Historical Cost Nominal Dollars	Inflation Rate	Historical Cost Constant Dollars
Bought Dec. 31, 19x0	$100	1.10	$110
Depreciation	$ 10	1.10	- 11
Bought Dec. 31, 19x1	$120	—	120
Depreciation	—	—	—
			$219

	Current Dollars
Property Bought Dec. 31, 19x0 is now valued at:	$120*
Depreciation at 10%	- 12
	$108
Property Bought Dec. 31, 19x1	120
	$228

*Given in the illustration. In practice, it is typically calculated by means of construction indices.

Step 5: Identify the monetary items at the beginning and end of the period and the change during the period:
These items were given at the outset. Net monetary liabilities at the beginning of the period were $100: at the end of the period they were $150, and the change during the period was $50.

Step 6: Compute the purchasing power gain or loss on net monetary items:

	Nominal Dollars	Inflation Rate	Constant Dollars
Balance, Dec. 31, 19x0	$100	1.10	$110.00
Increase in net monetary liabilities	50	*1.0476	52.38
			$162.38
Balance, Dec. 31, 19x1	150		150.00
Purchasing power gain on net monetary items			12.38

*Represents the price index at the end of the year 19x1 (1.10) divided by the average index for the year (1.05).

Step 7: Compute the change in the current cost of inventory and property, plant, and equipment and the effect of the increase in the general price level.

	Increase in Current Cost of Inventory		
	Nominal Dollars	Inflation Rate	Constant Dollars
Balance, Dec. 31, 19x0, 2 @ $30	$60	1.10	$66.00
Sales	-35	*1.0476	-36.67
Purchases	35	*1.0476	36.67
	$60	1.10	$66.00
Balance, Dec. 31, 19x1	80	—	80.00
Increase in current cost	$20		$14.00

*Represents the price index at the end of the year 19x1 (1.10) divided by the average index for the year (1.05).

The "specific price" component of the increase in current cost is the difference between the nominal dollar and the constant dollar measures:

Increase in current cost (nominal dollars)	$20
Increase in current cost (constant dollars)	$14
Inflation Component	$ 6

Increase in Current Cost of Property, Plant and Equipment

	Nominal Dollars	Inflation Rate	Constant Dollar
Balance, Dec. 31, 19x0	$100	1.10	$110
Depreciation	- 10	1.10	- 11
Bought, Dec. 31, 19x1	120	—	120
	$210		$219

Current Cost

	Nominal Dollars	Inflation Rate	Constant Dollar
Balance, Dec. 31, 19x1 ($240 - $12)	228	—	228
Current cost increase over nominal dollars	$ 18		$ 9

Increase in current cost (nominal dollars)	$18
Increase in current cost (constant dollars)	9
Inflation Component	$9

Final Result as Reported

Statement of Income from Continuing Operations
Adjusted for Changing Prices for the Year Ended December 31, 19x1

	As Reported in the Primary Statements	Adjusted for General Inflation	Adjusted for Changes in Specific Prices (Current Cost)
Net Sales	$50	$50	$50
Cost of Goods Sold	25	28*	40
Depreciation	10	11	12
Provision for Income Taxes (assumed)	5	5	5
Income (loss) from Continuing Operations	$10	$ 6	($ 7)
Gain from Decline in Purchasing Power of Net Amounts Owed		$12.50	$12.50

Increases in specific prices (current cost) of inventories and property, plant, and equipment held during the year.** ($20.00 + $18.00)	$38.00
Effect of increase in general price level ($14.00 + $9.00)	$23.00
Excess of increase in specific prices over increase in general price level ($6.00 + $9.00)	$15.00

*Rounded, exact figure is 28.205
**At December 31, 19x1 the current cost of inventory was $80.00 and the current cost of property, plant, and equipment, net of accumulated depreciation was $228.00

A comparison of the three statements reveals the effect of inflation on reported results. Employing conventional accounting procedures, based on historical costs, the company shows net income of $10. When general inflation is taken into account, costs are raised and net income falls to $6. When current costs are considered, however, a net loss of $7 is reported. This substantial change occurs primarily because the net loss excludes the $15 dollar holding period gain based on the difference between the FIFO cost of the toaster used in the conventional statement ($12 when adjusted for general inflation) and the current cost employed in the statement adjusted for specific prices. Results based on the latter statement are sometimes described as distributable income. This figure represents the amount of income a company can distribute in the form of dividends without impairing its capital maintenance ability. It highlights the significance of current cost statements in periods of inflation.

In its discussion of financial concepts, the FASB describes the return on capital as measuring inflows in excess of the amount needed to maintain capital. It refers to two concepts of capital maintenance, either of which can be measured in units of either money or constant purchasing power. Under the financial capital concept, holding gains or losses are included in return on capital. Under the physical capital concept, these changes are called capital maintenance adjustments that are included directly in equity from the return on capital.

Contributing to the size of the holding gain in the illustration is the fact that the company employed FIFO accounting. Companies that value inventories on a LIFO basis implicitly adjust reported earnings for the effect of inflation on inventories. On the other hand, this accounting convention results in the underpricing of inventories in the balance sheet.

Other than the influence of inventory valuation policies on the cost of goods sold, a major element affecting current pricing statements is the difference in depreciation. In the illustration, the depreciation differential was two dollars, or twenty percent of nominal dollar depreciation. For capital intensive companies, the difference between the amount of depreciation based on historic and current costs could be substantial.

An issue often noted by companies in their discussions of the effects of changing prices is that of taxation. During inflationary periods, income on a current basis is likely to be less than that reported on the conventional basis. The implication is that taxes are overstated. In the illustration, the company provides for taxes of 5 dollars even though it shows a current cost loss of 7 dollars.

A purchasing power monetary gain occurs when a company holds monetary liabilities in excess of monetary assets. The theory is that during periods of inflation, monetary liabilities can be repaid in dollars with less purchasing power than those borrowed. Acceptance of this notion too literally resulted in some companies overborrowing during periods of inflation. As a result, when the rate of inflation abated, the companies found themselves with the necessity of meeting heavy debt servicing requirements in cash that was not readily available. In the illustration, the purchasing power gain of $12.50 that was reported did not represent additional cash flow that the company could use to service its debt.

3.4   THE FINANCIAL MANAGER AND EXTERNAL FINANCIAL REPORTING

It has often been said that any large business keeps three separate and distinctly different sets of accounting books. The first set, so the story goes, is used for external profit reporting and management's primary objective in this case is to try to present the kind of picture it wishes to portray. Any and all accounting devices are fair game and tools to be used in order to present the desired picture. The Certified Public Accountant and the professional accounting associations, of course, act as a break on this activity. And, to the extent that the range of choice among "generally accepted accounting principles" is narrowed, the ability of the financial manager to "manage" externally reported profit figures is similarly reduced. This chapter was devoted largely to a consideration of these opposing forces. We looked at the desire on the part of the financial manager to increase or at least maintain the scope of his accounting discretion over externally reported earnings and the movement of the accounting profession as embodied in the FASB and as prodded by the SEC, to standardize and define accounting principles and their applications.

The second set of books is kept for tax reporting purposes to the government. The primary objective in this case is to minimize the firm's aggregate tax liability among the various taxing authorities to which it is subject. Chapter 24 considers this area.

Finally, the third set of books[45] is the one kept for internal corporate reporting purposes. As there is hardly any reason for a corporation to fool itself or distort this area of reporting, it is often said that this is the set of books in which the corporation presents the most accurate picture of its operations and financial position.

Where then does the annual report fall within the corporate reporting spectrum? The answer is decidedly within the first reporting sphere, the one in which management attempts to present whatever picture of the firm it finds most desirable. Moreover, this is certainly not limited to efforts with respect to the financial data and the financial statements. Annual reports now serve as vehicles for promoting sales of the company's products. They are used to enhance employee morale and also serve as a lobbying tool with the aim of favorably influencing governmental activity toward the firm. In short, the annual report constitutes a propaganda document for the firm which, within SEC and FASB constraints, is used to foster the interests of the firm as management sees them.

3.5   CHAPTER SUMMARY

In this chapter the accounting and economic concepts of profits were compared. The accounting concept of profits was then further developed in terms of its relationship to corporate funds. We then looked at the significant contemporary issues involved in the accounting measurement of profits. We stressed throughout, the degree of accounting choice prevalent in the determination of profits for external financial reporting. In the next chapter we will rely upon our understanding of external financial reporting and the environment in which it operates. We will consider the techiques of financial analysis which can be applied in order to gain an insight into the meaning of this external data.

FOOTNOTES

1. Angela Falkenstein and Roman Weil, "Replacement Cost Accounting: What Will Income Statements Based on the SEC Disclosures Show?—Part I," *Financial Analysts Journal,* January-February 1977, pp. 46-57.
2. The Financial Accounting Standards Board (FASB), now the rulemaking organization in the accounting profession, has since affirmed and slightly modified this APB ruling. See FASB News Releases October 3, 1979, February 29, 1980, and February 11, 1982.
3. See F.M. Scherer, *Industrial Market Structure and Economic Performance,* Rand McNally & Co., 1973, Chapter 19, "Price Fixing," pp. 443-453. There has been some empirical work done in this area directed at assessing the information content and capital market impact of social disclosure. For example, see Robert W. Ingram, "An Investigation of the Information Content of (Certain) Social Responsibility Disclosure," *Journal of Accounting Research,* Autumn 1978, pp.

270-285, and John C. Anderson and Alan W. Frankle, "Voluntary Social Reporting: An Iso-Beta Portfolio Analysis," *The Accounting Review,* July 1980, pp. 467-479.

4. The cash concept can be expanded to include near cash items (marketable securities) with only modest conceptual alteration.

5. Prepaid items will never be converted into cash; as they would have required a current expenditure of cash had they not been acquired and as they are normally small in amount, however, their liquidity need not concern us here.

6. Chapter 14 amplifies this point.

7. We shall have more to say below about accounting for non-consolidated subsidiaries and capitalization of interest during construction.

8. This is because of the so-called "fundamental accounting equation" (assets = liabilities + equities) which is actually not an equation but a tautology in that it always holds by definition.

9. Yuji, Ijiri, "Cash-Flow Accounting and its Structure," *Journal of Accounting, Auditing and Finance,* Summer 1978, pp. 331-348.

10. As evidence of movement in this direction see, *A Statement of Financial Accounting Concept #1, Objectives of Financial Reporting by Business Enterprises,* November 1978, pp. 3121-3138, Financial Accounting Standards Board. The profession in this release appears to be moving in a "cash flow" direction.

11. *op cit.,* Ijiri, p. 331.

12. AICPA Study Group on the Objectives of Financial Statements, *Objectives of Financial Statements,* New York: AICPA, 1973.

13. *op cit.,* Ijiri, p. 332.

14. *op cit.,* Ijiri, p. 331-348.

15. B.S. Yamey, H.C. Edey, and Hugh W. Thomson, *Accounting In England and Scotland: 1543-1800,* London: Sweet & Maxwell, 1963, pp. 170-171.

16. F.W. Cronhelm, *Double Entry by Single,* London, 1818, in A.C. Littleton and B.S. Yamey, eds. *Studies in the History of Accounting,* (Illinois: Richard D. Irwin, 1956), p. 310.

17. *Ibid.,* p. 310.

18. *Ibid.,* p. 338.

19. Alfred Marshall, *Principles of Economics,* 8th edition, London: Macmillan & Co. Ltd., 1962, p. 61.

20. Robert H. Montgomery, *Auditing,* p. 360, in *Changing Concepts of Business Income,* Report of the Study Group on Business Income (New York: The Macmillan Company, 1952), p. 25.

21. Jack L. Treynor, "The Trouble With Earnings," *Financial Analysts Journal,* September-October 1972, pp. 41-43.

22. Much of the beginning portions of this subsection are taken directly from *FASB*—"Description and Background," July 14, 1978.

23. Just prior to that time this function was performed by the AICPA. Accounting areas considered by the AICPA but not yet ruled upon by the FASB are governed by the AICPA pronouncement. (See FASB news release, October 3, 1979.)

24. *The Wall Street Journal,* June 14, 1978, p. 8. It has also been charged that the FASB is dominated by the "big eight"—the largest firms in the profession. See, U.S. Senate, *The Accounting Establishment,* a staff study prepared by the Subcommittee on Reports, Accounting and Management of the Committee on Government Operations, 94th Congress, 2nd Session, December 1976. Further, is has been claimed that accountants in general have a low degree of public spiritness. See, John C. Burton, "Where are the Angry Young CPA's?" *The New York Times,* April 13, 1980, p. F-13.

25. We present these areas in order of their relative liquidity, which is the order of their listing in the balance sheet.

26. Normally marketable securities are listed ahead of accounts receivable. Marketable securities are generally disclosed at "cost or market whichever is lowest." When the market value of the portfolio of current marketable securities temporarily falls below its cost, a loss is recognized to the extent of the decline and the balance sheet value of the marketable securities portfolio is reduced. Should the market value of the securities portfolio subsequently increase, it may be written back up. This will result in a gain and an appreciation in the balance sheet value of the portfolio of marketable securities. However, it should be noted that the "write-up" can never exceed the amount required to restore the portfolio to its original cost basis. (See Jon A. Booker and Bill D. Jarnagin, *Financial Accounting Standards: Explanation and Analysis,* Chicago, Commerce Clearing House, Inc., 1979, pp. 89-101.)

27. Some of these methods are the Base Stock Method, NIFO (next in first out—or replacement cost), and HIFO (highest in first out). It should also be noted that inflation accounting discussed later in this chapter, has an effect upon accounting for inventories.

28. We should keep in mind that although a firm may choose, for reporting to stockholders, any inventory costing assumption it wishes from among those which are "generally accepted," for taxation purposes it can use only LIFO if it uses this method for reporting to stockholders.

29. A detailed discussion and comparison of the various depreciation methods and the mechanics by which each operates is presented in Chapter 14.

30. It should be noted that the SEC normally requires purchase accounting for a business combination when the surviving company has reacquired its own common stock within two years of the merger. In this case, the SEC reasons that the merger was effectively made with cash (calling for purchase accounting) although common stock is nominally used. For more on corporate reacquisitions of their own common stock see Chapter 21.

31. In an opposite sense with respect to liabilities, it should be noted that due to limited corporate liability, total consolidated corporate debt, unless guaranteed, does not represent an obligation of the parent firm. Thus, consolidated statements may overstate the burden of the consolidated debt upon the parent firm. Conversely, companies frequently use trust agreements, joint ventures and subsidiaries to hide debt from their balance sheets. In November, 1983 this procedure was sanctioned with respect to trust agreements by FASB Statement No. 76, "Extinguishment of Debt." This statement deals with an in-substance defeasance by which a company deposits securities in an irrevocable trust dedicated to servicing one of its outstanding debt issues. For financial reporting purposes the debt is then treated as if it has actually been extinguished. It is removed from the balance sheet and any gain or loss on the transaction (usually there is a gain) is recorded as income. In effect, the debt is "in substance" retired and removed from the balance sheet. However, the debt actually remains outstanding, with debt service provided by the trust. This is an extremely controversial area and likely to remain so for some time.

32. Congress, in an unprecedented move, passed a provision that precluded any accounting rule-making body (principally the SEC and the APB, and then the FASB), from requiring firms to use the deferral method exclusively. The intent of Congress was to ensure that the ITC had the maximum favorable effect on reported net income in the year a firm acquires eligible property.

In pursuing this action, Congress demonstrated that it has, and is sometimes willing to undertake, the authority to directly regulate the accounting profession. Further, this episode highlighted the overriding concern of many sectors of the economy and interest groups with the reported earnings of business. In spite of the fact that cash flow is unaffected by the method used to account for the ITC, many influential individuals felt that the flow through method would provide a greater and more rapid stimulus to the economy by resulting in higher net income in the year of acquisition of the eligible property. This presumption flies in the face of the vast preponderance of the evidence collected in attempts at validation of the efficient market hypothesis. This hypothesis and some of the empirical studies relevant to it were discussed in Chapter 2.

33. Assuming a 10 percent credit.

34. $11,000 - $5,000 (tax before ITC) - $900 (annual depreciation) = $5,100.

35. $11,000 - $5,000 (tax before ITC) - $1,000 (annual depreciation) + $1,000 ITC = $6,000.

36. For an analysis of these effects of extraordinary items on the price of common shares see, Bertrand Horwitz and Allen Young, "Extraordinary Gains and Losses and Security Prices," *Quarterly Review of Economics and Business,* Winter 1974, pp. 101-110.

37. The accounting profession has sought to restrict management's options in this area somewhat through APB No. 30. This rule states that two criteria both must be met for classification of an event or transaction as an extraordinary gain or loss. First, that the item be of an "unusual nature," and second, that it possess an "infrequency of occurrence."

    (A) Unusual nature—the underlying event or transaction should possess a high degree of abnormality and be of a type clearly unrelated to, or only incidentally related to, the ordinary and typical activities of the entity, taking into account the environment in which the entity operates.

    (B) Infrequency of Occurrence—the underlying event or transaction should be of a type that would not reasonably be expected to recur in the forseeable future, taking into account the environment in which the entity operates.

    The Opinion further elaborates on the Infrequency of Occurrence criteria:

    Determining the probability of recurrence of a particular event or transaction in the forseeable future should take into account the environment in which an entity operates... The past occurrence of an event or transaction for a particular entity provides evidence to assess the probability of recurrence of that type of event or transaction in the forseeable future. (APB Opinion No. 30, "Reporting the Results of Operations," AICPA, 1973).

38. Among other things the following should be excluded from the determination of net income under all circumstances: (1) adjustments from transactions in the company's own capital stock (accounting for treasury stock is discussed at length in Chapter 21); (2) amounts transferred to and from accounts properly designated as surplus appropriations, such as charges and credits to general purpose contingency reserves; (3) amounts considered to represent excessive costs of fixed assets, and annual appropriations in contemplation of replacement of production facilities at higher price levels; and (4) adjustments pursuant to a quasi-reorganization.

39. Accounting considerations relevant to extra compensation costs, particularly pensions and stock options are dealt with in 26.2.

40. Direct costing cannot be used for external reporting or tax purposes.

41. FASB News Releases, December 21, 1978, October 22, 1979, January 28, 1980 and April 23, 1980. The FASB has come under some criticism for FASB No. 34 because of the many estimates needed for its application and because capitalizing is called for in this area, while expensing is required for a number of other areas they have recently decided, i.e., research and development costs. For more on this see, Michael P. Bohan and John Van Camp, "For Those With Interest—A Capital Idea," *Journal of Accounting, Auditing and Finance,* Fall 1980, pp. 72-83. Further, it should be noted that FASB No. 34 does not affect taxes payable or cash flow, only reported earnings.

42. For a study of the comparative accuracy of management's earnings forecasts, as compared with those of external financial analysts see, Bikki Jaggi, "Comparative Accuracy of Management's Annual Earnings Forecast," *Financial Management*, Winter 1978, pp. 24-32. In this article it was found that management's forecasts exhibited a smaller mean relative prediction error compared to financial analysts' forecasts. A similar conclusion is reached in Bart A. Bass, Kenneth J. Carey and Richard D. Twark, "A Comparison of the Accuracy of Corporate and Security Analysts' Forecasts of Earnings," *The Accounting Review*, April 1976, pp. 244-254. It should be pointed out that such studies suffer from an inherent sampling bias in that only companies which voluntarily disclose forecast data are subject to analysis.
43. Much of this section was taken from Lee J. Seidler, *Accounting Issues*, June 1978, Bear, Sterns and Co.
44. For an analysis of the effect of segment disclosure on security prices see, Bertrand Horwitz and Richard Kolodny, "Line of Business Reporting and Security Prices: An Analysis of an SEC Disclosure Rule," *Bell Journal of Economics*, Spring 1977, pp. 234-249; D. Collins, "SEC Product-Line Reporting and Market Efficiency," *Journal of Financial Economics*, June 1975, pp. 125-164; and Bertrand Horwitz and Richard Kolodny, "Segment Reporting: Hindsight After Ten Years," *Journal of Accounting, Auditing and Finance*, Fall 1980, pp. 20-35.
45. Of course, some firms, particularly those in regulated industries, keep additional sets of books as required by regulatory and other authorities.

SUGGESTED READINGS

Bohan, Michael P., and John Van Camp, "For Those With Interest—A Capital Idea," *Journal of Accounting, Auditing, and Finance*, Summer 1980.

Bonocore, Joseph J., "A New Era of Financial Reporting," *Financial Executive*, December 1981.

Borst, Duane R., "Accounting vs. Reality: How Wide is the 'GAAP'?" *Financial Executive*, July 1981.

Burton, John C., "Emerging Trends in Financial Reporting," *Journal of Accountancy*, July 1981.

Casey, Cornelius J. and Michael J. Sandretto, "Internal Uses of Accounting for Inflation," *Harvard Business Review*, November/December 1981.

Dearden, John, "Facing Facts With Inflation Accounting," *Harvard Business Review*, July/August 1981.

Denman, John H., "Corporate Reporting and the Conceptual Framework Issue," *CA Magazine*, April 1981.

Duff, C.P., W.H. Duff and R.P. Duff, *Duff's Common School Bookkeeping*, New York, Harper & Brothers, 1881.

Fama, Eugene, "Efficient Capital Markets: A Review of Theory and Empirical Work," *Journal of Finance*, May 1970.

Fahnestock, Robert T. and Russell F. Briner, "How to Use the Cash-Basis Funds Statement as an Analytical Tool," *Practical Accountant*, March 1981.

———, "A Cash Flow Model for the Future," *Management Accounting*, June 1981.

Financial Accounting Standards Board, *Examples of the Use of FASB Statement No. 33, Financial Reporting and Changing Prices*, 1980.

Grant, Edward B., "Financial Executive's Role in External Reporting," *Financial Executive*, February 1981.

Grivoly, Dan and Dan Palmon, "Classification of Convertible Debt as Common Stock Equivalents: Some Empirical Evidence on the Effects of APB Opinion 15," *Journal of Accounting Research*, Autumn 1981.

108

—— and ——, "Timeliness of Annual Earnings Announcements: Some Empirical Evidence," *The Accounting Review*, July 1982.

Gutberlet, Louis G., "Compilation and Review of Financial Statements by an Accountant," *Journal of Accounting, Auditing and Finance*, Summer 1980.

Horwitz, Bertrand, and Richard Kolodny, "Line of Business Reporting and Security Prices: An Analysis of an SEC Disclosure Rule," *Bell Journal of Economics*, Spring 1977.

——, and ——, "Segment Reporting: Hindsight After Ten Years," *Journal of Accounting, Auditing, and Finance*, Fall 1980.

——, and Allan Young, "Extraordinary Gains and Losses and Security Prices," *Quarterly Review of Economics and Business*, Winter 1974.

Ijiri, Yuji, "Cash-Flow Accounting and its Structure," *Journal of Accounting, Auditing, and Finance*, Summer 1978.

Kistner, Klaus-Peter and Tino Salmi, "General Price Level Accounting and Inventory Valuation," *Journal of Accounting Research*, Spring 1980.

Koch, Bruce S., "Income Smoothing: An Experiment," *Accounting Review*, July 1981.

Kreiser, Larry, "Toward a More Social Income Statement," *Financial Executive*, June 1980.

Littleton, A.C., and B.S. Yamey, eds., *Studies in the History of Accounting*, Illinois, Richard D. Irwin, 1956.

Short, Daniel G., "General Price Level Accounting—Dead or Alive?" *Financial Executive*, September 1981.

Smith, Gerald R., "Inflation, Accounting and the Financial Executive," *Financial Executive*, December 1980.

Smith, John L., "Improving Reported Earnings," *Management Accounting*, September 1981.

Strauss, Norman N., and Alex T. Arcady, "A New Focus on the Bottom Line and its Components," *Journal of Accountancy*, May 1981.

Szepan, Susan B., "Corporate Social Responsibility—An Update," *Journal of Accountancy*, July 1980.

Tipgos, Manuel A., "Reforming the Balance Sheet and the 'Window-Dressing' Hypothesis," *Financial Executive*, June 1981.

Tuthill, William C., and Al L. Hartgraves, "Restating the Statement of Changes for Price Level Changes," *Journal of Accountancy*, June 1982.

APPENDIX A: A GLOSSARY OF SOME DIFFICULT TO UNDERSTAND ACCOUNTING TERMS

Sometimes accountants use words that have a common sense or everyday meaning, but employ these terms in a far different sense. This seeming equivocation on the part of accountants makes an understanding of the work accountants do particularly difficult for the lay public.[1] Worse still, other professionals, such as lawyers or economists often use these terms in an entirely different sense from accountants. This makes for considerable misunderstanding. For example, it has been noted that the accounting provisions of the Foreign Corrupt Practices Act "are drawn from language used by accountants and clear enough for them but not clear enough for attorneys. Many lawyers have pointed out that the language is far too imprecise to constitute legal standards, according to the auditing firm of Peat, Marwick and Mitchell & Co."[2] Thus we offer a brief compendium of some selected terms which might at times cause some confusion as the result of a different meaning applied by the accounting profession than that generally employed by the lay public or other professionals.

(A) Goodwill

Most economists would understand goodwill as applied to a business as representing a strategic economic advantage for the firm. Perhaps a corner location for a retail outlet as opposed to one in the middle of the block. Or an economist might use the term goodwill to refer to a company's having particularly good customer relations. The standard dictionary defines goodwill as "the value of a business in patronage, reputation, etc., over and beyond its tangible assets."[3]

To accountants, however, goodwill is something entirely different. To an accountant goodwill can only occur in one way for a firm. It buys another firm, pays an amount greater than the net assets (assets less liabilities) and accounts for the transaction as a purchase rather than as a pooling of interests. The extent of the difference between the price paid and the net assets represents goodwill. The accounting assumption made is that all transactions are of an arm's length nature and that a firm would only pay more than the carrying value of an acquired firm's net assets if these assets had some additional worth or goodwill. Nevertheless, as demonstrated earlier in this chapter, goodwill is not something acquiring firms desire to have on their books. (It lowers returns on assets and subsequent net income as the goodwill is written off.) Thus, we have the seeming Alice in Wonderland contradiction in terms, wherein goodwill is not very good and is in fact considered very bad by those firms which have to record it on their books.

One wonders about an acquiring firm that shrewdly acquires a firm at a price less than its net assets as the result of effective negotiation, while a competitor pays more than net assets for a similar acquisition as the result of ineffective negotiation. If the ineffective negotiating firm acquires goodwill as the result of its ineffectiveness, does the shrewdly negotiating firm acquire badwill as the result of its effectiveness? Clearly this is an anomaly which accountants have attempted to obscure by using such terms for acquisitions at prices below net assets as "Surplus Arising on Consolidation."[4] As might be expected, however, the result is even more confusion for non-accountants.

(B) Depreciation

Depreciation is a particularly troublesome area because the economists' and the public's definition is so different from the accountant's. Most people define depreciation as the annual decline in the value of an asset. Indeed, economists and engineers look upon depreciation in this manner. In other words, to economists, engineers, and the general public, depreciation is a process of valuation or assessing the decline in value. Again, a standard dictionary is instructive; it refers to depreciation in the first meaning it offers as a "decrease in value of property through wear, deterioration or obsolescence."

The difficulty, however, arises in the second definition the dictionary offers for depreciation—"The allowance made for this (as given in the first definition) in bookkeeping, accounting, etc." For the allowance for depreciation, as seen by accountants, is not a process of valuation, as all other groups view it, but a process of cost allocation. To an accountant, depreciation is a process of allocating the original cost of a fixed asset over its useful service life. Yearly depreciation represents the portion of the original cost allocated to the current period. Moreover, there need be no attempt by accountants to have the yearly amount of the original cost allocated to a particular period conform to the physical decline in value during that period. In choosing a depreciation method for an asset all that is required of the accountant is that he select a procedure which is "systematic and rational." There is no necessity that the method conform to the physical decline in value an asset has undergone. Thus accountants view depreciation as a process of allocation, whereas others view depreciation as a process of valuation and therefore can misconstrue the meaning of the data accountants present. This will become even more apparent when we look at other definitional differences below.

(C) Valuation Account—as Allowance for Depreciation

Accountants use the term valuation account to represent an account which is offset against another account and thus alters the carrying value of the other account. The Allowance for Depreciation is an example of a valuation account in that it alters the carrying value of Plant and Equipment. Referring to the Allowance for Depreciation as a valuation account, however, only serves to exacerbate the confusion noted in the previous section as to the accounting meaning of depreciation. As indicated above, to accountants, depreciation is an allocation process and not a valuation concept. Thus, by making entries to the Allowance for Depreciation account in an allocation setting, yet referring to the account as a valuation account, the accounting profession is adding to the confusion which surrounds depreciation.

This can be further illustrated by means of a simple example. Assume 10 years ago a firm bought its present plant, which, at the time, was expected to have a life of 20 years. The original cost was $1,000,000. At the present time the disclosure of this information that the firm might typically make on its balance sheet is as follows:

Plant	$1,000,000
Allowance for Depreciation	$ 500,000
Book Value	$ 500,000

The term book value might lead some to believe that the current worth of the plant is begin represented. Of course, nothing could be further from the case. In no reasonable sense of the term is "value" being disclosed. The Plant account merely represents the original acquisition cost; the Allowance for Depreciation is that portion of the original acquisition cost which has been charged to past periods (as a deduction from revenue in those periods in computing net income); and the Book Value is the unexpired portion of the original cost which is awaiting future period matching against revenue.

(D) Reserve

The accounting use of the word reserve is also very frequently an unfortunate construction. In common usage a reserve represents a resource held back or withdrawn from use so that it can be employed at a later date should circumstances warrant. Some dictionary definitions of the term are as follows: "to keep back, store up, or set apart for later use or for some special purpose; to hold over to a later time; in business cash, or assets easily turned into cash, held out of use by a bank or company to meet expected or unexpected demands." Thus, when accountants, instead of using the title Allowance for Depreciation, refer to the account as a Reserve for Depreciation, as is sometimes the case, considerable confusion can arise. The same situation results when the Allowance for Bad Debts is referred to as the Reserve for Bad Debts. In neither case does the account represent a pool of resources held back which can be employed at the service of the company. Both are merely so-called valuation accounts, which itself, as noted above, causes some confusion. Yet some firms still use the term reserve to refer to such accounts.

An even more difficult problem is created by so-called Retained Earnings reserves such as a Reserve for Contingencies. When a non-accountant sees an account referred to as a Reserve for Contingencies, he might reasonably be led to the conclusion that it contains a pool of resources which can be placed at the disposal of the company to meet a general category of contingencies or perhaps a specified event. Again, nothing could be further from the truth. Actually, a company with a Reserve for Contingencies is not necessarily in any better condition to meet a general or a specific contingency than a firm without such an account. For Retained Earnings Reserves, such as Reserves for Contingencies, contrary to the common usage of the term, do not contain a pool of resources that the firm can call upon should a contingency arise, but merely represent a segregation of Retained Earnings which, in effect, limits the firm's dividend paying ability. (In most states, dividends can only be paid to the extent of Retained Earnings.) In practice, however, as cash is normally the limiting factor in the payment of dividends, rather than retained earnings, the creation of a Reserve for Contingencies rarely affects a firm's dividend paying ability. In essence, then, as there are no funds in the Retained Earnings account, since earnings themselves are not necessarily translated into funds, there can never be any funds in a Retained Earnings reserve such as a Reserve for Contingencies.

(E) Profits

As this term was developed at considerable length in the chapter, a discussion of it will not be repeated here. The reader is merely referred to the discussion of the historical development of the accounting meaning of the term profits, the practical accounting computation of business profits as accounting developed over the years, and the relationship between the economic and the accounting concepts of profits.

1. For example see, James C. Worthington, "Making Financial Statements More Readable," *CA Magazine,* September 1977, pp. 34-37. A quote from this article is particularly apropos. "Public accountants audit a corporation's records and express their opinion on whether the footnotes disclose the technical matters correctly. In the past, public accountants generally assumed the readers of the financial statements had technical training in accounting and the footnotes were written accordingly." Also see this article for some examples of changes which might make financial statements more readable.

2. Charles N. Stabler, "SEC's New Weapon: Foreign Bribery Act Imposes Tough Rules on the Bookkeeping of All Public Firms," *The Wall Street Journal,* July 28, 1978, p. 30.

3. All dictionary definitions in this appendix are taken from *Webster's New World Dictionary: College Edition.*

4. Of course, as in the case of purchases above net assets, the difference between the net asset and the purchase price must be assigned to specific assets if such a determination can be made.

4

TECHNIQUES OF FINANCIAL STATEMENT ANALYSIS

4.1 THE IMPORTANCE AND USE OF FINANCIAL STATEMENT ANALYSIS

In the prior chapter we stressed the importance of comparable external accounting principles in the derivation of financial statements in order that the analyst observing differences or similarities in two sets of data, may distinguish between those that are the result of real economic conditions rather than cosmetic accounting devices. In this chapter, on the assumption that the appropriate accounting corrections have been made, we take the discussion one step further by developing a series of analytical techniques for the better understanding of financial statements.

It is imperative that the financial analysis discussed in this chapter be based upon a set of financial statements which have been standardized or "corrected" to remove or at least mitigate the spurious effects of alternative accounting treatments which tend to distort the relationship between reported versus true economic earnings.

The predominant technique of financial statement analysis is ratio analysis to which most of this chapter is devoted. The ratio is a commonly used statistical yardstick that provides a measure of the relationship between two figures. In financial analysis, this relationship may be expressed as a rate (the change in costs per dollar of gross sales), as a percent at a particular time (cost of sales representing a designated percentage of gross sales), or as a quotient (current assets as a certain number of times current liabilities). Of these forms, the percentage is the most popular.

Ratio analysis may be used to keep close control over a product or process as well as for broader planning purposes. In the former case, the emphasis is on the preciseness of the ratios and on the comparisons between particular rather than general items. This bias toward the specific is not necessary for planning, where an overall portrayal of company performance is desired. As an illustration, to control profit margins, the sales manager may require exact information on the dollars and cents cost per unit of an individual product; top management on the other hand can gain an insight into operating efficiency by noting trends in the percentage relationship between costs of sales and total sales.

Because ratios are simple to calculate and easy to understand, there is a tendency to employ them at the drop of a hat. While such statistical alacrity may help stimulate thinking and develop understanding, it may also lead to the accumulation of a mass of data that obscures rather than clarifies relationships. Then, too, there is a tendency to compare figures through ratios whether or not a fundamental economic connection exists between the items being studied. Ratios are useful only when they bring to light a key economic relationship and their construction should place this relationship into proper focus. The financial manager must steer a careful course between the Scylla of too few ratios, which hinders analysis, and the Charybdis of an excess supply, which produces confusion.

In addition, the financial manager must look beyond the red flags which these analyses develop to the basic factors which have brought about the underlying conditions. Thus, the appropriate use of the techniques of financial statement analysis is to provide the financial manager with a starting point and some indication of where a more concentrated direction of his attention will prove fruitful.

4.2 SPECIALIZED RATIOS

Particular ratios may be developed to meet the needs of particular industries. As an illustration, it is important for companies with wasting assets to know their available reserves. To obtain the number of years of reserve availability at the current operating rate, a relationship may be determined between estimates of reserves and the current rate of output.

Where production is important, idle capacity becomes a significant cost factor. To gauge this condition, a ratio may be calculated which relates a measure of capacity to a measure of output. In the public utility field, a popular tool for this purpose is the load factor, which is a ratio between the actual net generation of kilowatt hours for the year and maximum net generation possible.

In the railroad industry, a number of specialized ratios are employed for analytic purposes. Of particular importance is a key ratio, which combines the two principal factors contributing to a railroad's efficiency—the speed of transportation and the weight of the load moved. These two elements are incorporated into a single ratio by multiplying the quantity of train miles divided by train hours (train speed) and gross ton miles divided by train miles (trainload), as follows:

$$\frac{\text{Train miles}}{\text{Train hours}} \times \frac{\text{Ton miles}}{\text{Train miles}}$$

The train miles cancel, of course, and the resulting ratio is ton miles per train hour, which measures the overall efficiency of a railroad's operations.

When revenue and cost data may be allocated to particular products and when output in units of production is available, a whole group of ratios may be determined which relate revenues and costs to production. In this category are the selling price, cost of production, and margin of profit per unit. These ratios are particularly helpful in assessing the effect on profits of changes in selling prices and costs.

The financial manager will, of course, be familiar with the specialized ratios applicable to the industry in which his firm operates. He will employ these ratios to evaluate the operating trends of his company and to compare his firm's operations with those of competitors. In addition, he will rely upon a more generalized approach which makes use of the income statement and balance sheet as discussed later in this chapter.

4.3   THE PERCENTAGE FINANCIAL STATEMENT

Percentage financial statements incorporate an additional column which shows the percentage relationship between each item and a selected base. In income statements, the base is generally net sales; in balance sheets, it is total assets or liabilities. Percentage income statements are often prepared monthly, together with comparative data for prior months in the same year and the same month in the preceeding year, for presentation to the board of directors or other management groups. Their wide use is traceable to their helpfulness in providing a picture of internal operating and financial changes. By expressing the figures in financial statements as percentages of a common base, shifts in the relative size of the different components may be readily observed. At a glance, management can determine the trend in profit margins, the growth or shrinkage in particular expense items, and the comparative importance of nonoperating income. The percentage balance sheet is employed in a similar manner to gauge the relative significance of specific assets and liabilities, but it is not as popular as the percentage income statement.

Relative figures measure the changing importance of the components of financial statements. This perspective is desirable to evaluate the significance of each item and to check the overall harmony of internal operations. However, analyzing the absolute data is also necessary to determine actual growth or decline. Thus, while the percentage statement may reveal that a larger portion of a company's sales is flowing into earnings, a deeper examination of the original statements is required to ascertain which particular areas are responsible.

4.4   SELECTING INDIVIDUAL RATIOS

The financial manager may not want to prepare a complete percentage statement, feeling that its comprehensiveness would obscure individual items that he wants highlighted. Or he may find it necessary to use ratios in order to investigate significant trends identified by the percentage financial statements. As a result, he may prefer to show only the figures that he feels are particularly significant. His experience will help him determine which of the ratios are most meaningful in his enterprise.

Appraising performance requires standards of comparison. In ratio analysis, these standards are usually a selected base year, a trend line over a period of years, industry averages, or the results in comparable firms. Average ratios for industries are prepared by government agencies, trade associations, the business research staffs of universities, and private organizations such as Dun & Bradstreet and Robert Morris Associates, an association of commercial bank credit managers. The analyst may want to select the ratios of particular companies or groups of companies that he believes are most appropriate. The ratios themselves are calculated from data in the income statement, the balance sheet, or both. While an abundance of ratios are conceivable, we present below those in general use.

[1] INCOME STATEMENT RATIOS

Ratios calculated from income statement data are used to evaluate a company's operations. For this purpose, the principal stages of profits— gross, operating, and net—are often compared with sales. These relationships are demonstrated on the basis of the income statement of Corning Glass Works for the year 1981 as shown in Figure 4.1.

FIGURE 4.1 *Consolidated Statement of Income (1981)*

Corning Glass Works
(In Millions)

Net Sales		$1,598.5
Cost of Sales		1,147.4
Gross Margin		$ 451.1
Selling, General and Administrative Expenses	$302.2	
Research and Development Expenses	91.3	393.5
Operating Margin		$ 57.6
Royalty, Interest and Dividend Income	$ 23.5	
Interest Expense	(29.3)	
Other Income, Net	11.3	5.5
Net Income Before Taxes on Income		$ 63.1
Taxes on Income		14.6
Income Before Minority Interest and Equity Earnings		$ 48.5
Minority Interest in Earnings of Subsidiaries	$ (1.4)	
Equity in Earnings of Associated Companies	50.3	48.9
Net Income		$97.4

Source: Corning Glass Works, Annual Report 1981, p. 26.

(a) Gross Margin Ratio

In general, the first profit stage shows the gross margin achieved after the cost of sales is deducted from net sales. As a ratio, it shows the percentage of net sales represented by gross profits and tells us something about the ability of a firm to control production costs in relation to sales. It is calculated by dividing the gross margin by net sales. In the case of Corning Glass Works,[1] the gross margin ratio for 1981 was

$$\frac{\$\ 451.1}{\$1,598.5} = 28.2\%.$$

In profitable operations, the gross margin must more than cover the portion of sales absorbed by all other expenses. Obviously, the ratio varies with both sales and production costs. When several products are sold, the gross profit margin may be affected by changes in the sales mix even though sales prices and unit costs are constant. And from year to year the margin will be influenced by accounting changes, such as the method of valuing inventories.

(b) Operating Margin Ratio

This is a common ratio that focuses on the percent of sales flowing into profits after allowing for all operating charges. These typically include costs of sales; selling, general and administrative expenses; and research and development expenses. (Thus the operating margin equals the gross margin, less these items as shown in Figure 4.1.) The operating margin ratio deals with the ability of a firm to control operating expenses in relation to sales. It is calculated by dividing the operating margin by net sales.

For Corning Glass Works, the operating margin ratio for 1981 was

$$\frac{\$ \quad 57.6}{\$1,598.5} = 3.6\%.^2$$

While the ratio serves an an index of overall efficiency, its usefulness is limited by its vulnerability to changes resulting from accounting decisions. For example, a high ratio could signify nothing more than a management policy of charging less maintenance and/or taking small depreciation charges. However, for purposes of internal analysis, it is useful in detecting areas of difficulty. Any major departures from the results of comparable companies or changes in prior trends are signals that call attention to the need for more detailed investigation.

(c) Net Income Ratio

The last profit stage, of course, is represented by net income, which is calculated by adjusting the operating margin to take into account such factors as financial income and expenses, equity in associated companies, minority interest, and taxes. The net income ratio tells the analyst something about the efficiency with which a firm is able to take down dollars of sales into final net income. The ratio is determined by dividing net income by net sales.

The net income ratio for Corning Glass Works for 1981 was

$$\frac{\$ \quad 97.4}{\$1,598.5} = 6.1\%.$$

A primary concern of management is the percentage of sales revenues taken down into final net income. This percentage, in conjunction with the operating ratio, casts light on the importance of a company's non-operating activities.

(d) Relationship Between Income Statement Ratios

Since each of the three ratios depicting the major profit stages is computed from a common base (net sales), a comparison of one ratio's movement with another throws light on a company's progress. For example, should the financial manager find that during a given period, the company's gross margin ratio increased while its operating margin ratio remained the same, he probably would want to explore the reasons for the improvement in controlling production costs and the deterioration in controlling administrative, selling, and research expenses. Because net sales is used as a common base, an improvement in the gross margin ratio should result in an improvement in the operating margin ratio, even if administrative and related expenses remained the same in relation to net sales. Thus, if the operating margin ratio is unchanged in the face of an improving gross margin ratio, the relationship of administrative and related expenses to sales must have worsened. Similar inter-income statement ratio comparisons can be made depending on the circumstances which prevail.

[2] BALANCE SHEET RATIOS

Balance sheet ratios indicate the financial condition or solvency and ability to carry debt of a firm. More specifically, they provide a gauge of the adequacy of the working capital structure. To illustrate the computation of balance sheet ratios the balance sheet of the Corning Glass Works as of January 3, 1982 is presented in Figure 4.2

FIGURE 4.2 *Consolidated balance sheet as of January 3, 1982*

Corning Glass Works
(In Millions)

Assets	
Current Assets	
Cash	$ 17.5
Short-term investments, at cost, which approximates market value	69.8
Receivables, net of doubtful accounts and allowances—$15.6	236.1
Inventories	261.5
Prepaid expenses including deferred taxes on income	58.3
Total current assets	643.2
Investments	
Associated companies, at equity	323.5
Other, at cost	15.0
	338.5
Plant and Equipment, at Cost	
Land	22.8
Buildings	248.4
Equipment	953.5
Accumulated depreciation	(635.3)
	589.4
Goodwill	20.2
Other Assets	22.1
Total Assets	$1,613.4
Liabilities and Stockholders' Equity	
Current Liabilities	
Loans payable	$ 45.2
Accounts payable	79.9
Taxes on income payable	58.2
Wages and employee benefits accrued	71.8
Other accrued liabilities	86.0

Total current liabilities	341.1
Accrued Furnace Repairs	27.3
Other Liabilities and Deferred Credits	36.1
Loans Payable Beyond One Year	200.1
Deferred Investment Credits and Deferred Taxes on Income	35.7
Minority Interest in Subsidiary Companies	7.7
Common Stockholders' Equity	
Common stock, including excess over par value—	
Par value $5 per share; authorized—	
25,000,000 shares (net of cost of 374,739	
shares of common stock in treasury—$20.3)	90.8
Retained earnings	874.6
Total common stockholders' equity	965.4
Total Liabilities and Stockholders' Equity	$1,613.4

Source: Corning Glass Works, Annual Report 1981, p. 27.

(a) Current Ratio

We calculate the current ratio by dividing current assets by current liabilities. Current assets and current liabilities are compared since the former represents items which either are cash or will be converted into cash within a period of one year, while the latter represents claims against the company which must be paid within one year.

In the case of Corning Glass Works, the current ratio at the end of 1981 was

$$\frac{\$643.2}{\$341.1} = 1.9.$$

The current ratio is one of the primary tests of a company's financial condition. Some financial managers and analysts feel that a company's current assets should be at least twice its current liabilities to avoid financial concern. In most instances, it is believed that this margin is sufficient to provide against a shrinkage in current assets or a rise in current liabilities. The present tendency, however, is to determine acceptable standards by prevailing conditions within the company's industry. Because an undue concentration of funds in any item (such as an overstocking of inventories), may also create financial problems, the current ratio is often supplemented by a breakdown of the composition of the current assets.

(b) Quick Asset Ratio

Since inventories and prepaid items are not as liquid as the other current assets contained in the current ratio, they are excluded when using a more stringent test of financial solvency—the quick asset ratio. This is generally considered to be the most effective measure of a firm's short-term solvency or liquidity. It's also known as the *acid test* or liquidity ratio. This ratio is determined by dividing cash, marketable securities, and accounts receivable (sometimes called the quick assets) by current liabilities. These items are assets which can be called upon for the quick payment of debts. Marketable securities, for example, can readily be sold and, as discussed in Chapter 9, accounts receivable can be used to raise cash quickly through a factor. The quick asset ratio is as follows:

$$\frac{\text{Cash} + \text{Marketable Securities} + \text{Accounts Receivable}}{\text{Current Liabilities}}.$$

The quick asset ratio of Corning Glass Works at the end of 1981 was

$$\frac{\$17.5 + \$69.8 + \$236.1}{\$341.1} = .9.$$

The traditional standard provides for a minimum quick asset ratio of 1 to 1, implying that current liabilities may be cleared by liquidating quick assets. Again, however, industry norms are the determining factor. Note also that while short-term creditors are quite pleased to see a very high quick asset ratio, management and the owners of the firm may find this a sign of declining corporate investment opportunities. Cash rich firms are often not able to uncover high rate of return capital investment opportunities. They are then left with large amounts of liquid, but low earning resources. Cash ordinarily brings a relatively low return and receivables none, and the return on even effectively managed marketable securities is usually well below that expected by most corporations on their asset investments. Thus an excessively high quick asset ratio may presage a take-over, cause workers to demand higher wages, or stockholders to require higher dividends and, in any event, probably represents a drain on earnings. For these reasons, the financial manager may not desire a high quick asset ratio.

The current and quick asset ratios are generally used to assess the corporation's short-term financial condition. We now turn to two additional ratios which look to the corporation's long-term financial condition and ability to carry long-term debt.

(c) Capitalization Ratio

This ratio is calculated by dividing the principal value of bonds by the sum of this value and the market value of preferred and common stock, as follows:

$$\frac{\text{Principal Value of Bonds}}{\text{Principal Value of Bonds} + \text{Market Value of Preferred and Common Stock}}.$$

This ratio distinguishes between that portion of long-term sources of funds provided by creditors and that portion provided by owners. Stock is taken at market rather than using owner's equity at book value because of the accounting inconsistencies discussed in the prior chapter.

For Corning Glass Works, this ratio at the end of 1981 was[3]

$$\frac{\$200.1}{\$200.1 + (18.3 \times 51\,7/8)} = 17.4\%.$$

A company ordinarily finances the acquisition of long-term assets with funds provided by either the long-term creditors or the owners. While conservative practice leans toward a low ratio, there is merit in keeping the maximum level that seems feasible in the light of the company's earnings record and financial strength. Firms maintaining a low capitalization ratio have less risk of loss in a business downturn but also have lower expected returns during a business upswing. Conversely, highly levered firms face higher risks of loss and higher expected gains during the course of business cycle downturns and upswings, respectively. For the financial manager, therefore, determining the appropriate level of the capitalization ratio requires a balancing of the increased expected returns versus the increased risks associated with greater degrees of leverage.

The national credit rating agencies, e.g., Moody's and Standard & Poor's, generally consider the fixed charge coverage (to be considered next) and capitalization ratios as the major determinants of corporate bond ratings. The financial manager, seeking guidance for his firm's leverage policy, should look to the levels of these two ratios which the agencies consider appropriate for various industries.

Use of long-term debt enlarges the amount of funds used for the benefit of the owner's of the company, thereby taking advantage of the well-known technique of "trading on equity" and adding leverage to the earnings that flow to the owners. Furthermore, leverage or debt financing magnifies the return on equity to the owners when the rate of return on borrowed funds exceeds the cost of borrowing. Finally, the capitalization ratio is important to bondholders who look to the equity or shareholder supplied funds as a margin of safety. In essence, determining the proper amount of capital to be raised from creditors is an important managerial decision. In making such judgments, the long-term budget is a major tool.[4]

(d) Fixed Charge Coverage Ratio

This ratio is based on the income statement, but is presented here because it complements the capitalization ratio in indicating something about a company's ability to carry long-term debt. It is computed by comparing the fixed charges a company must meet on its debt (interest) with the earnings the company has available for this purpose. Since interest is tax deductible, the earnings normally used in calculating the ratio are before income taxes (and, of course, also before fixed charges). In theory, minority interest should be deducted proportionately from both earnings and fixed charges. This amount, however, is usually small and rather than go to this trouble, it might conservatively be deducted from earnings available for fixed charges, or ignored entirely.

The appropriate expression is as follows:

$$\frac{\text{Net Income Before Taxes and Fixed Charges (Interest)}}{\text{Fixed Charges (Interest)}}.$$

The fixed charge coverage ratio at the end of 1981 for the Corning Glass Works was

$$\frac{\$97.4 + \$14.6 + \$29.3}{\$29.3} = 4.8.$$

Standards for the fixed charge coverage ratio vary by industry. Sectors having typically stable earnings (i.e., public utilities),[5] generally are allowed the lowest minimum ratio by security analysts; those sectors with somewhat more volatile earnings (i.e., retail concerns) are held to a slightly higher minimum standard; and those business areas that tend to have the greatest earnings volatility (i.e., industrials in general) are held to the highest mimimum ratio.[6]

The fixed charge coverage ratio is ordinarily used to evaluate the ability of a company to meet its recurrring interest charges. It also may be used to gauge the company's ability to meet both interest payments and sinking fund requirements. In this case, the sinking fund amount must be adjusted because it is paid after income taxes are deducted.[7]

[3] RATIOS FROM BOTH THE INCOME STATEMENT AND THE BALANCE SHEET, INTEGRATION OR TURNOVER RATIOS

The final set of ratios presented draw on data from both the income statement and the balance sheet so as to integrate key asset areas with a relevant income statement item. These integration ratios combine operating and financial items so as to shed light on company performance in managing key asset areas as measured by their turnover.

The turnover of an asset tells the financial manager something about the speed at which it is being used to generate profits. On the other hand, the income statement ratios presented previously measure various margins to show the profitability of sales in relation to costs. By revealing the rapidity of asset utilization, the turnover ratios assess the company's efforts at achieving these margins as often as possible. Both efforts affect profits. The extent of a company's margin and the frequency of its realization combine to determine overall corporate profitability.

For most companies the predominant asset investments are in the areas of accounts receivable, inventories, and plant and equipment. Accordingly, we look at the turnover of each of these items and total assets, as well, by matching each with the relevant income statement item.

(a) Turnover of Receivables

The turnover of receivables is determined by dividing net sales by the average amount of accounts and notes receivable outstanding (unless the notes do not arise out of sales). The ratio is used to get some idea of the rapidity of a company's collection of receivables and their conversion into cash. The expression reads:

$$\frac{\text{Net Sales}}{\text{Average Amount of Accounts and Notes Receivable}} .$$

The turnover of receivables for Corning Glass Works in 1981 was

$$\frac{\$1,598.3}{(\$236.1 + \$223.4)^8/2} = 7.0.$$

When trying to measure the average amount of receivables during the year, beginning and end of the year figures can be averaged. Alternatively, if the data is readily available, it would be better to average monthly figures.

To concentrate upon credit policy, cash transactions (if the data are available) may be excluded from net sales in evaluating the receivables turnover ratio. If this ratio is high it indicates a rapid conversion of receivables into cash. The significance of this figure must be interpreted in the light of the company's credit policy, because a high ratio may also reflect overly cautious credit standards.

Further insights into the appropriateness and effectiveness of the firm's credit policies as well as the collectability of its accounts receivable are obtained by evaluating the turnover of receivables in conjunction with the terms of sales. Dividing the receivables turnover ratio into 365 gives the average number of days sales which are outstanding as follows:

$$\text{Average Number of Days Sales Outstanding} = \frac{365}{\text{Receivables Turnover Ratio}}.$$

In the case of Corning Glass Works, the average day's sales outstanding for 1981 was

$$\frac{365}{7} = 52 \text{ days}.$$

Compared with the normal credit terms of the company of net 30 days for most products, this figure indicates that there are some past due accounts.

Further insights into the appropriateness and effectiveness of the firm's credit policy can be obtained for internal analysis by drawing up a schedule of receivables aged according to the length of time they have been outstanding (an aging of receivables). This schedule is desirable because it indicates something about the collectability of a firm's receivables.

(b) Turnover of Inventory

The inventory turnover ratio indicates the speed with which a company is able to convert inventory, held in various stages (raw materials, work-in-process, and finished goods) into final sales. The ratio is calculated by dividing the cost of goods sold by the average amount of inventory carried on the books of the firm during the year. The expression reads:

$$\frac{\text{Cost of Goods Sold}}{\text{Average Inventory}}.$$

As in the case of the receivables turnover ratio, the average inventory level for the year can be estimated by dividing by two the sum of the beginning and end of year inventory levels on the balance sheet. For highly seasonal businesses, the intrayear turnover may vary sharply and therefore averaging monthly figures is desirable. A sluggish rate of inventory turnover indicates that capital is being unnecessarily tied up and suggests that the financial manager should conduct a more comprehensive review of inventory.

The inventory turnover ratio of the Corning Glass Works for 1981 was

$$\frac{\$1,147.4}{(\$261.5 + \$230.3)^9 / 2} = 4.7.$$

(c) Plant and Equipment Turnover

The plant and equipment turnover ratio measures the effectiveness with which a firm's plant and equipment investment has generated sales and is calculated by dividing net sales by the value of the company's plant and equipment. This expression reads:

$$\frac{\text{Net Sales}}{\text{Plant and Equipment}}.$$

Gross, rather than net, plant and equipment is used in the calculation because varying depreciation policies across firms could make comparisons difficult and misleading. If the plant and equipment account has changed significantly during the year due to retirements and/or additions, an average figure is necessary. The average of the gross account at the beginning and end of the year usually suffices.

While a high ratio value suggests management's ability to effectively exploit its tangible assets, a low ratio value may be caused by large outlays for expansion and capital investments which will subsequently enhance operating efficiency and raise profit margins. Thus, the ratio values must be interpreted in the light of other important factors, including the firm's capital budgeting program.

The plant and equipment turnover for Corning Glass Works for 1981 was

$$\frac{\$1,598.5}{\$589.4^{10} + \$635.3} = 1.3.$$

As can be seen, accumulated depreciation is added back to net plant and equipment to produce the gross figure.

(d) Net Income to Total Assets or Net Return on Total Assets

The final ratio we consider is really not a single ratio but a combination of two individual ratios which measure the two component areas of profitability mentioned earlier—margin and turnover. To measure margin in terms of a company's ultimate ability to take dollars of sales down into net income and thus control costs in relation to sales and achieve a satisfactory margin, we looked earlier at the ratio of net income to net sales (net income/net sales). The turnover of a company's assets, in effect the utility of assets in generating sales, can be measured by the ratio of net sales to total assets (net sales/total assets). When the two components of profitability, net income/net sales (margin) and net sales/total assets (turnover) are combined, the net sales figure drops out, leaving net income/total assets. This latter ratio shows how profitable a company's total asset commitments have been on the whole and is a widely used measure of return. The expression is as follows:

$$\frac{\text{Net Sales}}{\text{Total Assets}} \times \frac{\text{Net Income}}{\text{Net Sales}} = \frac{\text{Net Income}}{\text{Total Assets}}.$$

For Corning Glass Works, the component figures and the final combined ratio for 1981 was

$$\frac{\$1,598.5}{\$1,613.4} \times \frac{\$\ 97.4}{\$1,598.5} = .99 \times .06 = 5.9\%.$$

Clearly, the higher net income is in relation to total assets the better. Using the two components to compute this ratio allows us to get behind the figures to the extent of an indication of whether improvement efforts should be directed toward margin or turnover.

[4] WHAT RATIOS DO AND DO NOT TELL US

It was mentioned earlier that caution must be exercised to employ ratio analysis only when a fundamental economic relationship exists between the items being compared. Similarly, one must avoid ascribing powers to ratio analysis which the technique simply does not possess. For example, one might assume that a quick asset ratio greater than one would insure a company's solvency, at least for the current period. Yet, that conclusion is not necessarily warranted. The preponderance of a company's short-term liabilities may be due within a few weeks, its receivables may be collectible only after that time, and any additional financing may prove difficult. Also, the firm may undertake ill-advised new short-term commitments during the current period which it may not be able to meet. Each of the above conditions could result in short-term insolvency for the firm despite the presence of a quick asset ratio greater than one. Further, companies can "window dress", in the sense of creating the appearance of a very favorable quick asset ratio just at the time the financial statements are computed. For example, a company with a quick asset ratio in excess of one could easily improve this ratio simply by paying off some of its current liabilities just prior to the statement date. It could even repay a short-term bank loan at that time and then reconstitute the commitment just subsequent to the balance sheet date. Management could thus create a spuriously high quick asset ratio.

In addition, as implied throughout this chapter, the astute use of ratio analysis necessitates an understanding that little in the way of conclusive evidence can be developed through this technique. Through ratio analysis alone we cannot determine the root causes of corporate difficulty; nor can we pinpoint the underlying factors creating success. Why then, some might ask, should this technique be employed at all? The answer is that it is probably the quickest means of spotting conditions which cry for more detailed and comprehensive analysis. In essence, the financial manager's use of ratio analysis is akin to the physician's initial diagnosis of a patient's condition through observation and measurement of symptoms. But just as complete diagnosis by a physician must contemplate the underlying conditions which gave rise to the readily observable symptoms, the financial manager must look beyond the flags which ratio analysis develops to the basic factors which brought about these conditions. Thus the appropriate use of ratio and financial statement analysis is to provide the financial manager with a starting point and some indication of where a more concentrated direction of his attention might prove fruitful.

Determining the appropriate level for a given ratio is perhaps the most challenging aspect of financial statement analysis. Where a firm has many divisions and multiple product lines, the concept of a single or composite ratio value is of limited use. A more realistic approach to ratio analysis involves using ratio standards for each distinct division or business area.

In general, the financial manager will not be able to assess the significance of specific ratio values without conducting further investigation. For example, a very high current or quick asset ratio can be symptomatic of a good liquidity posture or a poor cash management program. Similarly, a high sales to total assets ratio can be indicative of either an efficient firm or an undercapitalized one which has difficulty financing asset expansion.

4.5 INTERPRETING RATIOS

Once the percentage financial statements and individual ratios have been calculated, the financial manager's job is to analyze and interpret the results. Basically, two primary types of analyses are performed: (1) comparative analysis and (2) trends analysis.

[1] COMPARATIVE ANALYSIS

In the previous step, the financial manager has developed the percentage financial statements and calculated the values of the ratios which gauge the firm's profitability, liquidity posture, ability to carry debt, and ability to utilize assets. The values calculated must now be compared against a set of standards in order to assess the firm's effectiveness or "grades" in each of these areas. In general, we compare the calculated values against two sets of standards: (1) the average values of the ratios and percentages for the overall industry and (2) the average values for prominent competitors or firms of comparable size in the industry.

Comparing the firm's performance against that of the industry as a whole provides a good first impression of the firm's overall financial health. The industry averages, in essence, represent the fundamental or inherent characteristics of the business; however, where the industry is significantly diverse, the averages tend to be less useful. The more definitive picture is provided by comparison against the comparable ratio values and percentages for significant competitors. Section 4.5 [3] discusses the primary sources of information on industry ratio averages and the ratio values for individual firms in different industries.

[2] TRENDS ANALYSIS

The comparative analyses discussed above provide a good initial picture of the firm's overall operations and financial health. They are, however, deficient in one important aspect—they provide only a static picture at one point in time. As such, they given no information regarding significant trends in profitability, liquidity, etc. A static comparative analysis which shows firm ratio values close to industry averages may, in fact, be misleading if the performance in recent years is characterized by significant erosion in these values.

Trend analysis is performed by focusing on the trend in percentages and ratio values for the firm over the recent past, say the past three to seven years. These trends are then compared to the comparable trends for competitors and the overall industry. These kinds of comparisons provide a gauge of the firm's current position relative to competitors and the industry as well as demonstrate the trend or change in the firm's position relative to competitors and the industry as a whole.

[3] SOURCES OF DATA FOR RATIO ANALYSIS

The conduct of comparative and trend analyses with ratios and percentage financial statements requires data on industry averages and the values of ratios for competitors and other firms. Highlighted below are the most prominent sources of these data.

(a) Quarterly Financial Report for Manufacturing Corporations

Balance sheet and income statement data on manufacturing corporations are published quarterly by the Federal Trade Commission. The *Quarterly Financial Report (QFR)* presents analyses based on industry segment (defined in terms of a Standard Industry Classification (SIC) code) and by firm size (measured on the basis of total assets). The financial statements are presented in ratio and percentage forms and are frequently supplemented by more detailed, industry specific surveys and analysis.

The *QFR* represents, perhaps, the most important source of data for the conduct of ratio and percentage financial statement analysis.

(b) Dun and Bradstreet

In its publication *Key Business Ratios*, the Dun and Bradstreet Corporation provides the most comprehensive and widely used data base of ratio values for the large number of industries defined by the four digit SIC level. The data base, compiled on the basis of a sample of over 400,000 companies, presents the interquartile ranges for 14 major ratios for each industry. With each industry, the firms are grouped into three categories on the basis of asset size.

(c) Robert Morris Associates

In its annual *Statistical Studies,* Robert Morris compiles an extensive base of 16 ratios for manufacturing, wholesaling, retailing, contractors, and finance companies. The average values of these ratios and the sales, net income, and total assets are presented for the overall industry, for four industry groups based on firm size, and for the individual firms within the industry.

(d) Industry Associations

Industry and trade associations often compile comprehensive statistics, including financial data, on their members. Some of the larger associations also compile ratios, with industry averages and ratio quartile values calculated as well. Traditionally, these data have been the most comprehensive and detailed available.

(e) Moody's and Standard & Poor's

The Industry Surveys of Standard & Poor's and the various industry manuals (e.g., Industrial, Public Utility, Transportation) of Moody's Investors Services provide comprehensive balance sheet and income statement information on most industries. The financial data on individual firms are frequently supplemented with industry averages for key financial and operating variables and ratios.

(f) Individual Companies

Financial and operating information on individual firms can also be obtained from the annual reports to shareholders and the 10-k reports companies file with the Securities and Exchange Commission. These sources tend to be of limited value because the raw data has not been "scrubbed" or adjusted to remove the effects of the accounting veil previously discussed. Notwithstanding this caveat, the 10-k reports present a wealth of data on individual firms and can be extremely useful in the conduct of comparative analyses focused on competitors.

(g) Computer Tapes

The most important recent innovation in financial research has been the introduction of computer tapes that provide data banks as well as analytic results. The Compustat II tapes, introduced by Standard & Poor's, have applications in such varied areas as mergers and acquisitions, financial modeling, rate case studies, capital adequacy studies, market analyses, and both stock and fixed income security analyses. If Full Coverage Compustat II tapes are purchased, one can obtain annual financial data on over 6,000 companies including all New York Stock Exchange, American Stock Exchange, and over 3,500 Over-the-Counter industrials and non-industrials. A separate data file can be purchased covering close to 300 leading Canadian industrial companies.

These industrial files provide annual data for up to twenty years and quarterly data for up to ten years. The data base is updated weekly. The non-industrial files, although less broad in scope, provide the same degree of in-depth analysis as their industrial counterpart. The non-industrial files provide data on 135 leading U.S. banks and bank holding companies as well as 250 Class A gas & electric utilities. On this group annual data is provided for up to twenty years and quarterly data for twelve years. Armed with this information, the financial manager can prepare complete financial statements along with an array of derived ratios, margins, and growth rates.

Compustat II can help company management compare the firm's results with those of selected corporations with different product line/business mixes. It also allows management to make timely and detailed comparisons of its profitability, financial risk and growth with those of its competitors. Company financial characteristics can also be identified for use in marketing strategy. In addition, Compustat II aids in the evaluation of the credit worthiness of a corporation.

Various industrial firms and brokerage houses offer computer services, including a number of prepackaged programs. Tapes from other sources cater to macroeconomic studies. A very prominent example of this is the Citi-base system. Aggregate macroeconomic data such as national income, product accounts, leading, lagging and coincident indicators and the like, are compiled from 100 source agencies, both public and private, and are made available to subscribers on a weekly, monthly, or quarterly basis. This data base is also updated weekly.

4.6   CHAPTER SUMMARY

This chapter discussed the major steps in the analysis of financial statements by using two principal techniques: (1) percentage financial statements and (2) ratios. Analyzing a firm's strengths and weaknesses is a critical element in the overall corporate planning process. The analysis is performed prior to the planning for future financial requirements which have evolved from the forecasting and budgeting actitivies of the firm. The major purpose of the analysis discussed in this chapter is to identify important symptoms of financial and operating difficulty which require the financial manager's attention. Chapter 5 discusses volume-cost-profit analysis which is one of the primary techniques used by the financial manager to investigate the underlying conditions which give rise to the symptoms uncovered through financial statement analysis.

FOOTNOTES

1. The data for all ratios are in millions.
2. While this is not yet the time to make comparative evaluations, it should be noted in passing at this point that this figure is relatively low within the industrial sector.
3. At the end of 1981, Corning Glass Works had 18,276,883 common shares outstanding. The market price of these shares at that time was 51 7/8. The firm had no preferred shares then outstanding.
4. Leverage is discussed in Chapter 15.
5. Regulatory testimony has suggested that the fixed charge coverage ratio is the primary determinant of electric utility bond ratings. For a multiple discriminant analysis of the relative importance of various variables and ratios in predicting bond ratings, see George E. Pinches, J. Clay Singleton and Ali Jahankhani, "Fixed Coverage as a Determinant of Electric Utility Bond Ratings," *Financial Management,* Summer 1978, pp. 45-55. This paper also examines classification results using discriminant analysis and a number of univariate models. The results indicate that the fixed charge coverage ratio is not the primary determinant of electric utility bond ratings. Also, for a study of the relative importance of various ratios in determining electric utility bond ratings, see Edward I. Altman and Steven Katz, "Statistical Bond Ratings Classification Using Financial and Accounting Data," in *Proceedings of the Conference on Topical Research in Accounting,* ed. Michael Schiff and George Sorter, New York, New York University School of Business, 1976.
6. For investor owned electric utilities, Standard & Poor's and Moody's generally like to see the fixed charge coverage ratio in the range of 3.0 to 4.0 in order to bestow the quality credit ratings of "A" or "Aa". In general, they will not consider an electric utility's bonds "investment grade" if the ratio remains below 2.5 for an extended period of time.
7. The standard means of adjustment is to divide the sinking fund amount by the factor 1-t, where t represents the tax rate the company is currently paying. The resulting figure shows the income the company must generate to pay its sinking fund and the taxes theoretically applicable to the sinking fund amount. Earnings available for fixed charges are then divided by interest plus the adjusted sinking fund amount. See Chapter 15 for a discussion of sinking funds.
8. $223.4 million was the notes and accounts receivable balance for Corning Glass Works on January 1, 1981.
9. $230.3 million was the inventory balance for Corning Glass Works on January 1, 1981.

10. $535.9 million was the balance of gross plant and equipment for Corning Glass Works on January 1, 1981. This is close enough to the end of the year figure of $589.4 million not to require the averaging of these figures.

SUGGESTED READINGS

Abelson, H.R., "Research the Ratios," *Credit and Financial Management*, July/ August 1982.

Altman, Edward I., "Financial Ratios, Discriminant Analysis and the Prediction of Corporate Bankruptcy, *Journal of Finance*, September 1968.

——— and Thomas P. McGough, "Evaluation of a Company as a Going Concern," *Journal of Accountancy*, December 1974.

Beaver, William H., "Financial Ratios as Predictors of Failure," *Empirical Research in Accounting: Selected Studies*, 1966, Supplement to the *Journal of Accounting Research*, 1966.

———, "Market Prices, Financial Ratios, and the Prediction of Failure," *Journal of Accounting Research*, Autumn 1968.

Bhattacharya, K., "Management Ratios: The Dilemma," *Accountancy*, July 1981.

Burianek, Frank, "Using Financial Ratios to Analyze Pension Liabilities," *Financial Executive*, January 1981.

Chen, K.H. and T.A. Shimerda, "Empirical Analysis of Useful Financial Ratios," *Financial Management*, Spring 1981.

"Companies Facing Inflation May Be Stronger Than Ratios Indicate," *Journal of Accountancy*, September 1981.

Dambolena, Ismael G. and Sarkis J. Khoury, "Ratio Stability and Corporate Failure," *Journal of Finance*, September 1980.

Foulke, Roy A., *Practical Financial Statement Analysis*, 6th ed., New York, McGraw-Hill, 1968.

Gibson, Charles H., "How Industry Perceives Financial Ratios," *Management Accounting*, April 1982.

——— and Patricia A. Boyer, "Need for Disclosure of Uniform Financial Ratios," *Journal of Accountancy*, May 1980.

Graham, Benjamin, David L. Dodd and Sidney Cottle. *Security Analysis: Principles and Technique*, 4th ed., New York, McGraw-Hill, 1962, Pt. II.

——— and Charles McGolrick, *The Interpretation of Financial Statements*, 3rd rev. ed., New York, Harper & Row, 1975, Pt. III.

Graham, Lynford E., "Analytical Review Techniques: Some Neglected Tools," *CPA Journal*, October 1981.

Helfert, Eric A., *Techniques of Financial Analysis* 4th ed., Homewood, Ill., Irwin, 1977, ch. 2.

Johnson, James M., "Problems in Corporate Liquidity," *Financial Executive*, March 1980.

Lentini, Lawrence, "Using Ratio Estimation in Observing Inventories," *CPA Journal*, June 1981.

Ohlson, James A., "Financial Ratios and the Probablistic Prediction of Bankruptcy," Spring 1980.

Patrone, F.L. and D. duBois, "Financial Ratio Analysis for the Small Business, *Journal of Small Business Management*, January 1981.

Patton, J.M., "Ratio Analysis and Efficient Markets in Introductory Financial Accounting," *Accounting Review*, July 1982.

Pinches, George E., J. Clay Singleton and Ali Jahankhani, "Fixed Coverage as a Determinant of Electric Utility Bond Ratings," *Financial Management*, Summer 1978.

Schiedler, Patricia L., "Using Accounting Information to Assess Risk," *Management Accounting,* June 1981.

Seed, A.H., "Measuring Financial Performance in an Inflationary Environment," *Financial Executive,* January 1982.

Sienel, J.G. and M. Levine, "Appraising the Liquidity of a Business," *Accountant,* August 14, 1980.

von Furstenberg, George M. and Burton G. Malkiel, "Financial Analysis in an Inflationary Environment," *Journal of Finance,* May 1977.

Welsh, J.A. and J.F. White, "Small Business Ratio Analysis: A Cautionary Note to Consultants," *Journal of Small Business Management,* October 1981.

Wooller, J., "Ratio Analysis as an Indicator of Financial Strength," *Accountant,* February 28, 1980.

VOLUME-COST-PROFIT ANALYSIS

5.1 THE INTERRELATIONSHIP BETWEEN VOLUME, COSTS AND PROFITS

The controllers of most well run businesses today have worked out methods of analyzing costs in a decision-making framework and of forecasting profits at different volume levels. Costs are an important determinant of business decisions, as once sales are known, profits become a function of costs. An important segment of profit forecasting, therefore, revolves around a determination of how costs can be used for decision-making purposes and how they change with output.

Historically, the original aim of cost accounting was to provide a company's executives with the details of full product costs. As a considerable amount of new data was made available to financial managers, many were inclined to use the material more for planning than for recording historic results. Eventually, cost statistics were refined and employed with volume data to study the relationships between these two basic elements of profits. Management planning now relies heavily upon such volume-cost-profit sequences.

In this chapter, we first define the major categories of decision-making costs. We then analyze the effects of changing volume patterns on costs. With this background in mind the primary focus of the chapter is on break-even analysis and flexible budgeting as analytical tools for making managerial decisions based upon the interrelationship between volume, costs and profits.

5.2 MAJOR CATEGORIES OF DECISION-MAKING COSTS

The classification of costs in Chapter 3 was based upon their effects on profits appearing in current financial statements. Management, however, also needs to consider costs as they shape alternative investment opportunities and therefore future profits. These costs differ both in concept and nomenclature from the costs employed in financial statements and historical financial analysis. The more important of these decision-making costs are now analyzed.

[1] OPPORTUNITY COSTS

Management may find it helpful to consider as a cost of a present activity the benefits that are not experienced with other opportunities. For example, in judging whether to use a machine to make a current item or whether to have it make another product, the financial manager must analyze the potential revenues of the alternative use. These are the opportunity costs of continuing the machine in its present purpose.

Opportunity costs are important in capital budgeting where a decision must be reached on alternative long-term expenditures. Suppose, for example, that the financial manager discovers that the purchase of a new piece of equipment at a specified price would generate revenues of $1,500 per month against costs of $700 per month. It might appear that this difference between revenues and costs, representing a monthly income stream of $800, would be the basis for determining the rate of return on the new equipment. To make this calculation, however, the manager would have to determine those net revenues which would be lost by abandoning the old equipment.

If these net revenues amounted to $300 per month, the net inflow applicable to the new machine would be $500 per month. The $300 represents the opportunity cost of running the new machine.

[2] MARGINAL COSTS

The principle of marginal costs is based on the distinction between fixed costs, which in total are immune to changes in output, and variable costs, which in total move directly with changes in output. (Section 5.3 provides a detailed discussion of the composition and determination of fixed and variable costs.) Our present concern is to explain marginal costs which requires an understanding of the difference between marginal, fixed, and total costs.

Marginal costs may be defined as the change in total costs resulting from a change in the unit of output at a given level of capacity. In effect, therefore, the change in total costs occurs because of a change in the unit of output. To illustrate, let us assume that a company is producing three products. It has determined by means of cost accounting analysis that the total costs per unit of product A are $7, of B $8, and of C $9. One hundred units of each product are produced and sold at a price of $10 per unit to produce a total profit of $600. In order to round out its product line, the company contemplates a new product, D. It estimates that it can sell 200 units of D at a competitive price of $10 per unit, but that it would cost $12 per unit to produce D. Through methods described later, the financial manager ascertains that total fixed costs amount to $1,500 and that the variable costs of each product are distributed as shown:

| | Product | | |
	A	B	C
Fixed Costs per Unit	$ 5	$ 5	$ 5
Variable Costs per Unit	2	3	4
Total Costs per Unit	$ 7	$ 8	$ 9
Selling Price per Unit	10	10	10
Net Profit per Unit	$ 3	$ 2	$ 1

The company recognizes that if it produces 200 units of D, the fixed costs per unit of each product would decline, while the variable costs would remain the same. On this basis, the breakdown is as follows:

| | Product | | | |
	A	B	C	D
Fixed Costs per Unit	$ 3	$ 3	$ 3	$ 3
Variable Costs per Unit	2	3	4	9
Total Costs per Unit	$ 5	$ 6	$ 7	$12
Selling Price per Unit	10	10	10	10
Net Profit (Loss) per Unit	$ 5	$ 4	$ 3	($ 2)

It is true that the company incurs a loss of $2 per unit on product D, but as a result of manufacturing it, the fixed costs per unit of each of the other products are reduced, their profits per unit are increased, and the total profits from A, B, and C amount to $1,200. While this amount is offset somewhat, by the $400 loss on D, the net result is a rise of total profits to $800, compared with $600 prior to manufacture of D.

This illustration reveals the importance of marginal costs. By increasing production 200 units, the company incurs marginal costs of $1,800. Since it receives revenues of $2,000 for the additional production, it makes a marginal profit of $200. Added to the original profit of $600, this marginal profit results in the rise to $800 just described. It is clear, therefore, that in determining the advisability of expanding production within a given range of capacity, a comparison must be made between the revenues received on each additional unit, $10 in this instance, and the marginal costs per unit of $9, rather than the total costs per unit of $12.

[3] DIFFERENTIAL COSTS

When a company expands within existing capacity, the financial manager must compare the additional revenues against marginal costs as described above. When expansion occurs through changing capacity, for example by introducing new machinery or changing production methods, the entire cost structure is likely to be affected and fixed costs are likely to rise to a new level. In such a case, the manager needs to compare the growth of revenues and the change in total costs, both fixed and variable, at the two different capacity levels.

Often, however, the alternative course of action involves a change or modification of equipment that does not influence revenues measurably but directly affects costs. In such cases, the difference in costs between the two courses of action (differential costs) represents the relative income caused by substituting the new equipment for the old.[1] This differential in costs then may be measured against the expenditure on the equipment to obtain a gauge of the rate of return on the investment.

Marginal costs are related to differential costs, but the former concept is applicable within a given cost structure while the latter becomes significant as the cost structure changes.[2] Differential costs reflect both the added variable and fixed costs associated with an enlargement of capacity through basic operating modifications. Thus, differential costs are linked to shifts in output that occur at different levels of capacity.[3]

[4] SUNK COSTS

Suppose that prior to the antibiotic era, a pharmaceutical company had expended large sums on a serum against pneumonia. The discovery of antibiotics outmoded this whole line of research. Thus, the company had to decide whether to continue its research on the serum or to abandon it and concentrate on antibiotics. In reaching such a decision the temptation is strong to consider money already spent.

Succumbing to this type of temptation is a mistake because it is useless to spend money on a product that has clearly become outmoded. In this case, the only reasonable course open to the company was to resolutely write off the amount spent on the serum, regardless of how large it was, and to adapt its research facilities and efforts to the more effective area of antibiotics. Had it permitted its prior outlays to justify continued work on the serum, the company would have fallen even further behind in the competition for the new product. To describe this kind of situation, the term *sunk cost* has been coined; it signifies that the *prior* cost is irretrievably lost, and that decisions should be based on *future* outlays.

Sunk costs are ignored in financial decision-making for two important reasons: (1) they have little to no significant value in financial decision-making; and (2) when sunk costs do enter the decision process, they typically lead to incorrect decisions.

[5] SHUTDOWN COSTS

Sometimes a company is confronted with a decision which could lead to the closing of certain plants for a while. For example, it may be weighing the advisability of granting certain union demands in the light of shutdown costs that would materialize in the event of a strike. In making this determination, consideration must be given to *all the costs* which would arise from the temporary discontinuation of activity and which could be avoided if operations were sustained. Included in this category are such items as storing machines, bringing them back into production again, rehiring employees, market loss to competitors and possible adverse consumer reaction. Shutdown costs can be extremely expensive.

[6] CONTROLLABLE COSTS

These costs are relevant in connection with the formulation of a responsibility reporting system. In such a system costs are reported along lines, or according to cost centers, which follow paths of controllability. Controllable costs embody the idea of classifying costs into integrated groups for which different department heads may be held responsible. Clearly, decisions can only be made regarding costs over which the decision-maker has control.

[7] STANDARD COSTS

The principal use of the concept of standard costs is to provide some measure against which the adequacy of actual results may be gauged and controlled if considered unsatisfactory.

A standard cost accounting system ordinarily includes standard measures in the recording of transactions. As a result, variances are shown between the actual and standard prices paid for raw materials, the actual and standard wages paid direct labor, and the actual and standard usage of direct materials and labor in the production process. Management then may analyze these price and usage variances to ascertain the efficiency of the company's operations and to eliminate shortcomings. In addition to its value as a measure of accomplishment and as a control device, a standard allows information to be reported more quickly. In this sense, it may be considered a predetermined rather than a standard cost.

Standard costs are helpful in controlling costs because any variances that occur guide management's attention to operating efficiencies or inefficiencies. Variances, therefore, may be included in financial statements, such as the monthly reports going to management for internal purposes.

5.3   EFFECT OF VOLUME ON COSTS

Financial executives have gained considerable prominence in the corporate hierarchy as top management places more reliance on financial analysis for policy decisions. Underscoring this rise in status is the growing complexity of costs incurred by companies in their efforts to attain sales volumes that permit a desired level of profits. Complex cost structures obscure the movement of funds from sales through costs to profits. To help unravel these relationships, distinctions are generally made among three classes of costs:

- fixed costs;
- variable costs; and
- semivariable costs.

[1] THREE CLASSES OF PRODUCTION COSTS

In this section, we define and illustrate the three major classes of production costs, using a classification scheme employed frequently by accountants and economists as well as financial managers.

(a) Fixed Costs

Every business sells a product or service and experiences costs in doing so. Some of these costs are fixed, such as:

- financing outlays which must be met regardless of sales;
- depreciation charges;
- property taxes;
- insurance; and
- salaries of principal officers.

These costs arise because of the mere existence of plants, equipment and office space. They tend to be related to the creation of capacity rather than to the conduct of an activity within the existing level of productive capacity. Thus, these costs are also a function of time. They will be the same during any designated period regardless of the level of output attained during the period, because they are prescribed by contract or are incurred in order to insure the existence of an operating organization.

As the costs of capacity (facilities, personnel, and organization) grow, the potential for more production may also grow, but actual production increases may or may not result from the increased costs of capacity. Idle capacity represents that capacity which is not being productively employed at any particular time. The cost of idle capacity represents the cost of not producing rather than the cost of producing. Providing extra capacity to allow for growth is a top management decision, unrelated to the costs of current production. Moreover, such costs do not result in future cost avoidance. Accordingly, the costs of idle capacity may be regarded as an expense of the period in which they occur, chargeable directly to profit and loss.

The inflexibility of fixed costs is maintained within the framework of a given combination of resources. As a company increases its production potential by adding to its resources, depreciation becomes larger, more property taxes are paid, and a greater amount of insurance must be borne. From stage to stage of its capacity growth, therefore, the fixed costs of an enterprise rise. And so when they are considered over a long enough time, their seeming immobility vanishes. Within each capacity stage, however, they remain fixed, regardless of the changes in actual production that may occur.

(b) Variable Costs

Other expenditures move in close proportion to changes in output. For example, the number of items produced in a period directly determines the amount of material used in their production. Similarly, the volume of output establishes the number of workers required and the hours they must put in as well as the amount of certain supplies and other factory expenses. These costs are considered variable.

As we have indicated, all costs tend to be variable over the long-run. Within the time span embraced by an established level of capacity, however, valid distinctions may be drawn between costs that are relatively immune to the ups and downs of production and those that vary directly with these changes. Variable costs, then, are related to the activity itself rather than to the physical and administrative framework which makes the activity possible. Depending upon the nature of this relationship, these costs will expand or contract as the activity rises or falls.

(c) Semivariable Costs

Some financial analysts distinguish solely between fixed and variable costs; others recognize a family of semivariable costs as a separate category. When this is done, the minimal aspects of fixed expenses are emphasized, and their existence is identified with the need of a company to keep a portion of its physical facilities and personnel intact no matter how long business drops, unless it is contemplating liquidation. Thereafter, as operations grow, additional amounts of these charges are sustained.

A large portion of manufacturing expenses fall in this category. Even when a plant is closed down, for example, some light, heat, and maintenance are required. But as activity gets under way, the need for these items increases with rising production. In effect, therefore, the semivariable category is composed of both fixed and variable elements. In determining the fixed portion of these costs, some companies employ expected normal rather than zero activity as the measuring base, on the theory that normalcy provides a more realistic clue to the minimum organization that must be maintained over a period of time to meet future operations.

At a given level of output, the fixed element of semivariable costs is the same. As capacity changes, owing perhaps to the acquisition of additional equipment, the fixed element will also change. In other words, the minimum amount of maintenance required to keep two machines in good condition is greater than that required for one—although the amount may be fixed for either one or two machines.

[2] INTERRELATIONSHIP OF FIXED, VARIABLE AND SEMIVARIABLE COSTS

Because total fixed costs do not change with production, the amount per unit declines as output rises. Also, since total variable costs react proportionately with production changes, the amount per unit remains constant with output. However, because the fixed portion of semivariable costs shrinks, on a per unit basis, as output gains, while the variable portion remains unchanged, their overall unit variation depend upon the relative magnitudes of the two segments. The relationships between these total and unit changes as volume rises is illustrated in Figure 5.1.

FIGURE 5.1   *Relationship between total and unit changes in*
fixed, variable, and semivariable costs
(costs in dollars)

Production Level in Units	Fixed Costs		Variable Costs		Total or Semivariable Costs*	
	Total	Per Unit	Total	Per Unit	Total	Per Unit
0	20,000	—	—	—	20,000	—
1,000	20,000	20.00	5,000	5.00	25,000	25.00
2,000	20,000	10.00	10,000	5.00	30,000	15.00
3,000	20,000	6.67	15,000	5.00	35,000	11.67
4,000	20,000	5.00	20,000	5.00	40,000	10.00
5,000	20,000	4.00	25,000	5.00	45,000	9.00

*We are assuming for the illustration that the semivariable costs are the sum of the fixed and variable segments shown.

Fixed costs remain at \$20,000 as production rises from 0 to 5,000 units, resulting in a shrinkage in the fixed costs per unit from \$20, at the 1,000 unit level to only \$4 per unit, at peak output. Total variable costs grow by \$5,000 with each production gain of 1,000 units, leaving the costs per unit unchanged at \$5. Semivariable costs move up by 5,000, the amount of their variable portion, at each level of production, but their fixed segment is constant at each stage. The net result is that as production increases from 1,000 to 5,000 units the percentage decline per unit of semivariable costs from \$25 to \$9 is more moderate compared with that of each unit of fixed costs.

The movements of the three classes of costs are shown graphically in Figure 5.2. Fixed costs follow a straight line. Mathematically, they may be expressed as:

$$C = a$$

where C represents the total costs of the quantity produced and a is the amount of costs applicable to the period of time covered.

Variable costs rise at the rate of \$5 per unit. The mathematical expression for this curve is:

$$C = bX$$

where b is the slope of the curve which, in this case, is the cost of each unit of output, and X is the number of units produced.

Semivariable costs start from a fixed cost base of \$20,000 and then grow at the rate of \$5 per unit. Mathematically, this curve is expressed as:

$$C = a + bX$$

where a is the fixed element, and b is the slope of the curve representing the cost per unit of the variable portion of semivariable costs.

FIGURE 5.2 *Movement of the three major classes of costs with changes in volume*

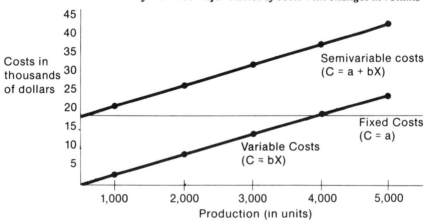

[3] IDENTIFICATION OF COSTS

Much of the analytical work of financial management is based on an understanding of how costs change with the volume of activity. The financial manager, by necessity, must make careful assessments of these relationships in order to classify costs properly. Comprehensive records should be kept, listing fixed costs and the appropriate ratios for variable costs.

Management should also be prepared to break-down semivariable costs to show their fixed component, as a dollar amount, and their variable component, as a ratio related to some direct measure of output. Without this basic material, subsequent analyses will necessarily be weak.

Companies with well established budget systems have the data to distinguish between fixed and variable costs. In those organizations where this information is not reported, the distinction may be drawn either from the company's chart of accounts or statistical studies of how varying levels of output influence costs. In the case of new plants or products, prior data are lacking, and industrial engineering studies of materials, labor, and overhead at varying volumes provide another approach.

Among the variety of simple analytical techniques used to examine the statistics of cost-volume-profit relationships, three which are extremely popular with financial managers include:

- scatter diagrams;
- high-low analysis; and
- sensitivity analysis.

(a) Scatter Diagrams

Scatter diagrams are a common device for conducting these statistical investigations. In order to eliminate distortion created by changing technologies and capacities, the production characteristics of the period under scrutiny should be reasonably uniform, or adjustments must be made to simulate such an environment. At the same time, there must be enough information available to reveal the effect of changing volume levels under conditions of stable capacity. Diagrams showing the three classes of costs and what happens to them when volume changes are constructed in Figure 5.2, by showing the number of units for each item of cost on the vertical axis of a graph and the number of units for the corresponding production yardstick on the horizontal base, and then portraying the relationship between the two factors by points (coordinates) on the graph.

As observed in Figure 5.2, the relationship between the different classes of costs and output characteristically follows a straight line. The line may be constructed algebraically through the use of a statistical technique called ordinary least squares regression[4] or may be approximated by observation. The latter method may save time and is usually of sufficient accuracy, although computers facilitate the expression of curves.

For the semivariable costs curve in Figure 5.2, a, the amount of fixed costs, is $20,000. Subtracting this amount from any point on the line of total semivariable expenses, let us say $35,000, and dividing by the corresponding number of units of production, 3,000, gives the variable costs per unit, which are $5. Similarly, the variable line intercepts the vertical axis at zero, which means that there are no fixed expenses. The unit costs may be calculated by directly dividing a point on the line, let us say $20,000, by the corresponding 4,000 units to yield $5. Or, in either curve, there is a rise of $5,000 of costs per

1,000 unit gain in production, which gives a growth of $5 per unit as the slope of the curve.

(b) High-Low Analysis

Another technique, called the high-low method, is also used to identify variable costs or to separate the fixed and variable portions of semivariable costs. In this procedure, the output measure is listed from the lowest to the highest levels together with the corresponding expenses. The increase in costs calculated for each unit advance in output represents the variable ratio, which is then applied to the number of production units to give the dollar amount of variable costs at this level. Deducting the variable from the total expenses leaves the fixed amount.

For example, looking at the variable segment of Figure 5.2, we find that as production moves from 1,000 to 5,000 units for a gain of 4,000 units, costs increase from $5,000 to $25,000, or $20,000. The cost per unit is then $5. Thereafter, we can apply this unit cost to any given level of production to obtain total variable costs. For instance, if we assume 5,000 units, the variable element is $25,000. Over the same production range, semivariable costs grow from $25,000 to $45,000, or $20,000; thus the cost per unit is still $5. Accordingly, at a level of 5,000 units, the variable element is $25,000, compared with known total semivariable costs of $45,000, producing a fixed portion of $20,000.

The high-low method yields the same results as the ordinary least squares solution when all the costs follow a straight line. Although this precise matching rarely occurs, the method is used because of its simplicity and because it will prove satisfactory when the scatter of coordinates is not too dispersed.

(c) Sensitivity Analysis

Through the use of computers, many companies employ a set of *ad hoc* techniques, generally referred to as sensitivity analyses, to assess the relationships between costs and volume. In order to avoid extensive analysis, some companies simply classify costs as fixed or variable depending upon their major characteristic. For example, one company uses as its measuring rod the degree to which costs would be affected by a drop in sales. On this basis, it counts as fixed such costs as advertising, rent, donations, professional fees, fuel for heat, travel and entertainment, experimental work, and salaries. The costs remaining are considered variable. These include: direct labor, direct material, indirect labor, tools, supplies, power, freight, and maintenance of equipment. While the company recognizes that there are some costs that should be classified as "mixed", it does not use this category because the amount involved would not be significant. Some companies use sensitivity analysis as a "rough first cut" technique in situations where detailed subsequent analysis is not required, while other companies use it as a prelude to more detailed analysis in situations where accuracy is of paramount importance.

[4] ADDITIONAL CONSIDERATIONS

In the discussion of cost-volume-profit relationships our curves and calculations have followed neat patterns which permitted easy and uniform results.

In practice, separating fixed and variable costs may prove trying. Relationships often are not clear cut or may be obscured by unusual circumstances. For example, technological changes of recent years have made it difficult to establish a static period when output and costs can be measured over time with a reasonable assurance that important residual influences are not present. As a result, when the financial manager attempts to determine the components of semivariable costs by means of historical data, he may find that derived total costs are different from actual total costs. In these circumstances, fixed costs may have to be estimated directly. Sometimes, too, decisions may have to be made by executive fiat, although in most cases reasonably satisfactory results are likely to be obtained through statistical or engineering analyses.

5.4 MAJOR TECHNIQUES FOR ASSESSING VOLUME-COST-PROFIT RELATIONSHIPS

We have now discussed several of the more popular and simplified techniques for identifying costs and for assessing the relationship between costs and volume. We now turn our attention to more sophisticated and potentially more effective techniques available to the financial manager when he attempts to understand how changing volume influences profits. Two of the more widely used of these techniques are break-even analysis and flexible budgeting.[5]

[1] BREAK-EVEN ANALYSIS

There is little doubt about the importance of distinguishing between fixed and variable costs to understand how changing volumes influences profits. There is considerable disagreement, however, about how this information can be used most effectively. A case in point is break-even analysis. Some companies rely on this technique, whereas others claim that it oversimplifies reality and steer clear of any formal calculations of this sort. The most ardent supporters of break-even analysis usually determine the break-even volumes for their operating divisions and graphically present this information to top management. Despite its limitations, the widespread use of break-even analysis attests to its popularity amongst practitioners and dictates its comprehensive coverage in this chapter.

(a) Determination of the Break-Even Point—Static Analysis

In this section, we discuss the concept and calculation of the break-even point under the conditions that the basic relationships between volume and costs remain constant over the levels of volume under consideration and a constant unit sales price is maintained. In a subsequent section, we will relax this assumption and focus on a "dynamic" break-even analysis concept. For purposes of explanation, the ensuing discussion differentiates between the determination of the break-even point for the single versus the multiproduct company.

[i] SINGLE PRODUCT FIRM: The break-even point, by definition, is the volume of output at which the firm's overall profit is zero. This occurs when sales produce a margin of income above variable costs that equals the amount

required for fixed expenses. Consider a hypothetical example involving a company that produces and sells each month 50,000 units of a product selling at $5 per unit. If the variable costs of manufacturing are $3 per item, it obtains a marginal income balance (or contribution toward covering fixed costs and generating profit) of $2 per unit, or $100,000. In addition, if fixed expenses of $100,000 must be met each month regardless of output, the company is operating at the break-even point. When monthly production and sales fall below 50,000 units, it incurs a loss because marginal income is insufficient to meet fixed expenses. As operations rise above 50,000 units monthly, the full amount of the marginal income from production and sales above this level flows into net profits for the period.

The break-even point in units is calculated from the following expression:

$$\text{Break-even Point (units)} = \frac{\text{Fixed Expenses}}{\text{Marginal Income}}.$$

To determine the break-even point in dollars, the denominator of the ratio is modified as follows:

$$\text{Break-even Point (\$ Sales)} = \frac{\text{Fixed Expenses}}{\text{Percent of Marginal Income to Sales}}.$$

Using the data of the previous example, we find that the percent of marginal income (contribution income) to sales is 40 percent ($5 - $3/$5). Fixed expenses are $100,000. Dividing this figure by 40 percent gives $250,000, representing 50,000 units sold at $5 each, and this, as we have seen, is the break-even point. If the maximum capacity of the plant is 200,000 units per month, the company's break-even point may be expressed as 25 percent of capacity, a monthly production rate of 50,000 units, or monthly sales of $250,000.[6]

[ii] MULTI-PRODUCT FIRM: A multi-product firm may apply break-even analysis to each of its independent activities. In addition to calculating the departmental or product break-even points, the firm is likely to require the overall break-even for its entire operation. In this case, changes in the items comprising the sales mix or in the proportions sold affect operating profits even though the dollar sales volume and selling prices do not fluctuate. Thus, management may reduce the break-even point by increasing the sales of a product with a high profit margin at the expense of a less profitable item. The problem in attempting to derive an overall break-even point is illustrated by the special circumstances required for the sum of individual products' break-even points to equal the company-wide figure calculated from total sales and costs. This equality occurs only when the ratios of fixed expenses to marginal income are the same for each product.[7]

Characteristically, firms that manufacture a number of products with common fixed costs determine the overall break-even point by extending the single product analysis. For example, suppose a firm has three products, x1, x2, and x3, with the following data:

	x1	x2	x3
Selling price per unit	$5	$6	$10
Variable cost per unit	3	3	5
Marginal income per unit	$2	$3	$5
Common fixed costs	$6 million		

The firm is planning a sales mix that provides for two units of x1 and two units of x2 for each unit of x3. Thus, x1: x2: x3 = 2:2:1 which, converted into percentage equivalence in terms of the sales units, becomes 40 percent for x1, 40 percent for x2, and 20 percent for x3. On the basis of this relationship, we may visualize a new "composite" product x, a physical unit of which consists of 40 percent product x1, 40 percent x2, and 20 percent x3. The marginal income per unit of "composite" product x, m_x, is represented by the weighted average of the unit marginal incomes of the component products:

m_x = $2(40%) + $3(40%) + $5(20%) = $3.

The break-even sales volume of "composite" x, in units, then equals:

$6,000,000/$3 = 2,000,000 units. This figure implies:[8]
    800,000 units of product x1;
    800,000 units of product x2; and
    400,000 units of product x3.

[iii] PRESENTATION OF RESULTS: It is common practice to portray break-even relationships graphically as profitgraphs. Figure 5.3 shows a conventional profitgraph. While the principle underlying these charts is the same, the details of construction may vary. For example, the horizontal axis represents volume, but the measuring rod may be physical units, the dollar value of production, percent of capacity, or any other index of output that is believed to control the changes in costs.[9] The vertical scale ordinarily denotes dollars, and is applicable to both revenue and costs.

The sales curve, which reveals the relationship between revenue and physical volume, is plotted as a straight line beginning at zero on both scales and inclining upward as volume increases. The area of fixed expenses is usually marked off by a horizontal line starting at the level of these costs on the vertical axis. The total cost line begins at this same point and moves upward to another point or through several points determined by plotting total costs at different volume levels.

FIGURE 5.3 *Conventional profitgraph (break-even chart)*

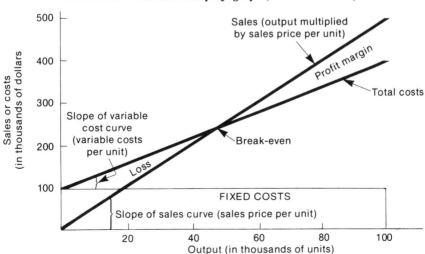

Sometimes variable costs are drawn first, beginning at the zero axis and sloping upward, while fixed costs are indicated by the size of the band between this line and a parallel one indicating total costs at the appropriately higher level, as shown in Figure 5.4.

FIGURE 5.4 *Profitgraph constructed with variable costs starting at zero axis*

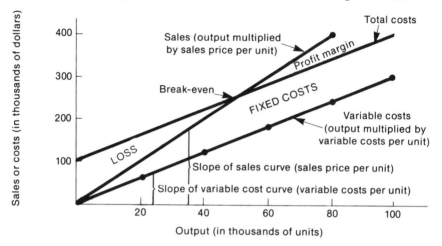

FIGURE 5.5 *Profitgraph showing major components of cost*

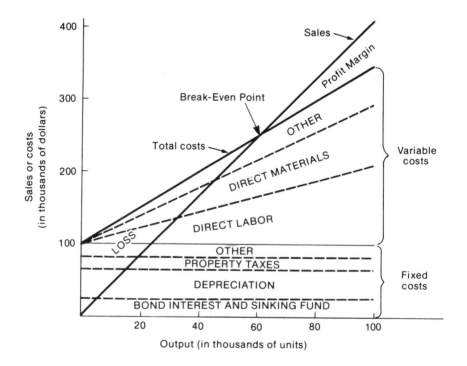

Management may desire to graphically judge the relative importance of the factors contributing to the variable and fixed costs. For this purpose, the cost areas may be subdivided into their principal components. Figure 5.5 illustrates this approach.

FIGURE 5.6 *Profitgraphs showing a direct relationship between sales and profits*

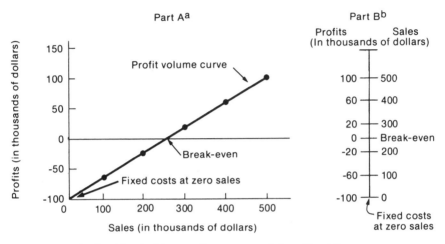

a   Profit = Marginal Income Percentage x Sales - Fixed Expenses.
b   Profit = .40 x Sales - $100,000.

The depth of each variable expense subarea grows as production mounts because a constant cost per unit is applied to a larger volume of output. The depth of each fixed expense subarea, however, remains the same regardless of the level of production because a declining fixed cost per unit is applied to a growing volume of output. The categories of subareas may be made as detailed as desired.

The profitgraph chart may also be constructed to show a direct relationship between sales and profits. Figure 5.6 indicates two methods of making this presentation. In Part A, a line is drawn to connect coordinates representing sales on the horizontal scale and profits on the vertical scale. The position of these points is determined by the profit formula in the chart, which allows for both fixed and variable expenses. It is a simple matter to read from the curve the amount of profits corresponding to any level of sales. The relationship is the same in Part B, but the chart shows at adjacent positions on the vertical axis, the profits corresponding to the different levels of sales.

(b) Determination of the Break-Even Point—Dynamic Analysis

Assuming an unchanging unit sales price and a prescribed relationship between production and costs, the profitgraph shows profits resulting from varying levels of output. Because this concept makes no allowance for the vigor of business activity it is static. If we allow for changes in the basic relationships, the analysis becomes more dynamic.

At any given level of fixed costs, the effect on the break-even point of adjustments in the unit sales price or unit variable costs depends on the relationship of these two items. When they are the same, the curves never cross and break-even is at infinity. A change in either one of them eventually results in a crossing. An increase in the unit sales price thereafter has no direct effect on costs, which are related to the volume of activity rather than price. A reduction in the variable cost per unit modifies the slope of this curve but does not directly influence sales. In either case, the point of intersection of the sales-cost curves, corresponding to break-even, is dropped; that is, if the slope of the sales curve is raised, it meets the cost curve at a lower point, and likewise, if the slope of the cost curve is reduced, it meets the sales curve at a lower point.

As the sales price is pushed farther upward or costs are lowered, the curves meet earlier, and the break-even point continues to decline. The drop is relatively rapid at first, but as the marginal income mounts, additional changes in either sales price or costs have an increasingly modest influence on the break-even point.

In making pricing decisions, it is helpful to visualize the effect of any given change in marginal income on the break-even point. The curve in Figure 5.7 demonstrates this relationship. The base of the chart shows marginal income; the vertical axis indicates the reciprocal of these figures, which we call the marginal income factor.

FIGURE 5.7 *Effect of changes in marginal income on the break-even point*

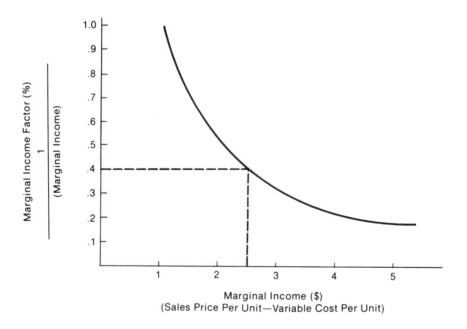

By applying this income factor to any given amount of fixed expenses, the break-even point in physical units is obtained.[10] As an illustration, in an earlier example it was determined that fixed expenses of $100,000, a unit sales price of $5, and unit variable costs of $3 produced a break-even sales volume of 50,000 units or $250,000. Let us assume that the financial manager desires to ascertain the effect on the break-even point of raising the sales price to $5.50. Referring to Figure 5.7, we observe that the new marginal income of $2.50 yields a marginal income factor of .4, which when applied to the fixed expenses of $100,000, results in 40,000 units. Note that the reduction occurs at a relatively steep point in the changing slope of the curve.

With respect to physical volume, it makes no difference in the break-even point whether the unit sales price is raised or variable costs are lowered. In the first case, however, the dollar volume break-even point is higher.[11] In the prior illustration, for example, we found that a $.50 increase in the sales price lowers the break-even point to 40,000 units or $220,000. A $.50 reduction in variable costs still drops the break-even point to 40,000 units, but the dollar value is $200,000.

The break-even point may also be adjusted by modifying fixed costs. A change in this area has no effect on the marginal income ratio which provides the mathematical lever for raising fixed costs to the break-even sales level. Once this factor is standardized, any change in fixed costs is reflected in a corresponding percentage change of the break-even point.

Certain principles may be drawn from this analysis of the effect of changing conditions on a company's operations. A high break-even point indicates that a precarious base underlies the earnings position of an enterprise. To reduce this level, the selling price may be increased, variable costs curtailed, or fixed charges reduced. If the variable costs per unit are large relative to the selling price, the first two measures may prove more effective. Under these circumstances, raising the selling price or lowering variable costs will cause a drop in the marginal income factor at the steep end of the curve. Whether it is more desirable to elevate prices or further restrict costs depends upon competitive market conditions, the elasticity of demand for the company's products, and the efficiency of its operations. When the marginal income pickup is relatively great, the firm may be better advised to concentrate its efforts on lowering the break-even point by dropping the level of fixed costs.

As a final issue, we will show how the profitgraph is used in the dynamic break-even analysis environment in which most companies operate. To circumvent the assumption underlying most profitgraphs of a constant selling price and variable costs per unit, a nonlinear relationship between revenue and costs may be portrayed, as in Figure 5.8. Here the revenue curve rises at a varying rate over the entire volume range, as the selling price per unit (the slope of the revenue line) is first stable (point O to point A) and then cut (point A to point B). The variable costs per unit, in turn, initially rise (point F to point A) and subsequently fall (point A to point D). Finally, they rise again (point D to point B).

The curves intersect at point A, the lower break-even point and at point B, the upper break-even point. Maximum profits occur at point C, where the distance between total revenues and total costs is greatest.

The nonlinear profitgraph of Figure 5.8 may more realistically portray many business situations because the demand curve of a firm's products is likely to have a downward slope. It introduces an added complexity into break-even analysis, however, which ordinarily is concerned with issues other than changing prices.

150

FIGURE 5.8 *The nonlinear profitgraph*

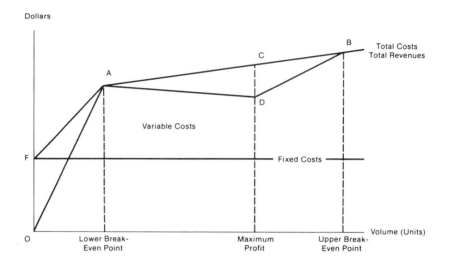

(c) Use in Profit Planning

Financial analysts use the break-even formula in a number of ways. As an aid in budgeting, they show the pretax profits generated at various volume levels above the break-even point base. When this information is charted, management may determine at a glance the expected profits relative to the break-even point at the budgeted volume and the effect of variations from this figure. A safety factor may be constructed from the relationship between actual production and the break-even volume over a period. Relative efficiency may be checked by comparing the dates during each year when the break-even production is reached. To ascertain the dollar volume necessary to meet a profit objective, the desired profit figure may be added to fixed expenses and divided by the marginal income ratio.

The use of break-even analysis in profit planning has important disadvantages and advantages, some of which are presented below.

[i] DISADVANTAGES: Many costs and their components do not fall into neatly compartmented fixed and variable categories, but rather overlap. Also, identifying costs with given output rates obscures the range of relationships that may exist and the assumption of constancy in unit selling prices, technologies, and the operating environment, is generally unreal. Another problem of break-even analysis is the existence of additional restraints, such as limitations in manpower and natural resources, that must be taken into account in determining levels of production for optimum profit. In other words, when the results of break-even analysis are presented as a graph, which is commonly done, the summary of diverse activities into a few neat lines oversimplifies the intricacies of business relationships.

[ii] ADVANTAGES: Despite the oversimplification inherent in the profit-graphs, the graphical display of information provides an easy to understand mechanism for portraying to top management the problems of volume-cost-profit relationships.

By focusing attention on marginal income, break-even studies avoid vexing problems of allocating fixed costs which do not change with volume or price variations.[12] By cutting the ties that link these analyses with the chart form and lifting the traditional emphasis on the point of no profit return, the technique is broadened to include the general area of volume-cost-profit investigations. In planning short-term strategies, these studies help determine the direction of sales efforts and establish volume requirements. Marginal income analysis emphasizes cost differentials, and these, rather than total costs, are influential in deciding alternative courses of action. Break-even studies cast new light on the profitability of product lines, and pricing problems may be resolved into policy measures. They also give management an administrative tool to flag high cost areas and to establish benchmarks for guidance in developing operating policies.

(d) Integrating Break-Even with Probability Analysis

In the broader context of profit planning, break-even presentations may be supplemented by probability analysis. The extent to which this dimension may be added depends upon the nature of the data and the reliability of expectations. When there is some reasonable basis for subjective extrapolations, probability analysis may provide the financial manager with helpful information.

This is particularly true if sales forecasts are characterized by a high degree of uncertainty, a situation leading the financial manager to want information about the likelihood of achieving the break-even level of sales. The break-even point in this case is no longer a known or deterministic constant; rather, it becomes an estimate from an underlying probability distribution associated with forecasted sales. Here is a hypothetical example:

Consider a product whose sales volume has historically been approximately normally distributed, with average or mean sales of 10,000 units and a standard deviation of 1,000 units. Figure 5.9 depicts the probability distribution characterizing the annual sales volume of this product. Because of the symmetry of the normal distribution, practically all of the annual sales volume can be expected to lie within a range of three standard deviations, plus or minus, the average or mean sales (i.e., 7,000 units to 13,000 units).

The product's contribution margin per unit (sales price per unit minus variable costs per unit) is $8 and the relevant fixed costs are $64,000. Based on the given probability distribution for annual sales, we can estimate the average or mean level of profits and the standard deviation as follows:

Average Profits = (Contribution Margin Per Unit) (Average Units of Sales) - Fixed Costs

= ($8) (10,000 units) - $64,000 = 16,000

Standard Deviation of Profits = (Contribution Margin Per Unit) (Standard Deviation of Sales)

= ($8) (1,000 units) = $8,000.

FIGURE 5.9 *Normally distributed sales volume for a hypothetical product*

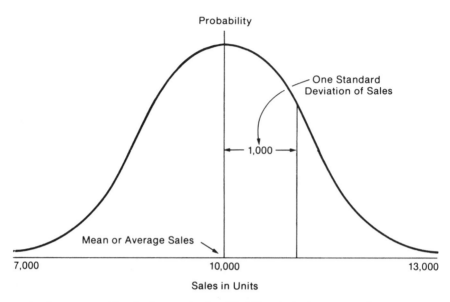

At the expected level of annual sales (10,000 units), the expected or average profit will be $16,000. This is depicted in Figure 5.10, where the probability distribution of Figure 5.9 is superimposed on the traditional profitgraph.

FIGURE 5.10 *Probability distribution of sales superimposed on the profitgraph*

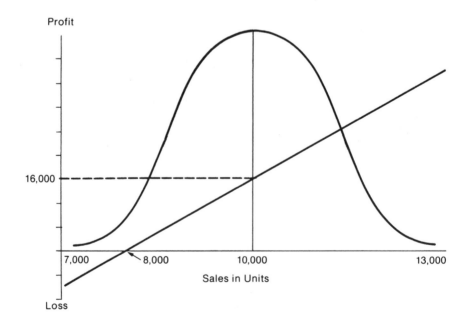

Note that the break-even point is 8,000 units ($64,000/$8) as shown in Figure 5.10. Based upon these data, the product's profit will be normally distributed with a mean of $16,000 and a standard deviation of $8,000. Figure 5.11 shows the probability is about 95 percent (two standard deviations) that the profit range will be between zero and $32,000.

FIGURE 5.11   *Profit range of normal distribution*

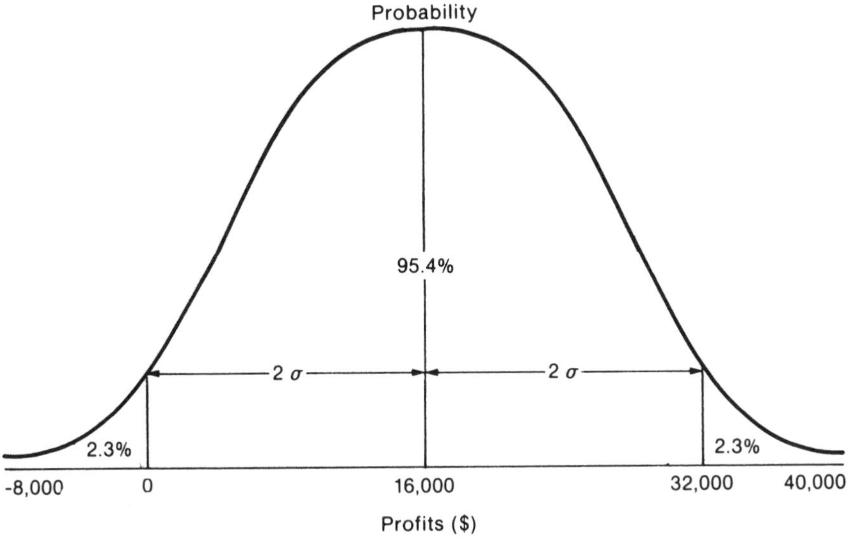

Given the profit description depicted in Figure 5.11, we can also calculate the probability of *not* reaching break-even. This probability is given by the shaded or cross-hatched area under the curve in Figure 5.11, which shows that there is a 2.3 percent probability of not reaching the break-even production level of 8,000 units.[13]

[2] FLEXIBLE BUDGETING

Preparation of a budget for the following year necessitates a forecast of the level of output that is expected. Overall budgeting is treated in Chapter 6, but we are now concerned with the effects on budgeted costs of the differential between the actual and projected levels of production. These effects are ordinarily handled and interpreted through the so-called flexible budget. Since the procedures implicit in this approach relate projected costs to different levels of production, we discuss this phase of budgeting in the present chapter as an aspect of volume-cost-profit analysis.

(a) The Flexible Budgeting Concept

In our discussion of budgeting, we point out that the sales forecast links together the individual budgets of a business. Even if the estimate proves inaccurate, the budget still affords certain benefits because its preparation directs management's thinking ahead and requires an evaluation of organizational responsibilities. These activities improve planning, coordinate functions, and permit management to exercise more effective jurisdiction over a firm's operations. Unreliable sales projections reduce rather than eliminate these advantages. Inaccuracies impair efforts to control costs, because the allowances permitted in the light of production schedules associated with the expected sales objective might bear little resemblance to those that would have been established on the basis of the level of output and of sales actually realized.

The flexible budget overcomes this deficiency by providing the means for gearing cost allowances to varying volumes of business. Firms which can estimate sales and production closely may find the traditional fixed budget, with its prescribed expense allowances, suitable for their purposes. In these cases, no large deviations between actual and budgeted figures are likely to occur from errors in estimating output, and variances will generally be attributable to performance. Where sales forecasting is difficult, involving the possibility of substantial inaccuracies, this assumption cannot be made and the flexible budget is an important planning tool.

A fixed budget does not mean a rigid budget. Any well organized system is subject to periodic revision, and incorporates procedures that permit expenditures to exceed original allotments when this is considered to be in the company's best interests. Although in this sense the term *fixed* is a misnomer, such a budget is not intended to be applicable to a range of production possibilities. The flexible budget is prepared with the objectives in mind of providing in advance for adjusting costs to changes in activity.

(b) Use of the Flexible Budget to Control Operating Expenses

The flexible budget principle applies to all the component budgets, but its widest application is in the control of manufacturing expenses or overhead. Cost analysis methods permit management to appraise charges for direct labor and materials regardless of the volume of activity. Manufacturing expenses require special attention, because these charges are so diverse that unless a special study of their fluctuations is undertaken, the appropriate allowances for varying production levels cannot be ascertained. Consequently, the financial manager may find that he must devote considerable time and effort to controlling manufacturing expenses and interpreting variances in these accounts to top management.

[i] GENERAL APPROACH: Manufacturing expenses cover many items: supervision and indirect labor, setup labor, or the time required to setup dies, tools, fixtures, or machines prior to initiating operations; and downtime, which is the idle time of productive employees for causes beyond their control, like the breakdown of equipment, waiting for job assignments, preparation for the job, the failure of utilities, or the lack of materials. There are also the costs of material handling, supplies used, spoilage and waste, maintenance, rent, insurance, depreciation, and property taxes. Regardless of short-term changes in production, some of these manufacturing expenses, such as rent and insurance, are fixed. Some, like material handling and supplies used, vary with plant activity and are absent when operations halt. Still others, and probably the bulk of these expenses, are semivariable.

When broken down into their fixed and variable elements, manufacturing expenses may be readily calculated for any given volume of business activity.

To make this breakdown, as we have seen, requires a measure of production activity. Various devices are used for this purpose, such as units of output, direct material costs, machine hours, direct labor hours, or direct labor costs. After the yardstick for gauging burden charges (to be defined below) has been selected, the behavior of the different manufacturing expenses may be studied against the background of this standard.

[ii] IMPLICATIONS OF THE USE OF PRE-DETERMINED BURDEN RATES: A complication in the analysis of manufacturing costs is created because the accounting for manufacturing expenses is usually based upon a predetermined ratio of estimated costs and production. Accordingly, to establish and interpret budgetary differences in manufacturing expenses, some understanding is needed of the use and significance of this predetermined burden rate.

In cost accounting, the actual material and labor costs experienced are applied directly to particular jobs or processes. Manufacturing costs though, present a different problem for two main reasons: first, the amounts of many of these costs are not known until the accounting period is over; second, it is often impossible or impractical to charge them directly to production orders. Nevertheless, to price inventories and make internal analyses, the costs must be distributed to products during the period as production occurs.

This distribution is made by means of predetermined burden rates calculated for different cost centers, which may be departments. The rates are based upon estimates of the manufacturing expenses which each department is expected to incur during the following period. When a company has a flexible budget, the estimates initially take into account the break-down between fixed and variable expenses. The predetermined burden rate, however, represents the relationship between the totals of manufacturing expenses, covering both the fixed and variable portions, and some measure of normal production.

During the period, manufacturing expenses are charged to the job by applying the predetermined burden rate for each department to the actual production. These estimated expenses are absorbed into inventory and become the basis of pricing and other analytical decisions. At the same time, the manufacturing expenses actually experienced by each department are recorded. At the close of the period, therefore, the accounts of the departments show both the estimated manufacturing expenses charged to the job and the manufacturing expenses actually incurred. The estimated expenses are said to be overabsorbed when they are greater and underabsorbed when they are less than the actual expenses.

Over or underabsorption exists for two major reasons. One is that the actual production for the period may vary from the normal level used to establish the predetermined burden rate, in which case the difference is attributed to volume: if actual production is higher, a greater amount of manufacturing expenses are charged to the job than were incurred, whereas if actual production is below normal, the manufacturing expenses charged to the job are less than actually incurred. The other reason is that the efficiency of performance in this area may be above or below that expected; differences arising for this reason are called efficiency or performance variances. Clearly, it is important that the financial manager be able to evaluate the significance of the over- or underabsorption of manufacturing expenses by ascertaining how much of this differential was caused by volume and how much by performance variances. The flexible budget permits this breakdown.

Let us assume, for example, that a company has a flexible budget which shows that at a normal volume of activity of 200,000 direct labor hours, fixed manufacturing expenses are $260,000 and variable manufacturing expenses are $480,000. After the period is over, it is found that actual production called for the expenditure of 180,000 standard direct labor hours and that manufacturing expenses amounted to $850,000. The predetermined burden rate originally used to distribute these expenses was calculated as follows:

Fixed manufacturing expenses	$260,000	
Variable manufacturing expenses	480,000	
Total manufacturing expenses	$740,000	
Normal level of activity	200,000	direct labor hrs.
Predetermined burden rate	$740,000	or $3.70 per
	200,000	direct labor hr.

During the period, the predetermined burden rate of $3.70 in manufacturing expenses per direct labor hour was applied to the 180,000 standard hours called for by production to give $666,000, representing the amount of manufacturing expense actually charged to the product. This figure, called applied manufacturing expenses, is used for costing purposes and invariably differs from the expenses actually incurred. In our illustration, the applied manufacturing expenses of $666,000 compare with the actual expenses incurred of $850,000. The difference of $184,000, reflecting at least in part, the amount of manufacturing expenses unabsorbed because actual production was less than normal, is eventually charged against profits for the period. If the amount applied had been larger than actual expenses, the overabsorption would have been subsequently credited to profits through appropriate accounting entries. In either circumstance, the portion of the variance attributable to volume differences and the portion attributable to operating efficiency must be ascertained. These relationships are portrayed in Figure 5.12. Direct labor hours are plotted on the horizontal axis and manufacturing expenses on the vertical axis. The company estimates that manufacturing expenses for the period will be $740,000 (H-J) at a normal capacity of 200,000 direct labor hours (A-J), which gives a predetermined ratio of $3.70. These manufacturing expenses are composed of $480,000 in variable expenses (H-I), obtained by multiplying the variable unit rate of $2.40 by 200,000 direct labor hours, and $260,000 in fixed expenses (I-J), equivalent to a fixed unit rate of $1.30 multiplied by 200,000 hours.

At the actual level of activity experienced during the period, only 180,000 direct labor hours (A-D) were called for. Actual expenses at this level amounted to $850,000 (E-D), budgeted expenses equaled $692,000 (F-D), and applied expenses were $666,000 (G-D). Points E and H cannot be compared because they fall along different vertical lines, but E, F, and G are comparable since they follow the same vertical line. The difference between actual and budgeted expenses equals $158,000 (E-F), the budgetary variance;

the difference between budgeted and applied expenses is $26,000 (F-G), the volume variance; the sum of these two variances, $184,000 (E-G), represents the overall difference between actual and applied expenses.

FIGURE 5.12 *Relationship among actual, budgeted, and applied manufacturing expenses*

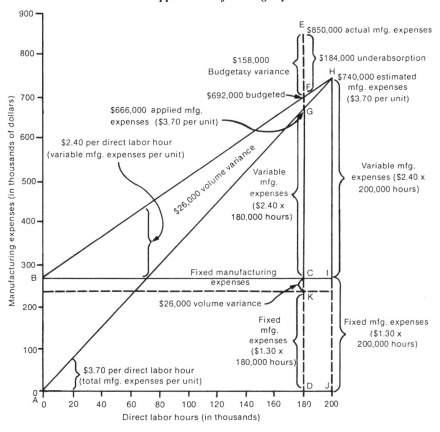

The original estimate of $740,000 may be visualized as falling along the line B-F-H or A-G-H. In the first instance, the line starts at $260,000, representing fixed expenses on the y axis, and runs upward at a variable expense rate of $2.40 per unit. In the second case, it starts at zero and moves ahead at an overall predetermined burden rate of $3.70 per unit. Since the latter rate is used to charge manufacturing expense to inventory, at 180,000 direct labor hours the $666,000 applied expenses consist of $432,000 of variable expenses ($2.40 x 180,000) and $234,000 fixed expenses ($1.30 x 180,000). The difference between the $260,000 of fixed expenses and the $234,000 absorbed at 180,000 direct labor hours is $26,000 (C-K), or the underabsorption caused by applying fixed charges to inventory at a rate based on a higher number of direct labor hours than was experienced. Graphically, it can be seen that the difference between budgeted and applied expense of $26,000 (F-G) is actually caused by this underabsorption of fixed expenses (C-K).

[iii] INTERPRETING THE VARIANCES: In our hypothetical example, the volume variance may be ascertained directly. To determine the applied manufacturing expenses, a predetermined burden rate of $3.70 per hour was employed. We have seen that this rate is composed of a variable rate of $2.40, which is the same at any level of production, and a fixed manufacturing rate of $1.30, assuming that fixed manufacturing expenses are spread over 200,000 hours. But the activity amounted to only 180,000 hours. Distributing the fixed expenses of $260,000 over this reduced volume of activity increases the rate to $1.444 per direct labor hour. Accordingly, at the level of production actually experienced, the rate of distribution should have been 14.4 cents higher ($1.444 - $1.30) or $3.844 instead of the predetermined figure of $3.70. Applying the 14.4 cent differential to the 180,000 actual hours gives $26,000, which is the same volume variance that was determined above. Stated differently, because production was 20,000 hours or 10 percent less than normal, the fixed expenses applied to production were 10 percent greater or $26,000.

Analyzing these variances shows that the largest part of the $184,000 difference between actual and applied manufacturing expenses is traceable to the inability of the company to reach budgeted allowances. Management is then justified in investigating the reason for this performance. Because each department head presumably may take corrective action within his area of responsibilities to rectify his part of the underabsorption, it is sometimes called the controllable portion.

The remaining difference of $26,000 shows that the company operated at a below-normal level, thereby incurring charges because a portion of its usable capacity remained idle. Generally, the disposition of the volume variance for product costing and financial accounting is made independent of the measure of production activity selected to determine the applying burden rate. If the variance is material, it probably will be treated as a product cost and allocated between inventories and cost of goods sold. Immaterial variances are likely to be considered a period cost and immediately directed to income.

In a more refined approach, the method of disposition is related to the production activity. If expected annual capacity is selected as the production activity, the resulting variances are assigned to income for the period. When normal capacity is employed to establish the predetermined burden rate for allocating the fixed overhead to products, one part of the volume variance may be attributable to the difference between normal and expected capacity, and therefore considered anticipated and carried forward on the balance sheet as a deferred item. The other part which results from the difference between the expected and annual capacity is unanticipated and may be assigned to income for the period. Since companies commonly plan to have some excess capacity, there is justification for not treating the volume variance arising from use of this measure as a loss due to idle capacity. Depending upon the point of view taken, therefore, the volume variance that occurs when practical capacity is used may result in three parts:

- one part would be treated as a product cost and apportioned between inventories and cost of goods sold;
- another portion can be handled through a balance sheet deferral; and
- a third portion may be written off as a period cost.

5.5 CHAPTER SUMMARY

Volume-cost-profit studies have helped spotlight the importance of marginal analysis. Management has found that decisions on product or price alternatives require emphasis on differential rather than on aggregate costs. With the marginal approach gaining headway, management has become interested in corollary aspects of volume-cost-profit relationships. Profit-graphs have been fashioned in various forms to show the minimum volume of sales required to report a profit. Also the flexible budget has been introduced to provide better control of elusive manufacturing expenses, and it has become commonplace to report performance and volume variances. As a result, management's analytic kit at present typically includes marginal analysis techniques, such as break-even point determination and the flexible budget.

FOOTNOTES

1. It is often difficult to determine the revenue applicable to a particular machine. Accordingly, the comparison is more likely to be between the two streams of costs, with the cost savings, in effect, representing the revenues generated by the new machine.
2. The reader is cautioned that the nomenclature is not standardized and that the terms *marginal costs, differential costs,* and *incremental costs* may be used to identify the same or different concepts by various authors.
3. For purposes of financial analysis, it has been found that within a given capacity, variable costs per unit do not change. This means that unit marginal costs are constant, and it is profitable for a firm to expand to full capacity as long as the sales prices per unit remains above unit marginal costs. In economic theory, on the other hand, it is traditional to state that profits are greatest where marginal revenue equals marginal costs, and to assume for this purpose a changing marginal cost curve per unit. But in financial analysis a rising unit marginal cost curve can only take place if additional equipment or other operating modifications are introduced, both of which change the variable costs per unit. In effect, therefore, a changing marginal cost curve per unit enters into the area of differential costs and presents another framework for analysis.
4. An ordinary least squares regression is a line connecting a number of points such that the sum of the squared deviations of the points from this line is less than that produced by any other line connecting these points.
5. A third such technique is direct costing in which internal financial statements are prepared on a basis similar to the concept of marginal analysis discussed in this chapter.
6. The concept of marginal analysis can also be used in the decision of which of two or more products the company should attempt to sell if the firm can sell one or the other product but not both.

	A per unit	B per unit
Selling Price	$5.00	$10.00
- Variable Costs	3.00	7.00
Contribution to fixed costs and profit (Marginal Income)	$2.00	$ 3.00

At first it might seem that product B is more desirable to sell than product A. Product B yields a marginal income of $3.00, while product A produces a marginal income of $2.00. However, the company must invest $7.00 to gain $3.00 in the case of product B—a risk:gain ratio of 7:3 or 30%, while it need invest only $3.00 to gain $2.00 for product A—a risk:gain ratio of 3:2 or 40%. Since A produces a higher marginal income relative to its variable costs than does B, it is a more desirable product to manufacture and sell. (See chapter 9 for an additional application of the concept of marginal analysis where it is used in the credit granting decision.)

7. For a mathematical proof of these relationships, see Sidney Robbins and Edward Foster, Jr., "Profit Planning and the Finance Function," *The Journal of Finance*, December 1957, pp. 451-467. This is an early article, but the mathematical relationships, of course, have not changed.

8. Alternatively, the following relationships may be established: Let x1, x2, and x3 be the units to be sold of product one, two, and three, respectively. Then, simple equations may be used to express the relationships among the products, as follows:

$(2)x1 + (3)x2 + (5)x3 = \$6,000,000$ [1]
$x1: x2: x3 = 2:2:1$ [2]

Equation [1] indicates that the sum of the contribution margins of all three products equals the amount of the common fixed costs. Equation [2] captures the relative weights embodied in the planned sales mix. To ascertain the number of units of x1 that must be sold in combination with x2 and x3 to break-even, the equivalence of x2 and x3 in terms of x1 is established from [2] to get a one-unknown, simple equation. Thus,

$x1:x2 = 2:2$ which means $x1/x2 = 2/2$ or $x1 = x2$, and
$x1:x3 = 2:1$ which means $x1/x3 = 2/1$ or $1/2\ x1 = x3$.

These values are put into [1] to get:

$(2)x1 + (3)x1 + (5)(1/2)x1 = \$6,000,000$.

Therefore, $7\ 1/2\ x1 = \$6,000,000$
    and $x1 = 800,000$
    so $x2 = 800,000$
    and $x3 = 400,000$.

9. Some analysts have suggested using production value realized, obtained by subtracting the cost of items that are purchased from outsiders—raw materials, power supplies—from the sales value of output. They argue that the internal funds a company has available for expenditures on output are limited to the value of its own productive effort, because the money going to other sources is not controllable by the company.

10. At any given unit sales price, the break-even formula may be expressed in terms of physical units. Let s represent the sales price per unit, n the number of units sold, v the variable costs per unit, and, F, total annual fixed costs. The break-even relationship then works out as follows:

$$sn = \frac{F}{1 - \dfrac{vn}{sn}}$$

$$sn = \frac{F}{\dfrac{sn - vn}{sn}}$$

$$sn = \frac{F(sn)}{n(s - v)}$$

$$n = \frac{f}{s - v}$$

$$n = F \frac{1}{s - v}$$

11. Since the break-even formula expressed in physical units is $F/(s-v)$, the same effect is obtained by raising the unit sales price(s) or lowering the unit variable cost (v). To convert to dollar values, the break-even point in units is multiplied by the unit selling price(s). Therefore, the dollar value break-even point is higher when the increased marginal income differential is derived by raising the unit selling price than when it is derived by reducing the unit variable cost.

12. Full product costs are still necessary for purposes of cost analysis and pricing.

13. This probability is calculated directly from a mathematical table that shows the area under a standardized normal curve. See Figure 18.4 for such a table. Also see the discussion in that chapter of finding the area under the normal curve. In our example, it is necessary to standardize the dollar units of profits in order to use the table. Thus, the zero level of profits is two standard deviations ($0-$16,000/$8,000) to the left of the mean, which is read from the table as .0227. Since the firm would break-even if sales were 8,000 units, the probability of having less than 8,000 units is 2.3 percent.

SUGGESTED READINGS

Bartenstein, Edwin, "Different Costs for Different Purposes," *Management Accounting*, August 1978.

DeCoster, Don T. and Eldon L. Schafer, *Management Accounting: A Decision Emphasis*, 2nd Ed., John Wiley & Sons, Inc., New York, 1979.

Finley, D.R. and Woody M. Liao, "A General Decision Model for Cost-Volume-Profit Analysis Under Uncertainty: A Comment," *The Accounting Review*, April 1981.

Grossman, Steven D., Charles W. Plum and Robert B. Welker, "New Dimensions in the Cost-Volume-Profit (Breakeven) Technique," *Managerial Planning*, March/April 1979.

Kottas, John F., and Hon-Shiang Lau, "Direct Simulation in Stochastic CVP Analysis," *The Accounting Review*, July 1978.

Kupper, Harold, "Break-Even Analysis with Variable Product Mix," *Management Accounting*, April 1978.

Lambrix, Robert J. and Surendra S. Singhvi, "How to Set Volume-Sensitive ROI Targets," *Harvard Business Review*, March-April 1981.

Lau, Amg Hing-Ling and Hon-Shiang Lau, "A Comment on Shih's General Decision Model for CVP Analysis," *The Accounting Review*, October 1981.

Louderback, Joseph G. and George E. Manners, Jr., "Integrating ROI and CVP," *Management Accounting*, April 1981.

Morse, Wayne J. and Imogene A. Posey, "Income Taxes Do Make a Difference in C-V-P Analysis," *Management Accounting*, December 1979.

Shih, Wei, "A Comment on Shih's General Decision Model for CVP Analysis—A Reply," *The Accounting Review*, October 1981.

———, "A General Decision Model for Cost-Volume-Profit Analysis Under Uncertainty," *The Accounting Review*, October 1979.

APPENDIX A: ANALYZING PROFIT DISCREPANCIES FOR THE MULTIPRODUCT FIRM

Volume-cost-profit analysis may also be used to decompose the difference between actual and budgeted profits in order to determine the portions attributable to changes in the sales mix and that which results from changes in unit variable costs. As an illustration, consider the firm described in 5.4[1](a)[ii] that has planned a sales mix providing for two units of x1 and two units of x2 for each unit of x3.

The firm's budget appears as follows:

Product	Unit Selling Price (dollars)	Unit Variable Cost (dollars)	Quantity (millions of units)	Total Sales Revenue (millions of dollars)	Total Variable Costs (millions of dollars)
x1	$5.00	$3.00	2.0	$10.0	$6.0
x2	6.00	3.00	2.0	12.0	6.0
x3	10.00	5.00	1.0	10.0	5.0

Subtotal
Variable Costs	17.0
Fixed Costs	6.0
$32.0	$23.0

After the year is over, the company finds that its results are as follows:

Product	Unit Selling Price (dollars)	Unit Variable Cost (dollars)	Quantity (millions of units)	Total Sales Revenue (millions of dollars)	Total Variable Costs (millions of dollars)
x1	$5.00	$3.00	3.0	$15.0	$9.0
x2	6.00	3.00	1.0	6.0	3.0
x3	10.00	3.00	1.1	11.0	3.3

Subtotal
Variable Costs	15.3
Fixed Costs	7.7
$32.0	$23.0

With respect to total sales and costs, $32.0 million and $23.0 million respectively, the company met its planning objectives. As a result, actual profits of $9.0 million coincide wth budgeted profits for the year. Within this framework, however, significant differences occurred between targets and outcomes. It is important to identify these differences in order to understand its underlying operations.

There is no special problem in analyzing fixed costs. Actual fixed costs of $7.7 million exceeded planning costs of $6.0 million by $1.7 million. Management could investigate the different elements of these costs to ascertain which were out of line. Having obtained this information, it could analyze the reasons for the discrepancies and establish the need for corrective action.

Actual variable costs of $15.3 million were less than the $17.0 million planned by $1.7 million. The reason for this differential is more complex. Part of it is due to the fact that the actual unit variable costs of each product were not the same as planned. Another part is attributable to the fact that the actual quantities of each product were not the same as those planned.

In this case, there are only three products involved, their unit sales prices were met, and only the unit variable cost of product x3 differed from plan; it was $2.00 per unit more favorable. Since 1.1 million units of product x3 were produced, $2.2 million dollars ($2.0 x 1.1 million units) of variable costs were saved. Comparing the $2.2 million favorable variable costs variance with the $1.7 million by which total actual variable costs were below those planned, we can readily see that $0.5 million of extra variable costs were incurred because of an unfavorable actual sales mix.

In most cases, the analysis would be much more complex and a simplifying procedure is desirable. For this purpose, use may be made of the concept of the "equivalent selling price per unit."[1] This figure is calculated in two stages. First, according to the budget, the planned average profit margin of all the company's products in percentage is determined. Then, the equivalent unit selling price of each product is calculated after the period is over, (the equivalent dollar margin by which the actual unit selling price of each product exceeds the standard unit variable costs divided by the average planned percentage margin.)

These relationships may be expressed in equation form:

$$M = \frac{R - V}{R} \qquad [1]$$

$$ESP_p = \frac{ASP_p - SVC_p}{M} \qquad [2]$$

where:

M = average planned profit margin in percentage;
R = total revenues in dollars;
V = total variable costs in dollars;
ESP_p = equivalent unit selling price of each product;
ASP_p = actual unit selling price of each product; and
SVC_p = standard unit variable cost of each product.

In the third stage, the equivalent unit selling price of each product becomes the means of obtaining the total equivalent sales revenue. This calculation simply involves multiplying the equivalent selling price of each product by the number of units of each product actually sold and summing the results.

$$S = \sum_{p=1}^{n} (ESP_p) \, Q_p \qquad [3]$$

where:

S = total equivalent sales revenue;
Q_p = the number of units of each product sold; and
n = the number of products sold.

Stage four provides a basic figure used in the final unravelling process. This figure represents the percentage deviation in actual gross profits (total sales revenue less total variable costs) caused by deviations in the sales mix. It is calculated by taking the product of two percentages: the average percentage profit margin (M) multiplied by the percentage of the total equivalent sales revenue (S) to the total actual sales revenue (R). This expression reads as follows:

$$\triangle P_s = M(S/R - 1)100 \qquad [4]$$

where:

P_s = percent deviation in gross profits due to deviations in sales mix.

Stage five provides another basic figure used in the unravelling process. It represents the percentage difference between the gross profits that actually were achieved and the gross profits that would have been achieved had there been no deviation in unit variable costs. The figure is calculated by subtracting the following percentages:

(1) the percentage of total equivalent sales revenue multiplied by the average planned profit margin to the total actual sales revenue; and

(2) the percentage of total actual variable costs to the total actual sales revenue. In equation form this expression reads as follows:

$$\triangle P_c = (1 - V/R - MS/R)100 \qquad [5]$$

where:

P_c = the percent deviation in gross profits due to deviations in variable costs.

The two basic percentage figures determined above are then converted to dollars by applying them to the total sales revenues. Thus, the product of the percent deviation in gross profits due to deviations in the sales mix ($\triangle P_s$) and the total actual sales revenues (R), yields the dollar amount by which actual gross profits differ from those planned because the actual sales mix was not in the same proportion as the original plan. The product of the percentage difference between the gross profits that were actually achieved and the gross profits that would have been achieved had there been no deviation in unit variable costs ($\triangle P_c$) and the total sales revenue (R), yields the dollar amount by which actual gross profits differed from those planned because of deviations in unit variable costs.

The description of these stages may seem complicated, but their application is quite simple, as may be seen by returning to the firm in our illustration. We may now apply the prior equations to decompose the difference between actual and budgeted profits into the portions attributable to sales mix and variable costs.

Applying equation [1], we obtain the average planned contribution margin in percentage (M).

$$M = \frac{\$32.0 - \$17.0}{\$32.0}$$

$$= \frac{\$15.0}{\$32.0}$$

$$= .4688$$

(M) may be used in equation [2] to obtain the equivalent unit selling price (ESP).

ESP Product One $= \dfrac{\$5.00 - \$3.00}{.4688} = \dfrac{\$2.00}{.4688} = \$4.27$

ESP Product Two $= \dfrac{\$6.00 - \$3.00}{.4688} = \dfrac{\$3.00}{.4688} = \$6.40$

ESP Product Three $= \dfrac{\$10.00 - \$5.00}{.4688} = \dfrac{\$5.00}{.4688} = \$10.67$

The ESP data may be used to obtain the total equivalent sales price (S) as indicated in equation [3].

Product	ESP (dollars)	Actual Quantity (millions of units)	S (millions of dollars)
x1	$ 4.27	3.0	$12.81
x2	6.40	1.0	6.40
x3	10.67	1.1	11.74
Total			$30.95

Equation [4] provides the percent deviation in gross profit due to deviations in sales mix.

$$\Delta P_s = .4688 \, [(\$30.95/\$32.00) - 1]100$$
$$= .4688 \, (-.0330)100$$
$$= (-.0154)100$$
$$= -1.54 \text{ percent.}$$

Applying -1.54 percent to the sales revenue of $32.00 million yields - $0.5 million, the amount (the same as determined previously) by which gross profits were reduced because of the difference between the actual and the planned sales mix.

Equation [5] provides the percent deviation in gross profits because of deviations in variable costs.

$$\Delta P_c = [1 - (\$15.3/\$32.00) - (.4688) (\$30.95/\$32.00)]100$$
$$= [1 - .4781 - (.4688) (.9672)]100$$
$$= [1 - .4781 - .4534]100$$
$$= [1 - .9315]100$$
$$= [.0685]100$$
$$= 6.85 \text{ percent.}$$

Applying 6.85 percent to the actual sales revenue of $32.0 million yields $2.2 million. This represents the amount (the same as determined previously) by which gross profit was increased because of deviations in the sales mix.

These simple formulae provide the basis for analyzing the reasons that actual gross profit exceeded planned gross profit by $1.7 million. Of this amount, $2.2 million was caused by a favorable variance in variable costs, offset in part by an unfavorable variance of $0.5 million in the sales mix.

FOOTNOTE:

1. The following discussion is based on Harold Klipper, "Breakeven Analysis with Variable Product Mix," *Management Accounting,* April 1978, pp. 51-54.

6

FINANCIAL PLANNING AND CONTROL THROUGH BUDGETING

6.1 ROLE OF BUDGETING IN THE OVERALL PROCESS OF FINANCIAL PLANNING AND CONTROL

The previous chapters in Part II discussed the primary techniques for analyzing the important characteristics of a firm's activities and the environment in which they are performed. In this chapter we show how to plan and exercise control over the firm's expenditures and the availability of funds. The budget itself serves as a major tool of financial analysis; the budgeting process, however, is also an integral part of overall corporate planning and control.

The objectives of financial planning and control are to attain the desired or targeted levels of profits and to ensure sufficient cash for meeting current obligations and financing future capital expansion. To a large extent, modern business firms conduct this financial planning and control through a series of budgets.

Figure 6.1 illustrates the relationship between budgeting and the overall process of financial planning and control. As previously discussed in Chapter 1, planning represents one of the most important activities conducted by the financial manager. Planning, and thus budgeting, as an integral component, begins with the statement of corporate goals or obligations. The profitability goal generally serves as the unifying principle for the firm's executives and supervisory personnel involved in the budgeting process because it represents the corporate objective common to all their activities.

From the statement of overall corporate goals evolves the long-term business plan which encompasses the firm's long-term sales forecast and its strategy with respect to the numbers and kinds of goods and services to be produced. Under the umbrella of the long-term business plan, corporate managers develop the short-term (6-12 months) sales forecasts and the individual operating budgets necessary to translate the sales forecast into the

FIGURE 6.1 *Relationship between budgeting and the overall process of financial planning and control*

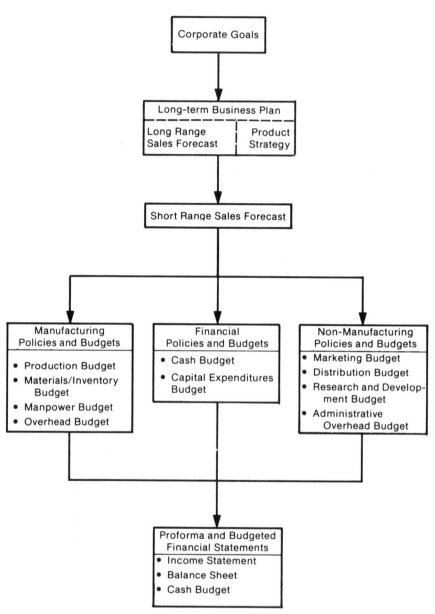

desired or targeted level of profitability. As illustrated in Figure 6.1, these operating budgets cover virtually every important area of firm activity-production, sales, marketing, research and development, etc.

Through a series of financial budgets, of which the cash and capital budgets are most important, the firm's managers can effect comprehensive control over expenditures. This is because the budgets serve as the basis for the critical comparison of planned versus actual expenditures. In addition, the short-term operating plans for all major division or departments—as found in the respective operating budgets—are integrated in proforma financial statements which indicate how closely the predetermined corporate goals will be achieved. If the results appear likely to fall short of corporate goals, budgetary levels may be revised during the fiscal year in order to integrate new developments into the budgeting process.

This chapter addresses the following important aspects of the budgeting process:

- primary objectives of budgeting programs;
- major types of budgets;
- ˙relationship between budgeting standards and costs;
- principles for effective budgeting; and
- fundamental issues in constructing budgets.

6.2   PRIMARY OBJECTIVES OF BUDGETING PROGRAMS

The benefits derived from a budget reflect the care and effort put into it. Loose and informal budgeting systems may be little more than administrative procedures to help in daily activities. Even more elaborate systems may have only restricted purposes, such as lightening the executive load by distributing responsibilities or solving particular problems of costs or sales. However, when the company installs a comprehensive budgeting system as an integral part of the process of overall financial planning and control, its purposes transcend any one objective. The budgeting system represents the functional standards that integrate and guide the firm's operations. In light of these broader goals, the primary objectives of a budgeting system may be described as follows:

[1] PLANNING FOR PROFITS

Profits are the outcome of many interlocking transactions. In a manufacturing concern, for example, sales depend upon production which requires floor space and equipment. Labor and materials put into the facilities are converted into salable units. This process entails engineering applications, record-keeping, supervising, servicing, maintenance, and other activities. Each of these elements contributes to a successful product, and if any important one is missing, the overall process suffers.

The producing selling process is complicated. A company cannot trust to chance, for example, that plant capacity will be available when necessary to meet an expected increase in demand; that the funds will be obtainable when a plant needs to be built; or that suitable machine tools and adequate labor and materials will be on hand to initiate and maintain the necessary manufacturing flow. A management that relies on the vagaries of fortune to arrange its operating scheme risks running into a wall of problems.

The budget establishes a plan of action that enables management to know beforehand the amounts and timing of the production factors required to meet desired levels of sales. The demand supply characteristics of these factors should be studied to judge their adequacy for schedule needs. There is little point, for example, in developing production schedules around materials that will be in short supply. Similarly, the company's ability to obtain funds must be evaluated to determine whether the program presupposes exaggerated financing capabilities. If weaknesses are detected in advance and appropriate steps are taken to eliminate them, financial difficulties may be avoided. Harm occurs primarily from coping with unexpected problems. A budgetary system thus provides an operating model which a company can use to work out its mistakes without reaping their consequences.

[2] COORDINATING PRIMARY CORPORATE FUNCTIONS

Planning enables management to anticipate problems and to revise programs should these problems appear insurmountable. But once operating goals are established and measures taken to eliminate potential blocks, the whole organization must work together as a team.

Unfortunately, operating heads sometimes consider themselves independent captains rather than members of a large group. Their major objective may be to build their own section, department, or division, and they may disregard its role in the overall organization. The budget combats this tendency. It establishes echelons of objectives which govern the activities of different functional units and integrates them into the company's goals.

By coordinating activities, the budget ideally reduces the danger of interdepartmental frictions. The sales department recognizes that its schedules must be developed in the light of manufacturing capabilities; the production department investigates whether certain materials or supplies are available before demanding them; the engineering department learns the importance of considering producability, costs and quality standards in its designs. The reduction of these typical intracompany difficulties, in turn, enhances overall efficiency.

[3] CONTROLLING COSTS

A budget establishes the amount of expenditures allocated to each function for the ensuing fiscal period. These allowances permit a ready comparison with actual accomplishments, so that any tendency for disbursements to run ahead of established limits may be spotted promptly.

To ensure that the detection of excesses leads to corrective action, various operating heads are given the responsibility for administering the budget's detailed segments. The nature of this accountability depends on the organizational structure of the company; assignments may filter down to low echelons when coordinate authority is similarly distributed.

Assigning certain individuals the responsibility of controlling designated segments of expenditures, furnishing them with guidelines to determine the amounts that may be spent, giving them the authority to change the flow of spending, and establishing policies which ensure that upper management will follow a uniform procedure of checking actual against allowable disbursements; all create the mechanism for controlling costs within a company. A budgetary program sets up and coordinates these tasks.

[4] LEVERAGING MANAGEMENT

The managerial group of a large organization is very small compared with the number of employees. It is impossible for these few individuals to closely follow all the interrelated activities of the business. To maximize its effectiveness, management must distribute its responsibilities so that it can maintain a broad perspective on the entire operation.

A budget program erects the framework for achieving this objective. It requires allocating projected expenditures to appropriate cost centers, thereby requiring management to attend to the organizational structure. To make this cost distribution effective, the program also necessitates a co-ordinate spread of operating responsibilities, and this encourages individual interest and initiative. This emphasis on organization and localized authority enlarges the management base, leads to the development of new administrative talent, and defines more clearly the levels of managerial responsibilities.

6.3 MAJOR TYPES OF BUDGETS

The corporate budget is composed of a number of written reports systematized in an overall program of financial planning and control. Each of these reports is an individual budget. These individual budgets are integrated by using the same standard, i.e., corporate profitability, as a goal. The various individual budgets, in turn, are classified into two primary categories: (1) budgets that coordinate operations and (2) budgets that control the financial aspects of the business.

[1] OPERATING BUDGETS

The principal components of the firm's operating budget include the sales, production, inventory, materials, and manpower budgets. Other components include the budgets for distribution, administrative, and research and development expenses. Figure 6.2 presents a simplified illustration of how these components of the overall operating budget are interrelated.

(a) Sales Budget

The sales budget provides the thread of uniformity throughout the entire budgeting process. Some companies employ elaborate statistical techniques to project sales and to test the accuracy of the results. In making a forecast, consideration is given to the conditions of the economy as well as the role of the industry within the economy, the portion of the industry's market that the firm expects to capture, and the distribution of sales, month by month, in the light of this estimated gross market. In many firms, the sales budget originates in the field and is reviewed by key personnel in the sales and other departments, especially planning. In this way, the sales budget incorporates conditions outside the firm as well as the expectations of key managers within the sales, marketing and planning areas. The sales budget subsequently serves as the first step in the development of the production budget.

FIGURE 6.2 *Interrelationships within the overall operating budget*

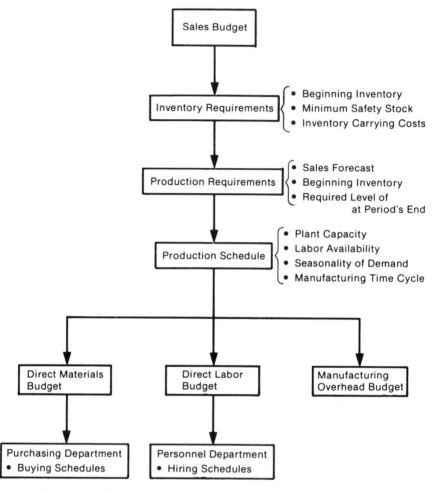

(b) Production Budget

The step from sales to production may be taken in different ways. Perhaps the most direct route starts with estimates of beginning inventory. For this purpose, consideration must be given to factors such as minimum safety stocks, carrying costs, and the optimum ordering quantities.[1] The sales forecast less the starting inventory plus the anticipated ending inventory yields the required production volume. The production department translates the output estimates into monthly schedules that take into account plant capacity, labor availability, seasonal patterns, and the manufacturing time cycle.

(c) Inventory, Materials and Manpower Budgets

Production schedules form the basis for the budgets of direct materials, inventory and direct labor. Material requirements for each product are stated in cost sheets developed by engineering studies. Materials and labor requirements are translated into quantity and dollar costs by applying the appropriate rates to the production schedule. After adjusting for lead time and the demands of the operating cycle, the purchasing department develops its buying schedules, while the firm's personnel department establishes hiring schedules.

(d) Overhead Budget

Manufacturing overhead or burden is generally composed of indirect labor, supplies and other manufacturing costs that cannot be directly assigned to any one product. Preparing the overhead budget is complicated by the number of items included, their varying patterns of fluctuation, and the lack of clear cut lines of responsibility for controlling them. For purposes of control it is important to classify carefully manufacturing overhead expenses so they may be distributed to the accountable department. In this allocation, the financial manager must make a distinction between those items that are directly controllable by the department and those assigned for costing purposes but outside its jurisdiction, such as plant depreciation, rent, utilities, etc.

Because it is relatively easy for inefficiencies to creep into the manufacturing overhead budget, companies often devote considerable effort to its control. For example, Figure 6.3 illustrates the importance given to the overhead budget by a large Midwestern manufacturing firm.

In general, most firms use daily, weekly and monthly reports to detect problem areas before they become serious. To provide standards of comparison, many firms expand the manufacturing overhead budget to include estimates of what each expense item would be at different levels of production. This is the flexible budget previously discussed in section 5.4[2]. As we have seen, it takes the form of a fixed expense base plus a variable expense ratio that is applied to actual production to obtain the budget for that level.

(e) Other Operating Budgets

Other operating budgets cover distribution, administration, and research and development expenses. Distribution expenses embracing salesmen's salaries, advertising, warehousing and storage, are closely related to the sales budget. The administrative budget, which includes salaries of executives and the costs of common service departments such as general accounting and law, is relatively fixed, and there is a tendency to relax the degree of review given it. The research budget, increasingly important in recent years, is particularly sensitive to the influence of competitive pressures.

(f) Interrelationship Within an Operating Budget

As a simplified illustration of how the components of the operating budget are interrelated, let us take as a starting point the physical volume of sales and associated inventories shown in Figure 6.4. These have been prepared by the budget department on the basis of information provided by various cooperating departments, as discussed above.

FIGURE 6.3 *Reports employed by a major midwestern manufacturing firm to prepare the manufacturing overhead budget*

MONTHLY ANALYSIS OF PLANT BURDEN
A summary of all expenses involved in
running of plant showing actual and
allowable levels

Weekly and Monthly Plant Cost Summary	Weekly Analysis of Departmental Budget	Weekly Manufacturing Efficiency Report
Gives production costs, inventory analyses, payroll statistics, and general production information. The production and inventory data show their materials, labor and burden components. The payroll data indicate the relationship between the nonproductive payroll and direct labor.	This is the most important form for control purposes. It is the nucleus of the operating budget. It decomposes the operating budgets to show all the expenses over which the foremen exercise primary control. To assist the foremen, detailed analyses are made of the following expenses.	This is a condensed summary of plant expenses, showing the allowable and actual expenses of the production and other departments. It also summarizes the other expense items affecting operations.

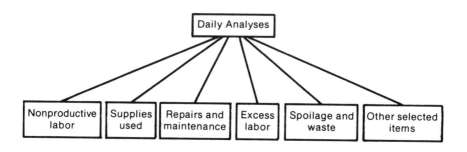

Daily Analyses

| Nonproductive labor | Supplies used | Repairs and maintenance | Excess labor | Spoilage and waste | Other selected items |

FIGURE 6.4 *Interrelationships within an operating budget*

	Sales	Opening Inventory (Thousands of units)	Production	Material (Thousands of lbs.)	Manpower (Number of employees)
January	100	110	125	375	63
February	120	135	125	375	63
March	130	140	125	345	63
April	140	135	115	315	58
May	115	110	105	330	53
June	105	100	110[a]	315	55

[a]July opening inventory and production are estimated at 105,000 units.

The company prepares monthly forecasts for the first half-year and quarterly forecasts for the final half; these forecasts are revised quarterly. For illustration, it is assumed that sales are made from stock, thereby eliminating the necessity of converting sales to orders. The production schedule is derived by adding the expected change in inventory to or subtracting it from the sales projected for the month. The bills of materials call for three pounds of raw material for each unit of production, and a lead time of one month is required to permit the processing. Manpower requirements are determined by applying one direct employee for each 2,000 units of production; no allowance has been made for the learning curve because the units being produced represent well-established items, only a short period is covered, and a small number of new employees are hired. In practice, as manpower requirements are developed over long periods of time and involve hiring, particularly on new processes, the effects of the learning curve could be very important and must be taken into account.

After these preliminary schedules are established, they must be reviewed for reasonableness and effectiveness. Turnover rates will be calculated to gauge the likelihood of achievement. The decline in production over April and May will be studied to assess the advisability of stabilizing output. For this decision, the need and cost of carrying additional stocks of inventory will be weighed against the problems and influences on costs of laying off and hiring direct labor to meet the changing production schedule.

(g) The Financial Manager and Operating Budgets

The responsibility for the entire budget system may fall to the financial manager, or it may be placed under an independent executive, reporting on a staff level to the president. Even when the financial manager has the administrative responsibility, he will probably not participate directly in the supervision and preparation of the operating budgets. Most of these functions are handled by operating and accounting officials. In matters involving policy decisions, the financial officer has a more direct role.

Since the reliability of the long-range forecasts rests upon the accuracy of the sales projections, the financial manager may play an important part in making this forecast. It is likely that he will be one of the executive team that gives final approval to the projections. More particularly, he will probably be requested to interpret the estimates of the sales department in the light of the outlook for the national economy. His opinions in this regard, as on expected levels of consumer purchasing power or the significance of particular financial events such as changes in the tax structure, may require adjustments in the original sales data.

The financial officer is often called upon to arbitrae budgetary conflicts. For example, the sales department may want production schedules that gear inventory levels to sales regardless of seasonal changes; the production department may prefer uniform schedules in order to stabilize employment and facilitate manufacturing flows. As another illustration, engineering has characteristically been the tail wagged by the marketing dog, but as it has gained strength in recent years, it has tried to do its own wagging. If engineering gets its way, the number of products is likely to be reduced while each one is probed in greater depth, whereas marketing ordinarily prefers broad product lines that cover the spectrum of customer needs. Decisions regarding the relative merits of these positions may be resolved through cost studies and profit forecasts made by the financial department.

Policy decisions underlying budgetary procedures require the attention of the financial officer. These include establishing projected levels of inventory and rates of inventory turnover; fixing the nominal operating capacity, which forms the basis of the budgetary allowance for manufacturing expenses; and approving final burden rates for allocating expenses to the products. In addition, he will probably determine the package of reports constituting the master budget for management, and will supervise the preparation of the accompanying budgetary analyses and recommendations.

Finally, the financial officer is responsible for advancing the idea of establishing formal budgetary procedures in firms that do not already have them. Before a program is put into effect, he will have to obtain the cooperation of the entire organization, and he must subsequently maintain their continuation of interest and support. For this purpose, the financial officer would do well to make certain that instructions are understandable, reports simple, and the information disclosed actually used.[2]

[2] FINANCIAL BUDGETS

The principal budgets required for financial control are the cash budget, the capital expenditures budget, and the pro forma balance sheet and income statement. In effect, these budgets reveal the influence of the operating budgets on the firm's financial position and earnings potential. They are thus concerned with problems for which the financial officer is primarily responsible, and are of direct interest to him.

(a) Cash Budget[3]

The cash budget demonstrates the net effect on cash resources of all the expected transactions of the firm during the budget period. The amount of cash available determines the firm's ability to take advantage of trade discounts; meet obligations falling due, such as interest payments; make pension fund contributions; pay income tax installments and dividends; as well as meet the firm's other financial obligations. The cash budget also projects cash deficiencies and excesses, thereby indicating the need for either borrowing or investing. Because these matters are vital to a company's operating success, the cash budget is one of the most important tools in the budgetary kit.

In general, companies prepare the cash budget in different ways depending upon the background of the financial officer and the firm's recording system. In principle, cash budgets can be developed by four methods: (1) adjusted net income statement; (2) projected balance sheet; (3) working capital differential; and (4) direct estimation. The Appendix to this chapter presents several examples of the wide variety of cash budgeting practices found in industry.

[i] ADJUSTED NET INCOME STATEMENT METHOD: Figure 6.5 illustrates the typical form used to project cash balances using the adjusted net income statement method. In this method, the cash budget often resembles a projected sources and uses of funds statement. Cash increases include net income, noncash transactions (such as depreciation, amortization, and accrued expenses), decreases in current assets (except cash), sales of fixed assets, increases in liabilities, and the sale of stock. Cash decreases result from increases in current assets (except cash), purchase of fixed assets, liabilities and equities (repurchases of common or preferred stock) and dividend payments.

FIGURE 6.5 *Form to develop the cash budget by the adjusted net income statement method*

Cash Balance at the Beginning of the Year

Additions: **+**

1. Estimated net income

2. Noncash transactions:
   - depreciation
   - amortization
   - accruals

3. Decreases in assets:
   - marketable securities
   - accounts receivable
   - inventory
   - fixed assets

4. Increases in liabilities:
   - accounts payable
   - notes payable
   - taxes payable
   - long-term debt

5. Increases in net worth:
   - sales of stock

Subtractions: **—**

1. Increases in assets:
   - marketable securities
   - accounts receivable
   - inventory
   - fixed assets

2. Decreases in liabilities:
   - accounts payable
   - notes payable
   - taxes payable
   - long-term debt

3. Decreases in net worth:
   - repurchases of stock
   - cash dividend payments

=   Cash Balance at the End of the Year

[ii] Projected Balance Sheet

With this method, an estimated balance sheet (excluding cash) is constructed by adjusting its components on the basis of the sales projection and expected capital changes. The cash balance is then derived by subtracting total estimated assets, less cash, from the total estimated liabilities, plus capital.

[iii] Working Capital Differential Method

In the working capital differential method, the working capital for the period is first projected by adding estimated income plus other receipts to the prior period's working capital and then deducting nonoperating expenses. By subtracting the required working capital for the period, exclusive of cash, from this projection, the financial manager can obtain the cash available for deposit or investment at the close of the period.

[iv] Direct Estimation Method

For short-term forecasting of cash balances, most firms directly estimate each item affecting cash because this method offers the opportunity for more detailed analyses. **Figure** 6.6 presents the form generally used to directly estimate the cash balance for the budget period. As can be seen from the table, the most important sources of cash are cash sales, collection of accounts receivable, and certain nonoperating transactions that generate cash such as interest, dividend receipts, and the sale of capital assets. Cash disbursements are made for accounts payable, salaries and wages, operating taxes, rent, light, heat, insurance, interest, income taxes, fixed assets, reduction of loans, pensions, and cash dividends.

In preparing the direct estimates of cash increases and outlays, the financial manager relies upon the operating budgets and studies of past years' experience. For example, by analyzing the sales budget and collections, the financial manager may translate credit sales into cash receipts for any designated period. In addition, the financial manager can list, by month, the actual receipts and expenditures of the previous year, segregating ordinary from unusual transactions. Using the sales budget as a point of departure, he can then adjust each item in accordance with the anticipated change in sales.

FIGURE 6.6 *Form to develop the cash budget by the direct estimation method*

	January	February	March	Remaining Months
Cash increases:				
Cash sales	$	$	$	$
Collections				
Interest received				
Dividends received				
Sale of capital assets				
Total increases	$____	$____	$____	$____
Cash decreases:	$	$	$	$
Accounts payable				
Salaries and wages				
Operating taxes				
Rent, light, heat				
Insurance				
Interest				
Income taxes				
Capital improvement				
Payment of loans				
Pensions and profit-sharing				
Dividends				
Total decreases	$____	$____	$____	$____
Cash balance, beginning of period	$	$	$	$
Net change				
Cash balance, end of period	$____	$____	$____	$____

(b) Capital Expenditures Budget[4]

The capital expenditure budget embraces a company's plans for replacing, improving, and adding capital equipment. Ordinary repairs to maintain a property represent overhead and are included in the manufacturing expense budget. Capital costs, on the other hand, are chargeable to the accounts for fixed assets and eventually appear in the income statement through depreciation allowances. Because capital expenditures tend to be large, special procedures are often used for controlling them.

Although ideas for major capital expenditures are likely to originate with top management, those for smaller outlays may come from lower level executives, and there is now a tendency to go farther down the line and invite suggestions from operating personnel as well. The actual responsibility for administering the budget is likely to rest with a financial officer, although some firms place it with production executives. In either case, capital expenditures impinge importantly on the financial program. For one thing, such outlays may seriously drain a company's working capital, leading to an impairment of its financial condition. Then again, the funds required to obtain large plant additions may not be available from internal sources, requiring a coordinated program of financing by means of securities. Moreover, the justification for a new factory or piece of equipment rests primarily in the relationship between its acquisition costs and the expected return from the new investment — a determination that is likely to be made by financial analysis.

Growth can lead to heavy outlays for facilities that require considerable time to build. To permit construction during periods of relatively low costs and to exploit favorable money market conditions, plans must be made well in advance of the requirement date. The long interval covered means that many changes will probably be necessary before these plans are effectuated, but this kind of budget helps to coordinate equipment and financial programs.

Companies often prepare both long- and short-term budgets. For the long-term budget, three to five years appears to be a normal planning period, although some big companies make extensions as long as 10 years. Because it is difficult to judge consumer demand, production methods, and economic conditions in the distant periods, shorter projections are required to develop more specific plans. The annual capital expenditure budget is likely to be geared to the economic outlook, and the amounts set aside are sensitive to changes in the forecasts of business prospects.

To ensure control, the budget procedure is likely to embrace several stages. First, operating or department heads report on replacements or additions they will require to meet anticipated sales and related production programs. In a large business, these requests are incorporated into an overall capital budget for management's consideration.

Ordinarily, approval of the capital budget signifies its acceptance only for planning purposes. As a result, in this initial stage, the budget is often presented in broad terms that describe the kind of undertaking contemplated and the general benefits to be derived. So that these budgets may be easily reviewed, they may be classified by organization unit and by function, as well as by whether the expenditures are for cost reduction, replacement, expansion, or some other purpose.

Authorization of actual expenditures may be done through a written appropriation for each item. These requests are often prepared on standard forms that show both the expected costs and savings from the project. Designated lower level executives may handle modest authorizations, but large expenditures will usually require the approval of a senior officer or a top level management committee, of which the financial manager often is a member. Sometimes, however, top management insists upon scrutinizing all capital expenditures regardless of amount, a policy which can cause a serious drain upon its time, as well as unnecessarily slow up the whole capital budgeting process. To follow the progress of these expenditures, a detailed record is helpful, showing authorizations, commitments, unencumbered balances, and a comparison of planned and actual expenditures. **Figure 16.2** in Chapter 16 presents a capital budget summary employed by the Mobil Oil Corporation in its capital budgeting process.

(c) Pro Forma Balance Sheet and Income Statement

Income statement and balance sheet forecasts are called pro forma financial statements and are intended to portray the effects of future circumstances on the financial condition of the firm. These statements fall into two categories: (1) those based on structural changes in organization or capitalization and (2) those based on operating or economic developments.

Statements in the first category are based on those events whose influence may be gauged with some accuracy. When a firm contemplates refinancing, for example, it may find it desirable to restate both the balance sheet and income statement for a prior period to show the effects of substituting new for old securities. These adjustments are largely mechanical and involve the application of prescribed accounting changes to known situations.

In the second category of pro forma financial statements, the future events referred to are operating or economic developments whose influence is more difficult to assess. The effects on earnings of a proposed expansion program, for example, may be demonstrated by an income statement which assumes that the construction has already occurred and that profits are flowing from the additional facility. Similarly, estimates of probable cash resources may be made by means of a pro forma sources and uses of funds statement that presents the cash expected to be available at the close of a designated period.

Pro forma statements in this latter category are the logical outcome of the budgeting process. They may summarize all the operating budgets into the familiar form that management is accustomed to using as the final measure of business success. Should the pro forma balance sheet growing out of the budgetary process show a deteriorating position, reflected in less favorable financial ratios, a reworking of operating plans or credit policies may be in order even though earnings appear satisfactory. Or, should the profit expectations disclosed in the pro forma income statement flowing out of the overall operating budget fall below the corporate target, a revision in the underlying budgets becomes necessary. By comparing monthly budgeted profits with actual results, the financial manager may observe how well the budget's preconceived targets are being met. Major variations suggest areas to investigate to determine whether the discrepancies are caused by inefficiencies in operations or inadequacies in the budget.

Pro forma statements are characteristically included in the financial analyses given to management to help in planning. They may also form the basis for procuring credit. A lending institution, for example, may insist that the borrowing corporation observe certain restrictions, such as maintaining a minimum relationship between cash and current debt at specified times during each year. In order to determine the company's ability to meet these requirements, it may be helpful to prepare pro forma balance sheets on a monthly basis.

Business decisions are based on management's judgment of the effects of future events on a company's activities. Pro forma statements illustrate these outcomes. By converting the abstractions of possibilities into the realities of concrete statements, they facilitate management's understanding and evaluation of alternative courses of action. Their usefulness has made them a standard item in any scheme of financial controls.

6.4 RELATIONSHIP BETWEEN BUDGETING AND STANDARD COSTS

The costs of particular jobs or processes may be calculated by reference to historical data. So that management may be able to use this information for control purposes, the achieved results must be compared with those attainable at desired levels of efficiency. Standard costs fulfill this purpose.

A standard costing system establishes standards for material quantity and price, labor time and wage rates, and overhead expenses. The extent to which actual results meet prescribed standards is a measure of efficiency. Departures from standards are summarized in variance accounts which are analyzed and distributed to appropriate company officials. Reports on direct materials, labor, and controllable burden (overhead) variances are given to the responsible operating executives who can take corrective action if necessary. Price and volume variances are reported to top management because they are likely to affect factors outside the jurisdiction of supervisory heads.

Standard costs provide predetermined levels of allowable expenses. In such a system, the budget is a summary of these standards applied to a designated operating base. Negative variances from standards indicate areas where a better operating performance may be attained if costs are reduced. Budgetary levels represent the goals that permit the company to earn a desired rate of return on its investment.

By applying estimated unit selling prices and standard manufacturing costs to the projected monthly sales volumes shown in Figure 6.4, the budgeted gross margin is obtained as indicated in Figure 6.7.

FIGURE 6.7 *Budgeted gross margin of profit*

	Sales Volume[a]	Cost of Goods Sold at Standard[b]	Gross Margin
January	$ 200.000	$100.000	$100.000
February	240.000	120.000	120.000
March	260.000	130.000	130.000
April	280.000	140.000	140.000
May	230.000	115.000	115.000
June	210.000	105.000	105.000
Total	$1,420.000	$710.000	$710.000

[a]Unit selling price is $2.

[b]Unit cost of goods sold at standard $1.

If any significant departures from standard are expected because of special conditions developing during the course of the year, these variances may also be included in the budget. The personnel department may anticipate some labor rate variances during certain months, for example, and the purchasing department may want to plan for some material price variances. Overhead costs may be forecast by means of the fixed-variable manufacturing expense breakdown obtained for the flexible budget, and absorbed costs may be calculated by multiplying the indicated burden rate by the monthly production schedule.[5,6] This information may then be incorporated into a pro forma income statement showing the budgeted gross margin based on standard costs and the variances from standard. Figure 6.8 illustrates how such a condensed statement might appear.

**FIGURE 6.8   Pro Forma Condensed Income Statement
showing variances from standard, January-June**

Sales		$1,420,000
Cost of goods sold at standard		710,000
Gross margin of profit at standard		$710,000 [a]
Less:		
Material price variances	$ 14,000	
Labor rate variances	10,000	
Underabsorbed burden	2,000	
		26,000
Gross margin, actual		$ 684,000
Less:		
Selling expenses	$140,000	
Administrative expenses	100,000	
		240,000
Net operating income		$ 444,000
Interest expense		40,000
Net income		$ 404,000

[a] Gross margin at standard is from Figure 6.7, the other data are assumed.

Developed in this fashion, a budget may easily be prepared at any volume level. As an integrated document designed to establish cost goals that must be met if certain profits are to be achieved, the budget unifies the entire operating sequence of a company. Like standard costing, it also helps control costs, a supporting benefit. To a limited degree, therefore, standard cost determinations and budgets both have the aim of cost control; from a broader viewpoint, standard costing contributes to better budgeting, which in turn provides management with a more effective vehicle for administrative planning and control.[7]

6.5   PRINCIPLES FOR EFFECTIVE BUDGETING

Companies typically develop budgeting systems and procedures which meet their unique requirements. Although these systems differ in detail, they usually possess certain important unifying features which, in effect, represent principles for effective budgeting. These are highlighted below.

[1] INTEGRATION OF FUNCTION AND RESPONSIBILITY

Whenever actual results exceed budgetary allowances by a substantial margin, an investigation is required to determine whether remedial measures should be instituted. To ensure that the necessary action is taken, budgets covering specific cost centers should be submitted to the responsible supervisors. This integration of function and responsibility is made possible by relating the accounting classification to the firm's organizational structure so that designated department heads are answerable for prescribed cost areas.

[2] COMMUNICATION OF BUDGET OBJECTIVES

Budgeting is a company function requiring the backing and interest of all echelons of management. This cooperation is best obtained when the purposes of the budget are explained to all supervisory personnel. As part of the same effort, each individual responsible for administering a package of expenditures should help determine the framework of allowances within which he will operate.

[3] DEMONSTRATION OF BUDGET'S EFFECTIVENESS AS A PLANNING AND CONTROL TOOL

To gain the continued cooperation of those participating in the budget system, the financial manager should show them its usefulness as an operating and planning tool. He should, for example, point out improvements effected by supervisors, following shortcomings revealed by the budget. Similarly, top level management should be provided with volume-cost-profit studies flowing from data made available in the budgets. General supervisors may be apprised of pricing and product mix decisions reached through these analyses.

[4] DEFUSING THE NEGATIVE CONNOTATIONS OF THE BUDGETARY PROCESS

It is imperative that company employees not come to consider the budget a restrictive device. To avert this attitude, management should make it clear that it does not regard penury in expenditures as an unconditional achievement. Rather, it must emphasize that the budget is a planning vehicle to permit all members of the management team to obtain their full share of the funds required for desired profit levels.

[5] CLEAR DEFINITION OF BUDGETARY RESPONSIBILITIES, FUNCTIONS, AND PROCEDURES

To enable each responsible official to carry out his budgetary responsibilities, functions and procedures should be outlined clearly. For this purpose, it is helpful to work up a manual describing the budget's procedural steps. Accounting techniques should be developed so that management can easily evaluate the operating facts. There is no virtue in achieving niceties of accounting theory that require considerable effort if they do not contribute usable results. At the same time, the records must provide the necessary sales, costs, profits, and performance measures.

[6] ASSIGNING OVERALL RESPONSIBILITY FOR THE BUDGETARY SYSTEM

Finally, most companies designate a particular organizational unit within the firm as responsible for implementing the budget, coordinating its various parts, putting budgetary information in the proper format, studying the procedures in use, and recommending changes. Traditionally, the task of supervising the budget mechanism has been assigned to the financial division, which already has access to accounting records and cost studies. Some companies, however, believe that the programming and planning elements of the budget require a special approach that disassociates the broader or overall budgeting program from the more restricted cost procedures. In these cases, the responsibility for the budget is given to an independent director on the staff level who reports directly to a high-ranking executive officer.

6.6 FUNDAMENTAL ISSUES IN CONSTRUCTING BUDGETS[8]

In addition to the above principles or guidelines, effective budgeting requires resolving several significant issues relating to constructing operating and financial budgets.

[1] TYPES OF BUDGETS AND LEVEL OF SOPHISTICATION REQUIRED

As mentioned previously, before the budgeting process can begin, management must decide what kinds of budgets are to be produced. In some small firms, construction of rudimentary cash budgets will suffice. Most large firms, however, regularly produce sophisticated cash budgets as well as other budgets and forecasted income statements and balance sheets. Large companies also generally develop operating, production, construction, and other budgets suited to their particular needs. It is important that a procedure be developed which produces those budgets required by the firm, but which does not generate excess and unnecessary paperwork. Thus, the question of which budgets are needed and which are not should be carefully considered.

[2] BUDGET TIME HORIZON

In some especially volatile industries, forecasting for excessively long periods seems a fruitless exercise. However, most firms could benefit from some considerable attention to long-range budgeting. Most small to medium sized firms budget one year in advance. However, larger firms generally conceive of at least some budgets that cover longer periods and normally develop construction and capital expenditure budgets as well as pro forma balance sheets and income statements for up to five years.

[3] TIMING OF THE BUDGET REVIEW PROCESS

Another consideration of some importance is the timing of the budget review process. Not only must the firm decide how often budgeted and actual results are to be compared and the variances developed, but it must also assess the appropriate time interval over which budgeting updates and revisions are to take place. Again, the decision is usually based on the level of effort the firm is able to devote to the entire budgeting process. As might be expected, large companies ordinarily undertake more frequent budget reviews, variance reporting and budget revisions than smaller enterprises. The Vice President of P & C Food Markets, Inc., stated that he spends approximately four days a month solely with the budget review process and considers this one of his most important responsibilities. At his firm, variances of actual from budgeted performance are developed monthly by department, with department heads called upon to justify departures under their jurisdiction. In addition, P & C engages in a quarterly update and revision of all budgets to account for new developments.

[4] BUDGETARY STANDARDS

Another important issue in constructing the budget is determining the appropriate individual or entity to set the standards against which actual performance is to be measured. Broadly speaking, there are two possibilities, standards might be set initially by low level operating individuals in terms of their own performance and then move up the organizational hierarchy, with each successively higher responsibility level developing a standard on the basis of the cumulative standards reported to them. Such a system is sometimes referred to as a "bottom up" approach to setting standards. Alternatively, in a "top down" approach, top management sets standards for those immediately below who, in turn, set standards for those reporting directly to them, and so on down the organizational hierarchy.

The advantages of the former approach are a frequent improvement in employee morale and a feeling of being "part of the process" and in control of one's destiny. Productivity may be enhanced by using this procedure. However, the "top down" approach usually offers a greater degree of coordination between departments, more conformity between actual and overall corporate objectives and a closer congruence of operating performance with external industry-wide and overall economic conditions. In addition, a "top down" approach often results in a more realistic setting of standards.

Of course, a middle ground between the above two methods of setting standards can be found.[9] For example, Niagara Mohawk Power Company, basically uses a "bottom up" approach for its operating budget. However, overall company policy, which must be closely followed as a guideline in setting standards, is set by top management and carefully transmitted down the organizational structure.

[5] BUDGETING INTERVAL

The appropriate budgeting interval must be determined in order for the firm to construct the type and quality of budgets necessary to effectively plan and control its overall operations. The budgeting interval is the time interval into which the budgeting period is to be broken down. A firm may decide to produce a cash budget for a period of six months. But, before it can do so, it must decide how broad a time interval is to be used in breaking down the six month period. The firm may decide upon a monthly breakdown and thus treat the next six months as six individual periods. Alternatively, a weekly or even a daily breakdown may be used.

The breakdown period is crucial because of the assumptions which must be made in all cash budgeting regarding the timing of inflows and outflows within the breakdown interval. In order to avoid a relationship whereby opposing cash flows are concentrated at the beginning and at the end of the period (thereby suggesting cash excesses or deficiencies during most of the period), it is generally assumed that either all inflows and outflows occur at the same point in time within the interval or that each occurs at the same rate during the interval. In assessing the validity of this assumption, the particular interval chosen is of considerable relevance. For example, the broader the interval (a week as opposed to a day or a month), the greater the likelihood of noncongruence of inflows and outflows within this time dimension. This may lead management to choose short budgeting intervals. However, we must keep in mind that ultimately budgeting is merely forecasting and that forecasting over a broader time interval is easier and likely to be far more accurate than budgeting over a narrower time span. For example, at the beginning of the year, the financial manager may be able to project overall sales reasonably well for the next six months. However, the level of accuracy undoubtedly would be reduced if he were required to make a forecast for each of these six months individually. A further deterioration in accuracy would occur if the forecast were required to be made by weeks and a still further departure from accuracy would undoubtedly result should daily projections be attempted. The vagaries of business conditions tend to smooth themselves out and the accuracy of the forecast is enhanced by broadening the budgeting interval.

In essence, then, in choosing a budgeting interval, a balance must be struck between the desire for accurate forecasts on the one hand, and the need for inflows and outlfows to be in harmony within this interval on the other. This balance must be suitable to the particular company, and indeed, firms often choose different budgeting intervals. For example, as a result of the considerable degree of predictability in both the use of its service and the rate of collection of its receivables, Niagara Mohawk Corporation employs a daily interval for its cash budgets. On the other hand, Fay's Drug Company, a discount drug chain, indicated that as a result of great uncertainty over disbursements, cash budgeting is done over three-month intervals.

6.7   CHAPTER SUMMARY

The prime objectives of financial planning are to attain the desired levels of profits and to ensure sufficient cash for meeting obligations and financing future expansion projects. To a large extent, modern business firms conduct this financial planning through a budget.

The bulk of a company's executive and supervisory personnel help develop the budget. In order for their efforts to be unified, it is important to establish a common objective. The desired net return on investment represents such a goal. In many instances, budgetary planning calls for the submission of annual forecasts of the rate of return expected to be reached during the year. The proposals of the various operating departments are eventually integrated into pro forma financial statements indicating how closely the predetermined goal will be achieved. If the results appear likely to fall short of the objective, budgetary allowances may be revised before the fiscal year ends in order to integrate new developments into the budgeting process.

A budget helps a firm to attain desired profit objectives not only by promoting more effective planning but also by requiring stern control over expenditures. Companies often refer to the cost benefits derived from introducing a thorough system of budgetary controls. All phases of a budget plan—sales, operating expenses, and capital expenditures—are eventually reflected in balance sheet changes. Therefore, the financial budget is sometimes called the master plan of the entire planning scheme. Using the cash budget and pro forma balance sheets, a company assembles all the anticipated transactions that will affect cash and working capital. Its management can then appraise the company's liquidity in the light of the budgeted volume of activity.

At different levels of operations, a company requires varying amounts of working capital. Within these levels, the composition of its working capital needs also changes. Introducing new products that require longer manufacturing cycles may demand that larger inventories be carried: undertaking new lines that traditionally entail generous credit terms will increase the amount of receivables carried relative to cash. Similarly, the amount of short-term liabilities reported will depend on management's policies with respect to financing methods.

To evaluate its financial status, a company may develop working capital standards based upon historical experience. It can then gauge the adequacy of budgeted results against these standards. If shortcomings are revealed, corrective action is called for or standards must be revised in accordance with the essential principles of budgeting procedure. The combination of working capital projections, cash analyses, and financial statements helps management determine the need for future borrowing or retrenchment of operating programs.

Budgeting represents an important and potentially valuable technique of financial analysis, and along with the other tools of analysis considered in this part of the text, can make a considerable contribution to the many tasks of the financial manager. Budgeting is also our first indepth examination of the management and administration of cash and other working capital items. It is for this reason that budgeting considerations are developed just prior to our analysis of short-term sources and uses of funds, which are dealt with in the next part of this text.

FOOTNOTES

1. See Chapter 10 for a comprehensive discussion of inventory management.
2. For a discussion of the effects of operating budgets on introrganizational conflict, see M. Edgar Barrett and LeRoy B. Fraser, III, "Conflicting Roles in Budgeting for Operations," *Harvard Business Review,* July-August, 1977, pp.137-146.
3. Chapter 8 presents a comprehensive discussion of cash management and the development of cash budgets.
4. Chapter 16 provides indepth coverage of capital budgets and the capital budgeting process.
5. Flexible budgeting is developed at length in paragraph 5.4[2].

6. Exponential smoothing techniques have also been applied to the problems of forecasting and the setting of standards. For example, see James O. Hicks, Jr., "The Application of Exponential Smoothing to Standard Cost Systems," *Management Accounting*, September 1978, pp.28-32 and 53. The author of this article finds that "exponentially smoothed standards move away from an over-emphasis on a prodding technique—employees must be carefully controlled—to a system based on proven statistical techniques that may have a more favorable behavioral impact."

7. For a discussion of the application of standard costs to the restaurant industry and an analysis of the contribution of standard costs to effective control and budgeting in that industry, see Matthew J. Mullett, "Benefits from Standard Costing in the Restaurant Industry," *Management Accounting*, September 1978, pp.47-53.

8. Although budgeting and the relationship of actual vs. budgeted performance in the development of employee compensation and motivation is not dealt with in this chapter, some reference to this area might be made here. In this connection, see Howard O. Rockness, "Expectancy Theory in a Budgetary Setting: An Experimental Examination," *The Accounting Review*, October 1977, pp.893-903; and J. Ronen and J.L. Livingstone, "An Expectancy Theory Approach to the Motivational Impacts of Budgets," *The Accounting Review*, October 1975, pp.671-685. For an extended analysis of the effects of budgets in influencing behavior and the interaction and relationship of budgets to organization structure, see William J. Burns and John H. Waterhouse, "Budgetary Control and Organization Structure," *Journal of Accounting Research*, Autumn 1975, pp.177-203.

9. For a third approach which combines elements of both the "top down" and "bottom up" methods, see Frank Collins and John J. Willingham, "Contingency Management Approach to Budgeting," *Management Accounting*, September 1977, pp.45-48; and Fred Luthans, "The Contingency Theory of Management: A Path Out of the Jungle," *Business Horizons*, June 1973, pp.67-72. Also see, R.J. Swieringa and R.H. Moncur, *Some Effects of Participative Budgeting on Managerial Behavior*, New York, National Association of Accountants, 1975.

SUGGESTED READINGS

Babcock, Richard and Mahmood A. Qureshi, "A Program for Integrating Budgeting and MBO," *Management Planning*, May-June 1981.

Benke, Ralph L., "Setting and Using Control Limits on Operating Budgets with Non-Standard Costs," *Management Planning*, July-August 1980.

Bergeron, P.G., "Budgeting in Managment — More Than a Balancing Act," *CA Magazine*, January 1980.

Brownell, Peter, "Participation in Budgeting, Focus on Control and Organizational Effectiveness," *Accounting Review*, October 1981.

———, "Role of Accounting Data in Performance Evaluation, Budgetary Participation, and Organizational Effectiveness," *Journal of Accounting Research*, Spring 1982.

Bullock, James H. and Virginia H. Bakay, "How Las Vegas Casinos Budget," *Management Accounting*, July 1980.

Chandler, J.S. and T.N. Trone, "Bottom-up Budgeting and Control," *Management Accounting*, February 1982.

Conn, Carolyn, "Budgets: Planning and Control Devices?" *Managerial Planning*, January/February 1981.

Dino, Richard N. and Lori Wrona Dino, "A Sure-Fire Method to Improve Budget Cycling," *Management Accounting*, January 1980.

Dobson, Chris, "Controlling the Facility Budget," *Industrial Development*, January/ February 1981.

Joiner, C. and J.B. Chapman, "Budgeting Strategy: A Meaningful Mean," *SAM Advanced Management Journal*, Summer 1981.

Magee, Robert P., "Equilibria in Budget Participation," *The Journal of Accounting Research*, Autumn 1980.

Merchant, Kenneth A., "Design of the Corporate Budgeting System: Influences on Managerial Behavior and Performance," *Accounting Review*, October 1981.

Miller, Leland B., "The Buck Starts Here: The Role of the Financial Officer in Corporate Expansion Planning," *Industrial Development*, July/August 1980.

Mosely, Owen B., "Some Thoughts on the Human Side of Budgeting," *Supervisory Management*, April 1981.

Newton, R.L., "Establishing a Rolling Budgeting Process," *Hospital Financial Management*, May 1981.

Valenta, J.R., "Planning — Budgeting Balance," *Managerial Planning*, May/June 1982.

APPENDIX A
EXAMPLES OF CASH BUDGETING PRACTICES FOUND IN INDUSTRY

Through experience, a company may learn to employ expediting techniques for its cash budgeting. For example, it may list by months the actual receipts and expenditures of the previous year, segregating ordinary from unusual transactions. Using the sales budget as a point of departure, it then adjusts each item in accordance with the anticipated change in sales. Thus, if a sales increase is forecasted, a proportionate rise in purchases, payrolls, and other related expenses is made to support this increased volume.

To estimate disbursements for its 12-month forecast, Pitney-Bowes has developed three categories for its cash forecasting: (1) payroll, (2) major expenses such as taxes, dividends, and profit sharing payments, and (3) vouchers, which include all other forms of disbursement except unusual capital expenditures. The company estimates payroll and the separate elements of major expense directly, but uses a formula to forecast the remaining disbursements, thereby eliminating the necessity for estimating a large number of individual items.

Longer-term budgets are characteristically coordinated with short-range forecasts and are defined further as more information becomes available. To this end, the Stromberg-Carlson Division of General Dynamics makes a detailed daily cash budget with a rolling forecast, updating it weekly, for a 12-week period. In addition, they forecast their operating plan by month and measure actual results against these forecasts. P & C Food Markets develops a budget for each coming fiscal year on a month-by-month basis and updates the budget quarterly to account for changing conditions.

American Telephone and Telegraph Company forecasts monthly its daily cash flows for a six-month period. Additionally, cash flow by month is forecasted and modified each month for a period of twelve to twenty-four months. Thus, a detailed daily cash flow forecast is developed for the first six months and monthly cash flows are forecasted thereafter, through the current year and the next calendar year. The Ford Motor Company has an elaborate system: it uses two-year, four-month, and one-month projections of cash flows supplemented by weekly forecasts of daily requirements to cover the following week's operations.

Gulf Oil Corporation utilizes its Comptroller Department's annual 5-year plan prepared each fall for planning its long-range liquidity position. However, since its

Treasury Department's operations require more detailed and timely information than is provided in the annual 5-year plan, the Treasury Department has developed a cash forecasting system for obtaining detailed updates each month on all operational and financial cash flows. Specific information provided includes the exact timing and dollar amount of major disbursements, crude oil receipts, and dailybased in Houston, London, and Bermuda is collected and summarized by the Treasury Departments in those locations and then forwarded to the home office. Other strategy centers and staff elements submit their cash forecasts projections directly to the home office, where all implicit strategy center assumptions are balanced and corporate adjustments made.

The system uses several cash flow models to predict routine monthly and daily cash flows. The models are based primarily on historic trends, recurring seasonal and intramonth cash flow patterns and other cash management considerations. In addition, there are several system balancing functions which ensure that all implicit strategy center assumptions (product prices, volumes, credit terms, etc.) are congruent.

As the result of all of this effort, Gulf prepares a forecast at the beginning of each month detailing all major corporate cash flows for the next three months. This forecast is supplemented by a 12-month forecast published at the beginning of each quarter. In addition, a forecast of daily net operating cash flows for the next 30 days is published several times each month for use by Gulf's Treasury Department in its cash operations investment functions.

A description of the distribution and use of Gulf Oil Corporation's cash forecasting reports is presented in Figure 6-9.

Companies often supplement their cash budgets by forecasts of cash made during the budget period. These nonbudgetary projections are likely to cover shorter terms and to contain greater detail than the regular budget. In those areas where cash is scarce or the company invests cash balances each day, forecasts of cash flows may be prepared by day for periods of from one to six months as a guide to financial management.

A good part of the receipts in the short-term forecasts will come from billings made or from shipments scheduled. A large portion of the expenditures, in turn, will be for purchase invoices received, payrolls determined from already established production schedules, and other reasonably well-known commitments. Accordingly, short-term cash flow forecasts can ordinarily be made with much greater accuracy than longer-term budgeted estimates, which start from the sales forecast, which is itself subject to considerable imprecision.

Since cash flows are constantly changing, continuous forecasting is desirable in order to provide guidance for daily and weekly cash management. By the same token, the financial officer responsible for its management requires regular reports of cash balances. Where daily or weekly cash forecasts are made, these balances may be entered in the cash forecasting form. More commonly, the daily cash report going to the financial officer provides a brief summary of bank balances and related data, such as receipts and payments for the day. Top level nonfinancial management also may want to keep abreast of the company's changing cash position in order to coordinate overall operations. This information is likely to be included in a daily report that covers other key operating statistics. The cash information will probably be limited to reporting current and expected balances without reference to the details of banking locations.

Large decentralized companies give considerable autonomy to the individual operating entities. In these cases, each department or division, as the case may be, prepares its own budgets, which are reviewed and consolidated with company-wide data on the corporate level. Special attention is given to the cash forecasts, because of both their importance and the difficulty of determining cash, which is the net result of

FIGURE 6.9 *Gulf Oil Corp*

Cash Forecasting Reports

Name of Report	Distribution of Report	Comments/Use

A. Monthly Cash Forecast
 	
- 3 month forecast
- 12 month forecast
	- Assistant Treasurer → CFO →
	  Executive Treasurer
	- Investment → Internal Management → Finance
	- Portfolio Investment Group-NYC
	- Corporate Finance
	- Other treasury and staff elements
		- Provides information necessary for upper
		  management to make strategic decisions
		- Used in setting long-range investment strategy
		  and planning major internal financings
		- Used in establishing financing strategy plans
		- As needed

B. Daily Cash Forecast	- Portfolio Investment Group-NYC
	- Cash operations, Pittsburgh
	- Investment management → Corporate Finance →
	  Internal Finance
		- Used in planning maturities of
		  marketable securities
		- Used in monitoring/controlling daily cash flows
		- Used in setting short-term investment strategies
		  and, if necessary, arranging for additional funds
		  via internal or external finance

C. List of Expected Major
Disbursements
	- Cash operations, Pittsburgh
	- Portfolio Investment-NYC
	- Used as a "long-range" guide in setting
	  maturities of marketable securities
	- Assistant treasurer and other management
		- Used in preparing for and monitoring
		  major payments
		- Used in monitoring major payments

all transactions. Department cash budgets are likely to be built up in some detail and discussions held to iron out striking differences among the results obtained at various organizational levels.

The Monsanto Company attributes the success of its cash forecasting procedure to its formulation on a decentralized basis. Each responsible company executive prepares forecasts covering the operations of his department which are eventually incorporated into the company-wide budget. Monsanto's current cash forecasting system distinguishes between the short and intermediate-term forecast horizon. The following summarizes the two types of cash forecasts utilized to satisfy different management requirements.

Tactical Cash Forecast—on a quarterly basis, Monsanto produces a twelve-month cash forecast. Each business group within the five Operating Units of the Company independently prepares profit and working capital projections (excluding cash) based on anticipated business conditions. These decentralized forecasts are aggregated with capital expenditure projections provided by the Corporate Planning group, data from the Tax Department and long-term financing plans supplied by the Treasury Department. If the forecast anticipates a decline in the cash position, the Treasury Department will establish plans for short-term borrowing to supplement internal cash generation. On the other end, surplus funds are targeted for investment in short-term marketable securities.

Financial Planning Cash Forecast—on a semi-annual basis, the Company produces a five-year cash projection. Using the tactical cash forecast for its first year, a "macro model" is utilized to simulate corporate financial results. The computer simulation is useful for analysis on strategic business growth plans based upon various econometric scenarios. If the model indicates a need for long-term funding, action will be taken to secure the required long-term cash at optimum cost.

PART III
MANAGEMENT OF
WORKING CAPITAL

This section examines how companies obtain and employ cash and credit, which provides access to cash, in their everyday operations. The common thread is the movement of cash from its short-term sources to its eventual uses. Cash is a fungible: a dollar received at any point in time is the same as any other dollar received or used at that same point in time. Thus, the flow of cash ties together the various short-term sources and uses of funds, all of which either result in a temporary increase (or decrease) of the firm's cash pool or the acquisition (or disposition) of an asset which will be converted into cash. The five chapters in this section of the book (Working Capital Policy, Cash Management, Credit Management and Policy, Inventory Management, and Short Term Sources of Funds) follow a balance sheet approach. The unifying theme is the cash and credit posture of the firm and the short-term circulation of these items through the business.

7

WORKING CAPITAL POLICY

7.1 WORKING CAPITAL MANAGEMENT— DEFINITION AND IMPORTANCE

The management of working capital encompasses all facets of the planning and administration of current assets and current liabilities. It embraces the recurring transition from cash to inventories to receivables that forms the conventional chain of business operations.

Primarily, the financial manager attempts to ascertain and maintain the level of current assets and liquidity necessary to achieve the firm's desired profitability as well as its growth, capital investment, and long-range financial goals. Toward these objectives, he adjusts the firm's working capital position to reflect its sales activity and its particular financial and operating characteristics.

The adjustment process is intended to maintain working capital at a minimum cost. Senior financial officers stress the importance of this factor in the formulation of working capital management policy. For example, if capital costs 10 percent, an extra $100,000 in inventory ties up $10,000 of profits and requires as an offset $200,000 in sales at a return on sales ratio of five percent.[1]

To help understand the analytic techniques presented in Chapters 8-11, this chapter highlights those aspects of working capital management that guide the financial manager in formulating an effective strategy.

7.2 UNDERSTANDING THE WORKING CAPITAL CONCEPT

The management of working capital requires an understanding of the concept not only by a firm's financial specialists, the controller and treasurer, but also by its various decision makers. Essentially, the concept — in terms of a dynamic activity — embraces the recurring transition, from cash to inventories to receivables to cash, that forms the conventional chain of business operations. While differences of opinion have existed in framing specific definitions, a reasonably standard meaning has emerged in stockholder annual reports, which, under the guidance of governmental and professional bodies, have been gaining greater reliability and uniformity. An integral part of the annual report is the Consolidated Statement of Changes in Financial Position (Source and Application of Funds Statement). This statement shows changes in working capital which flow from the interplay of current assets and current liabilities.[2] The outcome is shown by an increase or decrease in working capital, which is the difference between current assets and current liabilities. This same usage can be found in the text or financial highlights summary of annual reports, although there is a move to place greater stress on cash flows.[3] Accordingly, throughout this chapter and the book as a whole, we employ the terms net working capital and working capital interchangeably, defining them both as current assets less current liabilities. We feel this definition is most appropriate to the purpose of the financial manager.

7.3 THE APPROACH OF WORKING CAPITAL MANAGEMENT

By and large, management controls working capital through cash flows derived from budgetary projections with special attention given to each of the components of working capital. Consequently, management has been able to reduce the cash required to sustain operations, curtail losses, and cut inventory costs.

A fruitful approach has been developed through cost balancing analyses which are essentially minimization problems, where the decision variable is a particular current asset affected by costs moving in different directions. With respect to inventories, for example, the problem is to determine the minimum amount that optimizes the relationship between the ordering costs of accumulating inventory and the carrying costs of holding inventory.

In addition to the overall issue of optimizing values by reducing the firm's costs, mathematical techniques may be used directly to attack the interrelationships among different aspects of working capital. Financial simulation has been employed in these interrelationships so as to visualize the tradeoffs between different possible outcomes in the light of a firm's objectives. Considerations of risk and probability have also been introduced into these analyses.

7.4 THE FACTORS AFFECTING WORKING CAPITAL REQUIREMENTS

The breakdown of expenses into fixed and variable components has its counterpart in working capital. A company must always have sufficient cash or access to cash to meet its established obligations, such as principal maturities, interest charges, and property taxes; these requirements are known in advance and are independent of current activity levels. In addition, even when the business is at its ebb, the company must keep some inventory to ensure minimum operations. The working capital required for prescribed payments and for basic operations during slack periods is considered fixed.

Sales expand as a company enters its active months, causing larger amounts of inventories, receivables, and cash to move through the production sequence. These temporarily enlarged requirements for working capital represent the variable portion that recede as sales decline seasonally. Expanded capacity as a result of secular growth leads to growth in both variable and fixed working capital. At the new enlarged level, fixed working capital requirements remain relatively unchanged, whereas, the variable segment fluctuates with the seasonal swings. The amount and composition of a firm's working capital are constantly affected by criss-crossing economic currents. The nature of the firm's activities, the industrial health of the country, the availability of materials, the ease or tightness of the money market are all part of these shifting forces. It is important that the financial manager be able to identify and analyze the primary factors affecting all the working capital flows of his company because they provide the basis for selecting the appropriate working capital management techniques to control this movement.

Presented below are some of the factors which have characteristically been important influences on working capital flows and requirements.

[1] NATURE OF THE BUSINESS

Basically, a firm's working capital requirements are directly related to its kind of business. A company that sells a service primarily on a cash basis, such as a cleaning establishment or, on a larger scale, a railroad, does not have the pressure of keeping considerable amounts of inventories or of carrying customers' receivables. Cash turns over rapidly, receivables are modest compared to the volume of business transacted, and stocked materials are mostly for equipment repairs. In contrast, a manufacturing enterprise ordinarily finances its own customers, requires large amounts of cash to pay its own bills, and uses inventories of direct materials for conversion to end products. These conditions augment the working capital requirements.

Whenever special circumstances in a particular business threaten supplies of inventories, buildups are likely to occur. For example, a strike looming on the horizon can create fear that deliveries will be held up or price increases occur. As a result, in major labor intensive companies, large inventory increases often take place prior to the negotiation of nationwide labor contracts.

[2] DEGREE OF SEASONALITY

The degree of seasonality is one of the most important factors influencing working capital flows and requirements. Sharp seasonal movements necessitate the buildup of inventories to meet increased demand and subject the firm to the subsequent volatile interplay of receivables and cash as merchandise is liquidated. Companies with strong seasonal movements, therefore, have special current asset problems in controlling these internal financial swings. Aggravating this difficulty are the distortions that may occur in expected patterns. Although seasonality may lull a financial manager into developing fixed programs to meet recurring requirements, flexible arrangements are preferable to guard against unforeseen contingencies. An inability to cope with sharp working capital swings is one reason that companies undertake offsetting diversification programs.

[3] PRODUCTION POSSIBILITIES

Even without diversification, some companies may be able to offset the effect of seasonal fluctuations upon working capital by adjusting their production schedules. As a matter of policy, the choice will rest between the need to vary output in order to gear inventories to seasonal requiremens, on the one hand; and the need to maintain a steady rate of production, permitting inventories to build up during the off season, on the other. In the first instance, inventories are kept to minimum levels but the production manager must constantly adjust his working staff; in the second, the uniform manufacturing rate avoids accordion-like fluctuations of production schedules, but enlarged inventory stocks create special risks and costs.

Because the purchase of inventories is often financed by suppliers, the mere fact that a company carries larger amounts does not necessarily mean that its cash problem is more serious. If the financing is from banks, however, it could lead to greater costs.

[4] GROWTH

Increased working capital requirements are the logical and expected result of corporate expansion. More working capital is required to avoid interrupting the manufacturing sequence. Despite the apparent logical connection between sales growth and the need for working capital, it is not easy to formulate strict rules or firm policy concerning this relationship.

It is initially difficult because in many firms the relationship is constantly changing as the result of management's increasing sophistication in handling its current assets; companies are becoming more able to conduct their business with a smaller amount of liquid funds. It is secondarily difficult because changes in economic circumstances and business practices have resulted in significant shifts in the composition of current assets and current liabilities.

An important reason for the ability of American corporations to keep working capital in line with sales growth is their adoption of control procedures over the major components of working capital. Such procedures are discussed in Chapters 8-11.

[5] POSITION OF THE BUSINESS CYCLE

In addition to seasonal factors and the long-term secular trend, recurring movements of the business cycle influence working capital flows and requirements. As business recedes, companies tend to defer capital replacement programs. Similarly, curtailed sales reduce accounts receivable and modify inventory purchases, thereby contributing further to the accumulation of cash balances. This tendency for companies to become cash rich as the tide of economic prosperity runs out is a well known economic phenomenon.

Conversely, the sales, capital, and inventory expansions that accompany a boom produce a greater concentration of credit items on the balance sheet. Moreover, the pressure on company finances during boom years is reflected in the business drive for loans and the high interest rates of these years.

The financial implications of these movements may be deceptive. A weakening of the cash position in a favorable economic environment may suggest the need for or difficulty of raising capital for further expansion rather than a shortage of funds to take care of current needs. On the other hand, a strong cash position when the economic outlook is bleak may be the forerunner of actual financial difficulties. If the recession is sufficiently deep, a company's liquid status tends to evaporate, its cash inflows dry up, and it may be unable to take care of its obligations.

The financial manager must learn to look behind the obvious implications of the standard tests of corporate liquidity to interpret their meaning in light of a company's position in the industry, the prospects of new business, and the availability of external sources of additional capital.

[6] COMPETITIVE CONDITIONS

A corporation that dominates its market may relax its working capital standards because failure to fill customer's requirements promptly does not necessarily lead to a loss of business. When competition is keen, however, there is more pressure to stock varied lines of inventory to satisfy those demands and to grant more generous terms, which results in an expanded inventory and more accounts receivable. Such a problem is particularly serious when a company is in the same markets as larger enterprises with considerable resources. As an example, Sieberling,[4] prior to selling its tire division to Firestone, complained about a continuing working capital shortage. This was particularly "acute", the company noted, because of "competitive trends towards larger credit terms" and because of the requirements for "more product lines necessitating still larger inventories."

In general, highly competitive market conditions will create conflicting pressures on the financial manager. One of these pressures is to increase the working capital levels to provide "off the shelf" product variety and more liberal credit terms; a countervailing pressure is to maintain price competitiveness by reducing working capital costs through lower levels of current assets and current liabilities.

[7] CREDIT POLICY

Closely related to a company's competitive status are the credit terms it must grant. These arrangements may be the result of tradition, policy within the industry, or even carelessness in failing to carry out announced principles. And the arrangements, in turn, are part of the overall production-collection time sequence, that is, the time intervening between the actual production of goods and the eventual collection of receivables flowing from sales.

There are a number of influences on the length of this cycle. Purchases may be on a cash basis, but the manufacturing cycle may be prolonged and sales terms generous, causing a wide gap between cash expenditures and receipts and possibly placing heavy financing pressures on the firm. These pressures may be eased, despite a long manufacturing cycle, if the company can persuade its suppliers to bear a large part of the financing burden. Or the manufacturing cycle may be short, and the financing requirements of the company may be traced to the relation between purchase and sales credit terms.

[8] INFLATION

The record rate of inflation experienced by the U.S. economy during the 1970's had profound effects on corporate working capital requirements. The inflationary impact drove interest rates skyward thereby substantially raising the cost of long- and short-term borrowing, expanding carrying costs for inventories and accounts receivable, and greatly increasing the opportunity costs of corporate liquidity. Further upward pressure on working capital requirements occurred as suppliers and customers tried to tilt the balance of trade credit in their favor. The growing divergence between book and replacement costs significantly increased the expenditures for fixed assets, thus intensifying the internal competition for cash to meet dividend, capital, debt service, and working capital requirements.

The uncertainties engendered by high inflation induce corporate managers to shift toward planning horizons and projects with quicker payoffs. These uncertainties also encourage the managers to develop several inflation forecasts and to generate pro forma financial statements and budgets for each of the forecasts. This procedure enables them to evaluate the sensitivity of firm performance and financial health to the inflation outlook and to assess the "cost of guessing wrong".

[9] DIVIDEND POLICY

Corporate policy to maintain or increase an established cash dividend may affect working capital, or changes in working capital may bring about an adjustment of dividend policy. In either event, the relationship between cash dividend policy and working capital is well established, and very few companies declare a cash dividend without considering the effects on their overall cash position.

There is a constant tug between a corporation's desire to retain and use funds internally and its recognition of stockholder concern with cash dividends. Some companies insist upon low payouts in order to use their cash for non-dividend purposes. How long they can follow such a policy without adverse stockholder reaction depends upon their rate of return on the retained earnings and the price movements of their stock. The payout ratio is a sensitive barometer of corporate dividend policy and stockholders are not likely to indefinitely disregard limited dividend payments.

Once a company has established an annual cash dividend policy, it is usually reluctant to effect a cut, but may be compelled to do so because of cash shortages or declining earnings that boost payout ratios to lofty levels. A shortage of cash or working capital is generally a powerful reason for reducing or eliminating a cash dividend payment, even though such a move may be difficult in the face of a long-term record. Consolidated Edison's decision to forego a quarterly dividend payment in April, 1974, represents a classic example. A significantly deteriorating working capital position led to this decision that shocked the financial community.[5]

Other companies, confronted with a shortage of cash or working capital, have attempted to resolve their cash dividend dilemma by disbursing stock dividends. Mitigating against the continued use of stock dividends are the high handling costs involved, the negative attitude of investment companies requiring cash to maintain their own cash dividend payouts, and concern over stockholder reaction. Another limitation is an accounting requirement in which stock dividends of less than 25 percent need to be shown as a transference from retained earnings to permanent capitalization in an amount equal to the fair value of the additional shares issued. Growth companies, which often take the stock dividend route, have found that as the price of their shares advance, further payments of this sort become difficult because of the drain on retained earnings. Indeed, as a classic illustration of this point, International Business Machines Corporation once called attention to this condition in its annual report. Eventually, IBM abandoned its stock dividend policy, thereafter gradually increasing its cash dividend rate, as its internal fund generation exceeded financing requirements.

Still other factors may have an influence. Stockholder reaction when dividends are cut in the face of maintained or even increased executive salaries may be particularly important if a proxy fight is brewing. Or, management may find that the dividend decision affects its own compensation if the company has a bonus tied to dividends. Finally, state laws, federal regulations, and restrictions now commonly written into trust indentures bear directly upon dividend decisions.

All in all, corporate directors are likely to seek some compromise between the consistency of cash dividend payments—which satisfies stockholders, improves the firm's credit rating, and aids future financing—and flexibility— which enables management to reduce cash payments when necessary and to deflect cash to other purposes.[6] A popular solution has been to combine announced regular payments with year-end extras. Under any circumstances, a predominant consideration is the effect of dividend policy on working capital measured against the future cash needs of the company.

[10] THE INTERRELATIONSHIP OF SHORT- AND LONG-TERM CHANGES

The modern corporation frequently moves into new lines and products to meet competition. Conversely, should the corporation find some activities unprofitable, it typically displays a willingness, surprising in light of the tacit admission of prior error, to dispose of them. Such a policy contributes to the accountant's quite justifiable concern about identifying extraordinary items and the effects of discontinued operations in financial statements.

Perhaps in theory such capital operations of a firm should be separated from the firm's everyday functions. In fact, it is impractical to keep the financial effects of these two aspects apart. Embarking upon a new undertaking may draw down working capital to provide funds. Disposal of an existing plant produces cash that may be used to expand inventories of current products which, when sold, lead to receivables, thereby retaining these funds within the framework of working capital. Similarly, a portion of the funds from long-term financing may become a part of working capital.

7.5   THE CYCLE OF WORKING CAPITAL FLOWS

As a result of the intermingling of the factors just discussed, the working capital of a company is constantly changing in composition and level. Perhaps it is more appropriate to say that working capital, in its different forms, is always moving—as cash entering a business firm, as inventories going to customers, as receivables coming from customers, and as cash moving to creditors. An important day to day responsibility of the financial manager is to ensure that the flow proceeds smoothly through different stages. To fulfill this responsibility, he must have a keen grasp of the working capital cycle. He may find it helpful to visualize the operations of the business as movements of cash and credit along three major paths:

• *Current Cash and Credit Cycle*—the flow of cash through inventory, receivables, and back to cash once more, with a portion deflected to short-term investments;

• *Capital Cycle*—the two way stream of capital flows from the owners and long-term creditors to the business and back again; and

• *Fixed Asset Cycle*—the acquisition of plant and equipment and their preservation through outlays originating in revenues retained through depreciation.

Figure 7.1 illustrates these three major cash and credit paths for a firm and demonstrates their interlocking nature. In the figure, the current flows of cash and credit are represented by the curved arrows (shaded for cash and white for credit). These cover the passage of cash and credit through four major stages before coming back to their original cash form to be used for various purposes. The four stages include:

• raw materials;
• work in progress;
• finished goods; and
• accounts receivable.

The second cycle is shown in the figure by a single line. It encompasses the flow of funds to the firm, through the sale of securities or borrowing, and from the firm, through cash dividend and interest payments or stock and debt retirements. The capital cycle is joined to the cash and credit cycle when some of the original cash transfers go through the four transforming stages to be returned to the cash compartment and redistributed to the holders of financial instruments.

The third or fixed asset cycle is described by a path of wavy lines and is ordinarily indirect. It shows the flow of cash and credit from their original source to fixed assets, to cash once more via working capital, and eventually back to fixed assets again.

Special relationships in Figure 7.1 are shown by broken lines. These cover the links between the store of credit and creditors; between the expenditures on direct materials, labor and manufacturing expenses and the corresponding inventories of work in process and finished goods; and, as depreciation, between fixed assets and overhead. In order to activate the working capital credit line, the store of credit is converted into accounts payable. Thus, these

FIGURE 7.1 *The major cash and credit paths of a manufacturing company*

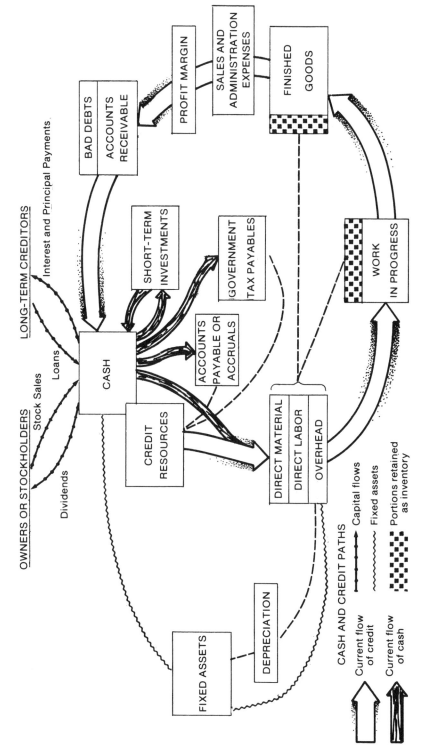

two compartments offset each other in size, one rising as the other declines thereby indicating that as the company increases its short-term debt (accounts payable), its store of credit shrinks correspondingly.

In the next sections, we present the important highlights of each of the three major cash and credit paths of the firm and discuss the relative importance of these paths to the financial manager.

[1] CURRENT CASH AND CREDIT CYCLE

In a manufacturing business, the corporation starts the current flow by applying its credit resources (in the form of payables or accruals) to the purchase of direct materials, the reimbursement of labor to work on these materials, and the expenditures for heat, light, and other items necessary to keep its plant in production. Through these operations, the credit is transformed successively into work in progress and finished goods, parts of which are retained as current inventory. For this latter reason, the amount of finished goods moving via sales to the accounts receivable stage is reduced; on the other hand, this amount may be increased by drawing upon the stock of finished goods. In order to ease the transfers and to guide the overall operations, expenditures are necessary for sales administration. If the eventual cash recovery by the company is to exceed its original outlays, a margin for profit must also be provided.

As the path continues through the sales stage, the finished goods are transferred into accounts receivable. The additions for selling expenses, administration, and profit margins are indicated by the fact that the finished goods station is larger than that of the component expenses. After customers pay their bills, the accounts receivable are converted to cash; those failing to pay are written off as bad debts. Having been returned to its starting point, the cash is used for various purposes:

• a minimum amount is maintained for operating purposes, while temporary excesses are placed in short-term securities;

• some is returned to the current flows;

• a portion is used to acquire fixed assets;

• another portion is paid to the government as income taxes, to creditors as interest and principal repayments, and to the original contributors of capital as dividends; and

• a final portion is used to reduce payables and accruals which were originally incurred when the company financed expenditures with credit.

[2] CAPITAL CYCLE

The capital cycle starts with the shift of cash from the stockholders to the corporation. Some of the funds remain in the form of permanent working capital, while another part moves through the ordinary operations of the business and eventually returns to the original cash compartment. Through its credit resources, the corporation also obtains funds from lenders. Part of this cash may be used to retire currently outstanding debt, while part is absorbed into the current flows. That portion moving into the working capital stream eventually returns as cash and may be used to pay dividends or interest or to retire capital.

[3] FIXED ASSET CYCLE

In the fixed asset cycle, the corporation channels some cash obtained externally from capital contributors and some obtained internally from its current flows to the acquisition of plant and equipment. The value of these fixed assets is recouped via depreciation charges, which add to the size of manufacturing overhead. The firm establishes a selling price covering all costs, including depreciation, thereby enlarging the current flows by an amount equivalent to the shrinkage in the value of fixed assets. Eventually, the retained cash represented by depreciation charges is poured back into fixed assets. Acquisitions of the fixed assets during a given period may be more or less than the amount of depreciation allocated to that period.

[4] RELATIVE IMPORTANCE OF THE THREE CYCLES

While the cash and credit resources of a business constantly move through the three paths of Figure 7.1, the current cash and credit flows represent the heart of the activity, linking the segments of the production-selling cycle into a circular path along which the components move swiftly. By accelerating the speed of this flow through redced manufacturing time, tightened delivery schedules, more rapid collection of receivables, or similar measures, working capital becomes more productive and the amount that must be kept on hand is reduced.

Financial managers, therefore, give careful attention to controlling the assets which represent the transitional stages in the current flows. To guide those working capital flows, they maintain close control over inventories, accounts receivable, and cash. The management of working capital rests upon the effective control of all its components.

7.6   CHAPTER SUMMARY

This chapter introduced working capital management and focused on several important aspects related to working capital policy, including: (1) the concept of working capital; (2) approaches to managing working capital, and (3) the major determinants of the level and composition of working capital. In addition, the chapter highlighted the overall process of working capital flows within the firm, with particular emphasis on the three predominant paths or cycles: (1) current cash and credit cycle, (2) capital cycle, and (3) fixed asset cycle.

The next four chapters elaborate on the main approaches and primary tools employed in the day to day management of the major components of working capital.

FOOTNOTES

1. Roy E. Doggett, "Managing Working Capital," *Management Accounting,* December, 1980, pp. 19-20.
2. Current assets are cash and items which will be converted into cash within a year, including marketable securities, accounts receivable, inventory, and prepaid items. Technically, prepaid items will not be converted into cash, but would have

required the use of current cash or credit had these items not been acquired. Current liabilities are debts of the firm which must be paid within a year.

3. For example, in the annual report of Burlington Industries for the fiscal year ended October 1, 1983 (p. 18), the statement is made "Format changes from a presentation of changes in working capital to a presentation of changes in cash and short-term investments in order to provide clearer reporting of funds flow." Similarly, in its Exposure Draft, *Reporting Income, Cash Flows, and Financial Position of Business Enterprises,* (November 6, 1981, p. xi), the FASB tentatively concluded "...that reporting meaningful components of cash flows is generally more useful than reporting changes in working capital."

4. The name was later changed to Seilon Inc.

5. In 1973, the firm's current ratio was 1.0 times compared with 1.6 times in the prior year. Cash and equivalents fell by \$14.0 million to \$19.1 million and represented only about 1. 4 percent of current assets. Net accounts receivable, on the other hand, comprised almost 70 percent of current assets. Moreover, over the previous years, accounts receivable had more than trebled because of deteriorating customer payments. By mid July 1973, about 20 percent of the company's retail and gas receivables were over six months old.

6. It is the unusual firm that has never effected a dividend reduction. Indeed, the Dow Chemical Company once stated that it is "...the only industrial company... never to have reduced its cash dividends since it began paying them regularly in 1911." (The Dow Chemical Company *Annual Report, 1975,* p. 4). In addition, a number of other companies can point to long-term records of continued cash payments of some amount. For example, at the beginning of 1984, W.R. Grace & Company had paid cash dividends on its common stock for 50 consecutive years; American Home Products for 65 years; Owens-Illinois for 77 years; and Nabisco Brands (formerly Nabisco) for 85 years.

SUGGESTED READINGS

Belt, B., "Working Capital Policy and Liquidity in the Small Business," *Journal of Small Business Management,* July 1979.

Cascino, A.E., "How to Make More Productive Use of Working Capital," *Management Review,* May 1979.

Doggett, R.E., "Management of Working Capital," *Management Accounting,* December 1980.

Goldman, Robert I., "Look to Receivables and Other Assets to Obtain Working Capital," *Harvard Business Review,* November-December 1979.

Heath, L.C., "Is Working Capital Really Working?", *Journal of Accountancy,* August 1980.

Johnson, James M., et. al., "Corporate Liquidity: A Comparison of Two Recessions," *Financial Executive,* October 1983.

Lambrix, R.J. and S.S. Singhvi, "Managing the Working Capital Cycle," *Financial Executive,* June 1979.

Maier, Steven F. et. al., "A Short-Term Disbursement Forecasting Model," *Financial Management,* Spring 1981.

Mallinson, Eugene, "Working Capital of Nonfinancial Corporations," *Federal Reserve Bulletin,* July 1978.

Miller, Ian S., "Accelerated Cash Management: Capital Ideas for Making Your Working Capital Work," *C.A. Magazine,* November 1980.

Miller, Jeffrey W., "Working Capital Theory Revisited," *Journal of Commercial Bank Lending,* May 1979.

Nordgren, Roger K., "The Cornerstone of Liquidity Analysis: Working Capital," *Journal of Commercial Bank Lending,* April 1981.

Richards V.D. and E.J. Laughlin, "Cash Conversion Cycle Approach to Liquidity Analysis," *Financial Management,* Spring 1980.

Thomas, Barbara S., "Deregulaton and Cash Flow Reporting: One Viewpoint," *Financial Executive,* January 1983.

Viscione, J.A., "Flow Concepts—Do You Know the Difference?" *Credit and Financial Management,* November 1978.

Yardini, Edward E., "A Portfolio Balance Model of Corporate Working Capital," *The Journal of Finance,* May 1978.

8

CASH MANAGEMENT

8.1 INTRODUCTION

Cash control is an important financial function, demanding systematic study and the careful attention of management. It starts with the cash budget, which highlights the timing and magnitude of the cash flow through the corporation. By means of monthly, weekly, or even daily forecasts of cash needs, the financial manager is able to determine when he requires additional funds and when he has excess supplies.

As a result of analyzing cash movements, the financial manager can take measures to regularize his flows, thereby reducing his financing costs and possibly contributing to a better integration of operating activities. To the extent that regularization is not practical, the financial manager may add to his company's income by investing short-term surpluses, an activity that necessitates specialized attention and close famiiarity with the money market.

The combination of a keener awareness of when funds will be required and a knowledge of the money market has made it possible for financial managers to invest funds required at different times and for different purposes in a variety of instruments. As a result, they have been able to raise their overall return from investment operations.

In this chapter, we divide our discussion of cash management into three parts: The first is concerned with regularizing cash flows by means of balancing the movement of funds into and out of a business; the second describes the principles developed to reduce the amount of cash required to support operations; and the third treats the sources available to invest for short periods of time whenever excess funds accumulate.

8.2 REGULARIZING CASH FLOWS

In conducting its every day affairs, a company generates a cash inflow and outflow. If operations are successful, net cash inflows will be positive and the company will gain cash that will be used for major expenditures and distributions to stockholders. But even if there is a long-run tendency for cash to accumulate from current operations, heavy drains may occur in the short-run as a result of seasonal pressures, scheduling conditions, or financing arrangements. Consequently, even within a given year, a company may seek bank loans at one time and invest cash excesses at another, depending upon the period in the cash cycle it is in. If the swings are rapid, the problems of being an efficient borrower and lender are aggravated, particularly since both types of financial transactions are likely to be outside the scope of the company's established business activities. By and large, it is desirable to smooth out these fluctuations so that a gradual buildup of cash occurs, or at least so that the number and depth of the swings are reduced, thereby helping to plan for cash use. But if adequate control is not exercised over these movements, the inflows and outflows will probably not be coordinated.

Thus, the regularization of cash changes—which are the outcome of many related activities—cannot be trusted to chance. Management must have a good idea of when and how much funds will be needed to carry out the firm's activities, because it may be difficult to quickly make suitable investment plans or to overcome cash shortages after they have occurred. Moreover, even if corrective action is still possible, the pressure of an already developed deficiency may not provide the time to examine all the various possible cures, particularly since the most effective remedy may not be to borrow money but to rearrange some phases of the operating cycle.

Frequently, actions are required to smooth out cash flow balances until a major restructuring of the firm's way of doing business can be undertaken. For example, seasonal sales patterns may require significant shifts in inventory management policy and rescheduling of production in order to mitigate cash imbalances. In other cases, it may be necessary to adjust the terms of materials purchasing and product selling. In the ensuing section, we present a comprehensive hypothetical example illustrating several of the major alternatives frequently employed by financial managers to ameliorate cash flow imbalances.

[1] EXPERIMENTING WITH THE CASH BUDGET

The cash budget is the crystal ball that enables management to observe future cash movements. It has been described as "...the most important step leading to a more sophisticated approach to cash management."[1] We have previously explained its role in the overall budgetary procedure and discussed the various methods of its presentation. At present, we shall illustrate its use in solving a problem requiring a reformulation of cash sequences. For this purpose, let us consider a hypothetical company in the following situation:

The company sells an item at $10 per unit, costing $1.50 per unit for labor and $4.00 for materials. To avoid any problem of inventory evaluation, it is further assumed that prices remain unchanged during the year, and that sales and administration expenses have a fixed base of $20,000 per month plus a variable component of 2 percent of sales. Depreciation of $360,000 annually is apportioned uniformly throughout the year. Manufacturing expenses (exclusive of depreciation) equal a fixed segment of $360,000 per year plus a variable portion of 50 cents per unit of output. (It is assumed that the expenses are paid each month.) Sales follow a seasonal pattern of 30,000 units per month during the first quarter, 40,000 units per month in the second, 100,000 units per month in the seasonal peak third quarter, and 50,000 units per month in the final quarter. Despite this characteristic sales buildup each year to a third-quarter high, the company maintains a steady production rate of 55,000 units per month, preferring to follow the practice of varying inventories rather than its labor force. Sales are made on the basis of 60-day terms, while purchases are cleared within 30 days. The capitalization includes $4 million of bonds bearing 10 percent interest payable January and July.

The company's quarterly profit and loss statement and the resulting changes in its working capital during the course of a typical year are shown in Figure 8.1. Cash declines during the first half-year, rises moderately in the third quarter, and spurts ahead during the last three months, reflecting the payment of accounts built up during the seasonal peak third period. These changes are influenced by the movement of receivables, which reach their maximum growth in the third quarter and then drop precipitously as customers pay their obligations. Inventories are accumulated in the first two periods in anticipation of the heavy concentration of sales in the third quarter, when a normal shrinkage takes place. This is followed by a resumption of the inventory buildup in the last three months.

FIGURE 8.1   *Changes in income and balance sheet items of a hypothetical company under certain operational conditions*

	First Quarter	Second Quarter	Third Quarter	Fourth Quarter
Income Statement Changes[a]				
Sales	$ 900[c]	$1200	$3000	$1500
Cost of goods manufactured, including depreciation	$1170	$1170	$1170	$1170
Plus or (minus) inventory	(532)	(319)	957	(106)
Cost of goods sold	$ 638	$ 851	$2127	$1064
Gross profit	$ 262	$ 349	$ 873	$ 436
Sales and administrative expenses	78	84	120	90
Bond interest	100	100	100	100
Net profit or (loss)	$ 84	$ 165	$ 653	$ 246
Balance Sheet Changes[b]				
Cash	$ (58)	$(164)	$ 400	$1330
Receivables	(400)	200	1200	(1000)
Inventory	532	319	(957)	106
Net change	$ 74	$ 355	$ 643	$ 436
Allowance for depreciation	$ 90	$ 90	$ 90	$ 90
Bond interest accrued	(100)	100	(100)	100
Net profit or (loss)	84	165	653	246
Net change	$ 74	$ 355	$ 643	$ 436

212

NOTE: Parentheses indicate a decline.

^a The income statements are based on the following calculations: dollar sales equal unit sales per month times selling price per unit: dollar cost of goods manufactured equals unit production per month times the sum of labor, materials, and manufacturing expenses per unit (manufacturing expenses per unit equals variable manufacturing expenses per unit plus fixed manufacturing expenses divided by units provided during year); change in inventory per month equals unit sales minus unit production times dollar cost of goods manufactured per month; sales and administrative expenses equal $20,000 per month plus 2 percent of monthly dollar sales; bond interest equals $100,000 per annum payable in January and July, but accrued during the period. The statements are shown prior to income taxes. It is assumed that the company starts with enough inventory to permit the large third-quarter sales.

^b The cash budget providing the basis for the changes in cash is shown in Figure 9.2 under budget A; no allowance is made for income taxes; because production is the same each month, no changes occur in the amounts of raw material ordered or in the resulting accounts payable which are cleared on a uniform basis.

^c All amounts in thousands of dollars.

Thus, at the close of the year, the financial manager finds the company flush with cash, but he knows that an erosion will set in shortly. Through the cash budget, he is aware that the amount of net cash expenditures during the first half of the year is likely to absorb less than a quarter of the probable cash buildup during the last part of the year. This leaves him with a substantial excess, but he also realizes the necessity of keeping a minimum cash balance to take care of current needs and provide protection against such contingencies as rising prices, a business recession, fires, or strikes. Similarly, he must anticipate enough cash "throw-off" to meet his own payment schedule and to provide funds for the expanding volume of inventories required to meet his seasonal demand pattern. He also wishes to know the amount of funds he can use for dividend payments, the acquisition of fixed assets, or temporary investments and how much he must keep in cash form. Finally, he would like some guidance as to the timing of these discretionary uses of cash.

The financial manager, studying the pro forma income statements and changes in working capital, in addition to the above concerns, is disturbed by the severe cash changes and steady net drain occurring during the first half of the year compared with the unusually rapid expansion during the second half. He recognizes that, at best, these drastic shifts pose a problem of investing the surplus funds of one period to take care of the deficiencies of another. If the seasonally excess funds fall below expectations or have to be used for another purpose, short-term borrowing will be required. He also wants to minimize his visits to the short-term investment market. He therefore decides to investigate alternative means of ironing out the bends in the company's net cash receipts curve. If we assume that the company is not in a position to take on supplementary products, the seasonal swings in cash may be eliminated through some combination of rescheduling production and adjusting the buying or selling terms. To explore these avenues, he prepares cash budgets under varying assumptions, as indicated in Figure 8.2.

Budget A reflects the conditions originally described and provides the basis for the working capital changes shown in Figure 8.1. Because the same level of production is maintained regardless of sales and payment terms are uniform, the cash expenditures on manufacturing are unchanged from month to month. Combining constant outlays for manufacturing in the face of varying cash receipts contributes to the sharp variations in cash.

In experimenting with modifications designed to stabilize the cash fluctuations, the financial manager decides that a closer relationship between sales and production would be desirable. To this end, he schedules output at the level of the following month's expected sales and buys materials against this program, using a one-month lead time; the result is budget B. Changing production introduces sharp variations in cash expenditures on manufacturing. By lightening the outlays during the first four months of the year, the number of deficit months is reduced, but the sharpness of the subsequent deficits is accentuated.

Believing he is on the right track, the financial manager goes one step farther by adjusting production to the expected sales of each month. In budget C, he continues to order materials one month in advance of production in order to avoid manufacturing difficulties, but he is able to persuade the suppliers of materials to accept payment in 30 days. All other suppliers are paid by the close of the production month. This program further reduces the number of deficit months, but the cash swings are still steep.

In the last budget, D, the financial manager attempts a new set of relationships. He still matches production to sales and continues to order materials one month in advance of production. He decides, however, to see what would happen if he could induce his suppliers to give him even more generous credit terms, while cutting down on those he grants to his own customers. The arrangements he makes are to reimburse materials suppliers in 60 days and all others in 30 days, while wages are paid as incurred; his customers pay in 30 days. In effect, the financial manager is interested in shifting the burden of financing from his shoulders to those of his suppliers. He also is able to convince his long-term creditors to move the bond interest dates to the months of cash plenty. The results of these adjustments are striking: cash builds up throughout the year, with only one deficiency incurred, and that a relatively moderate one. These contrasting movements are displayed in Figure 8.3.

Under the first set of conditions, the company has a cash deficit during most of the year. Under budget B, the earlier deficits are eliminated, but the severest cumulative shortage is experienced. The third situation is a more moderate replica of the second; the number and the sharpness of the changes under budget C are reduced, but the pattern is the same. Only under budget D is there a substantial difference. Here the cash rise is steady during the first six months of the year, swift for the next three months, and more moderate thereafter.

Based on the transactions in the last budget, a set of income statements and balance sheets are provided (Figure 8.4) to match those shown earlier. On a quarterly basis, all cash shrinkages are eliminated. The new balance sheets provide for the accumulation of inventories of raw materials because they are ordered one month in advance of production, which is scheduled at the level of the sales expected for each month. In addition, these balance sheets introduce the item of accounts payable, which helps considerably to stabilize the cash movements by shifting some of the company's financing needs to its suppliers.

FIGURE 8.2 Alternative cash budgets for the hypothetical company
(in thousands of dollars)

	JANUARY	FEBRUARY	MARCH	APRIL	MAY
BUDGET A					
Production unchanged; order materials in the month of production; pay suppliers by the end of the month; customers pay in 60 days.					
Cash from sales	$500.0	$500.0	$300.0	$300.0	$300.0
Wages	$ 82.5	$ 82.5	$ 82.5	$ 82.5	$ 82.5
Accounts payable:					
Materials	$220.0	$220.0	$220.0	$220.0	$220.0
Variable manufacturing expenses	27.5	27.5	27.5	27.5	27.5
Fixed manufacturing expenses	30.0	30.0	30.0	30.0	30.0
Total	277.5	277.5	277.5	277.5	277.5
Sales and administrative expenses	26.0	26.0	26.0	26.0	26.0
Bond interest	200.0	—	—	—	—
Total cash outgoing	$586.0	$386.0	$386.0	$386.0	$386.0
Net change in cash	- $ 86.0	+ $114.0	- $ 86.0	- $ 88.0	- $ 88.0
BUDGET B					
Production precedes sales by one month; order materials one month in advance of production; buying and selling terms are as previously.					
Cash from sales	$500.0	$500.0	$300.0	$300.0	$300.0
Wages	$ 45.0	$ 45.0	$ 60.0	$ 60.0	$ 60.0
Accounts payable:					
Materials	$120.0	$160.0	$160.0	$160.0	$400.0
Variable manufacturing expenses	15.0	15.0	20.0	20.0	20.0
Fixed manufacturing expenses	30.0	30.0	30.0	30.0	30.0
Total	165.0	205.0	210.0	210.0	450.0
Sales and administrative expenses	26.0	26.0	26.0	28.0	28.0
Bond interest	200.0	—	—	—	—
Total cash outgoing	$436.0	$276.0	$296.0	$298.0	$538.0
Net change in cash	+ $ 64.0	+ $224.0	+ $ 4.0	+ $ 2.0	- $238.0

Production adjusted to sales; order materials one month in advance of production; pay materials suppliers in 30 days and others by the end of the month as previously; customers pay in 60 days as previously.

Cash from sales	$500.0	$500.0	$300.0	$300.0	$300.0
Wages	$ 45.0	$ 45.0	$ 45.0	$ 60.0	$ 60.0
Accounts payable:					
Materials	$120.0	$120.0	$120.0	$160.0	$160.0
Variable manufacturing expenses	15.0	15.0	15.0	20.0	20.0
Fixed manufacturing expenses	30.0	30.0	30.0	30.0	30.0
Total	165.0	165.0	165.0	210.0	210.0
Sales and administrative expenses	26.0	26.0	26.0	28.0	28.0
Bond interest	200.0	—	—	—	—
Total cash outgoing	$436.0	$236.0	$236.0	$298.0	$298.0
Net change in cash	+ $ 64.0	+ $264.0	+ $ 64.0	+ $ 2.0	+ $ 2.0

Production adjusted to sales; order materials one month in advance of production; pay materials suppliers in 60 days and others in 30 days, except for wages, which are paid as incurred; customers pay in 30 days; bond interest is shifted to April and October.

Cash from sales	$500.0	$300.0	$300.0	$400.0
Wages	$ 45.0	$ 45.0	$ 60.0	$ 60.0
Accounts payable:				
Materials	$200.0	$120.0	$120.0	$160.0
Variable manufacturing expenses	25.0	15.0	15.0	20.0
Fixed manufacturing expenses	30.0	30.0	30.0	30.0
Total	255.0	165.0	165.0	210.0
Sales and administrative expenses	30.0	26.0	26.0	28.0
Bond interest	—	—	200.0	—
Total cash outgoing	$330.0	$236.0	$451.0	$298.0
Net change in cash	+ $170.0	+ $ 64.0	- $151.0	+ $102.0

	JUNE	JULY	AUGUST	SEPTEMBER	OCTOBER	NOVEMBER	DECEMBER
	$400.0	$400.0	$400.0	$1000.0	$1000.0	$1000.0	$500.0
	$ 82.5	$ 82.5	$ 82.5	$ 82.5	$ 82.5	$ 82.5	$ 82.5
	$220.0	$220.0	$220.0	$220.0	$220.0	$220.0	$220.0
	27.5	27.5	27.5	27.5	27.5	27.5	27.5
	30.0	30.0	30.0	30.0	30.0	30.0	30.0
	277.5	277.5	277.5	277.5	277.5	277.5	277.5
	28.0	40.0	40.0	40.0	30.0	30.0	30.0
	—	200.0	—	—	—	—	—
	$388.0	$600.0	$400.0	$ 400.0	$ 390.0	$ 390.0	$390.0
	+ $ 12.0	- $200.0	—	+ $600.0	+ $610.0	+ $610.0	+ $110.0
	$400.0	$400.0	$400.0	$1000.0	$1000.0	$1000.0	$500.0
	$150.0	$150.0	$150.0	$ 75.0	$ 75.0	$ 75.0	$ 45.0
	$400.0	$400.0	$200.0	$200.0	$200.0	$120.0	$120.0
	50.0	50.0	50.0	25.0	25.0	25.0	15.0
	30.0	30.0	30.0	30.0	30.0	30.0	30.0
	480.0	480.0	280.0	255.0	255.0	175.0	165.0
	28.0	40.0	40.0	40.0	30.0	30.0	30.0
	—	200.0	—	—	—	—	—
	$658.0	$870.0	$470.0	$ 370.0	$ 360.0	$ 280.0	$240.0
	- $258.0	- $470.0	- $ 70.0	+ $630.0	+ $640.0	+ $720.0	+ $260.0

$400.0
$ 60.0
‾‾‾‾‾‾
          $160.0
           20.0
           30.0
210.0
28.0
  —
$298.0
+ $102.0

$400.0
$150.0
‾‾‾‾‾‾
          $400.0
           50.0
           30.0
480.0
40.0
200.0
$870.0
- $470.0

$400.0
$150.0
‾‾‾‾‾‾
          $400.0
           50.0
           30.0
480.0
40.0
  —
$670.0
- $270.0

$1000.0
$150.0
‾‾‾‾‾‾
          $400.0
           50.0
           30.0
480.0
40.0
  —
$ 670.0
+ $330.0

$1000.0
$ 75.0
‾‾‾‾‾‾
          $200.0
           25.0
           30.0
255.0
30.0
  —
$ 360.0
+ $640.0

$500.0
$ 75.0
‾‾‾‾‾‾
          $200.0
           25.0
           30.0
255.0
30.0
  —
$360.0
+ $140.0

$400.0
$ 60.0
‾‾‾‾‾‾
          $160.0
           20.0
           30.0
210.0
28.0
  —
$298.0
+ $102.0

$400.0
$150.0
‾‾‾‾‾‾
          $160.0
           20.0
           30.0
210.0
28.0
  —
$388.0
+ $ 12.0

$1000.0
$150.0
‾‾‾‾‾‾
          $400.0
           50.0
           30.0
480.0
40.0
  —
$670.0
+ $330.0

$1000.0
$ 75.0
‾‾‾‾‾‾
          $400.0
           50.00
           30.00
480.0
40.0
200.0
$ 795.0
- $205.0

$ 500.0
$ 75.0
‾‾‾‾‾‾
          $200.0
           25.0
           30.0
255.0
30.0
  —
$ 360.0
+ $140.0

$500.0
$ 75.0
‾‾‾‾‾‾
          $200.0
           25.0
           30.0
255.0
30.0
  —
$360.0
+ $140.0

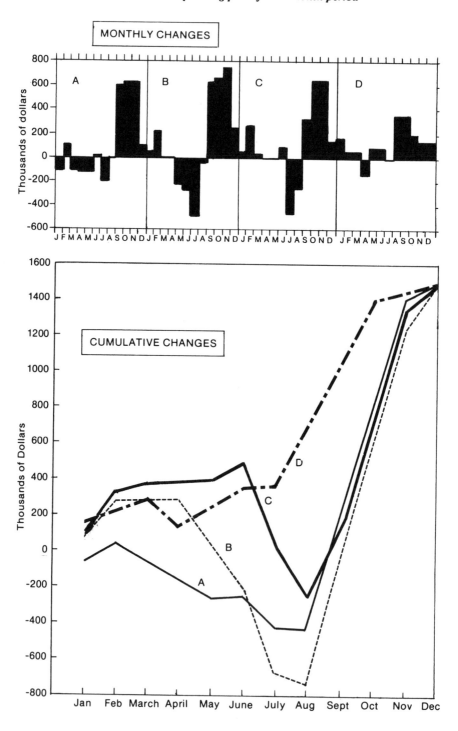

FIGURE 8.3 *Monthly and cumulative changes in cash under various operating plans for 12 month period*

FIGURE 8.4   *Changes in income statement and balance sheet items of
a hypothetical company under revised operating conditions*
(in thousands of dollars)

	First Quarter	Second Quarter	Third Quarter	Fourth Quarter
Income Statement Changes				
Sales	$ 900	$1200	$3000	$1500
Cost of goods manufactured, including depreciation	$ 638	$ 851	$2127	$1064
Plus or (minus) inventory	—	—	—	—
Cost of goods sold	$ 638	$ 851	$2127	$1064
Gross profit	$ 262	$ 349	$ 873	$ 436
Sales and administrative expenses	78	84	120	90
Bond interest	100	100	100	100
Over- or (under) absorption	(82)	(49)	147	(16)
Net profit or (loss)	$ 2	$ 116	$ 800	$ 230
Balance Sheet Changes[a]				
Cash	$ 298	$ 53	$ 672	$ 485
Receivables	(200)	100	600	(500)
Inventory (materials)	40	240	(200)	(80)
Net change	$ 138	$ 393	$1072	$ (95)
Accounts payable	$ (54)	$ 287	$ 82	$(315)
Allowance for depreciation	$ 90	$ 90	$ 90	$ 90
Bond interest accrued	100	(100)	100	(100)
Net profit or (loss)	2	116	800	230
Net change	$ 138	$ 393	$1072	$ (95)

[a] Parentheses indicate a decline.

Net profits now range from $2,000 to $800,000 a quarter compared with a range of $84,000 to $653,000 previously. This quarterly profit variability, however, must be evaluated in the light of the greater consistency of cash flows that has been introduced.

The preceding illustrations show the use of the cash budget for planning a company's operations. Without this tool, management would either have to guess at the effect of revised policies on cash flows or to place the policies into effect and observe their influence. The cash budget does away with both these procedures, enabling a company to anticipate cash changes resulting from certain policy decisions. But a decision must still be reached as to which policy is best for the company.

[2] THE NONFINANCIAL PROBLEMS INTRODUCED

The changes indicated by budget D regularize the movements of cash neatly. A consistent buildup occurs during the year; on a cumulative basis, in no month does the cash outflow exceed the cash inflow; and the company can probably operate without the need of short-term financing, thereby reducing borrowing costs. These are enormous advantages but they do not make the decision conclusive. The financial manager must still realize that the changes tend to weaken the firm's net current position because finished goods inventories are eliminated and there is heavy reliance on payables. Moreover, even though the present suppliers are willing to accept payment in 60 days, they may not grant discounts on this basis, which would raise the costs of materials and supplies. More important, the financial manager may find that if he tries to introduce the changes called for in budget D, the managers of other divisions will raise strenuous objections.

The production manager, who is likely to be more concerned with operating efficiei..ies may prefer long uninterrupted production runs in order to reduce setup costs. He may also be apprehensive that some of the present suppliers will object to being paid in 60 days, possibly forcing him to find new suppliers who might be less dependable or provide inferior materials. Additionally, the production manager may frown upon the greater purchasing, production planning, and scheduling problems that are bound to arise when production is geared to sales rather than maintained at a uniform level throughout the year.

The sales manager is likely to want a policy ensuring the swiftest delivery of products. He may favor a plan that involves building up finished goods inventories. Such a program might lead to overstocking, but from his point of view the costs of carrying more inventories might be outweighed by the goodwill generated. The sales manager also might be fearful that tighter credit and collection policies could lead to the loss of some customers who perhaps are slower payers but who nevertheless eventually meet their obligations.

The personnel manager's objectives are likely to be different as well. He is more directly concerned with maintaining an efficient work force. He may consider this aim thwarted by a policy of varying production, which could lead to substantial changes in employment levels. Seasonal hiring and layoffs would not only tend to raise labor costs but would probably have an adverse effect on employee morale. Thus, the personnel manager might well favor the original plan, which maintained an even production flow and was therefore more likely to minimize hiring and firing.

[3] THE FINANCIAL MANAGER'S DECISION

Nevertheless, from the financial manager's point of view, it is clear that the policies underlying budget D, which provides for the uniform buildup of cash, would help planning. The company's dividend policy and capital expenditures program, in addition, could be coordinated with these changes so as to keep the cash level reasonably uniform. He could not ignore, however, the difficulties created in other areas. Before the financial manager could introduce the changes called for in the last budget, he would have to work out with the production manager the feasibility of matching production and sales, convince the sales manager that the policies called for by the new budgetary plan are appropriate, and see if the personnel manager can handle the resulting employment problems. He would also need to arrange new credit terms with his customers and suppliers. Moreover, he would have to obtain authorization from the company's bondholders to alter the interest dates on their obligations. These are formidable modifications that may be out of his reach.

But at least the financial manager can do his planning on paper without the pain of empirical tests. He is now aware of how improvements can be obtained, and what he must do to get them. There is a final danger that his budgetary estimates providing the basis for his planning may be inaccurate. But this danger is common to all financial planning, and is best overcome through care in preparing budgets and experience in using them.

8.3   MAXIMIZING CASH AVAILABILITY

While regularizing cash flows permits more effective planning, greater sophistication in handling cash has enabled companies to cut down on the amount that must be kept in order to sustain any given level of operations. Operating with less cash and hence increasing turnover, benefits a company in two principal ways. It permits each dollar to earn more profits, and it reduces dependence on outside financing sources. This second result is particularly important in periods when interest rates climb and banks examine loan applications with greater care. Tight money means much less to a company which has discovered how to stretch the usefulness of each dollar. In order to attain this end, the flow of cash into the company must be accelerated.

[1] ACCELERATING THE CASH FLOW STREAM

If we visualize a company's cash inflow stream as starting from the moment the customer places his order, there are four major areas that can be controlled to speed up this flow.

- reducing the lead time required to manufacture the goods or to identify and ship them;
- drawing up and forwarding the invoice more quickly;
- reducing the time the customer takes to pay his bill and reducing delinquent accounts; and
- creating spendable funds.

(a) Reducing Manufacturing Lead Time

To the extent that manufacturing is required, reducing the lead time of this phase is a production problem, beyond the responsibility of finance, except to the extent that it could cause pressure on production. This is particularly so if a financial officer is on the executive committee. Caution must be exercised to avoid changes which accelerate the cash flow but add enough extra production costs to provide negative results. If goods come from inventory, certain characteristic operations are involved, including recording the order, checking the stock for availability, shipping as ordered and reordering if necessary. At any rate, the starting point is getting the goods to the customer as promptly as possible.

(b) Processing the Invoice More Quickly

Once the goods are dispatched, the second stage is drawing up and forwarding the invoice. Electronic processing has provided new opportunities to obtain even more information in less time at this stage. Manufacturing companies now can put an order into production promptly after receipt from the sales department and have materially shortened the time required for billing. As a result, inventories move out at a faster rate and customers are charged sooner.

(c) Speeding Up the Payment Cycle

With the customer billed, the third major focus of control is cutting down the time the customer takes to pay his bill and reducing delinquent accounts. This phase, commonly referred to as credit management, is now a well-established activity with a considerable body of widely accepted principles and techniques (see Chapter 9). A company which is able to get its customers to clear their accounts more rapidly and to reduce defaults can increase both the magnitude and the speed of cash inflows. To accelerate payments from customers, a company may offer more liberal discounts, require larger down payments, or it might shorten the payment period in return for providing more service, such as increased advertising or maintenance. The cost of these items may be an inexpensive way of obtaining greater use of capital. To avoid defaults, companies now pay more attention to formal credit rating services, reference sources, and past payment performance.

(d) Creating Spendable Funds

From the time a customer provides cash, as often occurs in retail transactions, or forwards a check to clear his account, to the moment the cash or check becomes spendable funds for the company, is still another interval subject to control. Once availability has been established in a particular locality, the funds still may have to be transferred substantial distances for use elsewhere. Unless these transfers are made quickly, companies may have to keep idle reservoirs of cash in different spots to permit prompt payment of local commitments. The current trend in industry toward diversification over wide geographic areas has both lengthened and complicated these funds movements. The economics of time and space have thus become extremely important in maximizing the availability of cash.

[2] MAKING FULL USE OF BANKING RELATIONS

The previous sections highlighted the emergence of cash flow controls as an important aspect of financial management. The heart of such a cash planning system is a carefully designed banking structure which may include for a large multinational firm several thousand banks scattered throughout the United States and the various foreign countries in which it does business. In such a structure, three kinds of banking relationships are ordinarily involved:

- at local levels, certain institutions are selected to service operating units in the area;
- at focal spots chosen to blanket different geographic sections of the country, second-level regional institutions are designated as concentration centers or "line" links; and
- at the top level, several "key" banks are selected to head up the entire system and work directly with the home office.

The three-layer system of banking relations, as well as the operating arrangements made with the different kinds of institutions, may be adjusted to suit the needs of individual corporations. Developing an overall system involves balancing the length of money flows with the clusters of funds tied up in different spots.

In general, five key elements enter into operating the banking relations system:

- a knowledge of the location of cash;
- methods of moving cash;
- lock box services;
- special procedures; and
- Electronic Funds Transfer System (EFTS).

These elements are discussed in the following subsections.

(a) A Knowledge of the Location of Cash

The financial manager stationed in a corporation's home office must know at all times the amount of his cash held in each of the firm's banks throughout the country so that he may be able to use those balances. This information is fundamental to cash control systems. The problem of obtaining it is particularly acute for a large corporation with many scattered branches; it is likely to have banking affiliations in the local areas served by branches or divisions, in concentration centers and in the home office city.

A principle commonly applied to keep the financial manager informed regarding the movement of cash is to impose limitations on the size of the accounts kept at certain institutions, while giving the responsibility for gathering and transmitting data to other banks. By establishing a working balance at the local banks, for example, the treasurer in the home office knows the amount of cash at each. Excess funds are remitted to the second-level line of concentration center banks. These institutions advise their banking correspondents in the home office city of the amount of deposits and balances at the close of business, which is available for immediate use or investment. Or, the second-level banks may also be given prescribed balances with excess amounts automatically transferred to the key banks. The latter institutions, in turn, keep the financial manager posted by telephone each day concerning the company's net cash position.

As modern communications technology evolves, the financial manager has sought more information to help in the development of his cash management strategy. In addition to knowing his cash balances, he can now obtain the details of debits and credits received on that day as well as useful statistics for prior periods. Moreover, through the use of inexpensive and readily available microcomputers, hooked to a banks mainframe, the financial manager is able to take advantage of the mainframe's power to provide information in the desired form for subsequent manipulation by the microcomputers.[2]

(b) Methods of Moving Cash

Within the framework of bank-corporation relations that we have described, three major procedural areas exist that govern the time required for converting the checks of widely scattered customers into spendable cash:

- length of the cash flow pipelines;
- transfers; and
- timing of movements.

[i] LENGTH OF THE CASH FLOW PIPELINES: To curtail the length of the pipelines through which the funds must flow, customers are requested to transmit payments to regional collection centers located sufficiently close to require only one day's mailing time. Companies with a network of sales outlets may use their own regional offices as collection points, from which the funds are routed to concentration centers.

[ii] TRANSFERS: The second area of control procedures involves transfers. Corporations may shift funds by means of check, wire, telephone, or depository transfer checks (DTC). The first three methods are obvious; the last is a specialized and less well-known instrument.

The DTC is employed only to transfer funds. It is addressed to a firm's local collection point or lock box bank, directing it to pay an indicated sum to a concentration center institution for credit to the corporation. The check is not signed by an officer or employee of the initiating corporation, but the lower right-hand corner bears the corporation's printed name, which is considered an official signature. The board of directors activates the arrangement by passing a resolution which is forwarded to a bank along with a letter of instruction. The DTC is a convenient means of making transfers because it does not require a signature, the name of the payee bank is already inserted, and its purpose is clearly defined. It is expected that eventually electronic DTCs will replace the paper DTC thereby further speeding the transfer of funds.[3]

Which method is selected depends upon the size of the balance the corporation desires to keep, the amounts of the transfers, and the extent to which the corporation wants the local office to administer the transfer of funds.

[iii] TIMING OF MOVEMENTS: The third area of control procedures is the timing of these movements. The frequency with which funds are shifted varies with the size of the business. Since it is uneconomical to effect movement in units of less than $1,000, a local office that does several hundred dollars worth of business each day may transfer deposits from a local to a concentration center bank only once a week, while a more active office may require daily transfers. Policies also vary concerning the party who initiates action. The responsibility for taking the necessary steps may be given to personnel in the local office, or provision may be made for automatic bank remittances.

(c) Lock Box Services

National companies that prefer to collect receipts at the home office may do so through the use of the lock box technique. Under these arrangements, a firm rents a lock box in its own name at the local post office servicing the bank designated to act as the company's collection agent in a defined region. It notifies its customers and indicates on its invoices that payments are to be forwarded to the box.

The company executes an agreement with the bank authorizing it to enter the box as an agent. Mail is picked up at frequent intervals, envelopes opened, and checks are removed, microfilmed, deposited to the firm's account, and processed for presentation. On the same day, the bank transmits to the company a deposit slip listing all remittances received together with the envelopes and their contents including microfilmed copies of the checks. Unpaid items, those which require special endorsements, and those for incorrect amounts are handled by prearranged methods. These might include making a magnetic tape of the day's regularly processed items and forwarding the information by dataphone to the company's computer center. Multinational firms may locate lock boxes in foreign countries and credit receipts to a dollar account with the foreign bank.[4]

Banks may be compensated for lock box services through the earnings they receive on the deposits maintained with them by the lock box customer or through fees. Careful analytical techniques have been worked out, including use of mathematical models, to ascertain the optimum number and location of lock boxes to maximize early cash availability of receivables relative to the costs of maintaining the lock boxes.[5] A rule of thumb in gauging potential lock box benefits is that accelerating collection time by one-quarter of a day produces $1,000 of savings for every one million dollars of sales, or $100,000 for a $100 million sales firm.[6]

Some companies have encountered difficulty in employing lock box systems. For one thing, there may be some diminution of credit control if a delay occurs in the time notice of payment reaches the corporate home office after the checks are deposited by the regional banks. This may be a disadvantage in the case of weak accounts where it is desirable to ascertain that checks are for the proper amount before further deliveries are made. Then again, some customers have objected to lock boxes because they reduce the float upon which they previously relied in making remittances.

(d) Special Procedures

Companies employ various devices to speed the availability of funds in their lock box programs. For example, some companies have a unique zip code to avoid substation processing by the Post Office. They use high speed equipment to sort the mail received and fully automated systems to process checks. Elaborate check clearing networks provide immediate availability to all major money centers throughout the country.

In addition to lock box systems and regional collection centers, companies employ other means of moving checks rapidly. As an illustration, checks can be routed directly from one city to another by airmail pouch service rather than sent through postal facilities. Or, messengers may be dispatched, if necessary by plane, to pick up a big check from a customer.

(e) Electronic Funds Transfer System (EFTS)[7]

The growth of business-to-business payments in an EFTS may make check movements obsolete. EFTS permits electronic payments between buyers and sellers. More broadly, it may be interpreted to mean any type of electronic transfers affecting money, whether it involves the actual movement of funds or of information regarding funds.

Thus far, the EFTS methods employed have primarily involved the individual consumer or retail transactions — automated teller machines and cash dispensers, direct deposits of payroll and social security checks, and point of sale systems. Attention now is shifting to the system's corporate applications.

Financial managers have found EFTS particularly helpful in formulating cash management programs. We expect corporations will develop a total system approach in computing cash movements and in transmitting information. Both banks and third-party services are working toward this end.[8]

[3] MANAGING THE PAYMENT OF FUNDS

Control over the outflow of funds is important for two major reasons. One is that a company obtains the maximum utility from its funds when it can keep them working as long as possible. To this end, an enterprise with decentralized activities must be able to shift funds to the spots where they are required at a moment's notice.

Thus, the same system that permits the more rapid flow of funds into a company's home office banks also enables a reverse movement to occur when desired. Assume, for example, that the financial manager located in New York City wishes to transfer funds to a branch office in Lexington, Kentucky. He notifies the New York bank of the amount and the transferee. The New York institution reduces the parent company's deposit account on its books, increases that of its correspondent—the transferee's bank—by the same amount, and wires its correspondent of the transaction. The Lexington bank increases both its cash account with the New York institution and the deposit account of the branch. The net effect is that funds available to the company in its New York bank are decreased while those at the disposal of its regional office are increased.

A second reason for controlling payments is that the company can determine which supplier's invoices may be deferred and which need to be paid promptly. A firm must strike a constant balance between the advantage of having more funds availability through invoice deferral and the benefit of enhanced supplier goodwill through prompt payments. Along these lines, companies have at times sought to delay paying bills by drawing checks on accounts in remote areas of the country. The Federal Reserve takes a dim view of this ploy.

Under the pressure of competition, corporations may find it expedient to take special measures to accelerate the collection time of checks paid to others for services rendered or benefits due. Such measures, of course, speed the outflow of cash and therefore cannot be introduced safely unless suitable controls are maintained over the inflows. As we have stressed, cash planning is a total approach which includes integration of the two streams.

[4] REQUIREMENTS OF A CASH MANAGEMENT SYSTEM

A fully planned cash control system aims to maximize cash usefulness by getting bills out faster, improving the collection process, accelerating cash flows, and finally, investing the surplus funds generated. Unless a company has thoroughly investigated the full scope of these activities, it can probably improve its operations in some of these respects.

In addition, a cash management system is likely to induce the financial manager to scrutinize more closely the caliber of the banks selected as depositories, the services they render, and the costs of banking activities. (The factors ordinarily considered in selecting banks in which deposits are kept are discussed in Chapter 11.) The effectiveness of a cash management system depends in large part on the cooperation of the participating banks and their efficiency in clearing and collecting checks and transferring funds. If particular institutions seem lax in these transactions, a firm can take steps to obtain improved performance or switch institutions. The cost-consciousness created by a cash management system may also lead the financial manager to investigate the cost implications of such practices as paying service fees, keeping compensating balances, directing customers to forward checks directly to bank depositories, and collecting payments through local sales offices.

Even without these positive gains, however, a company will often feel some pressure to install such a system because of the tendency of others to do so. As a firm's suppliers take steps to increase their own cash availability by speeding up the collection of the checks they receive, the firm will find that it has less use of cash from this source. Thus, corporations may observe that their cash availability is reduced even though no change has occurred in business conditions or trade terms. In order to prevent this condition and augment cash availability, the financial manager must study the direction taken by and time required for its own paid receivables to become converted into usable cash. He can exercise control over these movements.

The introduction of an overall cash control system also requires numerous planning decisions — locating depositories, selecting specific institutions in the area, keeping informed of their status, establishing minimum balances, transmitting instructions, taking advantage of unused funds, designing forms for the procedures, and coordinating the various activities. The system must be under constant surveillance to uncover new ways to maximize the utility of cash balances.

8.4 INVESTING SHORT-TERM FUNDS

Regardless of how carefully a company plans, it cannot balance the streams of cash inflow and outflow exactly. For one thing, the large tax liabilities and depreciation charges of recent years have led to accumulations that cannot be spent promptly. Then again, the financial manager may prefer differences to occur so that he can be sure of having certain funds when required. Corporations may have many reasons to accumulate short-term funds—for dividends, interest, or periodic bond retirement, or in anticipation of almost any kind of payment. To hold these funds as demand balances with a bank would be uneconomical, and logically they should be invested for the short period that they remain unused. As some gauge of the importance of this policy, investing $10 million for one week at a return of 10 percent would produce an income of over $19,000. In view of the time involved, not only is such a sum consequential even to a big corporation, but once the investing mechanism is understood and introduced, this income may be obtained at virtually no risk and with very little effort.

[1] DETERMINING MINIMUM CASH BALANCES

In order to invest excess funds, the financial manager must gauge the optimum amounts to be kept in cash at commercial banks and in petty cash funds. Seasonal factors and cyclical requirements make it difficult to estimate these amounts accurately, and therefore common policy is to deliberately err on the side of conservatism in order to avoid cash deficiencies. In an effort to seek more scientific approaches, mathematical models have been developed.[9] Financial managers have also attempted to adapt the Economic Order Quantity formula used for inventory control, (as discussed in Chapter 10) to ascertain optimum cash amounts. In accordance with inventory concepts, there are ordering costs arising from the clerical activity and brokerage in making transactions and carrying costs in the form of the income lost by holding cash to avoid the need of effecting transfers. Various proposals along these lines have been suggested, but in general, they tend to follow the pattern discussed below.

The point of departure is the total cash and securities portfolio that a company, through its budgetary procedures, has determined is required to take care of its ordinary payments (transactions motive) and which can provide a buffer against contingencies (precautionary motive). The problem is to determine the optimum division between cash and securities so as to hold to a minimum the ordering and carrying costs. Once the optimum amount of cash is established, the company draws upon these funds until a minimum level is reached; then the original amount is restored through liquidating the securities portfolio.

Certain decision rules have also been devised that might be formed through quantitative analysis for managing corporate cash and marketable securities. Still other techniques involving probability theory have been suggested. While these technical procedures are interesting, they are not widely used. However, the technicians may make some headway as more treasurers and controllers come to understand oprations research techniques. As a general policy, the following analytic pattern is more characteristic at present. First, cash is required to meet future payments. To determine this requirement, financial managers rely primarily on the cash budget and short-term cash projections. Some companies establish minimum targets, such as keeping a cash balance equal to three weeks' disbursements plus additional amounts for large periodic disbursements. Others establish maximum levels which, when reached, serve as a signal to the financial manager to investigate and determine what action should be taken. Second, cash is required to compensate banks for services rendered; this amount is usually ascertained through cost analyses. Finally, cash is required as a buffer against uncertainties. As mentioned, these amounts may eventually be determined by means of probability analyses; at present, decisions are reached for the most part by managerial judgment.

Once appropriate balances are established, they must be reviewed constantly because changing operations bring with them changes in cash requirements. Bank accounts may be kept active even though the need for them may have passed, and petty cash funds may be perpetuated simply because of inertia. Accordingly, examining all bank accounts and cash funds at regular intervals, as a number of companies do, appears to be a sensible procedure.

[2] PARTICIPATING IN THE MONEY MARKET

The increasing participation of corporations in the money market has been one of the striking financial developments of recent years. Corporations now are major buyers of short-term securities in which funds may be safely invested. Such investments are based upon daily estimates of surplus cash and the highest yield compatible with safety and liquidity. With experience, corporate treasurers have acquired considerable skill in placing short-term funds (see also 12.3[1], [3], [4] and [5]).

A well-run financial department of a large firm will probably include a money market specialist, who keeps careful track of the demand and supply factors influencing interest rate levels. These specialists study data on savings, the condition statements of the member Federal Reserve Banks, the weekly reports of Federal Reserve Banks, the indicated policy of Treasury and Reserve officials, and related information, in order to gain insights into the outlook for interest rates. Such information is vital to help the company, not only to plan its own financing requirements, but also to ascertain the most acceptable outlets for investing short-term funds. Thus, relatively high rates might induce money market specialists to recommend placing more funds in the marketable securities portfolio; rate differentials would lead to shifting the portfolio's composition; and an expectation that rates will rise could lead to reducing the portfolio in favor of cash or to shortening maturities.

The money market area has become so complex that a number of firms prefer to rely upon outside guidance which they may obtain from banks, securities firms, and investment counselors or consultants. Still, the final investment responsibility rests with the treasurer. For this reason, it is desirable to briefly review the major sources to which short-term funds can be committed. These are discussed below and include the following:

- U.S. Treasury securities;
- Federal Agency Securities;
- short-term non-government securities;
- interest rate futures; and
- special practices.

[3] U.S. TREASURY SECURITIES

A major form of corporate investment is the Treasury security. The safety, broad market, and great maturity range of these instruments provide them with a strong appeal. Income from Treasury securities is subject to the federal income tax, but is exempt from state and local taxes.

To finance its huge debt, the Treasury has instituted a variety of financing techniques for sale of notes and bonds. Since the Treasury's May, 1973, refunding, the auction method has become the primary marketing technique, with coupon issues generally sold on a yield basis, while bills are sold on a price basis. To help distribute a large volume of securities, fixed-price subscription-offerings may be used. Occasionally, the Treasury has resorted to the uniform price or "Dutch" auction. In this method, the Treasury makes awards for the competitive tenders at the price of the lowest accepted bid. This approach seeks to broaden participation by eliminating the risk of one investor paying more than another.

In the next section, we discuss the three major types of U.S. treasury securities:

- Treasury Bills;
- Treasury Notes; and
- Treasury Bonds.

(a) Treasury Bills

These instruments have been issued with different maturities up to one year to suit the government's financing needs. In recent years, three issues have been regularly employed. Thirteen and 26-week bills have been auctioned weekly and 52-week bills have been auctioned every four weeks. Cash management bills, ordinarily falling due shortly after tax dates, are offered irregularly. They have maturities from a few days to about six months and are used to bridge transitory cash gaps. Bills are sold on a discount basis and are paid in full at maturity. The discount represents interest. Because of the large amount outstanding and the regularity of new offerings, the market is active, the spread between bids and offers is narrow, and the instruments have proved particularly attractive for short-term corporate investment.

(b) Treasury Notes

These securities bear a fixed rate of interest payable semiannually and have maturities between one and ten years. The maximum length was raised from five to seven years in 1967 and to ten years in 1976. In recent years, the Treasury has regularly included one or more note offerings in its quarterly refundings. The short-term notes have some corporate appeal although they are not as popular as bills.

(c) Treasury Bonds

These instruments may be offered with any maturity but ordinarily it is over ten years. They bear a fixed interest rate payable semiannually, and may have a call option, meaning that upon four months' notice the Treasury may redeem them prior to maturity on or after specified dates. Because they represent the long-term segment of the government market, corporations hold relatively few of them. With the passage of time, however, these securities enter the short-term category and tend to sell on a yield basis which is comparable to that of the other short-term Treasury obligations.

The breadth of the market and the exact yield depend upon the outstanding amount and investor interest in a particular yield bracket. At any one time an issue may sell outside its normal yield curve, affording the financial manager relatively attractive purchase opportunities. The yields of the individual issues tend to fall back eventually to the normal pattern. This pattern, in turn, is largely determined by the yield relationships between short and long-term issues, a pattern that depends upon the outlook for interest rates, the amounts outstanding, and government policies. The quantity of publicly held bonds with coupons above 4½ percent is limited by law, but Congress ordinarily has increased such authorizations when considered desirable.

[4] FEDERAL AGENCY SECURITIES

In recent years, there has been a substantial increase in the volume of federal agency debt outstanding. A few of these instruments have the full faith and credit backing of the United States; some are guaranteed by the Treasury directly or implicitly by the issuing agency's right to borrow from the Treasury; others have no formal government backing. The Federal Financing Bank was established by the Federal Financing Bank Act of 1973 to consolidate the financing of the different federal agencies and other borrowers with debt guaranteed by the federal government. Many agencies now borrow from the bank which, in turn, issues its own debt or may borrow from the Treasury. (The bank tends to do the latter.) Corporations have shown some interest in the federal agency debt that matures within one year.

[5] SHORT-TERM NON-GOVERNMENT SECURITIES

When financial managers were less sophisticated, they tended to restrict the investment of their temporarily surplus funds to government securities. Occasionally, a more daring manager might have moved outside this area, but such forays could have been disastrous, particularly if the manager ventured into relatively risky areas, such as equities. At present, however, most financial managers have become sufficiently knowledgeable to avoid speculative pitfalls, while the variety and amount of high-grade short-term issues available have grown substantially. As a result, the managers have manifested growing interest in short-term non-government securities including:

- commercial paper;
- bankers' acceptances;
- repurchase agreements;
- negotiable time certificates of deposit (CDs);
- money-market mutual funds;
- Eurocurrency; and
- other types of short-term investments.

These are discussed below.

(a) Commercial Paper

Commercial paper is the name given to unsecured corporate notes issued to finance short-term requirements. Maturities may range from 1 to 270 days.[10] About half of all commercial paper outstanding is issued directly by a small number of large finance companies and commercial banks. The remainder is sold on behalf of many types of companies, principally through dealers such as Goldman Sachs, First Boston, A.G. Becker, Phibro-Solomon Inc., and Merrill Lynch.

The commercial paper obtained from dealers usually is bought and sold on a discount basis, although interest-bearing paper is often available. The finance companies ordinarily are willing to go to some lengths to tailor their instruments to buyer needs. By specifying the issue and maturity date, the corporate investor is assured that funds will be available to meet a tax, dividend, or other commitment. Dealers may transmit special orders to issuers who reserve the final decision and make no commitment to issue paper regularly.

There is no active secondary market in commercial paper. The major finance companies ordinarily will buy-back the paper if such a request is made. Buy-backs for paper purchased from dealers may also be arranged. Both dealers and direct issuers, however, discourage this practice.

The issuing firms generally obtain two ratings from services such as Moody's and Standard & Poor's Corporation. Commercial paper often is supported by bank letters of credit. This arrangement has facilitated the entrance to the market of relatively small industrial concerns. The return available on an issue is strongly influenced by its rating. Yields on the highest quality paper tend to be somewhat above those on Treasury bills and roughly equivalent to those on bankers' acceptances and CDs of leading banks, although relationships can change with market conditions.

By and large, investment experience in the commercial paper field has been good. In 1970, however, the market received a shock as a result of the bankruptcy of the Penn Central Transportation Company, which had received a "prime" rating by Moody's Investors Service. After a short period of hesitancy, the market recovered. To a large extent, reliance is still placed on ratings and the fact that the market generally is available only to credit-worthy firms.

(b) Bankers' Acceptances

Bankers' acceptances are instruments drawn on and accepted by a bank. They are an irrevocable primary obligation of the accepting bank and a contingent obligation of the drawer and of any endorsers. They have been used continuously since 1914 and there has been no known principal loss to an investor.

These instruments are used primarily to finance the movement of goods in foreign, and domestic trade. The Federal Reserve may discount qualified acceptances and makes purchases on behalf of foreign customers. While it no longer buys for its own account, the Federal Reserve engages in repurchase agreements with acceptance dealers.

(c) Repurchase Agreements

Repurchase agreements involve an investor purchasing securities and simultaneously selling them back to the dealer at a specified future delivery and payment date. The investor holds the securities as collateral and obtains an agreed-upon rate of return. The securities involved are ordinarily U.S. Treasury issues, but those of federal agencies, local governments or any of the popular money-market instruments may be used.

The repurchase agreement technique was developed by government secur-ities dealers to obtain additional means of financing their inventories. Alert to methods of exploiting existing investment and money needs, dealers have also undertaken reverse repurchase agreements, or sell backs, where they became the buyer and seller of the securities. By this means, the dealer obtains securities that he needs in his business, while the seller receives short-term funds. The dealer, in turn, may get the necessary funds by executing another contract with a different customer, thus arranging a double repurchase agreement. Suppose, for example, the dealer ascertains that Corporation X has accumulated excess funds that it is holding for a dividend payment date due in seven days, while Corporation Y requires funds for about the same period. The dealer may be able to execute a repurchase agreement with X under which it agrees to sell X a given money market security and to repurchase the security at the end of seven days. The dealer also makes a reverse arrangement in which he agrees to buy a money market security that Corporation Y holds and to resell the security to Y at the close of seven days. The dealer thus serves as a middleman in the transfer of funds from Corporation X to Corporation Y.

Repurchase agreements have become highly important to the U.S. financial market. Not only are these arrangements widely used by government securities dealers, but also the Federal Reserve employs them in the execution of monetary policy. Corporations as well as institutions find them very flexible investment outlets. Accordingly, failure in 1982 of Drysdale Government Securities and Lombard Wall, two relatively small dealers, sent shock tremors throughout the financial markets and led to a tightening of practices.

(d) Negotiable Time Certificates of Deposit (CDs)

A CD is a negotiable receipt given by a bank for the deposit of funds in denominations of $100,000 or more. It represents the bank's agreement to pay the bearer on a stipulated date the amount of the deposit plus interest. Most certificates have maturities of a year or less. Corporations, which hold the bulk of CDs, tend to prefer the large banks' instruments because of their relative liquidity and presumed greater security, a consideration arising from the limited protection afforded by the Federal Deposit Insurance Corporation. Moreover, the one-million dollar normal round-lot trading unit is a convenience to firms which have large sums to place. Then, too, some corporations only hold the CDs of banks in which they maintain demand deposits.

The yields on CDs which trade in the secondary market reflect prevailing money market conditions. The major banks customarily announce the rate at which they will issue certificates and adjust it only as money market conditions change. Rates offered by the smaller, non-money market banks tend to be somewhat above those of the so-called prime banks, although the latter designation has become more restrictive as the lending practices of some of the big institutions have been questioned at times.

The major banks also have issued variable rate and so-called "roly-poly" CDs. The latter type represents a series of conventional six-month instruments covering a period of two years or longer. The buyer contracts to purchase an equivalent dollar amount of new six-month certificates, which may bear a fixed or variable rate, upon each maturity date until the contract expires, but may at any time sell the current six-month CD in the secondary market.

A CD, denominated in dollars, but issued abroad by the foreign branch of a U.S. bank or by a foreign bank, is called a Eurodollar CD. A CD, payable in dollars issued by a branch office located in the U.S., usually New York, of a well-known foreign bank is called a yankee CD; secondary market trading has grown in these instruments. There is very little secondary market activity, however, in thrift institution CDs, issued mostly by savings and loan associations.[11]

(e) Money-Market Mutual Funds

For the financial officer who desires to invest excess funds in relatively risk-free instruments, but who does not have the experience to undertake this function directly, a useful vehicle might be a money-market mutual fund. This is an open-end investment company that typically sells its shares without a load charge, pays a management fee of about one half a percent, permits redemptions by checks drawn on the fund, and confines its investments to money market instruments, the nature of which depends upon the fund's policy as defined in its prospectus. Thus, some funds may limit their portfolio to short-term Government obligations, specified maturities, U.S. instruments, or to some combination of these elements.

Reflecting their conservative nature, it is common for a money-market fund to maintain its stated value at one dollar by following pricing practices stipulated by the SEC and adjusting dividend payments, which may be made monthly, as interest rates change. By wiring federal funds for purchases and redeeming by check, interest may be earned from the date of purchase to the date the check is cleared.

(f) Eurocurrency

Eurocurrency is a financial asset or liability denominated in one currency but traded outside that country. The principal instrument of the Eurocurrency market is the deposit which forms the basis of the market. Eurocurrency is initially created when a deposit, denominated in the currency of one country, is made in a bank located in another country. Thereafter, other instruments may be created such as CDs, bankers' acceptances, and commercial paper. A Eurocurrency denominated in dollars is a Eurodollar which constitutes the bulk of the market.

The foreign branches (mainly London) of major American and foreign commercial banks have substantial amounts of Eurodollar CDs that enjoy an active secondary market and ordinarily afford higher rates than those available at home offices. In recent years, floating rate Eurodollars also have been issued, as have conventional and floating rate Asian dollar CDs. These rates ordinarily are tied to the London Interbank offer rate, which is the rate at which major international banks are willing to offer term Eurodollars to each other. Most Eurodollar CDs are held by the same large corporations that buy domestic CDs in the U.S.

(g) Other Types of Short-Term Investments

A large number of state and municipal obligations are available which are issued on a short-term basis or become short-term over time. These have the advantage of exemption from federal income taxes as well as the taxes of the issuing agency, i.e., income from New York State bonds is exempt from New York income taxes. Much of the originally issued, short-term local government securities are general obligations sold in anticipation of revenues from the federal government or from future long-term bonds. These notes sell at yields that reflect the credit status of the issuer.

Corporations ordinarily do not issue short-term obligations other than commercial paper, but with the passage of time their outstanding securities enter into this category.

[6] INTEREST RATE FUTURES

Farmers and food processors have long used the futures market to hedge the price of the commodities they carry in inventory. The late 1960's introduced a period of high and volatile interest rates, a condition that both created new risks and new speculative opportunities for those dealing in interest-bearing securities. Since the interest rate is the price paid for money, changes in this price can be offset in a futures market, just like changes in the prices of agricultural commodities. Following the introduction in 1975 by the Chicago Board of Trade of a futures contract in certificates representing modified pass-through mortgaged backed instruments guaranteed by the Government National Mortgage Association, other exchanges as well as the Board of Trade made further applications to the Commodity Futures Trading Commission, the administrative governmental agency. A host of contracts was created covering stock indexes as well as securities and requests have been made to trade futures on such economic indicators as new car sales and housing starts.

An interest rate future is a standard contract to buy or sell a stated amount of a particular financial instrument at a designated date in the future at a price established in a central marketplace. A clearing-house intervenes as the party on the other side of a contract. Thus its credit is more important than that of the original buyer or seller and flexibility is provided to clear the contract by taking an opposite position. For example, entering an agreement to buy if the original commitment was to sell. In fact, it is relatively unusual to deliver or take delivery of the underlying security at the specified price.

Trading in interest rate futures, like any market of this sort, revolves around risk assumers (speculators) and risk avoiders (hedgers). The former hope to make profits in return for bearing the risk of future interest rate fluctuations. The latter desire to protect actual or expected cash positions against unforeseen interest rate movements. In the area of cash management, the financial officer is a risk avoider, and ordinarily would use the futures market to insure a current rate on funds that either will become available or will be required in the future.

To illustrate the first case, assume that on September 15, when the return on short-term Treasury Bills is 9 percent, the financial officer of a company engages in a transaction that will provide $5 million on December 10.[12] Observing that rates have been declining rapidly, the manager anticipates they will be substantially lower by the time the funds become available for investment. Accordingly, he desires to take measures so that at that time he will still be assured of obtaining the current 9 percent return.

Based on the 9 percent rate prevailing on September 15, the financial officer would have paid $4,886,250 for $5 million of Treasury Bills.[13] To lock in this rate, he buys five December Treasury Bill contracts at 9 percent amounting to $4,887,500.[14] On December 10, as the financial officer expected, rates fall to 7 percent. The funds from the September 15 transaction now become available and he buys $5 million of Treasury Bills at the then prevailing rate of 7 percent, resulting in a cost of $4,911,530.[15] At the same time, he closes out the five December contracts at 7 percent, receiving as proceeds $4,912,500.[16] Because he purchased the Treasury Bills on December 10, when the rate had dropped to 7 percent, the financial manager earns $25,280 less than he would have obtained had he made the purchase on September 15, when the rate was

9 percent ($4,886,250 - $4,911,530). On the other hand, he obtains a profit of $25,000 on the futures contract ($4,912,500 - $4,887,500). In effect, therefore, through the device of an interest rate future, the financial officer is able to earn the equivalent of the 9 percent rate that prevailed on September 15.

For the second case, assume that a financial officer on May 1, when the interest rate on 90-day commercial paper is 9.20 percent, plans to issue such paper on September 5. Desiring to lock in the current rate, he sells ten September Treasury Bill futures at the May 1 rate of 8.95 percent, receiving $9,776,250.[17] On September 5, when the financial officer actually issues the $10 million of commercial paper, he finds that he has to pay a rate of 9.90 percent, receiving $9,752,500.[18] At that time, however, he closes out his futures contract by purchasing $10 million of Treasury Bills at the prevailing rate of 9.75 percent, paying $9,756,250.[19] Thus, he earns $20,000 on the interest rate futures contract ($9,776,250 - $9,756,250). The financial officer's original interest cost when he issued the commercial paper on September 5 was $247,500 ($10,000,000 - $9,752,500). Accordingly, the net interest cost is $227,500 ($247,500 - $20,000), equivalent to an effective rate of 9.10 percent $\frac{($227,500 \times 4)[20]}{$10,000,000}$. By means of the futures market, therefore, the financial officer has been able to more than match the 9.20 percent rate that prevailed on May 1 when he initially contemplated the issuance of commercial paper.

In these illustrations, the futures market in Treasury Bills was used to hedge against changes in interest rates on such investments as well as on commercial paper. The underlying assumption, therefore, which seems reasonable, is that these rates will reveal similar movements. Possible discrepancies, however, could create a distorting condition. The Chicago Board of Trade did introduce a futures market in commercial paper, but it did not attract investor interest and was eventually aborted.

[7] SPECIAL PRACTICES

When they use the previously discussed instruments, corporations may engage in special practices, the more important of which are described below:

- direct bidding for Treasury bills;
- using the interest curve;
- using repurchase agreements; and
- paying by federal funds.

(a) Direct Bidding for Treasury Bills

Ordinarily, a corporate investment officer who wants to buy Treasury bills instructs his depository bank, presumably a money-market institution, to bid for a specified amount, and allows the bank to determine the bid price to establish. The bank then enters a "customer's bid" for the indicated amount.

The bank recognizes that it will probably receive little thanks for obtaining the lowest possible bid, but still will be criticized if its bid prevents the customer from procuring the desired amount of bills. Accordingly, a customer's bid is likely to be entered at a level higher than the low price at which full subscriptions are accepted by the Treasury and possibly even above the average price for which subscriptions are awarded.

FIGURE 8.5   *Typical yield patterns of U.S. Government securities*

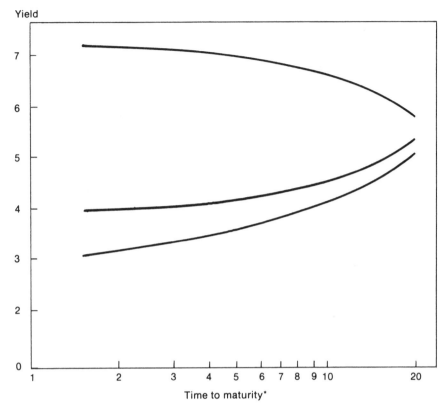

* Time to maturity is plotted on a logarithmic scale on which equal distances represent equal percentage changes in time to maturity.

Source: Morris Mendelson and Sidney Robbins, *Investment Analysis and Securities Markets,* Basic Books, Inc., 1976, p. 431.

Under these circumstances, an investment officer who is sufficiently close to the bill market to enter bids directly may well make his purchase at better prices than those the bank would submit. Over time, a policy of direct bidding not only could produce a fair amount of extra corporate income, but would also compel the investment officer to maintain an intimacy with the money market that may be helpful in the corporation's general financial program.

(b) Using the Interest Curve

When the maturities and yields of securities of comparable quality are plotted on a chart, an interest rate curve is obtained whose shape varies with economic circumstances. These differences create what is technically described as the term structure of interest rates, or more simply, yield curves, that are carefully studied by the investment community. As illustrated in Figure 8.5 these curves have taken different shapes. The most characteristic, reflecting the uncertainties of the future, is the ascending curve. The descending curve tends to appear when interest rates are relatively high, leading investors to buy long-term issues, thereby driving their yields down. Such curves were common in this country from about 1906 to 1929. When curves shift from one form to another, they may temporarily become flat, as has occurred in recent years. Sometimes a humped curve has also come on the scene. Changes in formulation occur as the whole spectrum of interest rates moves and because of the greater volatility of short as opposed to long-term rates.

When the yield curve has a pronounced upward tilt that is expected to persist, corporations with large holdings of short-term securities have been able to increase the effective yields on these obligations by "riding the curve." The corporations, for example, may buy on original offerings when an issue may be obtained at the relatively lower price of full maturity. Then, if the interest rate curve is shaped upward, the market price becomes proportionately higher (yield becomes lower) as maturity nears. The corporations sell the shorter maturities at the higher prices, promptly reinvest the proceeds in new offerings at the relatively lower prices, and continue the process. While particularly applicable to Treasury securities because of their breadth and liquidity, the procedure may be employed for other instruments as well.[21]

Corporations with dynamic investment policies will also be alert to buying securities that afford a yield above the interest rate curve and selling those providing a yield below the curve at comparable maturities. Unusual market conditions sometimes offer interesting opportunities for switches of this sort. Investors in certain geographic areas may be willing to pay premiums for issues maturing around the dates when local taxes fall due. Treasury bills maturing about income tax dates tend to sell at above-average prices. Savings banks often pay higher prices for securities maturing on the dates when Christmas Club disbursements must be paid. Conditions such as these afford favorable opportunities to dispose of securities; the investment officer may also be able to buy at propitious prices when others must sell under pressure.

(c) Using Repurchase Agreements

We have previously defined a repurchase agreement as a contract in which a corporation buys a security and simultaneously sells it to a dealer for delivery on a later date at a price that affords the buyer a specified return for the period held. To be on the safe side, corporations tend to provide for anticipated daily fluctuations in cash by keeping somewhat larger cash balances than the minimum level indicated by the cash budget. The repurchase agreement provides an excellent vehicle for the investment-minded financial manager to keep excess cash fully invested at all times. It allows him to make or terminate repurchase agreements regularly in order to smooth daily and weekly cash fluctuations. Suppose, for example, that a corporation obtains $10 million of surplus funds on Monday that it will have to spend on Friday. It might be disinclined to invest these funds in regular channels because the spread between buying and selling prices might cancel out the interest earned. Through a repurchase agreement, however, the funds could be readily invested at a specified rate for the exact period required.

(d) Paying by Federal Funds

Federal funds represent the reserves of Federal Reserve member banks and have immediate cash availability as compared with local funds which require one day clearance. Some companies are reluctant to use federal funds in their securities transactions because they feel that their depository banks might not care for continuing transactions of this sort. Most banks, however, do not object to providing this service to customers in good standing so long as they have enough notice to arrange their reserve position. Since the security dealer usually pays for his purchases in federal funds, he must buy them if he does not receive payment in this form from his customer. Under these circumstances, the dealer may add this cost to the price of the security bought by the customer. Accordingly, many large corporations arrange, as a matter of policy, for all transactions, on both the buy and the sell side, to be cleared in federal funds.

Using federal funds also makes it easier to arrange transfers. As an illustration, assume that the New York office of a large corporation instructs the home office bank to shift funds from the corporation's balances in a San Francisco bank to its account in New York City. The New York institution debits the account of the San Francisco bank, which keeps deposits with it, credits that of its client corporation, and notifies the San Francisco institution of the transfer. If the West Coast bank has insufficient interbank deposits to cover the transaction, its account will be overdrawn. To prevent this deficiency, it instructs the Reserve Bank in San Francisco to forward federal funds to the New York bank, thereupon increasing the balances of the San Francisco institution with it.

8.5 CHAPTER SUMMARY

In this chapter, we focused on cash management, one of the most important functions of the financial manager. By using the cash budget and regular forecasts of cash requirements the financial manager can determine the magnitude and timing of his cash needs. We also covered the principles and techniques currently used to smooth out cash flow and minimize cash requirements. Finally, we addressed the major types of money market securities available for the temporary investment of excess short-term funds.

FOOTNOTES

1. James E. Morley, Jr. "Cash Management — Working for the Extra 1% or 2%," *Management Accounting,* October 1978, p.18.
2. "The Electronic Treasurer," *The Banker,* March 1983, pp. 77-82.
3. Albert J. Fredman, "Accelerating Collections: Float Reduction Techniques," *Credit and Financial Management,* March 1981, pp. 27-29.
4. *Ibid.*
5. See, for example, Bruce D. Fielitz and Daniel L. White, "An Evaluation and Linking of Alternative Solution Procedures for the Lock Box Location Problem," *Journal of Bank Research,* Spring 1982, pp. 17-27.
6. Daniel M. Ferguson, "Optimize your Firm's Lock Box Selection's System," *Financial Executive,* April 1983, pp. 8-19.
7. For a discussion of this subject, see Coopers & Lybrand, "Electronic Funds Transfers — Current and Prospective Corporate Applications, *Special Report,* January-February 1979.
8. Westinghouse Electric Corp., which is doing considerable research in this area estimates a fully implemented electronic corporate payment system would result in annual savings of $1.4 million in processing costs on the receivable side,

$880,000 on the payable side, and provide a much better control of float. (Robert L. Caruso, "Paying Bills the Electronic Way," *Management Accounting,* April 1984, pp. 24-27.)

9. See, for example, Gary W. Emery, "Some Empirical Evidence on the Properties of Daily Cash Flow," *Financial Management,* Spring 1981, pp. 21-28 and L. Richard Keyser, "Corporate Demand for Cash Balances," *Business Economics,* Spring 1980, pp. 59-63.

10. Commercial paper with a maturity from 12 to 18 months and even occasionally up to 24 months has also been issued. Registration requirements on commercial paper with a maturity in excess of 270 days is normally avoided by placing such paper privately.

11. Brokers, including some giant securities firms, such as Merrill Lynch, Dean Witter Reynolds, a unit of Sears Roebuck & Co., and Shearson/American Express, have popularized programs of putting together small chunks of money and buying big CDs in banks and savings and loans around the country. These funds were sometimes directed to weak institutions which later failed thereby placing a financial drain on the federal guarantying agencies. As a result, these agencies put limits on the insurance available on brokered deposits, an area that may lead to congressional action.

12. The following illustrations are based on tables in Chicago Mercentile Exchange, "Opportunities in Interest Rates, Treasury Bill Futures," November 1977, pp. 20-21. In these illustrations, transaction costs are excluded.

13. Treasury Bills are quoted and traded on a bank discount basis. To convert the discount into dollars, the actual number of days involved is related to 360 days per year, according to the following formula:

$$\text{Cost} = \$1,000,000 - \frac{(\text{days to maturity x T-bill yield x } \$1,000,000)}{360}$$

Using the data of the illustration, we obtain:

$$\text{Cost} = 5[\$1,000,000 - \frac{(91 \times .09 \times \$1,000,000)]}{360}$$

$$= 5[\$1,000,000 - \$22,750]$$

$$= \$4,886,250.$$

14. The trading contract is for a $1 million, 90 day Treasury bill. Using the data of the illustration, we obtain:

$$\text{Cost} = 5[\$1,000,000 - \frac{(90 \times .09 \times \$1,000,000)]}{360}$$

$$= 5[\$1,000,000 - \$22,500]$$

15. $$\text{Cost} = 5[\$1,000,000 - \frac{(91 \times .07 \times \$1,000,000)]}{360}$$

$$= 5[\$1,000,000 - \$17,694]$$

$$= \$4,911,530.$$

16. $$\text{Proceeds} = 5[\$1,000,000 - \frac{(90 \times .07 \times \$1,000,000)]}{360}$$

$$= 5[\$1,000,000 - \$17,500]$$

$$= \$4,912,500.$$

17. $$\text{Proceeds} = 10[\$1,000,000 - \frac{(90 \times .0895 \times \$1,000,000)]}{360}$$

$$= 10[\$1,000,000 - \$22,375]$$

$$= \$9,776,250.$$

18. $$\text{Proceeds} = 10[\$1,000,000 - \frac{(90 \times .0990 \times \$1,000,000)]}{360}$$

$$= 10[\$1,000,000 - \$24,750]$$

$$= \$9,752,500.$$

19. Cost = 10[$1,000,000 - $\frac{(90 \times .0975 \times \$1,000,000)]}{360}$

    = 10[$1,000 - $24,375]

    = $9,756,250.

20. This rate reflects the bank discount basis. The "bond equivalent" yield would be somewhat higher since it involves 365 days and is based on the actual discounted proceeds received instead of the face amount of the underlying instruments.

21. If short-term interest rates rise during the period of "riding the curve," the return would be reduced.

SUGGESTED READINGS

Arak, Marcelle and Christopher L. McCurdy, "Interest Rate Futures," *Federal Reserve Bank of New York, Quarterly Review*, Winter 1979-80.

Austin, J. J., "Improving Cash Management with a Short Run Financial Planning Model," *Public Utilities Fortnightly*, September 10, 1981.

Cox, John C., Jonathan E. Ingersoll, Jr., and Stephan A. Ross, "A Re-examination of Traditional Hypotheses about the Term Structure of Interest Rates," *The Journal of Finance*, September 1981.

Fredman, A. J., "Accelerating Collections: Float Reduction Techniques," *Credit and Financial Management*, March 1981.

Freimuth, Richard C., "Cash Management for Smaller Business: A New Technique," *Management Accounting*, June 1982.

Gale, Bradley T., and Ben Branch, "Cash Flow Analysis: More Important Than Ever," *Harvard Business Review*, July-August 1981.

Goldstein, N. R., "Making Money Market Instruments Work," *Credit and Financial Management*, June 1981.

Hurley, Evelyn M., "The Commercial Paper Market Since the Mid-Seventies," *Federal Reserve Bulletin*, June 1982.

Koenig, Peter, "How Competition is Sharpening Cash Management," *Institutional Investor*, June 1982.

Mathur, Igbal and Penny J. Luisada, "Cash Management Services Offered by Banks," *Bankers Magazine*, July/August 1980.

McHenry, Wendell, "EFT in the 1980s," *Bankers Magazine*, May/June 1981.

Nauss, R. M. and R. Markland, "Theory and Application of an Optimizing Procedure for Lock Box Location Analysis," *Management Science*, August 1981.

———, "Solving Lock Box Location Problems," *Financial Management*, Spring 1979.

Oakley, R. J., "Putting Corporate Cash to Work," *Credit and Financial Management*, Spring 1979.

Pisani, Richard A., "Developing Electronic Cash-Management Systems," *Bankers Magazine*, November/December 1981.

Rappaport, Allen, James M. Murphy, and Arnold F. Parr, "Industrial Commercial Paper Ratings: A Discriminant Analysis," *Review of Business and Economic Research*, Spring 1982.

Stone, Bernell and Robert Wood, "Daily Cash Forecasting: A Simple Method for Implementing the Distribution Approach," *Financial Management*, Fall 1977.

——— and N. C. Hill, "Alternative Cash Transfer Mechanisms and Methods: Evaluation Frameworks," *Journal of Bank Research*, Spring 1982.

Westbrook, W. L. and C. O. Rawlings, "Bank Credit Commitments and Cash Management — Are Fees Really Cheaper Than Balances?" *Public Utilities Fortnightly*, August 27, 1981.

CREDIT MANAGEMENT AND POLICY

9.1 MANAGERIAL ASPECTS OF CREDIT POLICY

Credit management has emerged as a major part of business; its expansion has been paralleled by the growing professionalism of its practitioners. Credit managers now have their own professional publications, associations, and educational programs. Because of their enlarged managerial role and their intimate knowledge of the activities of important customers, credit managers can provide financial advice to customers who are having difficulty meeting credit standards or who do not have the managerial skills to develop their own corrective programs. This assistance not only creates goodwill but also may help these accounts to continue payments and eventually become sound once more.

[1] EXTENT OF MANAGERIAL ASSISTANCE

Managerial assistance may take different forms depending on the skills available at the credit department of the selling company, the nature of its customers, and its relationships with them. A professional credit department may be able to detect eroding finances before the customer. In these circumstances, the creditor company may take the initiative and provide the information to the customer, who is likely to appreciate the notification before more serious difficulties set in. Alternatively, the customer, recognizing the deteriorating position of his company, may request financial counseling.

Sometimes, too, a company may send a credit executive to a customer periodically to help manage different phases of the credit process. If the advice is broad gauged, such as how to develop an overall financing program, another financial officer, such as the company's treasurer, might accompany the credit manager.

On the other hand, it would be foolhardy for the credit department of a company to advise a customer on problems which the personnel of the credit department have no special expertise. Similarly, it is unnecessary to provide advice to financially strong customers who are professionally competent.

[2] CREDIT OBJECTIVES

As a general practice, those in credit determine whether or not a buyer's credit should be accepted in exchange for a seller's goods or services. Credit is, then, closely linked to sales. In some companies this link is quite strong, with credit policies oriented toward achieving the sales objective. If, for example, a firm wants to increase sales to make use of idle plant capacity, there is likely to be a relaxation of credit standards. On the other hand, if a firm is already operating beyond its capacity and no expansion of facilities is contemplated, the firm may accept only customers with high credit ratings. Moreover, shifting economic conditions may cause variations in a firm's objectives which can lead to a reformulation of credit policies.

The attitude of the sales department toward its customers also could influence credit policy. If a firm has a large number of relatively small accounts, the sales department may not feel that any one is particularly significant, and the credit department may not believe it profitable to spend the time and effort required to support close relations.

On the other hand, if there are a relatively small number of major accounts, the sales department may consider it desirable to maintain close contact with each to ensure the continuation of important orders. Or, the sales department may believe that the long-run interests of the business warrant cultivating a particular account. Motivated by such considerations, a company's credit department may overlook infractions of sales terms, help customers work out of financial difficulties, and advise them on how to handle impending problems. It depends on the firm's objectives.

Credit sales lead to receivables and generally to the need to institute collection procedures, because in most instances credit standards are not likely to be so rigorous or the reviewing procedures so exact as to eliminate all slow paying accounts and defaults. Here again, collection policies are likely to be geared toward overall firm objectives. The desire to increase sales may lead to permissive attitudes and a willingness to overlook missed payment dates. Conversely, a retrenchment program may be instituted by adopting stern collection policies which discourage orders from marginal accounts.

To push sales, a firm may not only relax its credit and collection standards but may also grant more generous repayment terms. Pressure for funds, on the other hand, may necessitate the adoption of only short payment periods. Or, continuing difficulties may call for a re-examination of the terms granted by suppliers compared with those given to the firm's own customers. Steps to bring about a better balance between receiving and offering terms may be adopted, even though competition and tradition limit the freedom of such changes.

Credit and collection policies designed to meet overall corporate objectives establish operating standards. To ensure that policy, objectives and operating standards mesh effectively requires careful planning.

9.2   COMPREHENSIVE CREDIT PLANNING

In this section, we focus on the overall aspects of credit planning and illustrate the use of marginal analysis in the planning process.

[1] KEY VARIABLES IN CREDIT PLANNING

Credit planning requires an understanding of how changes in sales, cost of sales, accounts receivables, and inventory affect earnings. The following two equations portray these relationships:

Accounts Receivable x Percent Profit Margin x Receivables Turnover = Earnings

or

$$R \times \frac{S-C}{S} \times \frac{S}{R} = E \qquad [1]$$

where: R = Accounts Receivable;
   S = Sales;
   C = Cost of sales; and
   E = Earnings,

and

Inventory x Percent Markup x Inventory Turnover = Earnings

or

$$I \times \frac{S-C}{S} \times \frac{C}{I} = E \qquad [2]$$

where: I = Inventory.

The first equation indicates that the average amount of receivables outstanding during the year multiplied by the percentage profit margin yields the profits resulting from a volume of business equal to the receivables. By multiplying this profit by the turnover of receivables, the earnings on the total volume of business actually done by the company are obtained. The second equation shows that the average amount of inventory outstanding multiplied by the markup gives the profits embodied in the inventory. When this profit factor is multiplied by the turnover of inventories during the year, the earnings are provided. It is clear that profits are directly affected by changes in sales and cost of sales. Profits are not directly affected by changes in receivables, but they may be indirectly affected if these changes lead to adjustments in the amount of inventory carried and therefore to changes in sales.

The first equation may be refined as follows to incorporate the effects of a company's collection experience:

$$\frac{SL}{360} \times \frac{S-C}{S} \times \frac{360}{L} = E \qquad [3]$$

where: L = average collection period for accounts receivable, which is typically represented by the number of days sales outstanding in receivables (DSO).[1]

The basis for these modifications is that the product of the average sales for one day ($\frac{S}{360}$) and the collection experience $\frac{360}{L = \frac{S}{R}}$ gives the average amount of receivables outstanding $(\dfrac{S}{360} \times \dfrac{360R}{S})$, and that the number of collection cycles during the year $(\dfrac{360}{L})$ is equivalent to the turnover of receivables $(360 \times \dfrac{S}{360R})$. In effect, therefore, the third equation merely revises the first to indicate that the profit on each collection cycle multiplied by the number of collection cycles during the year produces the earnings for the year.

We can now observe the effects of changes among the elements of our equation. The changes considered include:

- change in the average collection period (L);
- reduced cost of sales (C); and
- change in the level of sales (S).

(a) Effect of Change in the Average Collection Period (L)

If sales are unchanged, but a longer period is required for the company to collect its receivables (L increases), annual turnover $\dfrac{(360)}{L}$ down and the amount of receivables outstanding $\dfrac{SL}{(360)}$ rises. Theoretically, the company's profits are unchanged because it earns the same profit margin $\dfrac{(S-C)}{S}$ on a larger amount of receivables which turns over more sluggishly. The difficulty in this theory is that a company is likely to have limited funds, and if a larger portion is tied up in receivables, a smaller amount will probably be left in cash. The lesser amount of cash could mean that the company must carry less inventories (I). If turnover remains the same, sales and cost of sales will probably shrink proportionately with the decline in inventories. As a result, even though the percent markup is unchanged, the company's volume of business is less and earnings for the period fall. An inventory reduction of K dollars, for example, will cause profits to shrink by $\dfrac{K}{I}$ percent. In order to obtain the funds to keep inventory intact, the company may seek to convert its enlarged receivables into cash through borrowing from a commercial bank or factoring. Under these circumstances, its profits would still be reduced by the costs of the loan.

A reduced collection time (L) has no immediate effect on profits if the more rapid turnover only leads to carrying a smaller amount of receivables. But the reduction in receivables may release cash for inventories, which in turn permit more sales and higher profits. The process is the same as described previously but in the opposite direction.

(b) Effect of Reduced Cost of Sales (C)

Let us now assume that the company is able to reduce its cost of sales by K. The lowered cost of sales (C - K) increases the profit margin (S - C + K). Accordingly, as long as there is no offsetting decline in sales, profits are bound to rise. A sales reduction, as we have seen, may be induced by slower collections that curtail cash balances and lower purchases of inventories.

(c) Effect of Change in the Level of Sales (S)

A reduction in sales operates in a reverse way. Profits will be reduced unless offset by a greater or equal decline in the cost of sales. If greater, profits rise; if equal, a higher percentage $(\frac{S - C}{S - K})$ profit margin is applied to a smaller amount of sales (S - K), which could cut down on weak receivables and free cash for further profitable investment. Thus, credit planning may increase profits directly when it creates a higher total profit margin through enlarged sales, or indirectly when it frees cash for investment through an improved collections policy or a more balanced use of credit terms.

If sales rise and everything else remains the same, profits grow because the profit margin expands. If the cost of sales also rises, the profit margin is curtailed; the net effect on profits depends on the relationship between these two factors. Should the increase in the cost of sales (C + K) just equal the rise in sales (S + K), a lower percentage profit margin $(\frac{S - C}{S + K})$ is applied to more sales (S + K), and profits are unchanged. If the enlarged sales are made to weaker accounts, resulting in a longer collection period, growing receivables could cause a decline in cash. As a result, less funds will be available for inventories, leading to an eventual decline in sales and profits. To provide extra funds, therefore, the firm may have to borrow, an act which will create additional financing costs.

[2] USE OF MARGINAL ANALYSIS

Another way of employing credit management to enhance the profits of the firm is through the concept of marginal analysis developed earlier in our discussion of volume-cost-profit analysis (Chapter 5). Marginal analysis represents an attempt to match the sales price of a unit of production with the variable (another term would be direct or marginal) cost of production. This, in essence, is a matching of marginal revenue with marginal costs. It is, in a sense, the computation of the risk:gain ratio based upon production and sale of a single unit of the company's product.

We use a simplified hypothetical example to illustrate the use of marginal analysis in credit planning. Consider a product with a sales price per unit of $5.00 and unit variable costs of $3.00, the company would stand to profit $2.00 more or lose $2.00 less from each sale of its product. In effect, every time the company sells one unit of this product, its contribution toward coverage of its fixed costs and the generation of profits is $2.00. Thus:

	Per Unit
Sales Price	$5.00
Variable Costs	-3.00
Contribution to Fixed Costs and Profit	$2.00

For this product the risk:gain ratio is 60:40 (60 percent vs. 40 percent). In essence, every time the company produces and sells a unit of this production for $5.00, it risks $3.00 for the opportunity to gain $2.00.

The relevance of marginal analysis for credit management policy is in revealing the minimum collection percentage of receivables required to break-even on each item of sales. In the case above, where $3.00 is risked in order to achieve a gain of $2.00, the financial manager logically could extend credit to all customers who have a greater likelihood of paying than 60 percent. If, for example, an uncertain of paying group of customers cleared their accounts on this product 60 percent of the time and failed to pay 40 percent of the time, the company, as shown below, would be neither worse nor better off for having granted credit to these accounts.

Amount at risk x Percentage of time loss occurs =
Amount to gain x Percentage of time gain occurs
or
$3.00 (40%) = $2.00 (60%)
$1.20 = $1.20.

A financial manager, of course, grants credit to accounts he is confident will pay their debts. For this product, he should then continue granting credit successively to less certain accounts until he reaches the point where he believes there is a 60 percent likelihood of the account being paid. Although a precise determination of the likelihood of an account paying may be difficult, some of the techniques developed later in this chapter as well as the credit manager's own experience will provide guidance in this endeavor.

There is, in addition, other estimating elements in the credit granting decision which must be added to the relationship developed above. The amount of time the financial manager gauges it will take the customer to clear his account is also of consequence. Obviously, the time value of money (developed further in Chapter 17) and turnover of receivables considerations (developed just above in this chapter) dictate that a faster paying account is preferable to a slower paying one. With this in mind, the following additional relationship might be developed.

The financial manager would be indifferent to the granting of credit when:

| Risk:Gain Ratio | = | Likelihood of an account paying | x | Discount factor for the time to pay at the time value of money for the firm. |

Utilizing our hypothetical example, we see that the company should grant credit as long as the product of the likelihood of paying and the discount factor for the time to pay at the time value of money for the firm is above 60 percent. Thus, if it is decided that there is a 70 percent likelihood of a given account paying in a year, the firm should extend credit as long as the discount factor for the company is above .857 (60%/70%). In this case, assuming that the company's time value of money is 10 percent[2], reference to Figure 17.24 shows that the appropriate discount factor for one year is .909. The company would then extend credit since .909 x .7 is greater than .6.

We can take this framework of analysis one step further by placing specific probability parameters on the various payment patterns which the credit manager deems possible in the case of a given customer.[3] Consider the product described above with a sales price of $5.00 and a variable cost of $3.00 and thus a risk:gain ratio of 60 percent. The credit manager may then determine the following payment patterns and related probabilities for a particular customer:

Payment at the end of 1 year = 20% likely[4]
Payment at the end of 2 years = 40% likely
Payment at the end of 3 years = 30% likely
Payment never received = 10% likely.

If the time value of money is 10 percent, the following discount factors apply:

1 year = .909[5]
2 years = .826
3 years = .751.

Next, by multiplying the likelihood of each of the above payment schedules by its associated discount factor and summing the total, we can determine the appropriate overall figure to compare to the product's risk:gain ratio.[6]

1 year .909 x .2 = .1818
2 years .826 x .4 = .3304
3 years .751 x .3 = .2253
.7375

In this case the credit manager should extend credit since the risk:gain ratio on the product is .60. In effect, the overall probability and time adjusted likelihood of paying for this potential customer is still above .60.

While this decision may appear to represent an excessively lenient credit policy, keep in mind that credit granting decisions are made at the margin where coverage of total costs are not relevant. What counts is coverage of variable or marginal costs.

The obvious implication of this analysis is that different credit granting policies might properly be set for each of a company's products based on their relative risk:gain ratios. Even to the same potential customer, with the same likelihood and time of payment, a company should be more willing to grant credit on products with a more favorable risk:gain ratio.

Perhaps, this rationale helps explain why manufacturing firms may be willing to extend trade credit when banks are unwilling to grant loans. Assume, for example, a simple banking relationship where $100 is advanced with 10 percent interest deducted in advance. In such a transaction, $90 is given to the borrower and $100 is paid back in one year. (The actual interest rate is $10/$90 = 11.1%.) To the bank, the risk:gain ratio is 90:10 (90% vs. 10%). In effect, the cash advanced by the bank becomes its variable cost. But rarely do manufacturers have a variable cost as high as 90 percent of their selling price. Thus, they generally are more willing than bankers to grant credit to accounts which are uncertain to pay.

9.3   INCREASING SALES THROUGH THE CREDIT PROGRAM

Since most business sales are made on credit, a company's credit program is of great importance. Within the framework of company financial objectives, the credit manager usually has considerable leeway in developing such a program.

[1] THE APPROVAL POLICY

In part, the problem of credit management is to balance the benefits of greater sales volume with the risks of longer collections. But the problem is not really one of balance because there is a bias toward accepting the buyer's credit. After all, the primary function of business is to produce sales. In the process, certain risks are necessarily incurred. From a negative viewpoint, the function of credit management may be visualized as that of weeding out excessive risks, but more positively it is directed toward establishing principles that encourage new orders.

The credit manager may find, for example, that the expense of credit investigation and the losses from the resulting delays do not warrant any special checking procedures for small orders. He may therefore automatically recommend approving all orders below a certain amount. What this level should be depends upon the company's size, financial status, products, types of customers, and, as we have just seen, the risk:gain ratio for the product being sold. In general, the level will be determined by comparing the costs of credit analysis with the probable losses from a large number of small orders. A blanket approval limit will probably be set where the costs almost balance the losses. This arrangement is particularly adaptable to companies with diversified sales outlets, those with a large number of small accounts, and those with centralized record keeping. Only if a new order exceeds a customer's assigned credit limits will it be referred to the credit department.

A second way to cut costs and speed approval is to provide credit lines for new customers according to a schedule that relates allowable amounts to the ratings of a mercantile agency and to keep these lines up to date by periodic rechecks. As an example, when a policyholder of a major credit insurance company sells to accounts rated by one of the mercantile agencies, the coverage limit may be based upon the account's assigned rating, as indicated in Figure 9.1. The figure shows how these limits vary with Dun & Bradstreet's first and second credit ratings.

FIGURE 9.1 *Table of ratings and coverage*

Column One			Column Two		
Rating		Gross Amount Covered	Rating		Gross Amount Covered
5A	1	$100,000	5A	2	$25,000
4A	1	100,000	4A	2	25,000
3A	1	100,000	3A	2	25,000
2A	1	50,000	2A	2	25,000
1A	1	50,000	1A	2	25,000
BA	1	50,000	BA	2	25,000
BB	1	50,000	BB	2	25,000
CB	1	50,000	CB	2	25,000
1R	2	25,000	2R	2	15,000
CC	1	30,000	CC	2	15,000
DC	1	25,000	DC	2	12,500
DD	1	20,000	DD	2	10,000
EE	1	10,000	EE	2	5,000
FF	1	5,000	FF	2	3,000
GG	1	2,500	GG	2	1,500
HH	1	1,500	HH	2	750

Employing such a schedule, a company could make substantial initial sales to high rated buyers, and scale down the amounts as the ratings decline. As soon as the first order has been accepted, the credit investigation is launched, and a line can be established for succeeding orders.

A third way to speed approval is to provide established procedures for referring cases to the credit department which do not meet standard prescriptions. Rules may be laid down for granting approval to nonconforming accounts under certain conditions and on special terms. The computer has permitted flexibility to be incorporated into standard systems, thereby reducing the need for credit department referrals. Thus, points may be given for different factors, such as stability of employment, and a cut off total established to determine if credit should be given. If it is then decided to tighten credit standards as a result of changing economic conditions, the total required points need only be raised.

[2] TYPES OF CREDIT LINES

The kinds of credit lines that a company is willing to grant are an individual matter depending upon the activities and relations of the firms involved. These lines however, are often expressed in similar ways. One common method is to relate the credit limit to the customer's debt paying ability. The steps taken to determine this relationship range from a careful evaluation of his financial condition and earnings potential to the use of relatively arbitrary criteria such as a designated percentage of net current assets.

The limit can also be expressed in terms of the customer's estimated requirements. For this purpose, simple procedures may be used, like allowing the salesman to work out requirements with the customer or stating requirements as orders placed during a designated period.

When a customer's financial standing is very high and his payment ability unquestioned, the line may take the form of his normal requirements. The sales department simply is authorized to accept the orders given by certain customers. There is a tendency to extend this policy to others as experience is gained in working with them. Caution therefore must be exercised to prevent unwarranted abuses of the policy by customers whose financial status may have deteriorated.

In contrast to these simple approaches for determining requirements, a company may employ an elaborate procedure which considers such factors as the customer's annual volume of sales, the proportion of these sales in the company's own lines, the proportion of this business the company may expect to obtain and the number of days of credit sales the customer will be allowed. The following example illustrates such a procedure.

Let us assume that a drug wholesaler is establishing limits for a retail drugstore that has a sufficiently good financial condition to justify using estimated requirements. The wholesaler estimates that the drug company's sales for the coming year will be $160,000. Analyzing government data showing sales by commodities and the business of some of his other customers, the wholesaler further estimates that 75 percent of the retailer's business or $120,000 will be in merchandise that he handles. Because of the wholesaler's standing in the field, he will probably obtain one half of this business, or $60,000. The wholesaler's terms are such that his accounts are outstanding for 45 days on the average. Dividing 360 by 45 shows the number of times these days' sales will turn over during the year, and dividing this turnover figure, 8, into the estimated sales of $60,000 gives $7,500 as the credit limit at retail prices. In order to convert this figure into a wholesale amount, it is adjusted by the average gross profit margin of 36 percent to obtain a credit limit of approximately $4,800 ($7,500 x .64 = $4,800).

The monthly ledger balances of a customer with a good record of payments could also be used as the basis for assigning limits. For the sales department, however, a line expressed in terms of volume of orders over a given period of time is ordinarily easier to handle than one expressed in terms of balances. When a customer's payment record regarding his trade terms is sufficiently consistent, the credit department may therefore convert a line based on balances to its equivalent in terms of orders. If, for example, a customer invariably takes advantage of a discount by paying within the prescribed 10-day term, the sales department might be given monthly acceptable order limits that are three times the established balance limits (10 days are 1/3 of the month).

[3] WAIVING THE CREDIT LINE

It would be convenient if the financial standards of all of a firm's customers justified establishing credit lines and if these limits were always met within the prescribed time periods. Unfortunately, this is not common. There are invariably order-seeking firms which do not meet standards and established customers who fail to observe allotted terms.

When an established customer seeks more extended terms the financial manager must determine the reason. A request caused by a deteriorating financial position will probably be denied; a request that reflects expanding business, unusual seasonal developments, or other special circumstances, however, is likely to be given a favorable reception.

A new firm seeking to get established is a special case. On the one hand its potential may justify a line even if it does not at the moment meet the prescribed financial requirements. On the other, the current risks may be so great that even with promise of future strength, the credit department may prefer to sell on more stringent terms or even on a cash basis.

In all these cases, the credit department balances the possible gains and losses. It must also gauge the likelihood that future business will be worth the time and effort of working out special arrangements, the possibility that such extensions will become permanent, the effect of expected economic conditions on more generous policies, and the influence of either a stubborn or a flexible credit policy on competitors. While it is unrealistic to hold credit standards inviolate, it is equally unrealistic to relax them too easily.

9.4   CREDIT ANALYSIS

There is shop talk in credit circles about the intuition that a good credit man develops through experience so that he can reach decisions based upon his qualitative reactions to certain people and situations. There is no denying that at the very least, the credit decision depends on judgment, but one that is founded upon a core of solid facts. In our opinion, therefore, intuition or judgment is no more than a skilled interpretation of facts. The experienced analyst can read a statement faster, understand the relations better, and spot weaknesses more accurately than the novice. Regardless of how experienced he may be, however, his decision will need to be based on analysis in order to have any real merit.

Our discussion of credit analysis focuses on the two most important steps in this process, financial statement analysis and credit investigation.

[1] FINANCIAL STATEMENT ANALYSIS

The credit manager may formulate a plan without ever seeing the buyer's income statement or balance sheet. He does so when he authorizes all credit sales below a stated amount believing the costs of investigation not worthwhile, or when his preliminary checks reveal that the character of the buying firm's management is such that continued dealings are inadvisable. In the main, however, financial statements are viewed as an important basis for the final action.

(a) Obtaining a Statement

Financial analysts gain access to company financial statements in different ways. The controller already has them available; the bank lending officer will be given them before he opens a line of credit; the security analyst employs the regularly published information. But the initial contact between the buyer's and the credit manager's firms is likely to be through the sales department where interest is centered on closing the transaction. Additionally, the burden of time, the sensitivity of the parties, and the pressure of competition all may militate against the credit manager asking the buyer for a financial statement.

As a result, the manager might be tempted to rely on statements obtained through a mercantile agency or credit bureau. These organizations, however, usually service many accounts in different kinds of business and cannot be expected to develop data in the form and detail desired by the seller. Accordingly, the seller is likely to obtain better information if he asks the buyer directly for financial statements of the kind most useful for his purposes.

In credit analysis, the date of the financial statement is important, because the effects of seasonal variations should be taken into account. It would be unrealistic to make a judgment based upon data taken at a seasonal peak or trough. It may be desirable, therefore, to have interim statements covering operations throughout the year. Such statements are not likely to be audited, but the certification of an outside accountant is desirable for the annual reports. If the buyer is small and does not prepare interim statements, the financial manager must decide whether or not the cost of obtaining this information is worth the insights provided.

(b) Scope of the Analysis

The credit manager normally focuses on those items of the financial statements that throw light on a company's liquidity and earning power. In this process he is likely to cover the following:

- Ensuring that cash actually represents available funds, by determining whether any amounts are encumbered;
- Adjusting receivables to exclude advances to affiliated firms or persons, and breaking them down to show the amounts due on open accounts and on notes as well as those arising from merchandise and other transactions;

- Determining the method of pricing inventories and ascertaining the amounts represented by raw materials, goods in process, and finished goods;
- Identifying any inventories already subject to lien, and calculating the amount of inventory profits, especially during periods of inflation;
- Investigating the nature of the other assets, including investments, fixed property, intangibles, and deferred items;
- Noting current liabilities, particularly if any are overdue;
- Calculating the relationship between equity and debt;
- Assessing the ability of the firm to meet its fixed obligations;
- Ascertaining if there are any major off-balance sheet liabilities such as unfunded pension obligations and capital leases;
- Evaluating the significance of contingent liabilities in terms of both their amount and likelihood of occurrence;
- Analyzing the sales mix to reveal significant product lines;
- Distinguishing between recurring and non-recurring sources of income;
- Reviewing non-cash charges to ascertain their effect on both reported earnings and cash flows;
- Reviewing, when consolidated financial statements are provided, the methods of consolidation and obtaining independent statements from the parent company as well as its major subsidiaries; and
- Measuring the company's profit margin and rate of return on assets.

Once the analyst feels that he understands the prospective customer's financial statements, he will put the statements into the form most effective for his own study. To evaluate the buyer's present condition he might highlight the important current accounts, expressing them as percentages of some common base. For comparative evaluation, the statements might be listed over time in order to study changes in the significant ratios from year to year. How far back the analyst goes depends, of course, upon what he uncovers. If there were no unusual developments, the flow of transactions over the past several years might throw sufficient light on how the company reached its current status. If a more careful study is desired because of special developments such as an unusual growth of fixed assets, the accumulation of heavy inventories, or a major expansion of fixed charges, the data may be carried back through a complete business cycle. In such a study, he must carefully consider any basic changes during the period in the company's operations or product lines. We have already discussed some representative ratios and cautioned against using them haphazardly.[7] The same principles apply now, because the ratios employed for internal and credit analysis are similar, although differences may occur as a result of differing objectives. In general, the various ratios help the analyst determine how large a credit line may be given to customers without creating undue default risks.

(c) Qualitative Considerations

The credit manager must keep in mind that he is dealing with people, some of whom have a strong sense of financial responsibility and others of whom may seek to avoid their obligations. The trustworthiness of individuals assumes particular weight in credit decisions for new businesses, where there is no record of past performance. In such instances, a firm may be willing to accept the credit of the new enterprise on the basis of the character of its management, an essentially non-quantifiable factor.

[2] CREDIT INVESTIGATION

The heart of credit transactions is the seller's confidence that the buyer will meet his obligations on the due date, based on a knowledge of the buyer's financial statements, character, background, and payment record. As we have seen, this knowledge may be derived from an analysis by the credit manager, but information may also be available through a comprehensive network of credit agencies and interchange techniques that have been built up over the years.

(a) The General Mercantile Agency

Probably the most important single source of credit information is the mercantile agency, whose purpose is providing credit services. The best known of these agencies and the only one that covers all types of businesses is Dun & Bradstreet, Inc. Through its headquarters organization, district offices, sub-offices and reporting statistics, Dun & Bradstreet spans the country, and through subsidiaries and their ties with foreign mercantile agencies, it covers nearly the entire civilized world.

Prominent among its credit services are the reference books which, among other things, provide ratings on some three million businesses. The ratings describe a company's estimated financial strength and give Dun & Bradstreet's appraisal of its credit status. Some firms incorporate the ratings directly into their credit approval system, but more often the ratings serve as guides, and more detailed individual analyses are required before final credit decisions are made.

Dun & Bradstreet also maintains an up-to-date file of analyses or business information sheets prepared by its reporters through a variety of sources. These reports are furnished on request to clients who also automatically receive any revisions made during the course of the year. The regular reports follow a standard form and include information such as the names of the principal officers, the credit rating, the history of the company, the nature of its business, its location, its financial status, and its credit record with a number of suppliers. For larger companies, analytical reports are issued that follow the same pattern but are more comprehensive, including more comparative financial statistics as well as some ratio analyses. Subscribers may also obtain reports specially prepared for them to help resolve such issues as how to treat an unusually big order, evaluate substantial risks, or formulate important policy decisions.

In addition to providing certain other credit and collecting services, Dun & Bradstreet prepares and issues average credit ratios for a number of industries in different publications, including its own *Dun's Review,* which contains much statistical information as well as analytic articles. The company also conducts and publishes special studies concerning different business problems.

(b) The Special Mercantile Agencies

There are a number of other mercantile agencies that limit their activities by line of business, geographic operations, range of services, or some combination of these factors. Some of the agencies are specialized, working in particular fields and offering important and varied services. Among the largest of these is the National Credit Office, Inc. (NCO), originally established to work in the textile trades, but now, as a subsidiary of Dun & Bradstreet, it operates in a number of other fields as well. Although NCO does not issue a general rating book, its services include a reporting system, current comments on the various trades it covers, composite financial statements by industry, listings of marginal accounts and collections, and educational programs. Most of the other well-known specialized agencies, such as the Lyon Furniture Mercantile Agency, publish a general rating book and also offer some sort of reporting and collecting services. Several agencies, like Proundfoot's Reports, Inc. and Bishop's Service, Inc., concentrate on preparing more comprehensive reports geared to particular problems. A large number of national and regional trade associations also provide credit information of some type to their members.

(c) Exchanging Credit Experience

Of considerable help in evaulating the risk in making a credit sale is the experience with the customer which other creditors have had, particularly those who have been doing substantial business with the customer over a long time. By checking information such as the location of these creditors, the highest amount of credit they have been willing to extend the customer, the amounts he currently owes them, the amounts that are past due, the terms of sale, and the customer's payment record, a seller may gain a sound insight into the customer's reliability. Various agencies specialize in credit exchanges of this sort; among the most important of these are the credit interchange bureaus of the National Association of Credit Management (NACM).

A local bureau of the NACM accumulates information from participating creditors in its territory as well as from other bureaus. A member who makes an inquiry receives a copy of the latest report available, or if this is out of date, a fresh report is prepared covering the current ledger experiences of known creditors. The reports make no recommendations but provide the data from which conclusions may be drawn.

Most business firms have banking affiliations, and the experience of these institutions may be helpful to a seller in making decisions. The bank cannot be expected to perform credit analysis for an inquiring firm, but it can offer information on the average balances maintained by a client, the accommodations extended, and the client's payment records. This information will contribute to an overall picture of a customer's credit status. Additional sources of information are the company's own salesmen in the territory and other firms that have had business dealings with the customer.

9.5   REDUCING THE COLLECTION PERIOD

Any firm that sells on credit assumes the risk that the buyer will not meet his obligation when due. The firm's credit policy is calculated to distinguish between those who will meet their obligation and those who will not. The decision, however, sometimes walks a fine line, the outcome may be uncertain, the credit judgment may be inaccurate, or circumstances may change the status of a once financially strong customer. For any of these reasons the selling firm may find its customers extending their payment periods, thereby putting pressure on its own cash position. To curb such a tendency and to reduce the average payment date of its outstanding accounts, the firm will find it desirable to supplement its credit policy with an effective collection procedure.

[1] THE COLLECTION PROCEDURE

The initial question in collection is when to begin it. Ordinarily a specified number of days pass after the net due date before action is instituted. The number of days may be related to the nature of the account, with a more lenient period used for relatively consistent payers and a shorter term established for customers with more careless payment records. Some companies, however, with a particular need to maintain close and friendly ties to their customers, use the collection procedure as a means of extending the credit period on an accommodation credit basis.

In general, guidelines must be established to differentiate between current and overdue accounts. Figure 9.2 illustrates a typical form that ages accounts receivable for this purpose.

FIGURE 9.2 *Aging accounts receivable data*

Account	Total Amount	Current Amount	1-10	11-20	21-30	31-60	61-90	Over 90
				Days Past Due				
The Ace Company	$ 5,675	$ 5,000	$675	—	—	—	—	—
Shetland Corp.	4,300	4,300	—	—	—	—	—	—
Automatic Machines, Inc.	7,100	5,000	—	$1,600	—	$500	—	—
Total	$17,075	$14,300	$675	$1,600	—	$500	—	—
Percent of total	100	84	4	9		3		

When the company has established both a time sequence to ascertain when to start action and a method of relating this sequence to overdue accounts, it is ready to begin collection. Depending upon the size of the company, the number of customers, and their trade terms, this process may run the gamut from preliminary statements through collection letters, telephone calls, registered letters, wires, and personal visits, to end finally with collection agencies. Even though all these measures are available and used, their application in any particular instance is subject to the discretion of the credit department.

In general, however, it is important for a company to develop a policy that relieves it of carrying accounts for unduly long periods, resulting in the accumulation of receivables whose value is questionable.[8] In the long run, a "benevolent" attitude toward customers who are backward in paying bills may only lead to credit difficulties.

Periods of high interest rates are times when customers typically try to hold onto cash as long as possible, therefore delaying payments of their accounts.

During these periods, collection activities normally become more vigorous in order to combat the slower payment trend and to avoid having to borrow to offset retarded cash inflows.

[2] USING COLLECTION AGENCIES

There are a number of agencies specializing in the delicate task of collecting receivables for one business firm from another. These agencies function in a "last-resort" capacity charging a commission which may run 25 percent for the first $2,000 recovered, 20 percent on the excess up to $25,000, and at a negotiated rate thereafter.

Credit managers are likely to call a collector only after pursuing the debtor themselves for some time. Although the techniques of the collecting agencies differ depending on the size and age of the debt, in general, they rely on telephone and mail, and seek to maintain a businesslike approach, particularly to large accounts. If a debtor is not in a position to pay, the collection firm may offer advice on how to raise cash. Moreover, since the collector's request may be the last step prior to a lawsuit, the debtor may be stimulated to pay particular attention to such accounts.

[3] USING THE COMPUTER IN THE CREDIT PROCESS

The credit department is likely to be relatively small and staffed largely with professional personnel. Accordingly, reliance on the computer to perform the data processing and basic analytic work is highly useful. As a result, in a well automated operation, the computer is likely to take over such functions as:

- recording information;
- reporting information regularly or when called upon;
- determining if credit should be granted in routine cases;
- identifying delinquent accounts;
- establishing the time when collection activity should begin; and
- writing the collection letter.

It is efficient to integrate the automation of the credit activity into a company's management information system (MIS). Towards this end, the collaboration of the credit and MIS executives is desirable. The extent of credit automation then would reflect the nature of and be tied into the company's overall automation program.

In theory, the entire credit activity could be automated, as indicated by the range of credit functions listed above that are susceptible to automation. In practice, the credit automation process may be divided into certain stages, with some degree of personal judgment typically injected at each stage.

The basic function to be automated is the processing of information so as to provide a real time summarization of the status of individual accounts to be broken down and transmitted to users throughout the company for whatever action they deem desirable. Standards could be incorporated into the system at the next stage to filter accounts so that some are granted automatically, others granted after being subjected to further guidelines for risk evaluation, and still others reserved for personal judgment. At a final stage, the identification of delinquent accounts and use of collection letters and procedures could be similarly handled on the basis of predetermined guidelines, with filtered exceptions brought to the attention of credit executives for personal handling.

An important decision is how to introduce an on line credit and accounts receivable management system. Here, the choice is likely to be between developing such a system internally or adopting a system which is commercially available. The former approach permits the system to be specifically geared to the needs and characteristics of the company, but could entail considerable effort in researching, debugging, and continued maintenance as well as upgrading. Using a system which is commercially available may require some compromising of objectives, but offers the advantages of rapid installation, less in-house testing and the support of existing vendors. The experience of MIS executives, who may already have been exposed to this problem, would be helpful in reaching a decision on which route to follow.

9.6   THE RISK FACTOR IN ACCOUNTS RECEIVABLE[9]

The typical business sells goods or services on terms that permit future payment. During the period between sales and payment, the customer's obligations are represented on the company's books by unprotected accounts receivable, which are crucial to its financial success. To the extent that they are eventually converted into cash, the enterprise is capable of meeting its own expenses and of obtaining the necessary resources for continued operations and growth.

Accounts receivable represent assets against which a profit has already been anticipated. Should some of a firm's customers default, not only is the profit reduced, but a source of expected funds is lost. Accordingly, while a company is carrying receivables on its books, it is exposed to a pure risk, where the possibility of loss is not offset by any opportunity for gain.

[1] MEETING THE RISK

Most businesses recognize that even with proper diligence by their credit department, some customers who seemed capable of fulfilling their responsibilities will not be able to do so. These defaults may be the result of changed circumstances or oversights in credit evaluations. Accounting provision is made in advance for such expected losses, which enter into the prices established for goods sold.

A firm must figure that in the long run it will experience further sporadic losses, sometimes of large amounts, because extraordinary circumstances prevent customers from paying debts they ordinarily could handle. Unforeseen developments like crop failures, floods, strikes, fires, or other economic disasters, could exert severe pressures on individual debtors and lead to defaults. This risk in accounts receivable can neither be disclosed through normal credit tests nor, because of its nonrecurring character, be handled in regularly established accounts for bad debt losses.

Companies handle this risk problem differently. Some ignore it, either through ignorance, or because they are confident their own financial status is sufficiently strong to cope with losses from unpaid receivables. Others may attempt to soften the impact of any future blow by augmenting the amount of their ordinary bad debt allowances. In some cases, past successful collections may convince management that the problem does not warrant special consideration. Finally, some companies resort to insurance to guard against the risk of unexpected losses from defaults.

[2] CREDIT INSURANCE — ITS MEANING AND BACKGROUND

Credit insurance is a form of casualty insurance in which the protected property consists of accounts receivable arising from the sale, shipment, and delivery of merchandise to the debtor or his agent or from services performed, such as advertising. When an account is considered a loss, in accordance with the terms of the policy, the insurance company agrees to reimburse the policy-holder for the gross proven loss covered less stipulated deductions for such things as the amount collected from the debtor, goods returned, and sales discounts.

Two major companies write credit insurance in the United States:

- The American Credit Indemnity Company of New York, located in Baltimore, is a subsidiary of the Commercial Credit Company, the financial services unit of Control Date Corporation; and
- The London Guarantee and Accident Company of New York, an underwriting affiliate of Continental Corporation.

Both Companies use similar rates, underwriting rules, and provide similar forms of coverage.

[3] THE FUNCTION OF CREDIT INSURANCE

Heavy default can imperil a firm and, therefore, financial management must plan for the possibility of such an event. When a company is strong financially and its outstanding accounts are diversified, it may be able to self insure against these losses or to absorb them. Companies often do both. By establishing bad debt allowances, they regularize and distribute the effects of ordinary defaults over a period of time, while unusual losses are simply absorbed.

Many companies are not able to afford either a credit department sufficiently large to adequately evaluate their accounts or a collection department to pursue sluggish payers. Because of this inadequate followup policy, accounts may become delinquent, locking cash up in uncollectible receivables and thus forcing the company to seek more outside financing. If these circumstances persist, the added financing may eventually be denied, and cash shortages could lead to bankruptcy. Even an effective credit and collection policy, however, is no guard against unforeseen developments causing defaults. Should a firm be dependent upon relatively few large accounts, therefore, it may not be able to absorb unexpected losses developing in one or more of these accounts.

When a company sells to relatively few outlets or when its own resources are limited, credit decisions are particularly critical. The precise point at which the risk of selling to certain accounts outweighs the potential profit is shadowy. By insuring payment of covered accounts, the impact of potential losses on both capital and cash flows is reduced. This added financial security may help obtain bank lines because, through an endorsement, the lending institution may be named a beneficiary.

Credit insurance is particularly adaptable to small and medium sized firms. As a result, the amount written may never compare with that in other casualty lines. This form of insurance can nevertheless render an important service to firms which may suffer serious losses should certain of their customers default.

[4] HOW CREDIT INSURANCE OPERATES

Credit insurance companies cover manufacturers, jobbers, wholesalers, and certain service firms such as advertising agencies. A business firm desiring protection pays the required premium and submits an application (considered part of the credit insurance policy) which provides pertinent information concerning its business and the accounts to be insured. If the application is rejected, the premium is returned; if it is approved, the policy is completed. The original application becomes part of the policy which provides insurance against prescribed credit losses and includes supporting conditions such as, among other things, how to determine and settle claims. While individual policies may vary considerably, they contain the same basic features.

(a) Amount of Coverage

Most sales are made to customers with a mercantile agency rating which determines the amount of applicable coverage. While Dun & Bradstreet is ordinarily selected, other agencies are used as well. Tables are prepared for each of the major agencies showing maximum coverage limits for each credit category. The policy holder may evaluate the status of his own customers and buy the coverage required in each classification. As a protection to the insurance company, each policy provides for a maximum overall coverage, known as the policy amount.

Some debtors would not have any coverage under the Table of Ratings and Coverage because their rating either is too low or there is an absence of a rating. In these cases, the prospective policy holder submits the name of the debtor to the insurance company for a consideration of a credit limit and, if approved, the insurance company names the debtor specifically for coverage under the policy, indicating the credit limit approved for that debtor.

(b) Premiums

Premiums are determined primarily by the following factors:

- coverage for each rating;
- coverage for each debtor not covered adequately by rating;
- sales volume of the insured;
- maximum overall coverage; and
- special conditions incorporated into the policy.

On average, the cost varies between one tenth of one percent and one third of one percent of sales volume.

(c) Coinsurance

Coinsurance in credit insurance is not used in the same way as it is in fire insurance. In fire contracts, coinsurance provides for the insured to bear a portion of certain losses when the amount of insurance coverage is below a designed percentage of the value of the property insured. In credit insurance, the term refers to a specified percentage that is deducted from the net covered loss, regardless of the amount of insurance carried. The purpose is twofold: first, to require that the policy holder participate to the extent of the coinsurance in every risk, thereby encouraging the holder to screen risks more carefully, and second, to some extent, to approximate more closely the replacement basis of the merchandise. The coinsurance percentage ranges between 10 and 20 percent of the net loss, dependent upon the risk involved. Policies are also available without coinsurance and endorsements can be added to policies to eliminate coinsurance on accounts with preferred ratings. At present, complete coverage may be had on all accounts, and the insured can choose between having no coinsurance or accepting the deduction of coinsurance for a lower premium. Most credit insurance is now written without coinsurance.

(d) Primary Loss

Credit insurance is intended to protect against extraordinary losses arising from customers' defaults. The policy, therefore, provides for a deduction from the net covered loss of an agreed amount referred to as the primary loss. This amount is expressed as a fixed percentage of sales, subject to a minimum stipulated amount. The primary loss applicable to any given policy is determined in two ways:

- it may be found in tables which indicate the rates based on the company's line of business, annual sales volume, and the extent of coverage written into the policy; or
- it may be established by means of the company's individual loss experience, ordinarily over the immediately preceeding three years.

(e) Collection and Settlement

In general, a policy holder must file a claim within 10 days after learning of a debtor's insolvency. The account is then turned over to the insurer for collection. The policy lists the events that are considered causes of insolvency, such as the death, insanity, or bankruptcy of the debtor. The filing of past due accounts is voluntary, dependent upon the terms of the policy, but it must be done within a specific time. The insurance company provides a collection service and usually charges fees based on a schedule of rates stated in the policy.

(f) Types of Policies

The companies issue various forms of policies, which may be broadly classified as:

- back coverage type — covering losses occurring within the term of the policy; and
- forward coverage type — covering losses on sales, shipments, and deliveries of merchandise made within the shipment period of the policy.

Variations and endorsements can adapt the terms of the contract to individual cases, tailoring the protection to the client's needs. A firm may cover all its accounts or certain groups of debtors. Coverage may be purchased on a pay as you go basis, applicable only to amounts reported monthly; the primary loss may be adjusted, with corresponding changes in the premium paid; special agreements may be made with respect to filing claims or using the insurer's collection services; or other arrangements may be worked out.

9.7 ACCOUNTS RECEIVABLE FINANCING

A firm may be led to use accounts receivable as collateral for various reasons. Rapidly growing concerns which generate receivables more quickly than cash may be forced to use these assets as security for a loan to replenish their cash reserves, to purchase more inventory as a result of increasing sales, or to maintain their credit status. In order to carry out the full production cycle from cash to cash, a firm may have to go through a double financing process, first using inventory as collateral and then receivables after the inventory is sold. When warehouse receipts are used as security, for example, the borrower may not be able to give the bank the cash required to release covered goods that are sold on credit terms; he therefore obtains a new loan by assigning the accounts receivable in order to repay the former loan secured by inventory. Or, in floor planning, the dealer may require a secondary loan collateralized by accounts receivable to pay the bank in cash for floor planned goods sold on a credit basis.

Even though receivables are a step closer to cash than inventory, commercial banks until about the mid-1960's frowned upon accepting them as collateral.[10] This reluctance paved the way for the rise of business finance companies that specialize in this area of financing.

[1] USING BUSINESS FINANCE COMPANIES

We have mentioned business finance companies previously in connection with the issuance of commercial paper. Originally these companies grew rapidly because they developed financing techniques adapted to their borrowers' needs. Spurred by the competition of the commercial banks which have become active participants in the field as well as by the trend towards broadening the scope of financial services offered by individual institutions, the appearance of the modern business finance company has changed considerably.

The modern business finance company now functions as a financial service center. From an early concentration on receivables, its financing activities cover other areas such as equipment, leasing, and the consumer. Additionally, it offers a variety of services such as credit evaluation, collection, accounting, data processing, inventory control, sales analysis, and counseling. Indicative of these changes are the giant mergers that have occurred. In January 1984, as an illustration, Walter E. Heller, an old name in the factoring field, combined with the Fuji Bank Limited, the tenth largest bank in the world. Several months thereafter the Manufacturers Hanover Corporation announced its formal acquisition of the CIT Financial Corporation, another old name in the factoring field. In describing the advantages of the acquisition, Manufacturers Hanover pointed to its ". . . ten highly successful years of activity in the fields of equipment financing, factoring and consumer finance . . . (the) same three areas (that) are CIT's forte. We simply service different sizes and types of customers in different places."[11]

[2] CONVENTIONAL (OLD-LINE) FACTORING

Conventional factoring is the purchase of a firm's accounts receivable without recourse to the firm or notification to its customers. The factor assumes the credit risk and maintains a strong credit department which must approve each shipment of merchandise, or, in the case of stock shipments, may establish lines of credit within which a client may make prompt deliveries. The client's customer is told to pay the factor directly, who keeps receivables ledgers and collects the accounts.

A firm may be reluctant for its customers to know that their receivables have been sold to a factor, possibly because it is apprehensive that the customers would object to dealing with a third party or would gather the impression that the firm is financially deficient. Then, too, the firm may prefer to maintain its own bookkeeping and collection departments, while availing itself of the credit guaranty and funding services of the factor. These objections may be overcome through a method that does not involve informing the customer of the arrangement.

Non-notification factoring, as it is called, is similar to conventional factoring except that the information is not passed on to the firm's customers unless underlying invoices remain unpaid for a long period, usually 90 days. Checks received by the firm are forwarded to the factor in their original form ("in kind") or the firm's invoices may instruct customers to remit to a lock-box, owned and controlled by the factor. The factor endorses the checks in code to minimize the possibility of customers becoming aware of the arrangement. Reflecting the intent of preserving the direct relationship of the firm to its customers, the firm maintains the required records and is expected to perform a reasonable collection effort, as defined in the factoring agreement.

In the conventional factored arrangement, whether on a notification or non-notification basis, the factor is reimbursed in two ways. First, on the receivables bought, the factor earns a service fee or commission, which runs about one percent, varying somewhat below or above this level depending on such things as the volume of business, the terms of sales, the financial status of the customer, and the average size of the invoice. Second, he receives an interest charge for money advanced prior to the average date that the receivables acquired were supposed to be collected, after allowing a specified period of time, say 10 days, for mailing and clearing checks; this charge ordinarily is several percentage points above the prime rate and probably not much different from this rate after allowing for compensating balances.

The average due date is a weighed average of the individual maturity dates of all the invoices. If a firm does not want the cash advances for its receivable prior to the average due date, it incurs no interest charge. On the other hand, if the firm requests advances immediately after a sale is made, its total cost consists of the sum of the fee for the factor's services and the interest charge for the money obtained prior to the average collection date.

The financial manager who is contemplating use of conventional (old-line) factoring must keep the two cost elements (commission and interest) separate. For the fee his firm pays, he receives billing, ledgering, and collection services, as well as a guaranty against credit losses. He must therefore compare the cost of using the factor, measured by the amount of the fee applied to the volume of receivables sold, with the costs of running a credit and collection department, including salaries, office space, equipment, supplies, and postage, plus bad debts incurred. After making this comparison, he should also consider the psychological advantage of shifting the burden of credit decision-making to the factor and the greater freedom he would have for other phases of the firm's activities.

In comparing the interest charge, consideration must be given to the fact that a borrower will not have to renew lines of credit constantly or will not have to pay a commitment fee; moreover, the charge is applicable only to the number of days the money is used. Also, when a firm factors its accounts receivable, it substitutes a factor, who is likely to have a very high credit standing, for a number of different accounts. Should the firm simply draw upon its funds at the average maturity date, it has decided, in effect, to use the factor's credit position rather than its own. In this case, the firm's credit standing is likely to be enhanced. On the other hand, a bank would investigate closely the circumstances that lead a firm to constantly draw cash in advance of its accounts' maturity date and also to seek a bank loan.

There are only a handful of established institutions functioning as old-line factors, and they are concentrated largely in New York City, where this form of activity originated. Factoring has played a particularly important part in financing the textile industry, and it has also found acceptance in other fields characterized by a large number of small or medium sized manufacturers. Examples of this are the shoe, furniture, equipment, and appliance trades as well as certain hard goods lines.

[3] COMMERCIAL FINANCING

Rather than a sale, as in conventional (old-line) factoring, commercial finance represents a loan, where the client's accounts receivable are pledged or assigned to the lender as security for short-term borrowing. Since the basic transaction is a loan, it is made with recourse to the client, and it is not necessary to obtain prior approval of the customer's credit which created the receivable. The customer pays the invoice amount directly to the client, who then forwards the payment to the lender for processing. Reflecting the lending character of this arrangement, the client undertakes the necessary credit, collection and bookkeeping activities. Finance companies will also grant loans on inventory and through chattel mortgages on income producing marketable machinery and equipment on which there is no existing mortgage.

The costs of a regular bank loan are likely to be less than those of nonnotification financing which may involve a marginal borrower. In view of the relatively high costs of commercial financing, the financial manager of a large, well established firm which can meet all its financing requirements through bank lines, is not likely to seek this type of arrangement. On the other hand, the financial manager of a firm less well situated, may find that this method is the most effective available to him, since it permits him to obtain the required funds without informing his own customers of the nature of the financing arrangements. Accordingly, the method is likely to be employed by companies which are relatively new, undercapitalized, seeking additional lines, expanding rapidly, or desiring a continuing supply of funds for current operations, and which cannot qualify for traditional bank loans.

If the financial manager has decided upon nonnotification receivables financing, a basic question is whether to make these arrangements through a commercial bank or a commercial finance company. If conditions are appropriate, most large banks in big cities will grant a nonnotification loan, in part because they hope that the customer will eventually be able to become an unsecured borrower. There has also been growing interest in participation loans between a bank and a business finance company. Indeed, financing on the basis of accounts receivable, inventory or plant and equipment, by business finance companies in conjunction with banks may produce a lower net cost than would have been the case otherwise. The big business finance companies have offices that blanket the country, and are staffed with experts in finance, sales, and management who can assist clients in working out individual problems and who stand ready to take advantage of new opportunities. In recent years, for instance, as firms became merger minded and began looking for businesses to acquire as subsidiaries, the finance companies helped plan methods of financing buyouts, mergers, and consolidations, and assisted clients in determining the most advisable kind of expansion to pursue.

[4] SALES FINANCING

In sales financing, the finance company works with dealers and functions primarily by purchasing the credit instruments of the dealers or their customers. The dealer usually takes the initiative, and the selling and lending operations are closely tied together. These transactions occur on both the wholesale and the retail level.

A consumer durable goods dealer must keep his floor stocked with enough inventory to carry on his business. These goods, such as automobiles or appliances, are expensive, and the dealer ordinarily does not have the funds on hand to pay for them. He may therefore arrange for a finance company to meet the manufacturer's charges as each shipment is made and to be reimbursed as the dealer clears his stocks.

In order to dispose of consumer durable goods, the dealer must often enter into an installment contract with the buyer. If the dealer needs the funds from the contract prior to maturity, he may discount it with a finance company. In this case, the finance company may assume all the risk, or it may provide for assigning all uncollected contracts back to the dealer. This leaves him with the responsibility of collecting the balances due or of repossessing the property. This arrangement is often used in the purchase of appliance paper. In the automobile field, in the case of default on an installment contract, the more common practice is for the finance company to bear the cost of repossessing the car and to sell it to the dealer, who is obligated to take it back for the amount of the net unpaid balance if the return is accomplished within a designated period.

Large manufacturing or retail firms often have their own sales financing subsidiaries. Typically, the firms sell their receivables to these subsidiaries but do not include their operations in the firms' own consolidated statements. Accordingly, there may be a tendency for the firms to overlook the bad debt loss experience of these receivables.

Some finance servicing subsidiaries of large manufacturing corporations have extended their activities to outside financing. General Electric Credit Corporation, for example, with assets of $16 billion, is the largest diversified financial services and leasing company in the United States. The company advertises that it ". . . tailormakes a (financing) package from our vast storehouse of financial options for companies of $10 million and up."

9.8 CHAPTER SUMMARY

In this chapter, we have seen that credit planning contributes to the firm's well being by accelerating the flow of funds into and slowing the flow out of the company. The credit manager's ability to carry out his plans is limited by competitive pressures, custom, and the relative bargaining strength of customers and suppliers.

We have emphasized the managerial aspects of the credit activity, high-lighting important elements, including: (1) credit planning and analysis, (2) management of the risk factors in accounts receivable, (3) use of the computer, (4) and financing by means of accounts receivable.

FOOTNOTES

1. Various analysts, pointing to the distortions created in the DSO by fluctuating sales and changes in the sales averaging period, have suggested modifications in the calculation, such as determining a "weighted DSO" and developing new measures, such as the dollar cost of the number of days invoices overdue. See, Michael D. Carpenter and Jack E. Miller, "A Reliable Framework for Monitoring Accounts Receivable" *Financial Management,* Winter 1979, pp. 37-40; Robert M. Eichorn, "Dollar Days Outstanding, Determining the Age of Your Receivables," *Credit and Financial Management,* January 1983, pp. 13-15; Douglas H. Harknett, "Aging by DSO the Role of Future Datings," *Credit and Financial Management,* October 1982, pp. 24-25; and Robert R. Hunter, "The True Cost of Credit," *Credit and Financial Management,* May 1982, pp. 25-26.
2. Generally speaking, a company faced with a credit rationing situation would use its cost of capital (see Chapter 19) as the discount rate, while a firm with excess funds would use its opportunity cost rate (the rate at which it could invest in an alternative project).
3. Probability parameters are developed further in Chapter 18.
4. In this example we assume that if payment is made it is done so in full. However, probabilities for partial payments can readily be added to the analysis if desired.
5. Monthly payment expectations are easily handled by using a table of monthly discount factors.
6. Note that as there is a 10% chance of payment never being received, the probabilities applied now sum to only 90%.
7. A system of ratio analysis is presented in Chapter 4.
8. For an analysis of the effects of a lenient credit and collection policy on the cost of additional financing required to carry a higher level of accounts receivable and the opportunity cost on funds tied up in accounts receivable, see Tirlochan S. Walia, "Explicit and Implicit Cost of Changes in the Level of Accounts Receivable and the Credit Policy Decision of the Firm," *Financial Management,* Winter 1977, pp. 75-78.
9. The authors are grateful to Mr. J. E. Simms, Senior Vice President of the American Indemnity Company, for his helpful comments on this section.
10. David Rubin, "Bank Factoring Crossroads," *Credit and Financial Management,* Dec. 1981, p. 26.
11. *The Wall Street Journal,* May 1, 1984, p. 117.

SUGGESTED READINGS

Barrett, Keith A., "Set a Useful Accounts Receivable Model," *Credit and Financial Management,* August 1983.

Bruder, C. W., "Credit Seesaw: Striking a Delicate Balance in the '80s," *Credit and Financial Management*, November 1980.

Clark, Jack, "How to Improve Your Credit and Collections Act," *Credit and Financial Management*, March 1982.

Durkee, J. and I. Sharlit, "New Tools for Dealing with Problem Debtors," *Credit and Financial Management*, March 1982.

Engelke, W. J., "Past-Due Accounts: How to Use an Investment Banker," *Credit and Financial Management*, July-August 1981.

Fredman, A. J., "Accelerating Collections: Float Reduction Techniques," *Credit and Financial Management*, March 1981.

Heckman, Christine R., "The Effect of Trade Credit on Price and Price Level Comparisons," *Review of Economics and Statistics*, November 1981.

Hunter, Robert R., "The True Cost of Credit," *Credit and Financial Management*, May 1982.

Kimes, J. D., "Credit Management's Vital Role in Business Today," *Credit and Financial Management*, January 1982.

Landsberg, J., "Managing the Accounts Receivable Portfolio," *Credit and Financial Management*, April 1980.

Miller, Gregory, "The Emerging Art of Credit Management," *Institutional Investor*, November 1982.

Miller, J. E., "Monitoring Accounts Receivable with Varying Credit Terms," *Credit and Financial Management*, October 1982.

Sartoris, W. L. and N. C. Hill, "Framework for Credit Policy Decisions," *Credit and Financial Management*, October 1980.

Savoye, R. A., "Tools for Measuring the Quality of Receivables," *Credit and Financial Management*, April 1981.

Sibley, M. and A. Drews, "Investment Approach to Credit Policy," *Credit and Financial Management*, November 1980.

Snyder, D. S., "How to Handle Past Due Balances on Large Volume Accounts," *Credit and Financial Management*, November 1981.

Snyder, H. M. Jr., "Risks and Profits in Your Receivables," *Credit and Financial Management*, December 1981.

Volk, D. A., "Managing Accounts Receivable — Systematically," *Management Accounting*, July 1980.

Wemple, W. Barent, "Troubleshooting Accounts Receivable," *Financial Executive*, November 1980.

INVENTORY MANAGEMENT

10.1 INTRODUCTION

Inventories generally comprise a significant portion of the firm's total assets and often require sizeable investments. They are a critical link between the production and sales of a product, and as such, they often approach the level of importance attributed to capital assets. The major difference between the two categories of assets is that inventory usually involves a continuous investment process, while capital assets generally entail discrete investments.

This chapter addresses the role of the financial manager in the inventory management and control process. In addition, it focuses on the major classes of inventory and their valuation, as well as the principal types of inventory control systems.

10.2 ROLE OF THE FINANCIAL MANAGER IN INVENTORY MANAGEMENT

Included within the general area of inventory management are a number of individual activities such as: (1) determining the size of the inventory to be carried; (2) establishing timing schedules, procedures, and lot sizes for new orders; (3) ascertaining minimum safety levels; (4) coordinating sales, production and inventory policies; (5) assigning responsibilities for carrying out the inventory control function; and (6) providing the necessary reports for supervising the overall activity.

Historically, inventory management has not been the direct operating responsibility of the financial manager. In recent years, however, the enhanced importance of the financial aspects of inventory management has resulted in the financial manager playing an increasingly more important role in determining the general nature of the controls exercised, the methods for balancing the costs involved, and the pricing policies adopted. In many firms, the financial manager supervises these areas, or he may be a member of an inventory policy committee, which has broad responsibilities. In smaller firms, he is likely to participate even more directly in the management of inventories. Since the financial manager is concerned about efficient allocation of funds, he must be cognizant of the inventory control systems and tools which are utilized in the balancing of inventory benefits, costs, and risks.

10.3 MAJOR CLASSES OF INVENTORY

The types of inventory problems likely to be encountered vary with the form in which the inventory is held. As companies acquire raw materials, process them, and eventually turn them into finished goods, they create different sorts of inventories which are discussed below.

[1] RAW MATERIALS INVENTORY

As the name implies, raw materials inventory encompasses the basic ingredients which enter at the beginning phase of the production process. Important elements that contribute to the determination of the *raw materials* inventory a company carries are the type of business in which it is engaged, the variety of activities undertaken, and the possibility of shortages. The influence of each of these elements is illustrated below.

Kellogg Company and Campbell Soup Company are essentially engaged in a single industry — convenience foods. The nature of this business requires holding substantial inventories of raw materials and supplies that underlie the final products. As a result, for both companies, this category of inventory, at the close of 1980, constituted over half of total inventories.[1]

ACF industries is engaged in transportation, energy, and industrial plastics. This range of activities contribute to its large holdings of raw materials and supplies, which, on December 31, 1980, was 40 percent of total inventories, the biggest single component.[2]

The lines of Olin Corporation are also varied, including chemicals, brass, paper, and firearms. For these activities, the company purchases a great many raw materials. At times, the corporation has experienced interruptions in delivery of certain items when suppliers' operations were disrupted by electric power curtailments, materials shortages, and rail or barge transport problems. The company indicated that the frequency and severity of such interruptions cannot be predicted. It is probable that these conditions have contributed to increasing the amounts of raw materials and supplies that Olin keeps on hand.[3]

In contrast to these companies, where raw materials and supplies are an important segment of total inventories, Hueblein shows relatively small amounts in this segment. On June 30, 1981, raw materials constituted only 11 percent of total inventories. The largest single component that the company reported, reflecting the nature of the business, was in bulk whiskey and wine, which represented 54 percent of the total.[4]

[2] WORK-IN-PROCESS INVENTORY

Inevitably, some inventory is tied up as operations move from raw material to finished goods. Inventory in this in-between stage is broadly described as work-in-process. By and large, the amount carried is a reflection of the company's business and is related to the various schedules for production, delivery, and machine loading. It is also affected by the efficiency of operations, involving such factors as congestion, back-up, reservoir building and losses incurred along the way. Indicative of the range of differences that may occur, at the end of 1981, work-in-process constituted only 5.5 percent of W.R. Grace's inventories, reflecting the relatively short manufacturing cycle of the company's principal business, specialty and agricultural chemicals, as well as its relatively large general merchandising lines.[5] In contrast to this condition, much of the work of Combustion Engineering represents long-term contracts. Costs associated with these contracts are accumulated in work-in-process inventory. As a result, overall in-process costs comprised 66 percent of the company's total 1980 inventories.[6]

[3] FINISHED GOODS INVENTORY

Finished goods represent the product that is finally sold. When this product consists primarily of stock items, the amount carried may be large. On the other hand, if a company manufactures to order, the product is likely to be shipped promptly to the buyer and the amount of finished goods will be small. Between these two extremes, the amounts carried will depend upon such factors as competition, the length of the manufacturing cycle, perishability, storage facilities, and marketing considerations. Company policies may also vary in using inventory stocks to provide a buffer between production and sales.

As a result of these disparate conditions, companies report sharp differences in the proportion of their inventories represented by finished goods. For example, H.H. Robertson primarily is in the business of developing, manufacturing and erecting metal building products for non-residential construction projects. Most of its products are undertaken for specific contracts and shipment is made to the job site as construction progresses. Accordingly, the company keeps a minimum inventory of finished products; at the close of 1981, this segment represented only 14.5 percent of total inventories "at current costs."[7] On the other hand, end items represent the principal inventory of the Hoover Company, which is the undisputed leader in the U.S. vacuum cleaner industry; at the close of 1981, finished products composed 62 percent of the company's total inventories.[8]

10.4   VALUATION OF INVENTORY

An important function of the financial manager in the inventory management area is to establish the underlying policies concerning the valuation of inventories. During any accounting period, a stream of goods is constantly flowing into a firm through purchase or manufacture, while another stream is moving out as a result of sales. Since the two streams rarely match in size, a residue or residual in the form of inventories remain. The problem is what price to assign to the goods sold and to those still on hand.

In determining the valuation method to use, consideration is given to the size and turnover of inventories, the price outlook, tax laws, and prevailing practice in the field. The method selected could importantly affect ending inventory valuation and earnings.[9] Highlighted below are the most important inventory valuation methods.[10]

[1] SPECIFIC IDENTIFICATION

Where the physical units may be identified and suitable data are available, the cost of goods sold may be charged with the actual cost of these units and the remaining inventory priced at the actual cost of the units retained. While in certain industries, such as shipbuilding and real estate development, this may be possible, for most mass produced products, determining the cost of goods sold by specific identification is not feasible and some kind of inventory costing assumptions must be made.

[2] INVENTORY COSTING ASSUMPTIONS

In situations where it is difficult to identify individual units or lots, where joint costs must be allocated among many units, and where inventory items represent tangible goods that are indistinguishable from one another, it is common practice to price each unit on the basis of one of three major inventory costing assumptions: (a) first-in, first-out (FIFO); (b) last-in, first-out (LIFO); and (c) average cost.

(a) First-In, First-Out (FIFO)

Pricing the units sold on a FIFO basis results in ending inventory valuations that are based on the most recent purchase prices. Goods usually tend to move in this manner because companies will logically try to dispose of their oldest inventory to guard against obsolescence. Declining prices in a period of high tax rates enhance the attractiveness of the FIFO method because profits are curtailed when the cost of goods sold is charged with the earlier, higher prices.

(b) Last-In, First-Out (LIFO)

Pricing the units sold on the LIFO basis results in freezing inventories at original cost. A combination of rising prices and high tax rates favors the LIFO method because of its moderating effect on reported profits.[11]

(c) Average Cost

Instead of assuming a price for each unit of goods sold based upon the physical flow of inventory, values may be calculated on some average basis, such as a weighted or moving average.

[3] MARKET VERSUS COST VALUATION METHOD

Accounting proprieties call for departing from the cost basis of valuing inventories when their market values fall below this level. This writing down of inventories reduces current earnings, but the lowered opening inventories that follow add correspondingly to the income of the next period. The cost or market, whichever is lower principle, has the sanctity of tradition, although some accountants question its validity because of its exaggerated influence on profits during periods of price changes and the special importance it gives to balance sheets.

[4] OTHER VALUATION METHODS

A number of other methods have been used to determine the valuation of ending inventory and the cost of goods sold. These are either less popular or have a more specialized application than FIFO, LIFO, or average cost methods.

Retail stores are permitted to deduct an average percentage markup from the selling price of final inventories to value them. Other firms apply inventory valuation reserves to reduce inventory accounts to levels that reflect the possibility of future price declines. These reserves are based on assumptions regarding the extent and severity of potential shrinkages. Accordingly, reserves are ordinarily created by charges to retained earnings rather than to current income.

Finally, in the base stock method, a company establishes a minimum quantity that it considers essential for operations, and prices it at not more than the lowest cost experience. Then, as in the LIFO method, units sold are priced at the most recent acquisition costs; the base stock method may differ from LIFO in the way the values of ending inventories are determined.

10.5   CONTROL OF INVENTORY

The first step in the management of inventory is recognizing the different types of problems associated with each major class of inventory. The second step entails the assessment of inventory usage and the development of specific controls appropriate for particular inventory classes and usage levels. In this section, we discuss the issue of relating controls to usage and highlight several of the more popular control measures. In addition, we discuss in detail, the concept of comprehensive inventory management—a concept predicated on the idea of balancing all relevant inventory costs, returns and risks.

[1] RELATING CONTROLS TO USAGE

In many firms, thousands upon thousands of different items comprise the stocks of inventories that are held, and these items may receive widely varying usage. Clearly, it would not be sensible to devote the same degree of care and effort to controlling rarely used items as opposed to those that are constantly entering into the manufacturing operation. General Electric, for example, is purported to have been one of the first major companies to observe this condition and to apply it in developing an inventory control scheme. This system has been described as the ABC classification of inventories. Category A embraces the top smallest percentage of items that account for the biggest percentage of sales balance, category B includes the next most active group, and C represents the largest number of items with the least usage.[12]

In another case, a series of tests made at a plant of Reynolds Industries revealed that in one area, out of 876 inventory bins containing relatively low cost items, 246 had 2,441 units with a total value of $254.50, and in another instance 82 bins were found that contained 1,076 units with a total value of $168.70. Based upon this analysis, the policy was adopted of expensing items upon receipt where the unit cost was 50 cents or less or if it had a total value carried in inventory of $5 or less.

As a rule, by concentrating on several hundred instead of many thousands of items, companies have been able to introduce more effective control measures and bring about better overall supervision. Studies of inventory usage, therefore, provide the base upon which simplified and effective inventory management systems can be constructed.

[2] TYPES OF CONTROLS EMPLOYED

The ultimate goal of an inventory control program is to provide maximum customer service at a minimum cost. For this purpose, certain typical inventory procedures have evolved over time and are in use today. Some of these are as follows:

(a) Min-Max System

The min-max system establishes a minimum safety level to avoid inventory stockouts in excess of company policy and a maximum inventory level that is greater than normal demand. An order of sufficient size to bring the inventory to the maximum point is placed when the minimum level is reached.

(b) Two Bin System

As the name implies, the two bin system divides each item of inventory into two groups or bins. In the first, a sufficient supply is kept to meet current demand over a designated period of time. In the second, enough additional items are available to meet the demand during the lead time necessary to fill the order.

(c) Order Cycling System

Some companies employ an order cycling system in which the inventory condition is reviewed periodically through physical counts or estimates. The critical items in Group A have relatively short review cycles. On the other hand, the lower cost non-critical items in category C are given longer review cycles since stockouts would be less costly and order quantities larger. At each review date, the required amount is ordered to bring the inventory to the predetermined supply level.

(d) Materials Requirements Planning (MRP)

A method of inventory control that has gained increasing attention is materials requirements planning (MRP), which is described as a "... tool for planning and controlling a great number of products and parts that may interact with one another." An important aspect of this approach is that it takes into account both the quantity of items and the timing of their requirements. In essence, the system starts with a master schedule that determines when delivery of a particular end item is required. From the bill of materials, the parts applicable to the end item are ascertained. A check of the inventory status file reveals if these parts are in inventory or on order. Based on procurement lead and assembly planning schedules, the necessary information is then available to develop appropriate ordering points.[13]

[3] COMPREHENSIVE INVENTORY MANAGEMENT

A comprehensive inventory management system is predicated on the idea of balancing all the relevant costs, returns and risks. In terms of returns or benefits, large inventory levels allow economies of scale in production and procurement; they also enable the firm to fill orders quickly. In addition, larger levels minimize the risk of stockouts and the incurrence of substantial costs associated with production line shutdowns or slowdowns. On the other hand, large inventory levels incur opportunity costs as funds are tied up in current assets as opposed to more lucrative fixed assets. Also, larger inventory levels bring with them increased storage, handling and insurance costs.

Through the application of operations research techniques, the financial manager is currently able to assess the effects of alternative inventory management and control techniques or systems on overall and component inventory costs.

The successful application of operations research techniques, however, depends upon the availability of suitable information for cost comparisons. Costs, such as taxes on inventory or insurance, are explicit and readily obtainable from accounting records. Other costs, such as the cost of capital invested in inventory, are implicit and usually require management estimates of minimum benchmarks.

Once the cost breakdown is available, the solution to the different kinds of inventory problems lies in balancing the relative costs incurred under the alternative possibilities. For example, typical operating procedures which will cut inventory carrying costs but which will increase related costs are as follows:

Operating Procedure	Cost Increased
• Placing orders for inventories	• Ordering costs
• Changing production lines	• Changeover costs
• Taking on overtime labor	• Labor costs
• Adjusting production	• Production costs

These relationships are shown graphically in Figure 10.1 below.

As a company buys inventories in smaller lot sizes, it increases the number of times that it must place orders, but cuts down the costs of carrying inventories. As a company changes its production lines for different products more frequently, it increases the costs of changeover but lowers the costs of carrying inventories. In addition, as a company increases the overtime it pays to obtain more production during peak seasons, it increases its costs of output but reduces the costs of carrying inventories over longer periods of time. Finally, as a company makes more production adjustments to match inventories and needs, it increases its production costs but reduces the costs of carrying inventories. The optimum level of activity represents that point where declining inventory carrying costs meet the rising operating costs, or the flat bottom of the total variable cost curve.

The next two sections illustrate mathematically the determination of the optimal order quantity and the optimum reorder point.

276

FIGURE 10.1 *Relationship between typical operating procedures and inventory carrying costs*

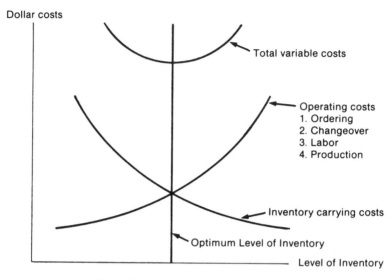

Dollar costs

Total variable costs

Operating costs
1. Ordering
2. Changeover
3. Labor
4. Production

Inventory carrying costs

Optimum Level of Inventory

Level of Inventory

Operation
1. Placing orders for inventories
2. Changing production lines
3. Taking on labor
4. Adjusting production

(a) Determining the Economic Order Quantity (EOQ)

Among the most basic inventory control problems are the determination of the optimal inventory level or, economic order quantity (EOQ) and the establishment of the optimum reorder point (ROP). Of these two, the EOQ appears to be the more frequently utilized tool in industry.

The basic decision in an EOQ procedure is to determine the amount of inventory to be ordered at a particular time so that the total of ordering and carrying costs is reduced to a minimum. The following formula has been developed for this purpose:[14]

$$EOQ = \sqrt{\frac{2AS}{iC}} \, ,$$

where:
A = the estimated annual usage of the inventory items in physical units;
S = the cost of handling an inventory order expressed in dollars per order;
 i = the cost of carrying the inventory expressed as a percent of the cost of goods on hand; and
C = the cost price per unit of inventory.

Thus, if the annual usage of item A is 20 units, the ordering cost per unit, S, is $49, the percentage carrying costs of the goods on hand, i, is 10 percent, and the cost of each unit, C, is $100, then the EOQ would be determined as follows:

$$EOQ = \sqrt{\frac{2(20)(49)}{.1\,(100)}} = \sqrt{\frac{1960}{10}} = \sqrt{196} = 14 \text{ units.}$$

A company may find that several factors in the equation are the same for all the items of inventory that it carries, a condition that simplifies determining the EOQ. If, for example, both carrying charges and ordering costs are the same for all inventory items, only two variables would have to be considered — annual usage and cost per unit — and the equation could then be expressed as follows:

$$EOQ = K\sqrt{\frac{A}{C}}$$

where $K = \sqrt{\dfrac{2S}{i}}$

To illustrate this case, suppose that an ordering cost of $10 per unit and a 10 percent carrying cost on goods on hand are the same for all the items of a firm's inventory. The EOQ for each item may be determined simply by taking the square root of the annual usage divided by the cost per unit and multiplying the result by 14.1 ($K = \sqrt{2S/i} = \sqrt{2(10)/.10} = \sqrt{200} = 14.1$) as shown below.

$$EOQ = K\sqrt{\frac{A}{C}} = 14.1\sqrt{\frac{A}{C}}.$$

Some companies have prepared EOQ tables or nomographs which show the EOQ under different assumptions. For example, if the ordering and carrying costs are the same for all inventory items, as described above, the table might show the EOQ corresponding to different annual usages and costs per item purchased. Such simplifying procedures are particularly useful where the inventory consists of a great number of stockkeeping items, say 10,000 or more, and where the inventory clerks are unskilled.

(b) Determining the Reorder Point (ROP)

In addition to knowing the EOQ, the inventory manager must know when to place an order; he must strike a balance between carrying costs and stockout costs. Obviously, the more inventory the firm keeps, the less likely it is to run out of stock but the greater are the carrying costs; on the other hand, the less inventory carried, the lower the carrying costs but the greater the likelihood that deficiencies will occur. While stockout costs are often hard to measure, they are real, and include such things as the cost of preparing and following up backorders, the profit on an order that is lost, and the potential of future sales because of a customer's dissatisfaction.

If one could tell exactly what the demand for a product would be during a designated future period, it would be possible to ascertain with relative ease the optimum inventory level at which to place an order. For example, assume a retailer knew that he would sell exactly 50 units of stock each week, that two weeks were required to replenish inventory, and that his EOQ was 200 units.

If he did not want to run out of stock, he would place an order each four weeks (to allow for sales) when his inventory dropped to 100 units (to allow for the replenishment period). Figure 10.2 illustrates the resulting pattern of the retailer's inventory.

FIGURE 10.2 *Economic order quantity for retailer*

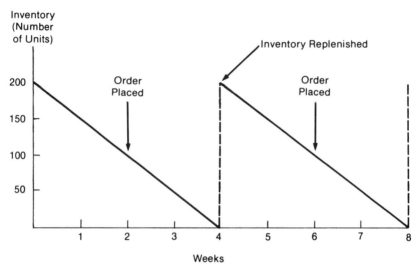

In most cases, future product demand cannot be forecasted exactly. Therefore, many companies develop forecast ranges or probability distributions of future sales based on experience, market research, or educated guesses. As an illustration, suppose that a firm analyses sales orders received during the previous 100 inventory reorder periods, and finds that they follow the pattern shown in the first two columns of Figure 10.3.

The company believes that this pattern is normal and will continue indefinitely into the future. The firm thus decides to use this pattern as the basis for gauging the probability or likelihood of receiving future orders. According to our table, no units will be ordered in three out of 100 reorder periods; one unit in four periods; two units in five periods; and so forth. When each of these frequencies is expressed as a percentage of the total number of reorder periods, 100, it is converted into a probability factor, as shown in the third column of the table. These probabilities, in turn, are expressed in cumulative form in the last column. Thus, the probability of receiving orders of less than four units in a reorder period is .22 (representing the sum of the probabilities of having no units ordered, one unit ordered, two units ordered, and three units ordered).

One technique of ascertaining reorder points is to compute the ratio of stockout costs to the total of stockout plus carrying costs and determine which cumulative probability in Figure 10.3 falls just below this critical ratio. The number of units at the cumulative probability represents the ROP, which means that the company should continue to augment its safety stock as long as the probability of not using the last unit is below this critical ratio. Thus, if

FIGURE 10.3 *Probability distribution of units ordered during the previous 100 reorder periods*

Units Ordered	Number of Reorder Periods	Probability	Cumulative Probability (Less Than)
0	3	.03	.00
1	4	.04	.03
2	5	.05	.07
3	10	.10	.12
4	11	.11	.22
5	12	.12	.33
6	14	.14	.45
7	8	.08	.59
8	7	.07	.67
9	6	.06	.74
10	6	.06	.80
11	5	.05	.86
12	4	.04	.91
13	4	.04	.95
14	1	.01	.99
	100	1.00	

the stockout costs relative to the period between restockings is $100 per unit and the carrying cost per inventory cycle is $23 per unit, the ratio of stockout to total costs, $100/$23 + $100, is .81. According to Figure 10.3, the probability of receiving new orders of 9 units or less during the period between restockings is .80; the ROP, therefore, is 10 units. The tenth unit is the highest one for which the probability of not receiving an order, .80, is less than 0.81.

In practice, firms rarely carry enough safety stock to eliminate stockouts completely, but rather attempt to reduce stocks to a desired degree. In such a system, reordering would be based upon an accepted standard of stockout frequency. For example, the ROP might occur at the level which would produce no more than one stockout per inventory item in two years. Through these methods, inventory managers have been able to help management evaluate the reasonableness of existing or proposed inventory policies. As in the case of the EOQ, tables have been developed to permit stock clerks to select the optimum ROP under designated assumptions.

In a complete inventory control program, provision would be made to determine both the optimum EOQ and the optimum ROP. Thus, the consideration might be to order 14 units of inventory (EOQ) whenever the inventory level falls to or below 10 units (ROP). With an expected usage of six units during the reorder period, a safety stock of four units would be carried. On the basis of the amount ordered, the physical quantity of inventory during each cycle period would be seven units ($Q/2 = 14/2$); but, with the addition of the safety stock of four units, the average inventory on hand, would amount to 11 units.

(c) Conducting the Follow Up

A comprehensive inventory management system should also include a follow up program to evaluate its effectiveness and should contain specific procedures to avoid excess and obsolete inventories. For the purpose of follow up, general tests such as the widely used inventory turnover ratio may be inadequate. This particular ratio obscures differences between individual inventory items and could be distorted by accounting changes such as writing down inventories or changing the costing methods. The effectiveness of inventory practices may be more accurately gauged by directly measuring the costs that the inventory management system is designed to minimize.

The avoidance of excess and obsolete inventories is also an important objective of inventory management. For this purpose, many companies have established an "obsolescence committee" consisting of representatives from sales, engineering, manufacturing and the controller's department. Important decisions are likely to be subject to review by the chief operating officer.

A typical system for controlling excess and obsolete inventories starts with the development of a suspect inventory list, which includes those inventory quantities in excess of expected usage over the next 12 months. Special attention is given by the engineering department to high cost items that represent a designated percentage of the suspect list. These items are checked to ascertain if conversion to or substitution for an active part is feasible.

The marketing department then reviews the list to eliminate new items and those with expected sales increases. What remains are primarily those items which may no longer be salable because of demand changes or contract expirations. For this category, reserve requirements are established by the finance department. Finally, the obsolescence committee evaluates the suspect list to determine whether specified items should be retained, disassembled, or scrapped.

Despite the scientific advances in the field of inventory management, rule of thumb and intuition are still commonly relied upon to reach inventory decisions. For many firms, these decisions are still very likely to be made at the clerical level. Nevertheless, the trend is toward increased utilization of the refined concepts. Companies already employing them are extending their use to new decisions, while other companies are beginning to experiment with these tools.

10.6   CHAPTER SUMMARY

In this chapter, we discussed the increasingly important role in inventory management that the financial manager is called upon to play in many corporations. The effective allocation of funds to inventory has become a major responsibility of financial management. As a result of this trend, the financial manager has found it necessary to be increasingly cognizant of the alternative control systems and tools which are utilized to balance major inventory costs, risks and returns.

FOOTNOTES

1. Kellogg Company, *1980 Annual Report,* p. 24; Campbell Soup Company, *1980 Annual Report,* p. 21.
2. ACF Industries, Incorporated, *1980 Annual Report,* p. 14.

3. Olin Corporation, *1981 Annual Report*, p. 29, *1975 Annual Report*, p. 28. The Company indicated that "Because inventory costs are determined principally by the use of the dollar value LIFO method, it is not practicable to separate the inventory into its components (raw materials, work-in-process and finished goods)."

4. Heublein, Inc., *1981 Annual Report*, p. 30.

5. W.R. Grace & Co., *1981 Annual Report*, pp. 52 and 54.

6. Combustion Engineering, Inc., *1980 Annual Report*, pp. 10, 14, and 15.

7. H.H. Robertson Company, *1980 Annual Report*, p. 4 and *1981 Annual Report*, p. 14.

8. The Hoover Company, *1981 Annual Report*, p. 16.

9. For example, the current replacement cost of FMC's inventories at the close of 1981 exceeded the value of inventories carried at the lower of cost or market by approximately $366 million; this figure was 76 percent of total inventories. FMC Corporation, *1981 Annual Report*, p. 36. Standard Pressed Steel liquidated certain LIFO inventories carried at lower costs prevailing in prior years. When compared with the higher current year costs, this differential provided net income benefits of approximately 51 cents per share; in the same year, the company reported a net loss of 62 cents per share. Standard Pressed Steel Co., *1977 Annual Report*, pp. 17 and 22 (on April 21, 1978, the Company changed its name to SPS Technologies, Inc.).

10. Regardless of the valuation method employed, the Financial Accounting Standards Board, as discussed in Chapter 3, requires that companies meeting specified size tests, include in their annual reports supplementary information on the basis of "current cost" accounting. Among the items to be shown on the new inflation adjusted basis are inventory and cost of goods sold.

11. Inventory enters directly into the cost of goods sold and therefore into reported profits. The substantial changeover from FIFO to the LIFO method of accounting for inventories that occurred in the 1970s because of rising prices, adversely affected the reported earnings of many companies but improved cash flows as taxes were reduced.

12. The importance of making this segregation was dramatically illustrated by an official of Honeywell in an address at the Conference of the National Association of Accountants some years ago. In his hand he had a list from one of the company's factories showing the parts with top dollar usage, amounting to $1 million. On the aisle of the conference hall he had rolled out the bottom part of the list showing the parts having the lower $1 million of usage. The list in his hand was 6 feet long; the one on the floor extended the grand length of 165 feet.

   Attempting to provide the same controls for the parts in both lists would inevitably have led either to inadequate overall supervision or to mountains of unnecessary paper. In general, therefore, tight controls with frequent ordering governed the 2 to 4 percent of the items with half the dollar usage; loose controls with infrequent ordering was the policy for the items at the bottom of the list; and an intermediate system was applied to those in the middle.

13. See Jeffrey G. Miller and Linda G. Sprague, "Behind the Growth in Materials Requirement Planning," *Harvard Business Review,* September-October, 1975, pp. 83-91. For a more detailed development of Materials Requirements Planning, see Appendix A to this chapter.

14. This formula may be derived as follows. The average amount of goods on hand (assuming a relatively constant usage rate) equals half the quantity ordered on each purchase order, Q, or $Q/2$; the cost of this investment in inventory is $(Q/2)C$; the carrying cost is $(Q/2)iC$. The number of orders placed each year is the annual usage, A, divided by the quantity ordered on each purchase order, Q, or A/Q; and the ordering cost is $(A/Q)/S$. Total costs equal carrying costs plus ordering costs,

or $(Q/2)$ iC + (A/Q) S. By taking the first derivative of total costs with respect to quantity and equating the result to zero, the minimum value is obtained. This equation $(iC)/2 - [A/(Q^2)]S = 0$, is solved for Q to obtain the formula expressed as an "economic order quantity."

SUGGESTED READINGS

Burton, Terence T., "Get Back to Basics with MRP," *Management Focus*, Peat, Marwich, Mitchell & Co., September/October 1978.

Cascino, A.E., "How to Make More Productive Use of Working Capital," *Management Review*, May 1979.

Doggett, R.E., "Managing Working Capital," *Management Accounting*, December 1980.

Dudick, Thomas, *Inventory Control for the Financial Executive*, NY, Wiley, 1979.

Fancher, D.O. and Beasley, D.B., "Inventory Control-Cost Cutting Through the EOQ," *Hospital Financial Management*, November 1981.

Fuchs, Jerome H., *Computerized Inventory Control Systems*, Engelwood Cliffs, NJ, Prentice Hall, 1978.

Fuerst, William, "Small Businesses Get a New Look at ABC Analysis for Inventory Control," *Journal of Small Business Management*, July 1981.

Jaggi, Bikki, and Richard Kolodny, "Selection of the LIFO Method of Inventory Valuation: Management's Motives and Investor's Reaction," *Financial Review*, Spring 1977.

Phillips, T.E., and K.R. White, "Minimizing Inventory Costs," *Interfaces*, August 1981.

Shaughnessy, T.E., "Aggregate Inventory Management: Measurement and Control," *Journal of Purchasing and Materials Management*, Fall 1980.

Silver, A., "Inventory and Taxes, or LIFO; Summing Up," *Industrial Distribution*, January 1979.

Smith, Keith V., *Guide to Working Capital Management*, NY, McGraw Hill, 1979.

"Working Capital of Nonfinancial Corporations," *Federal Reserve Bulletin*, July 1978.

Yardini, Edward E., "A Portfolio-Balance Model of Corporate Working Capital," *The Journal of Finance*, May 1978.

APPENDIX A: USING A MATERIALS REQUIREMENT PLANNING (MRP) SYSTEM

Twin Disc Inc., a Wisconsin-based manufacturer of power-transmission gear used in a large variety of products made by other companies was an early inaugurator of MRP. In 1979, one of its senior officials served as president of the Washington, D.C. based, American Production and Inventory Control Society, a professional organization involved in development of the monitoring techniques of MRP. Through a computer terminal in his office, this official is in close touch with the status of the company's inventories. "Now up to 11 o'clock last night we know exactly where we stood. Before, we were three weeks behind" (Before means before 1965 when the company began using its computerized inventory systems which has been substantially extended since that time.)[1]

[1] ELEMENTS OF THE SYSTEM[2]

An MRP system is based on three major building blocks integrated into a computer controlled planning program. These are:

FIGURE 10.4 Master production schedule development

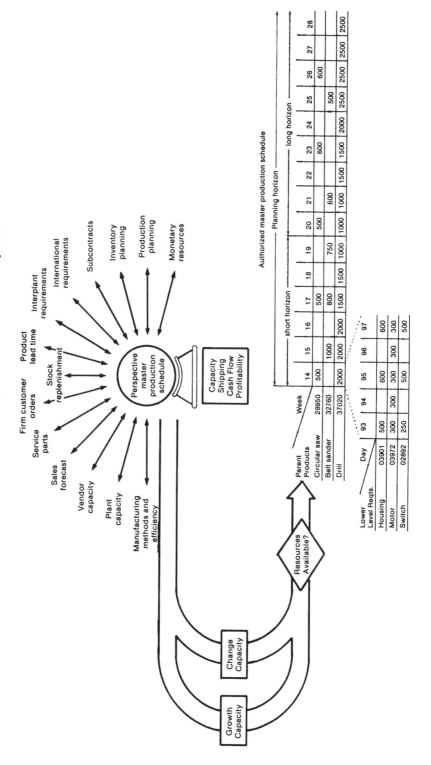

- the Master Production Schedule;
- Bills of Material; and
- the Human Element.

(a) The Master Production Schedule

As one analyst has observed, "an MRP system is a slave to the master production schedule," and it is "probably the weakest link in most MRP systems."[3] The schedule sets forth the requirements for end-items by date and quantity. It is neither a forecast nor a statement of objectives, but rather a realistic assessment of what can and will be produced. It is a planning document that over the near-term establishes the basis for material ordering priorities and over the long-term for the allocation of the company's resources.

Preparation of the master production schedule involves a constant interplay among the factors of existing capacity, operating routines, vendor/subcontracting arrangements, financial condition, and company goals. These factors, illustrated in Figure 10.4 lead to schedule revisions and/or capacity changes that culminate in the implementing master schedule, itself subject to change, until production is completed.

At Twin Discs, control starts with five-year sales projections made by a staff of economists and market researchers. "We've come up with our own leading indicators that apply to the markets we serve," observed the official in charge of this area, "and we've built them into a composite. It gives us 15 to 18 months advance warning.[4] The forecast is submitted to the production department, which determines either that the schedule can be met within existing capacity or that it cannot be met; in the latter case a policy decision must be made regarding a change in the schedule or in capacity. In either event, through computer facilities that use stored, up-to-the-minute information on inventories, orders, and output, a detailed master plan is formulated. This plan shows, for example, for each machine on the production line, a schedule of the material it will handle for each item manufactured.

(b) Bills of Material

Conversion from a production schedule to end-use requirements is done by means of the bill of material. Because this document originates in engineering, it often requires considerable redesign to define the end product's technical specifications, in order to accommodate its adaptation to the planning needs of an MRP system.

While still relied upon by engineering to evaluate design changes, the bill of material in an MRP system also serves as the means of determining inventory replenishment schedules. As such, it enters into the preview of different organizational sectors: production to translate the master production schedule to lower level requirements; manufacturing to identify and issue material to the shop; and finance to determine product costs and evaluate cost relationships.

An important step in the creation of an MRP system, therefore, is to make certain that the bill of material both serves its MRP purpose and conforms to the automated MRP environment. Thus, the bill must identify all end-products, assemblies, sub-assemblies, and component inventory items with a part number, the quantity required per unit produced, and the unit of measure. These requirements must be related to both all structural levels of assemblies and finished goods and defined to reflect the timing sequences of the manufacturing operation. Eventually all the information must be adapted to computer processing and evaluation.

(c) The Human Element

Commentators on MRP assert a refrain that runs "the system is only as good as those who use it."

The people involved in MRP, however, extend throughout the entire organization including production, engineering, marketing, purchasing and finance. Moreover, all hierarchial levels participate from top management to operating clerks. A broad-gauged educational program, therefore, must be fashioned to meet the differing needs of personnel who both contribute to and use the system in different ways.

MRP is a dynamic system that must be adapted to new technological developments. These developments, in turn, may demand changing personnel functions, and roles. Accordingly, the educational program must be continuously fashioned to convey a sense of new responsibilities as well as to assure technical competence.

[2] THE SYSTEM IN PROCESS

MRP may be conceived as a system that integrates its different elements with an overall planning program. As such, it permeates all the major operations of a company.

The basic inputs cover a wide range of information regarding the status of inventory items and product structure. These enter into the processing module to determine gross timing requirements, net out available inventory stocks, establish ordering schedules, explode these schedules to lower level requirements, and align these requirements, through appropriate lead times, with final production. Introduced into these processing arrangements are a series of MRP outputs that facilitate effective control.

The final test of MRP is the system's success in gauging the material and capacity needs of the company. This success should be reflected in improved cash flow; enhanced manufacturing efficiency; and lowered inventory obsolescence, carrying costs and stockouts.

[1] *The Wall Street Journal,* March 7, 1979, pp. 1, 16.
[2] The charts in this appendix and much of the material are from: Terence T. Burton, "Get Back to Basics with MRP," *Management Focus,* Peat, Marwick, Mitchell & Co., September/October 1978, pp. 29-34.
[3] *Ibid,* p. 34.
[4] *The Wall Street Journal, op. cit.,* p. 16.

11

SHORT-TERM SOURCES
OF FUNDS

11.1 INTRODUCTION

Credit is a commonplace notion, but it is used in different ways: the accountant makes a credit entry; the banker appraises a prospective borrower's credit standing; and the merchant is said to give credit to a customer. In its own context, each of these meanings is supported by custom and permits the communication of specific ideas. In this chapter, we review the various sources of short-term credit available to the firm or short-term sources of funds.

11.2 THE CONCEPT OF CREDIT

For our purposes, we find it convenient to regard potential credit as akin to an asset, even though it does not appear as such on the balance sheet. Alternatively, actual credit utilized does appear as a liability on the balance sheet and represents a source of funds through which assets (or one of the uses of funds) are acquired. From this viewpoint, the owner of credit has an important intangible property that he may use as he does cash to acquire goods or services. And if the owner overspends, the credit asset may be exhausted just as his stock of cash may be depleted.

In dealing with the short-term sources of credit of the firm, we divide our discussion into two basic parts: those sources of short-term credit which come to the firm spontaneously or through the normal course of business practice (we call these items spontaneous sources of credit), and those sources of short-term credit which must be negotiated and prearranged in some detail with the credit granting agency (we call these items negotiated sources of short-term credit). Our discussion of spontaneous sources of short-term credit will include such items as trade credit, wages payable, and taxes payable. Under the broad heading of negotiated sources of short-term credit we deal with, among other things, the issuance of short-term promissory notes and commercial paper by the firm, bank credit, business finance companies, and public agencies.

11.3 SPONTANEOUS SOURCES OF SHORT-TERM CREDIT

Since spontaneous credit arises out of normal business practices, the lenders are typically not financial institutions but rather entities with which a firm conducts its business such as other firms, its employees and the Government. Of these, by far the most popular are other firms which ordinarily do not obtain immediate payment as a result of their sales transactions.

[1] TRADE CREDIT

Trade credit arises out of sales. Typically the supplier of goods does not expect payment until after a designated period. Thus, credit is granted. Although some negotiation may be involved, the arrangement is so well established and the terms so strongly influenced by industry custom that it may be considered a form of spontaneous credit.

(a) Importance to the Buyer

To the extent that a buyer can gain access to goods or services through trade credit, he reduces his need to obtain funds from financial institutions and therefore cuts borrowing charges. From the viewpoint of the buyer, therefore, purchasing goods by means of trade credit is at least a cost savings device, and when money is tight, it may actually be the buyer's only financing medium.

Some buyers may require no financing other than trade credit. Such an arrangement could prove very satisfactory. A seller is not likely to insist upon prompt payment if the buyer represents a reasonably good account. Moreover, the seller would probably be more willing than a financial institution to help the buyer work himself out of a temporarily tight financial condition; the seller's basic profit comes from the sales transaction, whereas the bank's profit rises out of the borrowing transaction.

Thus, the financial manager is likely to try to take maximum advantage of the trade credit available. Nevertheless, he may also have to seek funds from financial institutions if he must consistently make payments prior to obtaining collections from his own customers, or if seasonality, expansion, or other factors make borrowing desirable. The financial manager may even decide that it is advantageous to keep some bank lines open just to have additional sources available if the need for them should arise.

(b) Importance to the Seller

To the seller trade credit is a means of promoting sales. As such, it is a powerful tool that contributes to his volume of business and makes important economies of scale possible. In the light of these benefits, his decision to accept credit for his goods rests upon his evaluation of the buyer's eventual ability to pay, his cost structure, his own capacity to obtain funds, and the costs of acquiring them.

Clearly, the seller must be able to absorb his added costs or to pass them on through the selling prices that he has established, and if he cannot do so, his reduced profit margin may make the sales transaction undesirable. The longer the seller must wait for his customers to pay, the greater are his financing charges. Moreover, the seller's own suppliers may not be willing to give him such generous payment deferral periods as those he grants to his own customers. He also has numerous operating commitments, such as wages and taxes, which are other forms of spontaneous credit but which must eventually be paid. These cash needs create pressures that encourage the seller to seek means of obtaining faster clearances of his outstanding accounts.

(c) Using the Sales Discount

In order to induce earlier payments, sellers have often found it profitable to grant customers special discounts. This policy has led to the now traditional dual pricing system used in American business—one price representing the amount due if the payment is made after the full deferral period allowed, and the other the amount due if payment is made within a prescribed shorter period.

Business attitudes toward the implications of the sales discount differ. As a rule, if the expectation is that buyers will accept the shorter terms that allow the discount, management feels that the gross figure less the discount is their actual price. In line with this idea, their accounting policy is to record receivables and sales on a net basis; if customer than fails to take the discount, the differential is reported as other income.

More commonly, management prefers to consider the gross figure as its actual price and to bill on this basis. For reporting purposes, the discount is then likely to be shown as a deduction from sales. If this policy is not followed, it is felt, buyers may come to regard the discounted figure as the actual price and to pay this amount regardless of how long they take. Even when gross prices are used in billing, there is some tendency for customers to exceed the allowable earlier date but to take the discount anyway. Management, in turn, may be reluctant to enforce the exact terms if it feels the account is sufficiently desirable. The use of the two price system may at least underline the fact that the sales discount is a bonus for earlier payments, which it is hoped will influence customers to observe the rules more closely.

The cost of the sales discount may be measured against the savings resulting from the smaller amount of capital tied up in receivables. By shortening its collection experience from 30 to 20 days, for example, a company achieves dollar savings equivalent to the product of the return it is able to earn on its investment and the reduced capital requirements. Thus, companies have, at times, gone to considerable lengths to employ the sales discount as a competitive device.

The sales discount (also called cash discount) should not be confused with either the quantity or the trade discount. The former is granted for buying large amounts and the latter to firms occupying different spots in the distributive channel. For example, a company may issue a catalogue with base prices listed; it may then provide separate statements showing the discounts from these prices for quantity purchasers, for wholesalers, and so forth.

(c) Classification of Terms of Sale

Together, the credit period and the sales discount permitted for early payment are considered the terms of sale; these terms may be classified as follows:

• No discount or time period.

• No discount but time period included; and

• Discount combined with time period.

These terms are considered below.

[i] NO DISCOUNT OR TIMER PERIODL In this arrangement, no credit is granted. The typical provision is COD (cash on delivery), so that the only risk the seller assumes is the failure of the buyer to accept the merchandise. Even if this should occur, the potential loss is small—freight charges, possible deterioration of merchandise, and the opportunity costs of foregone interest on the funds that would have been received from a consummated sale. But if the seller distrusts the buyer's ability to pay and does not want to expose himself even to these minor risks, he could employ the rarely used (CBD cash before delivery) CWO (cash with order), or CIA (cash in advance) terms.

[ii] NO DISCOUNT BUT TIME PERIOD INCLUDED: Sellers may give their customers a time period within which to pay. This may be done in several ways. In some fields, where regular and frequent deliveries are made, as is the case with gasoline and certain end-food products, the buyer may be permitted to pay the driver or salesman on his next visit. When this method is employed, the credit extension usually runs for only a few days. A seller may find monthly billings convenient; a common arrangement is to call for payment thirty or sixty days after the invoice date, expressed as net 30 or net 60 days. Or, he may permit his customers to pay for all items bought in one month at an early date in the following month. For this purpose, he might quote terms of n/10 BOM, which means that all items bought in one month (commonly prior to the 25th day) must be paid for by the tenth of the following month. In lieu of EOM (end of month), sometimes use is made of the term *prox.,* an abbreviation of the Latin word *proximo* or next.

[iii] DISCOUNT COMBINED WITH TIME PERIOD: This is the standard arrangement, and calls for quoting the discount first and then the credit period. For example, 2/10, net 30, means that the buyer has a choice of paying within 10 days and taking a discount of 2 percent or of paying in 30 days at the full price.

Within this framework, variations in terminology — reflecting differences in credit practices — are often used. In the textile industry, a common arrangement has been 2/10 EOM, n/60, meaning that a discount of 2 percent is provided for payment made within the first 10 days of the following month, but that the full price is due by the end of the next month. When the credit period is measured from the beginning of the month after purchase, there is a tendency for buyers to avoid ordering during the last days of the month. To discourage this practice, companies may announce that all purchases made after a certain date, say the twenty-fifth of the month, will be assumed to have been made in the following month. Or the period may run from the middle of the month to the middle of the next month (MOM); in this approach the term is measured from the fifteenth of the month for sales made in the first 15 days and from the beginning of the following month for sales made in the last 15 days.

Ordinarily, the credit period originates with the date of the invoice or the shipment of the order which is usually the same. To help customers located far from the seller, the credit terms may start on receipt or arrival of the goods (ROG and AOG). Thus, 2/10 ROG, n/30 means that regardless of how long shipment may take, the count of the 10-day discount term begins when the goods arrive at their destination; the length of the net credit period, however, may still be determined from the date of shipment.

(e) Factors Affecting the Terms of Sale

As in most economic relationships, the existing pattern in credit terms is the outgrowth of many circumstances. Some are obvious, others less so. Moreover, their influence varies in particular cases and changes from time to time. Any given set of terms, therefore, may reflect special conditions, and a financial manager contemplating changing them would have to give careful attention to the following factors:

- tradition;
- economics of the firm;
- competitive conditions;
- the business cycle;
- inflation;
- the money market; and
- paying practices.

These factors are discussed below.

[i] TRADITION: In the trade credit field, tradition is a powerful force. The country's economic development has led to the emergence of trade terms shaped to meet prevailing needs and changes have occurred slowly. There is a strong tendency for a seller to provide the same terms as his predecessor in the distribution channel or others in the industry and for a buyer to expect these terms. As a result, there is an association of terms with industries, which is likely to affect individual situations.

[ii] ECONOMICS OF THE FIRM: Just as tradition is powerfully resistant to change, the economic requirements of the firm are a major influence in inducing change. As the needs of a buyer or seller shift, it is only logical to

expect him to seek corresponding modification of his terms of sale. A buyer may be perfectly willing to accept short credit terms on goods that turn over quickly, because the rapid inflow of cash permits him to render prompt payments in turn. A seller may be amenable to granting long credit terms in order to help develop a new line or when goods move slowly and have a high profit margin. If the buyer and seller are far apart geographically, the length of time required for transportation may cause long credit terms. During the Colonial period, for example, this factor, together with the difficulty of communication, led to terms of sale running to 12 months and longer. Or if a seller finds suppliers shortening their terms, he may seek similar adjustments from his own customers. In addition, the terms of sale are likely to reflect seasonal conditions; the number, length, and timing of marketing periods; and storage facilities.

[iii] COMPETITIVE CONDITIONS: A seller may grant generous sales terms as a marketing device to attract customers, or he may impose severe terms and enforce them firmly when he has little concern about competition. In a buyers' market, bargaining strength shifts, and buyers may demand more favorable terms or simply pay less attention to those that exist. In some cases, a firm may find that an adjustment in credit terms is an equally effective, but more flexible competitive device than direct price concessions.

[iv] THE BUSINESS CYCLE: A plausible case could be made for a company's firming its credit terms during business depressions in order to minimize credit losses and easing them when conditions are good because the danger of default is less serious. The reverse, however, is more likely to occur. When business is depressed, competitive pressures are likely to drive a company to ease its terms in order to obtain business. As the cycle rises and demand gains once more, the seller is generally better able to impose more stringent terms. Indeed, the growth of marginal companies under such circumstances may bolster the need for a stricter policy in order to avoid the danger of seriously lowering the caliber of outstanding accounts.

[v] INFLATION: Inflationary fears could cause sellers to try to induce buyers to accelerate payments. For the most part, the terms of sale currently in vogue were developed when inflation was not the major consideration. Should the inflationary issue persist, some reorientation of terms may occur, dependent upon the competitive strengths of buyer and seller, as one seeks to accelerate and the other to defer payment.

[vi] THE MONEY MARKET: Money factors generate conflicting pressures. Tight conditions cause banks to reduce their credit lines leading companies to seek help from their sellers. As interest rates rise, there is a tendency for companies to look upon their suppliers as bankers. In these circumstances, however, instead of being more lenient, suppliers also under financial pressures, want to accelerate the rate of collection from their customers. Tight money also makes it more difficult for customers to pay and may cause them to seek an easing of credit terms. Similarly, as sellers have to pay higher charges on the funds they borrow, they try to pass these costs along by lowering their cash discounts. On the other hand, buyers, under similar pressures, desire larger discounts to offset their lowered profit margins because of higher interest rates.

[vii] PAYMENT PRACTICES: A firm's operating procedures may have a bearing on the credit terms it desires. A company that uses mechanized accounting, for example, may find that the optimum use of its equipment requires writing checks at a given date. If this date falls outside the established credit period, the firm may desire a change of terms in order to match its operating requirements. Some sellers object to such requests because they feel that the discount is a reward for earlier payment and should be administered on that basis. To fashion the discount period for the convenience of their customers, they contend, would be to strip it of its economic purpose. Nevertheless, some firms have been able to modify paying practices when they could show that the usual terms imposed real hardships on them.

(f) The Costs of Trade Credit

From the seller's point of view, the cost of trade credit has two parts. The first arises from the fact that he must finance his customers for a period of time; this cost may be gauged by multiplying the average amount involved by the cost of money over that period. The second, is the discount; as we have indicated, whether or not this is a true cost depends to a large extend on how the seller visualizes his pricing policies. The discount may be regarded as a deduction from the true price when taken, or as profit when not taken.

From the buyer's point of view, the credit period represents free financing. In lieu of incurring charges by borrowing from a financial institution, he exercises the privilege of deferring payment. And in some instances, this practice may free the buyer completely from the need for outside financing.

When the seller provides a discount to accelerate payment, the buyer must determine the charges he incurs by not accepting the discount. To permit comparisons with other costs, this figure must be expressed as an annual amount. For the period covered, the cost of not accepting a discount is approximately equal to the discount that would otherwise be saved; to place this cost on an annual basis, it should be multiplied by the number of times it would be incurred if done throughout the year. For example, if the terms are 2/10, net 30, the buyer in effect may have the use of the money for 20 extra days by forfeiting the discount of 2 percent. If he does this throughout the year, the multiplier would be 18 (360/20) and his cost would be about 36 percent. Since he would only have to pay 98 percent of the amount owed if he accepted the discount, his actual cost should be increased proportionately, and would amount to 36.73 percent (36 percent ÷ 98 percent) per year. This rate may be compared with that charged by financial institutions in order for him to decide whether or not to borrow in order to accept the discount. Of course, it should also be noted, that if a seller is to calculate the difference between his receipt of $98.00 in 10 days vs. $100.00 in 30 days, his cost in terms of an annual percentage is also 36.73%.

(g) Evaluating the Role of Trade Credit

Although standard terms are still prevalant, the tendency is away from uniformity in the direction of variability, with individual firms determining their own arrangements. This trend has culminated in periodic efforts to drop the discount as a general policy in favor of a straight credit period, during which sellers would be willing to finance buyers.

In discussing the merits of trade credit, a distinction must be drawn between the credit period and the cash discount. The willingness of a seller to wait a specified period before the buyer is expected to pay is a logical outcome of our kind of economy. Conceptually, the ability to purchase goods by means of credit has become ingrained in our way of thinking. Practically, the organizational setup and procedures of today's large company have become so complex that, despite the computer, in most cases paying cash on delivery would not be feasible; some time is required to execute the paper work necessary to record the receipt of the goods and to provide for payment.

A more serious controversy has revolved about the cash discount. Opponents of the discount have pointed to the confusion that its use often generates; they have been critical of the complicated and seemingly illogical terms that sometimes appear; they note the difficulty of enforcement, and claim that the discount system can degenerate into a method for granting preferential treatment to larger customers with greater external borrowing capacity that can be called upon in order to accept the discount.

In specific instances these contentions are valid. It is equally true that a strong theoretical case can be made for the use of the discount. If the typical firm must grant a credit period during which it is compelled to finance its customers because conditions of the trade make such an arrangement mandatory, it is reasonable to say that the firm should also have the right to take legitimate measures to encourage accelerated payments. The distributive chain is closely knit, and once a supplier or wholesaler has established a discount policy, its influence tends to be spread to the other organizational links in the chain. Since the old saw "time is money" is as valid as it is aged, it would appear logical to give some reward to the customer for paying earlier; the cash discount serves this purpose.

From the point of view of the buyer, the advisability of accepting the sales discount is dependent primarily upon the relationship between the cost of non-acceptance and the cost of available financing. Clearly, accepting the discount is desirable if the buyer can borrow funds at a lower rate than that implicit in non-acceptance. One only has to compare the greater financing charges borne by firms to advance their payments with the penalty incurred by any company that finds the more favorable financing routes barred because of its poor financial condition.

The problem is more complicated in the case of the seller, because he cannot be certain of the effect of the discount upon such factors as the timing of payments, sales volume, the fraction of a credit sales that will be paid with the discount, and the bad debt ratio. By making assumptions about the effects of these factors, however, as well as the earnings rate implicit in the funds made available to him, the seller can determine the present value of the cash flows arising from a discount and non-discount policy. By this method, he can calculate a break-even policy, represented by that rate which equalizes these two flows, and an optimal policy, involving the rate that maximizes the present value of the sales discount cash flows.[1]

In an effort to assess the actual rather than assumed relationship between the costs and benefits of sales discounts, two analysts conducted a survey of

100 firms in six industries. They measured the dollar cost of the discount against the change in profits produced by the elimination of the sales discount. Although no positive conclusions were reached, the authors observed that "even a skeptic would agree that the results present enough evidence to suggest that more companies should look to the elimination of cash discounts as a device for improving profits."[2]

(h) Rationing Through Trade Credit

The large business firm serves as a sort of capital entrepot in our economy. Funds move to it from all parts of the country, are collected, and then are once more distributed. Some of these funds come from the firm's own operations and are kept as retained earnings; others come from banks or the capital markets. The firm itself plays a vital role in determining the direction of these outward routes. As a result, its decisions have an important effect on the financial status of other businesses throughout the country. These decisions are of particular significance to small enterprises which obtain the largest part of their required short-term financing through trade-credit. This trade-credit is used not only to finance a substantial portion of inventory needs but also to make operating cash available.

The evidence suggests that smaller firms have come to rely more heavily on the financial shoulders of the big companies than on standard banking sources. There seems to be a relationship, particularly in mining and manufacturing, between the size of a firm and its financing role. The percentage of receivables to payables seems to grow as firms become bigger.

(i) Trade Credit Decisions of the Financial Manager

The financial manager of the selling firm must establish workable standards for granting credit to its customers. Determining these standards is a problem of credit management that is discussed in Chapter 9. Once these standards are established, the financial manager has the responsibility for carrying them out in the light of the firm's overall objectives. The buyer's financial manager, in his turn, must ascertain whether it is advantageous to purchase the goods on the terms offered. Finally, both officers must try to develop the best balance of arrangements and determine the extent to which the costs involved may be absorbed or passed on.

[i] IN THE SELLING FIRM: Trade credit is a means of financing sales, and therefore, sales and other policy-making executives have taken an interest in the influence of trade terms. The entrance of nonfinancial management on the scene has augmented the financial executive's responsibilities. Because of the "new look" given to the usefulness of credit terms, the financial manager must pay greater heed to the effect of these terms on the other branches of a company's activities; at the same time, he must maintain his diligence in evaluating credit procedures to ensure that changed policies do not lead to greater credit losses.

As a member of the executive team responsible for fashioning terms that help meet overall objectives, the financial manager can show how these terms may be used as a subtle form of nonprice competition. If liquidity is no problem, he may recommend not only granting generous terms but also overlooking infractions of these terms. Customers recognizing the benefits of the lenient credit policy will hesitate to consider the products of a competitor which may provide an equally good item but which cannot match the financing arrangements.

Competing firms watch pricing practices attentively, and are aware of announced changes that one of them makes. But they are not so likely to be familiar with the details of trade terms, which the financial manager may therefore be able to change with less fear of competitive reprisals. For example, the financing charges imposed on buyers who do not pay within the discount period may be modified simply by shortening or lengthening this period. By reducing the terms of trade from 2/30, net 60 to 2/10, net 60, the pressure on the discount taking buyer is augmented, while conversely, the rate paid by the non-discount taking buyer is indirectly lowered by almost 10 percentage points.[3] Similarly, the stress of competition may persuade the financial manager to permit customers to take discounts after the discount period has expired, and thereby aid buyers without even formally changing the established terms of sale.

As we have emphasized, each time the financial manager of the selling firm increases or decreases the discount granted and the time within which payment must be made, he is adjusting the costs incurred. In effect, therefore, his decision must balance these costs against the benefits. The principal difficulty in making this comparison is that the quantitative value of the benefits incurred is difficult to gauge, although the costs of changing the trade terms are more easily measured. The same steps may lead to different results for different companies. For example, even though the weight of opinion indicates that cash discounts accelerate the rate of customer payment, others have found that such discounts create their own problems. One company has stated bluntly that "cash discounts for observance of stated terms follows a long outmoded business practice. Such discounts are no longer an incentive for prompt payment. Instead, they are a source of irritation. You get involved in dunning letters . . . the whole thing just generates ill-feeling. Cash discounts should be eliminated from the business scene!"

Then again, the seller may be dependent upon building and maintaining a strong dealer organization, as in the petroleum and automotive industries. In these cases, establishing reasonably generous terms and implementing them with understanding helps to create high morale, which could prove a vital competitive factor under trying conditions. Or, the seller may want to develop a diversified sales outlet so as to minimize its dependence upon single buyers. It may find it desirable to help build specific accounts through generous financing arrangements. If the selling company is dependent on a single account, it may have to grant the terms the buyer desires; the willingness of sellers to seek government business despite the severe terms sometimes required is a case in point. Or, the seller may be dependent on a single industry and be willing to work special terms to accommodate financially pressed firms in which the seller has long-term confidence.

The characteristics of certain types of accounts may make a discount appealing to them. As stated by the credit manager of one firm, "We use the cash discount to advantage in selling our marginal customers on the idea of paying within our terms to earn this added income." Also, the financial manager of the seller may have little alternative except to match the terms that his customers grant to their customers. In the machinery field, as an illustration, sellers have been willing to offer customers extended payment dates if they in turn sell on rental or installment terms. On the other hand, the financial manager may want to swing to the opposite extreme and recommend charging interest on accounts that are a designated number of days overdue.

These varying considerations have led to the great number of terms in use. Some firms even issue two or more sets of selling terms. The use of multiple trade terms by the same company may create special problems for the financial manager. In the case of one small steel company which used multiple terms, for example, it was found that when more than one product was sold on the same order, the accounting department had difficulty indicating which discount applied to each product, and customers applied the highest product discount to the whole order.

It is imperative that the financial manager follow the implications of changing or using multiple trade terms. Throughout the sales procedure, he will find himself constantly engaged in measuring tangible costs against relatively intangible gains. And the conclusions of one period may not necessarily be applicable to another. To help in this decision-making process, forward looking firms have come to use the modern tools of scientific management. For example, they undertake careful analyses of distribution costs in order to develop, among other things, terms of sale and discounts that contribute most effectively to market profitability. They also make simulation tests of different plans of action, including terms and discounts as well as other factors, in order to evaluate their overall and independent influence on the market.

[ii] IN THE BUYING FIRM: The financial manager of the buying firm has the responsibility of assessing the implications of the seller's trade terms. If different terms are available from different sellers, he will measure the relative costs of each to determine which set is most favorable; his conclusion may be affected by whether the buyer must borrow from a financial institution to take the discount or generate sufficient funds from internal operations to meet the payments when due. For example, assume that a buyer can purchase a piece of equipment from a manufacturer by means of regular monthly payments of $97 at the close of each month for a year, or two semiannual payments of $591, with the first payment due at midyear; also assume that he will have enough funds at year end to provide for the bank obligation and to pay the last monthly or semiannual installment on the equipment. To meet these terms, he is in a position to obtain a bank line of credit which calls for paying 5 percent on the monthly or semiannual amount owed until the end of the year.[4] Under these circumstances, financing through monthly payments would be cheaper, because the total annual costs amount to $1,191, compared with $1,197 if the semiannual requirement is taken. The higher interest costs incurred through monthly borrowing are more than offset by the lower principal payments necessary in the monthly financial plan.

On the other hand, let us assume that the buyer generates $97 monthly which he could either invest or use to pay for the equipment, and that he is not able or does not wish to borrow from the bank. If he uses his monthly income to meet the monthly payment requirements for the equipment, he does not earn any money by the close of the year. If, however, he elects the semiannual or more expensive method of payment, he may invest his monthly income during the first half of the year in order to obtain funds for the semiannual payment; he may then continue to invest his monthly income during the second half of the year to meet the last installment.

If his net rate of return is 12 percent per year, he will receive $14.55 income during the first half of the year. He will use $9 of this to make up the difference between the $591 semiannual payment due and the total of his monthly income for the six-month period. During the second half of the year he will invest this net income differential of $5.55 plus the remaining monthly income receipts to obtain $14.88 by the close of the year, from which the second $9 differential would have to be deducted to obtain $5.88. In total, therefore, he would have net earnings of $11.43 ($5.55 + $5.88) in excess of his principal payment for the equipment as a result of adopting the more expensive semi-annual payment schedule. While the difference is not great, it represents a reversal of the previous conclusion, and larger variations could result from alternative payment and interest schedules. These procedures, of course, also assume that the investment opportunities can be timed to coincide with payment requirements.

In addition to the actual costs of financing, a less liquid buyer also has to consider the seller's willingness to cooperate with him in working out of temporary financial difficulties. Sometimes the buyer may find that he is required to adopt specified management practices in order to obtain additional financing; in this case, the financial manager must make certain that his company has not bartered some of its business independence for this freedom from financing worries.

The financial manager of a very big corporation may be able to virtually dictate trade terms to the firm's suppliers. While competition may exert some restrictions, the economic giant could place considerable pressure upon its suppliers by threatening to shift accounts. In most instances, a supplier will be dependent upon a large firm for its existence, while the latter will probably have alternative sources to meet its needs. Yet, the financial manager may find that he does not have complete freedom even in this case, because the firm's policy may be to spread its business among a number of small suppliers; this policy could in turn be dictated by the fact that the firm is a prime contractor for a government agency which encourages use of small subcontractors.

(j) Who Pays for the Credit

It is not easy to answer the question who pays for the credit. For one thing, the cost of part of the credit arrangement may be absorbed, while the rest is not. In the expectation that its customers will take the cash discount offered, for example, a company may pass on the cost to them by establishing higher initial prices. On the other hand, the company may not recognize the higher financing charges it experiences as a result of its payment terms, and so may absorb at least part of these costs.

Then again, a firm's ability to pass on costs is influenced by other factors as well:

- by the elasticity of demand for the product — if a modest price increase substantially influences demand, the firm will more readily absorb the cost;
- by the policy of competitors, which may make absorption necessary; and
- by profit margins — a company would probably be more willing to absorb additional costs on a high profit-margin item.

Within the framework of such limitations, it is reasonable to assume that companies tend to pass on the credit costs they incur.

The seller may have a higher credit rating than the buyer and be able to acquire funds more cheaply. Moreover, the seller's scale economies from the expanded business obtained through the use of trade terms may be sufficiently great to permit a lower price for the goods sold. Even when the seller passes on some of the cost, therefore, the buyer may find that, on balance, he is the saver.

Thus, the financial manager of the selling firm is constantly studying its trade terms to ascertain how they may best be used to fulfill the firm's objectives and encourage sales; the financial manager of the buying firm is evaluating the available terms to discover which provide the greatest latitude at the lowest costs. Both officers assess the terms they give and offer, trying to find the optimum relationship.

[2] WAGES PAYABLE

Another form of short-term business credit which accrues spontaneously as the result of common business practice, rather than through negotiation, is wages. In the normal conduct of business affairs workers are paid subsequent to their performance of services. Thus, at any particular point in time prior to payday, workers have, in effect, made an advance to the corporation in the form of their services for which they have not yet been paid. This wage accrual will show up on the corporate balance sheet as wages payable as long as the balance sheet date is not a payday.

On its part, the corporation can use those funds advanced by its workers until payday arrives. While this credit is, in most cases, of short duration, the volume of funds involved can be substantial. Additionally, it should be noted, that funds from wage credit are cost free to the corporation and thus represent a very valuable source of credit.

In most instances, the use of wages payable as a financing mechanism is not a planned undertaking. Rather, it is the outcome of other factors such as the labor intensity of the company's business, the duration of the pay period, relative pay scales, and reliance on lending institutions. In specific instances, however, particularly when a company is experiencing financial problems, special arrangements may be made with the wage earner, thereby giving wages payable an aspect of negotiated credit.

These arrangements may take different forms, such as simply lowering the pay scale or lengthening the pay period. More sophisticated solutions have also been formulated. For example, confronted with the pressures of competition financially plagued companies have been able to formulate special plans with unions that tie workers compensation to company earnings in order to prevent layoffs. Such plans also have encouraged lenders to work out flexible financing programs.

[3] TAXES PAYABLE

The final form of spontaneous short-term credit to be considered is taxes. Perhaps it may seem odd, particularly in these days of mass public concern with the extent of the burden caused by taxes, to look upon them as a form of credit. But, nonetheless, to the extent that the services government provides demands that revenue sources be found to fund them; government is the partner of all business enterprises. Yet, the payment government requires as its partnership share need not be made at the instant that it is earned. Instead, tax payments are made at specified dates during the earning period, but at a lagged rate in relation to the generation of earnings by the firm. The effect is to create, for most firms, at any point in time subsequent to the tax payment dates, a tax liability and to this extent a form of credit. As in the case of wages payable, this credit flows to the firm in the normal course of business affairs and need not be negotiated. Also, as in the case of wages payable, it is a form of credit which is cost free to the firm.

While the credit is initially cost free, it must eventually be paid and is therefore a source of expense to the company. Accordingly, efforts are made to reduce this expense and in varying degrees companies have been able to bring the tax rate actually paid below the statutory rate. Moreover, they have also been able to take advantage of tax flexibility to lower the amount of earnings reported to the Internal Revenue Service below that reported to shareholders in order to defer their income tax liability. Such deferrals have, among other things, taken the form of timing differences between financial and taxable income due to such things as the excess of tax over book depreciation, inventory writedowns, the deferred margins on installment sales, and deferred compensation. Additionally, some companies typically do not make a tax provision for the portion of accumulated and undistributed earnings of foreign subsidiaries which are intended to be reinvested indefinitely or received free of additional tax. As in the case of accounts payable and wages, taxes arise from the ordinary operations of a business and therefore are considered a form of spontaneous credit.

11.4 NEGOTIATED SOURCES OF SHORT-TERM CREDIT

As we have said, some sources of short-term funds can be obtained only through negotiation between the relevant parties or their agents. The nature of these items and their implications are discussed below.

[1] THE PROMISSORY NOTE AND ITS FINANCIAL IMPLICATIONS

The promissory note is a much less popular method of financing business transactions than the open account, because the note permits less flexibility in handling frequent transactions. A promissory note represents formal evidence of debt; it establishes the time and amount of payment, reduces the possibility of legal disputes, facilitates prompt payment, and is more readily exchangeable for institutional credit. It is widely used in bank loans and is apt to appear in fields of activity characterized by generous credit terms, as in the sale of wholesale fur and jewelry or certain high cost durable equipment.

A creditor may also insist upon a promissory note to formalize the due date of an original loan. He may then discount the note, thereby obtaining immediate funds and the services of the bank to demand payment on maturity. In addition, as an acknowledgment of debt, the note reduces the possibility of litigation in the event some disagreement exists concerning the amount of the obligation. Sometimes a debtor may take the initiative and offer a note on the theory that its purported advantages justify an extension of terms.

Characteristically, a financial manager does not have important decisions to reach concerning the use of promissory notes. Prevailing practices largely determine whether the instrument is employed in a particular transaction. As we have noted, the open account is more widely used in this country to finance purchases and sales among firms, while the note commonly makes its appearance in obtaining bank loans. Sometimes the financial manager will have to decide whether to insist upon payment of an overdue account, overlook the matter for a further period of time, or require a note in order to have formal evidence of the obligation. (Also, post-dated checks may be used to show the willingness of the obligator to pay when he has funds.) Which course of action the financial manager takes will depend upon his credit evaluation of the customer, his desire to keep the account, and his own financial position. In general, it is questionable whether the written evidence provides added assurance for the collection of an open account which is posing payment difficulties. The danger of using the note to aid in the collection process is that it may merely delay tackling the problem of final settlement.

[2] COMMERCIAL PAPER AS A MEANS OF OPEN MARKET FINANCING

Commercial paper is a business firm's promissory note that we describe as an independent instrument because of its special characteristics. A company desiring to raise funds by this means executes a number of instruments made payable to itself which it endorses and sells in the open market. The big sales finance companies distribute their own paper directly rather than going through intermediaries.

Commercial paper spreads the lending burden among many lenders. The relationship between lender and borrower is impersonal, which means that only strong companies can employ this method since the lender is deprived of the opportunity of making a personal credit check. Moreover, dealers do not endorse these notes, and therefore their investment strength comes from the credit of the issuer. As a result, the roster of companies using this market reads like a blue list of American industry and includes some of the best-known business names. Lesser known firms, however, have been able to gain access to the commercial paper market by obtaining a letter of credit from a commercial bank or endorsement from an insurance company which substitutes the credit of the institution for that of the issuer.[5]

The cost of commercial paper financing is the discount to the dealer plus his commission, which has run about ¼ percent on an annual basis. The prime commercial paper rate has usually been somewhat below the prime rate charged by commercial banks to their better grade borrowers, without considering the benefits of not having to keep compensating balances.

Although commercial paper is a short-term instrument, it is not uncommonly grouped with long-term liabilities in corporate financial statements. This reporting procedure occurs when the commercial paper borrowing is supported by long-term financing arrangements. In these circumstances, the expectation is that the obligation will be refinanced and therefore will not require the use of the company's working capital during the ensuing fiscal year.[6]

In a large modern business firm it is imperative for the financial manager to have an understanding of the money market, which means that he will be familiar with commercial paper both as a borrowing and investment vehicle.[7] In reaching decisions to borrow by means of commercial paper, he will make the comparisons ordinarily undertaken in studying alternative financing routes. With respect to costs, as suggested above, he will find this method highly competitive. Unless his firm has a top credit rating, however, the method may not be available to him. Because commercial paper buyers are spread across the nation and dealers are vigorous in their activities, the financial manager can ordinarily rely upon funds being available should he desire to issue this paper. These reasons may be sufficient to induce him to finance as much of the firm's requirements as possible through this route. Against these advantages, he must weigh the absence of the personal attention of a commercial bank and the institution's cooperation in working out terms suitable to his own needs. These opposing benefits and drawbacks lead most companies to rely heavily upon commercial banks and to use commercial paper as a supplementary device. Despite this primary dependence upon commercial banks, it is important for the manager to preserve flexibility in effecting financing arrangements because both the availability and costs of funds from the different sources vary.

Reflecting the growing demand for their services, sales finance companies, which issue commercial paper directly, continuously tap the market. The other borrowers, who sell through dealers, including manufacturers, wholesalers, and more recently foreign companies and utilities, use the market differently. They are inclined to issue the paper when they need large amounts of funds for short periods and they do not want to resort to bank credit. These firms might therefore follow the practice of filling part of their short-term requirements with bank loans and relying upon the open market as an auxiliary source. Or, a large firm may find that the statutory ceiling on loans to a single borrower necessitates obtaining credit lines from additional banks, a step that the firm may be reluctant to take despite the relative ease of obtaining a participation agreement from a number of banks. Particularly important users of commercial paper among nonfinancial companies are enterprises with seasonal needs, such as can companies, flour mills, grain dealers, packers, and apparel manufacturers.[8],[9]

[3] BANKERS' ACCEPTANCES AS A MEANS OF OPEN MARKET FINANCING

A bankers' acceptance is a draft drawn on and accepted by a commercial bank; it runs from one to six months, although the most common maturity is 90 days. In using a banker's acceptance, a buyer recognizes that his credit standing is not sufficiently well known to rely upon as a medium of exchange, and he therefore substitutes a bank's credit for his own. Unlike commercial paper, which provides the basis for meeting general corporate financial needs, the bankers' acceptance is used to finance specific shipments of goods, most often in foreign trade. Most domestic acceptances are drawn to finance the storage of readily marketable staples, such as cotton, grain, wool, tobacco, vegetable oil, peanuts, and sodium nitrate. The merchant draws on the accepting bank and discounts the accepted draft in the open market, thereby obtaining the required funds.

A bank's acceptance draft makes it highly salable, and by this means funds may be shifted several times during the course of a single transaction. Since the buyer often pays prior to maturity, the bank may be able to finance the transaction without any pressure on itself. Indeed, a large percentage of the acceptances in the United States market have been bought for the account of foreign banks, thereby shifting to them the burden of financing.

The laws and regulations of the Board of Governors of the Federal Reserve System prescribe limitations on the amount of acceptance credit an individual bank may extend, the maximum maturity of the instrument, its purpose, and the security required. Historically, about ten to twenty big banks have accounted for the bulk of the activity in bankers' acceptances. This field has been growing at a much faster rate than bank lending generally.

If custom, convenience, and the desires of the parties involved allow the financial manager to choose between acceptance financing and a direct bank loan, the relative costs will undoubtedly influence his decision. In acceptance financing, a commission is paid by the firm on whose behalf the acceptance is created; this charge traditionally has run about 1½ percent annually but well-rated customers, particularly in the commodities area, have been able to obtain lower charges. In addition, a discount, measured by the dealer's buying rate on acceptances, is paid by the seller, who will probably pass this cost on through the terms of the transaction. In effect, therefore, the direct cost to the borrower is the sum of the acceptance commission plus the market discount rate.

In general, domestic acceptance financing has expanded most rapidly during periods when financing differentials favored this medium; conversely, when cost differentials have been unfavorable, acceptance financing has slowed. Often the overall costs of acceptance financing will equal the rate at which a company could borrow from its bank. Since a major reason for a bank creating an acceptance is to service its customer's needs when money is tight, an important customer may be able to negotiate lower commissions. Encouraging this possibility is the fact that the Federal Reserve will discount eligible acceptances to provide banks with liquidity.

[4] BORROWING FROM COMMERCIAL BANKS

By far the largest form of negotiated source of short-term funds consists of borrowing from commercial banks. Yet, while some companies look principally to commercial banks as a source of funds, others make scant use of them. The difference in practice may be explained in various ways. A company's officers or partners may frown upon a policy of bank borrowing perhaps because of the ancient notion that it is a sign of weakness. Some companies are sufficiently profitable to generate their own operating funds.

Others have alternative sources, such as their suppliers, with whom they can work out suitable arrangements. In the normal sequence of events, moreover, funds obtained for long-term purposes, say, for building a new plant, are temporarily available for short-term uses. Indeed, it is not at all unusual for companies to sell securities for working capital as well as for some long-term project. It is unusual, however, for companies to remain completely aloof from maintaining some commercial bank borrowing relations.

In general, big firms do not rely as heavily on banks as do smaller enterprises. Economic conditions may upset this pattern, however, and cause big companies to come to the fore as bank users while smaller enterprises, either by choice or by necessity, cut down their borrowing. The effects of monetary policy also contribute to the relative increases or decreases in the proportion of large vs. small firm bank borrowing. Tight money sometimes casts a blanket on long-term borrowing. Therefore, big companies may find it necessary to finance inventory and receivables growth as well as capital expansion through bank loans. They do this expecting more favorable opportunities for long-term borrowing in the future when interest rates shrink. There is evidence, however, that banks react to monetary restraint by favoring local businesses, including small ones, rather than outside concerns.

The pattern of business borrowing from commercial banks reflects not only changing economic and monetary conditions but also the attitude of the banks. Over the past several decades these institutions have become increasingly aggressive. They have tended to discard the time-worn notion of confining their activity largely to so-called self-liquidating loans, and they now participate actively in different kinds of business financing, including accounts receivable, equipment, and commodity loans; they are also more inclined to accept long-term credit. Commercial banks, therefore, have become a much more flexible source of financing for business firms.

(a) The Authorizing Corporate Resolution

Over time a bank may occupy different relationships with a corporation. Thus, among other things, it may serve as a depository, effect payments, lend money, pledge certain property for money borrowed, and discount bills. To assure that any such transactions have been properly authorized and are carried out by the appropriately designated officials, the bank will require a resolution from the board of directors. The corporate secretary files this resolution under seal; he names the individuals responsible for conducting the indicated relations with the bank; and he certifies that there is nothing in the charter or by-laws of the corporation that limits the authority given in the resolution.

(b) THE FINANCING PACKAGE

A company that borrows from a bank ordinarily works out a package arrangement that in part is molded by the bargaining capacities of the parties. When money is tight, the bank will ration its lending by adjusting the terms of this package, whereas easing monetary conditions lead to fewer restraints. The bank may also use the creditworthiness of the borrower as a rationing device and insists upon higher standards without adjusting the terms of the loan.

In arranging a package, consideration may be given to four principal elements:

- the general nature of the deal: it may be a line of credit, a revolving loan, or a term loan, for example, and each of these arrangements may embody certain commitments on the part of the bank to advance funds and obligations on the part of the borrower to maintain prescribed financial standards;
- the security demanded: this may take the form of collateral, endorsement, or guarantee (although banks ordinarily do not think of endorsement and guarantees as security);
- the interest rate charge: this may be used at any particular time to discriminate among different borrowers, and over time to influence the general level of borrowing (in evaluating the interest charge, account must be taken of the compensating balance the firm may be required to keep); and
- maturity.

Each of these elements is treated in the remaining subsections on borrowing from commercial banks.

(c) Lines of Credit

Both lines of credit and revolving agreements have the same general purpose—to provide assurance that the firm will be able to obtain funds when required. The primary difference between the two methods is the formality of the arrangements.

Ordinarily, a credit line is not a binding contract; it is rather an informal understanding between a bank and a borrower regarding the maximum amount of credit that the bank will extend the borrower at any one time. Banking practice is to honor an established line unless the borrower's position changes drastically. Credit lines usually last for no more than one year since they tend to be associated with the seasonal needs of business. However, such lines are generally renewed once the year has expired. On top of this, most banks require at least annual payoffs, while some insist on more stringent terms, such as regular prepayment schedules or the elimination of all debt for not less than one month during the year, perhaps even without loans from other banks.

A bank that grants a line of credit may also require or expect the borrower to keep a minimum deposit balance. Observance of this practice varies with monetary conditions. When money is easy, the bank is likely to be more interested in placing its funds than in building deposits and may therefore relax its insistence on having compensating balances. When money is tight and funds are fully committed, banks will be more concerned about the balances their customers keep with them. Similarly, the actual requirements for compensating balances vary with economic conditions and competitive pressures; in general, these requirements may be for average balances against average loans, average balances against the line granted, a higher balance against a line that is in use and a lower one against one not being used, or some combination of these methods. As would be expected, the percentages in vogue also vary. In a highly competitive environment strong companies (able to issue prime commercial paper) usually can command a "split" balance arrangement, such as a designated percentage of the line and an additional percentage of the amount borrowed. Moreover, a bank may agree to accept a fee rather than a compensating balance.

All kinds of businesses use credit lines, often for seasonal or special requirements, such as floor plan or equipment financing. In general, banks tend to extend credit lines to accommodate larger borrowers and well-established firms. Because of the enduring implications of a line, banks give careful attention to the creditworthiness of the borrower. They check such points as the basic relationships and trends in the balance sheet and operating statement, the growth of the business, management's background and experience, the general economic environment, and, if security is provided, the market value of the collateral. Before seeking lines of credit, therefore, the financial manager must make certain that his financial house is in order and that his statements can pass the tests ordinarily imposed in such analyses.

(d) Revolving Loans

If the firm wants to develop a financing program that eliminates uncertainty regarding the availability of funds, it will enter into a revolving credit agreement that spells out formally the responsibilities of the contracting parties.[10] Such an arrangement typically provides for a commitment fee on the unused borrowing and for converting the revolving credit into a term loan on termination. When a company anticipates a future need for funds, the flexibility of long-term revolving credit may justify the commitment fee that must be paid.

If the amount involved is too large for an individual bank to assume the burden independently, it may form a participating group with each member allotted a percentage of the total. Specific terms vary, of course, depending upon the borrowing company, the institutions, and prevailing conditions.

(e) Term Loans

These are generally unsecured and have intermediate maturities, say between five and ten years, although longer terms can be arranged. The loans may be negotiated directly or represent conversions from revolving credits. It is common practice to base interest charges at some percentage above the prime rate, with charges possibly escalated over time. The loan may be fully amortized over its term or provision may be made for a balloon payment at maturity. Options may be given to the corporation to repay and to the bank to redeem the loan, in both cases at specified prices and times.

In order to provide protection for the parties involved and a general stability for the loan relationship, an agreement probably will be drawn up between the bank and the borrower.[11] Through this agreement, the bank establishes a clear understanding of its relationship with the borrower. By means of certain covenants and by requiring periodic confirmation that compliance with the agreement is maintained, the bank also seeks to ensure regular communication with the borrower, thereby permitting an up-to-date assessment of the borrower's financial condition and general management philosophy. Where other debt exists, the agreement can coordinate any legal or procedural interface with the various creditors.

Where several banks are involved, the loan agreement sets forth the bank participation terms, which provide for the functions of an agent bank for the participating group and the obligations of each of the members. In general, the agent is responsible for obtaining all the necessary instruments, advising the other banks of the loans in which they have participations, issuing the participation certificates in accordance with their respective interests, remitting to the banks their proportionate amounts of principal and interest paid, and generally administering the agreement; the borrower reimburses the agent for the services provided at an agreed rate. The participating banks agree to remit their respective segments of the loan to the agent and to share proportionately in any excess payments they may incur.

(f) Protective Provisions

Before legally committing itself to a long-term loan, a bank is likely to require assurances that the financial condition of the borrower during the life of the loan will be maintained at a level satisfactory to the safety of the loan. This objective is typically accomplished through covenants that, among other things, provide early warning signals of trouble which allows the bank to take rapid remedial action, make the borrower aware of minimum performance criteria, and help the borrower set reasonable goals for its financial condition and growth. In some cases, a "growth formula" is created which states that until a specified set of financial conditions is met, the borrower may not incur further debt.

Term loans are normally expected to be repaid out of the projected cash flow from earnings and therefore restrictions may be imposed on expenditures for such purposes as plant, salaries, cash dividends, and optional prepayment of other debt. To preserve a balanced financial condition, both the quantity and quality of current assets are important. With respect to quantity, fixed dollar requirements may be provided as well as ratios, such as current assets divided by current liabilities; with respect to quality, current assets for purposes of the loan may be described and relevant ratios may be used, such as the quick ratio (cash + marketable securities + accounts receivable divided by current liabilities). To preserve the borrower's corporate characteristics, restrictions may be imposed on mergers, the types of business in which the borrower may engage, the sale of a substantial portion of assets, and substantial changes in management. Such action may not be allowed without the prior approval of the lenders. "Key man" insurance also may be required. To ensure capital adequacy, restrictions may be imposed on the ratio of total liabilities to net worth. To guard against unfavorable off balance sheet changes, restrictions may be placed against the creation of guarantees for obligations of others and the assumption of long-term lease commitments.

The following is a simple illustration of how a combination of leverage and working capital covenants can be used to strengthen a company's financial condition.

1. Upon requesting a loan, the company has the financial condition shown below:

Current Assets	$100M	Notes payable	$ 25M
		Other Current Liabilities	25
		Total Current Liabilities	$ 50M
		Long-Term Debt	50
		Total Liabilities	$100M
Non-Current Assets	100	Net Worth	100
Total Assets	$200M	Total Liabilities and Net Worth	$200M

Working Capital = $50M ($100M - $50M)
Current Ratio = 2.0 ($100M / $50M)
Total Current Liabilities / Net Worth = 1.0 ($100M / $100M)
(Leverage Ratio)

2. The bank imposes the following covenants:
   a. A leverage ratio of .80 with no retirement of debt;
   b. Minimum working capital requirements of $75M; and
   c. Minimum current ratio of 2.5.

As a result of these covenants, at the end of the year, the company's balance sheet appears as follows:

Current Assets	$125M	Notes payable	$ 25M
		Other Current Liabilities	25
		Total Current Liabilities	$ 50M
		Long-Term Debt	50
		Total Liabilities	$100M
Non-Current Assets	100	Net Worth	125
Total Assets	$225M	Total Liabilities and Net Worth	$225M

Working Capital = $75M ($125M - $50M)
Current Ratio = 2.5 ($125M / $50M)
Total Liabilities / Net Worth = .80 ($100M / $125M)
(Leverage Ratio)

The covenants indicated above force the company to retain an additional $25M of profits by the end of year one and cause a shift of capital resources to the current section of the balance sheet.

The type of covenants provided will reflect both the credit standing of the borrower and the company's indicated rate of growth. To the extent possible, the bank will respect the attitudes of the borrower towards particular covenants. While the bank desires the restrictions to protect its financial stake in the borrower, it does not want to usurp the right to make management decisions, unless the company is in a workout position. In that case, the bank must oversee management to protect its own position.

(g) The Security Pledged on Business Loans

Security is used in business lending for three principal reasons:

• to manage the risk where the credit standing of the borrower does not seem sufficiently strong to justify an unsecured loan;
• to permit the borrower to obtain a more generous financing package in the form of a larger loan and/or longer maturity; and
• to conform with customary arrangements.

Illustrative of the use of collateral to bulwark a marginal loan is the high percentage of small business loans that are secured. Compared with a big firm, the small company is likely to have been in business for a shorter period of time and to have a lower credit rating, poorer financial records, and less bargaining power. Also, it is likely that with large firms collateral is often used for the kind of loans and borrowers which carry a greater than average risk. Banks also tend to require security on a higher proportion of their longer-term loans, where the hazards of unexpected declines in the borrower's earnings are greater than on their short-term loans. A borrower is likely to pay a higher rate for secured than for unsecured loans because the secured loan probably involves greater risk and entails administrative or "control" procedure costs.

Certain businesses generate suitable bank collateral in the ordinary course of their operations and are therefore more likely to use the collateral to obtain loans. As an illustration, public utilities buy large amounts of equipment and real estate firms deal in buildings; in both cases, the assets acquired have relatively long-term stable values suitable for bank collateral. As a result, secured loans are comparatively important in these fields for companies of all sizes. In other instances, firms use borrowed funds for a high proportion of their operating capital and may be called upon to provide collateral as additional protection. Brokers and dealers, for example, typically use as collateral the securities flowing from their ordinary activities to collateralize their bank borrowings. In the case of companies which have exhausted their lending potential, officers may obtain personal collateralized loans that are used for business purposes.

In the granting of secured loans, certain standard practices have developed. Liens against inventories may be secured by bills of lading, warehouse receipts, or, field warehouse receipts. Field warehouse receipts have become relatively popular because borrowers find it more convenient to lease part of their premises as a field warehouse rather than go to the expense and bother of using a public warehouse some distance away. When inventories consist of many component items moving rapidly through the work-in-process stage, warehousing may be inconvenient. In these instances even simpler methods of blanketing goods as collateral for a loan without going through a third party exist in states that have a factors' lien act. There, a written agreement gives the lender a lien on certain goods that remain in the borrower's possession. The borrower files notice with a public authority like the secretary of state and may also be required to post a sign on his premises. The collateral may be general, referring to all the personal property of the borrower including bank deposits, goods, financial instruments, contract rights and any other property. In that case the underlying agreement is likely to provide for the borrower furnishing additional collateral or reducing his obligation if the bank believes that the present security has become unsatisfactory. If the borrower fails to take these steps or in the event any one of the various other enumerated eventualities occur, such as the borrower becoming insolvent, all the liabilities become payable. If the physical possession of the collateral has been transferred to the borrower, a trust receipt can be used to give the bank title to the security.

(h) Floor Planning

A form of secured financing that warrants special mention is floor planning.[12] In this arrangement a dealer can obtain high priced goods, like automobiles, refrigerators, and furnaces so that he can sell them. In general, the procedure calls for the manufacturer to ship the goods to the dealer while the title passes to a financial institution, which reimburses the manufacturer. The dealer is obligated to the financing agency and pays the principal and interest of this loan from the proceeds of the sales as they occur. The financing agency thus relieves both manufacturer and dealer of the financial burden of carrying expensive inventories.

Commercial banks participate in this form of financing. Typically, an automobile dealer initiates the procedure by applying to a commercial bank for such a loan arrangement. If required by state laws, the bank files a trust receipt financing statement with the designated public record agency. The manufacturer draws drafts upon the bank for the full cost of automobiles shipped. So that the automobiles may be released, trust receipts for which the dealer is responsible are deposited with the bank. As each car is sold, the bank is reimbursed and the amount of the dealer's outstanding loans is reduced. To make certain that the proceeds of automobiles sold from the trust are applied to the loan, the bank routinely inspects the covered cars on the dealer's premises.

(i) Interest Costs

The interest rates charged by commercial banks on their short-term business loans may vary sharply both over time and among borrowers. The prime rate represents the cost of bank borrowing to the firms with top credit ratings. Both its significance and use have been somewhat weakened, however, by the practice of some banks granting certain customers rates below the indicated prime rate.

The rates on the smaller loans are almost always higher than those on larger loans, although this margin is not uniform and has even evaporated in high interest rate credit crunch periods. While it might appear, therefore, that in general, periods of relatively low interest rates produce the largest differentials and periods of high interest rates the smallest differentials, this is not necessarily a meaningful conclusion for small businesses, as very little bank credit is normally available to them on any terms during periods of high interest rates.

In general, the rates charged in New York City are below those in other Northern and Eastern cities. These variations may be due both to scale economies that enable the big New York City banks to charge less as well as to the fact that big companies, with higher credit ratings, tend to borrow more heavily in the New York money market. Stated interest rates are only suggestive of what borrowers have to pay. In order to determine actual costs, consideration has to be given to other factors as well, such as compensating balances and service fees. Assume, for example that a bank grants a one year revolving credit of $100,000 at 9 percent interest and charges a fee of 1/2 percent per annum on the amount of the commitment; funds are advanced on 90-day notes, and the bank desires the borrowing firm to maintain an average deposit balance of 15 percent. If the firm writes and repays these notes, the cost of the annual commitment fee applicable to a nine month basis amounts to 2/3 percent. Since the firm only had 85 percent of the loan amount actually available, the net borrowing charge comes to 11.37 percent (9% + 2/3%) / 85%.

On the other hand, the firm probably does business with the bank regularly and is likely to want to keep a minimum balance anyway, while the commitment fee may be regarded as an insurance payment to make certain that funds are available during the period specified and at the rate indicated. Should interest rates rise in the interim, the fee actually could reduce borrowing costs, unless the arrangement was on a floating rate basis.

The net costs will depend not only upon money market conditions at the moment and the credit strength of the borrower, but also upon the negotiating abilities of the parties involved. In the case of a small firm that does not have alternative sources available, the lending policy of the bank could call for terms that result in a very high effective borrowing rate. If interest is calculated on the original amount of the loan, for example, but the principal is repaid on an installment basis, the effective rate is generally close to twice the nominal or stated rate. In many areas of the country usury laws and banking tradition prevent such a discrepancy between the nominal and effective rates; in some states, however, corporations are deprived of the defense of usury, and the financial manager of a corporation with a relatively weak credit standing may find that he has to pay very high effective rates to obtain loans.

Since costs change over time, the financial manager should seek the maximum flexibility for his loan commitments. He may consider converting a revolving agreement into a term loan, so that he can fix his interest cost if he expects rates to rise. Or he might try to incorporate liberal prepayment terms if he expects rates to decline. When rate costs are compared, the opportunity of obtaining these attendant features cannot be overlooked.

(j) Loan Maturity

One of the important banking developments of the past two decades has been that commercial banks have become more willing to grant term loans with maturities of more than one year. As a result, the financial manager's ability to work out a lending program that suits the needs of his firm has been greatly strengthened. He can now develop an arrangement wherein a commercial bank assumes the intermediate segment of a loan and an insurance company takes up the latter portion. In effect, the bank finances the preliminary phase of a project that requires long-term financing, while the insurance company takes over the later term financing. This arrangement may be compared to a commercial bank's warehousing a mortgage for a savings institution. It holds the mortgage temporarily as collateral for a loan granted to the savings institution so that it can meet other commitments.

In general, New York City banks have led in the development of term loans. The reason for the more important role of the New York banks in this area is the fact that they service large customers located throughout the country and abroad. These big firms with widespread interests have a substantial demand for long-term funds which the New York banks, with their large capital, are both in a position to handle and under competitive pressure to accept.

From the lenders point of view, the increased willingness of banks to grant term loans is part of the general relaxation of their once rigid insistence on granting only short-term, self-liquidating loans. From the point of view of the borrower, this new orientation fills a genuine gap in business finance. For large firms, such borrowing may be a faster, less costly, and more convenient means of raising long-term funds, particularly in the five to eight year maturity range, than by entering the capital markets. For small firms that do not have ready access to the capital markets, term loans may be the only practical and reasonable means of obtaining long-term funds. The usefulness of term loans is augmented by the fact that through direct negotiation with lending banks, these loans can be tailored to meet the individual requirements of borrowers.

[5] ADDITIONAL CONSIDERATIONS OF SHORT-TERM NEGOTIATED SOURCES OF FUNDS

A number of additional considerations of short-term negotiated sources of funds should be noted, such as:

- the significance of negotiability;
- loans from affiliated individuals; and
- guaranties to support a loan.

These considerations are dealt with below:

(a) The Significance of Negotiability

Since the consummation of credit transactions depends upon the ready use of credit instruments, it is imperative that they be easily transferable. As we have seen, the willingness of one party to accept an instrument rests primarily on his confidence in the financial status and prospects of the other; additionally, he is likely to want assurance that the transfer is free fom legal entanglements.

If an instrument is to pass readily from hand to hand, it is clear that lenders cannot be expected to bear the time and expense of separately investigating each transaction in order to determine its legal status. This problem has been resolved by the enactment of negotiable instrument laws which facilitate the transfer of credit instruments. These laws relieve the recipients of apprehension regarding the defenses that could be advanced against the prior transferor. The Uniform Commercial Code has been adopted by the states, sometimes with modifications, to replace the former Negotiable Instrument Law. The reason for this change was to update the law in conformity with current business practices and to provide a uniform law across the nation. Nevertheless, variations occur as different court jurisdictions interpret the statute differently.

At common law, an assignment of property transfers no better title to the assignee than that possessed by the transferor. For example, let us assume that A, a manufacturer, sells some cleaning equipment on open account to B, who owns a laundry. A, in turn, has bought some supplies from C and transfers his claim against B in payment. B finds that the equipment does not perform in accordance with contractual specifications, asserts a breach of the original contract, and refuses to pay C, who has no better right than A because his contract is nonnegotiable.

In contrast to this situation, if B gives A a promissory note conforming with the requirements of negotiability, and A endorses this note to C, who accepts it in good faith for A's debt to him, the breach of contract defense is no longer valid, and C may recover in full from B. However, with respect to the original participants, A and B, breach of contract creates a good defense which would have prevented A from enforcing his claim against B. Negotiability therefore has the singular property of endowing a third party with better title than that possessed by the transferor. It frees the transferee from personal defenses arising from the consideration or from negligence in creating or executing the instrument. These defenses include fraud in the inducement, such as offering worthless stock as consideration; want of consideration; payment before maturity or to the wrong person; and lack of delivery of a completed instrument. The transferee is still vulnerable to the real defenses (those relating to the fact that no instrument was created in the eyes of the law) of forgery; alteration to the extent of the alteration; incapacity of the maker; fraud in the inception, such as trickery in the signing of an instrument; or voidance by the state, as of gambling contracts.

The Uniform Commercial Code provides that to be negotiable, an instrument must:

- be signed in writing by the maker or drawer; and
- contain an unconditional promise or order to pay a sum certain in money and no other promise, order, obligation or power given by the maker or drawer except as authorized . . .; and
- by payable on demand or at a definite time, and
- be payable to order or to bearer.[13]

For the person in possession of a negotiable instrument to obtain rights superior to those of the former holder or owner, he must be a holder in due course, that is, he must take the instrument:

- for value; and
- in good faith; and
- without notice that it is overdue or has been dishonored or of any defense against or claim to it on the part of any person.[14]

The maker of a negotiable promissory note or check and the acceptor (after acceptance) of a bill of exchange (draft) are primarily responsible on the instruments; the drawer of a draft and each general endorser of a draft, check or note are secondarily liable. In order to fix liability, the law provides that a negotiable instrument must be presented in a prompt and proper manner. If payment or acceptance is refused, prompt and proper notice of dishonor must be given to those secondarily liable. In the case of foreign bills, protest, which is a formal notice of dishonor, is required.

(b) Loans From Affiliated Individuals

It is not unusual for closely held corporations or partnerships to obtain working capital from those close to the business. The officers or major stockholders of the corporation or the principals of the partnership lend the enterprise money in order to strengthen its financial position. Thus bulwarked, the firm seeks additional funds from a commercial bank. Lending institutions regard these arrangements with skepticism; they feel that the loans of affiliated individuals to so-called thin firms should more properly be regarded as equity to strengthen the capital base. Before approving the loan applications of such an enterprise, commercial banks are likely to request that the officer or stockholder creditors subordinate their claims on the company's indebtedness to the bank's. Nonaffiliated creditors may also be persuaded to subordinate their claims when they feel that this is necessary for the enterprise to obtain a bank loan and that the additional funds will improve their own status in the long-run.

Banks may insist upon the inclusion of certain protective covenants in such agreements, for instance, that the subordinated creditor be prevented from suing for payment until the indebtedness to the bank has been paid; that all payments which would have been made to the subordinated creditor be diverted to the benefit of the lending bank, until the debt owed to it is satisfied; and that in the event of default the rights of the subordinated creditor be transferred to the bank and placed on the same plane as those of the other creditors.[15]

(c) Guaranties to Support a Loan

A lending institution that is reluctant to accept the credit of a business in exchange for a loan may be willing to do so if the business obtains the guaranty of other parties. This step may be considered necessary for various reasons:

- Creditors may make claims against all the property, both business and personal, of the members of a general partnership, but are only able to proceed against the business assets of a corporation. In a closely held enterprise, therefore, stockholders may make withdrawals that weaken their firm's position without exposing themselves to any personal financial risk. To safeguard against this, banks not uncommonly request that the officers or stockholders of closely held corporations guaranty any loans that are granted;
- A new business often has trouble obtaining capital. The father or close relative of a young person interested in such a venture may be willing to guarantee the loans until the undertaking is on a firm basis; and
- An established enterprise may experience a period of difficulty and require additional funds to help resolve its problems. Because of the company's deteriorated status, banks may be averse to granting a loan unless an outside guaranty can be obtained.

In order to evaluate the strength of the guarantor, the lending institution will probably request that he submit a personal financial statement which gives a summary of his assets, liabilities, and sources of income. The institution will also want to know any other contingent liabilities that he has outstanding and to have information on his banking relations and a description of his business activities. Since the loan is granted on the strength of the guarantor as well as on that of the borrower, this analysis is likely to be thorough.

Guaranties may be restricted to a particular note covering a prescribed period of time. An accommodation endorsement, for example, does not pass title but gives additional security to the instrument by means of the contingent liability of the endorser. Guaranties also may be continuing, applicable to all the borrower's debts to the lending party, or the amount of the guaranty may be limited.

A guaranty agreement is likely to contain provisions to protect the lender in several ways. For example, the guarantor waives notice of non-payment by the borrower; the bank obtains a lien on the deposits and other money and instruments of the guarantor that come into its possession; and, in the event of default, the bank may sell any of this property.

The guaranty and subordination devices are both intended to strengthen sufficiently the credit status of a company to permit it to exchange its credit for a loan. The guaranty accomplishes this purpose by directly adding the credit backing of another party; subordination achieves it by reducing the rank of an already existing obligation to an equity position from the viewpoint of the lender to whom the debt is subordinated. Additionally, if the corporation is using property that belongs to another party a hypothecation agreement may be provided; this agreement is executed between the owner of the property and the bank, giving the borrower permission to pledge the property as security for payment of the debt to the bank.

11.5   CHAPTER SUMMARY

The financial manager must make a decision on the appropriate mix between spontaneous and negotiated sources of short-term credit. In the former category we have considered such items as trade credit, wages payable and taxes payable. Under negotiated sources of short-term credit we studied short-term promissory notes, commercial paper, bankers' acceptances, and bank loans.

If the corporation is large and has a top credit rating, the chances are that interest costs will dictate that the choice be between using established commercial banking connections and selling short-term paper. The firm is assured of obtaining the lowest available rates, but the differentials in this area are not fixed, and in recent years firms have shown a greater willingness to compare the prime rate with rates available on short-term paper. They also weigh the advantages of strengthening existing banking connections through expanded borrowing against the benefits from employing the more impersonal relations of the short-term paper market.

When the creditworthiness of a firm is good, it can be assured of ranking high on any program for institutional allocation of funds, even during periods of tight money. For such a company, the problem is not so much availability as costs and flexibility. But for the company that occupies a lower rung on the credit status ladder, the question of availability is more important. For one thing, certain avenues, such as commercial paper, may be closed, and during periods of money stringency the firm may find that it is shut off from prior banking outlets.

This chapter concludes our discussion of short-term sources and uses of funds. While funds can, and often do, flow freely throughout the enterprise, short-term sources and uses have both a natural and analytical relationship to one another. Similarly, long-term sources and uses of funds are related and are dealt with in the next part of the text.

FOOTNOTES

1. Ned C. Hill and Kenneth D. Reiner, "Determining the Cash Discount in the Firm's Credit Policy," *Financial Management,* Spring 1979, pp. 68-73.
2. Kenneth E. Frantz and Jerry A. Viscione, "What Should You Do About Cash Discounts?," *Financial Management,* May 1976, pp. 30-37.
3. 2/30, net 60 - 60 days less 30 days = 30 days
   360/30 = 12. 12 x 2% = 24%   24%/.98 = 24.49
   2/10, net 60 - 60 days less 10 days = 50 days
   360/50 = 7.2. 7.2 x 2% = 14.4%   14.4%/.98 = 14.69
   24.49 - 14.69 = 9.80%

4. Rates and amounts are illustrative and not reflective of prevailing conditions.
5. Federal Reserve Bank of Richmond, *Instruments of the Money Market,* 1981, p. 110.
6. Financial Accounting Standards Board, *Statement of Financial Accounting Standards No. 6,* "Classification of Short-Term Obligations Expected to be Refinanced," May 1975, p. 4. This statement provides that a short-term obligation shall be excluded from current liabilities if "The enterprise's intent to refinance the short-term obligation on a long-term basis is supported by an ability to consummate the refinancing . . ."
7. See Chapter 8 for a discussion of the investment aspects of this instrument.
8. Both Moody's and Standard & Poor's provide ratings on commercial paper that has an original maturity of not in excess of nine months. Moody's employs the following three designations, all judged to be investment grade, to indicate the relative repayment capacity of issuers:
   Prime-1 Highest Quality
   Prime-2 Higher Quality
   Prime-3 High Quality
   Standard & Poor's employs more refined classifications as follows:
   "A"—Issues assigned this highest rating are regarded as having the greatest capacity for timely payment. Issues in this category are further refined with the designations 1, 2, and 3 to indicate the relative degree of safety.
   "A-1"—This designation indicates that the degree of safety regarding timely payment is very strong.
   "A-2"—Capacity for timely payment on issues with this designation is strong. However, the relative degree of safety is not as overwhelming as for issues designated "A-1."
   "A-3"—Issues carrying this designation have a satisfactory capacity for timely payment. They are, however, somewhat more vulnerable to the adverse effects of changes in circumstances than obligations carrying the higher designations.
   "B"—Issues rated "B" are regarded as having only an adequate capacity for timely payment. However, such capacity may be damaged by changing conditions or short-term adversities.
   "C"—This rating is assigned to short-term debt obligations with a doubtful capacity for payment.
   "D"—This rating indicates that the issue is either in default or is expected to be in default upon maturity.
9. Agway Corporation, a farmer's cooperative in the Northeast, in addition to using commercial paper and bank lines has a third short-term financing source—The Bank for Cooperatives. There are thirteen of these institutions, organized under the Farm Credit Act of 1933, which provide loans to farmer owned eligible cooperative associations engaged in agricultural activities. Although commercial paper generally fills 30 percent to 35 percent of its short-term borrowing needs, Agway attempts to obtain the lowest cost blend of the three elements it uses, while at the same time maintaining relationships and credit lines with banks. Starting about the spring of 1985, evidence emerged about the deteriorating financial condition of the Federal Farm Credit System as a result of illiquid loans stemming from a severely impaired agricultural situation.
10. In the retail trade, the term *revolving credit* may refer to a special kind of installment charge account which stores have promoted with considerable success. The details of these plans vary, but in general, any customer with a sufficiently good credit standing opens a charge account which entitles him to make purchases as long as his total debt to the store does not exceed an established maximum limit. Interest at a fixed monthly rate is charged on balances outstanding after a specified period. The growth of revolving credit accounts markedly expanded the

amount of accounts receivable carried by many stores and led them to explore the possibility of selling receivables to banks.

11. This discussion of the term loan and the protective provisions are from an excellent in-house memorandum provided by the Chase Manhattan Bank that is used in its training program.

12. Another form of secured financing of particular significance is accounts receivable financing. Usually referred to as factoring, this arrangement can utilize the services of either a commercial bank or a business finance company. As the ability of a company to factor its receivables is, to a large extent, dependent upon the quality of these receivables, factoring is developed in Chapter 10, where accounts receivable management is treated in depth.

13. *Uniform Commercial Code*, Section 3-104.

14. *Ibid.*, Section 3-302.

15. For example, assume that a company in liquidation receives for its assets $100,000, against which it has outstanding obligations of $100,000 to trade creditors, $50,000 to subordinated creditors, and $50,000 to a commercial bank. By virtue of this last provision, the bank is entitled to receive one-half of the assets, representing its own claim as well as that of the subordinated creditor, instead of the one-fourth portion it would otherwise obtain.

SUGGESTED READINGS

Arnold, J. H., "Banker's Acceptances: A Low-Cost Financing Choice," *Financial Executive*, July 1980.

Ben-Harim, M. and H. Levy, "Inflation and the Trade Credit Period," *Management Science*, June 1982.

Boldin, R. J. and P. D. Feeney, "The Increased Importance of Factoring," *Financial Executive*, April 1981.

——— and S. J. Mulholland, "Banker's Primer on Factoring," *Banker's Magazine*, January/February 1981.

Boullianne, E. C., "Factoring—A Financing Alternative for Clients," *Journal of Accountancy*, December 1980.

Bruder, C. W., "Credit Seesaw: Striking a Delicate Balance," *Credit and Financial Management*, November 1980.

DelGrand, M. A., "Factoring—A Misunderstood Source of Financing," *CA Magazine*, June 1980.

Garrison, J. S., Jr. and D. J. Dohren, "Simple Way to Borrow at Less Than Prime," *Credit and Financial Management*, June 1982.

Gates, W. T., "Aging Invoices—A Valuable Tool in Belt-Tightening Times," *Management World*, December 1981.

Hekman, C. R., "Effect of Trade Credit on Price and Price Level Comparisons," *Review of Economics and Statistics*, November 1981.

Hill, Ned C. and Kenneth D. Reiner, "Determining the Cash Discount in the Firm's Credit Policy," *Financial Management*, Spring 1979.

Humphrey, D. B. and D. T. Savage, "Bank Use of Downstreamed Commercial Paper and the Impact of Reserve Requirements in Controlling Liability Usage," *Journal of Economics and Business*, Winter 1981.

Hunt, W. S., "Change, Stress, and Credit Management," *Credit and Financial Management,"* March 1981.

Knobel, L. R., "Controversy Over Short-Term Bank Lines of Credit," *Mortgage Banker*, July 1980.

Mathis, S. and T. Ulrich, "Small Business Credit: The Competitive Factor," *Banker's Magazine*, January/February 1982.

Pinto, M., "Accounts Receivable Financing," *CPA Journal*, February 1982.

318

Rubin, David, "Bank Factoring Crossroads," *Credit and Financial Management,* December 1981.

Sartoris, W. L. and N. C. Hill, "Framework for Credit Policy Decisions," *Credit and Financial Management,* October 1980.

Savage, R. A., "Testing the Markov Chain Approach on Accounts Receivable," *Credit and Financial Management,* April 1981.

Westbrook, W. L. and C. D. Rawlins, "Bank Credit Commitments and Cash Management—Are Fees Really Cheaper Than Balances?" *Public Utilities Fortnightly,* August 27, 1981.

Williams, L., "Case for Industry Credit Groups," *Credit and Financial Management,* November 1981.

Wulff, J. K., "Impact of Inflation on Credit Decisions," *Credit and Financial Management,* September 1980.

PART IV
MANAGEMENT
OF
INTERMEDIATE
AND LONG-TERM
SOURCES OF
FUNDS

This is the start of a new part of this book (containing four chapters) dealing with intermediate and long-term sources of funds. The first of these chapters analyzes the focal point where suppliers and users of these funds meet (Financial Markets). The next two chapters deal with the two basic methods of acquiring such funds—externally (Financing in the Primary Markets) and internally (Internal Funds and Dividend Policy). Finally, the last chapter in this part of the book integrates and puts much of the material from the first three chapters together and looks at considerations relevant to a firm's entire spectrum of intermediate and long-term financing decisions (Long-Term Financing).

12

FINANCIAL MARKETS

12.1 INTRODUCTION

Traditionally, the financial manager is internally oriented, concentrating on funds control. This myopic approach tends to yield, with experience and advancement to a greater awareness of the markets for external funds. Whether the stimulus comes from the desire to place surplus funds or from the need to obtain additional financial resources, the modern higher echelon financial manager now finds it useful to have a sound understanding of the facilities and functions of the money and capital markets.

Financial managers are concerned with money, and it is in the financial markets that the forces of supply and demand for funds meet. Money is the stock in trade and the price of money—interest—is determined by the flow of funds into, among, and out of the financial markets. Often, the initial evidence of a change in economic activity, of a turn from boom to recession or from recession to recovery, can be perceived by the very sensitive movements in the markets for funds. Apart from the operating need to invest surplus funds or borrow money, the financial manager, who closely follows and understands trends in the money and capital markets, has his finger on the pulse of the economy, and will be able to evaluate economic developments.

12.2 SAVINGS AND INVESTMENT

The total output of goods and services (Gross National Product or GNP) in a given period yields a money income to those who produce it (individuals, business and government) which can be spent (consumed) or saved. That part which is spent will call forth a volume of goods and services in the subsequent period. Whether the part that is saved makes a positive contribution to the economy depends on what is done with it.

If the savings are all put to work productively, the GNP will expand in the subsequent period. As output grows, employment increases, income levels rise, and further savings occur which, in turn, may be utilized for productive investment. Thus, the process of capital formation takes place in a sort of cycle—but clearly a beneficial one.

If, on the other hand, as in a time of recession, such savings as occur are held idle, hoarded, and not invested productively through fear or lack of opportunity, output, employment, and income will fall. Savings will decline thereby further restricting the investment potential. Thus a downward economic cycle results until equilibrium is restored and the base is established for business to explore investment opportunities once more.

12.3   THE DIMENSION OF THE FINANCIAL MARKETS

A complex arrangement has been formulated to provide for the smooth and rapid flow of funds from savers to users through the facilities of the financial markets. Funds are moved so readily in these markets that their customary division into money and capital segments seems to have lost much of its meaning. Nevertheless, for purposes of exposition, we will maintain this traditional distinction which is based on the period of time over which the claims to funds change hands.

[1] THE MONEY MARKET

The money market is an amorphous constellation of institutions, arrangements, and communications, all aimed at lending and investing funds for relatively short periods. It is many faceted. It is the market in which banks set up riskless one day loans to each other; the market where large corporations use their excess liquidity to buy Treasury bills or negotiable time certificates of deposit; the market in which commercial banks make 180 day loans to small firms; the market where corporations buy U.S. Government securities from dealers who agree to repurchase the securities several days later; the market in which some commercial banks borrow from the Federal Reserve; and the market where the Federal Reserve buys or sells U.S. Government securities.

The money market is local, national, and international, where acceptance credit helps finance foreign trade. It is a personal market in which a speculator borrows to buy securities on margin. It is an open, impersonal market where corporations issue commercial paper directly or through dealers. Transactions range from the billion dollars which change hands for 24 hours in the federal funds market to the $10,000 loan by a small commercial bank to a belt manufacturer.

[2] THE CAPITAL MARKET

In the capital market, the users of long-term debt or equity funds obtain them from investors such as individuals, other corporations, commercial banks, insurance companies, pension funds, and others—who have surplus funds on which they wish to earn a return. The users are mostly corporations and government units which desire additional funds either to expand output or to undertake capital improvements. Funds transfers are made by means of instruments such as stocks, bonds, notes, and mortgages.

The capital market may be viewed in various ways. A common distinction is between the primary market, where the instruments are originally issued and the secondary market, where they are subsequently traded. Within these sectors, other differences may exist, depending upon whether the issuer is the Treasury, a Federally sponsored government agency, a local government, or a corporation.

In general, the primary market is a market only in the loosest sense; it has no definable geographic dimensions and its organization and components vary widely. Parts of the secondary market are similarly broad based and interconnected through communications systems, while others, such as the organized securities exchanges, conduct their transactions in specified localities on trading floors.

[3] INTERRELATIONSHIPS IN THE MONEY AND CAPITAL MARKETS

As mentioned previously, the distinction between the money and capital markets is not firm. We have already seen that short-term loans may be constantly renewed, thereby becoming intermediate or long-term obligations. On the other hand, long-term borrowers characteristically like to reserve the privilege to convert a long-term debt into a relatively short-term one.

The extent to which institutions straddle both markets tends to blur differences. Commercial banks, for example, usually regarded as pre-eminently money market institutions, also participate extensively in the capital markets. The growth of their time accounts have encouraged an interest in term credits of various sorts. In their trust functions, they are active in both the new issue and secondary securities markets. They underwrite Treasury offerings and a substantial volume of state and municipal issues. They arrange private placements, own discount brokerage houses and, if Congress relaxes Glass-Steagall restrictions, will further extend their activities in the securities field.

Corporations also straddle the two markets. They enter the money market on both the supply and the demand side. Short-term working capital financing may ultimately be consolidated by floating a long-term debt issue. Some companies borrow from banks; others, like sales finance companies, sell commercial paper directly. On the other hand, corporations generating large volumes of funds internally are able to extend substantial short-term trade credit, and in many cases, invest surplus amounts in U.S. Treasury bills, commercial paper, or negotiable certificates of deposit. Through repurchase agreements, corporations also provide funds to Government securities dealers. When interest rates are low, there is an incentive for corporations to borrow at long-term in the capital markets; when interest rates rise significantly, it is expedient to borrow temporarily in the money market.

Securities firms—in granting margin loans, holding their customers' credit balances, serving as dealers in short-term instruments, and borrowing from commercial banks—have played a major money market role for a long time. They have added to this role by creating money market funds, issuing credit cards, and directly acquiring limited functioning commercial banks. The securities firms have also been long-time participants in the capital market through providing advice to their corporate clients, underwriting their securities, and executing transactions.

The Federal Reserve, which has a major impact on the money market as it conducts its responsibility to control credit and the money supply, also influences the capital market. While the Fed's initial impact is felt on commercial bank reserves, this effect spreads rapidly to the capital market both because of the commercial banks' role in the capital market and because of the structure of interest rates. In a period of brisk expansion, if the Fed is tightening credit and thus squeezing member bank reserves, the commercial banks will sell off part of their bond portfolios to maximize available short-term funds to business. They will also cease to be securities purchasers at such times. The rise in short-term rates quickly spreads to the long-term structure. The price of high-grade bonds will fall as yields rise and coupons on new issues will have to be adjusted upward. Since so much of the flows and shifts between money and capital markets is caused by interest rate changes and differentials, it may be well to explore briefly once more the structure of interest rates in the money and capital markets (see also 8.4[7](b)).

[4] THE STRUCTURE OF INTEREST RATES

Interest is the price of money, and interest rates reflect the relative forces of supply and demand for the type of funds the particular interest rate is pricing. There are a large number of rates in the money and capital markets. These rates are sensitive, among other factors, to the following conditions:

- inflation;
- Federal Reserve policy;
- money supply;
- business loan demand; and
- Federal deficits.

Interest rates are varying and volatile. A focal rate because of the riskless character of the instrument is that on Treasury bills; this rate, as seen in Figure 12.1 has fluctuated sharply in recent years. The prime rate, presumably the rate commercial banks charge their most credit-worthy customers, has been used as a base to which other rates are related. Since banks frequently lend money to large corporations below their posted prime, this rate has lost much of its significance. Smaller companies often find themselves paying more for bank loans than their larger competitors.

Shifting conditions in the different money and capital market sectors, as well as movements of the business cycle, often cause changing relationships among various interest rates. It might be expected that short-term rates would run lower than long-term rates since liquidity has value and presumably the more distant the future, the greater the risk. Yet, there have been times, as discussed previously and portrayed in Figure 12.2, when short-term rates have been higher. Generally, towards the top of a boom short-term rates tend to rise proportionately more than long-term rates and the spread between the two tends to narrow.

Changing interest rate differentials cause funds to be shifted from short-term to long-term markets or vice versa. To a large extent, this condition is true because corporations often have considerable latitude in meeting their funds needs. They may postpone long-term debt issues by short-term borrowing if short-term rates are substantially lower than long-term; or, if the reverse is true, they may sell bonds and use the new funds to finance inventory increases or even to invest the loan proceeds in short-term assets. These funds shifts if massive enough, may in turn cause further changes in the interest rate structure.

FIGURE 12.1 *Short-term interest rates in the money market*

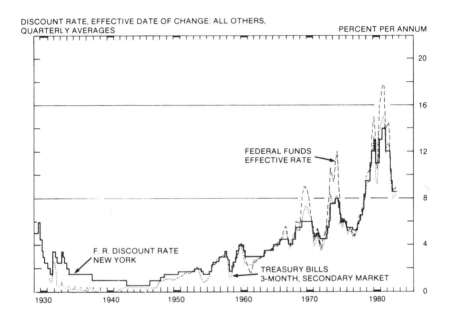

Source: Board of Governors of the Federal Reserve System, *Historical Chart Book,* 1983, p. 98.

The Federal Reserve is the primary influence on interest rate levels in the money market. Through its open market operations and rediscount policy, it can raise or lower rates by the impact on the reserve position of banks. Since the 1970's the Fed has sought to attain its policy objectives through achieving targeted growth rates of the money supply. For this purpose, it links the movements in its policy target to designated policy instruments which have varied over the years. Thus, if the money supply, its policy target, is growing at more than a desired rate, the Fed could use its policy instruments to put upward pressure on interest rates which, in turn, would decrease the demand for money and decelerate the growth of the money supply. Throughout the 1970's, the Fed used the federal funds rate as its principal policy instrument to achieve its policy target. On October 6, 1979, it announced a major shift whereby it focused more attention on nonborrowed reserves and less attention on day-to-day fluctuations in the federal funds rate.[1] While the Fed makes considerable use of these quantitative measures, it has not abandoned the application of interpretive judgment.

FIGURE 12.2 *Long- and short-term interest rates*

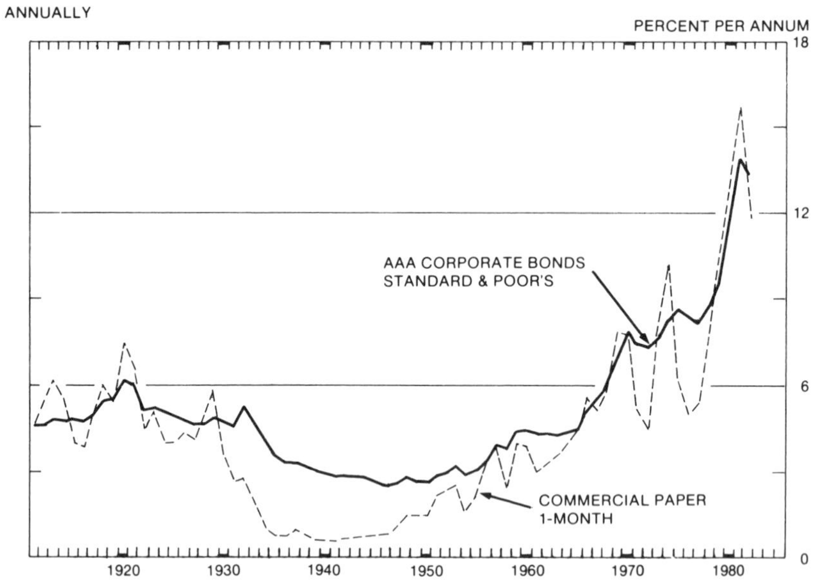

ANNUALLY

PERCENT PER ANNUM

Source: Board of Governors of the Federal Reserve System, *Historical Chart Book,* 1983, p. 96.

[5] THE INTERNATIONALIZATION OF THE FINANCIAL MARKETS

At one time, a U.S. corporation desiring to issue long-term securities would consider only the U.S. capital market. Presently, though, it may look as well to overseas markets which have become sufficiently international to permit financing on a relatively favorable basis and in substantial amounts. For example, when Texaco Inc. desired to fund the huge short-term debt it ran up as a result of its 1983 purchase of Getty Oil Co., it found that slumping U.S. securities markets prevented it from making suitable arrangements. As a result, it turned to the international market, offering $800 million of convertible Eurobonds; the bonds sold out quickly and the issue was raised to $1 billion. Reviewing the success of the offering, Texaco's senior assistant treasurer commented, "I don't want to demean the U.S. capital markets, but we felt Europe was the place to go."[2]

Between 1973 and about the first five months of 1984, U.S. corporations borrowed $32 billion abroad, $7.4 billion of it in 1983. Almost 80 percent of these Eurobonds were denominated in dollars.[3] Not only may such securities be made payable in different currencies, but they also can take many different forms.

In the first quarter of 1984, floating-rate notes represented 53 percent of the $15.3 billion of new Eurodollar offerings.[4] Contributing to the rapid growth of the Eurobond market was the substantial absence of regulation, the interest of syndicate managers in developing good relationships with issuers, and the freedom from the U.S. 30 percent withholding tax.[5]

A new element was injected into the picture by the repeal of the U.S. withholding tax in the Tax Reform Act of 1984. This change enabled all overseas investors, for the first time, to purchase bonds of the U.S. Government, its agencies, and U.S. corporations on a tax-free basis. As a result, U.S. corporations no longer found it necessary to issue bonds through such places as the Netherlands Antilles in order to circumvent the Internal Revenue Service. More significantly, the tax change creates new competition to the Eurobond market, although U.S. corporations are still likely to find financing opportunities abroad.

Reflecting expanding activity in U.S. Government securities, 24 primary Government dealers were operating abroad in June 1984 and it was expected that the rest would follow because of the repeal of the withholding tax. It was also believed that the growth in the U.S. Treasury market would buoy activity on the London International Financial Futures Exchange (LIFFE) which started trading futures contracts on Treasury bonds in June 1984.

Portfolio managers in the U.S. have manifest interest in introducing geographic diversification into their portfolios. Formerly, the only practical means of accomplishing this objective to any extent had been through the purchase of American Depository Receipts (ADRs), representing foreign securities listed by this means on U.S. exchanges. Improved communication systems and the expanded liquidity of various foreign exchanges, however, now enable portfolio managers to purchase securities directly on these exchanges.

Foreign governments and exchanges have also shown a desire to develop closer relations with the U.S. markets. Thus, with the concurrence of the finance ministries of the various foreign governments, there have been introduced into the U.S. securities markets, different investment companies that specialize in the purchase respectively of Japanese, Mexican, and Korean securities. A further tie between the U.S. markets and those of a foreign country is seen in the linking of the Chicago Mercantile Exchange (MERC) and the Singapore International Monetary Exchange. The MERC is the first U.S. exchange to enable traders to buy and sell contracts interchangeably on its own floor and on an exchange in another country. Further movements in this direction may eventually lead to round-the-clock trading.

12.4   THE SECONDARY MARKETS

The secondary markets have recently been experiencing such dramatic changes that it is difficult to keep abreast of developments. We divide our presentation into (1) the markets for securities (stock and bonds) including the development of the national market system, the futures market and the options market; and (2) the market for mortgages.

[1] THE MARKETS FOR SECURITIES

The secondary market for securities—the stock exchanges and the over-the-counter markets—are important elements that supplement the primary market. They provide the trading forums, the liquidity, the familiarity with issues and companies, and the price and value determining arena which encourage public interest in security investment and which aid new financing.

When an institution purchases a security it is buying a claim to assets or to income, and its faith in this claim will be enhanced or diminished depending on the ease or difficulty of liquidating the investment on short notice. Doubtless many investors would be hesitant to buy securities if they did not feel reasonably confident that a ready market was available in which they could dispose of their holdings. It seems reasonable to conclude that the development of the now elaborate machinery for trading in securities came about in response to a felt need. Indeed, the history of the secondary market's growth bears out this observation. Often, prices for new issues in the primary market are determined by prevailing prices in the secondary market. Mergers and acquisition take place by exchanging shares, the ratio for which is usually determined in the secondary market.

The secondary market provides facilities for the maintenance of free, close, and continuous prices. They are free in that any security's trading price, in the absence of illegal manipulation, is governed by the freely competing forces of supply and demand. They are close in that the spread between the price bid for a security and the price at which it is offered for sale normally is relatively narrow. They are continuous in that successive sales ordinarily are made at relatively small price variations.

(a) The Stock Exchanges

A stock exchange must be registered with the SEC as a national exchange unless its limited number of transactions makes it exempt. Once registered, an exchange falls within the authority of the SEC which has issued a substantial number of regulations to fulfill its responsibilities under the Securities Exchange Act of 1934.

The major stock exchange dealing in stocks and bonds (although most bond trading occurs in the over-the-counter market) is the New York Stock Exchange (NYSE). The American Stock Exchange (Amex) is a distant second followed, in the latter part of 1985 by the Midwest Stock Exchange, the Pacific Stock Exchange, the Philadelphia Stock Exchange, the Boston Stock Exchange, and the Cincinnati Stock Exchange.

The gateway for trading on an exchange is the listing standard which is most stringent on the NYSE. To obtain a listing a company submits an application to the exchange. Trading in the stock exchanges is by means of auction. Thus, a broker who has a sell order cannot simply match it with the buy order of another customer. Any lower price submitted by the specialist (discussed below) or by a competing customer of another firm will displace the stock of the first broker's selling customer. The sell order also will be matched against the highest bids that have been submitted. The auction process is continuous so that the completion of one auction may be followed by the immediate start of another in the same stock. The auction is also two sided with buyers competing by raising their bids and sellers by lowering their offers.

In general, trading on the stock exchanges revolves around the specialist who is expected to maintain a fair and orderly market in the stocks assigned to him. He does so by purchasing or selling shares for his own account, when there is a wide disparity between the prevailing bid and offered prices, thereby serving in the capacity of a dealer. The specialist also serves as a broker, buying and selling for others. Thus, customers may submit orders to purchase a stock below the prevailing price or to sell above it. These orders that cannot be executed currently are typically left with the specialist, who enters them in his "book" on the basis of price and time priorities. This combined broker dealer function has often been criticized as representing an inherent conflict of interest. In contrast, the London Stock Exchange traditionally separated these functions by permitting orders to be taken only by brokers, while actual executions were handled by dealers, termed jobbers. In July 1984, however,, the London Stock Exchange's ruling council unanimously approved plans to allow the same firm to both take orders from investors and execute trades on the stock market.

Except for certain inactive and very high priced stocks, the unit of trading on the stock exchanges is a "round lot" consisting of 100 shares. This traditional basis is being breached in several ways. For one thing, institutions, which are a dominant market factor, typically trade in thousands rather than hundreds of shares. Such so called "block" transactions must be handled with care because otherwise they could seriously upset the market for the stock being traded. In these cases, the executing broker will seek to find parties on the other side before bringing the order to the floor of the stock exchange. If the institution desires to sell the stock and the bro'.. is unsuccessful in finding buyers for all of the shares, he will either position that portion of the block which remains (that is, purchase it for the brokerage house's own account) or request the seller to accept a lower price. Then again, to expedite transactions, the various exchanges have developed special methods for handling relatively small orders.

These methods are of interest because they indicate the competitive pressures on the exchanges to speed their trading operations and the concern of the SEC that these accelerated approaches do not breach the auction system. Of these methods, three represent automatic execution systems. These include the Pacific Stock Exchange's SCOREX, the Philadelphia Stock Exchange's PACE, and the Midwest Stock Exchange's MAX. All three systems provide small order automatic executions at prices based on the inside consolidated quotation and account for a significant portion of the trading volume on the three exchanges. SCOREX and MAX afford specialists and other floor trading interests an opportunity to improve on the proposed automatic execution price, while the failure of PACE to provide such an opportunity has been criticized by the SEC. The Boston Stock Exchange has developed a Guaranteed Execution System whereby the specialist guarantees executions at the best consolidated quotation to all agency orders up to a designated size. This system does not afford the advantages of an automatic execution and therefore has not received the same volume of small orders as other regional exchanges. The NYSE's Designated Order Turnaround system and the Amex's Post Execution Report system directly route to specialists those orders that would not benefit significantly from individual broker handling and are thereafter executed by the traditional auction process. The NYSE has also been operating on a pilot basis its Registered Representative Rapid Response Service (4R) which allows a registered representative in a participating broker dealer firm to execute in its office an order up to a designated size at the prevailing consolidated quotation and then to report the execution to the NYSE specialist in the stock who guarantees that price for the customer. The SEC has expressed concern about this approach because it does not include any mechanism for such orders to interact with buying and selling interests on the floor.[6]

The Cincinnati Stock Exchange is a tiny market. In the latter part of 1985, its trading volume was only a fraction of one percent of that of the NYSE. Nevertheless, it is of special interest because the Cincinnati Exchange operates an electronic communications network through which its members can compete on an auction basis by entering bids and offers without appearing on the floor of the Cincinnati or any other exchange. The Instinet system, operated by the Institutional Networks Corporation, in the latter part of 1985 also accounted for a fraction of one percent of the transactions volume on the NYSE. But like Cincinnati, it is of interest for special reasons. Instinet, through its computer network, permits direct execution of orders on some 3,500 exchanges listed and over-the-counter securities at the 1,000 share level or below. The significance of these tiny operations is in the possibilities they present for further automating securities trading.

(b) The Over-the-Counter (OTC) Market

Perhaps the OTC market may be best defined negatively as representing securities transactions executed outside the stock exchanges. There is no defined physical location to this market. Purchases and sales are effected through the facilities of a large number of securities firms of varying sizes which keep in touch with each other through an intricate network of private wires, telephone lines, and a sophisticated electronic system. While members of the stock exchanges are included among these firms, most of them are not members of any registered exchange. Dealings are subject to the rules of the National Association of Securities Dealers (NASD), which is the self-regulating organization in this area, under the jurisdiction of the SEC.

There are approximately 28,000 stocks solely in the OTC market. Trading is centered in the market maker, who serves as a wholesale dealer, indicating a willingness to buy or sell by maintaining quotations on both sides of the market. The liquidity of a specific stock depends upon the market maker's role which may range from the sporadic activity of individual dealers to continuous competition among 30 or more dealers in the large, active issues. Unlike the specialist, the OTC market maker is not assigned the formal responsibility of maintaining a fair and orderly market, but competitive pressures lead him to keep reasonable pricing standards in the stocks for which he holds himself responsible.

The OTC market has been experiencing dramatic changes. Historically, it was conducted through a cumbersome process based on a package of sheets that show the dealers making a market in each stock and their current quotations. Trading in the great bulk of the nation's stocks, representing primarily small companies, is still conducted in this archaic fashion. Since the sheets are colored pink, it is customary to apply the designation "pink sheets" to this sector of the OTC market. Activity in these stocks differs markedly, ranging from those in which no transactions have occurred for some time and a dealer may show only a bid or offer, to stocks in which there is current interest and various dealers may be providing competing bids and offers.

In February 1971, the NASD introduced its National Association of Securities Dealers Automated Quotation (NASDAQ) System, which enables price quotations to be displayed on a real time basis on terminals located in subscribers' offices. As a result, the market for the several thousand OTC stocks admitted to the System has been improved considerably. Nevertheless, NASDAQ is a pricing system, and a subscriber still has to communicate directly with the market maker to complete the transaction. Accordingly, the NASD introduced a program, called the Computer Assisted Execution System (CAES), to enhance NASDAQ by providing it with order routing and execution capability. On April 21, 1981, the SEC mandated the establishment of an automated interface between CAES and the Intermarket Trading System (ITS) which, as discussed further below, is a communications arrangement for the nation's securities markets. On May 27, 1982, the linkage between CAES and the ITS got underway on an experimental basis.[7] In a deregulatory move designed to promote competition, the SEC, in September 1985, approved a plan to enable each of the nation's stock exchanges to begin trading on January 1, 1986 in 25 national market system stocks currently traded through NASDAQ.

(c) The National Market System

In the letter of transmittal accompanying its Institutional Investor Study on March 10, 1971, the SEC for the first time introduced the concept of a "central market system." The following year, the Commission put some flesh on the skeleton of its initial idea. "The term 'central market system' refers to a system of communications by which the various elements of the marketplace, be they exchanges or over-the-counter markets, are tied together. It also includes a set of rules governing the relationships which will prevail among market participants."[8]

Several years thereafter, the Securities Acts Amendments of 1975 introduced into the Exchange Act Section 11A which, among other things, directs the Commission ". . . to facilitate the establishment of a national market system for securities . . ." In carrying out this directive, the SEC expressed the belief that development of the system ". . . should remain essentially an evolutionary process," but at the same time cautioned that "continued uncertainty as to the . . . principles upon which a . . . system must be based, and the role the Commission will assume in shaping that system, is not in the best interests of the securities industry or the investing public." Accordingly, the Commission also ". . . set forth with some particularity its views as to those steps which it believes must be taken . . . to facilitate development of the kind of national market system envisioned by the Congress . . ."[9]

This combined policy of prodding the securities industry to act while allowing these actions to take place in an evolutionary fashion resulted in much give and take. By the early 1980's, however, the major elements of a national market system had been put together. These included:[10]

- A Consolidated Transaction Reporting System, which collects and reports last sale data on all stocks listed on the seven major U.S. stock exchanges and the third market (the OTC market in exchange listed stocks);

- A Composite Quotation System, which collects and displays in each participating market center the prices and the number of shares currently bid and asked for each listed stock in each of the market centers;
- A National Clearance and Settlement System, which permits single account clearance and settlement for brokers and dealers in the clearing organization of their choice; and
- An Intermarket Communication System, which is represented by ITS. This system is operated jointly by certain national securities exchanges and the NASD, and is authorized by the SEC as a national market system facility.[11] The system enables brokers and dealers in any of the participating markets to seek an execution in any of the others when a better price is available there.

Section 11A of the Exchange Act also directs the SEC to designate by rule the securities that are "qualified for trading in the national market system." It was clearly the congressional intent that such securities should be actively traded and represent relatively big companies. In seeking to develop the standards, however, the SEC found that there was disagreement as to whether over-the-counter securities that met the standards should automatically be included or should be included at the request of the company's management. Eventually, in February 1981, the Commission adopted a rule that incorporates a compromise between these two points of view. The rule provides two sets of standards, based upon such things as the size of the company, number of shareholders, and the trading activity of its stock. Tier one stocks that meet the higher standards are automatically included; tier two stocks meeting less stringent standards are included at the option of the issuer. Following adoption of the rule, a substantial increase occurred in the number of issuers applying for inclusion.

The national market system has not significantly changed the framework of the U.S. securities markets; the NYSE still does over 80 percent of share volume in its listed stocks. The increased competition engendered, however, has led to new operating methods. For example, the most frequently offered explanation for the loss of small order flow by the NYSE is that the small order handling systems operated by the exchanges in Chicago, Philadelphia and California as well as the NASD's Computer Assisted Execution Systems, that were described previously, have been siphoning business away from New York. This condition led the NYSE to develop its 4R system that provides a more competitive and cost effective small order service.

(d) The Futures Market

We have previously described the rise of a market in interest rate futures and illustrated how the financial manager could use this market to hedge against possible advancing interest rates (when embarking on a financing program) and to lock in current rates (when implementing an investment program in a period of expected declining rates) (See Chapter 8). The introduction of futures in stock indexes provides the financial manager with an additional tool that could be used in the management of the equity portion of his company's pension fund portfolio. Thus, he could immediately participate in a bull market by purchasing the desired amount of a stock index future. Similarly, he could hedge an existing equity portfolio against a possible market decline through the sale of a stock index future. Having illustrated the uses of financial futures previously, in the present section we provide a general description of how this market operates.

[i] STANDARDIZING THE TERMS OF THE CONTRACT TRADED: The traditional means of hedging commodities, including money, is through a forward contract which is entered into between the specific contracting parties. Such an arrangement has the clear benefit of being able to tailor the contract to the needs of the participants. On the other hand, it suffers the serious disadvantages of illiquidity because of the possible difficulty of locating a buyer or seller.

Through standardizing the terms of the contract, an instrument is created that may be traded on an impersonal basis in an open market, thereby providing the opportunity to attract the multitude of buyers and sellers that makes liquidity possible. The futures contract accomplishes this objective. It is a binding agreement to make or take delivery of a designated type and grade of commodity, during a specified future month, at a currently agreed upon price, and in accordance with the terms specified by the exchange where the commodity is traded.

The one variable in the contract that still has to be established is that of price. This is determined through the typical auction process by open outcry in a futures exchange that functions as a self-regulatory agency. The major domestic exchanges that currently trade financial futures include: the Chicago Board of Trade; the Chicago Mercantile Exchange, operating through its two divisions, the International Monetary Market and the Index and Option Market; the New York Futures Exchange; and the Kansas City Board of Trade.

In the latter part of 1985, the most active contract by far was that for Treasury bonds; the open interest (outstanding contracts not offset by opposite transactions or fulfilled by delivery in these bonds traded on the Chicago Board of Trade on September 16, 1985 was for 224,969 contracts. The most actively traded futures index was that on the Standard & Poor's 500 Composite Stock Index traded on the Chicago Mercantile Exchange; its open interest was for 73,444 contracts. In contrast, the open interest for the Composite Market Futures Index, traded in the New York Futures Exchange, a unit of the NYSE, was for 11,196 contracts and that for the Kansas City Value Futures Index, traded on the Kansas City Board of Trade was for 12,393 contracts.

The Chicago Board of Trade (CBOT) made its entry into the market for stock index futures with the Major Market Index futures contract which closely tracks the Dow Jones Industrial Average. The CBOT began trading the Major Market Index (comprising 20 stocks of major corporations) on July 23, 1984. This contract was the result of a joint agreement between the CBOT and the Amex which calls for cooperative efforts between the two exchanges for the trading of options and futures on the Index. The Amex introduced options on the Index in 1983.[12] Several of the smaller commodity exchanges, such as the Commodity Exchange and the MidAmerica Commodity Exchange, have also introduced contracts in financial futures. The various exchanges have been actively seeking to develop new products that they hope will attract investment attention.

The self-regulatory functions of the futures exchanges are conducted under the jurisdiction of the Commodity Futures Trading Commission (CFTC), established in 1974 by amendment to the Commodity Exchange Act, the legislation that provides for regulation of futures trading. In administering this Act, the CFTC is required to maintain communications with the SEC, Treasury and the Federal Reserve. The authority of the CFTC covers all futures as well as financial futures and options on securities which are traded for future delivery. The National Futures Association, under the jurisdiction of the CFTC, provides a self-regulatory program for firms that are not members of an exchange but are engaged in soliciting futures accounts from the public.[13]

[ii] ENSURING CONTRACTUAL INTEGRITY: In a forward contract between two specific parties, there is some uncertainty regarding the possibility that one of them might not live up to the required terms. To a large extent, this uncertainty is eliminated in the futures contract by the interposition of the clearing house between them. Accordingly, the linkage between the original parties is severed and the clearing house becomes the party on the other side to both the buyer and the seller. This arrangement achieves two major results: (1) each party may engage in subsequent transactions without concern about the attitude of the original buyer or seller; (2) the clearing house becomes the guarantor of the opposite side of the transaction while the positions remain open.[14] Most U.S. clearing houses are separate affiliated corporations although a few futures clearing houses are organized as departments within the exchange.

Additionally, all open futures positions are "marked to the market" on a daily basis. At the close of each day's trading, the clearing house notifies each member firm of its net gains or losses in open positions and debits or credits the firm's margin account accordingly. These changes are determined by settlement prices established by the exchanges on the basis of the transactions executed at the close of each trading day. The member firms, in turn, make similar adjustments to the margin accounts of their customers.

To help provide price stability, the exchanges impose limits on the extent to which prices may change from one day to the next. Presumably, these limits afford market participants the opportunity to reflect on situations provoking unusual price movements. In special circumstances, an exchange may widen its limits.

[iii] THE SIGNIFICANCE OF MARGIN: In the futures market, the margin concept is different from that in the securities market. In the latter case, margin represents a partial payment for a security, with the securities firm loaning the difference to its customer, on which interest is charged, so that full payment can be made against current delivery. In the futures market, margin represents a good faith deposit to ensure performance of the contract. Since a loan is not involved, no interest is called for and, indeed, the futures position is likely to be reversed rather than actually paid.

Each futures exchange establishes and may change the minimum amount of margin that a customer must deposit initially and thereafter maintain with the securities firm with which it does business. Each firm, in turn, must deposit and maintain margin with the clearing house of which it is a member as determined by that organization. Changes in market volatility may induce requirements for market adjustments.

Investors may withdraw amounts that are in excess of the initial margin required. Conversely, they must post additional margin if the account falls below the prescribed maintenance level (marking to the market). Reflecting the fact that margin is primarily an indication of good faith, the requirements are very low, running to a very small percentage of the size of the contract. As a result, the leverage potential is considerable.

[iv] DELIVERY: For all current futures contracts, except those on stock indexes, a seller may obtain delivery by submitting a request to his securities firm which notifies the clearing house. That organization, in turn, makes an assignment to the member with the oldest position in the contract and submits its name to the selling member. The two firms then deal directly with each other. A buyer, on the other hand, who still holds a futures contract at the last delivery date, will automatically be assigned delivery.

Delivery procedures are essentially similar among the different contracts and exchanges, with the major difference being that on some contracts, such as those on Treasury bonds and notes, a variety of issues may be delivered. For example, the deliverable grade of a Treasury bond provides for a maturity of at least 15 years, if noncallable, and at least 15 years to the first call date, if callable. The delivery price is based on the settlement price converted to a standard eight percent 20-year bond. Since a number of different issues meet the deliverable grade, conversion factors are worked out which permit the ready calculation of the delivery price. The availability of a range of deliverable issues also means that the buyer may assume that the seller will deliver the one which is least costly to obtain in the cash market.

Only in a very small percentage of cases, however, is delivery actually made. The great bulk of contracts are terminated by the participant taking an offsetting position. Thus, to cancel his contract, the buyer will execute a sale, while the seller will enter a purchase contract. With respect to stock indexes, delivery, of course, is impossible and settlement on contracts held at the last day of trading is made on the basis of the difference between the price level of open positions and the closing price of the index on that day. Up to that time, contracts would have been marked to the market daily.

[v] RELATIONSHIPS IN THE CASH AND FUTURES MARKETS: To some extent, prices in the futures market may be influenced by investor expectations regarding economic conditions at the specified future dates. Primarily, however, these futures prices are based on prices in the cash market, with the differential for the most part dependent upon the so called "cost of carry," which represents the net income received or net cost incurred by holding a cash position. The carry is positive if the income received exceeds the costs involved; the carry is negative if costs exceed income. In general, costs are represented by the short-term rate at which it is assumed the buyer borrowed funds to acquire his investment in the cash market, while the income is that derived from the investment.

The term, "basis," is used to describe the difference between the price of an instrument in the cash market and its indicated cash equivalent price in the futures market. As the delivery date approaches, the basis narrows and eventually disappears when that date is reached (convergence). In order to permit hedging to take place, the basis must remain reasonably in line. At any particular time, however, deviations may occur which give rise to a sort of arbitrage opportunity that tends to keep the prices in line.

Changing economic conditions affect price relationships in the futures market and create opportunities to benefit from these changes if they can be correctly anticipated. A typical technique is spreading which involves the simultaneous purchase and sale of different but related futures contracts. Spreading may be done in different ways, such as between: nearby and deferred delivery months of the same instrument on the same exchange (March and December Treasury bonds on the CBOT); different but related instruments on the same exchange (December Treasury bills and December bank certificate of deposits on the International Mercantile Market); and different but related items on different exchanges (September NYSE Composite Futures on the NYSE and September S&P 500 Futures on the Chicago Mercantile Exchange).

As an illustration of spreading, assume an unusual downsweeping interest rate curve with long rates below short rates. In such circumstances, there would be a negative spread. Accordingly, let us say that March Treasury bonds were selling at 61 and the December bonds at 63. Expecting the curve to change shape as interest rates peak and begin to decline, an investor buys the March contract and sells the December contract. His expectations are realized and as the curve moves to a more normal pattern the spread between the two contracts strengthens and by November becomes positive, with the March bonds selling at 66 and the December bonds at 64. As a result, the investor could close out both contracts at a net gain of four points; his profit on the long March contract of five points is reduced by the loss of one point on the short sale of the December contract.

(e) The Options Market

In general, a financial option represents a contract whereby the seller (writer) grants the privilege of obtaining a financial instrument to the buyer at a designated price (the striking price) for a specified period of time in exchange for a fee (premium). The Securities Exchange Act of 1934 gave the SEC broad powers under Sections 9(b) and 9(c) to regulate options trading. For 40 years following passage of the Exchange Act, such trading was concentrated in the over-the-counter market where it attracted little attention. Largely overlooked by the SEC, the market was primarily self-regulated by some 20 specialty firms which functioned as middlemen between option buyers and sellers.

This desultory scene was changed by the inauguration of the Chicago Board Options Exchange (CBOE) in April 1973, the nation's first organized and still dominant options exchange. The major contribution of the CBOE was to make the option a fungible instrument that could be readily bought and sold. This feat was accomplished by standardizing the striking prices and expiration dates, leaving only the premiums to be established through competitive bids and offers on the floor of the exchange.

Thereafter, trading grew rapidly and other exchanges, including the American, Philadelphia, and Pacific stock exchanges entered the picture. Competition became vigorous and a stream of new instruments was introduced such as options on interest rates, stock indexes, sub-indexes (like computer technology, oil and gas, transportation, gaming/hotel, and gold/-silver), interest-rate futures, and stock index futures. The NYSE was a late entry into the field with options on its composite index, futures index, and a telephone sub-index. The introduction of options on futures created a regulatory squabble between the SEC and the CFTC. This disagreement resulted in the enactment of legislation that essentially gave the SEC jurisdiction over options on securities and the CFTC jurisdiction over options on financial futures, although some further regulatory dust was stirred up by the inauguration of options on subindexes.

Changes have been persistent. To enhance speculative interest, some exchanges created an enlarged image of an existing index by doubling its base value. In mid-1984, the Philadelphia Stock Exchange proposed a new entity, called the Philadelphia Board of Trade, to deal in options on Eurodollar futures and an index of over-the-counter stocks. The CBOE and the Amex entered into a joint agreement that calls for cooperative efforts to deal in trading of options and futures on the American's major market index. Like the futures area, the options market is in a state of ferment with the exchanges constantly seeking new instruments and ways to enhance activity.

The Options Clearing Corporation (OCC) is the party on the other side in the case of options. At its expiration, an option is worthless. Accordingly, if a holder does not liquidate an "in the money" option by a closing transaction, he must exercise it before expiration to obtain some value. He does so by notifying a member firm which submits exercise instructions to the clearing corporation which, in turn, assigns an exercise notice to another clearing member, acting on behalf of a writer of the same series (options of the same class such as a put or call on the same underlying instrument having the same exercise price, expiration date, and unit of trading). The assigned member is then obligated to execute the terms of the contract and will obtain the required funds or instruments from a buying customer. Options of the same series which are listed on different exchanges may be bought and sold in opening transactions and thereafter liquidated in offsetting closing transactions on any of the exchanges on which that series of options is listed.

[i] THE QUALITY OF OPTIONS: The basic factors determining the size of the premium at which an equity option is traded are its duration, the difference between the exercise price and the market price of the underlying instrument, the level of interest rates, and the characteristics of the underlying instrument such as its volatility. These factors may not necessarily have the same effect on the premiums of options on other types of instruments. In general, for example, it is expected that rising interest rates will raise the value of a call option on a stock; have a slightly negative or indifferent effect on options on stock index futures because of the cost of carry; but have an adverse effect on options on bond futures because rising interest rates imply declining bond prices. Various formulae, executed through computers, have been developed to ascertain whether the premium of an option is too high or low based on its indicated intrinsic value.

There are various types of options. A call gives a holder the right to buy a designated amount of a particular stock at an indicated price within a limited period of time. A put is the other side of the coin, giving a holder the right to sell the stock under similar arrangements. Combinations of these types may be arranged. A straddle, for example, consists of a put and call with the same striking prices and expiration dates; the holder presumes to benefit by a sharp price change in either direction. As in the case of the futures market, option spreading is common. There are different strategies for this purpose, such as the simultaneous purchase and sale of options of the same class but with different expiration dates, or with the same expiration dates but different striking prices.

The premium on an option is substantially less than the cost of the applicable underlying instrument. As a result, the option provides access to a much larger quantity of the underlying instrument than would be possible through direct purchase. This condition represents the typical leverage opportunity, where the holder of the option could benefit from price changes in the underlying security to a greater extent than could be obtained through a direct position in the underlying instrument. As indicated previously, the futures market also provides significant and possibly even greater leveraging opportunities. But the holder of an option has known limited risks whereas the holder of a futures position may have unknown future risks.

[ii] THE USES OF OPTIONS: Options on securities may be used for certain reasonably well defined situations. Thus, purchase of a call may be used to maintain a long position in a security at a limited risk, anticipate the future purchase of a security, or to limit the risk of a short position. Purchase of a put may be used to limit inroads into a market gain an investor has earned, limit the size of a potential loss on a stock that he has acquired to the premium paid plus the difference between the purchase price of the stock and the striking price of the put, or to anticipate a price decline in the underlying security with limited risk.

Writing a call may be used by the holder of a stock to increase his return (a covered call). This approach is conservative since if the stock is called, he may deliver the instrument he holds. While his income is increased by the premium received, the opportunity of earning a substantial gain is sacrificed because if the stock advances beyond the striking price, it will be called away from him so long as his writer obligation continues. Writing a call on a stock not owned (an uncovered call) is risky because of the uncertainty of the price at which the writer might have to purchase the security to meet a call. Writing a put places an obligation on the writer to buy the stock with the ultimate decision resting on the purchaser. Presumably, the writer would use this approach to acquire a security in which he is interested at a net cost that is below the current market price.

The uses of options on indexes is much the same as those described for futures indexes. Such put options may be used to protect existing portfolios against potential market declines, while calls provide the means of locking in current market prices during the time individual securities are being acquired. Whether the option or futures market approach is more desirable depends on such factors as the cost of the relevant instruments and the risk return trade offs.

Options are useful to hedge risks of an uncertain potential transaction. For example, suppose a U.S. firm is bidding competitively in a foreign currency on a contract. The firm may be reluctant to use the futures market to hedge the implicit currency risk because of the uncertainty as to whether or not it will be awarded the contract. The firm can, however, create a hedge against the contingent receivable by purchase of a put option in the foreign currency. If the firm is awarded the contract, the foreign currency received can be "put" to the option seller; if the bid fails, the firm will not exercise the option and the only cost involved in the currency hedge is the premium on the put.[15]

Options can also keep costs within known modest limits. Consider, for example, a financial officer who negotiated a three-month bank loan of twenty million dollars. The interest rate on the loan is 12.5 percent, tied during its term to the prime rate, which at that time is 11.00 percent. Apprehensive of rising rates, the financial officer buys 20 large put option contracts on 13-week Treasury bills (a large contract is one million dollars, while a small contract is two hundred thousand dollars) at a premium of 1.20, equivalent to 120 basis points (each basis point represents 1/100 of one percent of the principal amount of bills covered by the option). His expense on the purchase is $60,000 (.012 x $20,000,000 x 13/52). At that time, the discount rate on 13-week bills is nine percent and the strike price of the options is 90.6 (exercise or strike prices are expressed as 100 minus the annualized discount rate of a hypothetical 360-day Treasury bill). At the end of the first month, the prime rate rises to 12 percent and the interest rate on the loan accordingly is adjusted to 13.6 percent (12.5% x .12/.11). This rate prevails for the next two months when the term of the loan expires. The total cost of the loan is:

First month (.125 x $20,000,000 x 1/12)   = $208,333.30
Second and third months (.136 x $20,000,000 x 2/12)   = 453,333.30
                                               $661,666.60

If the interest rate on the loan had remained constant, the total cost would have been $625,000,000 (.125 x $20,000,000 x 3/12). The extra cost resulting from the change in rates, therefore, is $36,666.60 ($661,666.60 - $625,000,000). The financial officer, however, finds that he is able to avoid this additional charge by exercising his put options upon expiration of the term of the loan. At that time, the discount rate on 13-week bills is 10.00 percent, representing a market price of 90. The financial officer, therefore, buys $20,000,000 par value of bills, paying $18,000,000 and puts them at the strike price of $18,120,000 (90.6 x $20,000,000). Disregarding commissions and certain minor adjustments, he realizes $120,000. After reducing this amount by the $60,000 premiums paid for the options and the additional interest charge of $36,666.60, he realizes $23,333.40. Accordingly, his net interest cost is $601,666.60 ($625,000 - $23,333.40) and his effective annualized interest cost on the loan is 12.03 percent ($601,666.60/$20,000,000 x 4). Thus, by utilizing the options mechanism, the financial officer was able to more than match the extra interest payment resulting from the unfavorable movement of interest rates.

[2] THE MORTGAGE MARKET

Over the past 15 years or so, a secondary mortgage market has been developing rapidly in the United States. In the 1970's, mortgage originators sold only about a third of all residential loans into the secondary market. By 1980 that proportion had risen to almost 50 percent and since then the market has continued its swift growth.

Traditionally, local lenders, which provided housing money, had no ready means of replacing the funds loaned to home buyers. Largely through the instrumentality of the Government, an outlet was created whereby these loans could be liquidated. The Federal National Mortgage Association (Fannie Mae), created in 1968 by the partitioning of an original agency, in 1981 began packaging pools of conventional mortgages, acquired from participating lenders, in pass-through securities which could be sold to the public. The Federal Home Loan Mortgage Corporation (Freddie Mac), created in 1970, has been active for a longer period of time in issuing mortgage participation certificates representing undivided interests in conventional mortgages previously purchased by the agency. This explosive growth has attracted to the pass-through mortgage market private competitors such as General Electric Credit Corp., a unit of General Electric, and Residential Funding Corp., a subsidiary of Norwest Mortgage Inc. of Minneapolis, while still others are entering the field.

The pass-through technique has enabled mortgages to be bundled into securities that bear competitive rates and possess liquidity. In effect, the financing burden is shifted to a variety of institutional and individual investors, as is the function of a financial market. As a result, it is expected that this increasingly steadier flow of mortgage funds from the capital market will provide substantial support to the housing industry.

12.5   CHAPTER SUMMARY

In this chapter, we presented an overview of the U.S. financial markets with emphasis on the dramatic changes these markets are experiencing, their broadening scope that facilitates entry into foreign markets, and the variety of new types of instruments being introduced as well as their uses. The point of view was that of the financial manager. In order for him to be able to use these markets effectively, it is necessary that he understand how they operate and the interrelationships of the various segments. Accordingly, we highlighted those aspects that seemed desirable to gain such an understanding. Using this background as a framework, we discussed how the financial manager employs the money and capital markets for both investment and financing purposes.

FOOTNOTES

1. James Parthemos, "The Money Market," p. 6; Seth P. Maerowitz, "Federal Funds," p. 49, Federal Reserve Bank of Richmond, *Instruments of the Money Market,* 1981.
2. *The Wall Street Journal,* May 29, 1984, pp. 1 and 16.
3. *The Wall Street Journal,* June 25, 1984, p. 3.
4. *op. cit., The Wall Street Journal,* May 29, 1984, pp. 1 and 16.
5. *Ibid.*
6. See, Securities and Exchange Commission, "In the Matter of the New York Stock Exchange, Inc.," Securities Exchange Act of 1934, *Release No. 19858,* June 9, 1983; *Release No. 20350,* November 4, 1983.

7. Securities and Exchange Commission, "Request for Comment on Off-Board Trading Pursuant to Rule 19c-3," Securities and Exchange Act of 1934, *Release No. 20074*, August 12, 1983.

8. Securities and Exchange Commission, "Statement of the Securities and Exchange Commission on the Future Structure of the Securities Markets," February 21, 1972.

9. Securities and Exchange Commission, Securities Exchange Act of 1934, "Development of a National Market System," *Release No. 14416*, January 26, 1978.

10. The New York Stock Exchange, "Automation of Stock Trading Facilities in the United States," *A Presentation by the New York Stock Exchange, Inc.*, Amsterdam, The Netherlands, May 14, 1982, pp. 2-3.

11. Securities and Exchange Commission, Securities Exchange Act of 1934, *Release No. 20074*, August 12, 1983, *op. cit.*

12. Chicago Board of Trade, *The Financial Futures Professional*, June 29, 1984, p. 1 (This is a monthly marketing bulletin).

13. Nancy H. Rothstein, editor in chief, and James M. Little, *The Handbook of Financial Futures, A Guide for Investors and Professional Financial Managers*, McGraw-Hill Book Company, New York, 1984, p. 498 and pp. 506-509.

14. Chicago Board of Trade, *A Guide to Financial Futures at the Chicago Board of Trade*, undated, p. 18.

15. Laurie G. Goodman, "New Options Markets," *Federal Reserve Bank of New York, Quarterly Review*, Autumn, 1982, p. 38.

SUGGESTED READINGS

Allen, P. R., *Asset Markets, Exchange Rates, and Economic Integration*, Cambridge University Press: New York, 1980.

Coats, Warren L., Jr., "The Weekend Eurodollar Game," *The Journal of Finance*, June 1981.

Cole, G. A., "The Financial Futures Market: An Analysis of its Strengths and Weaknesses," *Journal of Commercial Bank Lending*, March 1982.

Cornell, Bradford, "A Note on Taxes and the Pricing of Treasury Bill Futures Contracts," *The Journal of Finance*, December 1981.

——— and Marc R. Reinganum, "Forward and Futures Prices: Evidence from the Foreign Exchange Markets," *The Journal of Finance*, December 1981.

Cox, John C. et al., "A Re-Examination of Traditional Hypotheses About the Term Structure of Interest Rates," *The Journal of Finance*, September 1981.

Craven, John A., "Eurobanking in an Era of Volatile Interest Rates," *The Banker*, February 1981.

Curtin, D., "Are the Euromarkets Ready for Financial Futures?" *Euromoney*, March 1982.

Dougall, Herbert E. and Jack E. Gaumnitz, *Capital Markets and Institutions*, Prentice-Hall, Foundations of Finance Series, 4th ed., Englewood Cliffs, New Jersey, 1980.

"Eurobond Markets: Lessons for Investors," *The Banker*, February 1981.

"Eurocredits: Differentials Widen at Last," *The Banker*, September 1981.

Feder, G., and K. Ross, "Risk Assessments and Risk Premiums in the Eurodollar Market," *The Journal of Finance*, June 1982.

"Financial Futures: A Hedge for Euroloans," *The Banker*, January 1982.

"Financial Futures: Stock Exchange Rules," *The Banker*, March 1982.

Fitzgerald, H. Desmond, "Using the Financial Futures Market," *The Banker*, April 1982.

Folks, William R., Jr., and Ramesh Advani, "Raising Funds With Foreign Currency," *Financial Executive*, February 1980.

Garrison, J. S., Jr. and D. J. Dohren, "The Simple Way to Borrow at Less Than Prime," *Credit and Financial Management,* June 1982.

Holliday, J. E., "Mortgage Banker: Investment Hedge Technician," *Mortgage Banker,* May 1982.

Keyzer, Marinus W., "International Financial Markets in the 1980s," *The Banker,* March 1981.

Krasker, W. S., "Hedging on Loans Linked to the Prime," *Harvard Business Review,* May/June 1982.

Lomas, E. J. and P. Rozsa, "Impact of Changes in Capital Markets," *Dun's Business Month,* June 1982.

London, A., "Stability of the Interest Parity Relationship Between Canada and the United States," *Review of Economics and Statistics,* November 1981.

Loosigtan, Allan M., *Interest Rate Futures—A Market Guide for Hedgers and Speculators,* Dow Jones Books, Homewood, Illinois, 1980.

Mackenzie, M. A. and J. L. Playfair, "Interest Rate Futures—Not for Idle Speculation," *CA Magazine,* November 1981.

Mendelson, M. S., *"Money on the Move,"* *The Modern International Capital Market,* McGraw-Hill Book Co., New York and London, 1980.

Mercaldo, E. L., "Are the Euromarkets Too Competitive?" *Euromoney,* October 1981.

O'Leary, James J., "Revaluation in the Long-Term Markets," *Bankers Monthly,* December 1980.

Oppenheimer, Allan M., "Selecting an Asset Financing Alternative," *Financial Executive,* May 1980.

Park, Y. S., "Devaluation of the U.S. Prime Rate," *The Banker,* May 1982.

Picon, Glenn C., "Interest Futures," *Financial Executive,* August 1980.

Raier, S., "Disappointing Debut of Eurodollar Futures," *Institutional Investor,* May 1982.

Robinson, Roland I. and Dwayne Wrightsman, *Financial Markets: The Accumulation and Allocation of Wealth,* McGraw-Hill Book Co.; New York 1980.

Stapleton, Richard C. and M. G. Subrahamanyam, *Capital Market Equilibrium and Corporate Financial Decisions,* Greenwich, Conn.; Jai Press 1980.

Taylor, David G., et al., "Prospects for Financial Markets," *Bankers Monthly,* December 1980.

FINANCING IN THE PRIMARY MARKET

13.1 INTRODUCTION

The primary market for security sales refers to the aggregation of structural and administrative arrangements that enables a company to distribute its securities to the public. The purpose of this distribution is to assist the firm in meeting its financing needs. Primary markets may thus be distinguished from secondary markets (sometimes called trading markets) in which the participants buy and sell the securities that have been issued. Thus issuing firms are normally not directly involved in secondary market transactions.[1] Primary markets, however, directly relate firms attempting to finance their capital needs with investors seeking to purchase the securities of these firms.

In this chapter we look at the various approaches to financing in the primary market covering the activities of investment bankers or underwriters as well as the other significant operatives in this market.

13.2 INVESTMENT BANKERS AS A MEDIUM OF LONG-TERM FINANCING

Investment bankers or underwriters act on behalf of publicly held companies to sell debt or equity securities either to the general public or in a private placement. The financial manager contemplating the utilization of an investment banker must consider a number of factors, among the most important of which are:

- security sales method—private placement versus public offering; and
- underwriting process—if a public offering is employed the method of handling the underwriting.

These factors are discussed below.

[1] SECURITY SALES METHODS

The private placement and the public offering represent the two major categories of security sales methods. The private placement of stocks and bonds has increased in relative importance over the past several decades.

(a) Private Placements

A private placement entails a corporation selling its equities or debt to individuals or institutions, either directly or through an underwriter. Where an underwriting firm is used, it generally serves only as an agent, receives a fee based on services rendered, and assumes no risk.

[i] ADVANTAGES: A major advantage of a private placement is the elimination of the complexities of a registration with the SEC. As a result, the financing can normally be conducted more rapidly and the issue can be tailored to meet the specific needs of the borrowing firm and the lender. For a private issue, it is relatively easier to renegotiate the debt contract in response to unexpected developments. Added flexibility is provided because the actual borrowing does not have to take place all at once. Additionally, both corporate borrowers and private placement lenders develop a close working relationship that lasts through many transactions to their mutual advantage. Arrangements can be made so that funds can be drawn as needed. Flotation costs tend to be lower for private placements compared with public offerings, but these differences lessen as the size of the issue increases. Small firms may have little choice but to use private sales because of difficulties they experience in seeking to distribute their securities publicly.

[ii] DISADVANTAGES: It has been said that management is at a disadvantage in dealing with institutional investors who are skilled in lending and, indeed, there is some evidence that, in general, indenture provisions for private arrangements may be more restrictive. In addition, although the overall costs associated with a private placement are generally less than those for public issues of long-term debt, special costs may be involved in public issues such as equity "sweeteners", to compensate the buyers for holding illiquid securities.

(b) Public Offerings

Public offerings typically are made on an interstate basis to a relatively large number of investors. These issues are likely to be underwritten by investment bankers who purchase the securities from the issuer for resale to the public.

[i] ADVANTAGES: Companies use the public capital market for a variety of reasons. Some prefer it to private financing because of the extensive publicity involved. The company and its products become better known. A successful financing not only helps sales, but also gives the company greater assurance of future reentry into the capital market when it again needs funds. A public issue also offers a possible form of savings for a company should interest rates rise substantially, by enabling it to buy in the open market publicly held bonds which have fallen below par. Companies with excellent financial standing may find they can at times get somewhat more favorable terms in a public offering. There are companies whose need for funds is so great that they must utilize all sources, public and private. And finally, there are some very large companies whose demand for funds are so insatiable at any given time that they can only be satisfied by public sales.

[ii] DISADVANTAGES: The major disadvantages of public offerings are the advantages of private sales. Public offerings tend to be more costly and the private route may be barred to small firms. Of primary significance is the inflexibility incurred because of SEC registration requirements which hamper the ability to take advantage of changing market conditions.

The SEC has recognized the marketing difficulties created by its registration procedures. Accordingly, it has adopted rules that provide for considerable changes in these procedures and thus significantly altered the traditional underwriting process.

[2] THE TRADITIONAL UNDERWRITING PROCESS

The basic purpose of SEC registration is to provide a full, fair, and accurate disclosure of the character of the securities, the terms of the offering, and the nature of the distribution arrangements. Since both civil and criminal penalties are provided for failure to disclose all essential and relevant facts, any misstatement or omission is punishable and all those signing the registration statement become liable for its accuracy. Thus, the traditional registration statement is a lengthy and costly document. The issuer's expenses for printing the statement, filing fees, transfer agent and lawyer's bills, and underwriter's out-of-pocket expenses vary with the size and complexity of the distribution.

(a) The "Cooling Off Period" and the Prospectus

Section 8(a) of the Securities Act of 1933 (The Securities Act) provides that registration statements become effective twenty days after filing but that the SEC may "accelerate" the effective date based on the adequacy of the information available to the public. The twenty day period is renewed each time an amendment is made to the registration statement. In practice, statements are often amended and therefore the waiting period can be several months between filing and effective dates.

This intervening time span has been viewed as a "cooling-off period" during which the market can assimilate the new information about the security. During this period, also, the SEC staff can review and comment on the registration statement, while the underwriter performs its "due diligence" examinations to avoid the liability imposed by the Act for material misstatements and omissions. Since the contract is not signed until just before the effective date, the underwriter is in a position to insist on desired disclosures.

Section 5(b)(2) of the Securities Act makes it unlawful to sell in interstate commerce a registered security unless accompanied or preceded by a prospect that meets the requirements of Section 10 which, in turn, states that the prospectus contain the information provided in the registration statement. For first-time issuers, the SEC usually requires a full recitation of the risks involved in the offering. The SEC is empowered, however, to permit such information to be omitted from the prospectus when it judges that the information is not necessary for the public interest or the protection of investors.

A preliminary version of the prospectus, known as a "red-herring", is used to disseminate information regarding the issuer. The red-herring prospectus describes the forthcoming issue but does not indicate the price at which the security is to be sold or the underwriting commission. It is furnished to security dealers some days before the end of the waiting period. The term "red-herring" comes from the fact that each page of the document contains a statement, printed in red ink, to the effect that the document is not an offer to sell or a solicitation to buy, since no such offer may legally be made until the effective date of the registration statement. The red-herring prospectus, however, facilitates the efforts of the investment banking house which is negotiating or working up the issue to form a distributing group.

(b) Establishment of Purchasing and Selling Groups

The investment banking firm which works up or negotiates the issue is known as the originating house; later, when it forms a purchase group to buy the issue, it becomes the managing underwriter. Many issues are so large that they are beyond the capital resources of any one house. Even in the investment banking firm's capital were adequate to purchase the issue it would not want to tie up all its resources in one security. There would be undue and unnecessary risk and a lack of diversified offerings for its customers. Consequently, the originating house usually invites other leading investment banking house, known for their financial strength, to join it in purchasing the issue from the company, thereby forming an underwriting syndicate. Formal relationships among the purchasing underwriters are established by the execution of an "agreement among underwriters", which authorizes the managing underwriter or underwriters to represent the group in purchasing the issue and fixes the obligations among the members of the syndicate. Acting through the managing underwriter or underwriters, the syndicate members also enter into an underwriting agreement with the issuer that specifies the amount each of the underwriters in the purchase group is to take as well as the terms and conditions of the offering.

In order to secure the widest possible distribution and to dispose of the issue quickly, it is customary for the managing underwriter to arrange for the participation of additional houses in the sale of the issue. This may be done by organizing a selling group which may include members of the syndicate who agree to distribute more than their assigned portion of the underwriting. Participants in this group receive a concession for the securities they actually sell and ordinarily execute a "selected dealer agreement" that describes their rights and obligations in connection with the offering.

An underwriting syndicate is structured on the basis of the importance of its members. The status of each member is indicated in the typical "tombstone", (so-called because of its terse character), which is an advertisement appearing in newspapers announcing the offering. Leading the enumeration of participants is the managing underwriter, or if there are more than one, the co-managers as well. Behind this lofty spot on the list appears the secondary national firms, grouped in the order of their importance, followed by the smaller national and then the regional houses.

Ordinarily, the managing underwriter does not release all the securities to the other underwriters, but places a portion in a general syndicate account, known as the "pot". The managing underwriter then allocates and reallocates these securities among the syndicate and selling group members to assist in the distribution process. An institution interested in buying the underwritten securities may also request the managing underwriter to credit its purchase to a designated underwriter or dealer, who may cover the transaction from the securities released to it or may seek to have it covered from the "pot". So-called "swap transactions" may also be arranged whereby a syndicate member takes securities in trade from a customer, in lieu of cash, in exchange for the offered securities.

The gross spread between the price paid to the issue by the syndicate and the initial public offering price is composed of (a) a management fee for the leading underwriter, (b) the rest of the underwriting compensation, and (c) the selling concession. In recent years, the selling concession has grown as a percentage of the gross spread because of the increased importance of the selling effort to a successful underwriting.

Behind the cooperative facade of the listing in a tombstone announcement of all the institutions named in an underwriting lies fierce competition for position in an implicit investment banking hierarchy. Solomon Brothers was the leading manager of underwritten public securities offerings in both 1983 and 1984. In 1984, it was lead manager for 186 domestic underwritings with a dollar volume of $21.2 billion, representing more than 25 percent of all issues offered during the year.[2]

(c) Pricing the Issue

The price the underwriters can afford to pay for an issue is, of course, governed by their best estimate of what they can sell it for in the public offering they are about to make. They reach this estimate largely as a result of examining the prices at which comparable issues are selling in the market just prior to the price determination date. The financial manager can also do this, though perhaps not with the same degree of skill and experience as the underwriters, and, therefore, he too can come up with an estimate of how the issue should be priced. The process is somewhat less difficult for a bond issue than for a stock issue. Since the financial manager will lean towards high pricing while the underwriters tend to prefer lowering the price in order to assure sale, negotiations may be required to reach a final settlement.

In the case of common stock, a degree of underpricing may be necessary to provide an incentive to absorb the new shares. If the stock to be priced is that of a company just going public or of a new venture, considerable personal judgment regarding the merits of its product and the future progress of the company is involved. As a result, during so-called "hot-issue" periods such as occurred in 1983, when speculative interest is keen, the need to underprice may be placed on a back-burner and the stocks of presumed high growth companies could be driven to extraordinary levels. For example, Diasonics which makes medical diagnostic equipment, went public at a per share price equivalent to 70 or more times its current earnings at the same time that General Motors was selling at about six times its net profits per share.[3] If a new corporation's growth expectations are not realized, however, the subsequent decline in the price of its stock could be very steep.

Once the estimated price at which the issue can be sold to the public has been determined, the expected costs of flotation, including the underwriter's spread, are subtracted, and the resulting figure is the price which the underwriters will offer the company for the issue. In an effort to make the proposed offering price stick during the marketing period, most underwriters will engage in pegging operations.

(d) Pegging

To minimize the risk of price fluctuation during the marketing period, many syndicates will arrange to have the managing underwriter peg the price at the public offering figure until the termination of the syndicate. SEC regulations provide that the prospective investor must be informed that this is being done because when the marketing period ends and pegging is discontinued, the price of the security may fall below that at which it was recently sold to investors.

In pegging, two techniques ordinarily are involved—overallotment and stabilization—though they blend into one in practice. Assume, for example, that $200 million of bonds are to be marketed at an agreed upon price of 99 ($990 per bond) and that the underwriter's spread is $20 per bond (or a net sale price to the issuing corporation of $970). If the marketing period is 10 days, within that period some nervous purchasers may have second thoughts about the advisability of their purchase and decide to resell the issue immediately for whatever price it will bring. If such distress selling is allowed to push the price down to say 97, the remainder of the issue—and it may be the great bulk of it—will have to be sold at this price, thus wiping out the underwriters' margin. To prevent such a development, the managing underwriter will place a standing order with security dealers to buy for the syndicate account, at the agreed upon public offering price, any part of the issue reoffered during the marketing period. Obviously, this pegs the price of the issue, since anyone wishing to sell during the marketing period will find that he can get his purchase price back. The price is thus maintained at least until the end of the marketing period.

In cases where the underwriters anticipate that they may have to buy back any significant part of the issue in order to maintain the price, they will overallot in the original selling group assignment so that at the end of the marketing period not only the original issue but the extra amount they have had to buy back to stabilize the price may also have been sold. For example, assume that in the case of the $200 million bond offering, 100 houses comprise the selling group, each with a $2 million participation. It is estimated that $1 million of the issue may have to be bought back in the stabilization process. Each member of the selling group may be asked to take an extra $10,000, that is, to sell $2,010,000 each, so that by the end of the agreed upon marketing period, the $1 million of the issue that has had to be repurchased to maintain the price will have been resold.

(e) Selecting the Underwriter

Major corporations that desire to sell securities publicly ordinarily do not have difficulty in obtaining the services of an investment banker to undertake the distributions arrangements. Such corporations are not only well known to the financial community, but are also likely to have established prior relations with some investment banks which probably are among the leading houses in the field.

The problem is different for the smaller less prominent corporations, particularly those going public for the first time. In these cases, their ability to obtain an investment bank may depend upon the economic environment. If speculative fever is high, such firms may actually be sought after by investment bankers who are willing to take advantage of the receptive public attitude. Ordinarily, however, the banker chooses carefully. A fledgling firm, therefore, may have to approach several investment banks before it reaches a final agreement, although care must be exercised not to gain the reputation of "shopping around."

Fundamentally, a corporation that desires financing through the sale of securities should get more than a marketing effort from its investment banker. Such a corporation should obtain guidance through the entire financing process covering an evaluation of the need for funds, the type of security to be issued, and the timing of the sale, as well as the actual distribution steps.

For this purpose, it is desirable for a business firm to seek an investment bank that has the capability of providing the required services. While a small firm cannot expect to engage a leading institution, there are competent modest sized investment banks to match the quality of the expected issuer. A large, well established business firm, on the other hand, ordinarily has the option of selecting an underwriter on one of two primary bases: (1) the negotiated public offering and (2) the competitively bid offering.

[i] NEGOTIATED PUBLIC OFFERING: In the negotiated transaction, the company seeking to obtain funds calls in an investment banking house, usually one with which it has had previous dealings or some long-standing relationship. If a company does not have such a relationship, it may ask its commercial bank to recommend an investment banker, or one of the company's outside directors may be acquainted with an investment banking house and bring it into the picture. Or, the financial manager may visit two or three investment banking houses, telling them the purpose of his visit and indicating that he has also talked to several others. If, as a result of the initial discussions, the investment banker believes the undertaking promising, it probably will make a more careful evaluation before concluding arrangements.

A competent investment banker will not only provide guidance on the type and timing of the financing, but will also advise on whether the financing should be undertaken at all. The capital market is a tricky arena, and to a company utilizing its facilities infrequently and perhaps not close to trends and developments in it, the hazards of error are considerable. Timing the flotation, for example, unless expertly handled, can make a material difference in costs or may even cause the issue to be withdrawn or fail. During periods of unsettled market conditions the investment banker may be helpful in developing innovative issues to induce sales. This has been particularly prevalent in recent years.

[ii] COMPETITIVELY BID PUBLIC OFFERING: In competitive bidding, the issuer announces that until a given date, sealed bids will be received from interested groups; that at an appointed place and hour the offers will be opened; and that the issue will be awarded to the highest acceptable bidder, provided the bid is agreeable to the issuer.[4] In response, several of the larger houses may determine to form syndicates to bid for the issue. They invite other houses to meet with them, discuss the issue and endeavor to come to an agreement on the bid to be submitted. Often this price is not finally set and submitted until the morning of the day that the bids are to be opened.

The prime factor which has led regulatory authorities to espouse competitive bidding, and which is its chief advantage for management, is the demonstrated saving to the issuer through lower coupon rates or higher prices, as compared with negotiated transactions. When investment bankers compete for an issue they tend to narrow the spread, and this reduction usually is passed on as savings to the borrowing company.

If there is a clear savings through competitive bidding, why have relatively few industrial companies utilized the method in traditional underwritings? Several reasons suggest themselves. For competitive bids, the company's financial officials must themselves decide upon the amount and type of the issue, work it up on their own without the help of an investment banker, and know enough about trends in the money and capital markets to time the issuance of their invitation to bid so that bids will be forthcoming. To avoid this burden, many financial managers, particularly of industrial firms, have chosen to let the investment banker do the work and pay for it by foregoing the possible saving. Also, there is less uniformity and standardization in industrial issues. As a result, they are harder to judge. Probably, too, since there is no regulation to the contrary, the extra sales effort the investment bankers make to persuade industrial issuers to use a negotiated transaction has had its impact. Moreover, some industrial companies of lesser credit standing may fear public embarrassment through a dearth of bids or unpleasantly low bids should they go the competitive route. Accordingly, they seek safety in the closed door, nonpublic discussions which characterize the negotiated transaction.

(f) Compensating the Underwriter

The underwriting arrangement may be a firm commitment, where the investment banker purchases the offering from the issuer at an agreed upon price, assumes the market risk, and hopes to sell the securities to the investing public at a higher price. Or, the arrangement may be on a "best-efforts" basis, where the investment banker acts as an agent, earns a commission on the securities sold, and assumes no market risk. The investment banker is likely to prefer such an arrangement when the market risk is particularly high. Underwriting compensation, which may include nonmonetary payments such as options, are subject to regulation by the NASD.

(g) A Classic Distribution

High drama marked the IBM public financing of October 1979. It was not only the initial debt offering by a very distinguished corporation, but it also represented the biggest corporate borrowing in U.S. business history. Added to these "firsts" were the interesting developments that occurred as the distribution evolved.

At the very outset was the question of the managing underwriter. IBM wanted a comanagement arrangement to ensure an effective distribution and to provide ample capital. Despite the corporation's interest in having Morgan Stanley serve in this capacity, Morgan refused because it had the established policy of not sharing the top underwriting slot with any other firm.

The offering covered two different securities—notes and debentures, for an impressive total of one billion dollars. The comanagers were Salomon Brothers (now a subsidiary of Phibro) and Merrill Lynch. There were 225 other syndicate members. The underwriting spread on the notes was 5/8 of 1 percent or $6.25 per issue, with 20 percent going to the comanagers and 20 percent to the underwriters, while 60 percent represented the selling concession. The underwriting spread on the debentures was somewhat higher, 7/8 of 1 percent or $8.75, with 20 percent going to each of the comanagers, 22.86 percent to the underwriters, and 37.14 percent to the sellers. These spreads were reasonably standard.

Pricing was a sensitive issue. Reflecting characteristically different views in this process, IBM leaned towards pricing both notes and bonds only 5 basis points above the yields on comparable Treasury obligations, while the syndicate members preferred substantially higher yields. A compromise was reached at yield levels 7 basis points above Treasury notes for the IBM notes and 12 basis points above Treasury bonds for the IBM debentures. The considerable attention given to this area was rendered fruitless, however, by the sharp rise of interest rates that ensued and caused sales to dry up. The syndicate was disbanded, freeing prices to move with the market and sharp drops occurred.

Gauging individual losses was rendered difficult by uncertainties as to the amounts of securities returned to the "pot" and the amounts exchanged in "swap" transactions. In general, however, syndicate members caught with heavy inventories experienced severe losses. A conspicuous exception was First Boston which actually achieved a small profit by shorting government securities in the interest rate futures market which had been formed a short time previously. First Boston's action at this juncture focused attention on the use of futures by underwriters to hedge inventory positions.

[3] THE MOVE TO INTEGRATED DISCLOSURE AND SHELF REGISTRATION[5]

As originally enacted, the disclosure provisions of the Securities Act were designed to provide investors with information on offerings (transactional reporting), while the provisions of the Securities Exchange Act of 1934 (The Exchange Act) were intended to furnish periodic information on already issued securities traded in the secondary market (continuous reporting).

Starting around the mid-1960's, interest began to grow on integrating the two approaches. The SEC took various hesitant steps in this direction, culminating in the formal integration of the two disclosure systems in 1982.[6]

(a) Factors Leading to the Move

Several factors combined to influence the move to integration. On the economic side, a considerable demand for capital, high interest rates, and volatile market conditions all pointed to the need for timing flexibility in public offerings. On the theoretical side, the widely held concept of the efficient market maintains that new information about a security is promptly impounded into its price, implying, therefore, that the market already has the information about companies that file regularly with the SEC (see 2.5). On the practical side, in reaction to an increasing work load on its staff, the SEC has already curtailed its review of registration statements. In 1972, it adopted a policy that involved varying review levels and in 1980 shifted to a selective policy, whereby registration statements receive either a full review or no staff review at all.

(b) The Integrated Disclosure System

The information called for in the integrated disclosure system is spelled out in a revised regulation S-K. The centerpiece of the system is a three tier structure for Securities Act registration based primarily on the extent to which information is already available in Exchange Act reports and the indicated investor interest in the registrants' securities. Thus, a company that has filed all Exchange Act reports for three years and is widely followed may use the shortest form, S-3, which permits incorporation by reference to essentially all issuer-oriented information contained in current or future Exchange Act filings. In this case, the company may satisfy the disclosure requirements of the Securities Act by delivering a prospectus that contains a description of the transaction. Substantially all the remaining required information may be incorporated by reference to the Exchange Act filings. Under integrated disclosure, the SEC has routinely granted acceleration requests to registrants using the short form and has reduced the waiting period in a number of cases to 48 hours between filing and the effective date, a minimum period based on unwritten staff policy.

A company that has filed all Exchange Act reports for three years but is less widely followed may use Form S-2, which permits incorporation of certain issuer-oriented information from Exchange Act filings but no prospective filings. This form allows issuers the option of either providing investors with a copy of the annual report to shareholders or presenting the required information in the prospectus.

All new issues and those that do not qualify to use the other forms must use Form S-1. This does not permit any incorporation by reference and must disclose all information in the prospectus.

The specific eligibility requirements for use of these forms are outlined in Appendix A.

(c) Shelf Registration

Of considerable importance in the new system is Rule 415 which is concerned with the registration of securities for continued or delayed offering over time. An outline of Rule 415 appears in Appendix B. Initially proposed in the integrated reporting package on an experimental basis, the Rule was made permanent in November 1983. At that time, the SEC limited its use to only those companies eligible for the Form S-3 registration statement. While other companies may not use Rule 415 for conventional underwritings, they may continue to use shelf registration for such purposes as dividend reinvestment plans, employee stock options, and secondary sales of securities.

The primary significance of Rule 415 lies in permitting large, well established companies in which there is a trading interest to raise capital quickly for any purpose provided the shelf registered securities are expected to be sold within two years. In a typical procedure, the issuer files a registration statement containing the basic prospectus that provides a description of the securities to be issued periodically, the various possible methods of distribution, and perhaps a list of potential managing underwriters. All significant new information already will have been filed in Exchange Act reports and incorporated by reference so that post effective amendments will not have to be filed. At the time of pricing, the basic prospectus will be supplemented by a prospectus supplement or sticker that reflects the actual terms. As stickered, the basic prospectus will be delivered to purchasers, while the prospectus supplement will be filed with the SEC as a matter of record. This procedure enables shelf registration issuers to bring securities to the market without any waiting period.

(d) The Effects of the Move

The move to integration and shelf registration has opened a number of new financing avenues to issuers, such as the following:

- So called "bought deals", a European approach, may be arranged whereby one or several investment bankers buy an entire offering for subsequent sale, usually to institutional investors. For example, on May 3, 1982, American Telephone & Telegraph, one of the first firms to use this approach, placed 10 million shares on the shelf, naming 21 possible investment bankers in its prospectus. Twenty firms, singly and in groups, responded with bids. By May 6, Morgan Stanley, through virtual continuous and aggressive bidding, was allotted 2 million shares from the shelf at a price of $55.40, somewhat above the level at which the stock closed that day. Within 24 hours, the firm sold all 2 million shares, mostly at $55.67.
- "Bought deals" may be sold subsequently at fixed or variable prices and with or without the help of other investment bankers.
- The securities could be sold directly to institutions without any intermediary.
- Securities may be distributed on a continuous basis through a securities firm acting as agent.

The move to integration and shelf registration has resulted in a number of advantages and disadvantages which vary with the particular situation.

[i] ADVANTAGES: Those in favor of integration and shelf registration point to the following advantages:

- An issuer eligible to use shelf registration may take this route or opt for the traditional approach. Indeed, in offerings geared to individuals, issuers have included both major bracket and regional firms in their syndicates to preserve traditional ties. Thus, the choices available to the issuer are broadened.
- SEC sponsored studies conducted after shelf registration had been in effect for somewhat over a year indicated that the debt issues under Rule 415 sold at yields between 30 and 40 basis points less than comparable negotiated issues; 30 basis points less than comparable competitively bid issues; and about 29 percent below comparable equity securities.[7]
- Including information by reference reduces registration costs.
- Securities may be sold to take advantage of so-called "market windows", which are brief market intervals when interest rates fall only to experience a prompt reversal. One of the SEC sponsored studies, however, questioned the ability of issuers to detect such "windows."[8]
- Greater financing flexibility permits tailoring distributions more closely to current market conditions.
- By specifying a number of potential managers, issuers encourage them to submit competing bids.
- Increased competition also spurs investment bankers to devise innovative proposals for issuers, who, in turn, have evidenced a willingness to deal with investment bankers with whom they have not had previous relationships.

[ii] DISADVANTAGES: Critics of the move to integration and shelf registrations cite the following disadvantages:

- To absorb the virtual instantaneous financing demands of issuers requires large underwriting capital, which, in turn, creates a chain reaction of more investment banking concentration, lower capital market efficiency, and eventual higher issuer costs.
- The information provided investors about securities is less complete than under the traditional approach.
- Deprived of the "cooling off period" between filing and registration, investment bankers are not able to fulfill their "due diligence" responsibility.
- Financial managers may not have the time or ability to evaluate the proposals submitted by investment bankers and therefore reach incorrect decisions.
- In a similar vein, financial managers are deprived of the advice provided by investment bankers under traditional procedures.
- "Bought deals" could produce serious losses for underwriters and undermine their financing capabilities.
- The overhang of a shelf registered equity represents potential dilution that dampens its price. Another of the SEC sponsored studies does not support this contention.[9] On the other hand, in the AT&T first shelf registration offering mentioned previously, Morgan Stanley determined that the huge registration represented an "overhang" that depressed the stock's price and therefore provided that the company refrain from issuing more shares for 30 days.

13.3   FINANCING BY RIGHTS AND STANDBY UNDERWRITING

While most debt issues are marketed under one or another of the types of arrangements described previously, a considerable share of common stock financing (and of convertible bonds) is accomplished by the issuance of rights to existing shareholders to subscribe to the new common (or convertible security). At times this use of rights to sell common is the deliberate choice of the company. In many cases, however, it is a forced decision because of the existence of pre-emptive rights of existing shareholders.

[1] PRE-EMPTIVE RIGHTS

Under common law a shareholder has a pre-emptive right to maintain his proportionate interest in the company. Should management offer additional common for sale, therefore, unless pre-emptive rights have been waived, existing shareholders must be allowed the opportunity to obtain enough new stock to maintain their proportionate interest (see also 19.2[3](b)). Assume in a company with 100 shares of common outstanding, for example, shareholder A owns 25 shares, representing a one-fourth interest in the company. Should the company now sell another 100 shares, it must offer shareholder A the opportunity to buy at least 25 more, in order for him to retain his proportionate one-fourth interest. If he exercises this right and acquires the additional 25 shares, giving him a total of 50 shares, he maintains his one-fourth ownership interest in the new total of 200 shares. If he were not given the right to buy the extra 25 shares (or, if given the right, he failed to exercise it), he would hold only 25 of a total of 200 shares, thereby reducing his interest from one-quarter to one-eighth.

Some states have embodied the common law doctrine in their general incorporation acts. A few have negated it by stipulating that no shareholder may have the pre-emptive right unless it has been so provided in the corporate charter. Others, while recognizing the common law right, have provided in general incorporation acts that the right may be waived by a provision in the individual corporate charter or by a later amendment.

[2] FACILITATING A RIGHTS SALE

Other firms, particularly large ones with many shareholders, welcome the existence of pre-emptive rights to existing shareholders. Such shareholders, or those to whom they sell the rights if they do not care to exercise them, use the instrument to buy additional securities in the company, thus providing it with a special source of funds. If a firm has a relatively small number of shareholders, or is uncertain that its existing shareholders will exercise their rights and subscribe to the new stock, or that those who may buy the rights in the open market will subscribe, it can employ the services of investment bankers who will agree to "stand by" and take up whatever part of the issue remains unsold after the rights expire. The investment bankers, of course, charge for this service. For the issuing company such a charge is similar to an insurance fee. It is paid to ensure that the whole issue will be sold and that the company will raise the entire sum it needs.

Pre-offering pressure on the market price of the outstanding shares may occur when it becomes known that a rights offering is likely. In addition, during the subscription period itself, downward pressure on the market price of outstanding shares may develop. Accordingly, it is customary to set the subscription price of the new shares at a significant discount below the then current market level of outstanding shares.

13.4 THE NEW APPROACHES TO FINANCING

In addition to the traditional methods of financing in the primary market, the changed environment of highly volatile interest rates has led financial managers to make use of new markets, such as those in options and futures, and to develop new methods that involve the interlacing of a variety of tools. These methods have become sufficiently identified to be categorized under the broad heading of "asset-liability management".

Important among these new methods are interest rate and currency swaps, whereby a firm can gain substantial financial flexibility in matching its assets and liabilities. For example, in the transaction described in Figure 13.1, an international bank matched its floating-rate income priced off LIBOR (the London Interbank Offered Rate) with an interest payment based on LIBOR, while the fixed-rate interest it received offset the fixed-rate payment required on its Eurodollar bond issue. Similarly, the large thrift institution, which was on the other side of this arrangement, hedged the fixed-rate earnings from its mortgage portfolio with the fixed-rate payment to the bank, while the floating-rate income it received from the international bank provided some match against its floating-rate cost of borrowing.[10] It was estimated, in the spring of 1985, that the market for interest rate swaps amounted to about $80 billion annually.[11] Five years previously, it was virtually nothing. In another type of swap, a company raises funds in one currency but pays interest and principal in a different currency.

A financial manager that is reluctant to handle the complicated hedges involved in these techniques may, for a fee, turn over the job to an institution. Indicative of the interest in this area, in the summer of 1985, the Prudential Insurance Co. announced that it had formed a subsidiary, Prudential Global Funding, to be managed by its brokerage unit, Prudential-Bache Securities, for the purpose of acting as a principal in interest rate swaps valued at $10 million or more.

FIGURE 13.1 *How a swap works*

The following example is based on an actual transaction that was arranged by an investment bank between a large thrift institution and a large international bank; it is representative of many swaps that have been arranged since 1982. "Thrift" has a large portfolio of fixed-rate mortgages. "Bank" has most of its dollar-denominated assets yielding a floating-rate return based on LIBOR (the London Interbank Offered Rate).

On May 10, 1983, the "Intermediary," a large investment bank, arranged a $100 million, 7-year interest rate swap between Thrift and Bank. In the swap, Thrift agreed to pay Bank a fixed rate of 11 percent per year on $100 million, every 6 months. This payment covered exactly the interest Bank had to pay on a $100 million bond it issued in the Eurodollar market. Thrift also agreed to pay Bank the 2 percent underwriting spread that Bank itself paid to issue this bond. In exchange, Bank agreed to make floating-rate payments to Thrift at 35 basis points (.35 percent) below LIBOR. Intermediary received a broker's fee of $500,000.

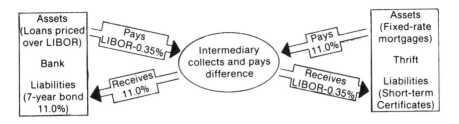

Twice a year, Intermediary (for a fee) calculates Bank's floating-rate payment by taking the average level of LIBOR for that month (Col. 2), deducting 35 basis points, dividing by 2 (because it is for *half* a year), and multiplying by $100 million (Col. 3). If this amount is larger than Thrift's fixed-rate payment (Col. 4), Bank pays Thrift the difference (Col. 5). Otherwise, Thrift pays Bank the difference (Col. 6).

1	2	3	4	5	6
Date	LIBOR	Floating-rate payment ½ (LIBOR-0.35%)	Fixed-rate payment ½ (11%)	Net Payment from Bank to Thrift	Net Payment from Thrift to Bank
May 1983	8.98%	—	—	—	—
Nov 1983	8.43%	$4,040,000	$5,500,000	0	$1,460,000
May 1984	11.54%	$5,595,000	$5,500,000	$95,000	0
Nov 1984	9.92%	$4,785,000	$5,500,000	0	$ 715,000
May 1985	8.44%	$4,045,000	$5,500,000	0	$1,455,000

The swap allows both Bank and Thrift to reduce their exposure to interest rate risk. Bank can now match its floating-rate assets priced off LIBOR with an interest payment based on LIBOR, while the fixed-rate interest payments on its bond issue are covered by Thrift. At the same time, Thrift can hedge part of its mortgage portfolio, from which it receives fixed interest earnings, with the fixed-rate payment it makes to Bank. However, the floating-rate payment that Thrift receives is linked to LIBOR while its cost of borrowing is more closely linked to the T-bill rate. Since LIBOR and the T-bill rate do not always move in tandem, Thrift is still exposed to fluctuations in the relation between LIBOR and the T-bill rate.

Source: Federal Reserve Bank of Philadelphia, *Business Review,* May-June 1985, p. 19.

Companies can perform other maneuvers with balance sheets and financings. Several years ago, Exxon Corp. pioneered in a transaction that removed $515 million of debt from its balance sheet without an actual cash outlay by putting Treasury securities into a trust that is repaying the debt. In a variant of this transaction, in the fall of 1984, Exxon sold zero-coupon bonds in Europe, although it did not need the money. The intent was to earn a profit, which it did, amounting to about $20 million, by using the proceeds from the sale of the zero-coupon bonds to buy lower-priced Treasury securities.

Desiring to raise funds to automate operations but reluctant to show more debt on already heavily loaded balance sheets, corporations have resorted to different ways of undertaking off-balance sheet financing. They may lend to a specific project and make payments from cash generated by the project; because the general credit of the company is not involved, the loan does not appear on its balance sheet. Many leasing transactions are not reported as liabilities. Often selected receivables represent a better credit risk than the company itself, enabling the company to sell such receivables to a bank at a better rate than it could borrow on its own credit. Financial institutions compete vigorously in this area as indicated by the full page advertisement of the Mellon Bank in *The Wall Street Journal*, announcing the availability of these services through its corporate banking offices in a number of cities throughout the country.[12] After The Fuji Bank acquired Heller International, it formed Heller Financial and Heller Overseas Corporation, as operating companies, "to win in asset-based financing, factoring, equipment financing and commercial real estate financing."[13]

In the extraordinary efforts of corporations that have been taking place to adjust to new conditions—through such methods as diversifying, slimming down, rediversifying, merging, and effecting acquisitions—financial restructuring has loomed important. In a study of 850 of North America's largest corporations from January through mid-July 1984, *The Wall Street Journal* identified 398 restructurings, of which 103 were financial, involving such activities as buying back common stock, issuing debt, and swapping securities, many of which involved working out arrangements with financial institutions.[14]

At one time corporate financing, at least as practiced by large corporations, was a relatively tranquil operation involving primarily developing relations with established institutions and making periodic forays into the primary market for the issuance of securities. The scenario has changed. Corporate financing has become a lively undertaking in which the financial manager has a variety of options in which to obtain the desired funds in a flexible manner, at the least cost, and so as to make a minimum impact on the corporation's balance sheet. Thus, John C. Pope, the chief financial officer of AMR Inc., the parent of American Airlines, is able to observe that the financial officer who once could not do much damage to his company, no matter what he did, now realizes that the former, passive approach to corporate finance would be terribly dangerous . . . The new tools have turned a bad thing—volatile interest rates—into an opportunity.

13.5 UNREGISTERED AND SIMPLIFIED OFFERINGS[15]

The Securities Act of 1933 and SEC rules provide certain exemptions from and simplifications of the registration statement. Principally, these apply to private offerings, small businesses, and intrastate offerings.

[1] PRIVATE OFFERINGS

Section 4(2) of the Securities Act of 1933 exempts from registration the "transactions of an issuer not involving any public offerings." This statutory exemption is available to issuers who comply with applicable judicial and administrative determinations. Although these determinations have been inconsistent and vague, they tend to cover the following factors:

- *Offeree qualifications*—The prevalent view appears to be that the qualifications of the offeree is not an independent standard but rather primarily pertinent in determining the extent and form of the required disclosure;

- *Manner of the offering*—The offering should be made through direct communication with the offerees rather than through general advertising;
- *Availability of information*—General categories of registration statement material seem sufficient such as relevant financial statements and basic financing data;
- *Number of offerees and purchasers*—While no fixed ceiling is imposed, it seems prudent to hold the number of offerees and purchasers to a reasonable limit; and
- *Absence of redistribution*—The statutory law does not require overt indications, such as legends, but good practice seems to encourage use of such devices.

The vagueness of these standards created continuing doubts and led the SEC to experiment with various rules in an effort to find a path out of the woods of uncertainty. In March 1982, it adopted Regulation D, which is a comprehensive set of six 1933 Act rules—501 through 506—to simplify and codify existing regulations. Rule 506, issued under Section 4(2), does not have any limit on the dollar amount of the offering, the number or qualifications of the offerees, or the number of accredited investors (such as major financial institutions) as defined in Rule 501. There is, however, a limit of 35 purchasers who are nonaccredited investors; there are also certain qualification requirements related to these nonaccredited purchasers.

If securities are sold only to accredited investors, Rule 502, which is concerned with general conditions, does not mandate any specific disclosure, presumably because these accredited investors can fend for themselves. If the securities are sold to nonaccredited investors, the degree of disclosure depends on the size of the offering and is related to the disclosures required by 1933 registration forms.

[2] SMALL BUSINESS

In adopting the Securities Act of 1933, Congress recognized that the imposition of extensive reporting requirements could be burdensome to small companies and inhibit them from going to the public market for funds. Since Congress also felt that these companies contribute to the country's capital formation, it provided in Section 3(b) that "The Commission may . . . by its rules and regulations . . . add any class of securities to the securities exempted . . . if it finds that the enforcement . . . with respect to such securities is not necessary for the protection of investors by reason of the small amount involved or the limited character of the public offering . . ."

Over the years, Congress has continued to manifest a sensitivity to the needs of small business through enactment of various easing provisions. At the very outset, the Securities Act contained a limitation on the amount that a firm could offer under Section 3(b) to $100,000. Through amendments, this amount was eventually raised to $5,000,000 in 1982.

Rule 505 of Regulation D provides an exemption under Section 3(b) of the 33 Act of offerings that do not exceed $5 million to an unlimited number of offerees and accredited investors but to no more than 35 nonaccredited investors. The disclosure pattern follows that of Rule 506 up to an aggregate offering of $5 million.

Rule 504 of Regulation D exempts limited offerings of not more than $500,000. There are no specific disclosure requirements for these offerings because of their small size and the fact that state regulation may provide some investor protection.

Rule 503 requires a Form D notice of sale to be filed for all offerings made under the Regulation.

Outside of Regulation D, there are certain other avenues provided by the SEC under the 33 Act that a small business may take to reduce its registration requirements. Regulation A is the body of rules created by the SEC under Section 3(b) of the Securities Act to provide a general exemption for small distributions. The attraction of Regulation A, once the principal alternative to full registration for small issuers, is on the wane. Its major use appears to be for the offer of sale by private companies of securities in connection with employee stock option programs.

Form S-18 is an optional simplified registration statement adopted by the SEC in 1979 to facilitate the entrance of small companies to the capital market. Since its adoption, the SEC has modified its requirements on several occasions and, in the fall of 1983, raised the aggregate offering price permitted from $5 million to $7.5 million. The net effect of the Form is to permit more timely and less expensive registration procedures for small issuers seeking to enter the public capital market.

[3] INTRASTATE OFFERINGS

In adopting the Securities Act, Congress incorporated the policy of not superseding state control, but rather injecting Federal supervision only when state regulation did not seem adequately able to meet a national need. Reflecting this policy, Section 3(a) (11) exempts from Federal registration requirements "any security which is part of an issue offered and sold only to persons resident within a single State or Territory, where the issuer of such security is a person resident and doing business within, such State or Territory".

The section is intended to permit a company whose operations are confined to one area to raise money from investors in that area without having to register the securities with a Federal agency. Continuing uncertainty existed in interpreting the meaning of the provisions concerned with the requirements of residency and doing business within the state. Accordingly, in early 1974, the SEC adopted Rule 147 which established objective standards to facilitate compliance with the Section.

The Rule 147 standards are strict in order to provide assurance that the intrastate exemption is used only by local companies engaged in local financing. Thus, the determination that the issue has been sold only to appropriate residents can be made only after the securities "have come to rest" within the state or territory and not only must the business be located in the state, but the predominant business must be carried out there.

It is clear that the legislative boundaries surrounding the intrastate exemption are tight. As a result, it appears to be applicable primarily to so-called local "mom" and "pop" operations.

13.6   THE MARKET FOR VENTURE CAPITAL

There is an allure (which may be measured by potential return) about converting an idea into an operating business. The economic outcome is so uncertain, however, that the traditional financing sources are not likely to be available for such an undertaking. From where, then, will both starting and continuing funds come to keep the fledgling enterprise alive during its formative stages? The answer may lie in a diverse area that is broadly described as "venture capital" and includes such sources as wealthy individuals, pension and endowment funds, banks and insurance companies, corporate venture divisions or subsidiaries, small business investment companies, and private limited partnerships. Foreign money has become a growing presence. In the first half of 1985, such funds accounted for $355 million or 27 percent of the total money committed to provide venture capital funds, compared with $360 million or 28 percent provided by pension funds, traditionally the largest source.[16]

These sources operate in different ways. A large corporation, for example, may form a venture capital unit both as an investment and as a means of developing new technology. In another approach, a wealthy individual or pension fund may form a private limited partnership by placing funds, usually more than one million dollars per investor, with a venture capital firm that acts as the general partner. The firm then commits these funds as it locates suitable investment opportunities preferably in diversified areas to minimize risk. It is hoped that these investments will blossom into suitable gains that eventually will be distributed to the limited partners. Foreign investors can help a young U.S. company penetrate overseas markets.

Several venture capital firms have established small business investment companies to take advantage of low cost government financing. The firms can also leverage their commitments because the government lends multiples of the equity the firms provide.

The venture capitalist ordinarily wants to make an equity investment only for a limited time and looks forward to the public market to furnish the funds for the company's next stage of growth. The initial investment is withdrawn to be recycled into another new venture. There is little interest in becoming a long-term stockholder.

The money invested in the venture capital area of new products, ideas, and systems has gone through accordion like movements generated by the changing speculative moods of investors. To an increasing degree, corporations, through venture capital subsidiaries and pension funds, have been moving into the field. Their entrance has not changed the risk characteristics of the field, however, and the probability of failure remains high for venture commitments.

There are ways to diminish the odds of failure, cautions a management consultant firm that specializes in this area. "The underlying cause of error is a confusion of motives between the investing company's urge for new technological insights and positioning. We opt for the primacy of technological knowledge transfer, with financial gain viewed as a by-product of the process." Furthermore, continues the firm, "Our experience shows us that technology should be geared to a company's goals. For most firms, 10 percent improved yields for ongoing technology strategies will have a far greater impact than a 100-1 winner that doesn't fit."[17]

13.7   CHAPTER SUMMARY

The focus of this chapter was the need for and the alternatives available for long-term external financing by the corporation. Attention was given to the new financing techniques that have been developed. As discussed, the major sources of long-term capital include public and private offerings of securities, rights and direct offerings, unregistered issues, and the venture capital market. The operations of investment bankers were also reviewed.

FOOTNOTES

1. Exceptions are noted in Chapter 21 and elsewhere.
2. *The Wall Street Journal,* January 2, 1985, p. 23.
3. *Time,* January 23, 1984, p. 48.
4. In competitive bidding an issuer need not accept a bid which it believes too low, even through it is the high bid or the only bid. All bids may be rejected if the highest one is not acceptable. As a result, the issue may be withdrawn and reoffered later, negotiated privately, or perhaps dropped entirely.
5. See, John Paul Ketels, "SEC Rule 415—The New Experimental Procedures for Shelf Registration," *Securities Regulation Law Journal,* Winter, 1983, pp. 291-338; and Lynn Nichols, "The Integrated Disclosure System and Its Impact Upon Underwriters' Due Diligence: Will Investors Be Protected?" *Securities Regulation Law Journal,* Spring 1983, pp. 3-44.
6. See, SEC Act Release No. 6383, (Exchange Act Release No. 18524), "Adoption of Integrated Disclosure System," March 3, 1982.
7. Memoranda to the Commission from the Office of the Chief Economist: Summary of "Rule 415—The Ultimate Competitive Bid", June 30, 1983; "The Rule 415 Experiment: Equity Markets," September 9, 1983.
8. Summary of "Rule 415—The Ultimate Competitive Bid," *Ibid.,* p. 5.
9. "The Rule 415 Experiment: Equity Markets," *op. cit.,* p. 3.
10. Federal Reserve Bank of Philadelphia, *Business Review,* May-June, 1985, p. 19.
11. Coopers and Lybrand, *Executive Alert Newsletter,* May 1985, p. 12.
12. *The Wall Street Journal,* June 15, 1985, p. 57.
13. *The Wall Street Journal,* May 3, 1985, p. 7.
14. *The Wall Street Journal,* August 12, 1985, p. 12.
15. For a discussion of private offerings, see: Standard & Poor's Corporation, *The Review of Securities Regulation,* B. W. Nimkin, "Offeree Sophistication in Private Offering," August 25, 1982, Carl W. Schneider, "The Statutory Law of Private Placements," August 26, 1981. For a discussion of Regulation D, See: Warren, Gorham, Lamont, Inc., *SEC Accounting Report,* "Regulation D Integrates Rules on Exemptions from Registration," May 1982, pp. 3-5, "New Regulation D Will Replace Most Limited Offering Exemptions," November 1981, pp. 2-4, *Securities Regulation and Transfer Report,* "Small Businesses: New Regulation D Consolidates Several Limited Offering Exemptions from Registration," April 15, 1982, pp. 1-5, Standard & Poor's Corporation, *The Review of Securities Regulation,* Carl W. Schneider, "Introduction to Regulation D," January 13, 1982. For a discussion of Regulation A, see: Standard & Poor's Corporation, *The*

Review of Securities Regulation, Larry W. Sonsini, "Regulation A," December 8, 1983; Warren, Gorham & Lamont, Inc., *Securities Regulation and Transfer Report*, "Small Offerings: Use of Regulation A is Declining," June 1, 1982, p. 6, "SEC Adopts Major Revisions of Regulation A," October 1, 1981, p. 4. For a discussion of Form S-18, see: Warren, Gorham & Lamont, Inc., *Securities Regulation and Transfer Report*, "Small Business: SEC Raises Form S-18 Aggregate offering price to $7.5 million," November 1, 1983, pp. 4-5, "Small Business: SEC Proposes to Raise Form S-18 Aggregate Offering Price to $10 million," August 15, 1983, pp. 5-6, "Form S-18: Now Available for Use by More Issuers," July 15, 1982, pp. 5-6, *SEC Accounting Report*, "SEC Proposes Increase in Form S-18 Dollar Ceiling," September, 1983, pp. 1-2.

16.   *The Wall Street Journal*, September 18, 1985, p. 10.
17.   Management Practice Consulting Partners, *Management Practice*, Fall 1983, "Fool's Gold: The Corporate Venture Capital Craze," p. 4.

SUGGESTED READINGS

Altman, Edward I. and Paul S. Tubiana, "The Multi-Firm Bond Issue: A Fund Raising Financial Instrument," *Financial Management*, Summer 1981.

"An Analysis of the Use of Regulation A For Small Public Offering," *U.S. Securities and Exchange Commission*, Directorate of Economic and Policy Analysis, April 1982.

Baron, David P. and Bengt Holmstron, "The Investment Banking Contract for New Issues Under Asymmetric Information: Delegation and the Incentive Problem," *Journal of Finance*, December 1980.

Block, Stanley and Marjorie Stanley, "The Financial Characteristics and Price Movement Patterns of Companies Approaching the Unseasoned Securities Market in the Late 1970s," *Financial Management*, Winter 1980.

Downes, David H. and Robert Heinkel, "Signaling and the Valuation of Unseasoned New Issues," *The Journal of Finance*, March 1982.

Friedman, Benjamin M., "Post War Changes in the American Financial Markets," *National Bureau of Economic Research*, Paper No. 458, February 1980.

Gumpert, D. E., "Venture Capital Becoming More Widely Available," *Harvard Business Review*, November/December 1980.

Hayes, III, Samuel L., Michael A. Spence, and David Van Praag Marks, *Competition in the Investment Banking Industry*, Harvard University Press, Cambridge, Massachusetts, 1983.

Hess, Alan C. and Peter A. Frost, "Test for Price Effects of New Issues of Seasoned Securities," *The Journal of Finance*, March 1982.

Killeen, Dennis, "Considering the Private Market for Institutional Investing," *Financial Executive*, January 1980.

Lee, Jevons, C., "The Pricing of Corporate Debt," *The Journal of Finance*, December 1981.

Marcus, Bruce W., *Competing for Capital in the '80s, An Investor Relations Approach*, Quorum Books, Westport, Connecticut, 1983.

Melicher, Ronald W., and J. Ronald Hoffmeister, "Issuing Convertible Bonds," *Financial Executive*, June 1980.

Piliero, R. J., "How the SEC Has Simplified the Disclosure System," *Euromoney*, May 1982.

"Requirements for Typical Filings of Small Issuers," *CPA Journal*, May 1982.

"SEC Proposes Major Changes to Registrations," *Financial Executive*, October 1981.

"SEC Proposes Ways to Pare Costs and Paperwork for Companies Selling Securities," *Journal of Accountancy*, September 1981.

Stricklan, D. Gordon, "How an Investment Banker Prepares a Company for a Tender Offer," *Management Accounting,* February 1980.

"Syndicate Relationships in the Bond Markets," *Euromoney,* March 1981.

Timmons, J. A. and D. E. Gumpert, "Discard Many Old Rules About Getting Venture Capital," *Harvard Business Review,* January/February 1982.

Tobin, Robert F., "Private Placement Market for MBS," *Mortgage Banking,* September 1981.

"Venture Capital Adventure," *Institutional Investor,* September 1981.

"Wall Street After 415," *Dun's Business Month,* April 1982.

Wittebort, S., "Tips for Playing the Venture Capital Game," *Institutional Investor,* July 1980.

APPENDIX A: ELIGIBILITY REQUIREMENTS FOR USE OF FORMS S-1, S-2, AND S-3

FORM S-3

The eligibility requirements are broken into two classifications, "Registrant Requirements" and "Transaction Requirements." A company using Form S-3 must meet the registrant requirements and at least one of the transaction requirements.

- Registrant requirements:
  - Must be a domestic corporation;
  - Must be a reporting company under the '34 Act;
  - Must have filed all required reports for at least 36 months and been timely in filing for the preceding 12 months;
  - Must not have had a material default that occurred since the last filing of a '34 Act report containing certified financial statements; and
  - Certain other requirements for specialized situations.

- Transaction requirements:
  - For primary and secondary offerings, an issuer must have a minimum float of $150 million of voting stock;
  - Issuers may register primary offerings of investment grade debt securities, as defined;
  - Resale of securities acquired under a Form S-8; and
  - Rights offerings, divided or interest reinvestment plans, and conversions or warrants are eligible for Form S-3 if the registrant requirements are met.

FORM S-2

The registrant requirements for the use of Form S-2 are the same as for Form S-3. There are no transaction or float requirements.

FORM S-1

There are no requirements for Form S-1 and it may be used by all registrants including first time filers.

Source: Warren, Gorham & Lamont, Inc. *SEC Accounting Report,* Volume 8, Number 6, May 1982.

APPENDIX B: SECURITIES SALES COVERED BY SEC RULE 415

The following is a review of the eligibility requirements of SEC Rule 415.

(1) Securities may be registered for an offering to be made on a continuous or delayed basis in the future, provided that the registration statement pertains to:

- An amount of securities that is reasonably expected to be offered and sold within two years from the initial effective date of the registration statement by or on behalf of the registrant, a subsidiary or its parent; or
- Securities which are to be offered or sold solely by or on behalf of other persons (a secondary offering); or
- Securities which are to be sold pursuant to a dividend or interest reinvestment plan or an employee benefit plan of the registrant; or
- Securities which are to be issued upon the exercise of outstanding options, warrants, or rights or upon conversion of other outstanding securities, securities pledged as collateral, and securities which are registered on Forms S-12 or C-3.

(2) The registrant must agree to file, during any period in which offers or sales are being made, a post-effective amendment to the registration statement that will keep the prospectus up to date. Registrants that are eligible to incorporate their periodic reports by reference need only file any material change to information in the registration statement. The registrant must also agree to remove from registration any securities which remain unsold at the termination of the offering.

(3) In the case of a registration pertaining to an "at the market offering" of equity securities by or on behalf of the registrant:

- Where voting stock is registered, the amount of securities registered must not exceed 10 percent of the aggregate market value of the float (calculated as of a date with 60 days prior to the filing date);
- The securities must be sold through underwriter(s) acting as principal(s) or as agent(s) for the registrant; and
- The underwriter(s) must be named in the prospectus.

The term "at the market offering" means an offering of securities at other than a fixed price through a national securities exchange to or through a market maker otherwise than on an exchange.

(4) Rule 415 does not apply to sales by companies under the Investment Company Act of 1940 or foreign government units.

Source: Warren, Gorham & Lamont, Inc. *SEC Accounting Report,* Volume 8, Number 6, May 1982.

INTERNAL FUNDS AND DIVIDEND POLICY

14.1 INTRODUCTION

A recurrent problem facing financial management is what percent of net profits after taxes should be paid out in dividends and what percent should be retained in the enterprise, thereby reducing the pressure to raise funds externally. The level of internally generated funds, external fund needs and dividend policy are highly interrelated. In the chapters on capital budgeting (16-19) we deal with the financing requirements of the firm. In the present chapter we discuss internally generated funds and dividend policy.

14.2 FACTORS AFFECTING DIVIDEND POLICY

The dividend payout ratio is the percent of earnings paid out in cash dividends (cash dividends/net income). Naturally, policy varies with respect to dividend payout and earnings retention, not only from industry to industry but among companies within a given industry. Variations between industries may reflect not only different payment policies, but also different economic factors. Variations within the same industry, where companies tend to be affected by similar economic considerations, are likely to be more heavily weighted by the special factors affecting the individual companies. The more rapid the growth of a firm, the greater the demand for additional funds for expansion; the higher the profitability, the more logical it will seem to retain funds and employ them to earn higher returns than would be obtained if they were paid out to stockholders and invested by them elsewhere. The variations between companies are sharp because of their different stages of development and particular circumstances. Companies in the field of consumer goods, such as soft drink, tobacco, gum and textiles, normally tend to have relatively high payout ratios. Presumably, they can exercise relatively good control over expenditures and do not require heavy capital outlays. On the other hand, firms with stable earnings tend to have stable payout ratios. When earnings are stable, there is less need than in the case of cyclical industries, to build up retained earnings in good years so as to maintain dividends in poor years when current earnings may not be sufficient to cover the established dividend rates.

On the average, the payout ratios are higher for electric utilities and telephone companies than for industrials. The greater dependence of utilities on external financing, as well as market acceptance of the fact that their capitalization ratios are significantly higher than those of most industrials, reduces the need for utilities to have as much retained earnings. While utilities do have substantial expenditures, the nature of their business facilitates long-term planning and minimizes the need for working capital. When conditions force the curtailment of payout ratios by utilities, higher payout ratios are usually later resumed.

American Telephone and Telegraph has paid out somewhat less than the average of other utility and phone companies because of its voracious need for capital. Were it not for its stockholders, most of whom are primarily interested in a stable income, a still lower payout ratio might have been pursued. On the other hand, its large continuing need for new capital and its reliance on rights offerings, make it imperative that its dividend policy not impair the confidence of its shareholders. Thus, a neat balance is required—a payout ratio as low as is consistent with dividend stability and stockholder serenity. Had it unduly lowered the payout ratio, the company would have defeated its own purposes because it might have dried up its shareholders as a major source of needed new capital. The nature of AT&T's dividend policy depends upon the relationship between its operations and financing needs. According to the David L. Babson & Co. Staff Letter, although dividends have been moving up for American companies as a whole, steadily, the payout ratio has been declining.[1] This statement is confirmed in a study by Dun's review of 234 companies which raised their payments during each year of a recent ten year period. Despite these increases, the estimated payout ratio for the end of the period was 40 percent, below the 44 percent average of the preceding five years, and well under the 57 percent average at the beginning of the period.[2] Payout ratios, whether based on cash flow or earnings, were higher a decade ago than they are at the present time.

The setting of dividend payments is a matter of carefully weighted financial judgment rather than of precise mathematical determination. One may say theoretically that the financial manager's payment policy should be directed toward maximizing the market value of the common stock over the long-run. But practicalities bring him to a balanced judgment between the needs of the company for additional capital and the requirements of shareholders for income. There are different viewpoints concerning this balance. Some financial managers contend that dividend policy should not be based on stockholder reaction, but should be planned as an integral part of the company's investment and financing options. More specifically, the viewpoint of a vice president of Chase Financial Policy is that the relationship between dividends and free cash flow (FCF), should be determined by a company's *sources* and *uses* of funds. FCF is the difference between cash operating profits after taxes and new investments. The latter, in turn, is defined to include working capital, leased assets, and investments in affiliated companies as well as plant and equipment. According to this thinking, the higher the return on investment, the more FCF and therefore the greater the ability to pay dividends.[3] On the other hand, a Conference Board study concludes that companies now give much greater weight to the needs and expectations of shareholders and the practices of other companies either in the same industry or the same invest-ment quality.[4]

Probably the major reason for these conflicting viewpoints is the difficulty of generalizing about dividend decisions. As indicated previously, policies tend to vary both by industry and company. In determining these policies, consideration must be given to both the requirements of the firm and the desires of shareholders. The weight that should be given each, in turn, is a judgment that the financial manager must base on the conditions applicable to his own firm. Nevertheless, most large companies do pay some cash dividends. One has to go back a long way, to the severe depression year of 1935, to find a time when less than half the companies listed on the New York Stock Exchange (NYSE) paid some cash dividend.

Financial managers appear to give much consideration to the maintenance of consistent dividend records. Almost 70 percent of all NYSE firms have paid some cash dividend for ten or more of the past years. To achieve this stability, companies have to maintain payouts, even when earnings fall during a recession. In these circumstances, dividends are kept intact by pushing up payout ratios, or if necessary, even by drawing down retained earnings for several years. If it is anticipated that the slump in income is to be short-lived and the recession brief, then the policy is logical since a reduction in a dividend rate shakes investor confidence, may impair the investment status of the company in the eyes of institutional investors, such as pension funds and investment companies, and may even precipitate proxy fights and other moves by outsiders to oust management. A dividend reduction may also affect executive compensation. In some companies the executive bonus is tied to the total cash payout to shareholders. Even when this is not the case, if the directors do cut dividends and do not cut high executive salaries, there may be some stockholder protest. The value of stock options is reduced, of course, if a dividend curtailment results in a decline in the market price of the common stock, as is usually the case.

In determining the current year's dollar dividend payment, the amount paid in the last year is of prime importance, for, as mentioned, managers are reluctant to institute dividend cuts. Should earnings rise in the current year, it is likely that management will consider a dividend increase, depending on the internal need for funds, the availability of outside financing and the preceived permanency of the earnings increase. Management will likely tend toward a dividend increase if the increased earnings appear likely to continue for some time. Otherwise, the payout ratio of the firm will fall, to the possible dissatis-faction of stockholders. Should a dividend increase be decided upon, the raise may be to a level short of the company's historical payout ratio. For if the earnings increase proves to be short-lived, the firm wants to be able to avoid dividend cuts. Another way around this problem is for the firm to institute the dividend increases through a year-end extra dividend rather than by increasing the quarterly rate.[5] In essence, firms seem to have a target payout ratio (which is greater than the actual payout ratio) that they move toward as earnings increase, internal needs and external fund availabilities allow. But, in most cases, the rate of return the firm feels it will likely earn vis-a-vis the rate of return stockholders can earn on their own is a prime consideration in determining whether to pay out earnings to stockholders in dividends and how much this payout should be.

In sum, there are a whole variety of considerations and influences in the dividend payout earnings retention decision. These include stockholders' demands for income or preferences for capital gains, the need for additional capital for growth, profitability, the cost of capital, the ability or inability to obtain funds externally, a desire to avoid raids, a desire to avoid diluting equity, the need for funds for debt reduction or working capital, a desire to maintain dividend stability, and the tax impact. It is sometimes said that, on a theoretical level, paying a dollar in cash dividends versus retaining the dollar within the firm ought to make little difference to stockholders other than serve as the basis of a management signal. This view seems as foolhardy as it is purely theoretical. The degree of control a stockholder has over the one dollar in his pocket (other than in a closely held company) is surely far greater than his control over a dollar not paid out in dividends and retained by the company instead. Thus in dividend policy, as elsewhere in financial management, theoretical constructs must give way to practical reality.

14.3   SHARE DISTRIBUTIONS: STOCK DIVIDENDS AND STOCK SPLITS

A company that uses stock as opposed to cash dividends gains the use of the retained funds for expansion or other profit making ventures.[6] There is an added advantage to a company that keeps cash, when borrowing costs are high. A study[7] evaluating the purpose and results of stock dividends questioned financial officers in firms that paid them and those that did not. The study found that the majority of both groups believed that issuing stock dividends conserves cash. The authors of this study said this is only true if stock dividends replace cash dividends. The researchers stated that only four out of the 80 firms they surveyed that paid stock dividends actually reduced their cash dividends. One interesting observation made was that even if the financial managers were aware that financial literature (journal articles and finance textbooks) on the subject was generally negative, they were hesitant about changing the company's historical stock dividend practice.

Fashioned after the stock dividend study, an investigation of stock splits[8] revealed that the financial officers using this route believe that splits facilitate purchases by small investors and keep the price of the stock in an optimal range; the stock dividend users did not feel that these smaller distributions achieved the same purpose. On the other hand, officials of the stock splitting companies did not think that splits conserve cash, whereas, as indicated above, the other officials believed they obtained such conservation through stock dividends. Similarly, the majority of the stock split group did not see that splits provided any tax benefits whereas the other officials felt that stock dividends do provide certain tax advantages.

There are certain basic similarities between the stock dividend and the stock split. In both cases, the issuing corporation distributes to the recipient stockholders additional shares in proportion to the amount currently held. Accordingly, the relative interest of the stockholders in the corporation remains the same. They do not gain any real values, nor, does the corporation obtain funds. On the other hand, the two methods differ with respect to both their financial implications and their accounting treatment. Those differences are explained below.

[1] STOCK DIVIDENDS

Ordinarily, management prefers to maintain dividend payments because such a policy suggests good performance and contributes to stockholder goodwill. Despite this preference, management may be in a quandary if the corporation is confronted with a cash shortage. To get around this difficulty, management may decide to pay all or a portion of the dividend in shares of stock.

A stock dividend used to replace a cash dividend is likely to provide for the issuance of a small number of shares relative to those already outstanding. In these circumstances, it seems logical to assume that the payment would have only a minor effect on the price of the stock. This notion appears to underlie the definition of a stock dividend framed by the American Institute of Certified Public Accountants (AICPA) which stated that a stock dividend's purpose is

> ... to give the recipient stockholders some ostensibly separate evidence of a part of their respective interests in accumulated corporate earnings without distribution of cash or other property ... [9]

The recipients of stock dividends, in turn,

> look upon them as distributions of corporate earnings and usually in an amount equivalent to the fair value of the additional shares received. Furthermore, it is to be presumed that such views of recipients are materially strengthened in those instances, which are by far most numerous, where the issuances are so small in comparison with the shares previously outstanding that they do not have any apparent effect upon the share market price and, consequently, the market value of the shares previously held remains substantially unchanged. [10]

As a guideline to determine a stock payment that is "small in comparison with the shares previously outstanding," the AICPA indicated an upper range of 20-25 percent. [11] When the number of shares to be issued relative to those already outstanding falls below this range, the accounting treatment calls for a transfer from retained earnings to capital stock of an amount equal to the market value of the number of shares distributed.

To exemplify this treatment, assume that a company has 100 shares of common stock outstanding selling at $10.00 per share and has paid a 10 percent stock dividend. This would result in $100 (10 shares X $10/share) being transferred from retained earnings to capital stock as follows:

Before the stock dividend

Capital stock, par value $5 outstanding: 100 shares	$ 500
Retained earnings	1,000
Total stockholders' equity	$1,500

After the stock dividend

Capital stock, par value $5 outstanding: 110 shares	$ 600
Retained earnings	900
Total Stockholder's Equity	$1,500

If the market price of the shares to be distributed is high, even a small stock dividend can result in transferring a large sum out of retained earnings. IBM provides a classic illustration of such a case. In 1958, the company reduced its usual 5 percent stock dividend (the company at that time had paid a stock dividend of 5 percent in 18 of the past 31 years) to 2½ percent as a result of this accounting provision, also embodied in the rules of the NYSE. Even the "reduced" 2½ percent dividend resulted in the transference from retained earnings to the capital stock account of nearly $26 million more in 1958 than the net income for that year. The annual report for that year observed: "While the Board of Directors believes that stock dividends can be in the best interests of our company and the stockholders, they wish to emphasize that the Corporation cannot continue to reduce retained earnings in this manner. Depending upon the future market value of IBM stock, therefore, further stock dividends may be declared on a less frequent basis or in amounts less than 2½ percent." After 1959 IBM ceased paying stock dividends and at this writing the company still has not resumed this policy.

There is some evidence that stock dividends, even those involving relatively modest increases in the number of shares outstanding, tend to exert pressure on the price of the stock.[12] In these circumstances, a question may be raised about the justification for requiring a transfer out of retained earnings, as in the case of a cash dividend. It may be more appropriate to reserve this treatment, as well as to apply the term "stock dividends", only to the very small distributions, say those not exceeding 3 percent of the shares outstanding.

Under the tax laws, stock dividends ordinarily are not considered income to the recipients and therefore not taxable. Instead the basis of a stockholder's shares is adjusted in proportion to the distribution. Accordingly, these dividends may be of particular interest to upper tax bracket stockholders.[13] Tax regulations provide, however, that when a stockholder has a choice between stock and cash, he pays a tax.

[2] STOCK SPLITS

The AICPA refers to the purpose of a stock split as increasing ". . . the number of shares for the purpose of effecting a reduction in their unit market price and thereby of obtaining wider distribution and improved marketability of the shares."[14] Then, employing the same guidelines as for stock dividends, it states that ". . . few cases will arise where the aforementioned purpose can be accomplished through an issuance of shares which is less than, say 20 percent to 25 percent of the previously outstanding shares."[15] In effect, therefore, the conditions characterizing a stock split are the reverse of those applicable to a stock dividend. In the case of a split, a large number of shares are issued relative to those already outstanding and it is expected that the price of the stock will reflect this distribution.

As would be expected, therefore, the accounting treatment called for differs from that required for the stock dividend. There are two ways of accounting for a stock split. One simply involves a change in par value. Using the same illustration as for the stock dividend, a two for one stock split would be shown as follows:

Before the stock split:

Capital stock, par value $5 outstanding: 100 shares	$ 500
Retained earnings	1,000
Total Stockholders' Equity	$1,500

After the stock split:

Capital stock, par value $2.50 outstanding: 200 shares	$ 500
Retained earnings	1,000
Total Stockholders' Equity	$1,500

The second method involves charging a capital surplus account (if one exists) for the par value of the additional shares distributed and crediting the same amount to capital stock, as follows (for a two for one stock split):

Before the stock split:

Capital stock, par value $5 outstanding: 100 shares	$ 500
Capital surplus	500
Retained earnings	500
Total Stockholders' Equity	$1,500

After the stock split:

Capital stock, par value $5 outstanding: 200 shares	$1,000
Retained earnings	500
Total Stockholders' Equity	$1,500

The net effect of both these methods of accounting for a stock split is the same. In the first method, however, the par value is changed. In the second, the capital surplus account is capitalized. Among the benefits a company may derive from a stock split, the following are considered most important:

- *Increased stock marketability*—This results from the possible increase in shareowners, the gain in number of shares on the market, and the reduction in price which places the issue in a popular price range. There is some evidence that this latter point (reduction in price to a popular price range) is perhaps the primary reason for most stock splits, although this benefit may be diminished because of the large amount of stock now held by institutions.

- *Rising volume*—This, in turn, helps to stabilize market conditions, permitting orders to be executed quickly and efficiently with minimum price change between transactions. This benefits the company as well as the shareowners, since a small supply of outstanding stock may cause unwarranted price fluctuations.
- *Broader base for future equity financing*—Stock splits also may provide added authorized but unissued stock which can be used in mergers and acquisitions. This objective can also be accomplished by simply increasing the authorized common.
- *Reduction in reported large earnings per share*—This may tend to improve the public image of the company although, quite obviously, such a reduction would not represent any real economic change.

On infrequent occasions, reverse stock splits are utilized by management's seeking to rehabilitate or resuscitate the value of stock which has fallen to a low point in the market. It is an embarrassment both to the exchange on which the shares are traded as well as to the company to have its shares traded at very low prices. In addition, in terms of achieving a better market for the security, it may be desirable to avoid large and dramatic percentage price swings which can occur in very low priced stocks. Because exchange prices are denominated in eighths of a point, very large percentage changes can occur when a stock selling at $1 or $2 changes by only a few eighths. Therefore, reverse stock splits are sometimes asked for by the exchange in order to bring the price of the stock into a desired or more normal trading range.

[3] EVALUATION OF STOCK DIVIDENDS AND STOCK SPLITS

In bull markets, the hoopla that accompanies an announcement of a stock split or a new stock dividend continually surprises sophisticated investors. Some investors seem to react as if they are getting something for nothing and often push the price of the stock up for a time. However, sophisticated investors maintain that stock dividends *per se* are of no value to investors. They simply represent a division of the company into additional pieces of paper. The individual shareholders have no larger share of the pie, nor has the pie increased. While the stock dividend can be sold for cash, this is offset by the expected decline in price of the holder's remaining shares, resulting from the larger number of shares now on the market.

The same conclusion applies to stock splits. They are valueless, adding nothing to the worth of the corporation or to the relative share of the stockholder. They have no more substance than stock dividends. A two for one stock split and a 100 percent stock dividend are the same thing. Neither increases any real values, either of the corporation or of the shareholder.

Why, then, do investors appear to desire share distributions? The answer may be that just prior to a share distribution announcement, a price increase may occur. Moreover, when earnings and/or cash dividend increases accompany the share distribution, the increase is likely to be lasting; otherwise, returns tend to fall back to what they were before the announcement of the share distribution.[16] Apparently, therefore, the earnings and cash dividends of a firm are the considerations which affect the market returns of a company's stock, rather than the number of common shares it has outstanding as the result of a share distribution. This is so regardless of whether the share distribution is large or a small percentage of outstanding shares.

14.4   THE DIVIDEND REINVESTMENT PLAN

In a dividend reinvestment plan shareholders are offered the opportunity to reinvest their dividends in the common shares of the firm paying the dividend. More than 800 firms listed on either the NYSE or the American Stock Exchange offer such a plan. In addition, there are hundreds of over-the-counter companies and mutual funds that seek additional equity capital through this approach, without spending a penny in underwriting fees. The shareholder is also attracted to a double bargain in some companies' offers which not only provide for payment of brokerage fees, but also for the purchase of shares at a discount from the market price. In the year before AT&T began its purchase offer of 5 percent off market price, it raised $184 million from its reinvestment program. In the nine months after its discount offer, AT&T collected $273 million. In 1979 its dividend reinvestment and employee savings program provided $1.7 billion in new equity. Companies without AT&T's large number of shareholders also find these plans a good internal source of funds.

Most of the stock purchased in these plans has been authorized, but not previously issued. Another interesting aspect of such plans and a growing trend is the opportunity to make monthly limited cash payments in addition to the reinvestment of dividends. The company gains market price support from these purchases and the investor has the advantage of dollar cost averaging.[17]

14.5   DEPRECIATION

Machinery and equipment, plant and buildings, indeed, all fixed assets except land, wear out over time, and in a going concern, need to be replaced, usually by more expensive and improved facilities. It is customary to deduct this depreciation as an expense from gross income each year to allocate the original cost of the fixed asset over its useful life. This is the classic accounting definition of depreciation. According to presently accepted accounting principles, this deduction is based on the historical cost of the properties acquired. As discussed in Chapter 3, the FASB, recognizing that these costs tend to understate the value of the properties during periods of rising prices and therefore to understate the annual depreciation charge to income, required among other things in FASB Statement No. 33, that depreciation expense calculated on a current cost basis be included in supplemental information. General Instrument, for example, disclosed that under the current cost inflation adjusted method, depreciation expense for the fiscal year 1980 was some 22 percent greater than that reported in the traditional income statement.[18]

[1] THE DIFFERING CONCEPTS OF DEPRECIATION

From a purely accounting point of view, depreciation is the allocation of the original cost of a fixed asset to the periods comprising its useful life. It is a noncash expense, chargeable to current operations. The accountant understands that depreciation, in itself, generates no funds. It is operations that generate funds, and depreciation is merely an expense entry on the books of the firm. It is true that if a firm has more depreciation in a given period it has more funds. But this is only as the result of the firm having lower taxable income and thus less taxes to pay. In a tax-free world (or to a firm with no income taxes to pay) depreciation can never be a source of funds. In this view, the accountant stresses the term *allocation,* as his concept of depreciation.

The concern with inflation, as indicated above, has broadened the concept of depreciation from one based only on original costs to embrace, as well, one based on higher replacement costs. As defined by the SEC, this is the "lowest amount that would have to be paid in the normal course of business to obtain a new asset of equivalent operating or productive capability." Based on this concept, Boise Cascade estimated that the total replacement costs of its facilities would be 240 percent of original cost.[19] Replacement cost, in turn, cannot exceed recovery measured by the amount that would be realized if the asset is to be sold.

But just as the accountant views depreciation as a process of allocating original cost in a systematic and rational manner, and not as a process of *valuation,* to the economist, it is just that. An economist looks upon depreciation as a means of expressing the decline in value of fixed assets which has taken place during a given period. In this sense, depreciation is akin to "wear and tear" and is employed as a deduction from original cost in order to express the current value of a fixed asset. Alternatively, an accountant deducts accumulated depreciation from original cost in order to indicate the portion of the original cost which has been allocated as an expense to past periods and to show the difference which represents the portion which is to be allocated to future periods. To the economist, it is possible that in a given period an asset may have appreciated in value. To the accountant this could never occur.

The financial manager, on the other hand, looks upon depreciation as a means of preserving cash flow. This point of view was expressed by Citicorp of New York in one of its monthly letters: "Apart from their influence on reported earnings, depreciation charges are important because they constitute an increasing 'internal' source of funds for financing business. This is due to the fact that they are an expense item involving no cash outlay at the time but representing instead the recovery, in piecemeal fashion, of the original capital investment in plant and equipment. In other words, even if a company reported no net profit (after the taking of depreciation) on operations it would, theoretically at least, experience a gain in cash holdings by the amount of its depreciation charge—assuming no capital outlays or other special transactions affecting the cash flow . . . Industrial rebuilding and expansion have been financed to a major and still rising extent by these mounting depreciation charges. They hold down the amount of outside money required for growth and permit a large portion of current earnings to be paid out in dividends."

[2] DEPRECIATION POLICY

Depreciation policy is a matter of considerable importance to the financial manager because if its impact on profitability, its size in relation to total deductible expenses of operation, its relationship to replacement policy, its effect on the rate of return on investment for the enterprise, its impact on the company's ability to meet tax liabilities and on the firm's competitive condition in terms of modernization or obsolescence of plant and equipment. Moreover, for many companies, depreciation charges are larger than net income.

The significance of depreciation policy varies for different industries. Thus, in the case of Allegheny Corporation, which is principally in the financial services business, depreciation represents less than one percent of the funds provided from operations, whereas for Mohawk Data Sciences, depreciation represent some 40 percent of such funds. Reflecting the vital role of depreciation in the computer field, a prominent observer of the financial scene noted, in effect, that the depreciation process receives paramount attention from these (computer leasing) companies because, for all intents and purposes, depreciation is really their stock in trade—they are, in essence, selling off each year that year's utilization of computer installations.[20]

Policy variations also exist within the same industry and even among equipment types in the same firm. The financial manager must consider whether to defer taxes and increase cash flow or improve the reported earnings picture. This policy, in turn, is implemented through depreciation deductions which are affected by both the method of depreciation and the assumption of asset lives.

[3] METHODS OF TAKING DEPRECIATION

A basic distinction may be made between straight line and accelerated depreciation methods. There are also minor variations on these themes, such as an approach that relates depreciation to usage.

The financial manager's choice of method will have an important impact on reported profitability, tax liability, and costs. It is, of course, possible to use one method for tax purposes and a different method for internal company operations and reports to stockholders. Also, different methods can be used for assets acquired at different times as well as for different classes of assets. In economic theory, the method chosen should reflect the cost of the service which the company received from the asset during the current period; the firm should carry forward as an asset to the end of the period only that part of the original cost which can be expected to provide a further service benefit. Other objectives may be to recover costs as quickly as possible, to minimize taxes and to maximize funds retained from current operations for future use. Alternatively, a method may be chosen which maximizes current reported net income.

(a) Straight Line Depreciation

The most common and easiest method to understand is straight line depreciation. Assume that a complex of machines to produce steel is purchased by a steel company at a cost of $25 million. The company knows that operating the machinery regularly and steadily each year will wear it out, will "depreciate" it a little each year until at the end of 25 years, it will be useless. Under straight line depreciation, the theory is that it will wear out an equal amount each year over the 25 years, and thus the company allocates as depreciation, $1 million of the original cost to each of the 25 years. Therefore, at the end of 25 years, when the machinery is worn out, the company has written off the entire purchase price of $25 million.

Many companies still use straight line depreciation. It is a simple, clear way of taking depreciation, but from a management point of view, it has several limitations. Assets depreciate more rapidly in the first few years of use than in the later years. Even after a year of use, equipment is second hand and in most cases will bring, if it can be sold at all, a considerably smaller sum than the initial cost less a year's straight line depreciation. There is the ever present danger, in this age of automation and rapid scientific progress, that a competitor will come up with new, improved and more efficient equipment, which makes relatively recently acquired machinery, only two or three years old, too expensive to operate or obsolete.

(b) Taking Usage Into Account

While the straight line method of depreciation is simple and clear, it charges an equal amount of cost against each year of the asset's useful life without regard to the actual productivity rendered annually by the asset. It assumes the service benefits are distributed evenly or equally over each year of useful life. Such is rarely the case, however, with many types of equipment. For example, machinery in a cyclical industry, such as steel, is used very actively in a boom year and relatively less in a recession year. Or a truck owned by a construction firm may be operated almost continuously in good years and much less so in poor years. To meet situations like these, depreciation methods based on the relative use of facilities have been developed. The useful life of an asset is expressed in terms of units of operating activity rather than time, such as the number of hours operated, number of items machined or produced, or the number of miles driven.

For example, we may express the useful life of a vehicle as 100,000 miles driven rather than in terms of time—two to five years. On the basis of a useful operating life of 100,000 miles driven, the vehicle cost $5,000 and after it is driven 100,000 miles it is to be scrapped (no salvage value), then the depreciable cost is 5 cents per mile. Assuming that in the first year of its use the vehicle is driven 12,000 miles, the depreciation to be taken that year is 12,000 times 5 cents, or $600. The cost will be allocated to accounting periods at the rate of 5 cents per mile driven over the 100,000 mile useful life of the vehicle, regardless of the number of accounting periods this takes. In short, depreciation is based on use and not on a predetermined time span of useful life.

It is common for companies in the extractive field to base their depreciation on units of production. For example, Pennzoil uses this method for its mining properties, except that those with an estimated life less than the estimated life of the mineral deposits are depreciated on a straight line method.[21] Boise Cascade provides for the depreciation and amortization of property and equipment on the units of production method at certain wood products and paper manufacturing facilities. Other facilities are depreciated on the straight line method.[22]

(c) Accelerated Depreciation Method

Several alternative methods of accelerated depreciation are in current use. One is the double declining balance method which may be switched over to straight line depreciation at any time during the useful life of the asset. If we assume the acquisition of a machine at a cost of $10,000 with a useful life of 20 years, straight line depreciation will be at a rate of 5 percent (one twentieth) of the original cost each year over a 20-year period. At the end of the twentieth year, the entire cost will have been written-off, as indicated in Figure 14.1. Also shown is the double declining balance method, which is applied each year at twice the straight line rate (10 percent in this case), not to the total original cost but to the declining balance of the undepreciated cost. This method has both an advantage and a disadvantage for tax purposes. The advantage is that a more rapid write-off of cost occurs in the earlier years. The disadvantage is that an unallocated balance of cost remains at the end of the 20 year period. In Figure 14.1 for example, the unallocated balance is $1,216. For this reason the tax law permits a shift to straight line after an initial depreciation period under the double declining balance method. The firm could obtain the advantages of accelerated depreciation through double declining balance and at the same time, by switching at some point to straight line, could write-off the entire cost over the stated useful life.

Another method of accelerated depreciation permitted under the tax laws is the sum-of-the-years-digits method. Figure 14.1 shows the sum-of-the-years-digits depreciation for a machine which costs $10,000 and which has a useful life of 20 years. During the first year the depreciation charge will be $952 or 20/210 of the original cost. The second year 19/210 of $10,000 will be charged off as depreciation. In short, the depreciation rate is a fraction whose numerator is the years of remaining life of the capital asset and whose denominator is the sum of the digits of the total number of years of useful life of the asset. In this example, the sum of the digits is 210, while at the beginning of the first year of useful life there are 20 years of operation remaining. The numerator is therefore 20, the denominator 210. If an airplane with an expected life of five years were depreciated by this method, the rate of depreciation the first year would be 5/15, with 15 being the sum of the digits (1, 2, 3, 4, and 5). The great tax advantage of this method is that it permits a rapid write-off of the cost of the asset without leaving an undepreciated balance at the end. Thus, the years-digits method is especially useful in writing-off assets subject to sudden obsolescence.

Figure 14.2 compares the depreciation patterns of the three basic methods. It shows that for an asset with a 20 year life a firm may write-off one half the cost over the first half of its useful life by straight line depreciation. Under the double declining balance method, two-thirds of the original cost can be written-off over the first half of the asset's useful life. Sum of the years-digits permits a company to write-off about three-fourths of the original cost in the first half of the asset's useful life.[23] Thus, if a rapid write-off of the cost is the financial manager's main objective, he will wish to choose sum of the years-digits depreciation.[24]

In general, straight line depreciation will give higher profits in the early years of an asset's life, as opposed to the accelerated method. This, of course, assumes that a switch in depreciation methods does not take place. For a firm

FIGURE 14.1 Four depreciation methods

End of Year	Straight Line 5%		Double Declining Balance		Double Declining Balance 10 Years, Then Straight Line		Sum of the Years— Digits	
	Deduction	Balance	Deduction	Balance	Deduction	Balance	Deduction	Balance
1	$500	$9500	$1000	$9000	$1000	$9000	$952	$9048
2	500	9000	900	8100	900	8100	905	8143
3	500	8500	810	7290	810	7290	857	7286
4	500	8000	729	6561	729	6561	810	6476
5	500	7500	656	5905	656	5905	762	5714
6	500	7000	591	5314	591	5314	714	5000
7	500	6500	531	4783	531	4783	667	4333
8	500	6000	478	4305	478	4305	619	3714
9	500	5500	431	3874	431	3874	571	3143
10	500	5000	387	3487	387	3487	524	2619
15	500	2500	229	2059	349	1743	286	714
20	500	0	135	1216	349	0	48	0

which is making net acquisitions of fixed assets at a greater rate than it is taking depreciation, however, the depreciable balance is constantly rising. In such a situation, the accelerated methods will continue to give greater depreciation deductions and lower profit figures. Inflationary pressures and rising prices for fixed asset acquisitions, as well as corporate expansion, tend to bring about this situation of continually higher reported profits under the straight line method.

FIGURE 14.2 *Depreciation methods on facilities having a 20-year life*

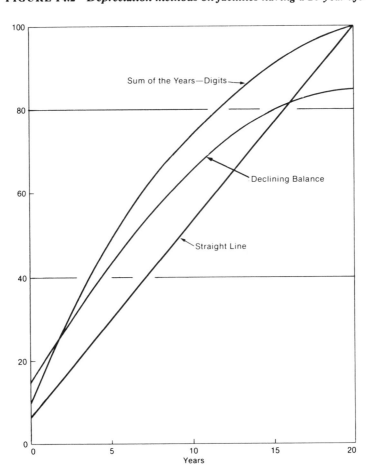

Since the method of taking depreciation has an important effect on both profits and tax liabilities, the Internal Revenue Service promulgates strict rules for and checks carefully on corporate depreciation policies. Business demands for more realistic and liberal depreciation allowances, therefore, take the form of pressure either on Congress to change the applicable law or the Internal Revenue Service to change the relevant regulations. (Some of the tax complexities of depreciation are discussed in Chapter 24.)

382

(d) The Impact of Depreciation on Financial Management

Choosing the method of depreciation has important consequences for fiancial management, affecting both the flow of internal funds and the uses of these funds. If allowances for depreciation exceed current capital expenditures, the excess may add to working capital and eliminate the need for short-term borrowing. Or the funds may be used to pay off term-loans or retire outstanding callable bonds. On the other hand, if depreciation allowances are less than current capital expenditures, the company will need either to draw on its own working capital or to use funds from current earnings, causing a greater retention of earnings than otherwise might be the case. As a third possibility, the firm might turn to outside borrowing.

The impact of alternative depreciation policies on profitability and tax liability is never insignificant. Overdepreciation results in an understatement of earnings and may be particularly useful in a period when large capital expenditures are necessary. For example, at one time Eastern Air Lines, on its stockholders' reports, depreciated its planes in four years instead of the seven years allowed at the time for tax purposes. This, plus a limited payout of earnings, enabled Eastern to purchase planes with funds supplied mostly from internal sources. The company switched to a seven year useful life for depreciating planes when it found that depreciation on a four year useful life would have caused it to report a $3.7 million net loss for a certain fiscal year, whereas by using a seven year useful life it was able to report a $7.1 million net profit.

Taking inadequate depreciation, on the other hand, overstates earnings if the company is operating in the black, and tends to minimize losses if it is operating in the red. During a recession a company may charge off less than it is legally permitted to do in order to maintain earnings so that stockholders will not be aroused.

Depreciation methods have differing impacts on the investment decision. Liberalized depreciation may have a significant effect on the "discounted cash flow" rate of return calculations (see, Chapter 18). Liberalized depreciation increases net cash receipts during the early years of an asset's life by decreasing income tax flows. A stream of declining annual receipts has a greater present value than a uniform stream which provides the same total for a given period of years. Liberalized depreciation, then, provides a higher rate of return than straight line depreciation using discounted cash flow methods.

Accelerated depreciation may be desirable if the company is expanding rapidly and can maximize both its rate of return and its tax savings by large depreciation deductions. Financial managers who anticipate lower earnings or less rapid growth, though, may prefer more conservative depreciation techniques because of the smaller impact they will have on stated profitability. Management must also determine whether or not taxes are likely to be reduced in the future.

A final word of caution with respect to depreciation is in order. While depreciation in excess of current capital expenditures may generate working capital, this does not necessarily mean that funds will be available for the replacement of capital assets when needed. The company may be holding large amounts of current assets in the form of illiquid accounts receivable or inventory, rather than cash, at the time the capital expenditures become necessary. Higher prices may have necessitated larger working capital and now may prevent its being drawn down for capital replacements. Depreciation allowances help a company limit its dividends, but they do not necessarily provide cash for replacing capital assets unless management policy is to set up a replacement fund, held in cash or short-term government securities and expendable only for that purpose. Only a minority of companies do this, however.

14.6   OTHER SOURCES OF INTERNAL FUNDS

Typically, the great bulk of a corporation's internal funds come from operations (net income plus depreciation.) The other most common internal source in concerned with taxation, either through the investment tax credit or deferred income tax provisions.

[1] THE INVESTMENT TAX CREDIT

Since the investment tax credit is a direct offset against taxes owed the federal government, it represents a source of funds to the corporation. The credit may be accounted for by the flow through method as a reduction in the current income tax provision or it may be amortized over the productive life of the acquired property. According to studies made by Price Waterhouse & Co. and the American Institute of Certified Public Accountants, nearly 90 percent of all big industrial corporations use the flow through method.[25] However, AT&T, General Electric, General Motors and DuPont amortize investment credits. Commenting on this, an AT&T financial officer said, we are of the opinion that the "amortization" method is the proper accounting for the investment credit because it spreads the effect over the life period of the equipment which gave rise to the investment credit, thereby, relating the tax benefit to the years in which equipment is used to produce income and not to the year in which the equipment was acquired.

The credit is based on the acquisition of property. To qualify, the property must be depreciable and tangible (except buildings or their structural components). It must be used in manufacturing, production or extraction and have a useful life of at least three years.

The amount of investment in qualifying property that is eligible for the investment tax credit depends upon the useful life of the property and whether it is new or used. Moreover, the amount of credit allowable against the tax liability in any one year is limited, although any excess may be carried back or forward.

The credit allowable is the sum the investment tax credit carry forwards, 10 percent of the current year's investment eligible for the regular investment credit, 10 percent of the current investment eligible for the business energy credit, plus the investment tax credit carry backs. The regular investment credit is limited to the income tax liability shown on the return, or $25,000 plus 90 percent of the tax liability in excess of $25,000, whichever is less.

[2] THE DEFERRED INCOME TAX PROVISION

Deferred income taxes arise from recognizing revenue and expense in different periods for tax and financial reporting purposes. For example, a corporation may employ accelerated depreciation for tax purposes but straight line depreciation for book purposes. It may then recognize the tax effect by a charge to expense and a counter balancing credit to a deferred tax account in the balance sheet. Through this charge, the corporation, in effect, delays the timing of the increase in book net income which results from lower taxes through use of the accelerated method for tax purposes.

Overall, book depreciation below tax depreciation is probably the most common reason for the deferred income tax provision. There are, however, other factors. Thus, of more importance for Sunbeam in 1979 was inventory appreciation relief for tax purposes; this was made available in the United Kingdom.[26] For General Instrument, the principal item in the deferred income tax provision for 1979 was unremitted earnings of foreign subsidiaries.[27] And the main component in the 1979 deferred income tax account of Allied Stores was the installment method of accounting for sales.[28]

The deferred income tax provision is typically included among the internal sources of working capital reported by corporations, but it is not likely to be significant. As an illustration, for the year ended 1979, Boise Cascade obtained slightly more than half of its working capital from internal sources. Of these about 57 percent came from income, 36 percent from depreciation, and 7 percent from the deferred income tax provision.[29]

[3] THE PURCHASING POWER GAIN FROM HOLDING NET MONETARY LIABILITIES

The conversion of the source and application of funds statement to a constant dollar basis produces several other sources, most common of which is the purchasing power gain from holding net monetary liabilities. Monetary items represent assets or liabilities—such as cash, accounts receivable or payable, and long-term debt—which are or will be turned into a fixed number of dollars, regardless of changes that may occur in the general price level. Nonmonetary items, on the other hand, are assets or liabilities—such as inventory, plant, and equipment—that are expected to retain their purchasing power regardless of changes in the price level.

A company that holds net monetary liabilities during periods of rising prices will presumably be able to pass on a portion of this inflation to its creditors and vendors because it will be making payments in dollars of declining purchasing power. This gain is excluded from income but added directly to retained earnings. While it does not produce a current cash flow, it does permit the clearing of debt with cheaper dollars and, therefore, in effect, preserves cash.

In the sense of preserving cash, the purchasing power gain may be regarded as a source of funds. It does not, however, contribute directly to cash flow. Accordingly, companies have tended to view its implications differently. Thus, the GAT Corporation and PepsiCo regard it as an offset against interest expense. Chessie System considers it an offset against depreciation. Still other corporations, apparently concerned that their shareholders might regard the purchasing power gain as a source of funds for the payment of dividends, specifically state that it does not serve this purpose. For example, Seaboard Coast Line Industries points out that "This gain does not represent a receipt of cash and, therefore, should not be considered as providing funds for corporate purposes such as reinvestment or dividend distribution."[30] In a similar vein, Wheelabrator-Frye states, "during periods of inflation, the holding of monetary assets (cash and receivables) results in a loss of general purchasing power. Conversely, the holding of liabilities results in a gain as less purchasing power is needed to satisfy such obligations. The amount has been calculated based on the average net monetary liabilities for the year multiplied by the change in the Consumer Price Index for the year. Such amount does not represent funds available for distribution to the shareholders."[31]

14.7   CHAPTER SUMMARY

In this chapter we looked at the factors affecting dividend policy. The use of a stock dividend as a supplement or alternate to a cash dividend was also analyzed. Stock splits and their purposes were reviewed as well. In analyzing internal sources of funds—funds generated by operations—our primary concern centered on depreciation. We looked at depreciation policy in terms of differing depreciation concepts and methods of taking depreciation. In addition, some other, less important, sources of internal funds were briefly reviewed.

FOOTNOTES

1. David L. Babson & Co., *Weekly Staff Letter,* January 3, 1980.
2. *Dun's Review,* December 1979, pp. 64-73.
3. Dennis S. Soter, "The Dividend Controversy—What It Means for Corporate Policy," *The Financial Executive,* May 1979, p. 38.
4. Vincent Massaro, "The Equity Market: Corporate Practices and Issues," *The Conference Board, Inc.,* Report No. 764, 1979.
5. Most firms pay cash dividends on a quarterly basis. But some firms supplement their quarterly payments with a year-end extra payment.
6. Stock dividends are dealt with in this chapter rather than one devoted to capital structure reorganizations and rearrangements (Chapter 21) because they are often used as a supplement or an alternative to a cash dividend.
7. Peter C. Eismann and Edward A. Moses, "Stock Dividends: Managements' View," *Financial Analysts Journal,* July-August 1978, pp. 77-80.
8. H. Kent Baker and Patricia L. Gallagher, "Management's View of Stock Splits," *Financial Management,* Summer 1980, pp. 73-77.
9. *AICPA, ARB No. 43,* Chap. 7B, paragraph 1. The Financial Accounting Standards Board (FASB) has supplanted the AICPA but the ruling on stock dividends and stock splits still stands.
10. *Ibid.,* paragraph 10.
11. The 20-25 percent region is purposely imprecise to provide an approximate division. Distributions within the region could be treated either as a dividend or as a split.
12. Sherman Chottiner and Allan Young, "A Test of the AICPA Differentiation Between Stock Dividends and Stock Splits," *Journal of Accounting Research,* Autumn 1971, pp. 367-374; and Allan Young, "The Effects of Share Distributions on Price Action," *Financial Review,* 1974, pp. 11-16.
13. For a method of determining stockholders' cash dividend preferences see, David F. Scott and J. William Petty, "A Note on the Relevance of Dividend Policy," *Financial Review,* Winter 1979, pp. 59-65.
14. ARB No. 43, *op. cit.,* paragraph 2.

386

15. *Ibid.*, paragraph 15.
16. Eugene Fama, Lawrence Fisher, Michael Jensen and Richard Roll, "Adjustment of Stock Prices to New Information," *International Economic Review*, February 1969, pp. 1-21; W. H. Hausman, R. R. West, and J. A. Largay, "Stock Splits, Price Changes and Trading Profits: A Synthesis," *Journal of Business*, January 1971, pp. 69-77; James A. Millar and Bruce D. Fielitz, "Stock-Split and Stock-Dividend Decisions," *Financial Management*, Winter 1973, pp. 35-45; and Lawrence Ingrassia, "Sign of the Bull: Recent Increase in Share Prices Has Led to Flurry of Stock Splits, Stock Dividends," *The Wall Street Journal*, January 27, 1983, p. 56.
17. In dollar cost averaging, an investor who systematically buys shares by investing equal dollar sums over a long period of both high and low prices, obtains more shares during periods of low prices and fewer shares during periods of high prices, thus paying a lower average price per share than if the shares were all purchased at their average (mean) price.
18. General Instrument Corporation, *Annual Report Fiscal 1980*, pp. 27-34.
19. Boise Cascade Corporation, *Annual Report, 1979*, p. 50.
20. Abraham J. Briloff, *More Debits Than Credits*, Harper & Row, 1976, New York.
21. Pennzoil Company, *Annual Report, 1979*, p. 24.
22. Boise Cascade Corporation *op. cit.*, p. 39.
23. Of course, the precise nature of the relationship between the double declining balance and the sum of the years-digits methods depends upon the number of years of useful life of the fixed asset.
24. When using the straight line and sum of the years-digits methods, salvage value is deducted from the depreciable balance before applying the appropriate rate. In the double declining balance method, however, salvage value is not directly considered. Since double declining balance depreciation will never result in a complete write-off, the difference taken at the end of an asset's useful life is presumed to approximate the salvage value.
25. *Business Week*, February 18, 1980, p. 3.
26. Sunbeam Corporation, *Annual Report, 1979*, p. 26.
27. General Instrument Corporation, *op. cit.*, p. 29.
28. Allied Stores Corporation, *Annual Report, 1979*, p. 16.
29. Boise Cascade Corporation, *op. cit.*, p. 37.
30. Financial Accounting Standards Board, "Examples of the Use of FASB Statement No. 33, Financial Reporting and Changing Prices," 1980, pp. 65-68.
31. Wheelabrator-Frye, Inc., *Annual Report, 1979*, p. 29.

SUGGESTED READINGS

Auerbach, A. J. and D. W. Jorgenson, "Inflation-Proof Depreciation of Assets," *Harvard Business Review*, September/October 1980.

Baker, H. K. and P. L. Gallagher, "Management's View of Stock Splits," *Financial Management*, Summer 1980.

——— and W. H. Seippel, "Dividend Reinvestment Plans Win Wide Currency," *Harvard Business Review*, November/December 1980.

Blume, Marshall E., "Stock Returns and Dividend Yields: Some More Evidence," *Review of Economics and Statistics*, November 1980.

Caks, J. "Sense and Nonsense About Depreciation," *Financial Management*, Autumn 1981.

"Can High Dividends Actually Hurt a Stock Price?" *Institutional Investor*, March 1981.

Eggitton, D. A., "Distributable Profit and the Pursuit of Prudence," *Accounting and Business Research*, Winter 1980.

Fama, Eugene, et al., "Adjustment of Stock Prices to New Information," *International Economic Review*, February 1969.

Gehrlein, W. V. and T. K. Tiemann, "Optimal Depreciation Policies for Regulated Firms," *Engineering Economist*, Winter 1980.

Hankansson, N. H., "To Pay or Not to Pay Dividends," *Journal of Finance*, May 1982.

Hess, P.J., "Ex-Dividend Day Behaviour of Stock Returns: Further Evidence on Tax Effects," *Journal of Finance*, May 1982.

Kalay, Avner, "Earnings Uncertainty and the Payout Ratio: Some Empirical Evidence," *Review of Economics and Statistics*, August 1981.

Kee, Robert and Oliver Feltus, "Role of the Abandonment Value in the Investment Decision," *Management Accounting*, August 1982.

Kolb, Robert, "Predicting Dividend Changes," *Journal of Economics and Business*, Spring/Summer 1981.

Litzenberger, Robert H. and Krishna Ramaswamy, "Dividends, Short Selling Restrictions, Tax Induced Investor Clienteles and Market Equilibrium," *Journal of Finance*, May 1980.

McInish, Thomas H. and Donald J. Puglis, "Ex-Dividend Behavior of Preferred Stocks," *Review of Business and Economic Research*, Fall 1980.

Michaud, R. O. and P. L. Davis, "Valuation Model Bias and the Scale Structure of Dividend Discount Returns," *Journal of Finance*, May 1982.

Modigliani, F., "Debt, Dividend Policy, Taxes, Inflation and Market Valuation," *Journal of Finance*, May 1982.

Raboy, D. G., "Depreciation Policy and Economic Efficiency," *Business Economics*, January 1982.

Ramaswamy, K., "Effects of Dividends on Common Stock Price: Tax Effects or Information Effects?" *Journal of Finance*, May 198_.

Rappaport, Alfred, "Inflation Accounting and Corporate Dividend," *Financial Executive*, February 1981.

Reilly, F. K. and E. F. Drzycimski, "Short Run Profits From Stock Splits," *Financial Management*, Summer 1981.

Roizen, J. A. H., "New Approach to Depreciation of Corporate Vehicles for Tax Reduction Purposes," *CA Magazine*, August 1982.

Schneid, Daniel L., "Packaging the Dividend Reinvestment Plan, *Financial Executive*, June 1981.

"Tax Shelters—Averaging Conventions Under CLADR System," *CPA Journal*, May 1981.

Wittebort, S., "Do Investors Really Care About Dividends?" *Institutional Investor*, March 1981.

15

LONG-TERM FINANCING

15.1 IMPORTANCE OF LONG-TERM FINANCING

In Chapter 1 we described the financing decision as one of the most important made by the financial manager. A wide variety of funding sources are available. After carefully evaluating cost, availability, risk, control, and other factors, the financial manager must determine the appropriate financing mix. Subsequently, in Chapter 19, we shall discuss another significant aspect of the long-term financing decision—whether a firm's choice of financing mix or capital structure over time can affect the value of its common stock.

In actual practice, there is a wide range of financing mix between debt and equity for many firms and industries. For example, Briggs & Stratton, Campbell Soup, Chemed Corporation and General Steel Industries have little or no debt in their capital structure. On the other hand, companies such as American Airlines, LTV, and a number of public utilities have a preponderance of debt. In this chapter, we discuss the factors that influence the firm's choice between debt (bonds) and equity (common and preferred stock). In addition, we highlight the principal bond and stock instruments available to the firm.

15.2 FACTORS INFLUENCING THE CHOICE OF DEBT

As we indicated in Chapter 14, companies normally find it expedient to finance by means of retained earnings; this approach, however, is often difficult to follow exclusively over a long period of time. Moreover, a moderate amount of debt may provide some benefits to earnings available for stockholders without exposing the company to undue financial risk.[1] Accordingly, the number of firms without any long-term debt in their capital structure is disappearing.

To a large extent, management's decision on financing methods hinges on the field in which the company operates. The considerable fixed capital requirements of public utilities lead these companies to do much of their financing through long-term debt. Similarly, railroads, which also have a substantial need for fixed capital, are relatively large long-term borrowers. In general, however, railroads borrow somewhat less than public utilities. Industrial companies may have more volatile earnings than either public utilities or railroads and, therefore, place relatively more emphasis on equity financing.

Various factors, which will be discussed later, tend to place upper limits on the degree of debt a firm can absorb. Consequently, companies usually follow self-imposed debt guidelines. We now consider a number of factors that favorably influence companies toward the use of debt. Then, in the following section, we address those factors that tend to limit the firm's use of long-term debt.

[1] FIRM PREFERENCE FOR DEBT

Among the more important factors encouraging a corporate preference for debt are the following:

- tax savings;
- ease of selling;
- lower costs of flotation and servicing;
- advantage of financial leverage; and
- additional factors.

These are discussed in the ensuing sections.

(a) Tax Savings

It is a very simple fact of corporate financial life that interest on bonds is deductible for income tax purposes as a business expense, whereas, dividends, on preferred or common stock, are not. Thus, to service a $1,000, 10 percent bond would take only $100 out of gross income; whereas, the dividend cost of $1,000 of 10 percent preferred stock, at a 50 percent marginal federal tax rate, would take $200 out of gross income, since dividends are paid after taxes.

The financial manager must decide whether the advantage of the tax savings justifies the more stringent financial requirements of bond interest as compared with preferred dividends. In general, payment of bond interest is a legally enforceable management duty; whereas, payment of preferred and common stock dividends are prerogatives of corporate management—within bounds.

In the case of common stock financing as an alternative, another aspect arises. It is possible that the common can be sold at a sufficiently high price to make the aftertax cost of common stock less than that of bond financing, or at least provide greater earnings per share. For example, assume a company has 100,000 shares of common stock outstanding, no debt, and is contemplating raising $2 million of new funds. With the new $2 million it expects its total gross income to be $500,000. If the company decided to raise the $2 million by selling bonds on which it paid 10 percent interest, it would incur annual fixed charges of $200,000. Assuming a tax rate of 50 percent, the company would have net earnings of $150,000 after taxes and interest, or $1.50 per share as follows:

Gross Income	$500,000
Less Bond Interest	200,000
Taxable Income	$300,000
Less Taxes (At 50% Rate)	150,000
Net Income After Taxes	$150,000
Shares Outstanding	100,000
Earnings Per Share	$1.50 ($150,000/100,000).

On the other hand, if the company decided to raise $2 million by the sale of common stock, it would incur no fixed charges and its net profit after taxes would be $250,000 as follows:

Gross Income	$500,000
Less Taxes (At 50% Rate)	$250,000
Net Income After Taxes	$250,000

The resultant earnings per share would depend on the number of shares of common stock the firm had to sell to raise the $2 million, and this, of course, would depend on the stock's sale price. With bond financing the company's earnings per share, as we have seen, would be $1.50. To obtain the same earnings per share, by common stock financing, the company would have to sell an additional 67,000 shares, bringing the total shares outstanding to 167,000. The additional share amount is determined by solving the following equation:

$$\frac{\text{Net Income After Taxes}}{\text{Total Shares Outstanding}} = \frac{\$250,000}{100,000 + \text{Additional Number of Shares}}$$
$$= \$1.50 \text{ earnings per share.}$$

The selling price for these additional shares is approximately $30 per share ($2 million/67,000 shares).

The financial manager, therefore, knows that if he can sell stock at more than $30 per share (a price/earnings ratio of more than 20/1), not only can he avoid the creation of fixed charges (bond interest payments), but as compared to the bond financing, he can also raise the per share earnings of the common stockholders. To the extent that he must sell common below $30 per share, as contrasted to using bond financing, the per share earnings of the stockholders are reduced and the financial manager must decide whether the reduced earnings per share are worth the avoidance of fixed charges. In the case at hand, if the common stock will bring only $25 per share, then 80,000 ($2 million/$25 per share) new shares would have to be sold to raise the $2 million. With net income after taxes of $250,000 and a new total of 180,000 shares outstanding, the earnings per share would fall to $1.39—a lower level than the $1.50 if bond financing were used.

(b) Ease of Selling

Investment bankers say that their most demanding underwriting task is to float a new issue of common stock where there are already common shares outstanding. In this case, stabilizing transactions to maintain the price of the common stock are difficult because of the increased number of shares available on the market. Bonds may often present an easier underwriting job for a variety of reasons. Institutional investors can absorb more bonds than stock. Life insurance companies, for example, have approximately 40 percent of their resources devoted to corporate bonds, but only about 10 percent in common and preferred stock. The range of bond types and the various specific features usually make it possible to tailor offerings that are attractive to institutional investors regardless of prevailing market conditions.

(c) Lower Costs of Flotation and Servicing

Not only is it less difficult to sell bonds; it is also less expensive. The average cost of a bond flotation is usually the smallest percent of gross proceeds, the cost of a preferred stock issue is more and the cost of common stock is greatest of all. Stock flotation costs are higher, of course, because of the greater risks and the more extensive selling effort often required. Apart from costs of flotation, servicing debt capital over time is ordinarily less expensive than meeting stockholders' dividend expectations out of earnings. While some corporate officials assume that retained earnings do not have a measurable cost, this, as we will see in Chapter 20, is inaccurate. There is a cost attached to retained earnings, and it usually exceeds the cost of debt capital.

(d) Advantage of Financial Leverage

Financial leverage is a simple concept, sometimes obscured and made difficult. Essentially, it represents the use of debt in a firm's capital structure. Positive leverage occurs when a business benefits by obtaining relatively low cost, fixed payment capital and uses it productively to obtain a higher return, with the differential going to benefit the owners (stockholders). Thus, the increment earned on debt capital, above its cost, accrues to the firm and enhances stockholders' return. (Negative leverage occurs when the cost of debt capital is above the return earned on these funds.) If a company pays 12 percent for debt capital and earns 20 percent on it, the 8 percent increment over cost is retained and serves to enhance the profitability of the company. Leverage has sometimes been called "trading on the equity".[2] Basically, it involves the impact of changing debt/equity proportions on the rate of return on common stock. Accordingly, it may be defined as the percent of debt in the capital structure.

A simple illustration (which ignores taxes) may make this clear. Figure 15.1 depicts three firms with varying degrees of financial leverage.

The total capitalization of Company A amounts to $1 million, consisting entirely of 100,000 shares of common at $10 par. Company A earns 20 percent on its capital, or $200,000. This amounts to $2.00 per share. Now, consider Company B. It, too, has a total capitalization of $1 million, consisting of $500,000 of debt (12 percent bonds) and 50,000 shares of common stock at $10 par. Since Company B also earns 20 percent on total capital, but must pay 12 percent interest on $500,000, its $200,000 gross revenues are reduced by $60,000 (debt service), leaving $140,000 for the 50,000 shares, or $2.80 per share. Finally, Company C also has a $1 million total capitalization, consisting of $800,000 of 12 percent bonds and 20,000 common shares at $10 par. It, too, earns a 20 percent return on its total capitalization. Debt service reduces gross revenues available to common stockholders by $96,000. The resulting net revenues of $104,000 for the 20,000 common shares produce earnings per share of $5.20.

FIGURE 15.1   *Illustrative example of the effect of financial leverage on earnings per share*

	COMPANY A	COMPANY B	COMPANY C
Debt (12% Interest)	$ 0	$ 500,000	$ 800,000
Common Stock ($10 Par)	$1,000,000	$ 500,000	$ 200,000
Total Capitalization	$1,000,000	$1,000,000	$1,000,000
Gross Revenues (20% Return on Capital)	$ 200,000	$ 200,000	$ 200,000
Less Interest Expense	$ 0	$ 60,000	$ 96,000
Net Revenues	$ 200,000	$ 140,000	$ 104,000
Shares of Common Stock	$ 100,000	$ 50,000	$ 20,000
Earnings Per Share	$ 2.00	$ 2.80	$ 5.20

It should now be clear why many companies prefer some degree of bonded indebtedness. As the proportion of stock in total capitalization is reduced, earnings per share can be increased, but also increased is the risk that the equity is assuming as the burden of fixed charges rises. As long as earnings are stable or grow, and as long as debt funds are used to earn a larger return than is paid in interest on debt, both the company and its shareholders benefit. Should the earnings fall far enough, however, or if the return on the debt funds is below its interest rate, then negative leverage would set in and the decline in return on common shares would be more rapid than in the case of a nonleveraged (no debt) company. As mentioned above, these two conditions are referred to as positive and negative leverage and combine to increase the variability of earnings per share for levered as opposed to unlevered firms.

(e) Additional Factors

There are other financial and psychological factors which tend to favor debt. Diluting the equity, for example, may have an adverse effect upon shareholders and may impair management control. Assume, for example, that management holds 51 percent of the one million shares a firm originally has outstanding. What will its position be after an additional million shares have been sold? (Assume management buys none of these new shares.) The original million shares, which had 100 percent of the voting power before the new issue, would now have only 50 percent. Thus, management will have only .51 x .50 = 25.5 percent of total voting power after the sale of the additional million shares. While the figures are merely illustrative, the principle is clear. Dilution may pose a threat to management or to any group exercising majority control of a company.

A bond issue also is a logical method by which to consolidate and fund short-term indebtedness. The net cost of long-term debt may actually be less than that of the short-term debt, since the latter may involve leaving minimum compensating balances at commercial banks, whereas, the former does not. Thus, if interest costs are comparable, say, 10 percent for both short-term bank loans and long-term bonds, the latter may be less costly. Furthermore, the bond issue may be useful in a period of rising interest rates since it sets the cost at the time of the issue. Accordingly, later rate increases which may affect the cost of short-term turnover borrowing can be avoided by means of the consolidation through the long-term issue. In a period of falling interest rates, presumably a call provision in the bonds may be exercised and the cost of debt thereby decreased. In addition, long-term borrowing, by reducing the need for frequent use of short-term funds, may make the current ratio look better.

[2] LIMITATIONS ON THE USE OF DEBT

In this section we address those factors that tend to limit the firm's use of long-term debt. The policy concerning debt usage is decided by management and, therefore, tends to be conservative. Benchmarks may be established by loan agreements or trust indentures that add to the pressure for restraint. Typical provisions, for example, may limit the payment of dividends when disbursements would reduce the working capital of the corporation to less than a specified amount; they may require the net current assets of the corporation to bear a specified relation to the outstanding bonds; and may stipulate that common stock plus surplus must represent a minimum percentage of the total capitalization.

In addition to the above limits on debt, it should be noted that as debt edges up to and perhaps beyond conventionally acceptable limits, various sanctions come into play which suggest caution and which have a breaking effect. Banks reduce lines of credit; bond ratings are lowered; interest costs rise; and investment bankers suggest preferred or common stock to raise additional capital rather than more debt, when such debt would place the firm beyond industry norms. The company itself may also study the practices of other firms in its industry and seek to achieve an industry standard. Finally, there are some firms which simply adhere to tradition.

Outside of such practices, there are two significant approaches that provide debt usage guidelines based upon financial relationships within the firm:

- the capitalization standard; and
- the earnings coverage standard.

These approaches are described in the ensuing sections.

(a) The Capitalization Standard[3]

In the widely used capitalization standard, debt capacity is expressed in terms of the balance sheet relationship between long-term debt and the total of all long-term resources, that is, total capitalization. It is widely held, for example, that debt should not exceed 25 to 30 percent of the total capitalization of industrial companies.[4] This is especially true for companies that are regarded as cyclical. At one time railroads freely incurred large bonded indebtedness. When it developed that railroads were among the most cyclical of industries, with freight car loadings (the real base of earnings) falling sharply during business declines, analysts suggested that indebtedness and fixed charges that could be carried in prosperity would bring receivership and reorganization in recession. As a result, railroads have attempted to retire debt in an effort to bring down the disproportionate amount they once used. Cyclical companies such as Ford Motor Co. (11 percent debt to total capitalization), General Motors (12 percent), American Smelting and Refining Co. (13 percent), Borg-Warner Corp. (15 percent), McGraw-Edison Co. (10 percent), and Armstrong Cork (19 percent), tend to hold debt to relatively low levels.

Some of the highest ratios of debt to total capitalization are generally found in investor owned electric utilities and in investor owned natural gas distribution companies. For telephone companies, the figure is also high. For General Telephone, the ratio is 57 percent, for Pacific Telephone and Telegraph, 51 percent, for New England Telephone, 43 percent, and for United Telecommunications, Inc., 59 percent.

Both the relative stability of earnings and the need for heavy investment in generating and distributing facilities have led to the acceptance of a heavier debt ratio for utilities. The permissable debt range for utilities is generally considered to be between 45 and 55 percent of total capitalization. Since bond ratings are importantly influenced by the debt ratios, incurring too much debt will increase the cost of capital because lower rated bonds require higher yields.[5] The cost of borrowing increases as the quality of the bond declines, and the debt ratio is an important determinant of quality.

(b) The Earnings Coverage Ratio

It has become customary to express the limits of debt in terms of income statement data. The earnings coverage ratio relates the net income before taxes available for debt servicing to the total of annual interest plus sinking fund charges.[6] By relating fund requirements for long-term debt to net earnings available for servicing of debt, light is shed on the question of whether earnings will be adequate under varying conditions to meet debt service requirements. No new long-term debt will be issued if net income available for debt servicing is not equal to or in excess of some multiple of total debt service requirements (for existing debt *plus* for the prospective new debt). This is because there needs to be a margin of safety to allow for a decline of earnings and yet still permit the firm to continue to service its debt. It is difficult to specify an appropriate ratio since it will vary with the type of company and status of the economy. In general, the greater the fluctuation in earnings, the higher the ratio should be to provide a large enough cushion to meet debt service under adverse circumstances. It is also logical to expect a higher coverage in boom periods.

The rating accorded a new bond offering will influence the price the underwriters are willing to bid and investors willing to pay. The basic evaluative criteria employed in the determination of quality ratings are earnings protection for fixed charges and asset protection for long-term debt.

Generally speaking, financial managers find that the higher the earnings and the more rapidly they are growing, the greater the financial incentive to finance by debt rather than by stock. This may be demonstrated in an extension of an earlier illustration. Recall the company that needed $2 million of additional capital and whose gross income after the acquisition and use of the capital was estimated at $500,000. It was shown earlier that if common stock could be sold at $30 share, it would be immaterial, (in terms of earnings per share) whether the $2 million were raised by debt or by common stock. Now, consider three possible levels of income, one at, one above, and one below the assumed $500,000 gross income. If the $2 million were obtained by selling common stock, resulting in a total volume of common stock outstanding of 167,000 shares, earnings per share at the three income levels would be as follows:

Income before taxes	$500,000	$800,000	$300,000
Taxes (at 50%)	250,000	400,000	150,000
Net Income	$250,000	$400,000	$150,000
Earnings per share (on 167,000 outstanding)	$1.50	$2.40	$0.90

If 10 percent bonds had been used to raise the $2 million, the impact on earnings per share would have been as follows:

Income before taxes	$500,000	$800,000	$300,000
Interest	$200,000	$200,000	$200,000
Income after interest	$300,000	$600,000	$100,000
Taxes (at 50%)	$150,000	$300,000	$50,000
Net Income	$150,000	$300,000	$ 50,000
Earnings per share (on 100,000 outstanding)	$1.50	$3.00	$ .50

Clearly, whenever income before taxes exceeds $500,000 in the case of the two alternative capital structures, the earnings per share of the one with the bond component will exceed those of the one with only common stock. In these circumstances, all the income differential above the break-even point, when net earnings are equal for the two types of capitalization, flow to the benefit of common stock. This differential, in turn, may be translated into a higher price of the common stock, as long as the bond component is within the limits which are considered acceptable for the particular company. In this case, the risk of holding the common stock does not increase at a pace faster than the increase in earnings per share.[7]

15.3   THE CORPORATE BOND

The corporate bond ordinarily consists of two separate instruments. The bond itself, which represents the evidence of the debt, is the document typically given to the lending investor and may be made out to his name or to bearer. In it, the issuing corporation promises to pay both interest when due and principal at maturity. Besides specifying the terms of the obligation, the bond characteristically refers to the indenture, which is the document setting forth the detailed stipulations and conditions of the loan.

[1] ROLE OF THE TRUSTEE

Since there are many bondholders, one or more trustees must be appointed to represent them. An important function of the trustee is to see that all the terms of the indenture, the governing contract between the borrowing company and the creditors, are fulfilled by the debtor corporation. The responsibilities and obligations of trustees are set forth in the Trust Indenture Act of 1939, administered by the Securities and Exchange Commission. The Act protects bondholders by providing for adequate indentures and qualified and responsible trustees.

[2] THE TRUST INDENTURE

The bond is merely the legal evidence of indebtedness. It is to the indenture that one must look for the detailed terms of the issue, the protective features, and the default provisions. The indenture spells out in full the payment requirements, sinking fund or serial provisions, call features, lien provisions, limitations on additional debts or on dividend payments, insurance and maintenance requirements and procedures for foreclosure, possession and sale. What does or does not get written into the indenture is a result of the relative bargaining power, strength or weakness of the borrower.

Below are some of the important protective features and requirements that may be provided:

- the property, if a mortgage is provided, must be fully maintained in first class condition;
- insurance must be adequate;
- taxes must be paid and not allowed to accumulate;
- no prior liens may be created;
- dividends either may not be paid or may be disbursed in only a limited fashion unless fixed charges are earned in excess of certain specified levels;
- annual or semi-annual payments to sinking funds may be required;
- limitations may be imposed on the right to add additional debt; this debt may be contracted only up to a specified percentage of the value of new property acquired;
- total debt may not exceed a stated percentage of total capitalization or of total assets;
- interest on outstanding or proposed debt must be covered a specific number of times, or the new financing may not be undertaken; and
- working capital must be maintained at more than a specified level or current assets must exceed current liabilities a specified number of times.

If these requirements are not met, no more debt may be contracted, or dividends may not be paid, or past accumulated retained earnings may not be able to be drawn upon to pay dividends.

[3] ROLE OF THE FINANCIAL OFFICER

The variety of restrictive covenants is as extensive as human ingenuity can devise; and while the chief financial officer is, of course, interested in maintaining the sound credit standing of his company, he needs also to recognize his duty to resist the imposition of inflexible restraints that circumscribe future freedom of action. An institutional investment officer looking to buy current debt is usually in the driver's seat here because he is constantly in the market, conferring with investment bankers and reviewing issues, proposed or actual, while the corporation's financial officer may have been involved in only several financial offerings over as much as a decade. He may therefore be uncertain, and not know how far or how vigorously he can move in opposing the imposition of conditions and limitations in a debt financing operation. He does not want the negotiation to fail, and he may therefore accept more restraints than are ordinarily needed. If extensive protective covenants and prohibitions must be accepted, a clause should be inserted that they may be waived with the consent of a majority of the bondholders.

15.4 BOND CHOICES

If, after all the relevant factors are examined, the decision is made to undertake bond financing, the next question is what kind of bond will be issued. Most bonds, of course, are backed by the general credit of the company, but they may also have a specific pledge of collateral as additional backing. The volatility of the bond markets has spawned various innovations that modify the traditional bond form. The major types of secured obligations include:

• mortgage bonds;
• collateral trust bonds; and
• equipment obligations.

Important types of unsecured obligations include:

• debentures;
• subordinated debentures;
• convertible debentures; and
• income bonds.

Among the innovative types are:

• Eurobonds;
• industrial development revenue bonds;
• variable rate bonds;
• original issue discount (IOD) bonds;
• compound interest bonds; and
• bonds with special features.

Whether a company will use a secured obligation or not depends on a variety of factors, including, but not limited to, the expected use of the proceeds, existing capitalization, the state of the bond market, the credit of the firm and the character of the business. For example, if the proceeds are to be used for a new plant, a mortgage bond may be appropriate. If, however, they are to be used for working capital purposes, a debenture may be logical. The state of the securities market may dictate the type of security to be issued. If stock prices are depressed and a company's shares are selling at a low earnings multiple, it may be wiser to issue bonds than try to sell more equity. Yet to make bonds salable it may be necessary to secure them or perhaps to offer sweetners, such as attached warrants. If, on the other hand, the firm's stock is selling at a high earnings multiple and it has a margin for additional debt, it may logically sell convertible debentures with the conversion feature set so that, in effect, common shares are being sold at above current market prices. To overcome investors' reluctance to buy long-term bonds when interest rates appear to be on the rise, floating rates may be desirable or possible tax benefits may encourage the issuer to employ deep discount bonds. In this and the next section we present a comprehensive description of the major types of secured and unsecured debt available to the financial manager as well as some of the primary bond innovations.

[1] MORTGAGE BONDS

Flexibility is desirable in formulating financing arrangements. Accordingly, if the borrowing corporation uses a mortgage bond, it will want an open-end mortgage, one under which additional bonds can be issued backed by the same conditional lien on the same property. The institutional investor, on the other hand, will want a closed-end mortgage, reserving the pledged property as exclusive backing for the given limited bond issue. The institutional investor may press for an after-acquired property clause, specifying that any additional plant built later must be pledged under the existing mortgage to back the outstanding bonds. Naturally, the company will hold out against such a clause, and will provide for it only if there is no possibility of obtaining the financing without it. From the corporate point of view, maximum flexibility with minimum restrictions must be the basic objective.

More and more, the mortgage bond with its retinue of iron clad safeguards has become the hallmark of the company with the lesser credit standing. It is increasingly being recognized that continued healthy earning power is the best backing for a creditor instrument. The company with steady, stable, and growing earnings can therefore escape the fetters of the mortgage bond with its protective and restrictive covenants, and utilize instead the more advantageous debenture.

[2] COLLATERAL TRUST BONDS

These are secured by personal property, usually stocks or bonds. The securities are deposited with a corporate trustee, who is ordinarily empowered to liquidate them in the event of default. The indenture is likely to include provisions that prevent any deterioration of the collateral, such as that the market value of the collateral must not fall below a minimum level in relation to the principal value of outstanding obligations.

[3] EQUIPMENT OBLIGATIONS

Traditionally used by the railroads to purchase rolling stock, these obligations have been employed by other industries such as airlines to acquire flying equipment and oil companies to obtain tank cars. Ordinarily, financing is done through the so-called Philadelphia plan, whereby title to equipment ordered by a corporation is transferred by the manufacturer to a trust company, which pays the manufacturer by issuing trust certificates. The trust company leases the equipment to the corporation in exchange for an initial down payment and a contract for periodic rentals sufficient to pay interest and amortize the principal.

[4] DEBENTURES

The use of debentures does not, of course, free the corporation from covenants and restraints. In many leading industrial companies, debentures constitute the senior debt. Accordingly, to protect bondholders from the possibility that obligations, with specific liens or prior claims to assets may subsequently be issued, which take precedence over and are detrimental to the debenture holder, an "equal and ratable" or "negative pledge" clause is customarily employed. Such a clause provides that if at any time the corporation creates a lien on all or any part of its property, the debentures must be secured "equally and ratably". It is also customary to provide for a sinking fund in most debenture issues.

A debenture is based on the general credit of the company, and its real security is the firm's earning power. Because this must be adequate and sufficiently assured to permit the flotation of the debentures, they may be rated as high if not higher than mortgage bonds, and therefore afford yields no more costly or perhaps less so.

[5] SUBORDINATED DEBENTURES

A subordinated debenture is a junior issue, just as a second mortgage bond would be junior to a first mortgage bond. Some feel that subordinated debentures are no more than glorified preferred stock. From management's point of view, however, there is a big difference. Interest on the subordinated debentures is tax deductible, while dividends on preferred stock are not. In the event of insolvency, subordinated debentures rank after other unsecured debt, such as bank loans or debentures, because of the indenture rather than because of the priority of liens.

[6] CONVERTIBLE DEBENTURES

The convertible debenture, often issued as a subordinated obligation, gives the holder the option of exchanging his bond for common stock at a fixed rate for a stated period. A firm may issue convertible debentures for a number of reasons:

- They enable management to raise equity capital indirectly, without diluting the stock, until the proceeds are earning an added return to support the additional stock.
- They permit equity capital to be obtained at higher prices for the stock than current market levels would allow.
- They attract the funds of the nonstock purchaser since some institutions which may only hold small percentages of their total investment in common stock, may invest in convertible obligations with fewer restrictions.
- Until the debentures are converted, the company has a tax advantage because interest payments are tax deductible.
- Convertibles can be sold at times when other bonds cannot. In periods of tight money, corporations may not be able to sell straight debt issues except at excessively high coupons. The addition of the stock privilege will permit a lower coupon and may make the issue salable when high grade bond prices are falling due to rising interest rates.

- The convertible debenture is usually unsecured, often subordinate to all other debt and generally has only limited and loose protective provisions. Its issuance will ordinarily not impair the issuer's borrowing power unless it has been pushed to the limit by the convertible issue.
- In some difficult or speculative situations, or in the case of a new growth company, a firm may find it impossible to sell a debt issue and too costly or impractical to market a stock offering; yet by combining debt with stock in a convertible, it will have a marketable security.

Thus, convertibles have advantages for issuing companies. Their use tends to avoid the underpricing of equities, which is often necessary when a straight new issue of common stock is sold in the face of already outstanding common. Straight bonds are subject to an interest rate risk. They will decline in price in a period of boom when interest rates often rise. It may be difficult, impossible, or too costly to sell straight bonds in such a period. Yet this is just the time when the market is most receptive to convertible bonds because investors stand to gain by investing in them in such periods. A generally rising stock market, high margin requirements for stocks, and the willingness of financial institutions to lend liberally on bonds used as collateral, make convertible issues especially attractive in such periods.

On the other hand, from the investor's perspective, it is sometimes said that "if the common stock of a company is a good buy, the convertible bond is a better one." Of course, this can be a gross oversimplification, among other reasons, because of the premium, above stock value, at which convertibles often sell. Nevertheless, some of the advantages to investors in addition to those already implied, of convertibles over common stock are as follows:

- Usually lower commissions on purchase and sale;
- Normally a higher current interest rate than the dividend yield on common stock;
- Downside protection (from the bond feature) in the event of a sharp decline in the price of the common stock;
- Lower volatility as the result of the downside protection;
- A better risk-return relationship as the result of lower volatility and the fact that, once the bond and stock sell on conversion parity, price increases in the common will result in equal percentage price increases in the convertible.

[7] INCOME BONDS

Just as the convertible bond has come into increasing favor recently as an alternative to preferred, the income bond has achieved some degree of interest for the same reason. An income bond is a debt instrument whose interest need by paid only if earned. Yet, despite the fact that interest is a contingent rather than a fixed charge, interest payments are tax deductible. Most income bonds require sinking funds; interest must be paid if earned, in contrast to preferred stock dividends; and interest is often cumulative for three years or longer, depending on the terms of the individual bond issue.

15.5 BOND INNOVATIONS

A combination of volatile interest rates and persistent inflation discourages investors from buying bonds. To overcome this resistance, corporate managements developed innovative instruments which modified the conventional bond.

[1] EUROBONDS

These are bonds offered for sale in a country other than the one in whose currency the bonds are denominated. Typically Eurobonds are simultaneously distributed in various countries through international selling syndicates. The principal currency is the dollar although other currencies have been used.

In order to protect against changes in exchange rates, Eurobonds have also been denominated in so-called baskets of currencies. In these cases, the relative changes in the rates of the constituent currencies are averaged, which results in a smaller overall change than that of any of the individual currencies. For this purpose, the special drawing right has also been used, which is a basket of the five major currencies of members of the International Monetary Fund.

By broadening their financing horizon to cover the international market, U.S. corporations have been able to obtain better borrowing terms. For example, in March 1982, American Telephone and Telegraph announced that it intended to finance abroad for the first time by selling $400 million of seven-year debentures managed by Credit Suisse First Boston Limited. One analyst estimated that the company could save ¼ percentage point by borrowing outside the United States.[8] In the first seven months of 1982, U.S. companies issued $8.7 billion of Eurobonds compared with $2.9 billion for the full year 1979.[9]

[2] INDUSTRIAL DEVELOPMENT REVENUE BONDS

These bonds are typically issued by state and local governments to provide facilities that encourage corporations to stay in or move into the area. Prior to the 1969 revisions of the Internal Revenue Code, all such bonds were free of federal income taxes (they can also be exempt from state and local taxes); but since then, the exemption had become more restrictive unless the issue is for less than $10 million, raised from $5 million in 1978.

In recent years, businessmen have recognized that these revenue bonds provide an inexpensive means of financing smallscale ventures. Many states also have broadened the corporate purposes for which tax exemption will be granted. As a result, use of these bonds has grown rapidly, and for a wide range of purposes, such as supper clubs, shopping centers, bowling alleys, bank branches, dentists' offices and racquet clubs.

Concern has been expressed that the public subsidy implicit in the industrial development revenue bond has been exploited by private interests to finance undertakings that do not warrant the tax exemption privilege. The area has been under congressional investigation for some time.

[3] VARIABLE RATE BONDS[10]

The interest paid on these bonds is periodically adjusted to reflect prevailing rates. As a result, their prices tend to remain at about par. An investor, therefore, incurs little risk of capital loss should interest rates rise. At the same time, he gives up the opportunity of benefiting if rates decline. An issuer, in turn, obtains a long-term commitment of funds, but is uncertain of future borrowing costs. In the United States, floating rate notes, with maturities up to about ten years, have had some popularity, but long-term bonds of this sort have not been used much. Floating rate bonds, on the other hand, have been relatively common in the Eurobond market.

[4] ORIGINAL ISSUE DISCOUNT (OID) BONDS

Two types have been used. One bears low coupons and is offered at a sufficiently deep discount to offset this feature (deep discount bonds). The other has no coupons and must be offered at an even greater discount (zero coupon bonds).

The bonds have generally been callable at par at any time but, because of their low or zero coupons, interest rates would have to fall precipitously to make redemption profitable to an issuing corporation.[11] Since such a drastic rate reduction is unlikely, an investor has the advantage of increased protection against redemption. The primary disadvantage of these bonds to the investor has been the requirement to amortize the discount at which they were originally issued on a straight-line basis and to treat this amortization as interest income each year for tax purposes.

The position of the issuer is reverse to that of the investor. Thus, the call advantage to the investor is a disadvantage to the issuer because the present value of the interest expense amortized on a straight-line basis is higher with deep discount or zero coupon than with conventional bonds.[12] This amortization provision may be modified by Congress to have it approximate the accrual of interest expense under a normal bond with stated interest.

U.S. corporations have issued zero coupon notes primarily purchased for Individual Retirement Accounts, Keough plans of self-employed persons, IRA rollovers, pension plans, and certain other investors not subject to federal income taxes. For the sale of zero coupon, long-term bonds, U.S. corporations have favored the international market where the bonds have appealed to investors in countries that recognize the price appreciation as a non-taxable capital gain.[13]

[5] COMPOUND INTEREST BONDS

These bonds are sold at par, like a conventional bond. The issuer, however, does not pay interest to the investor during the course of the bond's life; but rather, reinvests the interest. At maturity, therefore, the issuer distributes the compounded accumulation of interest as well as the principal. Thus, like its zero coupon counterpart, the compound interest bond eliminates the investor's problem of reinvestment.

[6] BONDS WITH SPECIAL FEATURES[14]

Two types of special bond features are currently prevalent:

- special conversion of stock purchase features; and
- special maturity features.

(a) Special Conversion of Stock Purchase Features

As previously discussed, corporations have sometimes employed bonds, convertible into a fixed number of shares of common stock, as a financing device. To attract investor attention, unique conversion features have been devised. One such type is the commodity linked bond which may be converted, at the option of the holder, into a fixed quantity of some commodity, thereby, presumably providing some protection against inflation. HMW Industries, for example, issued an eight percent bond which, from May 1, 1983, could be converted into 43 ounces of silver, or redeemed for cash equal to the market price of the silver. Another novel conversion feature enables the holder to exchange his debt instrument for another debt instrument with different terms. As an illustration, Chase Manhattan Corporation issued $300 million floating rate notes due in 2009 which could be converted at the holder's option into 8½ percent fixed rate debentures with the same maturity. Chase Manhattan also developed an unusual combination of a fixed rate issue with a related "common stock equity contract." Like any debt issue with warrants, each contract grants the holder the right to buy a designated number of shares prior to maturity of the debt. Unlike the typical warrant, however, each contract also *obligates* the holder to buy the stock at maturity.

(b) Special Maturity Features

In their search for investor inducements, corporations have also offered bonds with maturity options. For example, BankAmerica Corporation put together an offering of zero coupon notes, each of which had a face value of one thousand dollars. Investors were given the option of buying them at $500, $333.33 and $250, with maturities of about five years, eight years, and ten years, respectively. Similarly, Ford Motor Credit Company, in July 1982, offered $250 million of 16 percent so-called one year extendable notes. These were repayable at the option of the holder on July 18, 1983, or July 18, 1984.[15]

15.6 STOCK CHOICES

A company must resort to equity financing under two very different circumstances. Initially, the small growing company will not find a market for its debt instruments. It must first build an adequate equity base to serve as a cushion for debt financing. At the other extreme, the company that has utilized debt financing extensively may find that it has approached the limit of what the market regards as its debt servicing capacity and that it must first expand its equity base before it can undertake any further debt financing.[16]

In the ensuing section, we present a description of the two major types of stock (common and preferred) available to the financial manager.

[1] COMMON STOCK

A frequent reason for the issuance of common stock is that a closely held family corporation goes public because the owner (key man) is nearing retirement and estate tax problems loom. By splitting the few closely held family shares and selling a significant number to the public, funds become available to the owner, whereas, previously everything was locked up in the business. In addition, by developing a market for the shares, the liquidity of the owner's remaining holdings is established.

In general, common stock financing may result under circumstances such as the following:

- Companies develop comparatively high debt ratios. New financing through equities will balance their capital structures;
- Companies are satisfied with existing debt ratios but want to save borrowing reserve for a rainy day;
- Companies suddenly have become speculative favorites on the market. If their shares are selling at high price/earnings ratios, the sale of additional shares may provide an economical means of obtaining more permanent capital; and
- Newly formed companies or closely held family corporations use opportune times to go public.

Most corporate treasurers tend to shy away from additional common stock financing because of the tax factor, the impact on the market price of the common, or the dilution involved. To them the debate between stocks and bonds is academic. They prefer debt, where it can be used, because interest payments are tax deductible, while dividends on stock are not.

This preference for debt, however, could lead to financial difficulties if not adequately controlled. Thus, encouraged by persistent inflation which suggested an ability to repay fixed commitments in cheap dollars, many corporations found themselves casualties of receding business and deflationary conditions, leading to reverse efforts to curtail debt and build up equity.[17]

A method of achieving this objective, undertaken by a number of corporations during this period, was to execute swaps with financial institutions. By this means, a corporation could cancel debt, priced at a substantial discount from par because of high interest rates, earn a profit on the transaction, and at the same time increase its equity.[18]

The most important characteristics of common stock include:

- *Nature of the voting right*—The stockholder typically has the right, for each share of common stock owned, to cast one vote at the annual meeting which may be called. Many states now either allow or require cumulative voting, whereby a shareholder may vote the number of shares multiplied by the number of directors to be elected, for one or more of the candidates. Thus, if a person owns 100 shares and nine directors are to be elected, 900 votes may be cast for one director or split in any way the shareholder sees fit.
- *Nature of the preemptive right*—Shareholders are given, through the preemptive right, the first option to purchase additional issues of common stock. Under common law, a shareholder has a preemptive right to maintain his proportionate interest in the company. In several states, this doctrine is made part of every corporate charter. On the other hand, some states stipulate that no shareholder has the preemptive right unless it is specifically inserted into the charter. At times, corporations have contended

that the preemptive right interferes with financing, flexibility and, where permitted by state law, have persuaded their shareholders to waive it.[19]

- *Variations in forms of common stock*—There are two common stock forms which are sometimes used: (1) classified shares and; (2) founders' shares. Classified shares ordinarily have been designated as Class A or B with one class having superior voting rights over the other. Founders' shares may be given to a firm's organizers. These are a form of deferred stock which do not receive dividends for a number of years or until the firm has established an earnings record.

[2] PREFERRED STOCK

Preferred stock in recent years has been declining in importance. There is a growing tendency among companies to regard preferred stock less as equity and more as an expensive form of debt. This is partly due to the fact that the preferred dividend, unlike an interest charge, is not tax deductible.

In 1935, when the corporate tax rate was 13.75 percent, there was not a great after tax difference between interest and preferred dividends. However, with a corporate tax rate of 46 percent on taxable income over $100,000, a considerable difference occurs. A preferred dividend rate of say, 10 percent, imposes a revenue requirement of 18.5 percent[20] to cover the dividend rate and income taxes.

This tendency to place preferred stock in a sort of debt category is also the result of the fact that preferred is usually something more than a stock, with priority over the common dividends and in liquidation. In practice it has developed into a complicated instrument with protective and restrictive provisions similar to those found in bond indentures. It has become customary to strengthen the preferred by providing sinking funds, market purchase funds, and cumulation features. It is usual to prohibit the creation of prior stock or to mandate against important alterations of the provisions of the stock without the consent of two-thirds of the preferred shareholders. Additional stock may not be issued unless certain earnings or asset tests are met. Some preferred shares limit debt and some provide for restrictions on common dividends.

Sweetening features like conversions and occasionally income participation may also be employed with preferred stock. As in the case of bonds, the conversion feature may be used as a financing device. The preferred is originally issued as a senior security, with a fixed dividend rate during the period when the funds obtained from their sale have not as yet provided additional earnings to the company. Later, as earnings presumably rise, the common stock advances in price and conversion takes place or may be forced.[21] On the other hand, the senior security holder is offered in addition to his fixed dividend rate, the right to participate in the company's earnings on some basis along with common stock. Since there is no automatic way of eliminating the preferred, participation is not used as a financing device but merely as a means of making the preferred attractive. It is probable, therefore, that a company resorting to the participation feature does so because it is apprehensive that its preferred will not otherwise sell. The chances are that the company is not in a strong financial position, and the holders of the participating issue may never obtain the benefits of the participating feature; indeed, it is entirely possible that the company may even have difficulty meeting its preferred dividend payments.

If these and other provisions are necessary to sell a preferred, financial managers often reason that it is better to use subordinated or convertible debentures or income bonds, accept whatever restrictions are involved, but at least gain the tax advantage of interest. Industrial companies have increasingly taken this approach, and it is principally utilities that have turned to issuing preferred stock when an apparent debt limit is being approached.

The after tax superiority, from the point of view of the issuer, of bonds over preferred stock has not only led many companies to issue less preferred or curtail the practice entirely, but has also resulted in a considerable amount of refunding of callable preferred issues, when interest rates made this step possible. On the other hand, corporations having considerable investment portfolios—chiefly non-life insurance companies—are attracted to the existing supply of preferred issues of good quality because of their tax advantage to corporate holders vis-a-vis bonds. In order to reduce the effect of double taxation, there is, with relatively few exceptions, an 85 percent exclusion applied to the dividends paid by one domestic corporation to another. Thus, if the corporate tax rate is 46 percent, $100.00 in interest will result in the retention of $54 ($100 - $46) by a corporate security holder. However, corporate security holders will, after tax, retain $93.10 for each $100 they receive in preferred dividends [$100 - ($15 x .46)]. Therefore, corporate holders require lower yields on preferred issues than they do on bonds of comparable quality and risk. Each of these trends, reluctance on the part of corporations to have preferred issues outstanding when bonds can be issued in their place, and a preference by corporate holders for preferred issues over bonds of comparable quality, have resulted in a lowering of yields on preferred issues relative to those on bonds.

15.7   CHAPTER SUMMARY

In this chapter we discussed the primary factors which influence the firm's choice of debt versus equity financing. Although a number of factors in recent years have increased management preference for debt, there are some important constraints on the use of long-term debt. Finally, we also reviewed the major categories or types of bonds and stocks available to the financial manager.

In Chapter 19, we will address the issue of whether or not a financing mix or capital structure can substantively affect the market price of common stock over the long term.

FOOTNOTES

1. As the firm increases its use of debt, the amount of fixed charges, in the form of interest payments, also builds up. For modest amounts of debt, investors tend to feel that the benefit of potentially increased earnings per share outweighs the increased financial risk—the likelihood that the firm will have insufficient funds to meet mandatory interest payments. Leverage (or the use of debt) is discussed in greater depth in 15.2[1](d).

2. Financial leverage may also be defined in terms of the degree of leverage employed. The degree of financial leverage is the percentage change in earnings available to common stockholders that is associated with a given percentage change in earnings before interest and taxes.
3. A discussion of the capitalization standard is also included in Chapter 4.
4. This ratio is usually calculated by dividing the total principal amount of bonds by the total stated amount of capital (bonds, preferred stock, common stock, and retained earnings). However, when the market price of stock is substantially different from its book value, this procedure may be misleading. In this case, market values appear more appropriate. The total capitalization is then computed as debt at book value plus equity at market value (outstanding shares times the market price per share).
5. In general, the major national bond rating agencies (Moody's and Standard & Poor's Inc.) consider the fixed charge coverage ratio and the capitalization ratio among the most important financial ratios used in the rating process (see Chapter 4).
6. Failure to meet sinking fund payments will rarely put a corporation into bankruptcy, but it is more conservative to include these payments with fixed charges. In this case, the sinking fund payments must be divided by 1 minus the tax rate to adjust for the fact that these payments are made from after-tax funds whereas the related income figure is on a before-tax basis. However, when fixed charge coverage standards are cited, sinking fund payments are often excluded.
7. In judging between the issuance of bonds or common stock, it is helpful to determine the break-even point in income before bond interest and taxes when the resulting net earnings per share are the same in both cases. This is found by the formula:

$$\frac{(1-T)(EBIT - BI)}{CS_1} = \frac{(1-T)(EBIT)}{CS_2}$$

where: T = Tax rate;
   EBIT = Earnings before bond interest and taxes;
   BI = Dollar amount of bond interest;
   CS_1 = Number of shares of common stock outstanding of corporation with the bond component; and
   CS_2 = Number of shares of common stock outstanding of corporation with only common stock outstanding.

In the example in the text, a corporation with 100,000 shares of common stock outstanding is contemplating financing either by bonds involving an interest cost of $200,000 or the issuance of 67,000 shares of common stock. The formula would work out as follows:

$$\frac{.50(EBIT - \$200,000)}{100,000} = \frac{.50\ EBIT}{167,000}$$

83,500 (EBIT - $200,000) = 50,000 EBIT
EBIT = $498,507.

8. *The Wall Street Journal,* March 3, 1982, p. 4.
9. Morgan Guaranty Trust Company of New York, *World Financial Markets,* August 1982, p. 15.
10. For an analysis of variable rate preferred stocks (another new type of security) see, Yla Eason, "Variable Rate Preferreds—The Tale of a Good Idea That Was Crippled by Wall Street Fervor," *The New York Times,* March 6, 1983, pp. F-6 and F-7.
11. See Chapter 21 for a more detailed analysis of bond redemption.

12. For example, a two-year conventional bond paying 10 percent interest issued at $100 affords a yield to maturity and cost to the borrower of 10 percent. To provide the same yield to maturity and the cost to the borrower as the conventional bond, a zero coupon bond would have to repay $121 at the end of the second year, representing $100 principal and $10 interest compounded for two years at ten percent. If the $21 accumulation could be amortized equally over the two year period, the borrower would be able to deduct $10.50 each year for tax purposes as opposed to only $10 in the case of the 10 percent conventional bond.

13. For an interesting analysis of original issue discount bonds in the context of the term structure of interest rates see, Jess B. Yawitz and Kevin J. Maloney, "Evaluating the Decision to Issue Original Issue Discount Bonds: Term Structure and Tax Effects," *Financial Management,* Winter 1983, pp. 36-46.

14. See Chapter 12 for an analysis of the use of the futures market in long-term financing.

15. *The Wall Street Journal,* March 16, 1982, p. 36 and July 22, 1982, p. 31.

16. The Haloid Company (now known as Xerox Corp.) is a good example of a firm that had to build an equity base before it could resort to bond financing. As a small enterprise, it had for many years sold photocopy machines, photocopy and photographic paper. After World War II, the company ran across a new invention which promised to become a major method of copy reproductions, and it undertook to develop the process, called xerography. At the time the company had a total capitalization of $2 million and assets under $4 million. The first financing step was the private sale of $1 million of preferred stock to provide needed funds and to avoid any dilution of the common prior to xerography's developing its anticipated promise. By 1950 more money was needed, and the company sold common stock amounting to $1.3 million under a rights offering of one new share for each three shares held. In 1952 an issue of convertible preferred was sold amounting to $2.3 million. By 1954 it was felt that sufficient equity had been built up to justify $3 million of long-term debt. Thus, between 1946 and 1955, some $7.6 million was raised for a company with a beginning capitalization of only $2 million. Over the same period the company's sales grew from $6.7 million to $21.4 million, an increase of 319 percent and its net income rose from $150,000 to $1,162,000, an increase of over 700 percent. These rather dramatic increases were accomplished with an increase in common stock outstanding of less than 60 percent. Thus, the company served its stockholders well and at the same time maintained a balanced and sound financial structure. The equity base was increased until it could support a debt structure.

17. For example, following its merger with Lykes Corp. in late 1978, the debt of LTV ballooned to $1.7 billion, more than triple its stockholders' equity. Concerned about mounting interest charges, the company took steps to curtail debt and expand equity. By the end of 1981, the company's debt/equity ratio improved from a dangerous three to one to a much stronger one to one relationship. (*The Wall Street Journal,* April 30, 1982.)

18. As an illustration, in March 1982, Exxon swapped 639,995 common shares, valued at about $18.5 million, plus about $17 million in cash for approximately $56 million face amount of its 6 percent debentures due 1997 and its 6½ percent debentures due 1998 held by First Boston. Exxon realized a profit of $22 million, while First Boston held the shares for its own account. (*The Wall Street Journal,* March 26, 1982.)

19. At the April 26, 1982 annual meeting of IBM, the shareholders approved an amendment to the company's certificate of incorporation eliminating the preemptive right. In reviewing the proxy statement, however, the company found that it was "technically defective" because it did not include a description of a shareholder's right under New York State law to dissent and set payment for his

shares. Accordingly, IBM had to resolicit a vote on the amendment, which was accomplished some months later. In support of the amendment, the company stated that the preemptive right procedure not only involved considerable delay and expense, but also limited the ability of the company to take advantage of certain financing options. (*The Wall Street Journal*, June 1, 1982, p. 35.)

20. The revenue requirement for preferred or common stock is determined as follows:

$$\text{Revenue Requirements} = \frac{\text{Dividend rate (percent)}}{(1 - \text{Marginal Federal Tax Rate})}$$

For a preferred stock with a 10 percent dividend rate and with a 46 percent marginal Federal tax rate,

$$\text{Revenue Requirement} = \frac{.10}{1 - .46} = 18.52\%.$$

21. See Chapter 21 for a discussion of forced conversion of convertible and callable bonds and preferred stock.

SUGGESTED READINGS

Agmon, T. "Variable Rate Debt Instruments & Corporate Debt Policy," *Journal of Finance,* March 1981.

Aivazian, Varouj A., and Jeffrey L. Callen, "Investment, Market Structure, and the Cost of Capital," *Journal of Finance,* March 1979.

Altman, E. I., "Multi-firm Bond Issue: A Fund Raising Financial Instrument," *Financial Management,* Summer 1981.

Booth, L. D., "Capital Structure, Taxes and the Cost of Capital," *Quarterly Review of Economics and Business,* Fall 1980.

Bowman, R. G., "Importance of Market Value Measurement of Debt in Assessing Leverage," *Journal of Accounting Research,* Spring 1980.

Copeland, Thomas E. and J. Fred Weston, *Financial Theory and Corporate Policy,* Reading, Mass., Addison-Wesley, 1979, Chapters 11 and 12.

Donaldson, Gordon, "New Framework for Corporate Debt Policy," *Harvard Business Review,* September 1979.

Ferri, Michael G. and Wesley H. Jones, "Determinants of Financial Structure: A New Methodological Approach," *Journal of Finance,* June 1979.

Johnson, D. J., "Behavior of Financial Structure & Sustainable Growth in an Inflationary Environment," *Financial Management,* Fall 1981.

Kim, E. Han, "A Mean-Variance Theory of Optimal Capital Structure and Corporate Debt Capacity," *Journal of Finance,* March 1978.

Knutson, P. H., "Application of Replacement Cost to Long Term Debt," *Financial Analysts Journal,* May/June 1981.

McCabe, G. M. and B. P. Helms, "Are Tender Offers Viable Options for Debt Management?" *Public Utilities Fortnightly,* January 15, 1981.

McConnell, J. J. and G. G. Scharlbaum, "Evidence on the Impact of Exchange Offers on Security Prices: The Case of Income Bonds," *Journal of Business,* January 1981.

Riener, K. D., "Financial Structure Effects of Bond Refunding," *Financial Management,* Summer 1980.

Sharp, G. R. and A. Guzman-Garzo, "Borrowing Interest Rate as a Function of the Debt-Equity Ratio in Capital Budgeting Models," *The Engineering Economist,* Summer 1981.

Taggart, R. A., Jr., "Taxes and Corporate Capital Structure in an Incomplete Market," *Journal of Finance,* June 1980.

PART V
CAPITAL
BUDGETING

Part IV looked at intermediate and long-term sources of funds; part V deals with long-term uses of funds—capital budgeting. The following chapters focus upon the corporate organization for capital budgeting decisions (Forecasting and the Capital Budgeting Process), the elements and criteria of the decision process (Rate of Return on Investment), the means of integrating risk considerations in the analysis (Risk Analysis in Capital Budgeting), and the determination of the benchmark figure against which the returns from prospective capital budgeting projects are matched (The Cost of Capital).

FORECASTING AND THE CAPITAL BUDGETING PROCESS

16.1 DEFINITION AND IMPORTANCE OF CAPITAL BUDGETING

Capital budgeting involves planning expenditures whose returns are expected to extend beyond one year. These expenditures represent corporate commitments for fixed, as opposed to current, assets and constitute some of the most important investment decisions made by the financial manager. Capital budgeting encompasses planning, evaluation, approval, and control.

[1] LONG-TERM EFFECTS OF CAPITAL BUDGETING DECISIONS

Since the results of capital budgeting decisions occur over the long-term, the financial manager must be cognizant of the potential loss of flexibility and the possible adverse consequences of incorrect decisions. In addition, he must recognize that he cannot assess the results of most capital budgeting decisions until a significant passage of time. Only after many years have passed, for example, will he be able to assess the "correctness" of a decision to expand product sales by investing in a new production facility with an estimated economic life of 15 years.

Because capital investment decisions are founded on long-term forecasts, they are susceptible to large error. A major consequence of this error is over-or underinvestment. Over-investment portends direct consequences because of large recurring costs which can adversely affect financial results and competitive position. Underinvestment results in important opportunity costs and might require substantial increases in capital expenditures in order to regain lost market share.

[2] GAUGING THE TIMING OF CAPITAL ASSETS' AVAILABILITY

In the planning phase of the capital budgeting process, the financial manager must address the issue of timing—when the firm requires the asset in place versus the time expected until the asset is functional. The most accurate market study demonstrating the significant potential profitability of rapid market penetration goes for naught if the required new plant can't be built in time and if the necessary equipment can't be procured within the critical time frame. The manager's knowledge of and ability to deal with the appropriate segments of the capital goods industry will increase the odds that the required assets will be in place when needed.

[3] THE CAPITAL BUDGET AS A CRITICAL ELEMENT IN FORECASTING FINANCIAL REQUIREMENTS

Capital budgeting is also important because the typical projects, especially asset expansion, entail large investments. Prior to ratifying a capital budget, management must be certain that the necessary funds can be obtained and must make arrangements for their procurement. Since these funds are generally substantial and may not be readily available, the financial manager may have to arrange for the financing several years in advance. In addition, forecasting and planning for the financing requirements associated with the firm's capital budget traditionally dominates firm-wide financial planning. This is because the amount of dollars devoted to most current asset or working capital decisions pale by comparison to the volume of funds devoted to the capital budgeting process.

[4] REQUIREMENT FOR MULTI-LEVEL AND CROSS CUTTING ORGANIZATIONAL INTERACTIONS

Capital expenditures are the life blood of the firm and the capital budgeting process encompasses most of the line operations and many of the staff organizations of the large corporation. The capital budget traditionally originates within the major divisions of the firm, moves for review across departments such as accounting, finance, and corporate planning and finally is passed up the organizational chain of command through the senior financial vice president, chief operating officer, and the board of directors for approval. The importance of capital budgeting is best seen in the considerable time and the diversity of inputs from key organizational members that it requires.

16.2   PURPOSE OF THE CAPITAL BUDGET

In essence, capital budgeting entails planning for the availability and controlling the allocation of long-term investment funds. To achieve this goal the financial manager must answer four questions:

- How much money in total will be needed for capital expenditures in the coming planning period?
- How much money is available in total for such prospective investment?
- How are available funds to be assigned to proposed projects whose combined investment requirements may exceed the prospective supply of funds? and
- How is the entire process to be monitored and controlled?

While the general purpose of a capital budget is to plan and control expenditures, it also achieves a variety of additional benefits as explained below.

[1] CAPITAL BUDGETING FACILITATES LONG-TERM FINANCIAL PLANNING

Capital budgets forecast requirements for funds and thereby enable management to assess long-term financial needs as well as plan to secure the necessary funds. Divisions can be notified either to go ahead or to discard plans for a given project depending on management judgement and the availability of funds. If the plans are scrapped, decentralized units receive advance notice so they can revise their operating budgets.

[2] IMPROVES INTERNAL COMMUNICATIONS

In decentralized companies, the capital budgeting process enables top management to gain familiarity and maintain liaison with the plans and operating targets of its divisions and plants. Where the close relationships of the small company are lost, the capital budgeting process gives top management the opportunity to appraise the proposals of operating people and, in turn, furnishes division and plant managers with a means of bringing proposals and justifications to the attention of higher officials. Capital budgeting also helps to eliminate duplication of projects among divisions and plants.

[3] HELPS ESTABLISH PRIORITIES AND EFFECTIVELY RATIONS LIMITED CAPITAL

A capital budget is an effective way of playing down demand for funds and establishing project priorities within the framework of overall company objectives. This is achieved by establishing companywide criteria for the evaluation of projects. Projects meeting the minimum criteria are judged worthwhile and will be undertaken if the necessary funding can be obtained.

Even if a company is willing to seek external funds, capital budgeting represents a basis for rationing. Some projects are rejected, either because they do not meet the minimum criteria or because of the high cost of external funds. As depicted in Figure 16.1, the capital budgeting process provides an overall view of fund availabilities and requirements.

FIGURE 16.1   *Capital budget summary*

Fund requirements (proposed after initial evaluation)			$120,000,000
Fund availabilities:			
Depreciation	$32,000,000		
Net income after taxes	38,000,000		
Funds generated internally	$70,000,000		
Less dividends	19,000,000		
Net internal funds available		$51,000,000	
Proposed external sources		40,000,000	
Total availabilities			$91,000,000
Further cutback required			$29,000,000

16.3   DETERMINANTS OF CAPITAL EXPENDITURES

Historically, economic circumstances have played a role in determining the level and type of capital expenditures undertaken by most firms. Thus, after a long period of corporate caution, a plant building binge occurred in the early 1970's that culminated in the widespread overcapacity of the 1974-1975 recession. Accordingly, during the subsequent period of economic recovery, capital spending programs rose sluggishly and at first were aimed primarily at improving the efficiency of existing plants or at providing required pollution controls. Starting about mid-1975, these expenditures took another turn and were increasingly directed towards enlarging capacity. Nevertheless, the cautious sentiment did not fade completely, as corporations refrained from building major new plants because of apprehension that adequate returns could not be obtained from big investments.[1]

In addition to economics, the character of management shapes the size and direction of capital expenditures. Aggressive companies will expend more effort to increase their share of the market. Innovative firms will attempt to develop new products and thereby create new markets, or find fresh and novel uses for existing products and thereby add to the market. A company that fails to plan for these causes is not effectively managed. In the properly managed firm, there is constant pressure for capital expenditures.

Across the corporate sector of the U.S., the major reasons for new capital expenditures fall into six principal categories:

- expanding existing products or markets;
- expanding into new markets or products;
- replacing worn out equipment;
- reducing costs and maintenance;
- meeting mandated health, safety and environmental standards; and
- upgrading or maintaining support facilities.

16.4   TYPES OF CAPITAL BUDGETS

Some firms use both long- and short-range capital budgets; others use only short-range capital budgets. Very seldom do we find a firm that uses long-range capital budgets alone.

[1] LONG-RANGE CAPITAL BUDGETS

Long-range capital budgeting is a planning tool which usually extends for three to five years, or less often from seven to ten years. When capital budgeting extends for longer periods it rarely covers specific individual project proposals for capital expenditures. Rather it is more concerned with the planning of magnitudes. Surveys of corporate practice suggest that the long-range capital budget is typically developed as follows:

- The financial manager (or the corporate economist or the special long-range planning committee) develops a forecast of the outlook for the industry as well as the firm's projected position therein, and its probable share of the market.
- Plant and division heads are informed of this forecast and are asked to evaluate it and estimate their prospective capital requirements. These estimates are then combined into a planning budget for the whole company.
- The long-range planning budget is continually revised as economic conditions change, as the company's position shifts, and as expenditure needs become more precise and are incorporated into the short-range capital budget.

[2] SHORT-RANGE CAPITAL BUDGETS

While the long-range capital budget is flexible and oriented toward future growth, the short-range budget is more precise and definitive. The short-range budget basically allocates and rations within one to two years. Traditionally, the short-range capital budget is developed as follows:

- The financial manager estimates the total amount of corporate funds which are likely to be available for capital expenditures during the forthcoming budget period.
- Plant and division heads submit project proposals about three months prior to the new budget period. These proposals include estimates of costs, benefits, and savings.
- The financial manager and his staff then consider these proposals and relate them to the funds available during the coming period. While the screening process differs from company to company, the net result is a paring down and a tentative apportionment to plants, divisions, and departments.
- Plant and division heads, submit during the budget year, appropriation requests (or authority for expenditure requests) approximately in line with the amounts apportioned to them in the capital budget. While in some firms requests are limited to the overall sums budgeted, a degree of flexibility and internal shifting is expected and permitted in others.

16.5 MAJOR STEPS IN THE CAPITAL BUDGETING PROCESS

As we have said, capital budgeting encompasses planning, evaluation, approval and control. In most companies, actual authorization entails two basic phases: (1) formal budget development and approval and (2) authority to commit funds. Proposed capital budgets are essentially lists of new projects for the coming year plus a forecast of expenditures for previously approved but as yet uncompleted projects. The common practice is to require, at budget time, only the minimum information necessary to understand the nature and cost of proposed projects. Full details are usually not required until later in the second phase, when the authority to expend funds is sought. In the following sections, we focus on the specific steps which comprise the capital budgeting process for most corporations.

[1] PROVISION OF CORPORATE LEVEL GUIDANCE

The first major step in the capital budgeting process usually involves top management through its provision of guidelines and formats for budget submissions to the operating divisions and units. The guidelines provided by management include:

- overall corporate strategy and objectives; and
- broad guidelines that deal with the economic environment, rates of return, overall level of capital investment, and categories of capital expenditures.

Indicative of a typical pattern, the NCR Corporation management sends guidelines and formats for budget submissions to the various reporting divisions in the early spring. These documents indicate the current overall management philosophy and both short and long-term objectives. NCR's long-range plan provides senior management with insight as to the detailed capital needs and major long-range capital projects of each division. The short-range plan represents the "operating" capital budget for the forthcoming year.

[2] DEVELOPMENT OF THE CAPITAL BUDGET SUMMARY

At this stage in the process, the proposed capital budget is basically a list of proposed projects. The capital budget tabulation usually contains estimates of project costs, the time to recover the investment or estimated annual savings, and the anticipated rate of return on the investment. In this tabulation—formally called a Capital Budget Summary—the proposed capital investment projects are also summarized by division or unit and by project type, e.g., asset expansion, replacement, environmental pollution control, etc. The projects are also ranked in terms of their overall economic attractiveness.[2] Figure 16.2 presents a Capital Budget Summary form of a major oil company, which is used to summarize the key characteristics of literally thousands of individual projects of varying complexities.

The development of the Capital Budget Summary generally follows one of two basic approaches: (1) bottom-up or (2) combination top-down and bottom-up. In the bottom-up approach, a foreman, division manager, or research department has an idea for a better product, a cheaper or more efficient work procedure, a cost-saving machine, or an entirely new product. These are proposed, discussed, analyzed, and, if found to have merit, cast into financial terms and included in the annual consolidation of proposed capital projects.

In the combination approach, the bottom-up results are integrated with the results of top management's larger overview and longer look ahead at capital

FIGURE 16.2 *Major Oil Company capital budget summary*

Units: $ Million

LINE	COMPARISON WITH OBJECTIVES: OBJECTIVES (A)	COMPARISON WITH OBJECTIVES: BUDGET MORE (LESS) (B) = (C) - (A)	CLASSIFICATION		NEW PROJECT BUDGET (C)	UNSPENT APPROPRIATIONS (CARRY-OVERS) (D)	TOTAL COMMITMENTS (E) = (C+D)	EXPENDITURES BY AREA				
1			FUNCTION									
2												
3												
4												
5												
6												
7												
8												
9												
10			TOTAL (LINES 1-9):(11-14)									
11			AREA									
12												
13												
14												
15	MEMO	EXPENSE INCLUDED ABOVE										
16												
17			TOTAL									

NOTES

COMPANY UNIT:	PREPARED BY:	BUDGET YEAR:	DATE PREPARED:	EDITION: ☐ PROPOSED ☐ FINAL	PAGE:

expenditure requirements across the firm. The most astute managements periodically audit facilities, survey comparative industry position, analyze industrial engineering, and research expenditures for new products and markets. The top-down view provides a sound basis for assessing the bottom-up results in terms of the appropriateness of the overall level of proposed expenditures, the composition of proposed projects, and the extent to which proposals are in line with overall firm objectives and strategies.

[3] APPROVAL OF THE CAPITAL BUDGET PLAN

In this step, the formal capital budget plan is presented to and approved by the board of directors. The approval, however, only signifies agreement in principle with management's proposed capital investment program; it does not grant authority to commit funds. Approval of the capital budget plan is generally taken to mean that sponsors of proposed projects can proceed to the more detailed engineering studies and economic and technical analyses necessary to support individual appropriation requests.

Indicative of the range of approvals that may be required for the capital budget plan, a major conglomerate requires the signatures of the division heads, group leaders, director of real estate and construction, group controllers, group vice-presidents, the corporate controller, the senior vice-presidents, the president and the board of directors. In addition, other large firms may also require the approval of an investment and/or management committee. Typically, the investment committee scrutinizes the plan for its funding implications and conformance to the evaluation criteria and guidelines established by the top management of the firm. The management committee generally considers the strategic implications of the plan, especially its relationship to overall firm objectives and strategy.

[4] DEVELOPMENT AND APPROVAL OF AUTHORIZATION REQUESTS

Before actual capital expenditures are authorized for projects in the approved capital budget plan, it is customary to require that appropriation requests be submitted for management approval. Although such requests vary in form and title from company to company, they usually contain the following basic information:

- date of request;
- project identification number;
- project description;
- purpose of and justification for the project;
- estimated total project cost broken down by currency, where applicable;
- estimated starting and completion dates;
- estimates of the amount and timing of expenditures;
- estimated cost savings or other economic justification when applicable;
- estimates of the amount and timing of cash flows generated by the project; and
- required approvals.

The authorization for Expenditures form of a major oil company is presented in Figure 16.3. There are three crucial elements in the appropriation request. These include: (1) the timing estimate, (2) the estimated total project cost, and (3) the estimated cash flow from the project. One of the most vital aspects of the capital budgeting process is the assessment of these estimates. This has received less attention in the academic literature than the traditional project evaluation criteria and techniques (e.g., payback, net present value, internal rate of return), not because it is less important, but primarily because of the difficulty and diversity of estimating procedures and techniques. No matter how carefully contrived and thorough the project evaluation tests, the seeming decimal point precision will be wholly illusory if any one of these three estimates is seriously awry. Should the amount of the investment be under-estimated, for example, not only will the rate of return or the profitability of the project be lower than calculated, but the need to provide additional investment funds may cause subsequent abandonment or postponement of projects with more favorable rates of return.

Even if the investment estimate is correct, should it take more time than projected to complete the proposed project, anticipated cash flows will be delayed. Because of the time value of money, the timing "delay" will result in a lower than estimated rate of return. The importance of accuracy in both the dollar dimension and the time dimension of the estimates in capital budgeting cannot be overstressed.

The complexity of the approval process for a project authorization request depends primarily on the type of project and the amount of capital investment required. A common characteristic in the review and approval process is to classify projects. For example, projects may be classified "by type" along the lines of the six principal categories delineated in Section 16.3.

At International Flavors and Fragrances (IFF), the degree of analysis required and the level of management that must authorize actual expenditures depends upon the project's classification as follows:

- *"A"projects* require the title, a concise description of their purpose, and a detailed economic justification. The projects are arranged in order of decreasing dollar value down to $50,000.
- *"B"projects* or those in the $10,000 to $49,999 range, require a single entry on the budget form. A list of the projects included and the investment cost of each is submitted with the capital budget form.
- *"C" and "D" projects* require the same information as "B" projects. However, "D" projects do not need to be listed individually. "C" projects range from $5,000 to $9,999 and "D" projects up to $4,999.

The IFF classification system not only provides the basics for the amount and type of analysis required, but it also determines the level of approval that must be obtained before funds may be allocated. In the case of category "D", approval of the authorization request by the Capital Appropriation Committee automatically constitutes management approval to expand this part of the capital budget. Accordingly, no request for appropriations is necessary as long as the fixed asset additions charged to this capital project do not exceed $4,999 individually or exceed the approved total of budgeted category "D" projects. Capital funds may not be committed to the other categories of projects without the prior signature of the designated level of management.

FIGURE 16.3 *Major Oil Company authorization for expenditures*

ORGANIZATION	DATE SUBMITTED	STARTING DATE	NO.
PROJECT TITLE	BUDGET YEAR	COMPLETION DATE	BUDGET NO.

TYPE OF APPROPRIATION
☐ ORIGINAL APPROPRIATION ☐ FIRST DEFICIENCY
☐ EXTENSION ☐ SECOND DEFICIENCY
☐ CANCELLATION ☐

PROJECT LOCATION	OWNERSHIP

A. AMOUNTS

			DESCRIPTION	LOCAL	U.S.
1		CHARGED	ADDITIONS TO FIXED ASSETS		
2		TO	OPERATIONS FOR THE FUTURE		
3		BUDGET	TOTAL		
4	APPRO–	TRANSFER FIXED ASSETS			
5	PRIATIONS	ASSOCIATED EXPENSE			
6		OTHER (Specify):			
7		TOTAL THIS APPROPRIATION			
8		PRIOR APPROPRIATIONS			
9		AMOUNT FOR APPROVAL			
10	OTHER	FINANCIAL LEASES			
11	APPROVALS	INVESTMENTS AND ADVANCES			
12		OTHER			
13	MEMO	WORKING CAPITAL			
14		OTHER MEMORANDUMS			
15	PROJECT TOTAL				

B. PRIOR APPROPRIATIONS					C. FINANCIAL INDICATORS			
NO.	DATE	BUDGET	OTHER	TOTAL		DESCRIPTION	ORIGINAL	REVISED
1					1	NET PRESENT VALUE ___%		
2					2	DCF RATE OF RETURN		
3					3	PAYOUT PERIOD, YEARS		
4					4	PROJECT LIFE, YEARS		
5					5	MAXIMUM CASH EXPOSURE		
6					6			
7					7			

D. PROJECT DESCRIPTION AND JUSTIFICATION

☐ CONTINUED ON SEPARATE SHEET

SIGNATURE	DATE	SIGNATURE	DATE

In the IFF procedure, the different categories of projects are further subdivided into the following classifications:

1. New type product or process;
2. Cost reduction;
3. Additional productive capacity;
4. Replacement of facilities;
5. Auxiliary equipment;
6. Statutory requirements; and
7. Safety and welfare.

This classification affects the reporting procedures. For example, as indicated previously, only category "A" projects require detailed economic justification. To obtain an actual appropriation of funds, all category "B" and "C" projects require justification, and for classifications one through five, this must be an economic justification. For classifications six and seven, only a descriptive justification need be provided for category "A" and "B" projects.

[5] PROJECT MONITORING AND CONTROL

The capital budgeting process does not end with the approval of the appropriation request and the allocation of required funds. Most financial managers utilize a follow-up procedure to assure that capital projects conform to their proposed dollar and time dimensions. Control of the capital budgeting program is maintained through a series of reports that appraise senior managers, the appropriate overview committees (e.g., Investment Committee, Management Committee), and the board of directors of the status of the program on an ongoing basis. These reports track actual project authorizations and expenditures, and can be used for making comparisons with the annual capital budget plan. In addition, they provide data for determining corporate sources and uses of funds and financing needs.

Among the many reports and procedures used to control the capital budget, the following have generally been found most effective and necessary:

- accounting control procedures;
- project progress reports;
- supplemental appropriation requests;
- project change notices; and
- project completion reports.

(a) Accounting Control Procedures

Project accounting records are generally established shortly after the appropriation request has been approved. A detailed record of costs is essential and falls within the responsibility of the controller. Often, the controller may delegate this responsibility to the cost accounting department. Typically, project cost control reports present a monthly breakout of capital expenditures, non-capital costs classified by major category (e.g., direct labor costs and overhead, material expense, administrative expenses, indirect costs), and project revenues. These categories are periodically compared to the capital budget targets or estimates. Significant divergences between budgeted and incurred levels of costs, expenses, and revenues are immediately highlighted in the project progress reports.

(b) Project Progress Reports

Monthly or quarterly progress reports are used for major capital investment projects to identify problems and difficulties in time for management action. They aid in cash planning, warn of actual or prospective overexpenditures and permit a review of the accuracy of project proposal estimates. The project progress reports generally contain the following information:

- date of project approval;
- authorized dollar level of capital expenditures;
- actual capital expenditures to date;
- estimated date of project completion;
- percentage of project completed; and
- estimated level of expenditures in excess of budgeted authorization.

(c) Supplemental Appropriation Requests

In cases where a project encounters both delay and overexpenditure, management has four basic courses of action available: (1) continuation and completion of the project regardless of cost, (2) change in project management, (3) abandonment of the project, and (4) re-evaluation of the project and request for supplemental funding. While policy varies from company to company, seldom is a major project totally abandoned. Frequently, management will require a re-evluation and a supplemental appropriation request if actual expenditures run either a given dollar or percentage amount above estimates. In many companies, for example, a supplemental appropriation request must be filed where actual expenditures run ten percent or more above the budgeted amount.

Normally, when the supplemental request is submitted, the principal reasons for the overrun must be detailed. Also, most companies require a revised calculation of project profitability (e.g., payback, rate of return, etc.). The supplemental appropriation request serves three primary purposes:

- *early warning*—it alerts management to the projected magnitude of the prospective overexpenditure for the project;
- *transition planning*—it enables the company to change the project management, if necessary; and
- *forecast quality control*—it tends to make those who propose and sponsor projects more careful and exact in their estimating and planning since they know they will have to justify overexpenditures in the face of management disfavor.

(d) Project Change Notices

Where any significant aspect of an ongoing project is to be changed, such as purpose, funds or time, the effective corporate management will require a notice of change and approval thereof. In view of the many extensive and intricate interrelationships in the modern company, a substantial project delay can cause slowdowns, idleness, extra expense, and losses elsewhere in the company. The monetary consequences of these charges should be measured against the project's prospective return.

(e) Project Completion Reports

Most firms require completion reports which serve as comprehensive project summaries and which also can be used to recapture any unexpended funds. Project completion reports are used in a variety of ways, including the following:

- providing the basis for proper accounting entries on the firm's books, as well as for recording and distributing the costs of the completed project;
- establishing a date from which depreciation can be calculated on new assets;
- providing a comparison between actual and estimated project costs; and,
- providing an understanding of the problems encountered and the reasons for any variances between actual and estimated costs, so that similar errors or difficulties can be avoided in the future.

[6] CONDUCT OF POST-COMPLETION AUDIT

Finally, in well managed firms, a post-completion audit is usually undertaken for larger projects. While some firms audit projects after six months or one year, most wait until two or three years. Earnings during the first year, which is usually a period of trial and development, are seldom indicative of the returns in later, more stable periods.

The primary purposes of the post-completion audits are threefold:

- maintaining the integrity of original cost estimates and preventing their inflation or down playing their importance;
- improving future forecasts through the identification and assessment of major errors in costing, technical and engineering estimates; and
- assessing the actual intrinsic merits of new capital projects.

The post audit process itself is complex. When appraising capital projects, management must realize that the very uncertain nature of estimated cash flows means that some projects will turn out unfavorably. Second, management needs to differentiate reasons for project failure. Some projects will fail due to factors beyond the control of the operating personnel. In many cases, these factors could not have been anticipated with any degree of confidence. In addition, certain types of projects, e.g., replacement projects, are often difficult to assess in terms of overall or system-wide cost savings. Finally, the post-completion audit process should be conducted in a manner which does not discourage the future choice of potentially high profit, high risk projects.

16.6   MAINTAINING A WAY OUT

Despite the reluctance to abandon a project once it has been undertaken, management must remain fully aware of the dangers that may arise when completion runs over long periods of time. Large new plants may encounter costly litigation from environmental sources, inflation may lead to serious errors in cost estimates, or the growing global economy may prevent accurate economic forecasting, thus throwing market projections seriously out of line. For these reasons, the option to terminate must be kept open as long as possible. Reflecting this attitude, the president of Ponderosa System, a national steakhouse chain, cautioned, "We have contingency plans to stop and cut back on a program of adding substantially to company operated and licensed restaurants in the event conditions do not develop as expected."[3]

Once a major program has proceeded for a sufficiently long time, however, contingency plans are no longer feasible and the company is virtually committed to moving ahead with its completion. As a result companies tend to move cautiously in their capital budgeting plans by adding to production facilities in increments or by stressing cost reduction rather than expansion. This approach, however, may limit a company's ability to meet a future growth in demand for its products. Thus, management is constantly confronted with the need to consider these alternative approaches to its capital program. Because of the large sums involved and the potentially serious consequences of wrong decisions, considerable care typically must be given to this area.

16.7   CHAPTER SUMMARY

This chapter introduced capital budgeting as a process for planning expenditures whose returns are expected beyond one year. We looked at the importance and purpose of capital budgeting, and the determinants and types of capital·expenditures. Next, we outlined the major steps in the capital budgeting process. Finally, we explored the need to maintain an escape valve from capital budgeting commitments. Throughout, we highlighted four major elements of the capital budgeting process, namely: planning, evaluation, approval and control. Chapter 17 discusses the principal economic criteria and techniques used to evaluate the profitability of prospective capital projects.

FOOTNOTES

1. Ralph E. Winter, "Taking the Plunge: Many Firms Step Up Spending to Expand Productive Capacity," *The Wall Street Journal*, June 11, 1979, pp. 1, 23.
2. Chapter 17 discusses the economic criteria and techniques employed to evaluate and rank prospective capital investment projects.
3. Ralph E. Winter, *The Wall Street Journal*, June 11, 1979, *op. cit.*, p. 23.

SUGGESTED READINGS

Bavishi, Vinod B., "Capital Budgeting Practices at Multinationals," *Management Accounting*, August 1981.

Bierman, Harold Jr., "Strategic Capital Budgeting," *Financial Executive*, April 1979.

Clark, John J., Thomas J. Hindelang and Robert E. Pritchard, *Capital Budgeting: Planning and Control of Capital Expenditures*, Prentice-Hall, Englewood Cliffs, N.J., 1979.

DeThomas, A.R., "Forecasting Cash Flows: The Practical Side of Capital Budgeting," *Managerial Planning*, May-June 1982.

Durand, David, "Comprehensiveness in Capital Budgeting," *Financial Management*, Winter 1981.

Gordon, L.A., et. al., "Informational Impediments to the Use of Capital Budgeting Models," *OMEGA*, 1979.

Grossman, Steven D., and Richard Lendhe, "Important Considerations in the Budgeting Process," *Managerial Planning*, September-October 1982.

Hayes, Robert H., and David A. Garvin, "Managing as If Tomorrow Matters," *Harvard Business Review*, May-June 1982.

Kim, Suk H., "Making the Long-Term Investment Decision," *Management Accounting*, March 1979.

―――, and Edward J. Farragher, "Current Capital Budgeting Practices," *Management Accounting*, June 1981.

Miller, Leland B., "The Buck Starts Here: The Role of the Financial Officer in Corporate Expansion Planning," *Industrial Development*, July-August 1980.

Oblak, David J., and Roy J. Helm, Jr. "Survey and Analysis of Capital Budgeting Methods Used by Multinationals," *Financial Management*, Winter 1980.

Petit, Thomas, and Tony Wingler, "Key Factors in Capital Budgeting," *Managerial Planning*, May-June 1981.

Raiborn, Debra D., and Thomas A. Ratcliffe, "Are You Accounting for Inflation in Your Capital Budgeting Process?" *Management Accounting*, September 1979.

Scudiere, Paul M., "Justifying Proposals to Save Energy," *Management Accounting*, March 1980.

Sharon, Ed M., "Decentralization of the Capital Budgeting Authority," *Management Science*, January 1979.

APPENDIX A:
A CORPORATE EXAMPLE OF CAPITAL BUDGETING PROCEDURES: GENERAL FOODS

General Foods' capital budgeting program is developed within the framework of the company's annual financial plan. The following description of the program illustrates the division that occurs in the typical budgetary process between the aspects of planning, evaluation, approval and control.

Planning

An effective capital budgeting program must be based upon a set of common principles that underly the work of all participating units. In the case of General Foods, these principles emanate from three corporate sources:

(1) The Management Committee endorses a corporate strategy that determines the classifications for the various resource allocation units.

(2) The Investment Committee sets broad guidelines that deal with the economic environment, rates of return, and the split between profit sustaining and profit increasing projects. These, in turn, may involve new developments, expansions, cost reductions, profit improvements, support facilities and environmental projects.

(3) Staff areas, such as Corporate Operations and Corporate Planning, provide additional perspectives which could involve such areas as energy and the environment.

This information is communicated to the Operating Unit president and Operations Manager. Within the General Foods structure, the major units include the Beverage & Breakfast Foods Division and International units. Each unit's president and operations manager consolidate the material, establish the planning guidelines for their unit and transmit these guidelines to the individual plants for the actual creation of the capital plan for that plant. The functional flow that follows is illustrated in Figure 16.4.

428

FIGURE 16.4 *General Foods Corporation operating unit capital plan development*

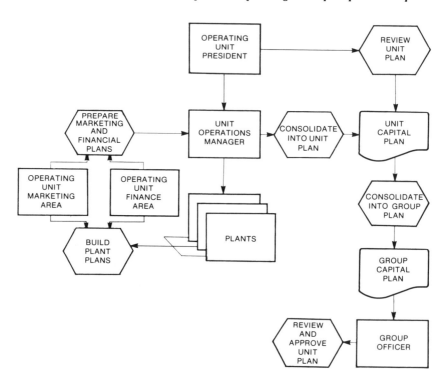

The responsibility for building the plan is given to plant operations personnel who know the needs of the plant and to personnel in marketing and finance areas within the unit who provide overall perspectives. The data emerging from each plant is consolidated into a unit plan that, in turn, is transmitted to a group officer. This officer reviews the capital plan of each unit within the group and gives his approval once he is satisfied that the unit capital plan meets the objectives and strategies of the group.

After the group officer has approved the unit capital plan, the unit forwards it to Corporate Financial Planning & Control (FP & C). That area consolidates the unit plans into a Corporate capital plan which becomes part of the Corporate Annual Financial Plan (AFP). In addition, a presentation "deck" is prepared which includes an assessment of the capital plan. This assessment provides historical background, a perspective of the total program, and expected ranges for appropriations and expenditures.

The corporate capital plan, embracing the plans of the individual units, now goes through the stages of final approval. The Investment Committee goes over the presentation "deck" to determine if the plan meets the prescribed guidelines. The Management Committee considers the plan from the point of view of its strategic implications, corporate guidelines, and conformance with the Corporate AFP. The finance committee of the Board of Directors reviews the capital plan separately with particular reference to the funding implications as they relate to the sources and uses of funds in the Corporate AFP. The Board of Directors finally looks at the AFP in total and the capital program as a specific component part. Board approval of the capital program provides General Foods' internal management with authorization to appropriate funds for individual projects smaller than $2,000,000 up to the approved amount.

FIGURE 16.5 *General Foods Corporation capital project evaluation and approval process*

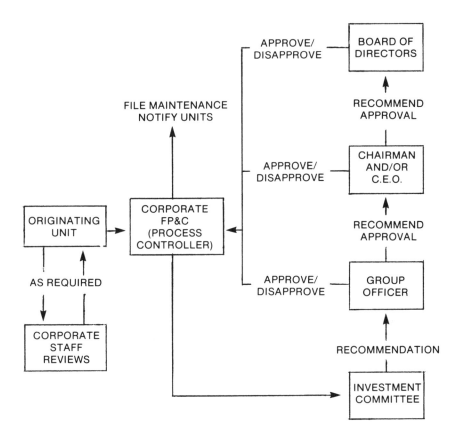

The *operating units* are responsible for preparing project proposals and obtaining written reviews from appropriate staff areas.

Evaluation and Approval

Once the plan has been approved, the operating units are responsible for preparing the proposals for particular projects. The steps to obtain final authorization are illustrated in Figure 16.5.

In order to prepare a project proposal, the originating unit obtains written reviews from appropriate staff areas on such things as projecting expenses and interpreting corporate requirements. All the necessary information is then forwarded to Corporate FP & C. Included in the project proposal is the following material:

(1) A description of the project;

(2) A list of the major components of the new funds required;

(3) A Financial evaluation that embodies analyses of the internal rate of return, return on funds employed, and payback; and

(4) Identification of the other investment alternatives considered and the reasons for rejecting them.

Corporate FP&C serves as a "process controller". In this capacity it acts as a focal point for all projects requiring corporate management approval. Upon receiving proposals, Corporate FP&C reviews the projects to ensure conformance with corporate policy, maintains files on the projects, identifies issues, and forwards the proposals to the Investment Committee.

The Investment Committee reviews every capital project, lease or asset disposal request that requires corporate management approval and forwards a recommendation to the corporate executive to whom the operating unit reports. The level of corporate management required for approval of a project proposal is dictated by the dollar magnitude of the total project cost as follows:

Less than $200,000   —Unit President
$200,000-$499,999   —Group Vice President
$500,000-$749,999   —Senior or Executive Vice President
$750,000-$1,999,999   —Chief Executive Officer or President
$2,000,000 and over   —Board of Directors
If the project is approved, Corporate FP&C notifies the appropriate area.

Control

Control of the capital budgeting program is maintained through a series of reports that apprise the Investment Committee, corporate management, and the Board of Directors of the status of the program on an ongoing basis. These reports provide the means for tracking actual authorizations and expenditures, and for making comparisons with the AFP. In addition, the reports provide data for determining corporate source and use of funds, financing needs, and so forth. The principal reports include the following:

- *The Monthly Latest Estimate of Capital Appropriations and Expenditures*
  This report is part of the Business Information System monthly reporting package. It provides data necessary for: a monthly update of annual appropriations and expenditures versus capital program; tracking changes to the capital program; the Board of Directors' report; and financial control.
- *The Annual Capital Authorization and Expenditures Status Report*
  This provides an annual summary of actual capital appropriations and expenditures by project and purpose and compares them with the plan. The report also serves as a basis for identifying projects which carry over to the following year.
- *The Annual Investment Status Report*
  This provides the latest estimate of financial returns on capital projects justified on a profit-increasing basis and compares them with the original objectives.

17

RATE OF RETURN ON INVESTMENT

17.1 INTRODUCTION

In Chapter 16, we discussed the process by which most corporations develop their capital budgets. One of the most important steps in this process is the determination of which of various investment opportunities is the most profitable. The size and composition of the firm's capital budget is primarily a function of the number of attractive investment opportunities available and the profitability of these alternative projects. The relative profitability among alternative capital investments is ordinarily determined by the employment of a rate of return analysis.

In addition to serving as a guide in making decisions on future financial commitments, the rate of return on investment concept can be used to measure the past performance of the company as a whole or its divisions. It can be used as an effective check on the performance and efficiency of the capital budgeting process as well as on the firm's forecasting ability.

This chapter presents the basic steps in rate of return analysis and discusses the most frequently employed analytical methods. In addition, the chapter highlights current industry practices and discusses additional factors which generally impact the typical rate of return on investment analysis.

17.2 CURRENT INDUSTRY PRACTICES

Academicians have paid considerable attention to the corporate capital budgeting decision process in recent years. Various surveys have been conducted to ascertain the extent to which business firms employ the different methods of calculating rate of return for decision-making purposes. In general, these surveys demonstrate the increased use of more sophisticated techniques among larger firms. Despite use of such methods as time adjusted rates of return, however, traditional methods such as payback remain popular. In addition, practitioners have criticized academicians and theorists for their perceived overemphasis on the refinements of the calculations involved in the more sophisticated methods. Practitioners advocate, instead, that the efforts be directed toward improving the overall capital budgeting process. They assign highest priority to dealing with the significant problems associated with cash flow estimation, important differences in perspectives of the key-decision makers in the capital budgeting process, and the tremendous difficulties involved in attempting to systematically identify attractive investment alternatives over time.

The aforementioned industry surveys also demonstrate many purposes for rate of return analyses. When applied to the past, the analysis is used to compare a firm's performance with either the industry average or with competitors; to gauge the relative profitability of product lines or divisions; or to check performance after the investment of capital in a seemingly desirable project. When applied to the future, it is used to screen proposed capital expenditures to see which should be undertaken and which should not; to rank projects in order of prospective return; or to decide whether and when to replace a piece of equipment. In addition, rate of return analysis is often employed in "make" or "buy" decisions, in "lease" versus "own" judgments, as a guide to optimum inventory volume, for pricing purposes, in bond refunding decisions, and to analyze prospective investments in other firms or in mergers and acquisitions. In summary, rate of return analysis has come to be one of the most important tools in financial decision-making.

17.3   BASIC STEPS IN RATE OF RETURN ANALYSIS

The conduct of a rate of return on investment analysis involves four primary steps:

(1) determining the amount and timing of projected cash outflows;
(2) determining the amount and timing of projected cash inflows;
(3) calculating the projected rate of return on investment; and
(4) deciding whether to undertake the project.

These steps are discussed in the ensuing paragraphs.

[1] DETERMINING THE AMOUNT AND TIMING OF PROJECTED CASH OUTFLOWS

The first two steps are the most difficult and time-consuming. In step 1, the total cash outflows of the prospective project must be estimated. This frequently necessitates detailed engineering and cost analyses. In the case of the original investment, for example, one must be careful to count not only the actual purchase outlays but also the transportation and installation costs as well as the increased amount of working capital that may be tied up as a result of the investment. It should be emphasized, however, that the cash flows used in the evaluation of a potential capital investment project should represent only those that relate to costs and revenues associated with that project and should exclude those related to the cost of its financing.

Often, it is difficult to recognize all the outlays that will be incurred. In the case of a decision to lease versus buy data processing equipment, for example, a comprehensive evaluation of costs would encompass the purchase price of the equipment, the costs of the manufacturer's federal excise and total sales taxes, maintenance costs, property taxes, and insurance premiums, as well as the timing of these prospective outlays.

[2] DETERMINING THE AMOUNT AND TIMING OF PROJECTED CASH INFLOWS

This step entails a significant amount of engineering, marketing, and financial forecasting. By cash inflow we mean the net cash difference between undertaking versus not undertaking the project.[1] Often this net change must be calculated on a relative rather than an absolute basis. That is, the cash inflow may be the result of cost avoidance or cost savings as well as the result of revenues generated by the project.

For example, consider the hypothetical situation in which corporate management is trying to decide whether to replace an existing piece of equipment (machine A) with a new piece of equipment (machine B) which has an economic life of 5 years and total purchase cost of $20,000. As shown in Figure 17.1 the costs of operating machine A are $10,000 in the first year; thereafter, the costs increase by $1,000 a year to $14,000 in the fifth year. Machine B will not change the existing gross revenue stream in any respect but will have lower annual costs than machine A. These costs are $5,000 in the first year of operation and increase thereafter by $1,000 a year to $9,000 in the fifth year. Accordingly, the replacement of machine A by machine B will reduce annual operating costs by $5,000 for each of the five years of the useful economic life of machine B. These savings in increased cash flow must be balanced against the $20,000 capital investment required for machine B.

FIGURE 17.1 *Relative measurement of anticipated cash inflow*

Annual Operating Costs

	YEAR 1	YEAR 2	YEAR 3	YEAR 4	YEAR 5
Machine A	$10,000	$11,000	$12,000	$13,000	$14,000
Machine B	5,000	6,000	7,000	8,000	9,000
Reduction in Annual Operating Costs if Machine B Replaces A	5,000	5,000	5,000	5,000	5,000

The previous example is an extremely simplified one. More often, the financial manager is confronted with projects entailing different useful economic lives and different total purchase costs. These and other important income measurement issues are discussed in 17.6.

[3] CALCULATING THE PROJECTED RATE OF RETURN ON INVESTMENT

In this step, the rate of return on investment for the project is calculated by comparing the level and timing of net cash inflows (i.e., cash inflows minus cash outflows) with the total original cost of the project. The actual calculation varies according to the particular rate of return analysis method utilized. There are three[2] major methods of determining the project's rate of return on investment, which include:

- Payback;
- Internal Rate of Return (IRR); and
- Net Present Value (NPV).

While all methods consider the level of projected net cash inflows and total original costs, only the IRR and NPV methods explicitly consider the timing of cash flows. The IRR and NPV methods are often referred to as time adjusted or discounted cash flow (DCF) methods. They provide a more discriminating rate of return on investment figure because they explicitly give effect to the difference between near versus distant cash flows. 17.4 predominantly discusses the payback method in detail. 17.5 discusses the IRR and NPV methods.

[4] DECIDING WHETHER TO UNDERTAKE THE PROJECT

Once the rate of return on investment is determined, the financial manager must decide whether or not to recommend the project for adoption. For this purpose, he must consider the calculated rate of return in comparison to the firm's established standards or cutoffs and its cost of capital. He must also keep in mind the level of capital investment funds available, the estimated rates of return on other prospective projects, and the anticipated risks involved. An important step is to weigh the estimated project rate of return against the anticipated risks. The financial manager, for example, may prefer a project that provides a higher but riskier rate of return. Chapter 18 discusses the primary methods of incorporating risk into the rate of return analysis. Finally, the financial manager is called upon to blend his judgment on additional qualitative factors such as competitive conditions, with the quantitative rate of return results to obtain a final decision.

Having discussed the fundamental steps in the conduct of a rate of return analysis, we now consider more closely the major methods of determining the rate of return.

17.4 NON-TIME ADJUSTED METHODS FOR DETERMINING RATE OF RETURN

[1] PAYBACK

As mentioned previously in 17.3, the payback method considers the level of expected net cash flows and the total original cost, but does not account for differences in the timing of these items. This procedure is essentially a yardstick which measures the number of years required for the net cash inflows of a project to return or "payback" the original capital invested. It is less a way of determining the rate of return on investment for a project than the time required to return the initial capital outlay.

FIGURE 17.2 *Estimated net income after taxes and net cash flows of a prospective press project.*

Year	Net Income (Before Depreciation and Taxes)	Depreciation[a]	Taxable Income[b]	Taxes	Net Income After Taxes	Net Cash Flow[c]
1	25,000	10,000	15,000	7,500	7,500	17,500
2	40,000	10,000	30,000	15,000	15,000	25,000
3	40,000	10,000	30,000	15,000	15,000	25,000
4	40,000	10,000	30,000	15,000	15,000	25,000
5	35,000	10,000	25,000	12,500	12,500	22,500
6	30,000	10,000	20,000	10,000	10,000	20,000
7	25,000	10,000	15,000	7,500	7,500	17,500
8	20,000	10,000	10,000	5,000	5,000	15,000
9	15,000	10,000	5,000	2,500	2,500	12,500
10	10,000	10,000	0	0	0	10,000

a. Depreciation is calculated on a straight line basis.
b. Marginal federal tax rate of 50 percent is used for illustrative purposes.
c. Net cash flow is equal to the sum of net income after taxes plus depreciation.

(a) Calculation of Payback

When the annual net cash inflows on a project are constant, the project's payback period can be calculated by dividing the total original capital outlay by the annual net cash inflow. In many cases, however, one needs to calculate the payback period when the annual net cash inflows are unequal. Consider the following example: A corporation is contemplating a giant press for a price of $100,000. The press has a useful economic life of 10 years, with zero salvage value at the end of the tenth year. Assuming depreciation on a straight line basis[3] and a marginal federal corporate income tax rate of 50 percent, we calculate the projected net income after taxes and net cash flows, as demonstrated in Figure 17.2. To calculate the payback period, we total the estimated net cash flows year by year until this cumulative sum equals the original total capital outlay of $100,000. To be exact, $92,500 will be recovered by the end of the fourth year, leaving $7,500 still to be recovered. Since $22,500 is recovered in the fifth year, it takes $7,500/$22,500 or one-third of year 5 to reach $100,000. Thus, the payback period is 4 1/3 years. Note that the only thing the financial manager learns from the payback calculation is that the corporation will recover its initial outlay in 4 1/3 years assuming all the underlying estimates are correct.

(b) Advantages of Payback

The widespread use of payback in the corporate sector is directly attributable to several of the significant advantages it offers the financial manager. The payback method is easy to calculate and relatively easy to use. The financial manager can judge the expected length of time funds will be tied up and thus readily assess the degree of commitment risk if a project is approved.

In a period of tight money, if funds are in short supply, a quick payback project may be preferable to one which may yield a higher level of profitability but tie up funds much longer. The payback method also can serve as a coarse screen for selecting clearly desirable and necessary projects. It favors short-term projects and, therefore, screens out riskier projects that extend farther into what may be a difficult to measure future with higher risks. Finally, as discussed below (17.5[2](d)), payback can, under certain circumstances, be used as a reasonably good approximation of the IRR.

(c) Disadvantages of Payback

The major disadvantage of the payback method is that it does not measure all the relevant dimensions of profitability. It does not measure rate of return, because no firm makes a capital expenditure just to get its funds back. Second, the payback method fails to take into account the time value of money. Thus, it fails to explicitly take into consideration that dollars received in the future are not equal in purchasing power to the same level of nominal dollars received today. Although each of the hypothetical projects A, B and C in Figure 17.3 has the same four year payback period, they differ markedly in the pattern of annual net cash inflows. Because of the time value of money, the financial manager is not likely to consider the three projects equally attractive.

FIGURE 17.3 *Comparison of payback period by project cash inflows*

	Initial Capital Outlay	Net Cash Inflows					Payback Period (Years)
		Year 1	Year 2	Year 3	Year 4	Year 5	
Project A	40,000	10,000	10,000	10,000	10,000	10,000	4
Project B	40,000	15,000	15,000	5,000	5,000	10,000	4
Project C	40,000	3,000	7,000	10,000	20,000	10,000	4

Payback also overemphasizes liquidity and fails to take into account the net cash inflows of a project after the payback period. Thus, in Figure 17.4 the payback method would deem both projects A and B of equal worth because the payback periods are exactly the same. Project B, however, has significantly higher forecasted net cash inflows in the two years after the payback period.

FIGURE 17.4 *Evaluation of payback period*

	Initial Capital Outlay	Net Cash Inflows					Payback Period (Years)
		Year 1	Year 2	Year 3	Year 4	Year 5	
Project A	10,000	3,000	4,000	3,000	3,000	3,000	3
Project B	10,000	3,000	4,000	3,000	10,000	15,000	3

Finally, the payback method does not take into account the effect of differing economic lives or the estimate of project profitability or rate of return. As an illustration, consider three prospective projects, A, B and C, each of which has an initial capital investment outlay of $125,000 and yields an annual net cash inflow of $25,000, but for differing periods of time. As depicted in Figure 17.5 the estimated useful lives of the projects are 10, 15 and 25 years.

FIGURE 17.5 *Factors involved in project analysis*

	Project A	Project B	Project C
Original Capital Outlay	125,000	125,000	125,000
Estimated Project Useful Life	10 Years	15 Years	25 Years
Payback Period	5 Years	5 Years	5 Years
Annual Net Cash Inflows	25,000	25,000	25,000
Excess of Total Net Cash Inflows Over Initial Capital Outlay	125,000	250,000	500,000

Although the payback period for all three projects is five years, the excess of total net cash inflows over the original capital outlay varies substantially from $125,000 for project A to $500,000 for project C. Obviously, the financial manager will not be oblivious to these differences in the selection process.

[2] THE ACCOUNTING RATE OF RETURN

The accounting rate of return method has most of the disadvantages of payback, without the advantage, during times of liquidity constraint, of favoring short-lived projects. Thus, our discussion of this procedure will be brief.

Basically, the accounting rate of return method normally calculates a ratio of average annual earnings over a project's life to its average investment. (Although there are a number of variations on this basic theme, all methods of computing the accounting rate of return suffer from most of the same deficiencies.) Based upon the net income after taxes and an original investment of $100,000 used in Figure 17.2, the accounting rate of return would be computed as follows:

$$\text{Accounting Rate of Return} = \frac{\text{Average Annual Earnings}}{\text{Average Investment}}$$

$$= \frac{\dfrac{\$7,500 + \$15,000 + \$15,000 + \$15,000 + \$12,500 + \$10,000 + \$7,500 + \$5,000 + \$2,500 + \$0}{10}}{\dfrac{\$100,000 + \$0}{2}}$$

$$= \$9,000/\$50,000$$

$$= 18\%.$$

The above calculation assumes an average annual earnings figure based upon a 10 year mean. The average investment is based upon the relationship between the original investment and a zero salvage value at the end of the tenth year. Other assumptions for computing the accounting rate of return are found in practice, but as noted, all such calculations are replete with deficiencies.

17.5 TIME ADJUSTED METHODS FOR DETERMINING RATE OF RETURN[4]

The time adjusted methods, often referred to as discounted cash flow (DCF) methods, are superior to the payback and accounting rate of return methods because they take into account both the level *and* the timing of projected cash flows. Moreover, the time adjusted methods discriminate between near term and distant cash flows in terms of their current purchasing power. Thus the DCF methods can deal effectively with projects of differing useful economic lives, differing initial capital investments and irregular cash flow streams.

There are presently available various types of electronic equipment, including sophisticated pocket sized calculators as well as personal and time sharing computer terminals with standard programs, that may be used to perform the mathematics of the time adjusted returns. These facilities make it possible for the financial manager to easily modify the inputs on which the calculations are based and to compare the varying results to help reach financial decisions. Accordingly, management can devote its time and efforts to evaluating the significance of the data inputs and outcomes rather than to concerning themselves with the mathematics involved.[5]

Nevertheless, a comprehensive appreciation of the value of the DCF methods requires a basic understanding of the "mathematics" of present value. Both the IRR and NPV methods are based on present value concepts. Accordingly, in the discussion which follows, we illustrate the basic principles of the present value concept.

[1] PRESENT VALUE CONCEPT

Suppose we know that by investing 56 cents today, we will receive $1 ten years hence. The rate of return is six percent and is determined as follows. The expression for the present value of a future payment is:

$$P = S(1 + i)^{-n}$$

where P = the present value of an investment;
i = the annual rate of interest;
n = the useful economic life of the project in years; and
S = the economic value to which the investment grows.

Thus, in our example the formulation is as follows:

$$\$.56 = \$1.00(1 + i)^{-10}$$
$$i = 6\%.$$

Instead of solving the present value equation directly, many analysts use tables where the results are already calculated. For example, in Figure 17-24 (Appendix B) .5584 appears at the intersection of the six percent interest row and the 10 year column.[6,7] This number represents the present value of $1 discounted for 10 years at 6 percent interest.

Conversely, the above expression can be reformulated to find the future value of a current payment as follows:

$$S = P(1 + i)^n$$

where each of the variables are defined as above. Figure 17.23 (Appendix B) contains these values. It shows that $1 growing at an annual rate of six percent will amount to $1.7908 in ten years. Multiplying that number by .5584 yields $1.00.

When a company switches to the use of time adjusted techniques, the importance of time in financial calculations is placed into focus. For example, by highlighting that at a 10 percent discount rate, a $1,000 cash inflow 20 years hence is worth less than $150 today, the emphasis tends to shift to shorter-term projects.

[2] INTERNAL RATE OF RETURN METHOD

The IRR method is defined as the particular discount rate that exactly equates the present value of a project's cash outflows to the present value of its cash inflows.

(a) Calculation of the IRR

The calculation of the IRR is illustrated through the use of a simple example. Consider the case of an investment requiring a cash outlay of $2.25 today and yielding net cash inflows of $1 next year, $1 five years hence, and $1 ten years hence. The IRR can be obtained directly by solving the equation for the value of the discount rate, i.

$$\$2.25 = \frac{\$1}{(1 + i)} + \frac{\$1}{(1 + i)^5} + \frac{\$1}{(1 + i)^{10}} .$$

This particular value of i is, by definition, the IRR. If electronic equipment is not available, this type of equation may be readily solved by means of present value tables such as Figure 17.24 (Appendix B) to solve for i through "trial and error". The trial and error approach is illustrated in Figure 17.6. In our first trial we use an i value of 5 percent to calculate the present value of the net cash inflows of $1 in each of years 1, 5, and 10. As seen in Figure 17.6, the present value factors for these three years are .9524, .7835, and .6139 respectively when i = 5 percent. The sum of the present values of the three net cash inflows equals $2.34 or 9 cents more than the present value of the original investment of $2.25.

A second trial is now made using an i value of 8 percent. As seen in Figure 17.6, this yields a total present value of $2.07 for the three net cash inflows or 18 cents less than the present value of the original investment. Since it is clear that the correct rate lies somewhere between 5 percent and 8 percent, we next try 6 percent. As seen in Figure 17.6, 6 percent is the actual IRR.

FIGURE 17.6 *Example demonstrating the trial and error procedure for calculating IRR*

Year	Investment Requirement	Net Cash Inflow	Trial No. 1 at 5%		Trial No. 2 at 8%		Trial No. 3 at 6%	
			Present Value Factor	Present Value	Present Value Factor	Present Value	Present Value Factor	Present Value
Now	$2.25		1.0000	$2.25	1.0000	$2.25	1.0000	$2.25
1		$1.00	.9524	$ .95	.9259	$ .93	.9434	$ .94
2			.9070		.8573		.8900	
3			.8638		.7938		.8396	
4			.8227		.7350		.7921	
5		1.00	.7835	.78	.6806	.68	.7473	.75
6			.7462		.6302		.7050	
7			.7107		.5835		.6651	
8			.6768		.5403		.6274	
9			.6446		.5002		.5919	
10		1.00	.6139	.61	.4632	.46	.5584	.56
				$2.34		$2.07		$2.25

The trial and error procedure quite often requires the use of linear interpolation to arrive at the IRR. This procedure is demonstrated in Figure 17.7 by the press example from 17.4[1](a).

FIGURE 17.7 *Calculation of the IRR for the prospective press project[a]*

Year	Net Cash Inflow	Present Value Factor: 15%	Present Value	Present Value Factor: 20%	Present Value
1	$ 17,500	.870	$ 15,225	.833	$14,578
2	25,000	.756	18,900	.694	17,350
3	25,000	.658	16,450	.579	14,475
4	25,000	.572	14,300	.482	12,050
5	22,500	.497	11,183	.402	9,045
6	20,000	.432	8,640	.335	6,700
7	17,500	.376	6,580	.279	4,883
8	15,000	.327	4,905	.233	3,495
9	12,500	.284	3,550	.194	2,425
10	10,000	.247	2,470	.162	1,620
	$190,000		$102,203		$86,621

[a] On original investment of $100,000.

At a discount rate of 15 percent, the present value of the net cash inflows equals $102,203, somewhat above the original investment of $100,000, while at a 20 percent discount rate, the present value of the net cash inflows is $86,621, somewhat below the original investment. Therefore, the IRR lies between 15 and 20 percent. The IRR can now be approximated by linear interpolation as follows:[8]

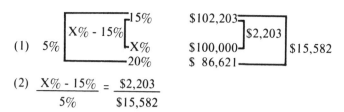

(2) $\dfrac{X\% - 15\%}{5\%} = \dfrac{\$2,203}{\$15,582}$

(3) X = 15.71%.

Thus, the IRR is 15.71 percent. It would have been sufficient to say 15 percent plus, since the precise accuracy of a two decimal point calculation should not obscure the fact that estimates of net cash inflows 10 years in the future necessarily have less than two decimal point accuracy.

(b) IRR Based on Equal Periodic Cash Flows

The IRR method can also be readily estimated for investment projects with equal periodic net cash inflows over a prescribed period of time. Such projects can be visualized as equivalent to annuities. Figure 17.8 illustrates an investment project with an initial capital outlay of $1,000 and annual net cash inflows of $250 for each of the next five years.

FIGURE 17.8 *Investment with initial capital outlay of $1,000*

Year	Net Cash Flow (1)	8% Discount Factor (2)	Present Value (1) x (2)
1	$250	.926	$232
2	250	.857	214
3	250	.794	198
4	250	.735	184
5	250	.681	170
		3.993	$998*

*The result should be $1,000; the difference is because the actual IRR is slightly under 8 percent.

As indicated above, these net cash flows, in effect, represent an annuity of $250 per year for five years. We can determine the present value of the annuity by adding the present values of the individual payments as done in Figure 17.8. Alternatively, we can add the discount factors and multiply that sum by $250, the annual net cash inflow. The summation of the discount factors for such annuity problems can be written as follows:

$$\sum_{t=1}^{n} (1+i)^{-t}$$

(which may be read as the sum of the present values at "i" rate of interest, of a sequence of payments of $1 per period over time, "t", which is equal to 1 through "n" periods.)

The actual calculation of such a sum is a special case of the formula for the sum of a geometric series, expressed as follows:[9]

$$\sum_{t=1}^{n} (1+i)^{-t} = \frac{1-(1+i)^{-n}}{i}.$$

In practice, it is much easier to use a table of annuity discount factors to look up the value rather than to solve what is called an Nth power equation. Thus, the IRR of the investment may be determined as follows:

[1] $\$1,000 = \$250 \sum_{t=1}^{5} (1+i)^{-t}$

[2] $\$6,000/\$250 = \sum_{t=1}^{5} (1+i)^{-t}$

[3] $4 = \sum_{t=1}^{5} (1+i)^{-t}.$

Referring to Figure 17.26 (Appendix B) which gives such values, we find that at 8 percent and 5 years, the summation is equal to 3.993. Thus, the IRR is slightly less than 8 percent.

Interestingly, the solution to an Nth power equation is sufficiently difficult that even the computer programs written for such solutions rely on the trial and error process.

(c) IRR of Projects with Deferred Equal Annual Cash Flows

Another useful concept in calculating the IRR is that of a deferred annuity. A deferred annuity is one whose term does not begin until some future date. For example, assume that an investment costs $48,770 and provides a net cash inflow of $5,000 for the first five years and $8,000 for the next five years. In order to determine the IRR we must find the interest rate producing a factor which, when applied to an annuity of $5,000 for the first through fifth years and $8,000 for the sixth through tenth years, yields a present value of $48,770. This relationship may be shown as follows:

$$\$48,770 = \$5,000 \sum_{t=1}^{5} (1+i)^{-t} + \$8,000 \sum_{t=6}^{10} (1+i)^{-t}.$$

We may obtain the last term in the equation (the present value of the annuity for the sixth through tenth years) by ascertaining the present value of an annuity for the first through tenth years and subtracting from it the present value of an annuity for the first through fifth years as follows:

$$\sum_{t=6}^{10} (1+i)^{-t} = \sum_{t=1}^{10} (1+i)^{-t} - \sum_{t=1}^{5} (1+i)^{-t}.$$

Thus, the present value of an annuity of $1 for five years discounted at 5 percent is $4.33. The present value of an annuity of $1 for ten years discounted at 5 percent is $7.72. Therefore, the present value of an annuity of $1 per year for the sixth through tenth years is $3.39 ($7.72 - $4.33).

The product of the annual cash flow of $5,000 received during the first five years and its related present value of 4.33 produces a total present value figure of $21,650; the product of the annual cash flow of $8,000 received during the sixth through tenth years and its related present value factor of 3.39 produces a total present value of $27,120. The sum of $27,120 and $21,650 gives $48,770, which is the cost of the investment. Therefore, a 5 percent IRR is obtained from an investment of $48,770, yielding an annual cash flow of $5,000 during the first five years and $8,000 during the next five years. Some experimenting with rates would have to be done before determining the 5 percent discount factor which brought about the required equality, but with familiarity, these trial and error calculations may be done rapidly.

(d) Employing Rules of Thumb to Calculate IRR

As a starting point in the calculation of the IRR, it is not uncommon to use the reciprocal of the payback period or the accounting rate of return, based on either the original or average investment, as a rough, initial proxy. Depending on the duration of the project and the actual IRR, each of these simpler measures varies in the accuracy of its approximation of the IRR.

In general, the IRR is less than the reciprocal of the payback. For any given rate, the deviation decreases as the project's economic life increases; while for any given duration, the deviation decreases as the IRR increases.[10] This relationship is shown in Figure 17.9.

FIGURE 17.9   *Percentage point deviations of the payback reciprocal k_p from the internal rate of return for selected values of k and n*

Internal Rate of Return k in Percent	Proposal Duration n in Years								
	2	5	8	10	15	20	40	60	100
5	+48.8	+18.1	+10.5	+8.0	+4.6	+3.0	+0.8	+0.3	—
10	+47.6	+16.4	+ 8.7	+5.3	+3.2	+1.8	+0.2	—	—
15	+46.5	+14.8	+ 7.3	+4.9	+2.1	+1.0	+0.1	—	—
20	+45.4	+13.4	+ 6.1	+3.9	+1.4	+0.5	—	—	—
30	+43.5	+11.1	+ 4.2	+2.4	+0.6	+0.2	—	—	—
40	+41.7	+ 9.1	+ 2.9	+1.4	+0.3	—	—	—	—
50	+40.0	+ 7.6	+ 2.0	+0.9	+0.1	—	—	—	—
60	+38.5	+ 6.3	+ 1.4	+0.6	—	—	—	—	—

Source: Marshall Sarnat and Haim Levy, "The Relationship of Rules of Thumb to the Internal Rate of Return: A Restatement and Generalization", *Journal of Finance,* June 1969, p. 481.

For long lived projects, say 15 years and over, the deviation between the payback reciprocal and the IRR is relatively small even when the IRR is modest. For projects with economic lives between five and twenty-five years, the deviations are relatively small when the IRR is high.

On the other hand, except for durations of one year, when the results are the same, the accounting rate of return based on total investment, as seen in Figure 17.10 is less than the IRR. The deviations follow a U-shaped pattern, initially increasing as the project duration rises from one year, reaching a critical maximum, and then declining once more. Thereafter, the accounting rate of return based on total investment asymptotically approaches the IRR as the project duration grows.

The accounting rate of return based on average investment tends to be greater than the IRR. For one year projects, this accounting rate of return is twice the IRR. The difference narrows thereafter, but remains positive, and then the average investment accounting rate of return asymptotically approaches twice the IRR once more as the project's duration moves towards infinity. Thus, the pattern is also U-shaped but reversed from that based on the total investment. For each IRR starting from one year, the deviations decline to a critical level, and thereafter rise once more.

FIGURE 17.10 *Percentage point deviations of the accounting rate of return on total investment, k, from the IRR, k, for selected values of k and n*

Internal Rate of Return k in Percent	Proposal Duration n in Years								
	1	2	5	10	15	20	40	60	100
5	0	- 1.2	- 1.9	-2.0	-2.0	-2.0	-1.7	-1.4	-1.0
10	0	- 2.4	- 3.6	-3.7	-3.5	-3.2	-2.3	-1.6	-1.0
15	0	- 3.5	- 5.2	-5.1	-4.6	-4.0	-2.4	-1.7	-1.0
20	0	- 4.6	- 6.6	-6.2	-5.3	-4.5	-2.6	-1.7	-1.0
30	0	- 6.5	- 8.9	-7.6	-6.1	-4.8	-2.5	-1.7	-1.0
40	0	- 8.3	-10.9	-8.6	-6.4	-5.0	-2.5	-1.7	-1.0
50	0	-10.0	-12.4	-9.1	-6.6	-5.0	-2.5	-1.7	-1.0
60	0	-11.5	-13.7	-9.4	-6.6	-5.0	-2.5	-1.7	-1.0

Source: Marshall Sarnat and Haim Levy, *Journal of Finance,* "The Relationship of Rules of Thumb to the Internal Rate of Return: A Restatement and Generalization," June 1969, p. 484.

The extent to which each of these simple measures of rate of return approximates the IRR is portrayed in Figure 17-11. The humped area, "A", encloses those combinations of project duration and IRR for which the accounting rate of return (based on average investment) provides the closest approximation to the IRR. The two outlying areas, marked "T" and "P" respectively, enclose the sets of the IRR and project duration for which the accounting rate of return (based on total investment) and the reciprocal of the payback period, provide the closest approximation of the IRR.[11] Appendix C shows how fairly precise relationships may be drawn that equate the payback or accounting rates of return with the time adjusted methods.

(e) IRR and the Cost of Capital

The IRR may also be defined as the maximum rate of interest that could be paid each period on the unrecovered amount of investment in order to permit the extinguishment of the total investment during its life. If capital could be obtained at less than this rate, the investment would provide a profit equal to the difference between the IRR earned and the cost of capital. If the cost of capital is higher than the IRR, the earnings generated from the investment would be sufficient to pay the required interest and amortize the investment during its life.

FIGURE 17.11 *Relationships between simple measures of rate of return and the IRR*

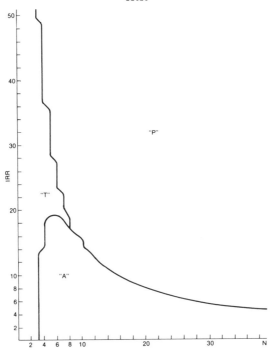

Investment Proposal Duration in Years

"A" = set for which the accounting rate of return based on average investment gives closest approximation to the IRR.
"P" = set for which the reciprocal of the payback gives closest approximation to the IRR.
"T" = set for which the accounting rate of return based on total investment gives closest approximation to the IRR.

Source: Marshall Sarnat and Haim Levy, "The Relationship of Rules of Thumb to the Internal Rate of Return: A Restatement and Generalization," *Journal of Finance,* June 1969, p. 486.

We illustrate this concept by referring to our prospective press project. In this case, if the firm borrowed $100,000 at an interest rate equal to the IRR selected, the annual payments required to both liquidate the loan during its life of 10 years and meet the stipulated interest rate would equal the cash inflows generation. This relationship is shown if Figure 17.12. Where the cash inflows are divided between the return on unrecovered capital at 15.71 percent and capital recovery, the initial $100,000 loan is fully paid off at the end of 10 years.

In addition, the IRR can measure the yield of a bond. The yield on a bond may be described as that discounted return which, when applied both to an annuity represented by the coupon payments on the principal value of a bond and to a single principal payment of $1,000 at the maturity of the bond, provides a present value sum that equals the price paid for the bond. For example, let us find, by this means, the yield on a 3¼ percent bond due in 27 years and selling at $1,075. The equation may be stated as follows:

(1) $\$1,075 = \$32.50 \sum_{t=1}^{27} (1 + i)^{-t} + \$1,000 (1 + i)^{-27}$

(2) at 2.75% interest: = \$32.50 (18.88) + \$1,000 (.48072) = \$1,094.32

(3) at 3.00% interest: = \$32.50 (18.33) + \$1,000 (.45019) = \$1,045.91.

We can see that the value obtained at 2.75 percent is too high, while that obtained at 3.00 percent is too low. Interpolating, we derive a yield of 2.85 percent, which is the same as that which would be obtained from a yield book.[12] Since the IRR calculated by this method is comparable to the rate used in finance on loans and on bond yields, the IRR can be compared directly with the cost of bond financing.

FIGURE 17.12 *Income and recovery of investment*

Year	Amount of Capital Unrecovered at Beginning of Year (1)	Annual Cash Inflow (2)	Return at 15.71% (3)	Amount of Capital Recovered During Year (2) - (3)
1	$100,000	$ 17,500	$15,710	$ 1,790
2	98,210	25,000	15,429	9,571
3	88,649	25,000	13,927	11,073
4	77,579	25,000	12,188	12,812
5	64,764	22,500	10,174	12,326
6	52,438	20,000	8,238	11,762
7	40,676	17,500	6,390	11,110
8	29,566	15,000	4,645	10,355
9	19,211	12,500	3,018	9,482
10	9,729	10,000	1,528	8,472
Total		$190,000	$91,247[a]	$98,753[b]

[a]The total should be $90,000.
[b]The total should be $100,000. These minor deviations are due to our earlier interpolation between the fairly wide bounds of 15 percent and 20 percent. (For example, had we interpolated between 15 percent and 16 percent, we would have computed our IRR as 15.64 percent and obtained return and capital recovery figures of $90,188 and $99,812, respectively.) Additional errors resulted from calculating return only to two decimals, interpolating linearly and rounding. Still, our IRR is sufficiently accurate for this type of calculation.

[3] NET PRESENT VALUE METHOD

The NPV method is the second major time adjusted rate of return method of evaluating capital expenditure proposals.[13] By definition, the NPV is simply the difference between the present value of net cash inflows and the present value of net cash outflows, including the original capital outlay, incurred during the life of the project.

(a) Calculation of Net Present Value

To determine the NPV of a project, the future annual cash inflows and outflows are discounted at a rate equal to either the firm's cost of capital or to the firm's minimum acceptable cutoff rate of return. Symbolically, we can represent the NPV calculation as follows:

$$NPV = -I + \sum_{t=1}^{n} C(1 + i)^n$$

where I = the initial investment or capital outlay;
C = the net cash flow for period t;
i = the discount rate; and
n = the number of years in the life of the project.

If the present value of the annual cash inflows exceed the present value of the cash outflows, including the initial capital outlay, then the project will return more than the cost of capital or more than the minimum acceptable cutoff rate of return. Projects for which the NPV is zero may be considered marginal, while projects with negative NPV's do not return the cost of capital and should generally be rejected as unprofitable.[14]

The NPV method provides a direct, one-step procedure for assessing project profitability because the cost of capital or discount rate is built right into the computation. If the NPV is greater than zero, the project is considered profitable. This contrasts with the IRR method which requires two steps to assess project profitability. The IRR value calculated in the first step is compared in the second step with the firm's cost of capital or minimum acceptable cutoff rate of return. If the IRR is greater, the project is considered profitable.

To demonstrate the computation of the NPV, consider a prospective project requiring machinery which has an initial capital cost of $1.5 million and a useful economic life of 5 years. As shown in Figure 17.13, the project has projected annual net cash inflows of $550,000 (year 1), $500,000 (year 2), $400,000 (year 3), $300,000 (year 4), and $250,000 (year 5). If the firm's cost of capital is 10 percent, we calculate the project's NPV as $73,500. (The IRR is 12.2 percent).

FIGURE 17.13 *Computation of a prospective project's net present value*

Year	Annual Net Cash Inflow	Present Value Factor at 10%	Present Value
0	$-1,500,000	1.000	$-1,500,000
1	550,000	.909	499,950
2	500,000	.826	413,000
3	400,000	.751	300,400
4	300,000	.683	204,900
5	250,000	.621	155,250
NPV	—	—	73,500

Whether this project should be undertaken would depend on a number of factors, such as total availability of capital, alternative opportunities on other proposed projects, and the mix of the firm's existing projects with this project.

This example highlights one of the limitations of the NPV method. If we computed the NPV alone, all we would know about the project is that, discounted at a 10 percent cost of capital, it would return a little more than its investment cost. We would know the absolute amount of the excess, $73,500

($1,573,500 - $1,500,000 = $73,500), but we would not have a rate that could be compared with rates on other projects. And the amount by which the present values of the cash inflows exceed the original investment cost could not be compared effectively with similar figures for other projects because of differences in the size of projects. For example, if another project discounted at the 10 percent cost of capital yielded a present excess of only $2,500 over the investment cost, we could not safely conclude that the project yielding a $73,500 excess was the preferred one. Why? Because the size of the excess is no basis for comparative judgments. We would have to know the investment cost of the second project and then work out a suitable method of comparison. The dilemma presented here is illustrated in Figure 17.14.

FIGURE 17.14 *A comparison of two projects*

Project	Initial Investment Cost	Net Present Value
A	$1,500,000	$73,500
B	10,000	2,500

Notice that while the NPV of A exceeds that of B by $71,000, it requires an additional $1,490,000 ($1,500,000 - $10,000) to generate the additional $71,000. The question arises here as to whether we might find alternative projects whose initial investment costs are less than $1,490,000 and which promise to provide NPV's in excess of $71,000.

This particular situation is frequently encountered in practice. Fortunately, we can systematically deal with it by using a present worth or profitability index. This index is simply an offshoot of the NPV and effectively facilitates the comparison amongst projects with substantial differences in both NPV's and initial investment costs. The profitability index is defined as follows:

$$\text{Profitability Index} = \frac{\text{Present Value of Net Cash Inflows (excluding the initial investment cost)}}{\text{Initial Investment Cost of Project}}$$

The index puts the million dollar and the thousand dollar projects in perspective. In our example, the index values are:

(1) Project A: $1,573,500/$1,500,000 = 1.05
(2) Project B: $12,500/$10,000 = 1.25

In this case, the profitability index demonstrates the superiority of the smaller project. As is the case with the IRR, the profitability index provides a similar basis for comparison of projects involving different capital outlays.

(b) Comparison of NPV and IRR Methods

The IRR method provides an actual rate that is both a convenient analytical tool and can be compared directly to the firm's cost of capital or minimum cutoff return for investment. However, those who prefer the NPV method point to two significant problems associated with the IRR method. First, when projects include negative net cash flows, the calculation may result in more than one IRR. This causes a problem in selecting the "correct" estimate. Second, the IRR method can give an incorrect ranking of projects when the actual reinvestment rate for funds generated by the project is significantly different from the project's IRR. The IRR calculation assumes that projected cash inflows are reinvested at a rate equal to the IRR.

Both these deficiencies are illustrated below. Figure 17.15 presents a prospective project calling for an investment in one of two new oil pumps. The larger oil pump entails an initial capital outlay of $11,600 and would provide savings of $20,000 in the next year. The smaller oil pump entails an initial capital outlay of $10,000 and would provide annual savings of $10,000 for each of the next two years.

FIGURE 17.15 *First deficiency of IRR method: negative cash flow causing two rates of return*

	Initial Capital Investment	Net Cash Inflow (Year 1)	Net Cash Inflow (Year 2)
Small Oil Pump	-$10,000	$10,000	$10,000
Large Oil Pump	- 11,600	20,000	0
Incremental Difference (Large Oil Pump- Small Oil Pump)	- 1,600	10,000	-10,000

As demonstrated in Figure 17.15, the incremental cash flows (large oil pump minus small oil pump) are negative in the current year *and* the second year. The result is that this investment project has two IRR's, 25 percent and 400 percent, as follows:

(1) $\$1,600 = \dfrac{\$10,000}{(1 + IRR)} + \dfrac{(-\$10,000)}{(1 + IRR)^2}$

(2) for IRR = .25,

$\$1,600 = \dfrac{\$10,000}{(1.25)} - \dfrac{\$10,000}{(1.25)^2}$

$\$1,600 = \$8,000 - \$6,400$

$\$1,600 = \$1,600$

(3) for IRR = 4.00,

$\$1,600 = \dfrac{\$10,000}{5.0} - \dfrac{\$10,000}{(5.0)^2}$

$\$1,600 = \$2,000 - \$400$

$\$1,600 = \$1,600.$

Mathematically, both 25 percent and 400 percent are IRR's for the proposed project. Figure 17.16 presents an illustration of the second IRR deficiency.

FIGURE 17.16 *Second deficiency of IRR method: incorrect ranking of projects*

	Project K	Project M
Initial Investment (the company's cost of capital is 10%)	$1,491	$1,491
Annual Net Cash Inflows (Years 1-10)	$200	$100
Annual Net Cash Inflows (Years 11-40)	$300	$512

In this example, a choice must be made between two projects. One provides a relatively high annual net cash inflow over the initial ten years and a relatively low inflow over the next 30 years of the project's life. Reversing this pattern, the other provides a relatively low inflow in the first ten years and a relatively high inflow in the ensuing 30 years. Inherent in this decision is the reinvestment opportunities that actually will be available during the life of both projects.

In calculating their respective IRR's, we find that project K has a rate of 15.0 percent and project M, 14.0 percent. At first glance, therefore, project K appears preferable to M. That is, on the basis of their IRR's, K would be ranked ahead of M. However, the 15.0 percent IRR calculated for project K implicitly assumes the reinvestment of generated cash inflows at that rate for the entire 40 year period. This assumption may or may not be valid. If, for example, the financial manager finds that investment opportunities have dried up and that the few available projects offer rates of return well below 15 percent, he should have selected project M.

Ordinarily, in the NPV method, the assumed reinvestment rate is either the cost of capital or the minimum acceptable cutoff rate, depending on which was used in the original calculation of the present value. In the absence of evidence to the contrary, this assumption is likely to be more realistic than the assumption underlying the IRR method, which is that the reinvestment rate is the calculated IRR. As a general proposition, therefore, the NPV method will provide a more realistic approximate ranking of projects than the IRR. Using the company's cost of capital of 10 percent as the discount rate, we find that project M's NPV is $985 ($2,476 - $1,491), while project K's NPV is $828 ($2,319 - $1,491). Accordingly, under the NPV method, project M is ranked ahead of project K.

The financial manager, however, may want to make an independent estimate of the assumed reinvestment rate. If he has to ration capital, for example, he may want to use the rate applicable to the projects expected to be foregone because of lack of funds (the opportunity cost of the marginal project). Accordingly, he may prefer an approach that permits the determination of an adjusted internal rate of return (IRR*) and an adjusted net present value (NPV*) under varying estimated reinvestment rates. The so-called terminal value (TV) method may be used for this purpose.

[4] TERMINAL VALUE METHOD

This method involves two basic steps. First, the TV of the project is calculated as,[15]

$$TV = \sum_{t=1}^{n} C_t(1 + r)^{n-t}$$

where: C_t = Cash flow for period t;
n = the life of the investment;
r = the assumed reinvestment rate; and
t = any period during the life of the investment.

Second, that rate is found which discounts TV to equal the present value of the investment; this is the IRR*

$$TV(1 + IRR^*)^{-n} = \text{Investment}$$
$$(1 + IRR^*)^{-n} = \text{Investment}/TV$$

or

the TV is discounted by the company's cost of capital (or the minimum acceptable cutoff rate). From this figure the value of the investment is subtracted. The result is the NPV*.

$$NPV^* = TV(1 + c)^{-n},$$

where: c = the cost of capital.

In 17.5[2](b), the formula was given for the sum of the present values of a sequence of $1 payments for "n" periods at "i" rate of interest. In determining the TV of a project, the formula used is for the sum of the future values of a sequence of $1 payments for "n" periods at "i" rate of interest, or:

$$\sum_{t=1}^{n} (1 + i)^{n-t} = \sum_{t=1}^{n} (1 + i)^{t-1} = \frac{(1 + i)^n - 1}{i}.$$

The values for this expression are shown in Figure 17.25 (Appendix B). For example, one dollar per year compounded at 10 percent per year for zero through 39 years will accumulate to $442.59 (shown at year 40 in the Figure) and compounded zero through 29 years will accumulate to $164.49 (shown at year 30 in the Figure). One dollar received during years 1-10 will compound for 30-39 years, amounting to $278.10 ($442.59-$164.49) at the end of the fortieth year. One dollar received during years 11-40 will compound for zero to 29 years, amounting to $164.49 at the end of the fortieth year.

The calculations of the IRR* and NPV* for projects K and M are illustrated in Appendix D. Project K, since it has substantially higher initial cash inflows than project M, will yield a higher IRR* than project M whenever the reinvestment rate is relatively high. As the reinvestment rate declines, however, the attraction of near term money diminishes when compared with long-term money. At some point, therefore, the larger amount of cash generated by project M in years 11-40 will result in its IRR* surpassing that of project K.

Figure 17.17 portrays this relationship between the IRR*'s of projects K and M as the assumed reinvestment rate moves between 8 and 16 percent. At an assumed reinvestment rate of 8 percent, the IRR* of project M is superior to that of project K — 10.20 percent compared with 9.82 percent. The IRR*'s

452

of project M remain above those of project K until an assumed reinvestment rate of 12 percent is realized. Then, a switch occurs. The IRR*'s of project K continue to rise above those of project M, reflecting the increasing benefits of its early larger cash inflows as the assumed reinvestment rate increases.

FIGURE 17.17 *Relationship between the assumed rate of reinvestment and the IRR* for projects K and M*

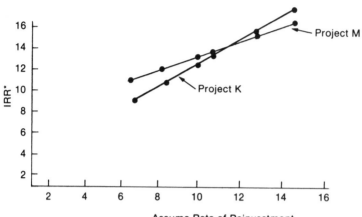

Figure 17.18 shows that the NPV*'s of projects K and M behave in the same fashion as their IRR*'s. Note that at assumed reinvestment rates from 8 percent through 11 percent, both the NPV* and the IRR* of project M are higher than those of project K. Thereafter, reflecting a reversal of the TV's of the cash flows of the two projects, both the NPV* and IRR* of project K exceed those of project M. As would be expected, at an assumed reinvestment rate of 15 percent, the IRR* of project K is also 15 percent, the same as the IRR that was originally determined. Similarly, at a reinvestment rate of 14 percent, the IRR* of project M is also 14 percent, the same as its originally determined IRR. By the same token, when the reinvestment rate of each project equals 10 percent (the cost of capital) the NPV of each project is the same as its NPV*.

The TV method is also useful in comparing projects with unequal lives. Figure 17.19 for example, recapitulates the data for project K and shows similar information for project Z that also costs $1,491 but provides heavy cash flows for ten years, after which its economic life expires.

Based on the data in Figure 17.19, the IRR of project Z, reflecting its large cash inflows during the years 1-10, is 19.55 percent, substantially greater than the IRR of project K, which was previously calculated to be 15.0 percent. On the other hand, using the company's 10 percent cost of capital as the discount rate, the NPV of project Z is $660, which is below project K's previously calculated NPV of $828. Which ranking is correct?

A fair comparison must place both projects on the same life span. To obtain a return of 19.55 percent, each of the cash flows of project Z must be reinvested at that rate. But, suppose that the financial manager gauges that these cash flows can only be reinvested at the company's cost of capital of 10 percent. What then? This question may be answered by the TV method.

FIGURE 17.18   *NPV* and IRR* of projects K and M at varying assumed reinvestment rates and a cost of capital equal to 10 percent*

Assumed Reinvestment Rate	Project K Terminal Values of Future Cash Flows	NPV*	IRR*	Project M Terminal Values of Future Cash Flows	NPV*	IRR*
8%	$ 63,139	$ -96	9.82%	$ 72,578	$ +113	10.20%
9	81,207	+303	10.51	89,946	496	10.79
10	104,968	828	11.22	112,030	984	11.40
11	136,267	1,520	11.95	140,179	1,606	12.03
12	177,552	2,432	12.69	176,139	2,401	12.67
13	232,062	3,636	13.45	222,169	3,418	13.33
14	304,084	5,228	14.22	281,199	4,722	14.00
15	399,294	7,331	15.00	357,025	6,397	14.68
16	525,183	10,113	15.79	454,565	8,553	15.37

Note: These values were obtained by means of a computer and therefore differ slightly from those obtained by means of the compound interest tables.

FIGURE 17.19   *A comparison of two projects with unequal lives*

	Project K	Project Z
Initial Investment*	$1,491	$1,491
Annual Net Cash Inflows (Years 1-10)	200	350
Annual Net Cash Inflows (Years 11-40)	300	—

*The company's cost of capital is 10 percent.

The TV of the 1-10 year cash flows of project Z may be calculated over the forty year life span of project K by the following formula:

$$TV = C_t \sum_{t=1}^{n} (1 + r)^{t-1}(1 + r)^{m-n},$$

where: m = the number of years of life of the longer-term project;
n = the number of years of life of the shorter-term project;
and all other values are defined as previously in this subsection.

For project Z the financial manager has determined that the annual cash flows (C_t) will be $350 for ten years and that the marginal opportunity investment rate, which ordinarily is used as the estimated reinvestment rate (r), will be 10 percent, the same as the company's cost of capital. In these circumstances, the TV of project Z is as follows:

(1) $TV = \$350 \sum_{t=1}^{10} (1.10)^{t-1}(1.10)^{30}$

(2) $TV = \$350 (15.937)(17.449)$

(3) $TV = \$97,330.$

The IRR* is then calculated by finding the rate that discounts the TV over m years to the present value of the investment (TV(1*IRR*)$^{-m}$ = Investment).

(4) $97,330 (1 + IRR*)$^{-40}$ = $1,491

(1 + IRR*)$^{-40}$ = $1,491/$97,330

(1 + IRR*)$^{-40}$ = .01532

IRR* = 11.01 percent.

Using the TV method, therefore, with an assumed reinvestment rate of 10 percent, we find that the IRR* of project Z falls to 11.01 percent. This rate is below the IRR* of project K which was previously determined to be 11.22 percent at an assumed reinvestment rate of 10 percent.

The NPV of project Z is calculated by discounting the TV of $97,330 by the company's 10 percent cost of capital over the 40 year life of the longer-term project and subtracting $1,491, the initial investment. This results in an NPV* of $660 which is the same as the NPV since the reinvestment rate equals the cost of capital. This amount is below project K's NPV* and NPV of $828. Thus, on the basis of the TV method, both the IRR* and the NPV* rank project K ahead of project Z.

[5] ADDITIONAL ASPECTS AND USES OF TIME ADJUSTED METHODS

It seems desirable to re-emphasize that the relatively mathematical overtones of the time adjusted methods should not obscure the important fact that the accuracy of these methods can be no better than the underlying data. Accordingly, much of the work in this area has been addressed to the development of effective means of forecasting cash flows.[16] But assuming that suitable forecasting techniques are in use, the risks attendant upon different ventures will still vary widely. Decisions regarding the future invariably entail uncertainty. The problem of taking uncertainty or risk into account is discussed in Chapter 18.

Time adjusted methods are also frequently used in the capital budgeting process to rank proposed projects in situations where the capital funds available are not sufficient to undertake all of the projects deemed desirable. As an illustration, consider Figure 17.20 which displays 10 projects proposed for a firm's capital budget.

FIGURE 17.20 *Capital budget proposals*

PROJECT	ORIGINAL INVESTMENT	INTERNAL RATE OF RETURN
A	$200,000	24.5%
B	600,000	20.0
C	450,000	18.4
D	700,000	14.0
E	150,000	17.5
F	250,000	21.0
G	275,000	27.0
H	350,000	16.5
I	155,000	27.5
J	500,000	22.0

The firm can approach the selection process in a number of ways. It can use a given rate of return as the cutoff point. If, for example, it has decided as a matter of corporate financial policy that it will undertake projects only if they have a projected rate of return of 20 percent or better, it would rank the projects according to their prospective rates of return and then choose projects I, G, A, J, F, and B and reject the others.

The second basis for project selection is the amount of funds available. If, for example, the company has $3 million to finance capital projects, it may choose to undertake all projects except D, for their total costs would amount to $2.93 million, as demonstrated in Figure 17.21.

FIGURE 17.21 *Ten proposed capital budgeting projects listed in order of rate of return*

PROJECT	RATE OF RETURN	ORIGINAL INVESTMENT	CUMULATIVE INVESTMENT
I	27.5%	$155,000	$ 155,000
G	27.0	275,000	430,000
A	24.5	200,000	630,000
J	22.0	500,000	1,130,000
F	21.0	250,000	1,380,000
B	20.0	600,000	1,980,000
C	18.4	450,000	2,430,000
E	17.5	150,000	2,580,000
H	16.5	350,000	2,930,000
D	14.0	700,000	3,630,000

The third and most frequently utilized method of project selection is to combine the first and second methods — that is, to set both a rate of return cut off and a maximum budget amount that can be expended. For instance, in the present example, the firm might decide that it has $2.5 million available to finance all capital projects whose original investment totals no more than that amount and whose yield is 18 percent or better. Thus projects I, G, A, J, F, B, and C would be undertaken.

No well run company, of course, ever puts itself in an absolute strait jacket in such decisions. Cut off points need not be arbitrary and inflexible. For example, if project E is highly desirable on other grounds, its 17.5 percent rate of return is very close to the 18 percent cut off level and the funds it requires will carry only $80,000 above the $2.5 million maximum so that it may well be included in the projects to be undertaken.

In addition to their use in the capital budgeting process to approve or reject projects, time adjusted rate of return methods also provide a firm foundation for financial decisions with respect to make or buy alternatives. The example in Figure 17.22 illustrates this application.

In this example, a steel company requires the annual replacement (for five years) of an essential part of one of its stamping presses. If it buys a machine for $25,000, (assuming no salvage value), it can make the part itself at an annual cost of $50,000. If it buys the part annually, it will cost $60,000. Thus, while manufacture of the part will tie up $25,000 of capital at once, it can achieve a savings, each year for five years, of $10,000. Should the company make the part or buy it?

FIGURE 17.22 *Time adjusted rate of return method applied in make or buy decision*

Year	Cash Inflow (Savings)	Present Value Factor 28%	Present Value	Present Value Factor 29%	Present Value
1	$10,000	.781	$ 7,810	.775	$ 7,750
2	10,000	.610	6,100	.601	6,010
3	10,000	.477	4,770	.466	4,660
4	10,000	.373	3,730	.361	3,610
5	10,000	.291	2,910	.280	2,800
			$25,320		$24,830

$$1\% \begin{bmatrix} & 28\% & \$25,320 \\ X\% - 28\% & X\% & \$25,000 \\ & 29\% & \$24,830 \end{bmatrix} \$320 \ \$490$$

Rate of return = 28.65%

$$\frac{X\% - 28\%}{1\%} = \frac{\$320}{\$490}$$

x = 28.65%

The question can be stated in terms of an IRR decision. What will the IRR be on the investment of $25,000 in order to realize an annual $10,000 cash inflow for five years? As indicated in Figure 17.22, the decision to acquire the $25,000 machine in order to make the part, rather than buy it annually, provides an IRR of 28.65 percent. If management has alternative investment opportunities which can provide a higher IRR than 28.65 percent, the decision may be to buy the part annually rather than to make it. On the other hand, assuming, of course, that the cost of capital is substantially less than 28.65 percent, and that the funds are available but that the alternative investment opportunities yielding more than 28.65 percent are not, then management should buy the machine and make the part. In the same fashion, decisions to lease or own can be worked out using the IRR calculation. Savings of owning over leasing can be determined and compared to the investment necessary for ownership. If the resultant IRR is less than the standard set for the company, or less than alternative investment opportunities available to the company, then a leasing decision is indicated. On the other hand, if the rate is sufficiently high, owning may be preferable. The IRR calculation gives a company a sound basis for decision. (See Chapter 22 for a discussion of the IRR in lease vs. buy decisions.)

The IRR calculation has also been applied usefully to the determination of inventory policy, to pricing practices and to setting an objective for a company's overall rate of growth. By calculating the IRR on the additional investment required to carry more inventory and comparing this with either the company's standard or with alternative investment opportunities, changes in inventory policy are suggested. Management has often found that high levels of inventory, designed to cover emergencies, show low returns when the number of such emergencies are put into proper perspective. Companies may also decide to sell overstocks when the sales price shows a present value greater than that attached to consuming the stocks over many years.

The IRR method has provided a systematic evaluation of projects mandated by government regulation to be in place by some undetermined future date.[17] Time adjusted capital budgeting methods which are modified to take inflation into account have also been developed.[18]

17.6 CHAPTER SUMMARY

This chapter discussed the use of the rate of return to evaluate the relative attractiveness or profitability among prospective projects in the overall capital budgeting process. Highlighted were the major steps in the rate of return analysis and the most frequently used rate of return methods. In addition, the chapter developed other factors which must be taken into consideration in the rate of return analysis. Chapter 18 discusses the methods used to assess the effects of risk and uncertainty on the rate of return in the context of the overall capital budgeting process.

FOOTNOTES

1. Cash inflow is measured in terms of net income after taxes plus non-cash outlays such as depreciation, amortization of bond discount, etc.
2. A fourth method, the accounting rate of return, is sometimes found in practice, but has little theoretical justification and is dealt with only briefly in this chapter.
3. The various depreciation techniques are discussed in Chapter 15.
4. The authors wish to acknowledge the help of Professor Lewis Freitas of the University of Hawaii in the preparation of the material on time adjusted methods.
5. Some of the major financial services make available time sharing programs without any charge. For example, Coopers & Lybrand, in introduction to the firm's booklet, *Library of Time Sharing Programs* (fourth edition), states, "Coopers & Lybrand time sharing programs were originally developed to help our professional staff to serve our clients. In time, it became apparent that many of these programs could be of direct benefit to clients and others; accordingly, we began making them generally available through commercial time sharing vendors ... Their use does not entail the payment of a fee to Coopers & Lybrand ... nor need the user be a client of our Firm."
6. Appendix 17A provides further treatment of the subject of present value mathematics.
7. Appendix 17B presents several of the more important compound interest tables.
8. Linear interpolation is an approximation because present value is an exponential function and exponential relationships are curved rather than linear.
9. To understand how this expression is obtained, we need to remember that the present value of $1 paid at the end of one year at an annual rate of interest of i is $(1+i)^{-1}$; the present value of $1 paid at the end of two years is $(1+i)^{-2}$; and the present value of $1 paid at the end of n years is $(1+i)^{-n}$. This sequence of values represents a geometric series where the first term is $(1+i)^{-1}$, the common ratio is $(1+i)^{-1}$, and the nth term is $(1+i)^{-n}$. The sum of a geometric series is:

$$\frac{\text{the first term} - (\text{the common ratio})(\text{the nth term})}{1 - \text{the common ratio}}$$

Substituting the previous terms in this expression, we obtain;

$$\frac{(1+i)^{-1} - (1+i)^{-1}(1+i)^{-n}}{1 - (1+i)^{-1}}.$$

After multiplying each term of the numerator and denominator by $(1+i)$, the expression is reduced to the form shown in the text:

$$\frac{1 - (1+i)^{-n}}{i}.$$

10. For two old, but well known articles on this relationship, see Myron J. Gordon, "The Payback Period and the Rate of Profit," *Journal of Business,* October 1955, pp. 253-260; and Marshall Sarnat and Haim Levy, "The Relationship of Rules of Thumb to the Internal Rate of Return — A Restatement and Generalization," *Journal of Finance,* June 1969, pp. 479-490.

11. The following equations show the relationship between the accounting rate of return and the reciprocal of the payback:

$$[1] \quad k_t = \frac{R - D}{P} = \frac{R}{P} - \frac{1}{n} = \frac{1}{B} - \frac{1}{n}$$

$$[2] \quad k_a = \frac{R - D}{P/2} = \frac{2R}{P} - \frac{2}{n} = 2\left(\frac{1}{B} - \frac{1}{n}\right)$$

where:

R = the pre-tax cash receipts before deducting depreciation, assuming equal annual net receipts;

D = annual straight line depreciation, i.e., P/n;

P = the current dollar value of the project;

B = the payback, i.e., P/R;

n = the economic life of the project in years;

k_t = the accounting rate of return based on total investment; and

k_a = the accounting rate of return based on average investment.

Equation [1] shows that the accounting rate of return based on total investment k_t, approaches the payback reciprocal, $1/B$, as a project's economic life approaches infinity. Equation [2] shows that the accounting rate of return based on average investment, k_a, approaches twice the payback reciprocal as the proposal duration increases indefinitely. Equations [3] and [4] express the two accounting rates of return as functions of N and the IRR, i, as follows:

$$[3] \quad k_t = \frac{i}{1 - (1 + i)^{-n}} - \frac{1}{n}$$

$$[4] \quad k_a = \frac{2i}{1 - (1 + i)^{-n}} - \frac{2}{n}.$$

Source: Marshall Sarnat and Haim Levy, *Ibid.,* pp. 482-483.

12. The desired amount of $1,075.00 falls between $1,045.91 and $1,094.32. To be exact, of the $48.41 difference between the two, it is .6 the way above and .4 below. That is, .6 x .25 = .15, which is subtracted from 3.00 percent, or .4 x .25 = .10 which is added to 2.75 percent. The rates shown are for illustrative purposes and do not reflect prevailing conditions.

13. To reconcile the NPV method of evaluating investments with the accounting incomes that occur if the investment is undertaken, see Harold Bierman, Jr., "A Reconciliation of Present Value Capital Budgeting and Accounting," *Financial Management,* Summer 1977, pp. 52-54.

14. Harold Bierman, Jr. and Vithala R. Rao, "Investment Decisions with Sampling," *Financial Management,* August 1978, pp. 19-24, however, argue that a company should not always reject an investment with a negative NPV in situations of uncertainty and when there is a possibility of replicating the investment. This situation would arise if there is some probability that the investment, perhaps in a piece of equipment, would have a positive NPV in any subsequent use. The general consideration of risk in capital budgeting is developed in the next chapter.

15. This step takes each periodic cash benefit (C_t) and calculates what it would be worth at the maturity "n" (or terminal point of the investment) by compounding it at the assumed reinvestment rate "r", for the number of periods remaining until maturity (n - t). Thus, with a 40 year life, the first year's cash benefit would be compounded over the remaining 39 years, the next one would be compounded 38 years, and so on, until the last one which would be compounded zero periods, or not at all, since it is expected to be received at the end of the investment's life.

16. For an interesting analysis of the effect that errors in data collection and the forecasting of cash flows can have on the calculation of the IRR, see William D. Whisler, "Sensitivity Analysis of Rates of Return," *The Journal of Finance,* March 1976, pp. 63-69. Also, Frank S. T. Hsaio and W. James Smith, "An Analytic Approach to Sensitivity Analysis of the Internal Rate of Return Model," *The Journal of Finance,* May 1978, pp. 645-649, provides qualitative and some quantitative information for the financial manager seeking guidelines for situations in which forecast errors are likely.

17. In this connection, see George W. Trivoli, "Project Investment Analysis and Anticipated Government Mandated Expenditures," *Financial Management,* Winter 1976, pp. 18-25.

18. For example, see Philip L. Cooley, Rodney L. Roenfeldt and It-Keong Chew, "Capital Budgeting Procedures Under Inflation," *Financial Management,* Winter 1975, pp. 18-27; Charles R. Nelson, "Inflation and Capital Budgeting," *The Journal of Finance,* June 1976, pp. 923-931; M. Chapman Findlay III, Alan W. Frankle, Philip L. Cooney, Rodney L. Roenfeldt and It-Keong Chew, "Capital Budgeting Procedures Under Inflation: Cooley, Roenfeldt and Chew vs. Findlay and Frankle," *Financial Management,* Autumn 1976, pp. 83-90; and Andrew O. Bailey, Jr. and Daniel L. Jensen, "General Price Level Adjustments in the Capital Budgeting Decision," *Financial Management,* Spring 1977, pp. 26-31.

SUGGESTED READINGS

Bartley, Jon W., "An NPV Model Modified for Inflation," *Management Accounting,* December 1980.

Bierman, Harold Jr., "Strategic Capital Budgeting," *Financial Executive,* April 1979.

———, and Seymour Smidt, *The Capital Budgeting Decision,* New York, Macmillan, 5th ed., 1980.

Crum, Roy L. and Frans G. J. Derkinderen, *Capital Budgeting Under Conditions of Uncertainty,* Boston, Nijhoff, 1981.

Dorfman, Robert, "The Meaning of Internal Rates of Return," *The Journal of Finance,* December 1981.

Durand, David, "Comprehensiveness in Capital Budgeting", *Financial Management,* Winter 1981.

Ekern, Steinar, "Time Dominance Efficiency Analysis," *The Journal of Finance,* December 1981.

Gahlon, James M. and Roger D. Stover, "Debt Capacity and the Capital Budgeting Decision: A Caveat", *Financial Management,* Winter 1979.

Gallinger, George W., "Capital Expenditure Administration," *Sloan Management Review,* Fall 1980.

Gitman, Laurence and John Forrester, Jr., "A Survey of Capital Budgeting Techniques Used by Major U.S. Firms," *Financial Management,* Fall 1979.

Kim, Suk H. and Edward J. Farragher, "Current Capital Budgeting Practices," *Management Accounting,* June 1981.

Larcker, David F., "The Perceived Importance of Selected Information Characteristics for Strategic Capital Budgeting Decisions," *The Accounting Review,* July 1981.

460

Martin, John D. and David F. Scott, Jr., "Debt Capacity and the Capital Budgeting Decision: A Revisitation," *Financial Management,* Spring 1980.

Nicol, David J., "A Note on Capital Budgeting Techniques and the Reinvestment Rate: Comment," *The Journal of Finance,* March 1981.

Perrakis, Stylianos, "Capital Budgeting and Timing Uncertainty Within the Capital Asset Pricing Model," *Financial Management,* Autumn 1979.

Petit, Thomas and Tony Wingler, "Key Factors in Capital Budgeting," *Managerial Planning,* May/June 1981.

Senbet, Lemma W. and Howard E. Thompson, "The Equivalence of Alternative Mean-Variance Capital Budgeting Model," *The Journal of Finance,* May 1978.

van Breda, Michael F., "Capital Budgeting Using Terminal Values," *Management Accounting,* July 1981.

Weston, J. Fred and Nai-fu Chen, "A Note on Capital Budgeting and the Three R's," *Financial Management,* Spring 1980.

APPENDIX A:
THE MATHEMATICS OF COMPOUND INTEREST

The concept of the time value of money as it is applied to capital investment proposals is important to financial managers. Simply stated, the concept of the time value of money means that a dollar received or spent in the future is worth less than a dollar received or spent today. For example, if a company can receive an after tax annual return of 5% on excess funds, paying $1 today would be the same as paying $1.05 in one year, $1.28 in five years, or $2.65 in 20 years. Thus, future expenditures and receipts of cash are discounted in order that the costs and benefits can be compared on an equal basis. Once it is agreed that future dollars must be discounted because of the concept of the time value of money, the next problem becomes one of determining how much to discount future dollars. This determination is a function of two things: (1) the mathematics of compound interest, and (2) the discount rate.

The mathematics of compound interest are expressed in the following function:

$(1 + i)^n.$

This indicates that money left for a period of "n" years to compound at a certain interest rate, "i", will grow according to the above mathematical expression. Discounted cash flow analysis, however, applies the concept of compound interest in reverse. That is, it discounts future cash flows to an equivalent present day value. The present value factors can be determined from the following expression:

Present Value Factor $= \dfrac{1}{(1 + i)^n}$ or $(1 + i)^{-n},$

which expresses the compound interest function in reverse. Using the above equation, we can establish a table of present value factors for any interest rate and time period as follows:

	i			
n	5%	6%	7%	8%
1	.9524	.9434	.9346	.9259
2	.9070	.8900	.8734	.8573
3	.8638	.8396	.8163	.7938
4	.8227	.7921	.7629	.7350

The use of the above table can be seen by an example. The .8163 under the 7% column and .he 3 year row means that the receipt of $1.00 three years from now at a discount rate of 7% is worth $.8163 today. This is because $.8163 invested today to earn 7% compounded annually will grow to $1.00 in three years.

The discount rate is the interest rate used to determine the discount factors from the above table. These factors are then used to determine the present day equivalent of future receipts and/or expenditures. The discount rate can also be viewed as the opportunity cost of funds. That is, if the funds were not tied up in the particular investment awaiting these future cash receipts, what return could the funds be earning? A minimum would be the after tax borrowing cost. In addition, the discount rate might include a premium to compensate for the inherent riskiness of the particular project. Chapter 18 analyzes risk in capital budgeting in much more detail.

APPENDIX B:
COMPOUND INTEREST TABLES

This appendix contains four standard compound interest tables. The first, Figure 17.23 shows the future value of one dollar left to accumulate for n periods in the future with an interest rate of i for each period, $(1 + i)^n$. The second, Figure 17.24 as discussed in the prior Appendix, applies the concept of compound interest in reverse. It shows the present value of one dollar that will be received in n periods in the future with an interest rate of i for each period, $(1 + i)^{-n}$. The third, Figure 17.25, shows the future value of an annuity of one dollar per period that will be received in n periods in the future at an interest rate of i for each period. It represents a summation of the outcomes in Figure 17.23 lagged by one year. For example, year one of Figure 17.25, 1.0000 (at 1%) equals the outcome of Figure 17.23 for year zero (not shown in the table); year two of Figure 17.25, 2.0100 (at 1%), equals the summation of the outcomes in Figure 17.23 for years zero and one, 1.000 + 1.0100; year three of Figure 17.25, 3.0301, equals the summation of the outcomes in Figure 17.23 of years zero, one, and two, 1.000 + 1.0100 + 1.0201, etc. Thus:

$$\sum_{t=1}^{n} (1 + i)^{t-1} = \frac{(1 + i)^n - 1}{i} \ .$$

The fourth, Figure 17.26, shows the present value of an annuity of one dollar per period that will be received for n periods in the future at an interest rate of i for each period. It represents a summation of the outcomes in Figure 17.24. Thus:

$$\sum_{t=1}^{n} (1 + i)^{-t} = \frac{1 - (1 + i)^{-n}}{i} \ .$$

APPENDIX C:
DEVELOPING TABLES OF RELATIONSHIPS BETWEEN PAYBACK OR THE ACCOUNTING RATE OF RETURN AND THE TIME ADJUSTED METHODS

Through experience, fairly precise relationships can be drawn that equate the payback or the accounting rate of return with the time adjusted methods. For example, some companies have prepared tables that contain horizontal rows showing the payback period, vertical columns showing how long a project will last, and intersection boxes giving the IRR for projects with uniform cash flows. In such tables, when the economic life is relatively long, the reciprocal of the payback matches rather closely the IRR. Thus, for a project that has a payback of five years and provides consistent benefits for over 20 years, both the reciprocal of the payback and the IRR are 20 percent; if the consistent benefits last only seven years, however, the IRR falls to 10 percent.

FIGURE 17.23 Future value of $1 n periods hence, with interest rate i per period = $(1 + i)^n$

n	1%	2%	3%	4%	5%	6%	8%	10%	15%	20%
1	1.0100	1.0200	1.0300	1.0400	1.0500	1.0600	1.080	1.100	1.150	1.200
2	1.0201	1.0404	1.0609	1.0816	1.1025	1.1236	1.166	1.210	1.332	1.440
3	1.0303	1.0612	1.0927	1.1249	1.1576	1.1910	1.260	1.331	1.521	1.728
4	1.0406	1.0824	1.1255	1.1699	1.2155	1.2625	1.360	1.464	1.749	2.074
5	1.0510	1.1041	1.1593	1.2167	1.2763	1.3382	1.469	1.611	2.011	2.488
6	1.0615	1.1262	1.1941	1.2653	1.3401	1.4185	1.587	1.772	2.313	2.986
7	1.0721	1.1487	1.2299	1.3159	1.4071	1.5036	1.714	1.949	2.660	3.583
8	1.0829	1.1717	1.2668	1.3686	1.4775	1.5938	1.851	2.144	3.059	4.300
9	1.0937	1.1951	1.3048	1.4233	1.5513	1.6895	1.999	2.358	3.518	5.160
10	1.1046	1.2190	1.3439	1.4802	1.6289	1.7908	2.159	2.594	4.046	6.192
11	1.1157	1.2434	1.3842	1.5395	1.7103	1.8983	2.332	2.853	4.652	7.430
12	1.1268	1.2682	1.4258	1.6010	1.7959	2.0122	2.518	3.138	5.350	8.916
13	1.1381	1.2936	1.4685	1.6651	1.8856	2.1329	2.720	3.452	6.153	10.699
14	1.1495	1.3195	1.5126	1.7317	1.9799	2.2609	2.937	3.797	7.076	12.839
15	1.1610	1.3459	1.5580	1.8009	2.0789	2.3966	3.172	4.177	8.137	15.407
16	1.1726	1.3728	1.6047	1.8730	2.1829	2.5404	3.426	4.595	9.358	18.488
17	1.1843	1.4002	1.6528	1.9479	2.2920	2.6928	3.700	5.054	10.761	22.186
18	1.1961	1.4282	1.7024	2.0258	2.4066	2.8543	3.996	5.560	12.375	26.623
19	1.2081	1.4568	1.7535	2.1068	2.5270	3.0256	4.316	6.116	14.232	31.948
20	1.2202	1.4859	1.8061	2.1911	2.6533	3.2071	4.661	6.727	16.367	38.338
21	1.2324	1.5157	1.8603	2.2788	2.7860	3.3996	5.034	7.400	18.821	46.005
22	1.2447	1.5460	1.9161	2.3699	2.9253	3.6035	5.437	8.140	21.645	55.206
23	1.2572	1.5769	1.9736	2.4647	3.0715	3.8197	5.871	8.954	24.891	66.247
24	1.2697	1.6084	2.0328	2.5633	3.2251	4.0489	6.341	9.850	28.625	79.497
25	1.2824	1.6406	2.0938	2.6658	3.3864	4.2919	6.848	10.835	32.919	95.396
26	1.2953	1.6734	2.1566	2.7725	3.5557	4.5494	7.396	11.918	37.857	114.475
27	1.3082	1.7069	2.2213	2.8834	3.7335	4.8223	7.988	13.110	43.535	137.370
28	1.3213	1.7410	2.2879	2.9987	3.9201	5.1117	8.627	14.421	50.065	164.845
29	1.3345	1.7758	2.3566	3.1187	4.1161	5.4184	9.317	15.863	57.575	197.813
30	1.3478	1.8114	2.4273	3.2434	4.3219	5.7435	10.063	17.449	66.212	237.376
35	1.4166	1.9999	2.8139	3.9461	5.5160	7.6861	14.785	28.102	133.175	590.668
40	1.4889	2.2080	3.2620	4.8010	7.0400	10.2857	21.725	45.259	267.862	1469.771
45	1.5648	2.4379	3.7816	5.8412	8.9850	13.7646	31.920	72.890	538.767	3657.258
50	1.6446	2.6916	4.3839	7.1067	11.4674	18.4202	46.902	117.391	1083.652	9100.427

Source: James E. Howell and Daniel Teichroew, *Mathematical Analysis for Business Decisions,* Homewood, Ill., Irwin, 1963, p. 309, Table I.

FIGURE 17.24 Present value of $1 to be received n periods hence, with interest rate i per period = $(1 + i)^{-n}$

n	1%	2%	3%	4%	5%	6%	7%	8%	9%	10%	12%	14%	15%	16%	18%	20%	24%	28%	32%	36%
1	.9901	.9804	.9709	.9615	.9524	.9434	.9346	.9259	.9174	.9091	.8929	.8772	.8696	.8621	.8475	.8333	.8065	.7813	.7576	.7353
2	.9803	.9612	.9426	.9246	.9070	.8900	.8734	.8573	.8417	.8264	.7972	.7695	.7561	.7432	.7182	.6944	.6504	.6104	.5739	.5407
3	.9706	.9423	.9151	.8890	.8638	.8396	.8163	.7938	.7722	.7513	.7118	.6750	.6575	.6407	.6086	.5787	.5245	.4768	.4348	.3975
4	.9610	.9238	.8885	.8548	.8227	.7921	.7629	.7350	.7084	.6830	.6355	.5921	.5718	.5523	.5158	.4823	.4230	.3725	.3294	.2923
5	.9515	.9057	.8626	.8219	.7835	.7473	.7130	.6806	.6499	.6209	.5674	.5194	.4972	.4761	.4371	.4019	.3411	.2910	.2495	.2149
6	.9420	.8880	.8375	.7903	.7462	.7050	.6663	.6302	.5963	.5645	.5066	.4556	.4323	.4104	.3704	.3349	.2751	.2274	.1890	.1580
7	.9327	.8706	.8131	.7599	.7107	.6651	.6227	.5835	.5470	.5132	.4523	.3996	.3759	.3538	.3139	.2791	.2218	.1776	.1432	.1162
8	.9235	.8535	.7894	.7307	.6768	.6274	.5820	.5403	.5019	.4665	.4039	.3506	.3269	.3050	.2660	.2326	.1789	.1388	.1085	.0854
9	.9143	.8368	.7664	.7026	.6446	.5919	.5439	.5002	.4604	.4241	.3606	.3075	.2843	.2630	.2255	.1938	.1443	.1084	.0822	.0628
10	.9053	.8203	.7441	.6756	.6139	.5584	.5083	.4632	.4224	.3855	.3220	.2697	.2472	.2267	.1911	.1615	.1164	.0847	.0623	.0462
11	.8963	.8043	.7224	.6496	.5847	.5268	.4751	.4289	.3875	.3505	.2875	.2366	.2149	.1954	.1619	.1346	.0938	.0662	.0472	.0340
12	.8874	.7885	.7014	.6246	.5568	.4970	.4440	.3971	.3555	.3186	.2567	.2076	.1869	.1685	.1372	.1122	.0757	.0517	.0357	.0250
13	.8787	.7730	.6810	.6006	.5303	.4688	.4150	.3677	.3262	.2897	.2292	.1821	.1625	.1452	.1163	.0935	.0610	.0404	.0271	.0184
14	.8700	.7579	.6611	.5775	.5051	.4423	.3878	.3405	.2992	.2633	.2046	.1597	.1413	.1252	.0985	.0779	.0492	.0316	.0205	.0135
15	.8613	.7430	.6419	.5553	.4810	.4173	.3624	.3152	.2745	.2394	.1827	.1401	.1229	.1079	.0835	.0649	.0397	.0247	.0155	.0099
16	.8528	.7284	.6232	.5339	.4581	.3936	.3387	.2919	.2519	.2176	.1631	.1229	.1069	.0930	.0708	.0541	.0320	.0193	.0118	.0073
17	.8444	.7142	.6050	.5134	.4363	.3714	.3166	.2703	.2311	.1978	.1456	.1078	.0929	.0802	.0600	.0451	.0258	.0150	.0089	.0054
18	.8360	.7002	.5874	.4936	.4155	.3503	.2959	.2502	.2120	.1799	.1300	.0946	.0808	.0691	.0508	.0376	.0208	.0118	.0068	.0039
19	.8277	.6864	.5703	.4746	.3957	.3305	.2765	.2317	.1945	.1635	.1161	.0829	.0703	.0596	.0431	.0313	.0168	.0092	.0051	.0029
20	.8195	.6730	.5537	.4564	.3769	.3118	.2584	.2145	.1784	.1486	.1037	.0728	.0611	.0514	.0365	.0261	.0135	.0072	.0039	.0021
25	.7798	.6095	.4776	.3751	.2953	.2330	.1842	.1460	.1160	.0923	.0588	.0378	.0304	.0245	.0160	.0105	.0046	.0021	.0010	.0005
30	.7419	.5521	.4120	.3083	.2314	.1741	.1314	.0994	.0754	.0573	.0334	.0196	.0151	.0116	.0070	.0042	.0016	.0006	.0002	.0001
40	.6717	.4529	.3066	.2083	.1420	.0972	.0668	.0460	.0318	.0221	.0107	.0053	.0037	.0026	.0013	.0007	.0002	.0001	*	*
50	.6080	.3715	.2281	.1407	.0872	.0543	.0339	.0213	.0134	.0085	.0035	.0014	.0009	.0006	.0003	.0001	*	*	.	.

*The factor is zero to four decimal places.

Source: James E. Howell and Daniel Teichroew, *Mathematical Analysis for Business Decisions*, Homewood, Ill., Irwin, 1963, p. 310, Table II.

FIGURE 17.25 Future value of $1 per period, n periods hence, at interest rate i per period = $\dfrac{(1+i)^n - 1}{i}$

n	1%	2%	3%	4%	5%	6%	8%	10%	15%	20%
1	1.0000	1.0000	1.0000	1.0000	1.0000	1.0000	1.000	1.000	1.000	1.000
2	2.0100	2.0200	2.0300	2.0400	2.0500	2.0600	2.080	2.100	2.150	2.200
3	3.0301	3.0604	3.0909	3.1216	3.1525	3.1836	3.246	3.310	3.472	3.640
4	4.0604	4.1216	4.1836	4.2465	4.3101	4.3746	4.506	4.641	4.993	5.368
5	5.1010	5.2040	5.3091	5.4163	5.5256	5.6371	5.867	6.105	6.742	7.442
6	6.1520	6.3081	6.4684	6.6330	6.8019	6.9753	7.336	7.716	8.754	9.930
7	7.2135	7.4343	7.6625	7.8983	8.1420	8.3938	8.923	9.487	11.067	12.916
8	8.2857	8.5830	8.8923	9.2142	9.5491	9.8975	10.637	11.436	13.727	16.499
9	9.3685	9.7546	10.1591	10.5828	11.0266	11.4913	12.488	13.579	16.786	20.799
10	10.4622	10.9497	11.4639	12.0061	12.5779	13.1808	14.487	15.937	20.304	25.959
11	11.5668	12.1687	12.8078	13.4864	14.2068	14.9716	16.645	18.531	24.349	32.150
12	12.6825	13.4121	14.1920	15.0258	15.9171	16.8699	18.977	21.384	29.002	39.580
13	13.8093	14.6803	15.6178	16.6268	17.7130	18.8821	21.495	24.523	34.352	48.497
14	14.9474	15.9739	17.0863	18.2919	19.5986	21.0151	24.215	27.975	40.505	59.196
15	16.0969	17.2934	18.5989	20.0236	21.5786	23.2760	27.152	31.772	47.580	72.035
16	17.2579	18.6393	20.1569	21.8245	23.6575	25.6725	30.324	35.950	55.717	87.442
17	18.4304	20.0121	21.7616	23.6975	25.8404	28.2129	33.750	40.545	65.075	105.931
18	19.6147	21.4123	23.4144	25.6454	28.1324	30.9057	37.450	45.599	75.836	128.117
19	20.8109	22.8406	25.1169	27.6712	30.5390	33.7600	41.446	51.159	88.212	154.740
20	22.0190	24.2974	26.8704	29.7781	33.0660	36.7856	45.762	57.275	102.443	186.688
21	23.2392	25.7833	28.6765	31.9692	35.7193	39.9927	50.423	64.002	118.810	225.025
22	24.4716	27.2990	30.5368	34.2480	38.5052	43.3923	55.457	71.403	137.631	271.031
23	25.7163	28.8450	32.4529	36.6179	41.4305	46.9958	60.893	79.543	159.276	326.237
24	26.9735	30.4219	34.4265	39.0826	44.5020	50.8156	66.765	88.497	184.167	392.484
25	28.2432	32.0303	36.4593	41.6459	47.7271	54.8645	73.106	98.347	212.793	471.981
26	29.5256	33.6709	38.5530	44.3117	51.1135	59.1564	79.954	109.182	245.711	567.377
27	30.8209	35.3443	40.7096	47.0842	54.6691	63.7058	87.351	121.100	283.568	681.852
28	32.1291	37.0512	42.9309	49.9676	58.4026	68.5281	95.339	134.210	327.103	819.223
29	33.4504	38.7922	45.2189	52.9663	62.3227	73.6398	103.966	148.631	377.169	984.067
30	34.7849	40.5681	47.5754	56.0849	66.4388	79.0582	113.283	164.494	434.744	1181.881
35	41.6603	49.9945	60.4621	73.6522	90.3203	111.4348	172.317	271.024	881.168	2948.339
40	48.8864	60.4020	75.4013	95.0255	120.7998	154.7620	259.057	442.593	1779.089	7343.853
45	56.4811	71.8927	92.7199	121.0294	159.7002	212.7435	386.506	718.905	3585.126	18281.297
50	64.4632	84.5794	112.7969	152.6671	209.3480	290.3359	573.770	1163.909	7217.711	45497.156

Source: James E. Howell and Daniel Teichroew. *Mathematical Analysis for Business Decisions.* Homewood, Ill., Irwin, 1963, p. 311, Table III.

FIGURE 17.26 Present value of \$1 per period to be received for n periods, at interest rate i per period = $\dfrac{1 - (1 + i)^{-n}}{i}$

n	1%	2%	3%	4%	5%	6%	8%	10%	15%	20%	25%	30%	35%	40%	45%
1	0.9901	0.9804	0.9709	0.9615	0.9524	0.9434	0.9259	0.9091	0.8696	0.8333	0.8000	0.7692	0.7407	0.7143	0.690
2	1.9704	1.9416	1.9135	1.8861	1.8594	1.8334	1.7833	1.7355	1.6257	1.5278	1.4400	1.3609	1.2894	1.2245	1.165
3	2.9410	2.8839	2.8286	2.7751	2.7232	2.6730	2.5771	2.4869	2.2832	2.1065	1.9520	1.8161	1.6959	1.5889	1.493
4	3.9020	3.8077	3.7171	3.6299	3.5460	3.4651	3.3121	3.1699	2.8550	2.5887	2.3616	2.1662	1.9969	1.8492	1.720
5	4.8534	4.7135	4.5797	4.4518	4.3295	4.2124	3.9927	3.7908	3.3522	2.9906	2.6893	2.4356	2.2200	2.0352	1.876
6	5.7955	5.6014	5.4172	5.2421	5.0757	4.9173	4.6229	4.3553	3.7845	3.3255	2.9514	2.6427	2.3852	2.1680	1.983
7	6.7282	6.4720	6.2303	6.0021	5.7864	5.5824	5.2064	4.8684	4.1604	3.6046	3.1611	2.8021	2.5075	2.2628	2.057
8	7.6517	7.3255	7.0197	6.7327	6.4632	6.2098	5.7466	5.3349	4.4873	3.8372	3.3289	2.9247	2.5982	2.3306	2.109
9	8.5660	8.1622	7.7861	7.4353	7.1078	6.8017	6.2469	5.7590	4.7716	4.0310	3.4631	3.0190	2.6653	2.3790	2.144
10	9.4713	8.9826	8.5302	8.1109	7.7217	7.3601	6.7101	6.1446	5.0188	4.1925	3.5705	3.0915	2.7150	2.4136	2.168
11	10.3676	9.7868	9.2526	8.7605	8.3064	7.8869	7.1390	6.4951	5.2337	4.3271	3.6564	3.1473	2.7519	2.4383	2.185
12	11.2551	10.5753	9.9540	9.3851	8.8633	8.3838	7.5361	6.8137	5.4206	4.4392	3.7251	3.1903	2.7792	2.4559	2.196
13	12.1337	11.3484	10.6350	9.9856	9.3936	8.8527	7.9038	7.1034	5.5831	4.5327	3.7801	3.2233	2.7994	2.4685	2.204
14	13.0037	12.1062	11.2961	10.5631	9.8986	9.2950	8.2442	7.3667	5.7245	4.6106	3.8241	3.2487	2.8144	2.4775	2.210
15	13.8651	12.8493	11.9379	11.1184	10.3797	9.7122	8.5595	7.6061	5.8474	4.6755	3.8593	3.2682	2.8255	2.4839	2.214
16	14.7179	13.5777	12.5611	11.6523	10.8378	10.1059	8.8514	7.8237	5.9542	4.7296	3.8874	3.2832	2.8337	2.4885	2.216
17	15.5623	14.2919	13.1661	12.1657	11.2741	10.4773	9.1216	8.0216	6.0472	4.7746	3.9099	3.2948	2.8398	2.4918	2.218
18	16.3983	14.9920	13.7535	12.6593	11.6896	10.8276	9.3719	8.2014	6.1280	4.8122	3.9279	3.3037	2.8443	2.4941	2.219
19	17.2260	15.6785	14.3238	13.1339	12.0853	11.1581	9.6036	8.3649	6.1982	4.8435	3.9424	3.3105	2.8476	2.4958	2.220
20	18.0456	16.3514	14.8775	13.5903	12.4622	11.4699	9.8181	8.5136	6.2593	4.8696	3.9539	3.3158	2.8501	2.4970	2.220
21	18.8570	17.0112	15.4150	14.0292	12.8212	11.7641	10.0168	8.6487	6.3125	4.8913	3.9631	3.3198	2.8520	2.4979	2.221
22	19.6604	17.6580	15.9369	14.4511	13.1630	12.0416	10.2007	8.7715	6.3587	4.9094	3.9705	3.3230	2.8533	2.4985	2.222
23	20.4558	18.2922	16.4436	14.8568	13.4886	12.3034	10.3711	8.8832	6.3988	4.9245	3.9764	3.3253	2.8543	2.4989	2.222
24	21.2434	18.9139	16.9355	15.2470	13.7986	12.5504	10.5288	8.9847	6.4338	4.9371	3.9811	3.3272	2.8550	2.4992	2.222
25	22.0232	19.5235	17.4131	15.6221	14.0939	12.7834	10.6748	9.0770	6.4641	4.9476	3.9849	3.3286	2.8556	2.4994	2.222
26	22.7952	20.1210	17.8768	15.9828	14.3752	13.0032	10.8100	9.1609	6.4906	4.9563	3.9879	3.3297	2.8560	2.4996	2.222
27	23.5596	20.7069	18.3270	16.3296	14.6430	13.2105	10.9352	9.2372	6.5135	4.9636	3.9903	3.3305	2.8563	2.4997	2.222
28	24.3164	21.2813	18.7641	16.6631	14.8981	13.4062	11.0511	9.3066	6.5335	4.9697	3.9923	3.3312	2.8565	2.4998	2.222
29	25.0658	21.8444	19.1885	16.9837	15.1411	13.5907	11.1584	9.3696	6.5509	4.9747	3.9938	3.3316	2.8567	2.4999	2.222
30	25.8077	22.3965	19.6004	17.2920	15.3725	13.7648	11.2578	9.4269	6.5660	4.9789	3.9950	3.3321	2.8568	2.4999	2.222
35	29.4086	24.9986	21.4872	18.6646	16.3742	14.4982	11.6546	9.6442	6.6166	4.9915	3.9984	3.3330	2.8571	2.5000	2.222
40	32.8347	27.3555	23.1148	19.7928	17.1591	15.0463	11.9246	9.7791	6.6418	4.9966	3.9995	3.3332	2.8571	2.5000	2.222
45	36.0945	29.4902	24.5187	20.7200	17.7741	15.4558	12.1084	9.8628	6.6543	4.9986	3.9998	3.3333	2.8571	2.5000	2.222
50	39.1961	31.4236	25.7298	21.4822	18.2559	15.7619	12.2335	9.9148	6.6605	4.9995	3.9999	3.3333	2.8571	2.5000	2.222

Source: James E. Howell and Daniel Teichroew. *Mathematical Analysis for Business Decisions.* Homewood, Ill. Irwin. 1963. p. 312. Table IV.

Flexibility can be introduced into such tables by creating models through computer programming that allow a variety of assumptions with respect to cash flows, economic lives, tax rates, salvage values, and costs of capital. For example, assume that the typical investment proposal of a company has a five-year productive life, a terminal net salvage value of 25 percent of the initial outlays, and a pattern of cash flows that is consistent in years two through five but one-half of this annual amount in the initial start-up year. If the company uses the sum of the years-digits depreciation, pays a corporate tax rate of 48 percent, and requires a 10 percent after tax rate of return, Figure 17.27 shows the calculation to determine the maximum amount that could be paid for the project and the corresponding payback to meet the minimum 10 percent requirement.[1] Thus, if the cash flows followed a pattern of $2,500 in the first year, and $5,000 in years two through five, the maximum outlay to permit the required 10 percent rate of return would be $18,950 (7.58 x $2,500)[2].

The higher the required rate of return, the larger the necessary cash flows relative to the investment and the shorter the related payback. The longer the economic life, the lower the necessary cash flows, and the larger the related paybacks. The higher the final salvage values, the lower the annual cash flows and the greater the payback. These relationships are portrayed in Figure 17.28.

FIGURE 17.27 *Breakeven IRR and payback analysis of a hypothetical investment proposal*

Year, i	PV Factor at 10%	Operating Cash Flows		Depreciation Tax Savings*		Net Salvage Value**	
		$C_i(1-t)$	PV	tD_i	PV	S	PV
1	0.909	$ 500(.52)	$236	$(.48)(5/15)(I)	.145I	—	—
2	0.826	1000(.52)	430	(.48)(4/15)(I)	.106I	—	—
3	0.751	1000(.52)	391	(.48)(3/15)(I)	.072I	—	—
4	0.683	1000(.52)	355	(.48)(2/15)(I)	.044I	—	—
5	0.621	1000(.52)	323	(.48)(1/15)(I)	.020I	$(.25)(I)	.155I
Project totals			$1,735		.387I		.155I

Thus, for a zero net present value, the condition is:

I = $1,735 + .387I + .155I or I = $3,788 and the payback requirement is 4.29 years.

*According to a sum of the years-digits depreciation schedule, for an initial investment of size I.
**Estimated equal to 25% of the initial investment outlay.

Source: Wilbur G. Lewellen, Howard P. Lanser and John J. McConnell, "Payback Substitutes for Discounted Cash Flow," *Financial Management,* Summer 1973, p. 19.

The underlying cash flow pattern is indicated at the top of Figure 17.28, where the form follows a two year initial buildup to a steady long-run level of earnings, followed by a two year decline to zero. For a project with zero salvage value and a fifteen year economic life, the required payback is 7.75 years if the cost of capital or required rate of return is 6 percent and 5.69 years if the rate is 10 percent. Within the 6 percent cost of capital or required rate of return requirement, the minimum payback is 3.52 years for a project with an economic life of 5 years, while the acceptable payback rises to 9.57 years for a project with an economic life of 25 years. Within each cost of capital or required rate of return and economic life category, the required payback rises as the salvage value increases. These tables are illustrative and appropriate relationships could be drawn for the accounting rate of return and prescribed changes in the other factors.

FIGURE 17.28 *Minimum payback period related to different factors*

Time Pattern of Projected Operating Earnings

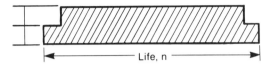

Parameters: 48% Corporate Tax Rate

SUM OF YEARS-DIGITS DEPRECIATION
TAX SCHEDULE

		A. Minimum payback standard (years) to match 6% cost of capital (or required rate of return)				B. Minimum payback standard (years) to match 10% cost of capital (or required rate of return)			
		For projected salvage value of					For projected salvage value of		
Project life, n (years)		0%	10%	25%	50%		0%	10%	25%	50%
	5	3.52	3.97	5.00	5.00	5	3.07	3.36	3.94	5.00
	10	6.08	6.64	7.71	10.00	10	4.81	5.07	5.54	6.57
	15	7.75	8.25	9.15	11.20	15	5.69	5.88	6.17	6.76
	25	9.57	9.88	10.39	11.38	25	6.33	6.40	6.51	6.71

Note: Salvage values expressed as a percentage of initial cost.

Source: Wilbur G. Lewellen, Howard P. Lanser and John J. McConnell, "Payback Substitutes for Discounted Cash Flow," *Financial Management,* Summer 1973, p. 21.

FOOTNOTES — APPENDIX C

1 This illustration is drawn from Wilbur G. Lewellen, Howard P. Lanser and John J. McConnell, "Payback Substitutes for Discounted Cash Flow," *Financial Management,* Summer 1973, pp. 17-23.

2 In the table, the maximum amount that could be invested to achieve the required 10 percent minimum rate of return is $3,788, which is 7.58 times the initial year's cash flow of $500. This relationship could be used to determine this investment regardless of the annual amounts of the flows so long as they follow the indicated pattern. The payback represents the cumulation of the first four years' cash flows and 29 percent of the amount in year five ($500 + $1,000 + $1,000 + $1,000 = $3,500; $3,788 - $3,500 = $288; $288/$1,000 = .29).

APPENDIX D:
ILLUSTRATING THE CALCULATIONS OF THE ADJUSTED INTERNAL RATE OF RETURN (IRR*) AND THE ADJUSTED NET PRESENT VALUE (NPV*) OF TWO HYPOTHETICAL PROJECTS, K AND M

As shown in Figure 17.16 in the text, both projects require an initial investment of $1,491 and have economic lives of 40 years. Project K, however, provides net cash flows in years 1-10 of $200 and in years 11-40 of $300. Project M provides net cash flows in years 1-10 of $100 and in years 11-40 of $512. The company's cost of capital is 10 percent.

On the basis of the IRR, Project K, with 15.0 percent, is ranked ahead of Project M, with 14.0 percent. On the basis of the NPV, however, Project M, with $985 is ranked ahead of Project K, with $828. Accordingly, the terminal value (TV) method is used to obtain consistency of results.

In the calculations of the adjusted internal rate of return (IRR*) and the adjusted net present value (NPV*) under the TV method for projects K and M which follow, it is assumed that the reinvestment rate equals 10 percent, the cost of capital.

Project K

Step One - Determination of the TV:

$$(1)\ TV = \$200 \quad [\sum_{t=1}^{40} (1+.10)^{t-1} - \sum_{t=1}^{30} (1+.10)^{t-1}] + \$300 \quad [\sum_{t=1}^{30} (1.10)^{t-1}]$$

(2) TV = $200 (442.59 - 164.49) + $300 (164.49)

(3) TV = $200 (278.10) + $300 (164.49)

(4) TV = $55,620 + $49,347

(5) TV = $104,967

Step Two - Discounting the TV to equal the present investment:

(6) $104,967 (1 + IRR*)$^{-40}$ = $1,491

(7) $\qquad$ (1 + IRR*)$^{-40}$ = $1,491/$104,967

(8) $\qquad$ (1 + IRR*)$^{-40}$ = .0142

(9) $\qquad$ IRR* = 11.01%

Project M

Step One - Determining the TV:

$$(1)\ TV = \$100\ [\sum_{t=1}^{40} (1+.10)^{t-1} - \sum_{t=1}^{30} (1+.10)^{t-1}] + \$512\ [\sum_{t=1}^{30} (1+.10)^{t-1}]$$

(2) TV = $100 (442.59 - 164.49) + $512 (164.49)

(3) TV = $100 (278.10) + $512 (164.49)

(4) TV = $27,810 + $84,219

(5) TV = $112,029

Step Two - Discounting the TV to equal the present investment:

(6) $112,029 (1 + IRR*)$^{-40}$ = $1,491

(7) $\qquad$ (1 + IRR*)$^{-40}$ = $1,491/$112,029

(8) $\qquad$ (1 + IRR*)$^{-40}$ = .0133

(9) $\qquad$ IRR* = 11.54%

The calculations of the NPV of Project K and Project M are as follows:

Project K

Step One - Determining the TV:

(1) - (5) Same as in the calculation of TV for Project K

Step Two - Discounting the TV at the cost of capital for the life of the project:

(6) NPV* = $104,967 (1.10)$^{-40}$ - $1,491
(7) NPV* = $104,967 (.0221) - $1,491
(8) NPV* = $2,320 - $1,491
(9) NPV* = $829

Project M

Step One - Determining the TV:

(1) - (5) Same as in the calculation of TV for Project M

Step Two - Discounting the TV at the cost of capital for the life of the project:

(6) NPV* = $112,029 (1.10)$^{-40}$ - $1,491
(7) NPV* = $112,029 (.0221) - $1,491
(8) NPV* = $2,476 - $1,491
(9) NPV* = $985

The following tabulation summarizes the results for projects K and M of the IRR* and the NPV* compared with the IRR and the NPV.

	Project	
	K	M
IRR*	11.01%	11.54%
NPV*	$829	$985
IRR	15.00%	14.00%
NPV	$828	$985

Both the NPV and the NPV assume reinvestment and discounting at the company's cost of capital of 10 percent. Accordingly, the outcomes are the same; any differences are caused by rounding.

Under the TV method, both IRR* and NPV* rank Project M ahead of Project K. Under the IRR method, Project K is ranked ahead of Project M, while under the NPV method, Project M is ranked ahead of Project K.

RISK ANALYSIS IN CAPITAL BUDGETING*

18.1 INTRODUCTION

In Chapter 17 we discussed the use of the rate of return to evaluate the relative attractiveness or profitability among prospective projects in the capital budgeting process. In this chapter, we expand that discussion to include the effects of risk and uncertainty on the rate of return in the capital budgeting process. Our focus includes: (1) definition of risk, (2) traditional approaches of incorporating risk in the capital budgeting process, and (3) use of modern portfolio theory as an alternative approach to managing risk.

18.2 CONCEPTS OF RISK[1]

The context in Chapter 17 within which we assessed the potential profitability of alternative capital investment projects available to the firm is limited because it failed to include risk or uncertainty. The typical business firm does not exist in the unreal world of certainty. Rarely do businessmen have all the information needed to make a decision. In the capital budgeting process, cash flows, their timing, and related data are usually estimates, each likely to take on any value within a specific range. Because future cash flows cannot be determined with certainty, management can never be 100 percent sure about its assessment of the prospective rate of return on capital investment projects under consideration. In fact, in some cases, the financial manager will assess as potentially profitable a prospective capital investment project which turns out to be unprofitable. The converse is also possible.

*Much of the material in the first three sections of this chapter is taken from Sidney Robbins, "Risk Analysis in Capital Budgeting," *Journal of Accounting, Auditing, and Finance,* Fall 1977, pp. 5-18.

[1] COMMON CONCEPTS

Before risk can be introduced into the capital budgeting analysis, we must understand its meaning. But individuals have different ideas of risk, depending upon the activity in which they are engaged, the particular problem at hand, and their own training. Among the more frequently encountered concepts of risk are the following:

- chance of "ruin";
- possibility of a loss; and
- variability of return.

These are briefly discussed below.

(a) Chance of Ruin

A business may be contemplating an investment in a politically troubled country where the potential return is very high because of a large untapped market, but where nationalization of properties might occur without reimbursement or insurance coverage. The firm undoubtedly would consider the risk that the entire investment might be destroyed. This is the chance of ruin.

(b) Possibility of a Loss

A common interpretation of risk is the possibility of "loss." A term often heard in the securities field, for example, is the "risk/gain" ratio, in which potential loss is measured against potential gain. In this sense, risk means the chance of getting a negative return on an investment.

(c) Variability of Return

The definition that academics have popularized is stated in terms of *variability* of return on an investment. In this sense, risk has to do with the chance of ending up with a return different from that anticipated. Suppose that a company is contemplating an investment in either of two projects, A or B. Its analysis indicates that the average or expected amount of cash flow from each project probably will be the same over a period of time. The pattern of the two flows is also likely to be the same, but the amount of cash flow received each year from B will vary more sharply than that from A. These relationships are portrayed in Figure 18.1.

The firm can be reasonably sure of the cash flows that it will obtain in any year from project A since it expects that these amounts will be centered at $6 million and range between only $4 and $8 million. It can be less certain of the flows from project B, which, although also centered at $6 million, vary more widely between $0 and $12 million. Planning and operating in the case of B will be clearly more difficult than A. Accordingly, the company would want to pay less for B than for A, and, to obtain a higher return on its investment in B. In general, most people, like most management, are risk averters, that is, they want higher returns to compensate for greater risks.[2]

FIGURE 18.1 *Comparison of the annual cash flows of two projects*

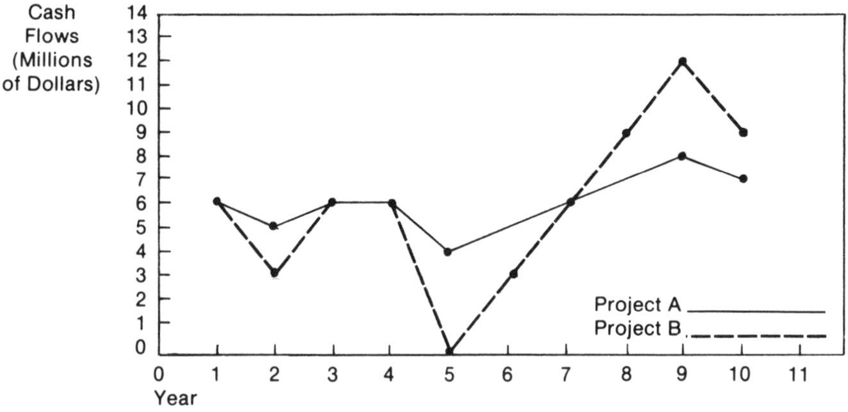

Year	Cash Flow A	Cash Flow B
1	6	6
2	5	3
3	6	6
4	6	6
5	4	0
6	5	3
7	6	6
8	7	9
9	8	12
10	7	9
Total	60	60

Data for Figure 18.1

[2] RISK AND PROBABILITIES

In the previous illustration, the firm's decision is that an investment in project B is worth less than one in A based upon its expectations of the cash flows to be received from each. Expectations are a common basis for human actions. On the other hand, in formal capital budgeting procedures, probabilities may be gauged and expressed in terms of a specific outcome relative to all outcomes for a given condition. As a result, differences in the degree of confidence management places in the outcomes of different projects may be compared quantitatively. For example, it was indicated that in Figure 18.1, the cash flows represented expectations of amounts to be received, and that in the case of both projects, the forecasts for years 1 and 7 were the same, $6 million. Yet it is unlikely that the firm could determine the figure for the later years with the same assurance as that for the earlier years.

Further analysis reveals the difference. Let us assume that, for long-range planning, the company's economist provided a forecast of the probable state of the economy over the next ten years. Based upon these forecasts, the cash flow estimates of the planning division for either project A or B of $6 million for years 1 and 7 were reached, as shown in Figure 18.2.

474

FIGURE 18.2 *A comparison of cash flow probabilities for two years for the same project (either A or B)*

State of Economy	Year 1			Year 7		
	Probability	Cash Flow	Weighted Cash Flow	Probability	Cash Flow	Weighted Cash Flow
Depression	.05	$4,000,000	$ 200,000	.10	$ 2,000,000	$200,000
Recession	.10	5,000,000	500,000	.20	4,000,000	800,000
Stable	.70	6,000,000	4,200,000	.40	6,000,000	2,400,000
Upturn	.10	7,000,000	700,000	.20	8,000,000	1,600,000
Prosperity	.05	8,000,000	400,000	.10	10,000,000	1,000,000
Overall	1.00		$6,000,000	1.00		$6,000,000

It can now be seen that although the firm expects the same cash flow for both years, it has different expectations about the likelihood of achieving these flows. The economist is much more confident about the prospects for stable economic conditions in year 1 than in year 7. As a result, in year 1 the forecast is for a 70 percent probability of obtaining cash flows of $6 million, compared with only a 40 percent probability in year 7. Moreover, because of internal developments within the firm and the changing nature of the market, the cash flows in year 7 are spread over a broader range than in year 1. The comparison, expressed in terms of a probability distribution is shown graphically in Figure 18.3.

FIGURE 18.3 *The probability distributions for years 1 and 7 for the same project (either A or B)*

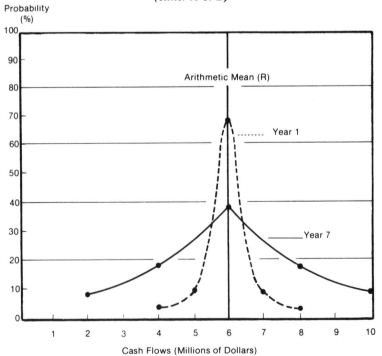

In capital budgeting, the probability distributions of cash flows, such as those in Figure 18.2, often resemble a normal curve. The equation of a normal curve is complex, but as will be seen in Section 18.3[5](b), the curve has certain properties, and it can be constructed with some simple statistical information about any particular project. Furthermore, the area within any portion of the curve may be easily ascertained. For these reasons, the normal curve lends itself quite readily to risk analysis in capital budgeting.

18.3   INCORPORATING RISK INTO CAPITAL BUDGETING—TRADITIONAL APPROACHES

Most firms are risk averters and therefore find it helpful to take variability of return or risk into account in estimating rates of return for prospective capital investment projects. In this section, we discuss the more popular traditional approaches used by financial managers to incorporate risk into the capital budgeting process. These techniques include the following:

- payback;
- scenario approach;
- risk adjusted discount rate technique;
- certainty equivalent approach; and
- mean-variance approach.

These techniques are discussed below.

[1] PAYBACK

We introduced the payback method of capital budgeting in Chapter 17 (Section 17.4[1]). Many firms expand on this use of the payback technique by using it to incorporate risk into capital budgeting decision-making. Basically, such firms develop, on a qualitative basis, different risk class categories for capital investment projects. To each category is assigned a minimum payback threshold which projects in that category must meet in order to be considered profitable. Shorter payback thresholds are assigned to the higher risk project categories. This technique suffers from two major deficiencies in practice:

- most firms are unable to develop their project risk categories on a systematic and quantitative basis; and
- few, if any, firms are able to quantitatively relate project risk category and minimum payback threshold.

At best, the payback technique provides a rough, first cut at project risk assessment.

[2] SCENARIO APPROACH

Simply stated, in the scenario approach the financial manager develops several forecasts of the prospective cash flows for a capital investment project and estimates, for each of these forecasts, the project's payback period, net present value and, rate of return. The approach is illustrated in Figure 18.4.

FIGURE 18.4 *Scenario approach to risk assessment in the capital budgeting process*

Cash Flow		PROJECT PROFITABILITY	
Scenario	Payback	Net Present Value	Internal Rate of Return
Pessimistic	5 years	-$50,000	8%
Most Likely	2 years	$350,000	25%
Optimistic	1 year	$475,000	34%

As seen in Figure 18.4, the scenario approach provides the financial manager with a clear picture regarding the sensitivity of project profitability to the assumptions made concerning prospective cash flows. This approach, however, provides no direct criteria for choosing among alternative risky capital investment projects.

[3] RISK ADJUSTED DISCOUNT RATE

In practice, the risk adjusted discount rate is a popular technique which is utilized as an integral part of the discounted cash flow approaches discussed in Chapter 17 (net present value (NPV) - internal rate of return (IRR) 17.5(2)). In theory, using this method results in an extremely straightforward adjustment process for risk.

In the NPV method, the discount rate used to discount cash flows and arrive at an estimate of NPV is computed by adding a risk premium component. This is based upon the degree of risk the project is considered to have relative to the level of risk inherent in the firm's typical or average capital investment project. Thus, the appropriate discount rate for a given project is determined as follows:

Discount Rate for	Firm's Discount Rate	Risk Premium for
a Specific Project	= for Typical or Standard	+ Additional Risk Inherent
	Projects	in Proposed Project.

As an alternative, many firms will use the weighted average cost of capital (see Chapter 19) as the base level of the discount rate and will adjust the rate upward on the basis of their assessment of the level of risk inherent in the specific capital investment project under consideration.

Using the IRR method, the adjustment process is the same as that just described except that the risk premium component is added to the minimum rate of return threshold against which the project's IRR is compared.

(a) Illustration of the Use of the Risk Adjusted Discount Rate

We now illustrate the use of the risk adjusted discount rate. In this example, the financial manager of a firm has estimated that a capital investment project costing $12,000 will generate cash flows of $4,000 annually over the next four years. Applying the firm's indicated discount rate of 10 percent to these cash flows, he finds that the project's NPV is $680.[3] Presumably, therefore, since the NPV is positive, the project is acceptable. The manager, however, is uncertain about future cash flow estimates on this particular project and believes that they may have considerably more variation than those ordinarily prevailing on the company's typical project. After taking into account the extent of these possible future variations, he decides that the project should provide a minimum return of 15 percent to reflect its added risk. As a result, the net present value of the project is reduced to -\$580,[4] and it no longer meets the desired rate of return.

(b) Evaluating the Risk Adjusted Discount Rate Technique

The amount that the discount rate should be raised to reflect the project's additional risk is largely a personal judgment based on the manager's assessment of the degree to which the market provides an allowance for risk. To gauge this allowance, he might start with the risk free rate available on short-term Treasury securities; he might note the gradual additions afforded by other marketable investments; he might determine where within the risk spectrum the company's typical project and the one under consideration fall; and on this basis he might determine a reasonable premium to be added to the company's overall 10 percent return. In effect, the manager works out to his own satisfaction the trade-off that he is willing to accept between risk and return.

At the theoretical level, however, the risk adjusted discount rate method suffers from the lack of a systematic and quantitative basis for:

- quantifying project risk (cash flow variability); and
- relating it to a specific risk premium to be added to the firm's normal discount rate.

[4] CERTAINTY EQUIVALENT APPROACH

Responding to criticisms of the risk adjusted discount rate technique, practitioners have often accounted for risk by opting to modify cash flows directly. In the certainty equivalent approach, each year's cash flow is multiplied by a coefficient and the resultant adjusted cash flows are discounted at the risk free rate of return to arrive at an NPV. In symbolic form, the certainty equivalent formulation is as follows:

$$NPV^5 = \frac{B_0 C_0}{(1+r_f)^0} + \frac{B_1 C_1}{(1+r_f)^1} + \frac{B_2 C_2}{(1+r_f)^2} + \ldots + \frac{B_n N_n}{(1+r_f)^n} = \sum_{t=0}^{n} \frac{B_t C_t}{(1+r_f)^t}$$

where:

C_t = cash flow in period t;
r_f = risk free rate of return;
B_t = certainty equivalent coefficient in period t; and
n = the number of periods in the project's life.

The B coefficient ranges from 0 to 1.00 and varies inversely with the degree of risk. Its function is to convert the risky cash flows into their certainty equivalents. This means that as the degree of risk perceived to be associated with the future cash flow rises, the value of the coefficient is lowered.

If any particular period the cash flow is anticipated at \$200, but the manager thinks that the associated risks suggest a certainty equivalent return of \$180, B is obtained as follows:

$$180 = (200)(B)$$
$$B = 180/200 = 0.9.$$

Thus, the determination of certainty equivalency directly incorporates the decision-maker's subjective assessment of risk. In this approach, a premium for risk must be excluded from the discount factor. The desired rate of return or cost of capital, however, embodies such a premium. To avoid double counting, therefore, the risk free rate is used as the discount factor.

Using the example from the previous section, we now illustrate the certainty equivalent approach. Suppose that the financial manager in question now decides that because of the increasing uncertainty with time, he should reduce each annual cash flow estimate by a factor (B_t) of 90 percent, 85 percent, 80 percent, and 70 percent to place them on a basis that is reasonably certain. Having converted the estimates to equivalent certainties, he applies, as the discount factor, the risk free rate, let us say, is 5 percent. After these adjustments, the NPV of the project is $419 as calculated below.

$$NPV = -\$12,000 + \frac{\$3,600}{(1.05)} + \frac{\$3,400}{(1.05)^2} + \frac{\$3,200}{(1.05)^3} + \frac{\$2,800}{(1.05)^4}$$
$$= -\$12,000 + \$3,429 + \$3,084 + \$2,764 + \$2,304$$
$$= -\$419.$$

Consequently, the project is rejected as unprofitable.

If the IRR approach is used, the discount factor that equates the certainty equivalent cash flows to the project's cost is calculated. This rate is compared to the risk free rate to determine if the project is to be accepted or rejected. In the preceding case, the equating discount rate works out to 3.5 percent, which is below the risk free rate of 5.0 percent and the project is therefore rejected.

[5] MEAN-VARIANCE APPROACH

In the mean-variance approach, the variability in forecasted cash flows is directly estimated and incorporated into the rate of return calculation. In Chapter 17, prior to any consideration of risk, we assumed that the cash flows were known with certainty and thus, IRR and NPV were calculated as specific numbers. Now, when we specifically recognize that the cash flows are variable and not known with certainty, our use of NPV or IRR methods is radically modified by several important factors:

- NPV or IRR for a project will no longer be one number, but also will be variable;
- the degree of variability in cash flows will be reflected in the variability of NPV or IRR; and
- the assessment of project profitability will no longer be a fairly straightforward process.

Focusing on these specific points, we recognize that the cash flows in any given year will have associated with them specific probabilities of occurrence. NPV, which in essence represents the discounted sum of these cash flows, will thus also have an associated probability distribution. The statistical properties of the NPV distribution will be used to estimate the average level of return and risk inherent in the capital investment project under consideration.

In the subsequent discussion of the mean-variance approach, we focus on the following important aspects:

- derivation of project mean (average) and variance of return;
- applying the normal curve;
- use of simulation; and
- simplification via decision trees.

(a) Derivation of Project Mean (Average) and Variance of Returns

As previously mentioned, the overall variability or risk inherent in a project is attributable to the variability of prospective cash flows. Standard practice in finance is to characterize prospective cash flows in terms of the mean and variance of their probability distributions. The more closely the projected probability distributions of cash flows are concentrated around their mean or expected value, the lower the variance and the less risky the project. In statistical terms, the mean or expected cash flow ($\overline{R}$) in any period is calculated as follows:

$$\overline{R} = \sum_{j=1}^{n} (R_j)(P_j)$$

where:

R_j = the specific values the cash flows may actually take on during the period;

P_j = the probability that the project takes on the "jth" flow value (R_j); and

n = the number of periods or years involved.

Thus $\overline{R}$ is the sum of the individual values the cash flow may take on, each weighted by its estimated probability of occurrence.

The formula for the variance (σ^2), of the cash flow distribution is given by:

$$\sigma^2 = \sum_{j=1}^{n} (R_j - \overline{R})^2(P_j).$$

The statistical properties of the individual year's cash flows for a capital investment project can be used to estimate the mean and variance of the project's NPV or IRR. Ultimately, we will measure project risk in terms of the variance of the project's NPV or IRR. Using the NPV method, the estimation of E(NPV) - Expected Net Present Value - and VAR(NPV) - Variance of the Net Present Value Distribution[6]—is based on the means and variances of individual year's cash flows, C. The relevant expressions are as follows:

$$[1] \ NPV = C_0 + \frac{C_1}{(1+K)^1} + \frac{C_2}{(1+K)^2} + \ \dots \ + \frac{C_n}{(1+K)^n}$$

$$[2] \ E(NPV) = C_0 + \frac{\overline{R}_1}{(1+K)^1} + \frac{\overline{R}_2}{(1+K)^2} + \ \dots \ + \frac{\overline{R}_n}{(1+K)^n}$$

$$[3] \ VAR(NPV) = \frac{\sigma_1^2}{(1+K)^2} + \frac{\sigma_2^2}{(1+K)^4} + \ \dots \ + \frac{\sigma_n^2}{(1+K)^{2n}}$$

where:

K = the required rate of return;

$\overline{R}_1$ = mean or expected cash flow in year 1;

σ_1^2 = variance of cash flow in year 1.

We now illustrate the calculation of the E(NPV) and VAR(NPV). Figure 18.5 presents the estimated cash flows for a simple capital investment project with a useful life of 3 years. The firm requires at least a 10 percent rate of return on its projects. In this example (for simplicity's sake), we assume that the cash flows are normally distributed and that they are independent from year to year.[7] Using the formula given above, we can estimate the E(NPV) and the VAR(NPV) for the project as follows:

$$E(NPV) = C_0 + \frac{\overline{R}_1}{(1+K)^1} + \frac{\overline{R}_2}{(1+K)^2} + \frac{\overline{R}_3}{(1+K)^3}$$

$$E(NPV) = -1,000 + \frac{2,400}{(1.1)^1} + \frac{2,200}{(1.1)^2} + \frac{1,000}{(1.1)^3}$$

$$E(NPV) = \$3,751.$$

$$VAR(NPV) = \frac{\sigma_1^2}{(1+K)^2} + \frac{\sigma_2^2}{(1+K)^4} + \frac{\sigma_3^2}{(1+K)^6}$$

$$VAR(NPV) = \frac{(2,154)^2}{(1.1)^2} + \frac{(1,077)^2}{(1.1)^4} + \frac{(2,683)^2}{(1.1)^6}$$

$$VAR(NPV) = \$(2,948).^2$$

FIGURE 18.5 *Example illustrating the mean-variance approach*

Year	Cash Flow (R_j)	Probability (P_j)	Mean or Expected Cash Flow $(\overline{R}_j)$	Variance of Cash Flow (σ^2)
0	-$1,000	1.0	-$1,000	$0
1	0 1,000 5,000	0.2 0.4 0.4	$2,400[a]	$(2,154)^{2}[b]
2	0 2,000 4,000	0.1 0.7 0.2	$2,200	$(1,077)^2
3	- 3,000 0 4,000	0.2 0.4 0.4	$1,000	$(2,683)^2

a. $\overline{R}_1$ is calculated as follows:
$\overline{R}_1$ = ($0)(0.2) + ($1,000)(.4) + ($5,000)(.4) = $2,400.
b. σ_1^2 is calculated as follows:
σ_1^2 = ($0-$2,400)^2(0.2) + ($1,000-$2,400)^2(0.4) + ($5,000-$2,400)^2(0.4) = ($2,154)

Thus the average return and level of risk inherent in this capital investment project can be described or quantified in terms of the mean or expected NPV and the variance of the resultant NPV distribution.

(b) Applying the Normal Curve

As mentioned previously, the normal curve has certain interesting properties that provide the basis for useful analysis in capital budgeting. We will first discuss the normal curve in terms of its important statistical properties and then demonstrate its usefulness via the previous example.

FIGURE 18.6 *Statistical properties of the normal probability distribution*

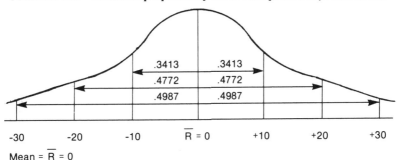

Mean = $\overline{R}$ = 0
Standard Deviation = 10

For the normal curve or normal probability distribution, there is a pre-scribed relationship between the arithmetic mean or expected value and the standard deviation. This relationship is illustrated in Figure 18.6. In the normal curve, one standard deviation (plus and minus) from the mean represents 68.26 percent of the area within the curve; two standard deviations (plus and minus) are 95.44 percent of the curve; and three standard deviations represent 99.74 percent of the curve. Thus, if the probability distribution of any series of expected values approximates the normal curve, there is a 68.26 percent probability that any particular value will fall within one standard deviation plus and minus from the mean. There is a virtual certainty that it will fall within three standard deviations plus and minus. Moreover, a normal probability distribution can be constructed once its mean and standard deviation are calculated. Knowing the normal distribution, the financial manager can determine the probability that the actual flows will be no less than a given amount or that they will fall within a specified range. But first the distribution must be standardized, which is done by subtracting the arithmetic mean from the value of concern and dividing the result by the standard deviation as follows:

$$Z = \frac{X - \overline{R}}{\sigma}$$

where:

Z = the standardized variable (the number of σ's from $\overline{R}$);
X = the variable whose distribution is to be standardized;

$\overline{R}$ = the arithmetic mean of the distribution of X; and
σ = the standard deviation of the distribution of X.

As a result of this process of standardizing, we convert any given normal distribution into a normal distribution which has a mean equal to zero and a standard deviation equal to 1.0. We can then refer to a table of values for the standard normal distribution to determine the probability corresponding to the calculated Z value.

We now demonstrate the usefulness of the normal curve in terms of the example in the previous section. In this example, we calculated that the project's E(NPV) and VAR(NPV) were \$3,751 and ($2,948)^2 respectively. Actually, the normal distribution of the project's NPV appears as depicted below.

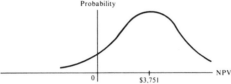

In reviewing this prospective project, the financial manager may wish to consider the probability that the NPV of the project will be less than zero, greater than a specific value (e.g., \$5,000), or between two values (e.g., \$2,000 and \$4,000). To make these determinations, the distribution must first be standardized as follows:

$$P(NPV < 0) = \frac{P(Z<0 - E(NPV)}{\sigma(NPV)}$$

$$= \frac{P(Z<0 - \$3,751}{\$2,948}$$

$$= P(Z< - 1.27).$$

The required probability is equal to the area under the Z curve to the left of -1.27, as depicted below.

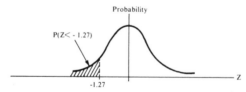

Figure 18.7 is a table of values for the standard normal distribution. It can be used to calculate the area under the Z curve corresponding to any specific value of Z. In this case, the table shows that 10.2 percent of the area under the curve lies to the left of - 1.27. Therefore, P(NPV<0) is equal to 0.102.

Similarly, we calculate the P(NPV>\$5,000) as follows:

$$P(NPV>\$5,000) = \frac{P(Z>\$5,000 - \$3,751)}{\$2,948}$$

$$= P(Z>0.42).$$

Using Figure 18.7, we find that 16.28 percent of the area under the Z curve lies to the right of .42. Thus P(NPV > \$5,000) = .1628. To illustrate the relationship of the distribution of NPV in both its nonstandardized and standardized form, we depict below the areas under both curves corresponding to P(NPV > $5,000).

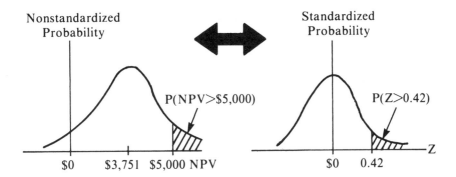

Another way in which the financial manager can utilize the normal curve in evaluating a project is to determine the probability that its NPV is at least a designated level. For this purpose it is easy to construct a cumulative probability distribution as shown in Figure 18.8.

Column (1) provides a range of estimated NPV's; columns (2) and (3) give the data for the determination of the Z values; and column (4) represents the cumulative distribution. Thus, in addition to knowing that there is a 89.8 percent probability that NPV>$0, the financial manager now sees that there is a 72.2 percent probability that NPV>$2,000, a 13.6 percent probability that NPV>$7,000, etc.

(c) Use of Simulation

For more complex projects, it is usually difficult, if not impossible, to derive the probability distribution of a project's NPV or IRR from a knowledge of the probability distributions of the project's annual cash flows as we demonstrated in Section 18.3[5](a) and (b). In such cases we may perform a useful analysis by using simulation techniques. This method ordinarily starts with the construction of an experimental model of the system (often represented by computerized mathematical models) which is then used to evaluate various alternatives by noting how well they fare in test runs of the (computer) model.

In a sense, computer simulation may be considered a live strategic planning experiment. The technique allows the analyst to understand complicated problems, identify dynamic interdependencies, evaluate risk factors, and choose final strategies from the results of the model run under selected variables and parameters.

In capital budgeting, a simulation approach would assume that key factors (e.g., initial investment cost, operating costs, selling prices and volumes, etc.) are random variables. Then the following procedure or set of steps would be employed to evaluate the project profitability and risk under subsequent dynamic situations. The financial manager would:

FIGURE 18.7 *Standard normal probability distribution*

Normal Curve Areas*

Z	.00	.01	.02	.03	.04	.05	.06	.07	.08	.09
0.0	.0000	.0040	.0080	.0120	.0160	.0199	.0230	.0279	.0319	.0359
0.1	.0398	.0438	.0478	.0517	.0557	.0596	.0636	.0675	.0714	.0753
0.2	.0793	.0832	.0871	.0910	.0948	.0987	.1026	.1061	.1103	.1141
0.3	.1179	.1217	.1255	.1293	.1331	.1368	.1406	.1443	.1480	.1517
0.4	.1554	.1591	.1628	.1664	.1700	.1736	.1772	.1808	.1844	.1879
0.5	.1915	.1950	.1985	.2019	.2054	.2088	.2123	.2157	.2190	.2224
0.6	.2257	.2291	.2324	.2357	.2389	.2422	.2454	.2486	.2517	.2549
0.7	.2580	.2611	.2642	.2673	.2701	.2734	.2764	.2794	.2823	.2852
0.8	.2881	.2910	.2939	.2967	.2995	.3023	.3051	.3078	.3106	.3133
0.9	.3159	.3186	.3212	.3238	.3264	.3289	.3315	.3340	.3365	.3389
1.0	.3413	.3438	.3461	.3485	.3508	.3531	.3554	.3577	.3599	.3621
1.1	.3643	.3665	.3686	.3708	.3729	.3749	.3770	.3790	.3810	.3830
1.2	.3849	.3869	.3888	.3997	.3925	.3944	.3962	.3980	.3997	.4015
1.3	.4032	.4019	.4066	.4082	.4099	.4115	.4131	.4147	.4162	.4177
1.4	.4192	.4207	.4222	.4236	.4254	.4265	.4279	.4292	.4300	.4319
1.5	.4332	.4345	.4357	.4370	.4382	.4394	.4406	.4418	.4429	.4441
1.6	.4452	.4463	.4474	.4484	.4495	.4505	.4515	.4525	.4535	.4545
1.7	.4554	.4564	.4573	.4582	.4591	.4599	.4608	.4616	.4625	.4633
1.8	.4641	.4649	.4656	.4664	.4671	.4678	.4686	.4693	.4699	.4706
1.9	.4713	.4719	.4726	.4732	.4738	.4744	.4750	.4756	.4761	.4767
2.0	.4772	.4778	.4783	.4788	.4793	.4798	.4803	.4808	.4812	.4817
2.1	.4821	.4826	.4830	.4834	.4838	.4842	.4846	.4850	.4854	.4857
2.2	.4861	.4864	.4808	.4871	.4875	.4878	.4881	.4884	.4887	.4890
2.3	.4893	.4896	.4898	.4901	.4904	.4906	.4909	.4911	.4913	.4916
2.4	.4918	.4920	.4922	.4925	.4927	.4929	.4931	.4932	.4934	.4936
2.5	.4938	.4940	.4941	.4943	.4945	.4946	.4948	.4949	.4951	.4952
2.6	.4953	.4955	.4956	.4957	.4959	.4960	.4961	.4962	.4963	.4964
2.7	.4965	.4966	.4967	.4968	.4969	.4970	.4971	.4972	.4973	.4974
2.8	.4974	.4975	.4976	.4977	.4977	.4978	.4979	.4979	.4980	.4981
2.9	.4981	.4982	.4982	.4983	.4984	.4984	.4985	.4985	.4986	.4986
3.0	.4987	.4987	.4987	.4988	.4988	.4989	.4989	.4989	.4090	.4090

* This table is reproduced with the permission of the publishers from J. Neyman, *First Course in Probability and Statistics*, Henry Holt and Company, Inc., New York.

(1) Estimate the range of values for each of the factors of a project and within that range the likelihood of occurrence of each value, thereby producing subjective probability distributions of these key factors.

(2) Select at random an individual value from the distribution of values for each factor. Combine the values for all the factors and compute the IRR or NPV.

(3) Repeat this process in order to obtain a range of IRR's (or NPV's) with corresponding likelihoods of occurrence, i.e., a probability distribution of returns.

(4) Use the results of (3) to evaluate the expected return and risk of competing projects.

This procedure, illustrated in Figure 18.9, develops the required NPV or IRR distribution by repeated computer sampling from the assumed distributions of individual year's cash flows. In addition, it also permits particular

FIGURE 18.8 *Cumulative probability distribution*

NPV	NPV-E(NPV)	$\dfrac{\text{NPV-E(NPV)}}{\sigma\text{NPV}} = Z^{*}$	$P(Z>Z^{*})$
-$7,000	$-10,751	-3.65	0.999
-6,000	-9,751	-3.31	0.999
-5,000	-8,751	-2.97	0.998
-4,000	-7,751	-2.63	0.996
-3,000	-6,751	-2.29	0.989
-2,000	-5,751	-1.95	0.974
-1,000	-4,751	-1.61	0.946
0	-3,751	-1.27	0.898
1,000	-2,751	-0.93	0.824
2,000	-1,751	-0.59	0.722
3,000	-751	-0.25	0.599
4,000	249	0.08	0.468
5,000	1,249	0.42	0.337
6,000	2,249	0.76	0.224
7,000	3,249	1.10	0.136
8,000	4,249	1.44	0.075

NOTE: E(NPV) = $3,751 and VAR(NPV) = ($2,948).[2]

values to be changed, and the new results to be calculated with the modified combinations (sensitivity analysis). Thus some insights may be obtained into the significance of specific factors.

(d) Simplification via Decision Trees

Another complexity the financial manager frequently faces in the application of the mean-variance approach or in the capital budgeting process, in general, is the fact that the decision to undertake a prospective project may depend upon a sequence of eventualities that occur over time. Each of these eventualities, in turn, could produce different outcomes with different probability distributions. As the process moves from eventuality to eventuality, therefore, the number of possible outcomes multiplies, creating the semblance of a tree with spreading branches. Hence, the term "decision tree."

FIGURE 18.9 *Use of computer simulation to estimate the probability distribution of a project's NPV*

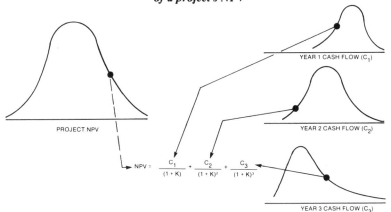

To illustrate decision tree analysis, assume that a manager is contemplating investing $50,000 in a plant. His analysis might follow the lines indicated in Figure 18.10. He believes that there is a 50/50 chance that the plant will produce sales of either $150,000 or $100,000. The initial eventuality, accordingly, is first year sales with a 0.50 probability of an outcome of $150,000 and a 0.50 probability of an outcome of $100,000. Thereafter, the manager estimates a 0.60 probability that sales will grow for 5 years at a 10 percent rate and a 0.40 probability of a 5 percent growth rate. Thus, the second eventuality is represented by sales in the fifth year. If the first year sales begin at the $150,000 level, then proceed at the higher growth rate, they will amount to $219,605 in the fifth year; at the lower rate, sales in the fifth year would total $182,326. The next eventuality is the cash flows that would result from either growth rate. The circumstances affecting the cash flows are believed to be similar, except for the variable/cost ratio incurred. The financial manager estimates that there is a 0.70 probability that the ratio will be 80 percent and 0.30 probability that it will be 60 percent. As a result, if sales begin at $150,000 and grow at a 10 percent rate, the resulting aggregate present value of the five year cash flows would be $68,180 if the variable cost ratio is 80 percent, and would increase to $136,360 if the ratio is 60 percent.

The calculation of these two flows and their present values, discounted at 10 percent are shown in Figure 18.11. Depending upon which sequence of branch development is followed, eight different cash flow outcomes are possible. To reach each of these flows, a series of probabilities is assumed. The product of each probability in each series represents the overall probability of attaining any of the flows for that particular sequence.

The expected present value of all the cash flows is $71,319, determined by weighing each present value cash flow by its indicated probability (for example, $68,180 x .21 = $14,318) and adding the resulting amounts. Comparing the expected value of the present value of the cash inflows with the cost of the original investment yields a profitability index of 1.43 times ($71,319/$50,000).[8]

This sequence may represent only part of the decision tree. Thus, the manager might want to compare the expected cash flow value and risk of the $50,000 investment with the results obtained if either a larger or smaller investment were made. In this case, the initial eventuality would be the size of the investment, with each amount producing a branch sequence as illustrated in Figure 18.10. Varying decision points could also be incorporated. For example, if the company made a big investment and sales grew at a high level, the upper branch would be pursued. If the company made a small investment, however, and sales grew rapidly, it might be confronted with a choice of staying with the small investment/high sales route or enlarging the investment, which would open another branch route.

There is a logical appeal to decision trees, and at least they provide a quantitative base for decision-making. They could be carried to complex extremes, however, and in these cases, the extent of required subjective estimates cast doubt on the validity of the quantitative outcomes and the need for such a meticulous approach. In practice, it is relatively unusual to find firms employing elaborate decision tree analyses in their capital budget programs.

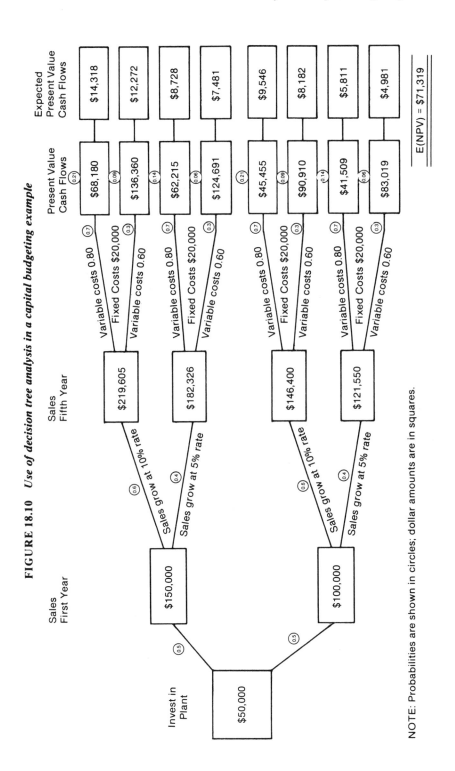

FIGURE 18.10 *Use of decision tree analysis in a capital budgeting example*

NOTE: Probabilities are shown in circles; dollar amounts are in squares.

FIGURE 18.11 *Illustrating calculation of the present value of cash flows for five-year period in decision tree*

Item	Years					1-5
	1	2	3	4	5	
Sales	$150,000	$165,000	$181,500	$199,650	$219,615	
Variable cost (0.80)	$120,000	$132,000	$195,200	$159,720	$175,692	
Fixed charges	20,000	20,000	20,000	20,000	20,000	
Earnings before taxes	10,000	13,000	16,300	19,930	23,923	
Taxes (50%)	5,000	6,500	8,150	9,965	11,961	
Net earnings	5,000	6,500	8,150	9,965	11,962	
Depreciation	10,000	10,000	10,000	10,000	10,000	
Cash flow	15,000	16,500	18,150	19,965	21,962	
Discounted at 10%	13,636	13,636	13,636	13,636	13,636	$68,180
Sales	$150,000	$165,000	$181,500	$199,650	$219,615	
Variable cost (0.60)	90,000	99,000	108,900	119,790	181,769	
Fixed charges	20,000	20,000	20,000	20,000	20,000	
Earnings before taxes	40,000	46,000	52,600	59,860	67,846	
Taxes (50%)	20,000	23,000	26,300	29,930	33,923	
Net earnings	20,000	23,000	26,300	29,930	33,923	
Depreciation	10,000	10,000	10,000	10,000	10,000	
Cash flow	30,000	33,000	36,300	39,930	43,923	
Discounted at 10%	27,272	27,272	27,272	27,272	27,272	$136,360

18.4   INCORPORATING RISK INTO CAPITAL BUDGETING—MODERN PORTFOLIO THEORY APPROACH

In this section, we address the potential uses of modern portfolio theory in the capital budgeting process, especially in assessing project risk. As discussed in Chapter 2, the theory was developed primarily in relation to securities markets and, in this area, has been applied to developing measures of risk and to aid in understanding market influences. While its direct application to capital budgeting is still extremely limited, an insight into the theory is desirable because of the basic issues it addresses. Our discussion here focuses on three related topics:

- projects with correlated returns;
- the Capital Asset Pricing Model (CAPM) and the risk adjusted discount rate; and
- modern portfolio theory and capital budgeting under risk.

[1] PROJECTS WITH CORRELATED RETURNS[9]

Not only must the financial manager be concerned with the risk of the specific project, but he must also be concerned with how the proposed project affects what the firm is currently doing, and is likely to be doing in the way of investment opportunities in the future. Intuitively, it seems reasonable to believe that some projects will provide an element of diversification and will, as a consequence, be more attractive to a firm than projects with a similar individual risk profile but without the same diversification feature. In short, a given project must be evaluated in terms of its effect on the firm's overall riskiness; because of diversification effects, it is conceivable that two projects from the same risk class could have markedly different effects on the firm's total risk exposure.

The mathematics of introducing project interrelationships into risk analysis can be highly complex so we will deal with this only in relatively simple terms. The expected net present value E(NPV), and the standard deviation $\sigma(NPV)$, of a combination of capital projects are given respectively by:

$$[4]\ E(NPV) = \sum_{i=1}^{n} E(NPV_i)$$

and

$$[5]\ \sigma(NPV) = \left(\sum_{i=1}^{n} \sum_{j=1}^{n} \sigma_i\, \sigma_j\, \varphi_{ij} \right)^{1/2}$$

where:

$E(NPV) = $ the expected net present value of capital project i;

$\sigma_i = $ the standard deviation about the expected net present value of capital project i;

$\varphi_{ij} = $ the correlation coefficient between the net present value capital projects i and j;[10] and

$n = $ the number of capital projects involved.

To exemplify equations [4] and [5], consider a firm that is committed to an array of capital projects with an expected net present value of $100 and a standard deviation of $20. Additionally, the firm has the opportunity to select one of the two proposed capital projects and add it to the array of capital projects that are currently underway. Both potential new projects have the same expected net present values, and the same standard deviations, $20 and $4 respectively. The correlations between each project's net present value and the net present value of the firm's current activities are, however, quite different. Project 1 has a correlation coefficient of +.75 and project 2 has a correlation coefficient of -.25.

To determine the expected net present value and standard deviation of project 1 and then project 2, each in separate combination with the firm's current activities, we use equation [4] to calculate the expected net present value of the combination and equation [5] to calculate the standard deviation. For the case where we have project 1 in combination with the firm's current activities, equation [4] becomes:

E(NPV) = E(NPV current activities) + E(NPV Project 1).
Substituting, we find

E(NPV) = $100 + $20 = $120.
Equation [5] becomes:

σ(NPV) = [σ^2 (NPV current activities) + σ^2 (NPV Project 1) + 2 φ (current activities Project 1) x σ (NPV current activities) x σ (NPV Project 1)]$^{1/2}$
and substituting, we find:

σ (NPV) = (20^2 + 2 x .75 x $20 x $4 + 4^2)$^{1/2}$

        = ($400 + $120 + $16)$^{1/2}$

        = $23.15.

Using the same procedures, we find that the expected net present value of project 2, in combination with the firm's current activities, is also $120, but the corresponding standard deviation is $19.39.

The financial manager would conclude that project 2 is preferred over project 1. Both result in the same expected net present value when combined with the firm's other activities, but project 2 gives the lower overall firm risk, and this is the case even though projects 1 and 2 have the same individual standard deviations. What has happened is that project 2 provides more diversification than project 1 because it is "less perfectly" correlated with the firm's current activities. All other things being equal, the lower the correlation between a firm's current activities and a given project, the more favorable the impact on overall firm risk from undertaking the project.[11]

The financial manager's problem in real life, of course, is more complex than that illustrated in this single example. Not only must he consider each possible new project in combination with the firm's current activities, but he must also introduce into the analysis the relationship between the new projects and the effects of abandoning some current activities.

[2] THE CAPM AND THE RISK ADJUSTED DISCOUNT RATE

In our discussion of the risk adjusted discount rate approach to incorporating risk into the capital budgeting process (Section 18.3[3]), we pointed out the difficulty in practice of quantifying project risk and translating it into a risk premium component to be added to the firm's normal discount rate for risk free projects. Modern portfolio theory, specifically the CAPM, offers a theoretical solution to these difficulties. Project risk is measured by the project's β (beta) coefficient[12] and the appropriate risk adjusted discount rate is calculated using the CAPM, as follows:

Risk Adjusted Discount Rate for Project X = $R_f + \beta_X [E(R_m) - R_f]$

where:

R_f = the firm's risk free discount rate;

β_X = the systematic risk or beta coefficient for Project X; and

$E(R_m)$ = the expected rate of return on the firm's total portfolio of capital investment projects.

While this approach appears conceptually straightforward, researchers and practitioners have made little headway in their attempts to estimate project betas. Unlike the situation with financial securities, firms do not have access to comprehensive historical data on rates of return for broad categories of capital investment projects.

[3] MODERN PORTFOLIO THEORY AND CAPITAL BUDGETING UNDER RISK

As had been mentioned, modern portfolio theory was developed primarily in relation to the securities markets, and its principal use has been in that area. Its most obvious application to capital budgeting is in visualizing the different projects undertaken by a company as a portfolio of projects. To some extent, many of them will have some degree of correlatiion with each other. If nothing else, the influence of the basic economy will tend to cause cash flows to move in the same direction. Moreover, a number of projects may relate strongly to the company's main line of business, which may also bring about similarity of movement.

On the other hand, there is a sufficient variation in different economic activities to permit firms to reduce the risk of their cash flows by diversifying the segments of their business. A firm that has a summer seasonal peak but is sluggish during the winter months, for example, might seek a counter-balancing line. Or, if the firm is heavily engaged in a cyclical business, it may seek a stable consumer line. There are various difficulties in undertaking such supplementary activities, including finding suitable candidates, obtaining adequate assurance of profitability, effecting the acquisition, and developing the internal know how to administer the acquired firm, particularly if the new undertaking is an unfamiliar area. Nevertheless, diversification of activity is an important means of reducing risk and one that most companies constantly have in mind.

The concept of the efficient frontier (See Chapter 2) has also been applied to capital budgeting where efforts are being made to develop models that permit the selection of optimal portfolios of projects.[13] Such a portfolio would be expressed in terms of the expected net present values of the constituent projects and the associated risk, measured by the variance of the net present values. While these models have appeal, their practical implementation has been difficult and the principal work along these lines is in academic circles.

18.5   THE RISKS OF RISK ANALYSIS

Modern management is fully aware of the need to evaluate risk in comparing the rates of return of different projects. Such evaluations, however, often are done informally. Specific procedures, to the extent used, are likely to involve determining the risk adjusted or certainty equivalent rates of return. These methods incorporate relatively modest modifications in basic discounted cash flow procedures and therefore are easy to understand.[14] The applications of the normal curve have some theoretical problems that stand in the way of their widespread adoption. The introduction of simulation models that assign probability distributions to critical values and permit determining the outcomes obtained from varying these values is a realistic approach. However, this method is elaborate, time consuming, and expensive. Accordingly, it would be desirable for management to know beforehand the circumstances under which simulation is likely to produce satisfactory results. Conclusions along these lines have been based upon a study of four major oil companies that decided to try the technique.[15]

In general, the following circumstances appear conducive to the effective introduction of formal risk analysis through simulation:

- the incidence of an important current issue that has to be resolved and seems susceptible to such analysis;
- a management staff responsible for implementing the approach within the division that has to use the results;
- continuous exchange of ideas between the management science and functional personnel;
- an effective training program for managers at each level of each division expected to employ risk analysis;
- an agreement on reasonable ranges and probabilities for all critical variables before their actual use in budget analysis and determination;
- developing the risk analysis approach through teams rather than through individual effort. Such a team might include management science "purists", finance experts, computer experts, and line engineers;
- encouragement of a management philosophy based on portfolio return and variability rather than concentration on individual projects; and
- educating personnel in the process of quantifying probability assessments.

Thus, the development of a risk analysis approach through a simulation model probably means that the company has a management science department seeking scientific solutions to business problems. It appears likely that such a department functions best in a strongly decentralized organization that encourages an exchange of ideas between the different categories of personnel involved in the implementation of projects.

18.6   CHAPTER SUMMARY

In this chapter, we expanded the discussion of capital budgeting to include risk—specifically, project risk. We defined risk and discussed the various traditional and modern approaches and techniques for assessing it in the context of capital budgeting. In Chapter 19, we further expand our capital budgeting discussion to include financial risk and the relationship between financial leverage and the cost of capital.

FOOTNOTES

1. A distinction sometimes is drawn between risk and uncertainty, the basis for which may have originated with Frank Knight, a distinguished economist, who defined risk as a measurable uncertainty. Reflecting the current tendency to involve probabilities in risk analysis, this concept may be narrowed to distinguish between risk, where the probabilities of a particular event are known, and uncertainty, where they are unknown. For practical purposes, however, risk and uncertainty may be considered similar concepts.

2. Assume two projects with the same average expected cash flows but with sharp differences in the amounts thrown off each year, as project A and B in the text. A risk seeker would prefer B; a risk averter, project A; and one indifferent to risk would have no preference. While various explanations may be given for risk aversion, a simple and reasonable one is that as persons accumulate money, they satisfy their most immediate needs first and their less urgent requirements subsequently. In technical language, money is said to have a diminishing marginal utility.

3. The actual NPV calculation is as follows:
   NPV = -$12,000 + $4,000 [PVAIF (10%; 4 years)] = -$12,000 + $4,000 (3.17)
   NPV = $680

   where:

   PVAIF = the present value annuity interest factor found in Figure 18.30.

4. The actual NPV calculation is as follows:
   NPV = -$12,000 + $4,000 [PVAIF (15%; 4 years)] = -$12,000 + $4,000 (2.855)
   NPV = -$580.

5. Note that in the certainty equivalent technique only the cash inflows are uncertain, the initial cash outflow is presumed to be certain.

6. According to established statistical theorems, if $y = a_1x_1 + a_2x_2 + a_3x_3 + \ldots + a_nx_n$, where x is a random variable, $a_1 a_2 \ldots a_n$ are coefficients, and the x's are independent, then the expected value of y, $E(y) = a_1E(x_1) + a_2E(X_2) + a_3E(x_3) + \ldots + a_nE(x_n)$, meaning that the expected value of y equals the sum of the expected values of x's, each multiplied by its corresponding coefficient; the variance (or standard deviation squared) of y, $V(y) = a_1{}^2V(x_1) + a_2{}^2V(x_2) + a_3{}^2V(x_3) + \ldots + a_n{}^2V(x_n)$.
   See P.L. Meyer, *Introductory Probability and Statistical Applications.* Reading, Mass.: Addison-Wesley Publishing Co., 2d ed., 1972, Ch. 7.

7. Statistical techniques also have been developed to handle cases where the cash flows between periods are correlated and where some of the flows are correlated and some independent. See Frederick S. Hillier, "The Derivation of Probabilistic Information for the Evaluation of Risky Investments," *Management Science,* April 1963, pp. 443-447.

8. See Chapter 17 for a discussion of the profitability index.

9. Much of this section is taken from John S. McCallum, "A Note on Professor Robbins' Paper on Capital Budgeting Under Risky Conditions," *Journal of Accounting, Auditing and Finance,* Summer 1978, pp. 373-376.

10. The concept of a correlation coefficient is discussed in Chapter 2.

11. In this connection, see Howard E. Thompson, "Mathematical Programming, The Capital Asset Pricing Model and Capital Budgeting of Interrelated Projects," *The Journal of Finance,* March 1976, pp. 125-131.

12. See Chapter 2 for a discussion of the CAPM and the concept of a beta coefficient.

13. For some examples of this work, see Dan J. Laughhunn and C. Ronald Sprecher, "Probability of Loss and the Capital Asset Pricing Model," *Financial Manage-*

ment, Spring 1977, pp. 18-25; Jerome S. Osteryoung, Elton Scott and Gordon S. Roberts, "Selecting Capital Projects with the Coefficient of Variation," *Financial Management,* Summer 1977, pp. 65-70, where the coefficient of variation (standard deviation of outcomes divided by the expected value of the outcomes) is suggested as an appropriate risk measure in capital budgeting, and Jerome S. Osteryoung, Rodney L. Roenfeldt, and Donald A. Nast, "Capital Asset Pricing Model and Traditional Risk for Capital Budgeting," *The Financial Review,* Spring 1977, pp. 48-58. However, some contend that the application of portfolio theory to capital budgeting problems is inappropriate. For an example of this debate, see Herbert E. Phillips, "Capital Asset Pricing Model and Traditional Risk for Capital Budgeting: A Comment," *The Financial Review,* Fall 1977, pp. 91-97 and Thomas J. Frecka, "Capital Asset Pricing Model and Traditional Risk Measures for Capital Budgeting: A Comment," *The Financial Review,* Fall 1977, pp. 97-99. In reply, see Jerome S. Osteryoung, Rodney L. Roenfeldt and Donald A. Nast, "Capital Asset Pricing Model and Traditional Risk Measures for Capital Budgeting: A Reply," *The Financial Review,* Spring 1978, pp. 90-93.

14. For a survey of the level of sophistication used in capital budgeting by the nation's leading firms, see Lawrence J. Gitman and John R. Forrester, Jr., "A Survey of Capital Budgeting Techniques Used by Major U.S. Firms," *Financial Management,* Fall 1977, pp. 66-71. The findings of this study suggest that major corporations in this country are tending to adopt more sophisticated tools of analysis in capital budgeting. J. William Petty and Oswald D. Bowlin, "The Financial Manager and Quantitative Decision Models," *Financial Management,* Winter 1976, pp. 32-41, find similar results.

15. See, E. Eugene Carter, "What Are the Risks in Risk Analysis?" *Harvard Business Review,* July-August 1972, pp. 72-82.

SUGGESTED READINGS

Abdelsamad, M. H. and J. E. Thornton, "What You Should Know About Risk in Capital Budgeting," *Management World,* January 1981.

Ang, J. S. and W. G. Lewellen, "Risk Adjustment in Capital Investment Project Evaluations," *Financial Management,* Summer 1982.

Benninga, Simon and Eitan Muller, "Maturity Choice and the Objective Function of the Firm Under Uncertainty," *The Bell Journal of Economics,* Autumn 1979.

Blatt, John M., "Investment Evaluation Under Uncertainty," *Financial Management,* Summer 1979.

Blocher, E. and C. Stilkney, "Duration and Risk Assessments in Capital Budgeting," *Accounting Review,* January 1979.

Brenner, Menachem and Seymour Smidt, "Asset Characteristics and Systematic Risk," *Financial Management,* Winter 1978.

Connie, Thomas E., Jr. and Maurry J. Tamarkin, "On Diversification Given Asymmetry in Returns," *Journal of Finance,* December 1981.

Cozzolino, John M., "New Method for Risk Analysis," *Sloan Management Review,* Spring 1979.

———, "Controlling Risk in Capital Budgeting: A Practical Use of Utility Theory for Measurement and Control of Petroleum Exploration Risk," *Engineering Economist,* Spring 1980.

Dorfman, Robert, "Meaning of Internal Rates of Return," *Journal of Finance,* December 1981.

Durway, Jerry W., "Evaluating Risk: Sensitivity Analysis and Simulation," *Infosystems,* May 1979.

Everett, J. E. and B. Schwab, "On the Proper Adjustment for Risk Through Discount Rates in a Mean-Variance Framework," *Financial Management,* Summer 1979.

Gehr, Adam K. Jr., "Risk Adjusted Capital Budgeting Using Arbitrage," *Financial Management*, Winter 1981.

Glahn, Gerald L., et. al., "How to Evaluate Mixed Risk Capital Projects," *Management Accounting*, December 1980.

Graver, Robert R., "Investment Policy Implications of the Capital Asset Pricing Model," *Journal of Finance*, March 1981.

Hederstierna, A., "Decisions Under Uncertainty: A Note on Skewed Uncertainty Distributions," *OMEGA*, 1981.

Hertz, David B., "Risk Analysis in Capital Investment," *Harvard Business Review*, September/October 1979.

Hoskins, C. G., "Capital Decision Rules for Risky Projects Derived from a Capital Market Model Based on Semivariance," *Engineering Economist*, Summer 1978.

Kim, Suk H. and Edward J. Farragher, "Current Capital Budgeting Practices," *Management Accounting*, June 1981.

Klotz, Ben P., "Portfolio Theory with Variable Risk," *Review of Economics and Statistics*, May 1979.

Markowitz, Harry M., "Portfolio Selection," *Journal of Finance*, March 1952.

Maxfield, M. W. and R. A. Pohlman, "On the Use of Certainty Equivalent Factors as Risk Proxies," *Engineering Economist*, Spring 1982.

Obel, Borge and James Vander Weide, "On the Decentralized Capital Budgeting Problem Under Uncertainty," *Management Science*, September 1979.

Osteryoung, Jerome S., Rodney L. Roenfeldt and Donald A. Nast, "Capital Asset Pricing Model and Traditional Risk for Capital Budgeting," *The Financial Review*, Spring 1977.

Perrakis, S., "Capital Budgeting and Timing Uncertainty Within the Capital Asset Pricing Model," *Financial Management*, Autumn 1979.

Schall, L. D. and G. L. Sundem, "Capital Budgeting Methods and Risk: A Further Analysis," *Financial Management*, Spring 1980.

Spahr, R. W., "Basic Uncertainty in Capital Budgeting: Stochastic Reinvestment Rates," *Engineering Economist*, Summer 1982.

THE COST OF CAPITAL

19.1 THE IMPORTANCE OF THE COST OF CAPITAL

Measuring the cost of capital indicates the relative cost of pursuing one line of financing rather than another. The present cost of financing by means of a given type of security may be compared with the estimated future costs of financing by the same method, to judge whether or not the present is an appropriate time to undertake such financing. The cost of capital also plays a major role in the capital budgeting process. As discussed in Chapter 17, a prospective project must generate returns in excess of the firm's cost of capital if the project is to be judged profitable. The cost of capital is used both as the minimum value of the discount rate in the net present value method and as the minimum return threshold in the internal rate of return method. The cost of capital is also useful in helping management move toward an optimum capital structure—one which minimizes the firm's cost of capital.

Despite the importance of this topic, however, there is no agreement in the academic literature or among financial managers as to how to measure the cost of capital.[1] Indeed, management is sometimes skeptical about the validity of such a figure, even though they calculate it. In determining the cost of capital, two separate procedures are involved. First, the financial manager determines the elements of a firm's capital structure. Costs are computed for debt, preferred stock, common stock, and retained earnings. Second, a means is found for combining the individual cost elements into an overall cost of capital. In addition, management must consider the potential effects of changes in the use of financial leverage (or changes in the extent of debt in the capital structure) on both the costs of the individual elements and the overall cost of capital. This chapter is organized into three primary sections which correspond to the three forementioned concerns, the cost of the individual elements, the overall cost of capital, and financial leverage and the cost of capital.

19.2 THE COST OF THE INDIVIDUAL ELEMENTS OF THE CAPITAL STRUCTURE

The cost of any element in the capital structure may be defined as the return required by holders of that element. The combined cost of capital of the firm might then be considered as the cost of each element weighted by the proportion that it bears in the firm's total capital structure. Presumably, this is the rate which the firm must earn on new investments in order to meet the return expectations of each of its security holders.

There is little disagreement about how to measure the cost of debt and preferred stock. On the other hand, there is considerable disagreement about how to measure the cost of common stock and retained earnings, and how to combine the elements into an overall cost of capital. In the ensuing sections, we discuss the cost of each element of a firm's capital structure.

[1] COST OF DEBT

One minor issue is whether to measure the cost of short-term as well as long-term debt. Since a company may borrow at short-term in the early stages of a new project and later refund this debt by floating a long-term bond issue, it may be logical to consider the cost of short-term debt as part of the cost of capital and to briefly examine its measurement.

(a) Short-Term Debt

If a firm borrows $150,000 from a bank for six months at 5 percent (a low figure under current conditions but used for illustrative purposes), what is the annual cost of the loan? Five percent of $150,000 is, of course, $7,500. But banks customarily discount loans, that is, they deduct the interest in advance and credit the borrower with the net proceeds. The company in this case initially receives not $150,000, but $150,000 minus ½ of $7,500, or $150,000 -$3,750 = $146,250. It pays $3,750 for the use of $146,250 for 180 days. The actual cost of the loan is:

$$\text{Cost of the Loan} = \frac{\text{Interest}}{\text{Proceeds}} = \frac{\$3,750}{\$146,250} = 2.56\% \text{ for 180 days.}$$

The true annual rate is 5.12 percent, not 5.00 percent. This is the pre-tax cost. The after-tax cost is obtained as follows:[2]

After-tax cost = before-tax cost x (1 - Tax Rate)

With a corporate tax rate of 46 percent, the annual after-tax cost of the loan is:

(5.12%)(1 - .46) = 2.76%

The true interest cost varies with the net proceeds so that different maturities will result in different interest costs. Although the credit is said to be a 5 percent loan, it will cost 5.042 percent annually before taxes for a 60 day loan of $150,000; 5.063 percent for a 90-day loan; 5.263 percent for a 360 day loan, etc. This is shown in Figure 19.1.

FIGURE 19.1   *A comparison of the specific costs of $150,000, 5 percent discounted loan of varying maturities*

	MATURITY (IN DAYS)					
	30	60	90	180	270	360
Face amount of loan	150,000	150,000	150,000	150,000	150,000	150,000
Interest charges	625	1,250	1,875	3,750	5,625	7,500
Net proceeds	149,375	148,750	148,125	146,250	144,375	142,500
Effective rate of interest (per annum)	5.020%	5.042%	5.063%	5.129%	5.195%	5.263%

Two added complications may be involved. First, if the bank, as is customary, requires that a minimum balance of from ten to twenty percent is maintained at all times during the life of the loan, the net proceeds may be calculated by substituting the minimum balance, since this amount is not available to the borrowing company. If a 10 percent minimum balance is required, the net proceeds of the 360-day, 5 percent loan becomes $127,500 rather than $142,500 and the true interest cost becomes:

$$\text{Cost of the Loan} = \frac{\text{Interest}}{\text{Proceeds}} = \frac{\$7,500}{\$127,500} = 5.88\%$$

Second, if the loan must be repaid in installments, the true rate of interest will be almost twice the stated rate, since the borrower will, on average, have the use of only half the amount of the loan over the full period. For example, if the 360-day, $150,000, 5 percent loan must be repaid in 12 monthly install-ments, the borrower has the use of $11/12$ of the loan during the second month, only $10/12$ of the loan during the third month, and so on, and during the final month only $1/12$, so that on average, the borrower would have had the use of $142,500/2$, or an average of $71,250. To calculate the true annual rate, the "constant ratio" formula may be used. In this case,

$$\text{true annual rate} = r = \frac{2MI}{P(N+1)}$$

where: I =   dollar cost of the loan;
M = the number of payments in one year (12 if repayment is on a monthly basis, regardless of the number of months taken to repay);
P = the net amount of the loan; and
N = the number of repayments actually made.
In our example,

$$r = \frac{2 \times 12 \times \$7,500}{\$142,500 \times (12+1)} = 9.71\%.$$

(b) Long-Term Debt
On a long-term bond issue, the interest cost to a definite maturity date is known and stated. This interest cost is related to the net proceeds to the

company of the bond issue. To determine the net proceeds, it is necessary to subtract from the price to the public, the underwriting spread and other costs of the issue.

The fact that bonds may sell at either discounts or premiums from par must also be taken into consideration. In other words, cost to maturity, not simply initial or current cost, must be considered. There is both an approximate calculation and an exact one which uses bond tables giving "yield to maturity."[3]

To illustrate the approximate method, assume that a company sells 10 percent, 25-year bonds to the public via underwriters at $1,010 for each $1,000 par value bond. Underwriting and other costs amount to $60 so that the net proceeds to the company are $950 per bond. The 10 percent coupon requires an annual interest payment of $100. Since the net proceeds are $950, but $1,000 must be paid at maturity, we may assume the difference of $50 per bond is set aside uniformly at the rate of $2 per year per bond over the 25 year life of the bonds. Thus, the total annual cost of the bonds is $102 ($100 + $2).

Only the actual interest ($100) is paid each year; the company holds the $2 it theoretically sets aside each year over the 25 year period. Thus, the company has the use of not $950, but $975—the average of the $950 originally received and the $1,000 which represents the final accumulated value of the bond-holder's investment at maturity. The cost of the bond is:

$$\frac{102}{975} = 10.46\%.$$

This same cost may be estimated via the following approximation formula:

$$\text{approximate cost} = \frac{I + \dfrac{(PV-NP)}{N}}{\dfrac{(PV + NP)}{2}}$$

where: I = the dollar amount of the annual interest payment;
PV = the amount payable at maturity (par value);
NP = the net proceeds of the issue to the firm; and
N = the number of years to maturity of the bond.

Using the figures from our preceeding example:

$$\text{approximate cost} = \frac{\$100 + \dfrac{\$1,000 - \$950}{\$25}}{(\$1,000 + \$950)/2} = 10.46\%.$$

The same formula can be used when the net proceeds provide a premium rather than a discount. Assume that the net proceeds were $1,025 instead of $950. Applying the approximation formula:

$$\text{approximate cost} = \frac{\$100 + \dfrac{(\$1,000 - \$1,025)}{\$25}}{(\$1,000 + \$1,025)/2} = 9.77\%.$$

In the exact method for computing the cost of a bond issue to the issuing firm, we recognize that the bond issue is similar to those simple capital investment projects we analyzed in Chapter 17 using discounted cash flow methods such as the internal rate of return or the net present value. In our example, the firm issues a bond and receives $950 per bond at the time of issuance. In return the firm must make annual interest payments of $100 for 25 years and repay par ($1,000 per bond) at the end of year 25 when the bond matures. The resultant cash flow stream (from the issuer's perspective) is as follows:

					-$100
					-$1,000
$950	-$100	-$100	-$100	....	-$1,100 .
ISSUANCE DATE	YEAR 1	YEAR 2	YEAR 3		YEAR 25

The exact cost of the bond to the issuing firm is the discounted rate which equates the present value of all the annual interest payments and the repayment of par value with the net proceeds ($950) received by the firm at issuance. This discount rate, as we have seen in section 17.5[2] is the internal rate of return for the bond. Algebraically, we calculate this discount rate (r) as follows:

$$950 = \frac{\$100}{(1 + r)^1} + \frac{\$100}{(1 + r)^2} + \frac{\$100}{(1 + r)^3} + \ldots + \frac{\$100}{(1 + r)^{25}} + \frac{\$1,000}{(1 + r)^{25}} .$$

Thus, the exact cost of a bond to the issuer is the bond's internal rate of return. In finance circles, we use the term yield to maturity in place of the term internal rate of return. In practice, we seldom go through the tedious algebraic calculations necessary to arrive at yield to maturity. Rather, we use bond value tables which provide the yield to maturity for varying coupon rates and maturities. These bond value tables makes quite simple, what otherwise would be an involved calculation.

The before-tax cost of long-term debt must be converted to an after-tax cost by multiplying by 1- the tax rate. The cost of capital to a firm in a bond issue is the after-tax yield to maturity on the net proceeds realized by the company. Finally, an adjustment must be made if interest rates have changed significantly from the time a bond was originally issued. Assume, for example, that 10 years ago a firm issued at par a 5 percent coupon bond maturing in 20 years and that at the present time interest rates have risen to the point where the present yield to maturity on the bond is 10 percent. The question is: should the historical 5 percent or the current 10 percent be taken as the before tax cost of debt? The answer, of course, is the current yield to maturity of 10 percent. The return expected by current creditors on the market value of debt is 10 percent, not 5 percent. Further, any additional debt floated at the present time will have to be paid for at current market rates. Thus, the current yield to maturity is the correct before-tax cost of debt, as the historical interest cost is a sunk cost and not relevant for current decision-making purposes.[4]

[2] COST OF PREFERRED STOCK

The cost of preferred stock, as is the case with the other elements of a firm's capital structure, is equal to the rate of return expected by the holders of preferred shares. The calculation of the cost of preferred stock is the least complicated of all capital structure elements because: (1) the dividend payment is specified in advance and (2) there is no stated maturity date. Thus, it becomes a simple matter to relate the annual cash outlay required to service the issue and the net proceeds.

Consider a preferred stock issue for which the annual cash dividend is $12.00 per share and the net proceeds after underwriting costs is $100 per share. The cost is calculated as follows:

$$\text{cost of preferred stock} = \frac{\text{annual cash dividends}}{\text{net proceeds}}$$

$$= \frac{\$12.00}{\$100} = 12\%.$$

This estimated cost is already an after-tax cost since preferred dividends are not tax deductible. Thus, no further adjustment need be made.

[3] COST OF COMMON STOCK

The cost of common stock is the equilibrium rate of return expected by common share owners. This is difficult to measure, however, for unlike fixed income securities (bonds and preferred stock), the return expected on common shares is dependent on unobservable expectations about future performance. Common stock can be issued either through a public offering or a rights offering. We consider each separately. In addition, we address the special problems in attempting to estimate the cost of common stock for growth companies.

(a) Publicly Offered Stock

According to one point of view, the cost of common stock may be seen as that rate that investors believe must be earned on incremental issues of stock in order to maintain the present value of their investment. For relatively stable companies, this rate is determined by dividing the earnings per share that investors expect will be earned in the future (which forms the basis for making their investment) by the current price of the share.

A more refined approach is to use, as the base, the price which investors are willing to pay for new offerings. In this approach, the cost of common stock is estimated as follows:

$$\text{Cost of common stock} = \frac{\text{Future earnings per share}}{\text{Net proceeds per share}}.$$

Using this approach commonly entails a one year time horizon to estimate future earnings per share. This estimate does not take into account the impact of any proposed projects that the firm may have under consideration. The application of this approach is demonstrated through the use of the following example.

Consider a company with prospective earnings of $10 million, 1 million shares outstanding, no debt, and a current market price per share of about $100. The market, then, is currently capitalizing prospective earnings at 10 percent, since $10/$100 = 10 percent. It decides to sell additional shares to raise $12,000,000. If it can sell new stock at $90 (10 percent underpricing) and underwriting and other costs combined come to another $10, it will net $80 per share. Thus, to raise $12 million, it will have to sell 150,000 new shares. We assume that management has estimated that it can earn at least $10 on each new share, and can thus avoid earnings dilution and maintain the investment of existing owners. Therefore the cost of the common stock is:

$$\frac{\text{Future earnings per share}}{\text{Net proceeds per share}} = \frac{\$10}{\$80} = 12.5\%.$$

The difference between the market capitalization rate and the cost of common stock is due to the underpricing and the cost of flotation. The extent of the dilution of share value because of these two factors can be measured as follows:

$$\text{Dilution factor} = \frac{\text{Market price - net proceeds}}{\text{Market price}} = \frac{100-80}{100} = 0.2.$$

The dilution factor can be related either to the market capitalization rate or to the market price of the shares to obtain the cost of common stock as follows:

$$\text{Cost of Common Stock} = \frac{\text{Market capitalization rate}}{1 - \text{dilution factor}} = \frac{10\%}{.8} = 12.5\%$$

or

$$\text{Cost of Common Stock} = \frac{E}{MP \times (1 - DF)} = \frac{\$10}{\$100 \times .8} = 12.5\%$$

where:

E = the expected earnings per share;
MP = the market price of common stock; and
DP = the dilution factor.

If the firm has not issued common stock recently, the analyst must estimate the net proceeds likely in the event of an issue. He may use, for example, a recent offering of a comparable company with a similar capital structure to gauge the cost of underwriting, other expenses, and underpricing. He could then adjust the market price of his firm's stock by these costs to estimate the net proceeds per share.

(b) Rights Offerings

The same technique may be applied in the analysis of the cost of capital involved in a rights offering. Indeed, whether shares are sold directly by means of a rights offering, the cost of capital will be affected only to the extent that different underpricing and issue costs are involved. Assume in the previous example, that management decides upon a rights offering to raise the required $12,000,000. After analysis, it decides to offer the shares at $64, a deep discount from the market price of $100, to ensure the success of the offering. Costs of issuance, including a standby underwriting, are estimated at $4 per share, making the net proceeds to the company $60 per share. Thus the company will have to sell 200,000 shares to raise the $12 million. Since there are 1 million shares currently outstanding, each shareholder will receive the right to subscribe to one new share for each five shares held.

The theoretical market value of a share after the exercise of rights is:

$$\frac{(\$100 \times 5) + \$64}{6} = \frac{\$564}{6} = \$94.$$

A shareholder who previously held 5 shares valued at $500 will now hold 6 shares valued at $564; the market value of the shares will fall from $100 to $94. The market capitalizes this company's earnings at 10 percent and it will therefore now require $9.40 per share rather than $10 in earnings to maintain the shareholder's position. Since the total earnings on the 5 shares originally held amounted to $50, the new investment will have to earn at least $6.40 per share. This may be shown as follows:

$(6 \times \$9.40) - (5 \times \$10) = \$16.40.$

The cost of common stock can now be computed as follows:

$$\frac{\text{Required earnings per share}}{\text{Net proceeds per share}} = \frac{\$6.40}{\$60} = 10.67\%.$$

A new project will have to earn this cost of capital of 10.67 percent to provide earnings of $9.40 per share for shares whose market value is now $94. This may be seen below:

- Total number of shares outstanding after sale of common stock   1,200,000
- Earnings per share needed to maintain a market price of $94 $9.40
- Total Earnings needed $11,280,000
- Earnings before expansion $10,000,000
- Minimum earnings required from new project $ 1,280,000
- Required rate of return on new capital $\dfrac{\$1,280,000}{\$12,000,000} = 10.67\%$

The application of this procedure produces results that may appear to be anomalous. When the publicly offered stock is sold at a price that provides the company with the cash receipts of $80 a share, the cost of the equity was determined to be 12.5 percent; but when it was sold, through rights, at a price that returned only $60 a share to the company, the calculated cost of common stock was actually lower, 10.67 percent. The reason for this diverse relationship is embodied in the differing influences of two of the major ingredients affecting the cost of common stock—underpricing and flotation costs.

The degree of underpricing is an important consideration with respect to a public offering of stock. This is so because to maintain the present value of the stockholder's investment, the company must sustain the same level of earnings on less money, thereby increasing the cost of capital. In the previous illustration, when the market price was $100 the company had to obtain $10 of earnings on the $90 ($80 after allowing for flotation costs) of proceeds from the sale of its stock. The degree of underpricing is irrelevant with respect to a rights offering because the earnings required on the new shares bear the same relationship to their original market price. In our illustration, the required earnings of $6.40 per new share subscribed at $64 provides the same ratio as the earnings of $10 per share on the previous $100 price of the old stock.[5]

From a different point of view, the stockholder, through a rights offering, is able to obtain another share of stock at $64 per share. If the company earns 10 percent on this price, it would have earnings of $6.40, the required amount. The company has a somewhat higher cost of capital than 10 percent because of the dilution factor, which results from the expenses of $4 per share involved in the rights offering. Thus, the dilution factor is

$$\frac{\$64 - \$60}{\$64} = \frac{\$4}{\$64} = .062.$$

When this dilution factor is related to the market capitalization rate of 10 percent, the result is 10.67 percent, as is seen below:

$$\frac{10\%}{1 - .062} = \frac{10\%}{.938} = 10.67\%.$$

In summary, while the degree of underpricing does not affect the cost of common stock in a rights offering, it does influence a public offering, thereby tending to keep the costs of rights financing relatively lower. Flotation expenses affect both rights and public offerings, but they are likely to be proportionately less in the former case, once more benefitting the costs of rights financing. The reason for this lower charge is that with a relatively successful corporation, stockholders are likely to respond favorably to a rights offering, thereby reducing the risks and cutting the relative costs of this form of financing.

(c) Growth Company Stock

Estimation of the cost of common stock for a growth company represents a complicated task which has challenged financial managers and academicians alike. The common stock of a growth company is likely to sell at a higher price relative to current earnings. The resultant earnings/price ratio would provide an unrealistic cost of capital criterion on which to evaluate investment opportunities. A paradox would result of an unusually low cost of capital target for growth companies that are earning unusually high rates on their investments. If such a procedure were followed, the growth company would shortly lose this characteristic as it took on low return investments made possible by the low cost of capital criterion. For example, a rapidly growing company with an earnings/price ratio of, say, 5 percent would, if it used this rate as its cost of capital, take on new investments as long as their expected return was above this figure. If it followed this policy, the firm would soon lose its "rapidly growing" status. In these circumstances, the earnings/price ratio is a poor expression of the cost of equity capital. Accordingly, an adjustment is necessary to take into consideration the element of growth. In such cases, it has been argued, that relying upon the dividend stream is desirable. This is because using earnings would result in a double counting of the contribution to retained earnings and the addition to the income stream from reinvestment of retained earnings. Others have suggested the use of the capital asset pricing model to estimate the cost of common stock for growth companies. In the ensuing paragraphs we discuss both approaches.

[i] Dividend Stream Approach: In the dividend stream approach, the cost of common stock is estimated to be the discount rate that equates the expected dividend stream, in perpetuity, to the current market price of the common stock.[6] The mathematical formula embodying this approach is as follows:

$$k_e = \frac{D_0}{P_0} + g$$

where: k_e = the cost of common stock;

D_0 = the current cash dividend per share;

P_0 = the current market price per share; and

g = the expected annual percentage rate of increase in future dividends expressed as a decimal fraction.

The following example illustrates this approach: Assume that a company's stock is selling at $80 per share, that the current dividend is $4 per share, and that the dividend is expected to increase by 3 percent a year. Then

$$k_e = \frac{\$4}{\$80} + .03$$

$k_e = .05 + .03$

$k_e = .08$ or 8%.

In this approach three important initial assumptions are made:

- dividends grow at a constant rate in perpetuity;
- investors value the common stock exclusively on the basis of the potential or expected dividends they will receive; and
- the payout ratio (i.e., the ratio of dividends to earnings) is constant.

The dividend stream approach also assumes a constant growth rate in expected earnings as well as dividends. Because the analyst usually relies on historical data to estimate future trends, it is advisable to focus directly on the earnings growth rate. Thus, the procedure for determining the cost of common stock for a growth company entails the following 3 steps:

- applying an estimated average dividend payout ratio to the current level of earnings to obtain the current basic dividend payment;
- dividing this basic payment by the current market price of the common stock to obtain the current dividend yield; and
- adding to the dividend yield a factor representing the expected future growth rate of earnings.[7]

[ii] Capital Asset Pricing Model Approach: The other method of computing the cost of common stock for growth companies is to use the so-called Security Market Line (SML). According to this method (see Chapter 2 for more details), the cost of common equity, K_e, can be estimated from the following equation:

$$K_e = R_F + [E(R_m) - R_F] \frac{COV(R_j, R_m)}{\sigma_m^2}$$

where: K_e = the required return on a given security;

R_F = the risk free rate of interest (usually taken to be the yield on 90 day Treasury Bills);

$E(R_m)$ = the expected return on the market portfolio of common stocks (usually estimated on the basis of a broad market index such as the Standard and Poors 500 Common Stock Index);

σ_m^2 = the variance of returns on the market portfolio of common stocks; and

$COV(R_j, R_m)$ = the covariance of the common stock's returns with the returns on the market portfolio.

The term $\dfrac{COV(R_j, R_m)}{\sigma_m^2}$ is often more popularly referred to as the beta (β_j) value of common stock j. The above equation can therefore be rewritten as:

$$K_e = R_F + \beta_j [E(R_m) - R_F]$$

In order to use this equation to estimate the cost of common equity for a growth company, we must know the following:

- the risk free rate of interest;
- the β value for the firm's common stock; and
- the expected return on the market portfolio of common stocks.

If we find the β value for a growth stock to be 1.5, the risk free rate .10, and the expected return on the market portfolio as .12, then the cost of common stock for the firm would be estimated as:

$$K_e = .10 + 1.5 [.12 - .10]$$
$$K_e = .13 \text{ or } 13\%.$$

This is to say that a rational, risk averse investor, would require a rate of return of 13% on such a security, and, therefore, that is the firm's cost of common stock.

It might be asked whether there are any advantages to making accept-reject capital budgeting decisions by means of the SML as opposed to the Weighted Average Cost of Capital (WACC) discussed later in this chapter. The WACC is a cost of capital figure provided by combining or weighting the individual costs to obtain an overall cost of capital. SML takes into account the risks of individual investment projects that the firm is considering, while the WACC does not. This can be seen by reference to Figure 19.2.

508

FIGURE 19.2   *The weighted average cost of capital (WACC) vs. the security market line (SML) in capital budgeting*

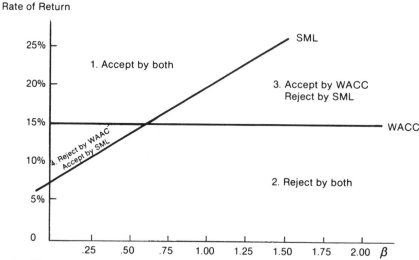

In Figure 19.2 both the SML and the WACC would come to the same decisions in the case of projects 1 and 2. (1 would be accepted and 2 would be rejected by each method.) Three would be accepted by the WACC, but rejected according to the SML, while project 4 would be accepted by the SML and rejected by the WACC. Evidently, the WACC does not account for variations in the riskiness of different projects. This method tends to reject some low risk projects, such as 4, that deserve acceptance because their rates of return adequately compensate for their low risk. Similarly, the WACC accepts some high risk projects, such as 3, whose expected rates of return are greater than the WACC, but not enough so in order to compensate for the high degree of risk on the project.

One of the primary problems with the use of the SML to measure the cost of equity capital is that as the result of the volatility of stock market returns over time, the computed cost of equity capital figure is considerably influenced by the choice of the observation period which is employed. For example, while a longer observation period for computing returns and risks will dampen out short-run fluctuations in stock market returns and risks, use of such a period will camouflage the changes which may be taking place in the relevant variables. This method can thus force one to choose between a short observation period, which often results in using relevant but inaccurate information, and a long period that can potentially result in an accurate measurement of irrelevant information.[8]

Another more serious problem with the use of the SML is the instability of β over time. This is particularly so since β is generally more stable over time for portfolios than for individual securities, and we must deal with an individual security in applying the SML to capital budgeting decisions. Nevertheless, there are a number of instances, particularly in the case of utility rate cases, of the SML being used by financial managers and regulatory authorities.[9]

[4] COST OF RETAINED EARNINGS

Companies raise equity capital by retaining earnings as well as by selling shares of common stock. Some managers regard retained earnings as cost free. The absurdity of this convention is clearly exposed when we recognize that there is an opportunity cost to stockholders. In essence, shareholders want the firm to retain earnings (as opposed to paying them out as cash dividends) only if the firm can earn a return which exceeds the after-tax return stockholders could themselves achieve by reinvesting the dividends. Were companies to retain earnings despited limited capital investment opportunities, investor displeasure would probably force a decline in the market price of the firm's common stock.

In the dividend payout approach to the "costing" of retained earnings, the marginal income tax rate of shareholders must be taken into account. For example, a company with a 10 percent cost of common equity strives to achieve a minimum rate of return on invested capital of 10 percent. Thus, the financial manager calculates the after tax rate at which shareholders would have to invest cash dividends in order to equal the 10 percent return that the firm could earn on the same funds. Unfortunately, since the marginal tax rates for individual shareholders vary broadly, this approach leads to a dead end.[10]

A more plausible approach is to recognize that the corporation might commit the retained earnings to external investments which offer an income-risk package similar to that of its existing assets. Based upon this view, it seems logical to assume that the cost of retained earnings is what could be earned in comparable uses outside the company—the company's opportunity costs, in the economist's terminology.

Another plausible alternative shifts the emphasis from opportunity costs to consideration of the sources of funds. In the hypothetical case of a company which has paid out all its earnings as cash dividends, the firm would have to undertake new external financing to replace distributed earnings. If this new financing were in the form of new equity capital, the cost would be equal to the cost of common equity. Since virtually all firms rely on equity capital to some degree, we are inclined to favor this approach. Thus, we feel that the cost of retained earnings is the same as the cost of financing by means of new common stock.

One might ask: If retained earnings should be regarded as having the same cost as new equity, why do companies apparently prefer the former? We believe that the answer lies in factors of convenience and availability rather than cost. When retained earnings are used, the uncertainties of a public financing are eliminated; the delay caused by preparing registration statements and prospectises is avoided; and the difficulty of gauging market conditions is bypassed. Management uses funds as part of its recurring activities. It does not draw fine lines of distinction between funds obtained directly from stockholders or from retained earnings. In effect, they both represent capital to be invested in the same type of projects at similar rates. Finally, as a practical matter, if the overall cost of capital is determined by using market values as weights, (as discussed below) the need for determining a separate rate and weight for retained earnings disappears, as both are embodied in common stock values.[11]

19.3 THE OVERALL COMPANY COST OF CAPITAL

Having determined the cost of each element of the capital structure, we might ask the question—can any of these costs be used individually to represent the company's cost of capital or must an overall cost figure be computed?

[1] SINGLE ELEMENT OF THE CAPITAL STRUCTURE

To presume that the cost of capital is the cost of the particular financing element employed, is to fall prey to what might be called the fallacy of the marginal cost of capital. While marginal analysis correctly employs a matching of marginal returns and costs, it is inappropriate to simply identify the cost of the element employed as the marginal cost of capital. When a company contemplates financing by using a particular capital structure element, the cost of which is perceptibly lower than all others (usually debt), it may be inclined to call the cost of this element the firm's cost of capital. Nevertheless, such a designation would be inaccurate. Use of any particular element in the capital structure may change the cost of the other capital elements. Since implicit costs are present that are apart from the explicit costs of the individual capital elements considered earlier in this chapter, by taking the cost of the lowest cost element in the capital structure as the cost of capital, one fails to consider such implicit costs. The cost measurements discussed previously are explicit costs for a particular degree of financial leverage. Once this degree changes, implicit costs result so that the cost of the lowest element is not the full cost of capital.

Senior debt may be used to raise capital for a particular project, but there is no justification for comparing the cost of capital for bonds alone with the projected rate of return of the project. Unless the company has an adequate equity base, the bonds cannot be sold. Earnings coverage, mainly derived from the equity base, must be adequate for the bonds to be marketed successfully.

[2] WEIGHTED AVERAGE COST OF CAPITAL

As discussed in 19.4, a firm's overall cost of capital and the costs of individual components of capital (debt, preferred stock, common stock, and retained earnings) may be affected by changes in a firm's capital structure. Hence, consideration should be given to the weights of the individual elements of capital in the calculation of the overall costs of capital.[12] Three basic possibilities exist for establishing the required weights:

- weighting by theoretical values;
- weighting by book values; and
- weighting by market values.

These are discussed below.

(a) Weighting by Theoretical Values

In this method, we could use as weights the proportions based on the desired (as opposed to the actual) capital structure or on the funds required to move from the present to the desired capital structure. The difficulty with each of these approaches is that they involve mixing amounts drawn from different time spectrums. In these methods, we use present costs for the individual components of capital structure and future values for the capital structure to establish the weights. The deficiency of this approach is apparent because the costs of individual components of the capital structure may change as the firm's capital structure itself changes. Therefore, we cannot match the future weights with current costs.

(b) Weighting by Book Values

In using book values as weights, one multiplies the proportion of each element in the firm's capital structure by its individual respective cost. The resulting formulation for the WACC is as follows:

$$\text{WACC} = \frac{D}{C}(Kd) + \frac{P.S.}{C}(Kp.s.) + \frac{C.S.}{C}(Kc.s.) + \frac{R.E.}{C}(Kr.e.)$$

where:

WACC = the weighted average cost of capital;
  D = the book value of debt;
 P.S. = the book value of preferred stock;
 C.S. = the book value of common stock;
 R.E. = the book value of retained earnings;
  C = the book value of total capitalization (C = D + P.S. + C.S. + R.E.)
 Kd = the marginal cost of debt;
Kp.s. = the marginal cost of preferred stock;
Kc.s. = the marginal cost of common stock; and
Kr.e. = the marginal cost of retained earnings

Consider a company whose balance sheet is presented in Figure 19.3. Given the firm's current capital structure and the following costs for the individual components of capital (10% cost of short-term debt, 15% cost of long-term debt, 14% cost of preferred stock, 15% cost of common stock and retained earnings), we can compute the WACC using book values as weights. The computation is as follows:

Despite the ease of calculation, the financial manager should be careful in the use of book weights to estimate the firm's WACC. Book values may be influenced by managerial choice among the various accounting alternatives. Thus two companies might be valued equally in the securities markets, yet a use of different accounting principles by each firm might make its respective costs of capital appear different when book values are the basis of weights.

Additionally, book values represent historical events, akin to sunk costs, and are not relevant for decision-making purposes. Moreover, the book value of common stock is influenced by both its market price at the time the company chose to go public and by the price at the time of subsequent common stock sales. Yet, the time in the past when a company chose to go public has little relevance in determining its present cost of capital. By using market determined parameters in computing the cost of each individual element in the capital structure and by using book values as the weighting

FIGURE 19.3 *ABC Corporation balance sheet as of 12/31/X1*

Assets		Liabilities and Stockholders' Equity	
Current Assets	$ 500,000	Short-term debt	$ 200,000
		Long-term debt	300,000
Fixed Assets	500,000	Preferred stock (10,000 shares outstanding, $10.00 par value)	100,000
		Common Stock (20,000 shares outstanding, $10.00 par value)	200,000
		Retained earnings	200,000
Total Assets	$1,000,000	Total Liabilities and Stockholders' Equity	$1,000,000

Component of Capital	Cost of Individual Capital Component	Book Weight		
Short-term debt	.10	x 0.2	=	.020
Long-term debt	.15	x 0.3	=	.045
Preferred stock	.14	x 0.1	=	.014
Common stock	.15	x 0.2	=	.030
Retained earnings	.15	x 0.2	=	.030
		WACC	=	.139

mechanism to combine them, one is matching and mixing unlike concepts—book and market values—and the outcome is not likely to be very meaningful.

(c) Weighting by Market Values

Market values are the true measure of the worth of a firm's investments. The returns on these investments, which are relevant to the company's owners and creditors, are based on market rather than book values. Therefore, it seems appropriate that the weighting mechanism when computing a firm's WACC should be based upon the market values of its outstanding securities rather than their book values.

In this approach the weights are simply determined by multiplying the current market price of each traded security by the amount of each security outstanding and then dividing the product by the total market value of a firm's capital structure. For untraded items, such as privately held debt or preferred stock, market prices must be approximated. For short-term liabilities, where market and book values are likely to be quite close, book values may be used. This weighting method results in changes in the cost of capital as market values change. This appears realistic because it reflects the changing market and environmental conditions to which all firms are subject.

We now illustrate the WACC computation using market values as weights for the ABC Corporation, whose balance sheet was presented in Figure 19.3. Assume that the market values of ABC's debt approximates its book value and that the current market price of both its preferred and common stock is $50.00 per share. The composite cost of capital would then be determined as follows:

Capital Structure at Market Values	$	%
Short-term debt	$ 200,000	10
Long-term debt	300,000	15
Preferred stock	500,000	25
Common stock	1,000,000	50
	$2,000,000	100

Component of Capital	Cost of Individual Capital Component	Market Weight
Short-term debt	.10	x .10 = .0010
Long-term debt	.15	x .15 = .0225
Preferred stock	.14	x .25 = .0350
Common stock[13]	.15	x .50 = .0750
		WACC = .1335

Thus, when market values are used as weights, the WACC of the ABC Corporation is 13.5 percent. When book values are used, the WACC is 13.9 percent.

19.4   FINANCIAL LEVERAGE

The financial manager can cause (within limits) his firm's WACC and component capital costs to rise or fall by changing the firm's capital structure. Most practitioners and academicians believe that the choice of financing mix (i.e. debt versus equity) significantly influences a firm's capital costs. In the financial literature, however, there has been a sharp controversy over the issue. The argument was initiated a number of years ago by Modigliani and Miller, who contended that the firm's WACC was independent of changes in its capital structure or in its degree of financial leverage (percent of debt in the capital structure).[14] Initially, this thesis won over a number of academicians, but the practical business community seemed never to have been persuaded by this position. Today, the academic community has, to a considerable extent, largely recognized that the Modigliani-Miller position is valid only under highly restrictive and unrealistic assumptions.[15]

We now proceed to illustrate and explain the relationship between capital structure and WACC. It is clear that, as a result of interest being tax deductible, the federal government, in effect, funds part of a leveraged firm's interest expense. As a result, the leveraged firm has more funds available for distribution to its creditors and shareholders (all other things being equal) than does the unlevered firm. In effect, interest payments provide a tax shield which inures to the benefit of the shareholders of the levered firm and, for low to moderate amounts of debt can be expected to result (other things being equal), in a higher share value and a lower WACC than for the unlevered firm. Figure 19.4 illustrates this concept.

FIGURE 19.4 *WACC at low to moderate levels of financial leverage*

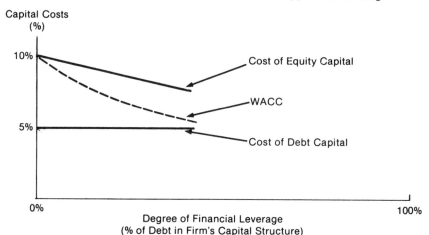

In Figure 19.4, the WACC declines as the degree of financial leverage in the capital structure increases for two reasons: (1) we are adding more "lower cost" debt which is replacing the "higher cost" equity capital in the firm's capital structure and (2) the cost of equity capital is falling with increasing use of financial leverage because of the positive effect that increased debt financing has on earnings per share.

At high levels of financial leverage, however, creditors and stockholders become significantly concerned about potential bankruptcy and its attendant costs. The benefits to earnings per share of the tax deductibility of interest payments becomes less important than the absolute level of debt service requirements facing the firm. Specifically, bondholders and stockholders become concerned that any subsequent downturn in sales revenues may jeopardize the firm's ability to meet debt service requirements with the necessary margin of safety. The bankruptcy costs of concern can be divided into two categories: (1) explicit costs and (2) implicit costs. Explicit costs include:

- trustee's fees;
- accountant's fees; and
- legal fees and other reorganization costs.

Implicit costs include:

- higher interest costs;
- higher cost of equity capital; and
- deteriorating relations with workers, customers, and suppliers.

Figure 19.5 demonstrates the adverse impact of high financial leverage on WACC. As shown, after the degree of financial leverage in the firm's capital structure exceeds what investors deem to be a prudent level, the WACC rises because investor concerns about bankruptcy costs exceed the benefits from the tax deductibility of interest payments. Notice that WACC rises because both the cost of debt capital and the cost of equity capital rise with increasing financial leverage beyond the prudent level.

FIGURE 19.5   *Relationship between WACC and the degree of financial leverage*

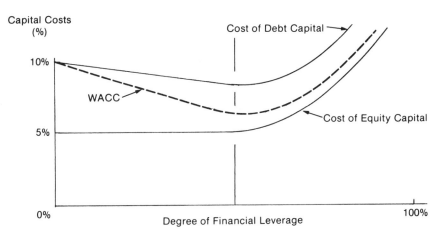

The significance of Figure 19.5 to the financial manager is that it suggests the existence of a specific capital structure (degree of financial leverage) which will minimize the firm's WACC. We refer to this specific capital structure as the firm's optimal capital structure. Recently, however, more and more academicians and practitioners are accepting a range of capital structures as opposed to a specific point, as being optimal.[16] Figure 19.6 illustrates such a range.

FIGURE 19.6   *Optimal range of capital structure for the firm*

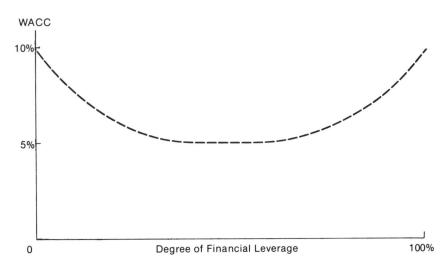

If such a shape is representative of a firm's financial leverage, cost of capital relationship, it gives the financial manager far more maneuverability in his capital structure decision than would be the case if a single point represented the firm's optimal capital structure.

Appendix A to this chapter provides a further illustration of the relationship between firm capital structure and WACC. This illustration consists of a numerical example.

The concept of an optimal range of capital structure is also supported by a good deal of empirical evidence. Most of this evidence shows that the degree of financial leverage for companies in the same industry cluster about a specific value and that there are statistically significant differences between the average financial leverage from one industry to the next.[17] If financial managers cluster their capital structures rather closely to their industry's means they are not behaving as though they are indifferent to their firm's capital structure and they thus seem to believe that this structure does indeed influence the cost of capital.

19.5   CHAPTER SUMMARY

In this chapter, we discussed the concept of a company's cost of capital and its importance to the firm's capital budgeting process. We analyzed the costs of the important individual components of capital and provided alternative methods for weighting these costs to arrive at an overall or weighted average cost of capital for the firm. Finally, we addressed the relationship between a firm's capital structure and its overall cost of capital. Specifically, we looked at the concept that the financial manager can minimize the overall cost of capital by maintaining the firm's capital structure within a limited range.

FOOTNOTES

1. In fact, the degree of debate surrounding this term has reached such a fever pitch that some authorities have suggested dropping the term "cost of capital" from the jargon of finance. (See Charles W. Haley and Lawrence D. Schall, "Problems With the Concept of the Cost of Capital," *Journal of Financial and Quantitative Analysis,* December 1978, pp. 847-853.

2. The tax rate is zero for a firm with a net loss for tax purposes. For a firm in this situation, the after-tax cost of debt is equal to the before-tax cost.

3. A further complication is added when the bonds are convertible. In this case the after-tax cost of the convertible bond can be found by the use of the following expression:

$$M = \sum_{t=1}^{n} \frac{C(1-t_c)}{(1+K_c)^t} + \frac{TV}{(1+K_c)^n}$$

where:

M = the price of the convertible bond;
C = the annual interest rate in dollars;
TV = the expected terminal value of the bond in year n;
n = the expected number of years that the bond will be outstanding;
t_c = the marginal corporate tax rate; and
K_c = the after-tax cost of the convertible bond.
(J. Fred Weston and Eugene F. Brigham, *Managerial Finance,* 6th ed., The Dryden Press, Hinsdale, Illinois, 1978, p. 697.)

4. For some additional complexities relevant to the cost of debt, see Fred D. Arditti and Haim Levy, "The Weighted Average Cost of Capital as a Cutoff Rate: A Critical Analysis of the Classical Textbook Weighted Average," *Financial*

Management, Fall 1977, pp. 24-34, and Andrew H. Chen, "Recent Developments in the Cost of Debt Capital," *Journal of Finance,* June 1978, pp. 863-877.

5. The degree of underpricing may become relevant, however, if price movements in the stock and the rights differ appreciably from the theoretical values suggested by traditional analysis.

6. See Harold Bierman, Jr. and Seymour Smidt, *The Capital Budgeting Decision,* New York. Macmillan 4th ed., 1975.

7. For an analysis of two alternate explanations of the cost of equity capital as equal to the common share yield or dependent upon the firm's investment rate of return, see Myron J. Gordon and L. I. Gould, "The Cost of Equity Capital: A Reconsideration," *Journal of Finance,* June 1978, pp. 849-861, and for additional detail on the cost of equity capital see, Myron J. Gordon and L. I. Gould, "The Cost of Equity Capital With Personal Income Taxes and Flotation Costs," *Journal of Finance,* September 1978, pp. 1201-1212.

8. Robert C. Higgins, *Financial Management: Theory and Applications,* Chicago, Science Research Associates, Inc., 1977, pp. 122-123.

9. In this connection see, Eugene F. Brigham and Roy L. Crum, "On the Use of the CAPM in Public Utility Rate Cases," *Financial Management,* Summer 1977, pp. 7-15.

10. Another possibility is to apply the expression

$$K_{RE} = \frac{D(1 - t_s)}{P}$$

where:

K_{RE} = the cost of retained earnings;

D = the current dividend;

t_s = the marginal tax bracket of the average stockholder, and

P = the current market price.

The rationale here is that retained earnings represent an opportunity cost to stockholders in the form of dividends foregone. Stockholders can always get P by selling. (The capital gains tax is disregarded because we assume there is an equal chance of incurring a capital loss.) Instead they accept $D(1 - t_s)$. Thus,

$$\frac{D(1 - t_s)}{P}$$

might be taken as the cost to them of remaining stockholders. However, the variability of marginal tax brackets of stockholders makes this method difficult to apply.

11. With respect to so called "free" capital, represented by the spontaneous sources of credit on which no interest is charged (accounts payable, wages payable, taxes payable and other accruals), it usually makes relatively little difference whether or not this item is explicitly included in calculating the cost of capital, provided appropriate adjustments are made. These "free" funds are normally netted out against the required investment outlay in the computation of the rate of return. In this case they can be ignored in the cost of capital calculation since we want to avoid double counting and they already have been employed in the calculation of the rate of return.

12. There is also controversy regarding the desirability of using the WACC. For example, in Raymond R. Reilly and William E. Wecker, "The Weighted Average Cost of Capital," *Journal of Financial and Quantitative Analysis,* January 1973, pp. 123-126, the authors attempt to show that the WACC is a biased estimate of

518

the true cost of capital (TCC). Linke and Kim (Charles M. Linke and Moon M. Kim, "More on the Weighted Average Cost of Capital: A Comment and Analysis," December 1974, pp. 1067-1080), however, correct an error in the logic of Reilly and Wecker and demonstrate the conditions for the use of the WACC as a proxy for the TCC. This is when the capital structure is kept constant. In addition, Nantell and Carlson (Timothy J. Nantell and C. Robert Carlson), "The Cost of Capital as a Weighted Average," *Journal of Finance,* December 1975, pp. 1343-1355) show that the WACC is usable for making investment decisions if the cash flows are consistently specified. However, Arditti and Levy (Fred D. Arditti and Haim Levy, "The Weighted Average Cost of Capital as a Cutoff Rate: A Critical Analysis of the Classical Textbook Weighted Average," *Financial Management,* Fall 1977, pp. 24-34) argue that the conventional WACC definition is wrong because it does not properly include interest tax subsidies. However, a number of subsequent articles all indicate that Arditti and Levy made the error of not maintaining their own constant capital structure assumption in their derivations. (Kenneth J. Boudreaux and Hugh W. Long, "The Weighted Average Cost of Capital as a Cutoff Rate: A Further Analysis," *Financial Management,* Summer 1979, pp. 7-14; John R. Ezzell and R. Burr Porter, "Correct Specification of the Cost of Capital and Net Present Value," *Financial Management,* Summer 1979, pp. 15-17; Moshe Ben-Horim, "Comment on the Weighted Average Cost of Capital as a Cutoff Rate," *Financial Management,* Summer 1979, pp. 18-21; and Alan C. Shapiro, "In Defense of the Traditional Weighted Average Cost of Capital as a Cutoff Rate," *Financial Management,* Summer 1979, pp. 22-23).

13. Retained earnings are reflected in the market value of the common stock.

14. See Franco Modigliani and M. H. Miller, "The Cost of Capital, Corporation Finance, and the Theory of Investment," *American Economic Review,* June, 1958, pp. 251-297 and "Corporate Income Taxes and the Cost of Capital: A Correction," *Ibid.* June, 1963, pp. 433-442.

15. Another difficulty with the Modigliani-Miller position is that it implicitly assumes that the capital markets possess full information about the activities of firms. But if managers possess inside information, then the choice of a capital structure signals information to the capital markets. As the markets move toward equilibrium, the inferences drawn from these signals will be validated. To the extent this occurs, the values of firms will rise with leverage since increasing leverage increases the market's perception of value. (Stephen A. Ross, "The Determination of Financial Structure: The Incentive—Signalling Approach," *Bell Journal of Economics,* Spring 1977, pp. 23-40.

16. J. Fred Weston and Eugene F. Brigham, *Managerial Finance,* 6th ed., Hinsdale, Illinois, The Dryden Press, 1978, pp. 757-758.

17. For a sample of such evidence, see Eli Schwarz and J. Richard Aronson, "Some Surrogate Evidence in Support of the Concept of Optimal Capital Structure," *The Journal of Finance,* March 1967, pp. 10-18; and David F. Scott, Jr. and John D. Martin, "Industry Influence on Financial Structure," *Financial Management,* Spring 1975, pp. 67-73; David F. Scott, Jr. "Evidence on the Importance of Financial Structure," *Financial Management,* Summer 1972, pp. 45-50; and Michael G. Ferri and Wesley H. Jones, "Determinants of Financial Structure: A New Methodological Approach," *The Journal of Finance,* June 1979, pp. 631-644.

SUGGESTED READINGS

Arzac, Enrique and Matityahu Marcus, "Flotation Cost Allowance in Rate of Return Regulation," *Journal of Finance,* December 1981.

Boudreaux, Kenneth J. and Hugh W. Long, "The Weighted Average Cost of Capital as a Cutoff Rate: A Further Analysis," *Financial Management,* Summer 1979.

Ben-Horim, Moshe, "Comment on the Weighted Average Cost of Capital as a Cutoff Rate, *Financial Management,* Summer 1979.

Bierman, Harold, Jr. and Seymour Smidt, *The Capital Budgeting Decision,* 5th ed., New York: MacMillan, 1980.

Booth, Laurence D., "Capital Structure, Taxes, and the Cost of Capital," *Quarterly Review of Economics and Business,* Autumn 1980.

Chen, Andrew H., "Recent Developments in the Cost of Debt Capital," *Journal of Finance,* June 1978.

Corcoran, Patrick J. and Leonard G. Sahling, "Cost of Capital: How High Is It?" *Federal Reserve Bank of New York Quarterly Review,* Summer 1982.

Dimson, Elroy and Paul Marsh, "Calculating the Cost of Capital," *Long Range Planning,* April 1982.

Ellitt, Grover S., "Analyzing the Cost of Capital," *Management Accounting,* December 1980.

Elliot, J. Walter, "Cost of Capital and U.S. Capital Investment: A Test of Alternative Concepts," *Journal of Finance,* September 1980.

Fizzell, John R. and R. Burr Porter, "Correct Specification of the Cost of Capital and Net Present Value," *Financial Management,* Summer 1979.

Fuller, Russell J. and Halbert S. Kerr, "Estimating the Divisional Cost of Capital: An Analysis of the Pure-Play Technique," *Journal of Finance,* December 1981.

Gordan, Myron J. and L. I. Gould, "The Cost of Equity Capital: A Reconsideration," *Journal of Finance,* June 1978.

——— and ———, "The Cost of Equity Capital With Personal Income Taxes and Flotation Costs," *Journal of Finance,* September 1978.

Gup, B. E. and S. W. Norwood III, "Divisional Cost of Capital: A Practical Approach," *Financial Management,* Spring 1982.

Haley, Charles W. and Lawrence D. Schall, "Problems With the Concept of the Cost of Capital," *Journal of Financial and Quantitative Analysis,* December 1978.

Kim, E. Han, "Miller's Equilibrium, Shareholder Leverage Clienteles, and Optimal Capital Structure," *Journal of Finance,* May 1982.

Kirsten, J.B., "Incremental Costs of Capital and a Reasonable Rate of Return," *Public Utilities Fortnightly,* July 5, 1979.

Maus, William J., "How to Calculate the Cost of Capital in a Privately Owned Company," *Management Accounting,* June 1980.

Modigliani, Franco and M. H. Miller, "The Cost of Capital, Corporation Finance and the Theory of Investment," *American Economic Review,* June 1958.

——— and ———, "Taxes and the Cost of Capital: A Correction," *American Economic Review,* June 1963.

Patterson, C. S., "Issue Costs in the Estimation of the Cost of Equity Capital," *Public Utilities Fortnightly,* July 16, 1981.

Schipper, Katherine and Rex Thompson, "Common Stocks as Hedges Against Shifts in the Consumption or Investment Opportunity Set," *The Journal of Business,* April 1981.

Schwartz, Eli and J. Richard Aronson, "Some Surrogate Evidence in Support of the Concept of Optimal Capital Structure," *Journal of Finance,* March 1967.

Shapiro, Alan C., "In Defense of the Traditional Weighted Average Cost of Capital as a Cutoff Rate," *Financial Management,* Summer 1979.

Solomon, Ezzra, "Leverage and the Cost of Capital," *The Journal of Finance,* May 1963.

Van Horne, James C., "An Application of the Capital Asset Pricing Model to Divisional Required Returns," *Financial Management,* Spring 1980.

FIGURE 19.7 *Effect of financial leverage on WACC*[a]

Stage	Market Value of Bonds (D)	Pre-Tax Average Cost of Debt Capital (Kd)	After-Tax Average Cost of Debt Capital[b] (1 − T)Kd	Average Cost of Equity Capital[c] Ke	Market Value of Common Stock (C.S.)	Total Market Value of Bonds and Stock[d] (C)	Financial Leverage (D/C)	After-Tax Combined Cost of Capital[e] (WACC)
0	$ 0	—	—	10.0%	$50	$ 50	0	10.0%
1	10	4.00%	2.00%	10.5	55	65	.15	9.2
2	20	4.00	2.00	11.0	60	80	.25	8.8
3	30	4.00	2.00	11.5	64	94	.32	8.5
4	40	4.25	2.13	13.0	63	103	.39	8.8
5	50	4.60	2.30	14.5	61	111	.45	9.0
6	60	5.00	2.50	16.5	58	118	.51	9.4
7	70	5.43	2.71	19.0	53	123	.57	9.7

[a] This table has been drawn without the specific inclusion of implicit bankruptcy penalties as debt increases. Greater debt means a greater risk of bankruptcy, in addition to the greater risk of fluctuating earnings.

[b] Assuming a corporate income tax rate of 50 percent.

[c] Equity capitalization rate after taxes.

[d] Dollars in millions.

[e] WACC = D/C [(1 − T)Kd] + (C.S./C) Ke.

1 Additionally, it is assumed that, internally, there is no change in the risk position of the firm within the industry or in the riskiness of the industry within the economy. It is also assumed that, externally, capital market conditions do not change the cost relationships between debt and equity at varying levels of leverage.

APPENDIX A:
EXAMPLE ILLUSTRATING THE RELATIONSHIP BETWEEN A FIRM'S CAPITAL STRUCTURE AND ITS WEIGHTED AVERAGE COST OF CAPITAL

As discussed in this chapter, the financial manager can raise or lower his firm's cost of capital by changing its capital structure. This situation is demonstrated in Figure 19.7. In this Figure we can observe the effect of increasing financial leverage on the WACC.

As we have noted, with an all equity capital structure, the WACC equals the cost of equity capital which, in this case, is 10 percent. As debt is added and the leverage ratio rises, the WACC falls. Management can achieve this effect in the range from pure equity to the optimal capital structure. Within this range, lower cost debt increments are being averaged in with higher cost equity, reducing the WACC.

In Figure 19.7 the point of optimality is 32 percent leverage. At this level $30 million of bonds have been added to the original $50 million of equity. The market value of the common stock had advanced to $64 million, the total market value of bonds and stock amounts to $94 million, and the WACC has been reduced to 8.5 percent. Beyond this point of optimum leverage, the cost of debt capital rises and, combined with the steadily increasing equity capitalization rate, causes the WACC to rise. Thus the WACC traces a U-shaped curve, falling from the all equity position to the point of optimum leverage and rising thereafter as further increases in debt raise its cost and concomitantly result in an increase in the equity capitalization rate. Thus borrowing will at first lower the WACC, but, if carried beyond the optimal leverage point, will increase the WACC.[1]

PART VI
SPECIAL
FINANCIAL
PROBLEMS AND
BASIC
CORPORATE
CHANGES

Using the principles developed in previous parts of this text, in Part VI we single out for some special analytical consideration some of the major contemporary problems facing the financial manager. We deal with Mergers and Acquisitions, Repurchasing and Other Capital Structure Rearrangements and Reorganizations, Leasing, Financial Aspects of Multinational Operation, Corporate Tax Planning and Management, and Financial Aspects of Employee Pension Programs and Other Forms of Extra Compensation. These areas are handled separately not so much because they do not readily fit within one of the prior segments, but rather due to their contemporary significance to the financial manager.

MERGERS AND
ACQUISITIONS

20.1 INTRODUCTION

The urge to merge has produced some improbable combinations over the
past two decades. During part of this period Charles of the Ritz, a leading
cosmetic maker and beauty salon operator, acquired the Venus Pen and
Pencil Co. Possibly the name attracted them. The report announcing the
merger stated that "Venus will be kept intact." I. Rokeach & Sons, Inc., food
manufacturers, and Exquisite Form Brassiere, Inc. merged to become
Exquisite Industries, Inc. And an operator of piers on the Brooklyn water-
front merged with a posh Fifth Avenue tobacconist when the New York Dock
Company and Dunhill International joined forces.

In more recent years, Time, Inc., a publisher and printer of newspapers,
periodicals, and magazines, acquired Inland Container Corp. Warner Lam-
bert, a drug manufacturer, acquired Entemann's, a bakery, and I.C. Industries, a manufacturer of iron and steel blast furnaces and foundries acquired
Pet Inc., a dairy products manufacturer.

Of course, not all combinations in recent years have been so exotic. Mergers and acquisitions in related fields, among many others, have included Seaboard Coast Line and Chessie System, Lykes Corp. and Youngstown Sheet & Tube, General Foods and Burger Chef, Pepsico and Pizza Hut, Kuhn, Loeb and Lehman Bros., Dean Witter and Reynolds Securities, and Touche Ross and J.K. Lasser. These, along with literally hundreds of other mergers, have led one observer to suggest a corporate what's my line quiz.[1]

20.2   REASONS FOR MERGERS AND ACQUISITIONS

While the motivations for mergers and acquisitions are diverse, they may be roughly divided into business and personal reasons.

[1] BUSINESS REASONS

Management may find that the merger or acquisition route is the easiest way for adjusting to changing economic conditions or for bringing new elements to the firm. These factors are reflected in the following business motivations:

- *Desire for Profits.* A company in a line of business which is dull, stagnant, or has been adversely affected, seeks more profitable and more rapidly growing lines. The severe shrinkage of brokerage rates following the elimination of fixed minimum commissions in May, 1975, contributed to the ensuing mergers in the securities field as companies sought more profitable sources of income to offset the declining profitability of the agency commission business.
- *Diversification.* A company dependent upon a particular line of business seeks to extend its activities.
- *Take Advantage of Low Stock Prices.* This motivation resulted in two types of specialized acquisitions in the late 1970's as the stock market remained depressed. Various financial firms, such as Oppenheimer & Co., arranged so-called leveraged buy-outs (LBO's) that are described in Appendix A. Also foreign firms took advantage of the low prices and deflated dollar at that time to acquire interests in U.S. firms.
- *Avoid A Deteriorating Financial Position.* A company that has encountered economic difficulties seeks to offset this condition by merging with a stronger company. Weeden & Co., for example, at one time the securities industry's premier "third market" firm, was absorbed by Moseley, Hallgarten and Estabrook, a Boston-based securities firm with 29 branches, because of Weeden's weakened financial condition which resulted from its heavy trading losses.
- *Obtain a Better Mix of Private and Federal Contracts.* This reason has come to the fore as the government has become an increasingly important business customer. Thus, when Beech Aircraft and Raytheon agreed to merge in late 1979, the chairman of the latter company said that the merger "is a significant step in achieving a better balance between commercial and government generated sales and earnings" for Raytheon.[2]
- *Stabilize Earnings.* To a large extent, RCA's interest in acquiring CIT Financial was for this reason. CIT's earnings tend to be cyclical, rising when RCA's electronic and broadcast oriented earnings decline.

- *Produce Additional Financing.* The smaller, rapidly growing company, like one in the electronics field, for example, reaches a point where it cannot expand unless it obtains additional financing and it cannot, by itself, obtain the financing on attractive terms.
- *Strengthen Managerial Personnel.* As a company grows, its normally one or two owner-managers find that it can no longer be run from the top of their heads, that more formalized procedures and techniques and additional key personnel are necessary. These may be difficult or impossible for the small company to obtain. Its solution may be to turn to the larger going concern with full operating departments and experienced line and staff personnel.
- *Achieve Operating Economies.* The wave of railroad mergers of the early 1960's stemmed largely from the desire to increase profitability by eliminating wasteful duplication, especially unnecessary empty runs, by means of merger.
- *Drive for Horizontal Integration.* Companies often are interested in broadening their activities in the same basic lines of business. For example, Ticor, a diversified financial services company, obtained a foothold in the life insurance area by the acquisition of Houston First Savings Association. Similarly, Reliance Group, an insurance holding company, with interests in container leasing and management services, diversified its interests by the acquisition of W.R. Berkley, a holding company in regional property and casualty insurance and reinsurance in the Midwest and Southwest.
- *Drive for Vertical Integration.* Many larger companies reach out and seek to acquire companies that either ensure sources of supply or provide outlets for the absorption of their products.
- *The Factor of Size.* A desire to expand its share of the industry's total may motivate a company. It may find expansion by merger easier and quicker than expansion by internal growth and a greater sales effort in the market. Coopers Industries, for example, a Houston-based maker of hand tools, engines and other products, consolidated its position in the area by acquiring Gardner-Denver, a Dallas-based equipment maker.
- *Acquisition of Assets.* In inflationary times assets can frequently be obtained more cheaply by merger than by direct purchase or construction.

[2] PERSONAL REASONS

Whatever may be the business issues involved, the primary motivation for a merger or acquisition may stem from the personal desires of management. These desires, as described below may be present under a variety of circumstances involving both private and public companies.

- *Managerial Succession.* In a family owned business, the key man may be approaching retirement and have no one to succeed him. This may provide the motivation to sell out.
- *Estate-planning.* The estate tax problem confronts every owner-manager. He may have a valuable income-producing business, but all his resources are tied up in it, and if he were to die suddenly, his heirs would be hard pressed to find the funds to pay the estate tax. By merging and taking shares in a larger, publicly held company, he liquefies his investment and renders it marketable.

- *Personal Diversification.* The owner-manager may become apprehensive about having his entire investment tied up in one business venture, frequently involving only one product. With the hazards of a changing market and changing technology, he may feel the need for the protection of being part of a much larger company with a more diversified product line.
- *Personal Growth in Business.* The owner-manager may feel that his talents and capacities are being limited by his successful but relatively small operation. He may feel that if he can be freed of continuous operating responsibility and obtain more liquid investment capital, he will be able to expand his personal activities in other and more profitable areas and channels.
- *Defend Against Takeover Attempt.* Often, when a company is threatened with an unwanted takeover attempt, its best strategy in fending off this action is to achieve a greater distribution of its shares in friendly hands through a planned merger.
- *Eliminate Minority Shareholders.* Mergers have been arranged with corporations controlled by a firm's major shareholders in order to eliminate the interests of the firm's minority shareholders.
- *Protect Incumbent Management.* In some cases, top management personnel seek to ward off an agressor firm when management realizes that its role is likely to be subordinated in the new organization. In these cases a friendly merger may be arranged.

[3] THE BASIC STANDARDS

The listing above is by no means complete, nor is it meant to imply that one factor alone is governing in any given situation. Several factors may motivate a given merger proposal, but the general climate of business activity will, from time to time, bring forth a rash of proposals. The trend toward automation, high labor costs, increasing expenditures on research and development, the structure of the tax laws, the high cost of funds, and the attractiveness of the tax loss company, all combine to increase the appeal of larger size in enterprise, and this in turn, stimulates mergers. Also, it seems to be generally recognized that growth by acquisition is more easily and more surely accomplished than growth through internal expansion.

20.3 THE HISTORY OF AMERICAN MERGER MOVEMENTS

Broadly speaking, American finance capitalism has had three separate merger movements. Not only were the kind of mergers different which took place during each of these periods, but also the means of financing them, the underlying motives, and the factors which brought each movement to an end also tended to be different.

The first recorded major merger movement, running in general from 1898 to 1903 was probably the most important of the three merger waves. It transformed many industries, formerly characterized by small and medium sized firms, into industries in which one or a very few large enterprises occupied leading positions. As a result this merger movement laid the foundation for the industrial structure that has typified most of American industry in the twentieth century.[3]

During this period, many major industrial aggregations of today were constructed through mergers, largely of a horizontal nature.[4] A partial list of the corporate giants which came into prominence during this time largely as the result of such mergers, includes U.S. Steel, DuPont, Bethlehem Steel, General Electric, International Harvester, Anaconda, American Tobacco, Republic Steel, International Paper, Eastman Kodak, Swift, American Can, Liggett and Myers Tobacco, and Allis-Chalmers.

Since at that time the United States was substantially a capital importing country, European capital (largely British) helped fund this initial movement. Its termination was largely caused by more vigorous enforcement of the early antitrust laws, as well as by declines in economic activity.

The second merger movement, generally encompassing the years 1925-1930, reached its height toward the end of that period. These mergers were predominantly of a vertical nature. The development of our anti-trust laws had not reached the stage where such mergers could be easily attacked. In addition, the predilection of government in that era was to refrain from a vigorous enforcement of the antitrust laws. Financing for the second wave of mergers was facilitated by the booming stock market of that era and came from domestic capital. This merger movement also saw the emergence of new industrial titans including RCA, American Cyanamid, National Dairy Products, Crown Zellerbach, General Foods, Borg-Warner, Caterpillar Tractor, and Owens-Illinois Glass. The sharp and protracted stock market slump of 1929 and the early 1930's, as well as the ensuing depression, contributed to the termination of this merger movement.

Whereas the earlier merger movements were first of a horizontal and then of a vertical character, the latest movement (beginning roughly in the mid-1960's) is of a different sort. The mergers of this period, in turn, may be classified into two categories. The first was of a conglomerate nature. These mergers reached their peak towards the end of the 1960's and involved, in one way or another, many of our major corporations. At the beginning of the 1980's conglomerate mergers of this type had not entirely disappeared, but the pace of the movement had subsided somewhat.

Financing for these mergers came about largely through the use of so-called "funny money" which refers to securities such as warrants, convertible bonds, convertible preferred stock, and classified common stock, which allowed conglomerate firms to achieve their merger objectives without impairing reported earnings per share. While these securities had been previously employed, the considerable extent of their use to finance mergers was a phenomenon of the conglomerate movement.

The sagging stock market of the 1970's and the decline of the price/earnings ratios of such conglomerate firms as LTV and Litton Industries, dimmed the attraction of their stocks. Additionally, passage of the Williams Act of 1968, requiring disclosure of sources of financing for certain kinds of consolidations, and the issuance of *Accounting Principles Board Opinion No. 15,* which provided for taking into account warrants and convertibles in the calculation of earnings per share, stripped the protective financial covering of conglomerate mergers. Accordingly, conglomerate firms changed the nature of their activities, began to concentrate on internal growth and adopted the now more fashionable "multi-product" title.

During this period, stock prices generally lagged behind inflation. As a result, various types of acquisition programs were unleashed, marking the second phase of the current merger movement. Business firms scanned the field to obtain enterprises that matched some profit objective. Financial firms, discouraged by sagging prices from buying stocks directly, embarked upon a program of buying companies. And foreign firms, attracted by low stock prices and a cheap dollar, substantially raised their direct investment in the United States. Reflecting this interest was Thomas Tilling Ltd., a two billion dollar British company. In the two and a half years following its entry into the United States market, that firm paid some $216 million for 11 companies in such diverse fields as medical supplies, pollution control, construction, and oil-industry equipment.[5] The ending tale of this current phase of the latest major merger movement cannot be recounted, for as of the time of this writing, mergers of the type just described are becoming more popular.

20.4 LEGAL AND ECONOMIC FORMS OF MERGERS AND ACQUISITIONS

Legal factors clearly play an important part in merger and acquisition procedures such as discussed below.

[1] LEGAL FORMS OF MERGERS AND ACQUISITIONS

Thus far we have been using the term merger in a general sense, to denote any acquisition or combination. However, merger has a more exact legal meaning, and the word acquisition should be used in the broad sense of any combination regardless of legal form. Legally, the following merger forms may be designated and defined.

(a) Sale of Assets

A sale of assets is a contractual procedure whereby Company A buys the assets of Company B either for cash or for stock. Generally speaking, in a sale of assets the buyer does not assume the liabilities of the seller (there are numerous exceptions). In a purchase of assets, in contrast to a merger, a resolution of the board of directors rather than the stockholders' approval is the only action which is needed to be taken by the acquiring corporation. In most states, the shareholders' approval by vote is necessary for the selling company. In a sale of assets, the selling company continues in existence, or at least the sale of assets does not constitute a dissolution requiring liquidation.

(b) Statutory Merger

Statutory merger is a tax free exchange between two companies, with one surviving and the other disappearing. The surviving company acquires not only the assets of the absorbed company but all its liabilities as well, known or unknown. At times certain liabilities, such as tax deficiencies, pension liabilities, executive compensation agreements, or outstanding stock options, may not be fully disclosed. Shareholders of both companies must approve the transaction. Often, the voting percentage required is greater for approval of a merger than for a sale of assets.

In a merger, which is statutory and not a contract procedure, several steps are accomplished simultaneously. Company A exchanges its shares for those held by Company B's shareholders. Company B shareholders now become shareholders in Company A and Company B goes out of existence. Dissenting shareholders ordinarily are entitled to rights of appraisal and payment at the appraised value. Which company is to survive in the merger may be determined by a variety of factors, such as tax loss considerations and the existence of valuable contracts or franchises which may not be transferred.

(c) Consolidation

Like a merger, a consolidation is a statutory proceeding. Companies A and B decide to join forces. They form a new company, C; shareholders of A and B receive shares in C; and Companies A and B cease to exist. As in the case of mergers, shareholders of A and B must vote affirmatively, and the liabilities of both A and B as well as their assets are taken over by C.

The usual procedure in both mergers and consolidations is for the board of directors of the companies involved, after preliminary agreement has been reached, to pass resolutions, often identical, stating the terms of the merger or consolidation, the basis and method for the exchange of shares, and so forth. The plan is then submitted by each company to its shareholders for ratification, usually at a special meeting called for this one purpose.

[2] ECONOMIC FORMS OF MERGERS AND ACQUISITIONS

Law and economics move hand in hand. There are various economic forms that mergers may take, each of which has its own legal implications.

(a) Horizontal

A horizontal merger occurs when one company acquires another in the same line of business. If Union Carbide proposed to absorb Dow Chemical, it would be a horizontal combination. This is perhaps the easiest target for government antitrust lawyers, because it can readily be shown that the number of competitors has been reduced and that the market share of the acquiring firm has been enhanced. Larger companies now usually tend to shy away from horizontal combinations because they are so legally vulnerable.

(b) Vertical

The attempt of a manufacturer to absorb a chain of retail stores would be a vertical combination. The usual line of government attack in such cases is that the elimination of retail outlets forecloses this part of the market to other manufacturers, or that the acquisition of an important source of supply shuts off competing manufacturers from this resource and thereby diminishes competition.

(c) Conglomerate

A conglomerate merger is one in which a company seeking diversification goes outside its own field to acquire a concern in another line of business, as when a snuff manufacturer acquires a bread and cookie maker or a coal company absorbs an underwear manufacturer. Such combinations might seem safe from antitrust molestation, since it would appear unlikely that they could be charged with substantially lessening competition or tending to create a monopoly. Yet Federal Trade Commission (FTC) action has penetrated the sanctity of the conglomerate merger. The government's position is that diversification by merger may have anticompetitive effects. The acquiring company may have such large financial resources that competitors of the acquired company could be overwhelmed by the new market power of their former manageable competitor. In view of these circumstances, it is not possible now to say that any particular kind of merger is free from possible antitrust action.

[3] ANTITRUST ASPECTS

As the merger movement accelerated in recent years, antitrust actions to block acquisitions or to secure divestiture have become more prevalent.

(a) The Basic Law

The Clayton Act reads as follows:[6]

No corporation engaged in commerce shall acquire, directly or indirectly, the whole or any part of the stock or other share capital and no corporation subject to the jurisdiction of the FTC shall acquire the whole or any part of the assets of another corporation engaged also in commerce, where in any line of commerce in any section of the country, the effect of such acquisition may be substantially to lessen competition, or to tend to create a monopoly.

Thus, the purchase of both stock and assets now comes within the purview of antitrust action if it can be shown that the merger or acquisition might tend to substantially lessen competition in any line of commerce in any section of the country. The aim of this law is preventive. Its purpose is to nip prospective restraints on competition in the bud, to prevent the growth of the market power of a company via the merger route if it appeared that the increase in market power might in the future substantially lessen competition.

(b) The Factors Involved

What are the chances that any particular acquisition will be attacked by antitrust action? The following factors might be examined in any analysis of the possible antitrust consequences of a proposed merger or acquisition:

1. The structure and behavior of the industry.
2. The extent and character of the markets affected.
3. The relation of the merging companies to those markets and to competition in the industry.
4. Are the buyer and seller directly competitive?
5. Are they selling the same or similar products in the same market?
6. What portion of the relevant market will the surviving company have?
7. Will the loss of one competitor mean a decline in the scope and vigor of competition in any line of commerce in any section of the country?
8. What are the conditions of new entry into the field? How will they be affected by the merger?

9. What has been the past history of the industry with respect to (a) mergers and (b) new entrants?
10. If the acquisition is to secure a continuous source of supply, will other competitors be closed off thereby from access to a significant source?
11. If the acquisition is to secure distributive outlets, are competitors thereby closed off from marketing channels?
12. Does the proposed acquisition give the acquired company significant additional market power vis-a-vis its competitors as a result of the great resources of the acquiring company?
13. How will this additional market power affect competitors?
14. Would the acquiring company have entered the industry of the acquired firm directly, thereby presumably adding to rather than detracting from competition?

This list, of course, is not complete. It is merely intended to provide some idea as to the extent of considerations that might be involved. The financial manager studying the underlying economic issues, however, might give attention to these factors to get an inkling of likely antitrust implications.

20.5   PUBLIC POLICY STANCE TOWARDS MERGERS AND ACQUISITIONS

This is perhaps the place for the authors to offer their view as to an appropriate public policy posture towards mergers and acquisitions. Our background leads us to stress economic rather than legal considerations. We are encouraged in this approach because the incidence of mergers has had considerable significance for the economy and therefore economic criteria are particularly relevant.

Over the years retained earnings have constituted an increasing proportion of the financing requirements of the country's giant corporations. Presently, the preponderance of the long-term funds needs of large American corporations is met from internal sources. Indeed, some corporations are able to obtain in excess of 100 percent of all their long-term fund needs from internal sources. Moreover, as will be further developed in Chapter 21 below, in some recent periods the corporate sector has been a net supplier (rather than user) of equity capital to the security markets through, in aggregate, spending more money to repurchase their own common stock than they have obtained from new equity issues. This condition has provided the management of large corporations with some insulation from the capital markets.

Our capitalist system is based on the presumption of competition, not only in the marketplace for goods and services, but also in the market for new corporate issues where users of capital bid against one another for the available supply of funds and obtain financing through the collective judgment of suppliers of funds as to the investment returns available relative to the risk involved. When management can satisfy its fund needs through retained earnings it need not approach the marketplace for new issues and the singular judgment of relatively few high placed corporate executives is substituted for the pluralistic and independent assessment of the marketplace in the raising of the capital at the nation's collective disposal.[7]

Certain kinds of mergers and acquisitions (primarily takeover bids) have lessened management's independence from the marketplace for funds. By threatening inefficient producers with a takeover bid, merger minded firms serve a useful social purpose in enhancing the vitality of American capitalism. They provide, in effect, an alternate constituency which inefficient producers must satisfy, and to this extent constitute a countervailing force to the insulation management has been able to achieve from the new issue marketplace. In this respect, we can expect that merger targets would, in the main, be less efficient producers. For it is such firms which can generally be expected to have lower price/earnings ratios and which are therefore easier targets.

We believe, therefore, that the type of mergers and acquisitions that has characterized the recent movement is in the public interest. The threat of a potential takeover can keep management on its toes to provide its shareholders with a competitive rate of return. Over the long-run, the ability of a management team to meet this test depends on a company's internal productivity. To the extent that merger targets are less efficient producers, their acquisition and replacement by other management probably is in the social interest of creating more efficient production. Such a situation also serves to enhance the vitality of the marketplace, both product and capital. The acquisition of an efficient producer, however, serves no social good and may result in less efficient production. An acquisition of this sort, therefore, runs the risk of substantial human and economic hardship through dislocations and other deleterious effects upon employees and businesses servicing the acquired firm as customer or supplier.

Accordingly, in gauging the desirability of mergers, the courts might give more attention to engineering and marketing efficiencies. When the market is limited relative to the number and size of firms involved, competition in itself, could lead to expenditures in relatively uneconomic areas such as excessive advertising. The more important direct criterion is production and operating efficiency measured in terms of cost per unit of output. In these circumstances, engineering judgments plus financial analysis will cast considerable light on the question of whether or not overall economic efficiency is being enhanced by a contemplated merger or acquisition.

20.6 FINANCIAL CONSIDERATIONS OF MERGERS AND ACQUISITIONS[8]

When a company sets out a program of mergers and acquisitions, three preparatory steps are usually involved:

- Screening of leads;
- Investigation; and
- Negotiation.

We deal with each of these areas below.

[1] SCREENING OF LEADS

In dealing with intermediaries such a financeers and investment bankers, it is useful for the company to have predetermined specifications indicating the kind of firm it would be interested in acquiring, product lines, size, degree of profitability, and preferred technique of acquisition. In the light of these criteria, an initial screening can be undertaken and an extensive weeding-out process developed, leaving a smaller number of more likely candidates to be investigated in more detail. For example, in the acquisition program of one domestic company over a three-year period 392 leads were screened, of these 52 companies were investigated, and negotiations were carried on with 12 firms resulting in 3 acquisitions. That is, only a little more than 13 percent of the leads were investigated, 3 percent were negotiated, and less than 1 percent were eventually acquired.[9]

[2] INVESTIGATION

A typical investigation usually has two stages. The first is obtaining whatever information is available outside the target company, including published balance sheets, income statements, funds statements, credit inquiries, a Dun & Bradstreet report, trade inquiries, and the like. The second phase involves an approach to the company, a face to face meeting of principals, and, if the meeting is encouraging, a look at the company itself, its books and its facilities. This task may prove difficult and delicate since most firms do not wish their employees, competitors, or customers to know that they are contemplating a merger or sale. Nevertheless, a company which is seriously interested in being acquired will realize that it must supply vital information. While many things must be reviewed, the following financial items will ordinarily be included:

1. Latest Audited financial statements.
2. Last available financial statements.
3. Ten year summary financial statements. (Product profit and loss statements essential, if more than one product.)
4. Projected operating and financial statements.
5. Full description of securities indebtedness, investments, and other assets and liabilities, other than day to day accounts.
6. Trial balance and chart of accounts and/or description of accounting practices relative to inventories, fixed assets, reserve accounts, etc.
7. List of bank accounts and average balances.
8. Credit reports from banks and Dun & Bradstreet.
9. Federal income tax status, i.e., credit carry forwards, any deficiency claims, etc.
10. Summary of state and local tax situation, i.e., applicable taxes, unemployment tax rate, any deficiency claims, etc.
11. Tax status of proposed transaction; recommendation of the best method of acquisition.
12. Complete list of insurance policies, including description of coverage and cost; workmen's compensation rate.
13. Statement of responsible officer of business as to unrecorded or contingent liabilities.
14. Statement of inventories.
15. Comparison of the last two physical inventories of sizable money items to reflect slow moving and obsolete materials. Note finished products

particularly. Determination of how physical compared with book at last physical inventory.

16. Aged list of accounts receivable, credit and collection policies, and trial balance of accounts payable.

17. Detailed statement of general and administrative expenses, selling expenses, and factory overhead on a comparative basis for three years.

18. Status of renegotiation and price redetermination.

19. Bonus and pension plans; salary and commission contracts.

20. Statement of unfilled orders, past and present.

21. Statistics regarding industry group (trends, return on investment, margin on sales, etc.)

22. If any defense contracts in backlog, a check of the margin of profit, and also whether any existing equipment is government owned.

23. Statements regarding company's break-even point, including details of product mix, costs, and fixed and variable expenses.

24. Status of production or other contracts requiring company performance for a fixed amount where work is yet to be accomplished.

25. List of outstanding capital asset items.

26. Status of patents, copyrights, royalty agreements, etc.

27. Details of corporate equity accounts.

28. Estimated costs and likely outcome of pending legal issues.

Not all this material may be available and in particular instances other items may be wanted.

[3] NEGOTIATION

Crucial to a successful merger or acquisition is reaching agreement on the commercial value of the company in question. There are a number of factors which, taken together, constitute evidence of and guides to commercial value.[10] The price/earnings ratio is a useful tool. In this case a value is placed on the earnings of a company based on the price in the security markets being paid for earnings of similar companies. For example, assume a stock is selling for $160 with annual earnings of $8 per share. The current price/earnings ratio is therefore 160/8 = 20. If this company is similar to the concern being valued, which is earning $1 million per year, the value of the latter is $20 million or 20 times its earnings of $1 million. This procedure requires study of the price/earnings ratios of comparable companies if available as well as the composite for the industry.

Capitalizing earnings is a traditional method of valuation. Annual earnings are divided by a rate of return to obtain a value figure. Selection of the capitalizing rate is open to debate. Should the company's own rate of return be taken? Should an industry average be used? Or should the acquiring company's rate be employed on the ground that its management can in due course attain this figure for the company to be acquired? Should the rate be one achieved over the past year, the past five years, or anticipated as a result of the merger?

Other factors which might be considered in the valuation process are nonoperating assets, such as land holdings; oil or timber reserves; goodwill; market value of the outstanding securities; book value or original cost of properties; reproduction cost appraisal; special conditions, such as high leverage with borrowed funds obtained at a low cost; the impact of the proposed merger itself on profitability; and liabilities.

In statutory mergers, where the exchange of shares is involved, the valuation process normally boils down to three considerations:

1. Market price of the shares;
2. Earnings and dividends per share; and
3. Book value of net tangible assets per share.

Each of these items is discussed below.

(a) Market Price of Shares

If the merging companies are both listed and there is a fairly active public market for the shares of each, the usual basis for the exchange of shares is the relative market price of each over a prior period. Why does market price figure so importantly in the determination of exchange ratios of listed companies? There are a number of reasons. First, buyers are seldom willing to pay more than the going market price and sellers are seldom willing to settle for less. Second, market price presumably entails thousands of impartial, objective evaluations, indicating a total concensus of the combined impact of all relevant and important factors playing upon the company's profit status, earnings and dividends outlook. Third, it is an easy benchmark for shareholders to use when evaluating a merger proposal. If they are offered less than the going market value, the number of dissenting shareholders may be so large as to block the merger. If the acquiring company, on the other hand, is offering too much, its shareholders may object. It is hard for management to argue with the seemingly irrefutable logic of the market.

Despite the logic of a balanced relationship between the share values of the acquiring and acquired companies, the terms will inevitably reflect the interests of the two parties. Thus, an acquiring company ordinarily will be willing to pay a premium for the acquired company, with the amount dependent upon the degree of interest that the former has in obtaining the latter.

The premium should be gauged in the light of the acquired company's rate of return and the acquiring company's cost of capital. Assume, for example, that Company A pays $50 per share for the stock of Company B, which sells at $45 per share. Company B earns $9.00 per share and its stock thus sells at a price/earnings ratio of 5. In effect, therefore, Company B provides a rate of return of 20 percent on the stock price, thereby justifying the acquisition of its stock provided that Company A's cost of capital is sufficiently below this rate to afford it an adequate margin of profit. In these circumstances, the opportunity costs to Company A involved in the expenditure of the premium are likely to be made up quickly by the relatively high rate of Company B's earnings.

Another question is what form the payment will take. As the takeover and merger movement got underway in the late 1960's, payment usually was in stock of the acquiring company. Thereafter, changes occurred and by the second half of the 1970's payment ordinarily was in the form of cash and preferred securities or bonds. The decision with respect to form is usually dependent upon negotiation in which such questions as taxation, financial position, and capital structure are likely to be involved.

(b) Earnings and Dividends Per Share

Where there is no public market for the shares of one or both parties to a merger, the focus of the exchange tends to center on earnings and dividends. While prospective rather than past earnings may be a more logical basis for valuation, past earnings are explicit and definitive, at least in the accounting sense, whereas estimates and forecasts of future earnings are, of course, uncertain, inexact, varying, and subject to controversy and disagreement. The parties to a merger often find it much easier to agree on what past earnings were than to come to a meeting of minds on what future earnings are likely to be. Yet past earnings may be poor clues to future performance. Despite this limitation, comparative earnings, present and prospective, play an important role in the valuation process in most mergers involving at least one unlisted firm.

(c) Book Value of Net Tangible Assets Per Share[11]

Assets or book values are usually, but not always, of minor importance in negotiating merger terms. By book value, of course, is meant the excess of assets over liabilities, or the net worth of the enterprise. The computation of this figure for acquisition purposes, can vary. Usually goodwill or other intangibles are excluded, but differing accounting techniques from company to company, including varying methods of charging depreciation and handling inventory, make book value an uncertain guide. While this condition generally applies to industrial companies, it has been less true in the case of banks and public utilities. Even for industrials, however, net monetary assets per share (monetary assets less liabilities, divided by outstanding shares) must be taken as the minimum per share value in the negotiation.

The larger company with considerable assets but low or stagnant earnings will attempt to place emphasis on book value in merger negotiations. On the other hand, the young and rapidly growing company with high and sharply increasing earnings will wish to give little attention to book value in merger proceedings. As between the two, earnings will generally control since in the final analysis assets are usually worth only what they can earn. In summary, then, book value is generally of lesser importance in merger valuations. Market price (for listed companies) or earnings are usually the controlling considerations.

20.7 RIGHTS OF DISSENTING SHAREHOLDERS

The proxy statement in a merger must clearly indicate the rights of dissenting shareholders; which usually are set forth in state law. Typically, a dissenting shareholder, provided that he has notified the company in writing of his opposition to the proposed merger and voted against it, has the right to receive an agreed-upon or appraised sum from the selling corporation for his stock. This is not his only remedy. He may sue to have the merger enjoined, but this is usually a more costly and often less successful remedy. Difficult problems of valuation arise in appraisal cases. The statutes say the dissenting shareholder is to receive "fair value" or "full market value", but this generalization must be reduced to specifics. A leading Delaware case used net asset value and capitalized earnings power.[12] In New York, however, the courts have favored "market value", and where a listed company has offered market price to dissenters, the institution of appraisal proceedings has been termed "arbitrary and vexatious."

20.8 THE TARGET COMPANY STRATEGY WHEN FACED WITH A TAKEOVER BID

Thus far we have looked at mergers and acquisitions largely from the point of view of the acquiring firm. However, there are occasions when an acquisition attempt is pursued by a firm (usually through a tender offer to the common stockholders of the target company) in spite of the hostility to the merger of the management of the target company. In this situation the management of the target company has a number of lines of defense which we consider below.

[1] REPURCHASE OF COMMON STOCK AS A TAKEOVER DEFENSE

In the following chapter we deal with corporate repurchases of their own common stock, which can be a powerful defense against an unfriendly takeover attempt. An important consideration in any proxy contest is what percentage of the outstanding stock each party controls. Clearly, the higher the percentage one of the contestants has, the stronger is his position. The proxy yield is defined as the percentage of the publicly held stock (shares not spoken for) that must be received to obtain some objective, say 51 percent control. When a target company repurchases its own stock, the proxy yield required by its management is reduced as long as the incumbent management begins the proxy contest with ownership of a larger percentage of outstanding shares than the company seeking to affect the acquisition.

Consider the following case. Target Company T has 100 shares of common stock outstanding. Its management either beneficially owns or has voting rights to 20 shares. Now assume the management of the firm fears an impending takeover attempt by firm A, which has not, as yet, begun to acquire its common stock position in T. Should a proxy battle for T erupt, either side would require the votes of 51 shares to obtain control. For the management of T the following situation prevails:

Shares outstanding	100
Shares controlled by management	20
Shares not yet spoken for	80
Needed for control of T	51
Shares controlled by management	20
Additional proxies needed by management	31

$$\text{Proxy yield required by management for control} \quad \frac{31}{80} = 39\%.$$

However, should T repurchase 40 of its common shares, the following improvement in the required proxy yield will occur:

Shares outstanding	60
Shares controlled by management	20
Shares not yet spoken for	40
Needed for control of T	31
Shares controlled by management	20
Additional proxies needed by management	11

$$\text{Proxy yield required by management for control} \quad \frac{11}{40} = 28\%.$$

In addition to an improvement in the required proxy yield, a repurchase is likely to afford the target corporation's management with another, more subtle, benefit. The shareholders who sell their stock back to a repurchasing corporation are likely to be less pleased with its management and less likely to vote in its favor if a proxy fight erupts than the shareholders who retain their securities. Thus, from a qualitative as well as quantitative point of view, the repurchase program should improve the survival chances of incumbent management.

Moreover, a dissident group seeking to unseat management must use its own funds (or any that can be borrowed) in order to finance the acquisition of the common shares of the target company. On the other hand, management defending the takeover attempt by repurchasing common stock can use general corporate funds for this purpose. Although reacquired or treasury shares, as is evident from the above illustration, are non-voting, they can reduce the proxy yield required by management.

[2] ISSUING COMMON STOCK AS A TAKEOVER DEFENSE

It may seem odd that issuing common stock can be an effective defense against a takeover attempt when the opposite procedure (repurchasing common stock) was just described as such a defense. Nevertheless, that is the case if appropriate circumstances prevail.

As described previously, a repurchase may help thwart a takeover attempt when incumbent management begins the struggle with control of more common shares than its adversary. In these circumstances, reducing the outstanding share base through a repurchase decreases the required favorable proxy yield. Conversely, if management begins the defense with control of fewer outstanding shares than the dissident group, a new issue of common stock not only gives management funds for the defense but will also increase the proxy yield required by the dissidents. Let us assume, for example, that in the case of target company T above, the dissident group, A, rather than management, has voting rights to 20 shares, and therefore, its proxy yield required for control is 39 percent. By issuing 100 additional common shares, management, as shown below, increases the proxy yield required by the dissidents. (This, of course, assumes that no additional shares are purchased by the dissidents.)

Shares outstanding	200
Shares controlled by dissidents	20
Shares not spoken for	180
Shares needed for control of T	101
Shares controlled by dissidents	20
Additional proxies needed by dissidents	81

$$\text{Proxy yield required by dissidents for control} \quad \frac{81}{180} = 45\%.$$

Similarly, as in the case of repurchase, the new shareowners are likely to vote with incumbent management since they had enough confidence to buy the firm's common stock.[13]

The offsetting strategy that the acquiring company might pursue in this situation is to buy some of the new stock. In these circumstances, however, the target company would still be getting its adversary to use more of its funds in the takeover attempt. As a result, if the new stock issue is large enough, the transaction may become too expensive for the acquisition-minded firm and cause it to lose interest.

Additionally, so long as it is not purchased exclusively by current stockholders, a new stock issue will increase the dispersion of shareholdings. This condition provides an advantage to incumbent management since it increases the difficulty an aggressor will find in seeking to contact existing shareholders.

[3] ACTIONS TO DELAY OR IMPEDE THE TAKEOVER BID

A firm may be faced with a takeover bid that it is unable to withstand financially. In this situation the target firm may resort to delaying tactics, hoping that the proceeding will become so costly and time-consuming for the acquiring firm that it will withdraw its bid. In this vein, a number of strategies have been used with some success.

(a) Filing Antitrust Actions

The target firm may seek to prevent the merger, or at least impede the takeover attempt, by filing an antitrust suit on the grounds that the merger would have anticompetitive effects. Target firms are frequently joined in this endeavor by similar antitrust suits brought by various branches of government or governmental agencies. Often, simply an indication that governmental agencies are looking into a proposed merger is sufficient to cause undesirable delays for the acquisition minded firm. For example, when American Express sought, in an unfriendly takeover attempt, to acquire control of McGraw-Hill, the transaction, in addition to being legally opposed on antitrust as well as other grounds by McGraw-Hill, was scrutinized by the FTC, the Securities and Exchange Commission, a House Banking subcommittee, the Federal Communications Commission, the U.S. Comptroller of the Currency, the Federal Reserve Board, the New York State attorney general and the New York State Banking Department. The considerable delays likely to have resulted from the involvement of such a large number of governmental agencies, as well as the opposition of McGraw-Hill, undoubtedly contributed to the withdrawal of the unfriendly bid by American Express.

(b) Filing Other Legal Action

There is also a wide range of other litigation that might be pursued by a target company depending upon the creativity and resourcefulness of its attorneys.[14] Again with respect to the McGraw-Hill-American Express situation, the defending firm through the ingenuity of its attorney, Martin Lipton, undertook an offensive posture in successfully warding off the unfriendly bid. McGraw-Hill, in addition to its other legal defenses, brought suit against Roger Morley, president of American Express, arguing that prior to an unfriendly bid, Mr. Morley sat on the Board of Directors of McGraw-Hill. The suit charged that Mr. Morley used his position as a director of McGraw-Hill to obtain inside information of value to American Express in making its takeover bid. But McGraw-Hill's legal maneuverings went even further. The company forced American Express to file a registration statement with the New York State attorney general under the New York Security Takeover Disclosure Act,[15] and requested that the attorney general investigate the takeover bid and call public hearings. McGraw-Hill said, "This tender offer is unique. It is the direct outgrowth of the breach by Mr. Morley of his fiduciary duties to McGraw-Hill for the sole benefit of American Express."[16] After the bid was dropped, all legal actions by McGraw-Hill were withdrawn.

(c) Acquiring a Firm in a Regulated Industry

This is not so much a defense against a takeover bid that has already been made as insurance against the success, or at least the rapid success, of future unfriendly takeover attempts. The relevant government agency must pass upon the appropriateness of any buyer of a firm under its regulatory supervision. Thus, some firms have acquired television stations as a method of discouraging unfriendly takeovers.

Acquisition minded firms have sometimes set up temporary trusts to hold property in regulated industries owned by target firms until approval by the appropriate regulatory agency is obtained. This process, however, may not be available with the Federal Reserve Board, which has rejected the trust route in hostile bank takeovers.

[4] A PUBLIC RELATIONS CAMPAIGN WITH A TARGET FIRM'S OWN STOCKHOLDERS

In the end it is the stockholders of the target firm who decide upon the success or failure of any tender offer the courts allow to be made. As a result, many firms, faced with an unfriendly takeover attempt, have sought a defense through appeals to their own stockholders. Such appeals ordinarily include: praise for the claimed success the management of the target firm has been having; contention that the tender price is inadequate as well as that the assets of the target firm are undervalued; and the claim that the prospects of the target firm are glowing. By these approaches, the management of the target company will try to convince its stockholders of the greater benefits to be derived by holding rather than selling their shares to the bidding firm.

The public relations campaign may get rough and even deal in personal attacks. For example, when Occidental Petroleum Corp. sought to acquire Mead Corp. in an unfriendly takeover attempt, Mead notified its shareholders by letter and double page newspaper ads that Occidental's offer should be rejected for many reasons. These ranged from Mead's own earnings prospects to the fact that Dr. Armand Hammer, Occidental's chief executive, was 80 years old and had pleaded guilty, in October 1975, of trying to cover up certain illegal contributions to Richard Nixon's 1972 reelection campaign. Indeed, the ferocity of Mead's counterattacks, among other factors, has made it a classic in this area that is likely to be examined by other managements hostile to takeover bids.

In addition to such rhetoric, some companies have bolstered their public relations campaign by the tangible gesture of increasing the cash dividend payment. For example, in the case cited above, shortly after Occidental made its offer, Mead's directors raised the dividend for the second time in the same year.

[5] USING STATE AND FEDERAL LAWS

Prompted by concerns with losing business, many states have passed laws which regulate corporate takeovers through tender offers. Needless to say, corporations fearful of takeovers and domiciled in any of the states with such laws have been pleased by them and have possibly even lobbied for their passage. Such legislation has been used to block or impede a number of takeover bids.

As the use of tender offers for takeover purposes mounted in the 1960's, Congress recognized a federal regulatory gap in this area. In 1968, therefore, it adopted and in 1970 modified, the Williams Act, which incorporates various amendments to the Securities Exchange Act of 1934. Section 14(d)(1) (of the revised 1934 Act) provides, that any person who, directly or indirectly, becomes the beneficial owner of more than five percent of any class of an equity security of a corporation must file with the SEC, at the time copies of a tender offer are sent to security holders, information specified in Section 13(d). This information is to include such things as the background and identity of the tender offerors; the source and amount of funds used in making the purchases; and if the purpose is to acquire control, any plans to make major changes in the corporation's business or financial structure.

An early question was the extent to which Section 13(d) was applicable to management seeking to fight a potential takeover. The answer was given in a 1975 federal court decision.[17] In this case, the management of LaFayette Radio and Electronic Corporation had formed a group to oppose Jewelcorp which had purchased 9.8 percent of LaFayette's stock. The court's opinion not only indicated that a management group is treated no differently under Section 13(d) than any other group, but also that such a group must make the requisite filing of information regardless of whether it agrees to purchase, hold, or dispose of securities.

Other federal legislation, the Hart-Scott-Rotino Act, establishes pre-notification and waiting period requirements which become effective after purchases exceed designated limits. If this measure is applicable, a purchase cannot be closed until 30 days after the bidder has filed the pre-notification form. The initial 30-day waiting period may be extended for an additional 20 days on the request of the FTC or the antitrust division of the Justice Department for additional information.

Companies which feel that they may be targets of future unfriendly takeover attempts have sought to ward off such bids by adopting a variety of bylaws and charter provisions designed to make a takeover tougher. For example, some companies set staggered terms for directors, which delay changes in the composition of their boards of directors.[18] Another such technique is to require shareholder approval of a potential merger by a percentage that is greater than the applicable state law requirement. Or, management may be given the option of either applying or waiving a "super-majority" provision. For example, several years ago, the shareholders of Gulton Industries, Inc. approved a requirement whereby an 80 percent vote would be necessary to approve any merger or consolidation of the company with another firm that had previously acquired five percent or more of Gulton's stock. The percentage would be reduced to a majority, however, if the board of directors approved a merger prior to the candidate obtaining a five percent or more interest. Dismissing a shareholder's complaint, the Delaware Court of Chancery indicated that recourse to such a defensive tactic was acceptable under the State's law. In general, there has been little litigation testing the validity of contingent supermajority provisions under state corporate statutes.

[6] FINDING A FRIENDLY MARRIAGE OR A "WHITE KNIGHT" TAKEOVER

In response to an unfriendly takeover attempt, some firms have sought to fend off their unwanted suitor by merging with another, more desirable firm, sometimes called a "White Knight." Often the terms of the desirable merger are more favorable or perhaps the officers of the target firm feel that they will obtain a better personal position for themselves in the new merged entity created with the desired partner than they would in the case of a combination with the undesired partner.

Daylin, Inc., used this strategy when they sought to merger with Narco Scientific, Inc., a Fort Washington, Pa., healthcare concern which was then involved in merger talks itself. At that time, Daylin was resisting the advance of W. R. Grace & Co. This case is interesting because a firm seeking a friendly marriage in response to an unfriendly takeover attempt normally approaches a firm larger than itself. Daylin, however, sought a merger with a smaller firm.

A more traditional friendly marriage with a larger firm to avoid an unfriendly one was arranged by Chemetron Corp., a specialty metal products and industrial gas producer. Crane Co. had made a tender offer for the common stock of Chemetron which the management of the latter firm resisted, first with the aid of investment bankers and then by seeking delays through the courts with the help of the Justice Department. But eventually, time began to run out on Chemetron. Therefore, the company contacted Allegheny Ludlum Industries which, oddly enough, had been considering 1,800 possible acquisition candidates for over a year and had by then narrowed its list to a relatively few firms, among which was Chemetron. In short order, a deal was hammered out which ultimately won out over the Crane offer.

[7] THE PAC MAN DEFENSE

The Pac Man defense against a takeover bid, of course, takes its name from the popular computer science game. This ploy is somewhat newer than the ones analyzed above and derives from the notion that frequently the best defense is good offense. Under this strategy, as in the Pac Man game, the target firm tries to "swallow up" the unfriendly would-be acquiring firm before that firm can acquire it. The Pac Man gambit which attracted the greatest notoriety was employed by Martin Marietta as a defense against an unfriendly takeover bid by Bendix. Martin Marietta responded to a Bendix offer to buy its stockholders' shares by counteroffering to buy Bendix's shares from *its* stockholders. A bitter corporate battle with complex legal entanglements ensued. United Technologies and then Allied Corp. eventually entered the imbroglio on the side of Martin Marietta and Bendix, respectively. Just when a seemingly absurd and surely legally intractable outcome was about to transpire (Bendix owning a controlling interest in Martin Marietta with the latter also owning a controlling interest in the former and the two managements bitterly in opposition), an eleventh hour agreement was struck. Allied acquired control of Bendix and a substantial investment position (though not a controlling one) in Martin Marietta. United Technologies bowed out, as eventually did William Agee, former chief executive officer of Bendix, who quickly resigned the post he was given in the combined Allied-Bendix entity. Mr. Agee had been the prime motivator behind the commencement of hostilities.

In the end for its efforts at undertaking the acquisition program, Bendix wound up a subsidiary of Allied which itself, though substantially larger, was considerably more debt ladened. This caused Moody's Investors Service Inc. to lower its ratings on Allied's securities. Martin Marietta also left the field of corporate battle a far more highly leveraged firm, though its Pac Man defense eventually did allow it to retain its corporate independence.

[8] THE GOLDEN PARACHUTE DEFENSE

Golden parachutes are not only a corporate defense against an unwanted takeover attempt, but can also be a personal defense by incumbent management against undesirable consequences flowing from a successful takeover bid. Golden parachutes are employment contracts given to a firm's top executives who may fear a takeover bid. Most such contracts provide that in the event of a successful takeover of their firm such executives are to receive from the acquiring firm cash settlements equal to several years' salaries as severance pay should they be fired or their status or responsibilities downgraded.

It is estimated that about 15 percent of the 1,000 biggest U.S. corporations have such agreements for their top management.[19] By making a successful takeover more costly, golden parachutes constitute a target company's defense. And the more generous the parachute, the better the defense.

It is interesting that the top executives of all four combatant firms in the Bendix-Martin Marietta-Allied-United Technologies takeover battle discussed in the prior subsection had handsome golden parachutes. One of the outcomes of this dispute, as mentioned in the prior subsection, was the resignation of Mr. Agee, formerly of Bendix. This action activated Mr. Agee's golden parachute, which provided him with a cash payment of $4.1 million.

[9] WHY SOME COMPANIES FIGHT A MERGER OFFER

Elements of price, power and personal prerogative may be involved in the decision to fight against a merger. It is logical to expect that the top executives of the target firm will not want to be reduced to division heads or even share authority. The response of James W. McSwiney, Mead chairman, to the overtures advanced by Joseph E. Baird, Occidental president, was "Joe, the combined company isn't big enough for both of us." But other than personal reasons, financial considerations can also come into play in the decision to oppose a merger.

The acquiring firm might not be thought an appropriate partner for financial, synergistic, marketing, managerial or other such considerations. Moreover, for many well run companies with considerable growth opportunities, undervalued assets and sound financial statements that are desired by potential buyers—a merger is really not a necessary course of action. These companies normally can develop the opportunities available to them with their own internal capital.

Fundamentally, an incumbent management does not like to have an outsider put pressure upon it to adopt any particular course of action. As an extreme case, management has at times decided that liquidation is in the interests of shareholders. For example, Martin Horwitz, chairman of UV Industries, presided over the dissolution of that company, on the grounds that the market was undervaluing the company's shares. J. Peter Grace, president of W. R. Grace & Co., announced that the board was considering splitting the company into as many as seven publicly held units to enhance stockholders' value. But when outsiders sought to gain control of SCM Corp. in order to dismantle it, management resisted the onslaught. In this case, dissidents, headed by H. Normal Muller, chairman and chief executive officer of MacMuller Industries, Inc., the privately held parent company of Petrocelli Clothes, put forth a slate of directors committed to liquidating SCM. Based on opinion by Bear, Stearns, and Co., the dissidents contended that holders could realize $36 to $47 a share from the sale of SCM's business. At that time, the stock was selling at about $20. On the other hand, Paul H. Elicker, SCM's president and chief executive officer, claimed that the way to enhance stockholders' value is to improve performance and referred to the dissident proposal for Mr. Muller to take over SCM as "a red-herring scheme".

[10] THE OVERALL DEFENSE PATTERN

When the management of a target company receives an undesired offer, it initially must find reasons, presumably made in good faith, that the offer is not in the best interests of its shareholders. Typical reasons that have been advanced are inadequate price, wrong timing, legal difficulties, and unfavorable economic consequences. The new state antitakeover laws plus federal regulations ordinarily provide sufficient time to formulate defense strategies.

The lawyers are then likely to take over, mounting antitrust and other suits, hurling subpoenas, and seeking depositions from the raider's top management. Such tactics may discourage the raider. But lawyers may become overly zestful. Thus, several years ago, when Monogram Industries offered to buy a controlling interest in Royal Industries, the latter company counterattacked on a number of fronts. These included nine separate lawsuits, an effort to purchase a company that had a pending antitrust suit against Monogram, and a proposal to require 90 percent shareholder approval of any business combination. A disenchanted federal judge ruled that Royal's extensive maneuverings raised "serious questions" about violations of securities laws and breach of fiduciary duty. However, the judge placed restraints on Monogram, which eventually lost out to another company.

Another common ploy on the part of a resisting company is to sell off the firm's best assets (called a "crown-jewel asset sale"), perhaps to a "friendly" third firm. Other defensive tactics include increased monitoring of trading in a company's own shares to quickly spot any takeover related accumulations.

The costs and uncertainties of fighting a resisting target firm have caused some companies to confine their acquisition efforts to potential corporate partners who are friendly. Nevertheless, some of the defensive tactics mentioned above may not appeal to crucial institutional shareholders who may fear a loss of marketability or value from their adoption and vote against the target firm as the result. This may perhaps be one of the reasons that a Kidder, Peabody & Co. study found that in 1982 raiders won 18 of 22 hostile tender offers.

20.9   CHAPTER SUMMARY

In this chapter we began our discussion of special financial problems and basic corporate changes by analyzing mergers and acquisitions. We first looked at the reasons for such activity and its history in this country. Then the legal and public policy aspects of mergers and acquisitions were developed. The many financial issues involved in this area were then analyzed. Finally, we reviewed the rights of dissenting shareholders and the defensive strategies of unwilling target firms. In the next chapter we discuss another area of special financial problems—repurchasing and other capital structure rearrangements and reorganizations.

FOOTNOTES

1. An interesting and opposite trend, the selling off of diverse divisions by conglomerate firms, has also emerged in recent years. Prodded by the feeling that a clear definition of a company's activities results in a higher price for its stock, many former acquisition minded firms sold off major divisions. For more on this see, Mitchell C. Lynch, "Slimming Down: Many Firms are Selling Off Acquisitions to Clarify Their Images, Lift Their Stocks," *The Wall Street Journal,* December 4, 1980, p. 54.
2. *The Wall Street Journal,* October 3, 1979, p. 3.

3. Ralph L. Nelson, *Merger Movements in American Industry, 1895-1956,* National Bureau of Economic Research, Study No. 66, Princeton, Princeton University Press, 1959.
4. Some of the terms used in this section are defined later in this chapter.
5. Lawrence Rout, "Buying American," *The Wall Street Journal,* August 21, 1979, page 1.
6. 38 B Stat. 730 (1914).
7. It is true that even when management can satisfy a corporation's financial needs through retained earnings, the management is not entirely free from competitive pressures of the marketplace. The reason is that the ability of management to use the company's retained earnings probably reflects the favorable performance of its stock in the secondary markets. In the case of such performance, investors would be amenable to disregard dividends in the expectation that management could use the retained earnings more efficiently. This relationship is indirect, however, and the ability of a company to curtail its use of primary market financing undoubtedly provides some diminution of the influence of investor judgment on management's behavior.
8. Tax considerations relevant to mergers and acquisitions are dealt with in Chapter 24.
9. For a look at RCA's acquisition program see *The Wall Street Journal,* March 8, 1979, pp. 1 and 10.
10. For an analysis of cash tender offers in a valuation setting, see Donald R. Kummer and J. Ronald Hoffmeister, "Valuation Consequences of Cash Tender Offers," *Journal of Finance,* May 1978, pp. 505-516. Also, for an analysis of the determination of the acquisition price, see M. S. Salter and W. A. Weinhold, "Diversification via Acquisition: Creating Value," *Harvard Business Review,* July-August 1978, pp. 166-176. And for a discussion of an acquisition strategy accomplished through the use of debt, see Frederick S. Gilbert, Jr., "Financing the Leveraged Buy-Out Through the Acquired Assets," *Harvard Business Review,* July-August 1978, pp. 8, 12, 16, and 20.
11. Accounting for mergers and acquisitions by the surviving firm is treated in Chapter 3.
12. Sporberg et al. v. City Specialty Stores, Inc., Court of Chancery of Delaware, 1956, 123 A. 2d 121.
13. An interesting case where common stock was issued to defend against a takeover attempt involved Unitrode Corp. which was being pursued on an unfriendly basis by Dynamics Corp. of America. By selling 400,000 new shares to Schlumberger Ltd., a "friendly firm" at $25 each, Unitrode increased its shares outstanding from 2,450,000 to 2,850,000 and provided Schlumberger with a 14 percent interest. The transaction, which reduced the interest of Dynamics in Unitrode to 11 percent from 13 percent, along with two lawsuits, was undertaken in order to stave off the unfriendly takeover attempt. Of the lawsuits, one charged Dynamics with violating federal securities law by "manipulation of Unitrode's stock and failing to disclose that Dynamics was conducting what Unitrode called an 'unconventional and illegal tender offer'." The other suit charged violations of Massachusetts securities laws in connection with the acquisitions of Unitrode stock. (*The Wall Street Journal,* March 27, 1979, p. 1.)
14. In an interesting case, Washington Steel charged that Chemical Bank, by offering to lend Tally Industries money for the purchase of the stock of Washington Steel, had breached its fiduciary duty, on the grounds that Chemical served as registrar for Washington Steel stock and had misused confidential information. In granting a 90-day injunction against Chemical, a Pittsburgh district judge indicated his concurrence with the charge. This decision, however, was overturned by a federal appeals court which said, "companies seeking to insulate themselves from take-overs ... could simply arrange for a series of loans from most of the major banks."

Although the appeals court decision cleared up a potential problem for bankers, it did not do Tally Industries much good, since the company withdrew its bid as a result of the court suit and a friendly or "white knight" bid by Blount, Inc. (*The Wall Street Journal,* July 24, 1979, p. 3.)

15. Under this act a tender offer cannot be made for 20 days after the filing and the attorney general has 15 days from the filing to schedule a public hearing. If a hearing is called, the acquiring firm cannot start its tender offer until it complies with any terms ordered by the attorney general. The hearing must begin within 40 days of the filing and the attorney general has 30 days after that to determine whether the acquiring firm has complied with the act. Thus, the calling of public hearings could cause a 70 day delay.

16. *The Wall Street Journal,* January 22, 1979, pp. 1 and 10.

17. Jewelcorp Inc. v. Pearlman 397 F. Supp. 221, 243 (S.D.N.Y. 1975). Dennis J. Block and Neal Schwarzfeld, "Management Groups Under the Williams Act," *Securities Regulation Law Journal,* Spring 1977, p. 82.

18. An example of the use of this tactic is Anheuser-Busch Inc., which set up a holding company as an anti-takeover device. Although the company said it was not aware of any takeover attempt, Anheuser-Busch felt it desirable to make such an attack more difficult. For this purpose, it effected a reorganization involving the elimination of cumulative voting (which enables minority holders to gain a foothold by electing some directors) and introduced staggered three years terms for directors (which facilitates keeping incumbents in office). The company noted that it also increased the number of authorized common shares so that in the event of a takeover attempt, they would be issued to friendly purchasers in order to make that takeover more difficult.

19. Frederick Klein, "A Golden Parachute Protects Executives, But Does it Hinder or Foster Takeovers," *The Wall Street Journal,* December 8, 1982, p. 56.

SUGGESTED READINGS

Abdelsamad, M. H. and T. L. Wheelan, "Corporate Capture: The Pros and Cons of Acquisitions," *Management World,* March 1982.

Austin, D. V. and W. Mandula, "Tender Offer Trends in the 1980's," *Mergers and Acquisitions,* Fall 1981.

Cummin, Robert I., "Unfriendly Corporate Takeover—Old Style," *Financial Analysts Journal,* July/August 1982.

Dobkin, Richard J., "Evaluating a Proposed Merger: The Accounting Trouble Spots," *Practical Accounting,* January 1982.

Emmet, Robert, "How to Value a Potential Acquisition," *Financial Executive,* February 1982.

Faber, Peter L., "How to Get the Maximum Benefit From Net Operating Loss Carryovers in a Corporate Acquisition," *The Practical Accountant,* December 1981.

Gilbert, Frederick S., Jr., "Leveraged Buyout Becoming Popular Financing Method," *Management Review,* August 1981.

Grossman, Sanford J. and Oliver D. Hart, "The Allocational Role of Takeover Bids in Situations of Asymmetric Information," *Journal of Finance,* May 1981.

Haight, G. T., "Portfolio Merger; Finding the Company That Can Stabilize Your Earnings," *Mergers and Acquisitions,* Summer 1981.

Hoffmeister, J. R. and E. A. Dyl, "Predicting Outcomes of Cash Tender Offers," *Financial Management,* Winter 1981.

Kapleau, Paul H., "Acquisitive Reorganizations: A Look at the Tax and Accounting Rules," *The Practical Accountant,* May 1981.

Keown, Arthur J. and John M. Pinkerton, "Merger Announcements and Insider Trading Activity: An Empirical Investigation," *Journal of Finance*, September 1981.

Kessler, J. and A. Gaines, "Spotting Takeovers," *Financial World*, March 1982.

Korn, Terry, "Structuring Corporate Acquisitions: A Profile of the Valuation Engineer," *Financial Executive*, March 1982.

Madden, Gerald P., "Potential Corporate Takeovers and Market Efficiency," *Journal of Finance*, December 1981.

Reier, Sharon, "Playing the Takeover Game," *Institutional Investor*, June 1981.

Reilly, Robert F., "Planning for an Acquisition Strategy," *Managerial Planning*, March/April 1982.

Sandler, L., "Wall Street Finally Discovers the Leveraged Buyout," *Institutional Investor*, August 1982.

Shue, G. H., "Valuation for Takeover Purposes—A 1982 Case Study," *Accountancy*, June 1982.

Strischek, Dev, "A Survey of Commercial Bank Activity in Merger-Acquisition Financing," *The Journal of Commercial Bank Lending*, October 1981.

Tarr, Herbert L., "A Basic Tax Guide to Acquisitions," *The Practical Accountant*, August 1981.

Weiss, J. M. and I. Blumen-Fruecht, "Tax-Free Reorganization," *Management Accounting*, October 1981.

APPENDIX A:
ACQUISITION THROUGH A LEVERED BUY OUT

An interesting form of acquisition which has come into prominence in recent years is called the "levered buy-out" (LBO). As expressed by George May, president of Firecom, Inc., an investment firm specializing in such acquisitions, an LBO is particularly attractive to Firecom since "as a group our investors have substantial incomes." The main interest of investors in Firecom is the potential for a substantial capital gain, which involves leveraging the firm's acquisitions to the greatest extent practical. Investment companies that have pioneered in this field are Oppenheimer & Co. and Carl Marks & Co. Kohlberg, Kravis, Robert & Co. arranged one of the biggest LBO's—Houdaille Industries for $355 million. The apparent success of these firms has attracted other well known names in the securities field such as First Boston Corporation and Lazard Freres & Co.

The basic elements that underly the construction of an LBO are the nature of the acquisition candidate, the price that is established, and the financing arrangements.

It is desirable that the acquisition candidate have the following characteristics:

- Established in a stable or growth industry;
- A track record of moderate earnings;
- A high proportion of total assets in tangible property, much of which may have a fair market value in excess of net book value;
- Middle management willing to remain with the company;
- A business that is basically manufacturing with a low technology and a non-obsolescent product line; and
- Problems that apparently will respond to normal, good management practices.

The price should be at or less than book value and low relative to earnings (generally under eight times earnings). In these arrangements, the buyer desires to minimize the cash outlay and therefore must be able to borrow a large portion of the purchase price, typically using the acquired firm's assets as collateral for the loan. Financing for LBO's normally is done by commercial finance companies and to a lesser extent by banks at relatively high rates. Insurance companies also have participated in this field. The income generated from the acquired assets is used to service the debt, a feature that makes it important for the acquired firm to have growing or at least stable earnings.

The discussion thus far has centered on the structure of LBO's from the standpoint of the buyer. From the point of view of the seller, the following types of businesses may lend themselves particularly well to the LBO format:[1]

1. Divisions of public companies that no longer fall within the companies planning framework of divestitutes forced by the government. (An LBO where the buyer is a privately held corporation with no other operations imposes no SEC, antitrust, financial reporting, or other legal restraints on the buyer.) Thus, the deal can be consummated quickly and with a minimum of regulatory difficulty.

2. Divisions of companies that do not meet required corporate return on asset measures. In these cases, the division typically has a large book value relative to its after-tax earnings and earnings growth may not be high. Thus, the parent company may find: (1) that it has assets invested at a yield below its own weighted average cost of capital, and (2) that the division is not salable to another public company except at a loss (discount from carrying value), since a publicly owned buyer will generally pay a price based on the growth rate of the business rather than its book value. The selling public company may be able to find a buyer who is willing to pay the asking price (i.e., the division's book value) if the seller provides a portion of the buyer's financing. The buyer believes that he can improve the earning power of the business, or reduce the assets employed in it, or both and is willing to bear the extra risk of higher leverage in the expectation of a significantly greater return. In such an arrangement, the seller may establish book value as the price and accept, say 70 percent in cash and 30 percent in medium-term notes. The buying group (often including the operating management of the division being sold) regards these notes as "soft" (i.e., less expensive and from a more benevolent source than an institutional debt) and is usually able to raise institutional debt in addition to the obligation to the seller. The seller records no gain or loss on the sale of the division and is able to receive the bulk of the purchase price in cash with an orderly liquidation program for the balance.

3. Privately owned businesses that are closely held. Because the LBO buyer has broad flexibility he is in a position to structure the deal to suit the particular objectives of sellers of private businesses. Many such private businesses lack sufficient secular growth to be attractive corporate acquisition candidates; however, the LBO depends more on stability of earnings than growth. Furthermore, the selling shareholders may be reluctant to sell their stocks for cash—the only acquisition medium offered by the buyer—because they are not anxious to recognize a taxable gain, establish a value for estate purposes, or both. In such cases, the shareholders may provide for their company's business and assets to be sold to the buyer for cash. The ownership of stock does not change, and, if the sale is at book value, no gain or loss is recognized. The remaining cash rich shell may then be operated as a personal holding company, investing its cash in preferred stocks (dividend income paid by one domestic corporation to another is 85 percent excluded for tax purposes), tax-exempt securities and tax shelter situations. The company can pay out substantial income to its shareholders, and, upon the death of a shareholder, his shares pass into the hands of his distributees at a stepped up tax basis (their December 31, 1976 value). Oppenheimer has developed imaginative programs on this basis. It buys the assets of the seller (primarily with funds borrowed against these assets). The former management continues to operate these assets under a term contract, while the seller's remaining corporate shell is converted to an investment company. The seller receives the cash payments except for the amount used to satisfy dissenters. These funds are used primarily to buy tax-exempt securities.

4. Public companies selling at low earnings multiplies and at a substantial discount from book value. These circumstances are sometimes prevalent in low (or no) growth companies. It may serve the best interests of the shareholders for the company to sell its business and net assets for a price exceeding the current aggregate stock market value, but still at a discount from book value. The difference between the book value and the sale price may, under the proper circumstances, represent an ordinary loss by the selling company for federal income tax purposes, which can be used to offset other income—or carried back as a net operating loss for refund of previously paid taxes. From the above we can see that the LBO can be an attractive undertaking for both buyers and sellers of businesses. To further illustrate the use and effect of this technique consider the following example:

Suppose a corporation wishes to divest itself of a division which operates in an area the corporation is not now pursuing. The firm might seek to sell this division through an LBO plan. Let's call this division B and assume it has highly stable sales and earnings and typically earns about $350,000 a year before taxes. If division B can be sold for a price equal to its book value of $1,300,000, a fruitful LBO might be arranged. Let's further assume that LBO Corp. agrees to such a transaction and pays 70 percent of the agreed price in cash and the balance in a five-year 9 percent subordinated note, which would be amortized fully over the last three years of its term. LBO finances the $910,000 down payment (70 percent of $1,300,000) by borrowing $850,000 from a finance company and using $60,000 in equity raised from the managers of division B who desire to stay on after the LBO.

The balance sheet of division B would look as shown in Figure 20.1, before and after the LBO.

FIGURE 20.1 *Division B balance sheet as of December 31, 19X1 (000's omitted)*

	As shown on books of selling corporation	Giving effect to acquisition by LBO Corporation
ASSETS		
Current assets:		
Cash	$ —	$ 50
Accounts receivable	275	275
Inventories	700	700
Other current assets	6	6
Total current assets	$ 981	$1,031
Property, plant & equipment, net of accumulated depreciation	450	450
Total assets	$1,431	$1,481
LIABILITIES AND SHAREHOLDERS' EQUITY		
Current liabilities:		
Notes payable*	$ —	$ 230
Current portion of long-term debt	—	134
Accounts payable	100	100
Accrued liabilities	31	31
Total current liabilities	$ 131	$ 495
Long-term debt, net of current portion**	—	926
Shareholders' equity	1,300	60
Total liabilities and shareholders' equity	$1,431	$1,481

*LBO financed $180,000 of the purchase price and generated $50,000 in operating cash by borrowing from a finance company.
**Giving effect to the acquisition LBO had the following Long-term debt:

	Current Portion	Long-Term Portion	Total
Term-loan payable to a finance company in 60 monthly installments of $11,167 plus interest, secured by inventories and fixed assets.	$134,000	$536,000	$670,000
Subordinated note payable to selling corp. in 36 monthly installments of $10,833 beginning 24 months after closing, plus interest payable monthly at 9 percent.	—	390,000	390,000
Totals	$134,000	$926,000	$1,060,000

A pro-forma cash flow statement for Division B giving effect to the acquisition by LBO would be as shown in Figure 20.2.

FIGURE 20.2   *Division B*

Pro-Forma Cash Flow Statement
Giving Effect to Acquisition by LBO
for the Year Ending December 31, 19X1
(000's omitted)

Sales	$2,500	
Cost of goods sold	2,000	
Gross margin		$ 500
Selling, general and administrative expenses		150
Operating margin		$ 350
Interest expense:		
Finance company debt	$115	
Subordinated debt	35	150
Income before taxes		$ 200
Taxes on income		95
Net income		$ 105
Add: Charges to income not requiring an outlay of cash:		
Depreciation		75
Deferred income taxes*		38
		$ 218
Less: Mandatory debt amortization		(134)
Additions to fixed assets		(40)
NET CASH FLOW		$ 44

*It is common for a corporation in LBO's position to have a sub-normal current tax outlay; allocation of the purchase price or acquired assets may result in a reduction of reportable income for tax purposes.

1   The following discussion is based on Hilary B. Miller, "LBO's—Trends and Techniques," *Business Horizons,* June 1978, pp. 73-78.

21

REPURCHASING AND OTHER CAPITAL STRUCTURE REARRANGEMENTS AND REORGANIZATIONS

21.1 INTRODUCTION

Seldom does a corporate financial structure remain static. In the course of its existence a company may retire some of its common stock, buy it up for use in mergers or acquisitions, refund or consolidate debt, recapitalize, retire preferred, exchange common for preferred, eliminate cumulative preferred dividend arrears, or place its common stock in a voting trust. These are only some of the rearrangements in which financial managements engage from time to time. In addition, firms running into extreme adversity may experience overall reorganization or even bankruptcy and liquidation. In this chapter, we discuss some of these rearrangement and reorganization changes, starting with one of particular current significance—common stock repurchasing.

21.2 COMMON STOCK REPURCHASING

Corporations buying back their own shares represent a big business. The practice came into the limelight as a result of studies which showed that in each year during the 1954-1965 decade, corporations increased the number of their own shares they acquired. The average increase during the entire period was about 19 percent. Moreover, there have been times when corporations were net suppliers of equity capital to the securities market rather than net users of such funds, as is thought to be the usual pattern.

There are a number of factors which come into play in management's decision to buy back its own company's stock.[1] Among the most important of these are the following:

- the motives in undertaking the repurchase program;
- the methods by which such a program can be accomplished;
- the characteristics of the repurchasing company;
- the overall economic conditions conducive to repurchasing;
- the applicable accounting principles;
- the legal environment; and
- the effects on security price performance and security market conditions.

While we deal with each of these considerations in turn, our objective is to paint a unified and comprehensive picture of corporate common stock repurchasing.

[1] MOTIVES OF MANAGEMENT

Financial managers have expressed different reasons for repurchasing stock but an underlying thread is the desire to improve the corporation's rate of return. Any time a company chooses to repurchase its common stock, it is selecting this use of its funds over competing alternatives. Thus, the question must always be asked; what is the rate of return on the repurchase of shares? The answer is indicated by the earnings/price ratio (the reciprocal of the more popular multiple or price/earnings ratio) of the firm.

In effect, the market price represents the approximate amount the firm will pay in order to repurchase a single share of stock, while the current earnings per share figure is the indicated income related to this amount. If, for example, a company's stock is selling for $10.00 and its earnings per share are $1.00, the return from repurchase would be 10 percent. Accordingly, in order to produce a more favorable effect on current earnings per share, an alternate use of funds must generate more income after tax than $1.00 for each $10.00 invested.

The return from repurchase is both risk free and net of taxes since there is no uncertainty attached to the outcome and no taxes need be paid. It is unlikely, therefore, that management will ignore the effect on earnings per share of a stock repurchase program. But other factors, such as those discussed below, may actually precipitate the decision.

(a) Provide a Store of Readily Issuable Shares for Residual Stock Issuing Needs

In recent years, the growth of employee stock benefit programs, as well as the increased issuance of securities with residual equity claims, such as warrants, convertible bonds and convertible preferred stock, have created a corporate need for a store of readily issuable shares. Further contributing to this need is the growth of mergers and acquisitions over the past two decades, as outlined in the last chapter, and the creation of shares as the result of stock dividends and stock splits. Repurchased shares remain as treasury shares and while they receive no dividends and are nonvoting, they can be readily reissued by management in satisfaction of these stock issuing needs.

One may wonder, why use treasury shares rather than authorized but unissued shares for this purpose. When a company reacquires its shares, the reason for avoiding the increased authorization route may be the time required before the new shares are available for issuance. Also, the stockholder vote to increase the authorization may result in unwanted publicity.

If the company has more authorized than outstanding shares, as well as funds available for repurchase, the route it chooses to follow is likely to depend upon its investment opportunities. Either it could issue more stock and use its current funds for investment purposes, or it could apply funds to repurchase its common stock and then reissue the shares. The better of the two alternatives depends, as stated above, upon the relationship between the company's earnings/price ratio and the rate of return the other investment opportunity will bring. If the return on the other investment, after risk and tax considerations, is below the company's earnings/price ratio, repurchase and subsequent reissuance will produce the better effect upon earnings per share.

The following hypothetical example illustrates this concept. Consider a company with the following characteristics:

- Net Income $100.00
- Shares outstanding   100 shares
- Earnings per share $ 1.00
- Market price of common stock $ 10.00
- Funds available for investment or repurchase $ 10.00
- Residual stock issuing needs   1 share

If the best available other investment opportunity will bring only 5 percent, the comparison between investment and repurchase looks as follows:

	Invest at 5%	Repurchase and Reissue
• Net Income	$100.50	$100.00
	($100.00 + $10.00 x .05)	
• Outstanding shares	100 shares	99 shares
• Earnings per Share	$1.005	$1.01

If, on the other hand, the best available other investment opportunity will return 20 percent, the comparison looks as follows:

	Invest at 5%	Repurchase and Reissue
• Net Income	$102.00	$100.00
	($100.00 + $10.00 x .20)	
• Outstanding shares	100 shares	99 shares
• Earnings per Share	$1.02	$1.01

This illustration is, of course, simplified. In practice, the company considering a repurchase program will need to go through a capital budgeting analysis of the type outlined in Chapter 17 and 18 in order to determine the risk adjusted after-tax rate of return on the use of funds. In any case, the basic question is still the same—will the company earn a rate that is greater or less than its earnings/price ratio on an alternate use of the funds?

(b) Assist Incumbent Management in a Control Battle

In this situation, the available rates of return and the firm's earnings/price ratio generally take a back seat to the control battle. The use of the repurchase technique depends upon the incumbent management having at the outset a greater proportion of the voting shares than the dissident group, thereby decreasing, through repurchase, the favorable proxy yield it needs in order to maintain control. (For an illustration of this principle see 20.9[1]).

If this condition does not prevail, an incumbent management still may seek to buy back the shares of a dissident group, often at a premium above the current market price, in order to avoid a control struggle. For example, in June 1978, Bache Group Inc., the securities firm holding company, repurchased from four large stockholders 560,000 shares at a $1.2 million premium above the then prevailing market price. The repurchase came shortly after a representative of one of the holders had indicated to Bache that all four were considering waging a proxy fight for control of the company. Bache indicated that it repurchased the shares in order to avert a proxy fight and asserted that it was within its legal rights to pay the premium to avoid discord within the company.[2]

Indeed, some managers view repurchasing primarily as a control device which can discourage a takeover attempt by sopping up the excess cash which frequently makes takeover targets attractive. Repurchasing can also make a target firm look less desirable if debt is used to finance the repurchase program.

(c) Save Stockholder Servicing Costs[3]

By reducing the size of its stockholder list, repurchasing firms may save stockholder servicing costs, which have ballooned in recent years. These costs include postage for frequent mailings; preparation and printing of annual reports, interim statements, proxy statements, post-meeting reports and other documents and materials sent to stockholders; running the annual meeting; bank charges for processing dividend checks; and fees of registrars and transfer agents. It is difficult to obtain good, current estimates of stockholder servicing costs, but the bulk of them do not depend on the number of shares owned. There is little difference between the costs of servicing the account of a stockholder owning 1 share and a stockholder owning 1,000 shares.

As a result, a company that has a large number of small stockholders and therefore a relatively large servicing bill, may offer to repurchase all the shares of small holders (normally those owning 25 or fewer shares). This situation may follow an unsuccessful takeover attempt when the bidding company distributes to its own stockholders the shares of the company it had sought to acquire. Usually such offers carry a small premium above the current market price in order to entice holders to accept. The offers also relieve tendering shareholders of the transaction costs which they would otherwise incur in liquidating their positions.

The presence of many small stockholders may also carry certain benefits. For one thing, they constitute both potential customers and unofficial salesmen of consumer oriented companies. They can also serve as a political force which might be particularly useful in highly regulated industries such as utilities or those in which government relations are important. Additionally, managerial control through the proxy system is facilitated if the company has its outstanding shares spread among large numbers of small stockholders. The cost savings of a shareholder reduction program may be measured without much difficulty, but the benefits of keeping shareholders are of a qualitative nature.

(d) Accommodate Insiders or Managers by Repurchasing Their Shares

The relationship between available rates of return and the earnings/price ratio is equally important in repurchasing shares from insiders or outsiders. The desire, however, to accommodate the former may, in some cases, become paramount. The estate of a deceased executive may need liquidity. If for any other reason a closely associated party desires to sell his or her shares and the public market for the securities is not broad and deep, a distribution of a large block of stock may lead to a significant price decline until this overhanging supply has been absorbed. In order to prevent this situation and also to accommodate a closely associated party, corporations have repurchased blocks of stock at or below current market quotations.

(e) Provide Support for the Market Price

It is unlawful for a company to intentionally manipulate the market price of its securities. Indeed, some firms have been accused by the Securities and Exchange Commission (SEC) of using repurchases to manipulate share prices in order to influence merger terms. Nevertheless, it is often stated that, at least in the short-run, repurchases will have a favorable effect upon price, primarily because they reduce supply and increase demand. To avoid legal complications, full and fair disclosure of any repurchasing program must be made and careful attention given to SEC regulations.

(f) Increase Book Value Per Share When Market Value is Below Book Value

Some managements tend to view book value per share as an important element in their decision-making. An impending full or partial liquidation may strengthen this attitude. Investment companies and holding companies, particularly, stress book value per share and have looked to repurchasing as a means of increasing it. Repurchases made below book value per share raised this figure. Interest has focused on this outcome in recent years as security analysts have given more attention to price-book value relationships.

(g) Increase Financial Leverage

Another motive for repurchasing is to increase the degree of financial leverage, that is, the proportion of debt relative to the amount of equity in the capital structure. If for some reason, such as high interest rates, a firm is reluctant to issue debt, it could still raise its financial leverage by repurchasing some of its common stock. As long as any debt is in the capital structure, the repurchase of stock lifts the debt proportion, or in other words, the firm's leverage.

A tandem program may also be undertaken. Thus, a firm may be able to issue debt but not enough to increase its financial leverage to the desired level. Repurchase of stock accompanied by some debt issuance (and perhaps even financed by the debt) could achieve the desired leverage.

(h) Reduced Equity and Cash Dividend Requirements as the Result of a Reduced Asset Base or Facilitate a Partial or Full Liquidation

Firms may at times have low return assets which they eventually sell or liquidate, thereby eroding the base from which they draw earnings to pay dividends. A firm in this situation may want to repurchase some of its outstanding common shares in order to reduce its dividend requirements. An offshoot of this motive for repurchasing was exemplified some years ago by Paramount Pictures. The company claimed it was able to maintain its cash dividends (when adverse industry conditions caused other film companies to cut their per share payments) by reducing the number of outstanding shares through regular repurchases of stock.

In addition, many firms have found that subsequent to a sale of some of their assets, the former capital structure is no longer required to support their reduced scale of operations. Accordingly, the funds obtained from sale of the assets often have been used to repurchase outstanding common stock.

The repurchase of outstanding common stock with cash obtained from the sale of some of the company's earning assets is somewhat akin to a partial liquidation. Repurchasing all outstanding common stock would, of course, represent a full liquidation. (The area of corporate bankruptcy and liquidation is discussed later in this chapter.)

(i) Technical and Miscellaneous Motives

A variety of technical or procedural difficulties have been resolved or eliminated through repurchases. Assets not qualified for ownership by regulated companies have been exchanged for common stock. Antitrust suits, because of intercorporate stockholdings, have been averted through repurchase. Court suits over voting rights, litigations by stockholders, and efforts to obtain favorable tax status have all been behind specific repurchase programs.

In addition, some researchers have maintained that the primary motive behind most repurchasing is to distribute cash to stockholders on a more favorable after-tax basis than in the form of dividends. Clearly dividends are taxed to individual stockholders at ordinary income tax rates, whereas repurchase dollars are taxed at the much lower long-term capital gains tax rates (assuming the shares were held for the required long-term holding period before repurchase) and then only at the amount that the repurchase price exceeds the stockholders' cost or other basis. Therefore, to the extent that management is trying to provide individual stockholders with greater after-tax returns—perhaps in order to increase the market value of the common stock—repurchasing may have been motivated by a desire to substitute a more favorable (in terms of individual tax rates) cash payment to stockholder than cash dividends.

Valid as to this point may be, however, with respect to individual stockholders, it does not take into account the tax status of dividends vs. repurchasing to corporate stockholders. With a few minor exceptions, dividends paid by one domestic corporation to another are includable for tax purposes in the income of the recipient corporation at the rate of only 15 percent. (In some cases there is a full 100% dividend exclusion.) In effect, $10.00 paid in dividends by one domestic corporation to another will result in a tax payment of only $.67 ½ (assuming a 45% corporate tax rate —— .45 x .15 x $10 = $.67 ½). However, $10.00 in long-term capital gains to a corporate stockholder would result in a tax payment of $1.80 (.45 x .40 x $10 = $1.80).

Moreover, when an increase in company funds available for distribution is felt to be short-lived, repurchasing permits the funds to be distributed so as to avoid the precedent of paying higher dividends that might not be able to be maintained. Designating particular payments as extra or extras might mitigate this problem, but the company would still be in the position of paying fluctuating dividends. Fluctuating dividends are generally considered less desirable for purposes of security valuation than a more constant and predictable dividend stream.

Often the burden of the greater disclosure and filing requirements for public companies makes them desirous of going private. This attitude is particularly prevalent when the current price of their common stock has fallen appreciably below its initial offering level and the firm does not contemplate a new common stock issue in the forseeable future. In this case some companies have repurchased stock in order to go private.

[2] REPURCHASING METHODS

An important step in the development of a repurchase program is the method of carrying it out, which must be in accord with the repurchase motive. The methods or techniques of repurchasing can be classified into several categories:

- open market transactions—general actions effected through the public markets;
- tender offers—limited programs conducted in the public markets;
- direct transactions with major holders—private programs executed away from the public markets; and
- special bids[4]—unique programs requiring special arrangements with members of the public markets.

In the ensuing sections, we discuss each of these four repurchasing methods.

(a) Open Market Transactions

By far the largest number of companies engaged in repurchasing, and the preponderance of shares reacquired, involve continuing programs undertaken in the auction markets of the major securities exchanges. The shares are reacquired through a broker, as is the case in any other security transaction on the exchange market. Companies often provide their broker with rules to guide their open market activity, such as: repurchases should be no more than a designated percentage of transactions in the stock exchange market; the timing of transactions during the trading day; the pricing of transactions; and whether large blocks of stock offered for sale call for responsive changes in the repurchase program. On the other hand, many companies prefer to provide their brokers with the widest possible discretion in meeting their repurchase objectives and merely require that they operate within SEC directives.

Generally, in open market transactions, shares are obtained at a moderate rate and at prices which are normally favorable compared with those paid in programs involving acquisition of a large number of shares in a short period of time, such as through tenders. Thus, if a company wants to meet a series of residual stock issuing needs over a moderate period of time (as in the case of expected conversion of convertible securities or for pension or stock option purposes) an open market repurchase program may be the most suitable device. However, when large numbers of shares must be reacquired quickly (as in the case of a control battle) or when the company wishes to reacquire the shares from a particular class of shareholders (such as small stockholders to save stockholder servicing costs), a tender offer may be the more suitable procedure.

(b) Tender Offers

Most tender offers are open to all stockholders (except when made to small holders) although management frequently exempts itself from participation. The tender usually specifies that the company will repurchase a certain number of shares, often within maximum or minimum (a minimum is usually designed for control purposes) limits, although the company ordinarily reserves some flexibility to penetrate these limits. The offer probably will remain open for a designated period of time (generally three weeks to one month), but may be extended at the option of the repurchasing company. Tenders generally carry market premiums which often are substantial (10 percent to 20 percent are common) in order to entice stockholders to accept the offer. Occasionally companies have announced they would buy back a given number of shares at the lowest prices indicated by selling stockholders. Cash is the predominant medium of exchange, although other assets are used such as preferred stock, convertible debentures, shares of other corporations held as investments, or a combination of securities and cash.

Since tender offers may involve large numbers of shares and dollar amounts, these decisions usually are made by senior corporate management. The company using this procedure is likely to be small or its securities may lack the deep secondary market desirable for open market purchases. Nevertheless, when a substantial number of shares is desired, some of the nation's largest firms have employed the tender device.

(c) Direct Transactions with Major Holders

Direct transactions are generally isolated from a general repurchasing program and vary widely. For example, suppose that a large financial institution seeking to diversify its portfolio, finds that the sale of a large block of a particular stock to the original issuing corporation is a convenient way of achieving this purpose. This was the case for the repurchase by Ford Motor Co. of 1,000,000 shares held by the Ford Foundation. The corporation reduced its outstanding shares and the foundation was able to effect the sale without commission costs and without upsetting the market for the stock. Direct transactions have also been used to eliminate the holdings of a major stockholder who had abandoned a control fight.

(d) Special Bids

Special bids utilize the facilities of the exchange market in a different manner than the open market transactions. A special bid is an offer to buy through any exchange member (typically at a special high commission) shares of a particular stock. The method has important limitations, such as a very brief offering period (usually one day), a modest premium and a sensitivity to current market conditions. On the other hand, this approach can sometimes produce a large number of shares in a short period of time. A variant of this approach is to enlist the cooperation of the exchange specialist in buying directly from him.

[3] CHARACTERISTICS OF REPURCHASING COMPANIES

As we have seen, the management of a corporation will have a motive in mind when repurchasing shares. It is logical to expect that this motive would be reflected in some characteristic of the corporation and research has confirmed that such a relationship, indeed, does exist.

We can flip the motive characteristic coin and say that corporations with certain characteristics are more likely to engage in a repurchase program. Perhaps the predominant characteristic is sluggish operating performance accompanied by the absence of promising investment opportunities to effect an improvement. All other things being equal, a company seeks to raise its earnings per share (ordinarily a major objective) through operating efficiencies and new investments. When the company is unable to achieve the desired efficiencies or uncover suitable investments, the incentive appears to better its earnings per share through repurchase of shares.

This incentive is strengthened if the corporation possesses the following characteristics:

- a high earnings/price ratio for its common stock;
- a high liquidity ratio;
- relatively low financial leverage; and
- a capacity of carrying and receiving additional debt.

In these circumstances, the company will either already have, or experience little difficulty in obtaining the funds to undertake the repurchase program.

Companies contracting through the liquidation of some assets or the spin-off of certain subsidiaries are candidates for repurchasing their own stock. They may seek to reduce their capital base to match the reduced scale of operations. A low dividend pay out ratio may reflect a desire to provide stockholders with a more favorable after-tax means of receiving corporate cash through repurchasing their shares rather than paying dividends.

Because of the increasing attention that has been focused on the relationship between market price and book value, tender offers not uncommonly are made when book value exceeds market value and when net assets are increasing. On the other hand, size of the firm generally is not a significant factor in repurchasing nor is the degree of operating leverage.

[4] ECONOMIC CONDITIONS CONDUCIVE TO REPURCHASING

At any time, particular circumstances may induce a company to buy back its own stock. In general, however, there are certain economic conditions that tend to produce in the typical repurchasing company the characteristics described above.

Stock prices generally lead cyclical business activity and, therefore, they tend to be relatively low as the economy moves into a downward cycle. At that time, too, a shadow is likely to be cast on future earnings prospects. In these circumstances, companies' stock will tend to sell at high earnings/price ratios. Then, too, because of sales declines, receivables (which by now have been collected) and inventories probably have been brought to modest levels, resulting in considerable corporate liquidity. It is thus shortly after the peak of economic activity that repurchasing may be expected to be at a high point.

Conversely, repurchasing may be expected to be at an ebb just after a low point in economic activity, as the upswing is taking place. At that time, stock prices are relatively high and rising, in anticipaton of increasing corporate profits. Furthermore, rate of return prospects are good and business liquidity is low since collections on prior sales are sluggish; receivables are rising and inventories are high in anticipation of rising sales. Thus, shortly after the trough, repurchasing can be expected to be at a low point.

These cyclical conditions are portrayed in Figure 21.1.

FIGURE 21.1 *Repurchasing and the business cycle*

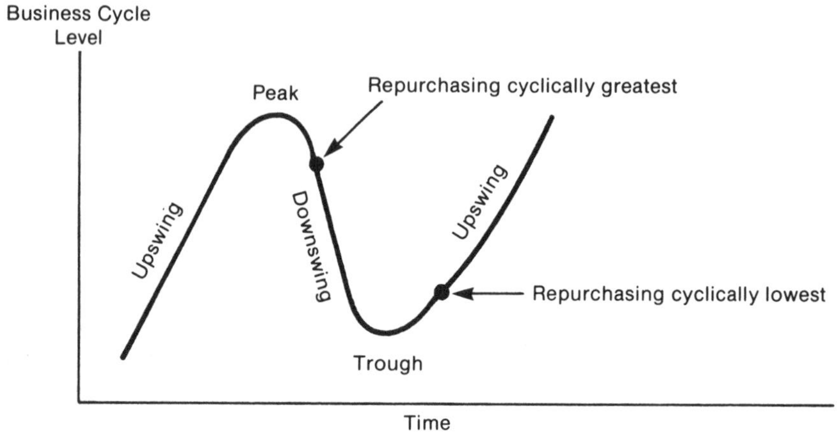

[5] ACCOUNTING FOR A REPURCHASE

The method of reporting treasury stock is interesting and has caused some controversy within the accounting profession. Broadly speaking, there are three methods of showing treasury stock in financial statements:

- reduction from paid-in capital;
- reduction from final stockholders' equity; and
- addition to assets.

The first two (which are by far the most popular) are so similar they will be discussed together. The third, a distinct and sometimes important departure, will be discussed separately. Since a company can choose any of these three methods, it normally selects the one which best presents the financial picture it wishes to portray.

Neither of the first two methods recognize gains or losses on trading in treasury stock. In both cases stockholders' equity is reduced by the same amount, resulting in the same improvements in the ratio of net income to stockholders' equity. Also, in both cases, the corporation does not distinguish between the treasury shares it intends to reissue and those it intends to retire, thereby depriving stockholders and the investment community of a valuable piece of information—the potential addition to supply resulting from a reissuance of the common stock. Since such disclosure might well depress the stock's price, corporations obviously prefer a reporting convention that does not require it.

Under the third method, treasury shares are disclosed as an addition to assets if the corporation intends to reissue them. This results in lower ratios of both sales to total assets and net income to total assets. It also recognizes in the income statement gains or losses upon reissuance of the treasury shares. Since asset disclosure of treasury stock informs the marketplace of the corporation's reissuance intentions, this method, although permissable, is not popular.

Traditionally, accounting theorists have favored reporting treasury stock either as a deduction from paid-in-capital or from stockholders' equity. The justification for this view is that repurchased shares have substantially the same status as authorized but unissued shares. An equity deduction for treasury stock which will be reissued has also been supported by viewing it as a temporary contraction of net worth.

The justification for viewing treasury stock as an asset is deeply rooted in the change which has taken place over the past three decades in the motives for and extent of repurchasing.[6] Corporate repurchasing has grown from a sporadic and infrequent occurrence of a relatively few companies to a major activity of a very large number, if not most, of the corporate giants.

When corporate reacquisitions were an infrequent occurrence and constituted an insignificant element in the corporate source and use of funds complex, the degree of managerial attention given to the treasury stock account was quite limited. Normally, when treasury stock was acquired, it was not done with the intention of satisfying a recognized corporate need for the treasury shares; nor was it part of a well conceived, overall corporate financial plan. When treasury stock acquisition was a sporadic occurrence, it usually resulted from some defensive action of the corporation.

Defensive repurchases of common stock often resulted from a corporation finding itself with unusually large liquid resources in comparison to the company's historical norm and/or the productive investment opportunities available to the firm. Such a situation could have resulted from either a decline in the rate of return the company expects on new investments or perhaps from a sale of one of the company's units of production. But in either case, the increase in liquid resources could bring about demands for wage and/or dividend increases that are particularly undesirable in light of the company's reduced productive capacity. In such a situation, a repurchase of common stock not only reduces the firm's liquid resources, but also its future dividend requirements. Occasional repurchasing also commonly resulted from a desire on the part of a company to assist in the liquidation of a large holder's position with a consequent tax benefit relative to ordinary dividends.

In these cases of defensive or occasional repurchases, the basic nature of the motivation of management in acquiring treasury stock was a defensive strategy for a situation which had arisen that was exogenous to the company's overall financial plan. In such a situation, it is entirely reasonable to maintain that treasury shares have substantially the same status as authorized but unissued shares. In this case, the treasury stock account is largely an inert element in the corporate balance sheet. When only defensive repurchasing is done, additions to the treasury stock account are normally of a sporadic nature and seem to have no discernible pattern of relationship to reductions in the account. Such is the nature of defensive repurchasing—it is not done with the aim of acquiring treasury shares for which the corporation has a specific purpose which is part of its overall financial strategy, but is rather exogenous to this strategy.

Yet while defensive repurchasing accounted for the preponderance of treasury stock transactions in the days when this phenomenon was small and sporadic, in recent years much of it has been undertaken with an entirely different aim in mind. Thus, while considering defensive repurchasing as resulting in an equity reduction is appropriate accounting treatment, it is necessary to rethink the assumptions used in the disclosure of treasury stock when the purpose of the reacquisition is quite different.

In the past two decades, corporate stock issuing needs have increased greatly, not only as a result of a need for capital injections at crucial intervals, but also in order to satisfy the greatly expanded contingent corporate common stock issuing commitments. Such commitments stem from an increased use of:

- stock options or stock purchase agreements with company employees;
- convertible corporate securities, both in the form of debt and preferred stock;
- warrants to purchase the common stock of the corporation;
- mergers and acquisitions requiring equity exchanges; and
- share distributions in the form of stock dividends and stock splits.

In this environment, the treasury stock account, in an increasing number of companies, has become a corporate tool which is now the subject of careful planning as a valuable corporate resource. A disclosure convention which treats reacquired shares as a reduction of corporate capital, or in a manner similar to unissued shares, does not seem to be consistent with current practices of corporate financial management. Equity disclosure for treasury stock is appropriate only when management treats the treasury stock account in a manner similar to a contributed capital item.

When changes in the treasury stock account were erratic, infrequent, often rather permanent, and usually only in the direction of increases, treatment as a deduction from the total capital element was meaningful. However, such a disclosure for treasury shares is misleading to the reader of the balance sheet when it is not in congruence with an environment in which management is treating the account as a frequently changing pool of corporate resource. That management is treating the treasury stock account in this manner can be seen from the changed motives for repurchasing and also from the available empirical evidence.[7] Thus if the intent, not the potential possibility, is to retire treasury shares, then these shares should be considered as a reduction of capital and are properly shown in the stockholders' equity section. If the reverse intent is true, however, and a reissuance is contemplated, then treasury shares are assets.

Splitting the treasury account into an equity disclosed segment and an asset disclosed segment would not only be proper but also necessary in those cases where the reissuance intention of management is different with respect to each segment. But, in either case, the prime consideration in determining the locus of disclosure should be the purpose of management in reacquiring the shares.

[6] LEGAL ENVIRONMENT FOR REPURCHASING

At one time purchase of its own stock by a corporation met with varying degrees of legal disapproval and restriction. This aversion was largely based on an antiquated British tradition of viewing corporate repurchases of their own common stock as a constructive fraud upon creditors. The belief was that a repurchase constricted the capital base and thus impaired the security or cushion upon which creditors could rely as a protection for their interests.[8] In the United States, the pendulum has now swung in the other direction. Over twenty years ago, a legal scholar observed:

> The "enabling" spirit of twentieth-century corporation statutes is well illustrated in the evolution of permission to a corporation to purchase its own shares. Its course can be seen in the swing from prohibition of purchase under an ultra vires analysis—in some jurisdictions at least, following the English precedent—to permissive purchase from surplus, and thence to purchase even out of capital in a few favored situations where apparently there were deemed to be overriding considerations of corporate convenience.[9]

At present, both U.S. courts and legislative as well as regulatory enactments have come to regard repurchasing in a far less restrictive light (perhaps reflecting the view that it is the earning power of a firm, rather than its capital or assets, which represents the real protection for creditors). The current tendency, therefore, is only to bar or restrict specific abuses of the practice, such as:

- actual or threatened fraud against creditors;
- stock price manipulation;
- obtaining or protecting management control;
- failure to adequately disclose repurchase intentions; and
- inobservance of fiduciary responsibility.

State laws concerned with repurchases vary as to the methods allowed and the authority needed, but, in the major jurisdictions, the statutes are generally broad and supportive. In practice, federal regulation tends to be primarily influential. Ordinarily, the major constraint on repurchasing firms and one which, if met, may be sufficient to obviate many of a firm's legal obligations, is to make full and fair disclosure of all material information which a prudent investor ought to have before purchasing a security and which might be expected to have an effect on the market price. Corporations ordinarily disclose their repurchasing activity in annual reports, shareholders bulletins, and general news releases.

Restraints on repurchasing apply to a variety of specifically regulated corporations such as national banks, closed-end investment companies, and public utility holding companies. Different rules pertain to transactions executed through the open market and through tenders.

[7] EFFECTS ON SECURITY PRICE PERFORMANCE AND SECURITY MARKET CONDITIONS

The effects of repurchasing on the subsequent price performance of the firm's common stock and on general trading market conditions have attracted considerable attention in recent years. We highlight below some of the available empirical evidence.

(a) Security Price Performance

The general conclusion is that, whether a comparison is made directly between repurchased security returns and returns on the Standard and Poor's 500 Composite Stock Index, or an explicit adjustment is provided for risk, the performance of repurchased securities subsequent to such programs has been rather unfavorable.[10] Similarly, the performance of common stocks subsequent to a repurchase program tended to be less favorable than that of the common stock of similar (in terms of size and industry) firms which did not repurchase their common stock.[11]

This conclusion is hardly surprising. It is to be expected that the securities markets would recognize the relatively poor earnings prospects of the typical repurchasing firm. Moreover, as we have pointed out, an important reason for repurchasing is that the company cannot find alternate suitable outlets for investment. Essentially, corporate share repurchasing is a financial transaction which cannot be relied upon to improve a firm's operating prospects.

(b) Security Market Conditions

With respect to tender offers alone, there is some evidence of a drying up of trading volume after the expiration of the offer; but for all repurchases taken together, little difference seems to exist in trading volume between repurchasing and non-repurchasing firms.

On the positive side, in repurchasing, a slow growing firm returns once used capital to the securities markets so that these funds can be reallocated by the marketplace to the faster growing segments of the economy. Stockholders whose shares have been repurchased will use some of the funds to invest in other securities; and, presumably, at least a portion will be directed towards more rapidly growing firms. Thus, repurchasing may help in the shift of funds from less to the more promising firms. Moreover, tender offers enable shareholders to liquidate their positions without the trade being upset by short-run imbalances between buy and sell orders. To this extent, tender offers constitute a source of competition to the trading market.

In general, the shares of repurchasing firms appear to have lower beta values than non-repurchasing firms. To the extent this condition exists, the reason probably is that the tender price acts as both a ceiling and a floor. If the market price falls too far below the tender price, arbitrage will push it up. But the company does not wish to see the market price above the tender price and investors may not want to pay more than the company is willing to pay. On a fundamental level, the greater liquidity and lower use of financial leverage by repurchasing firms seems to be reflected in their lower beta values.

On the other hand, the beta values of the stocks of repurchasing companies appear to increase as the result of a repurchase program. Repurchasing tends to raise a company's financial leverage as long as it has any debt in its capital structure. Furthermore, liquid assets are diminished in a repurchase program so that the mean volatility of the remaining asset portfolio tends to increase.

An aspect that has caused some regulatory concern is the effect of repurchases on stock exchanges. Repurchase programs, if pursued far enough, can be a successful means of "going private." In this process the number of stockholders, outstanding shares, and the number of stockholders owning round lots (100 shares) will all be decreased. As this process continues, far before the point of private ownership is reached, the firm will violate the standards for continued listing on any organized exchange on which its shares may have traded. Delisting, in turn, could work a hardship on the remaining public stockholders who may then only have available a limited public market in which to buy and sell shares. The firm may even have promised to achieve an exchange listing in first "going public", yet cause the delisting by its own repurchase policy. In such a case, legal as well as regulatory issues may be raised.

21.3   FINANCIAL REARRANGEMENTS— PREFERRED STOCK

Recapitalizations involving preferred stock can take a number of forms. Companies may retire preferred because it may be less expensive to substitute either income bonds or other forms of debt involving payments of tax-deductible interest in place of the non-tax-deductible preferred dividend. Some expanding companies with an insatiable demand for funds, particularly utilities, press against the effective outer limits of capacity to incur debt on occasion, and as a result have to retire debt and sell preferred. Because of the heavy burden of debt, the rate that must be paid to market the preferred may be high. Later, when some of the debt has been retired and the company has more financial flexibility, the high dividend preferred may be called, if this is possible, or a lower dividend rate preferred may be exchanged for it through some form of inducement, or new lower rate preferred and some common may be offered.

The most complicated recapitalization involving preferred usually occurs, however, when the company decides that it must eliminate accumulated arrearages on cumulative preferred. In some cases these mount up over the years and come to exceed the market value of the preferred. Either earning power has receded and the preferred dividend cannot be met, or while earning power may be adequate to meet current preferred dividend requirements, it cannot also cope with heavy prior dividend arrearages. Under the cumulative privileges of many preferred stocks, no dividends may be paid on common unless both the current preferred dividend and the arrears are paid.

Management, representing primarily common shareholders, may move to recapitalize to eliminate preferred arrears so that dividends may be resumed on the common, assuming earning power is available. Since at least a majority of the preferred shareholders must vote in favor of any recapitalization affecting them, why should they accept a plan which by itself does not increase earning power when they have a firm priority on whatever is earned? There are two answers. The accumulation of arrears may be so large that preferred shareholders will want to have them met so that normal dividends can be resumed. Or, if the preferred dividend is being paid currently, though past accumulated arrears have not been met, management may stop paying the current preferred dividend in order to pressure the preferred shareholders into accepting a recapitalization plan.

The crucial question in a recapitalization involving preferred stock arrears is what value to place on such arrears in the proposed exchange of shares. Management customarily argues that the preferred shareholder is entitled only to the discounted value of his arrears based on the time it would take to pay off such arrears. The disenchanted shareholder, on the other hand, pointing to the past interest free use of his arrears by the company, feels he is entitled to the full amount of the accumulation. Thus all such plans are open to differing interpretations of fairness.

There is no one right recapitalization plan. One must start with the premise that a recapitalization plan is the product of judgment applied to estimates of operating performance. In this approach there is no absolute scale to measure fairness in fixing terms of exchange of old stocks for new.

A final item that is worthy of note with respect to financial rearrangements concerning preferred stock is the forced conversion of this security into common stock, which management, under certain circumstances, can bring about. In order for management to be able to do this, the following conditions must prevail:

- the preferred shares must be convertible into common stock;
- the preferred shares must be callable; and
- the common stock value of the number of common shares into which the preferred is convertible must be greater than the call price of the preferred stock.

The following example illustrates the typical forced conversion situation. Company A has a preferred issue outstanding which is callable at a 5 percent premium above its par value of $100. The preferred is convertible into two shares of common stock which is currently selling at $60 a share. In this case, Company A could force its preferred stockholders to convert their position into common stock by threatening to call the preferred stock. On a share of called preferred stock, Company A would pay $105 ($100 + 5% x $100), whereas a preferred stockholder could convert each of his shares into common stock worth $120 ($60 x 2). The preferred stockholder would be better off converting into common stock than accepting a call of his preferred shares, even if he did not wish to become a common stockholder. He could probably still convert into common stock and sell the common stock and net more than the call price of his preferred shares even after paying commissions on the sale of the common stock. Before considering commissions on the sale of the common stock, the break-even point in the price of the common stock above which Company A could force conversion of its preferred shares into common shares, is $52½ ($52½ x 2 = $105).

In addition to being able to force conversion of its convertible and callable preferred shares into common stock under the circumstances outlined above, companies can, under similar circumstances, force conversion of their convertible and callable bonds into common stock.[12]

21.4   FINANCIAL REARRANGEMENTS— DEBT STRUCTURE

There are many financial rearrangements affecting the debt structure. Long-term debt may be issued to meet short-term debt maturities. Debt may be substituted for preferred or common in order to secure tax savings. On rare occasions, common will be sold to eliminate debt and reduce fixed charges. In addition, as mentioned previously, for a firm with debt, repurchase of its common stock results in restructuring the proportions and the degree of leverage in the capital structure. Our ensuing discussion of debt refunding focuses on the motives for refunding and the determination of refunding cost savings.

[1] REFUNDING MOTIVES

Refunding corporate debt can occur for a number of reasons. A cost savings can be achieved because a high interest coupon can be replaced by a lower one. Secondly, when debt is maturing, and it is not expedient to pay it off, new bonds may be offered in place of the maturing ones.[13] Bonds with objectionable features and technically disadvantageous or restrictive provisions can be replaced with more flexible issues. When a bond issue approaches maturity, when there has been no sinking fund arrangement and when the funds are not in hand to pay it off at its due date, the probable course is an extension of the maturity of the issue.

Usually a refunding has the intended effect of lowering interest costs. Timing is, of course, a big factor. Interest rates had been generally rising over most of the period from 1951 to 1981, whereas, over the previous 30 years, from 1921 to 1951, the trend had for the most part been downward. However, since 1981, interest rates have again started to decline, offering refunding opportunities. Unless the bond issue has a call provision, the company cannot, of course, take advantage of a decline in interest rates. Management will press for the earliest possible call provision at the lowest premiums, whereas investors will wish for either a remote or no call provision and high call premiums.

[2] DETERMINATION OF COST SAVINGS FROM REFUNDING

The calculation of the financial advantage from refunding at a lower rate of interest is not a simple matter based on a comparison of two levels of rates. It is complicated by additional factors such as:

- bond discounts and premiums;
- taxes;
- underwriting costs;
- legal fees; and
- present value of a stream of future cost savings over a large number of years.

However, in all such situations, the problem is one of comparing the future savings from refunding with the present cost of doing so. A variety of techniques have been employed in making the calculation. A rather straight-forward method is developed below and a more complicated technique used by a major telephone company is illustrated in Appendix A.

In the more direct procedure a rate of return is calculated which equates the present value of the future savings from the refunding to the present costs of the operation. The following example illustrates this technique. Assume that a company has a 30-year, $40 million bond issue outstanding, with 20 years to run. The coupon rate is 14 percent. Currently, the company finds that it can refund at 12 percent with a new issue which bears a 20 year maturity and can be issued at par. The old bonds are callable at 105, however, which represents a 5 percent premium. In addition, the company will incur certain under-writing costs and legal fees and will pay duplicate interest[14] for a short period because, for safety, management will not call the old issue until the new bonds are sold. Accordingly, the current costs that are created as a result of the refunding may be summarized as follows:[15]

• Call premium	$2,000,000
• Legal and other fees	800,000
• One month's interest on the old bonds	466,667
Total	$3,266,667

The major cash saving that the company will realize, of course, is the differential between the after-tax interest charges on the two issues. In addition, the current cash costs of the refunding will be treated as deferred charges to be written off over the life of the bonds. Accordingly, the company will also benefit from the tax savings as a result of these subsequent changes to earnings. These future cash flow savings may be summarized as follows:

• 14 percent of $40 million on the old issue	$5,600,000
• 12 percent of $40 million on the new issue	4,800,000
• Interest Savings	800,000
• After 50 percent taxes	400,000
• Future annual charge to earnings to write-off deferred charges ($3,266,667/20)	163,333
• Tax Savings	81,666
• Total after-tax savings	
—Interest	400,000
—From write-off of deferred charges	81,666
TOTAL	$481,666

The total cash flow savings, in effect, represent an ordinary annuity of $481,666 to be received for 20 years. The rate that results in the present value of this annuity equaling $3,266,667, the current cash costs of the refunding, represents the return from the operation. It may then be calculated as follows:*

$$\frac{\$3,266,667}{\$\ 481,666} = \sum_{t=1}^{20} (1 + i)^{-t}$$

$$\$6.78 = \sum_{t=1}^{20} (1 + i)^{-t}$$

$i = 13.6\%$[16]

*according to the methods and procedures developed in Chapter 17.5[2](b).

The financial manager may use this rate to compare with his minimum return on investment or with other investment opportunities. In deciding upon the final course of action, he may also be influenced by the fact that the return from the refunding is reasonably certain (although tax rates may change from time to time affecting the calculation). On the other hand, while the return from alternative investment opportunities may be higher, the risks may also be greater.[17]

21.5   FINANCIAL REORGANIZATIONS

Financial reorganization includes: [1] financial readjustments, [2] corporate reorganizations, [3] bankruptcy and liquidation. These topics are included in the same chapter as repurchasing since, as we have seen, repurchasing can be and often is the route by which a firm achieves an orderly death and liquidation. While the discontinuance of many companies results from simple liquidation or retirement, others die because of financial difficulties and ineffective management.

Among the basic underlying causes of failure as reported by Dun & Bradstreet are incompetence; unbalanced experience, that is, experience not well rounded in sales, finance, purchasing, and production; lack of managerial experience; and lack of experience in the line. These underlying causes of failure are evidenced by an inability to avoid conditions which resulted in inadequate sales, heavy operating expenses, receivables difficulties, excessive fixed assets, inventory difficulties, and other competitive weaknesses.[18]

In the technical parlance of finance, business failure may mean two different things. It may mean insolvency in the equity sense, that current liabilities exceed current assets and that the firm cannot at the moment meet maturing liabilities even though total assets exceed total liabilities. Insolvency in the bankruptcy sense, on the other hand, implies that both total and current liabilities exceed total and current assets. Failure thus, in the broad sense, may result in financial readjustments or corporate reorganizations, with the concern continuing in existence after necessary financial changes are made; however, it may also result in bankruptcy and liquidation. Most of the limited number of large firms which get into financial difficulties reorganize and continue. Many smaller ones go into bankruptcy and liquidate. We turn now to a discussion of each of the major types of financial readjustments.

[1] FINANCIAL READJUSTMENTS

The major techniques by which financial readjustments may be achieved, short of the more drastic measures of reorganization or even bankruptcy, include the following:

- extensions;
- compositions; and
- creditors' committees.

Creditors have often found that it is better to compromise and work out a mutually acceptable plan of financial readjustment for the embarrassed firm, than to throw it into bankruptcy and force liquidation. A hasty resort to the courts by one creditor has often in the past brought larger losses to all creditors than would have been the case had a quiet, relatively unpublicized readjustment plan been worked out, agreed to, and implemented. Where the embarrassed firm is not large, creditors relatively few, and management reputable, such readjustments can be developed more easily. At times outside mediation by a third party, such as a Credit Men's Association or an Adjustment Bureau, may be necessary, especially to persuade dubious creditors that it is to their ultimate advantage to go along with the proposed readjustment plan.

(a) Extensions

If the readjustment takes the form of an *extension*, giving the debtor more time to meet his obligations, it is necessary for all creditors to agree to it. If there are any dissenters, they will have to be paid off because they could otherwise throw the debtor into bankruptcy. On occasion, a large creditor who recognizes the value of helping the embarrassed firm over its present difficulties and keeping it in business may agree to pay off a smaller creditor in order to make the extension possible.

(b) Compositions

If the difficulties are more involved than those which can be met by a simple extension (e.g., if the debts are too large compared to probable capacity to repay in a reasonable length of time) the debtor may appeal to his creditors for an arrangement known as a *composition*. This is an agreement, usually in legal form, whereby creditors agree to accept a reduced amount in settlement for the full indebtedness. That is, creditors may agree to accept 70 cents on the dollar because they know the debtor cannot pay in full, that if they hold out he may be forced into bankruptcy, and that on liquidation by way of this time consuming and costly legal procedure, they may receive only 30 cents on the dollar.

(c) Creditors' Committees

To satisfy creditors that appropriate corrective steps will be taken in the future to meet obligations which are extended or reduced, the present management of the debtor firm may be asked to agree to step aside for a time and allow the business to be run by a creditors' committee or by someone nominated by the creditors. The present management may be forced to accede to this because the alternative, bankruptcy and liquidation, is even less palatable.

[2] CORPORATE REORGANIZATIONS

The United States Congress has the power, under the Federal Constitution, to establish uniform laws regulating bankruptcy. Under this authority various acts have been passed. The Bankruptcy Act of 1898, as amended in 1938 and again in 1978, is the basic federal legislation in this area.

(a) 1978 Amendments to the Bankruptcy Law[19]

Among the many changes brought about by the 1978 amendments, two stand out as particularly important:

- consolidation of Chapters X and XI; and
- added flexibility to creditors and stockholders in deciding upon a bankrupt company's value and negotiating a settlement.

The most fundamental change in the law brought about by the 1978 amendments is the consolidation of Chapters X and XI, as well as two other more specialized chapters, into a single procedure (new Chapter XI). As companies no longer have any choice of chapters disputes, which were formerly common, over which one is proper (X or XI) have been eliminated.[20] The new law also permits more informal negotiations between a company and its creditors and stockholders, and it gives the court more discretion to retain management instead of appointing a trustee. (The old Chapter X required the appointment of a trustee in cases in which the company's debt was $250,000 or more). It was intended at the time of the passage of this new law that the consolidation chapter would reduce squabbling, spread reorganizations, and improve the chances that unsecured creditors and stockholders would realize something on their claims. However, critics of the new legislation felt that if trustees were named less often, most reorganizations would be controlled by the corporation and by its senior creditors, usually including big lenders like banks and insurance companies. The law provides that a trustee will be appointed only for cause such as fraud, incompetence or gross misman-agement by the company, or if the court decides for some other reason that it is in the best interest of creditors and stockholders. Failing these considera-tions, incumbent management is to remain in office. However, the SEC is at liberty under the new law to file a motion to have a trustee appointed.

Another important provision of the new law has the effect of giving creditors and stockholders more flexibility in deciding upon a bankrupt company's value and negotiating a payoff plan. The old Chapter X absolute priority rule required that senior creditors must be fully compensated before anything goes to junior creditors, followed by stockholders. In practice, this often resulted in junior interests being completely frozen out. Yet in some cases under the old Chapter X proceeding some observers felt that this freeze out of junior interests occurred despite the willingness of senior creditors to take less than full value in order to expedite a reorganization. The new bankruptcy law eases the absolute priority rule to some extent. Corporate debtors are now permitted to negotiate a restructuring of debt with all creditors and stockholders. If the bankruptcy court finds that claimants will receive at least as much as they would under a straight liquidation, then a reorganization plan can be cleared by a vote of those affected.

(b) Financial Aspects of Corporate Reorganizations

If the court approves, drastic financial changes are possible through reorganization including:

- requiring junior bondholders to accept an equity interest in the reorganized company;
- changing the maturity dates and coupons on outstanding securities;
- amending the debtor's charter or certificate of incorporation;
- wiping out stockholders or permitting them to retain a proportionally smaller interest in the reorganized company;
- modifying or cancelling indentures;
- paying off creditors in whole or part;
- authorizing and issuing new securities;
- borrowing of funds with an overriding priority; and
- merging the debtor company with another firm or spinning off or selling a subsidiary or division.

In brief, the rights of secured and unsecured creditors and stockholders may be altered, leases and contracts abrogated, and property disposed of in any fashion that the court judges to be fair and reasonable. The more drastic the reorganization, the more severe may be the treatment of security holders, the essential financial aim of reorganization is to ensure that the company emerging from the procedure has been rehabilitated and can operate successfully on its own without recurrent financial embarrassment.

In the formulation of a plan of reorganization, three broad financial problems confront the court and the trustee; these include:

- What is the overall value of the proposed reorganized company?
- How is the new capital structure to reflect this value? and
- How are the proposed new classes of securities to be allocated to the old security holders?

These are difficult questions with no simple answers. The new law at least provides the opportunity for a more flexible solution than previously. In the ensuing sections, we discuss each of these three challenging issues.

[i] Assessing Value of the Reorganized Company

The starting point of any reorganization is the valuation of the company's assets. One technique frequently used is the capitalization of prospective earning power. If the reorganized company can be expected to generate annual sales of $40 million and it is estimated that it will earn 10 percent after taxes on sales, earnings will amount to $4 million per annum. If a price/earnings ratio of 10 times or a capitalization rate of 10 percent is applied (because this is the average experience of going companies in the industry) we arrive at a valuation of $40 million for the proposed reorganized company.

[ii] Establishing the New Capital Structure

Having established a valuation for the reorganized company, the focus turns to the revision of its capital structure. If the burden of fixed charges was the cause of insolvency, then the need to reduce the proportion of debt is clear.

One norm or standard that might be used to estimate the appropriate proportion of debt is the average for the leading companies in the industry. If this is 20 percent, for example, and the burden in the debtor company is 40 percent, then a halving of the company's debt is suggested. Reduction of the fixed charge debt may be accomplished by substituting income bonds or preferred stock. If part of the debt is secured by a senior lien on specific income earning property, it may be necessary to leave this lien untouched. Junior issues may have to incur the sacrifice of reducing debt and fixed charges, although this absolute priority is not required by the revised law. In the reorganized company, fixed charges should not be assumed in excess of those which the company can expect to cover in an adverse year. In a conservative reorganization, the same test should apply to the income bond contingent interest requirement and the preferred stock dividend. Any debt which is carried forward to the reorganized company should have a provision for sinking fund requirement, both to enhance the prospect that the company will not encounter another fixed charge crisis and to build new equity. If additional financing is required by the reorganized company, then a smaller volume of debt than might otherwise be the case can be carried forward in order to leave room in the capital structure for additional debt. If additional financing is not required, or if additional funds can be obtained by new contributions from the old equity holders, then less drastic sacrifices may be required of the old bondholders.

All these prescriptions and others which flow from them are based on the assumption that there will be a relatively stable flow of earnings. If, however, the outlook for prospective earnings is sufficiently uncertain or if profits are likely to fluctuate markedly, then a debt free capital structure may be the best, though more severe solution. If it is not clear that fixed charges can be met in future adverse years, then they should not be incurred. The proposed capital structure is a function of expected earnings.

[iii] Allocating Proposed Securities to Holders of Old Securities

Once the revised capital structure has been determined, the difficult problem of allocating the proposed securities to each class of old security holders can be addressed. In the Solomon-like decision-making task of allocating new securities to old, the court and the trustee must walk a narrow path between the requirement for fairness and equity with its now eased absolute priority dictum on the one hand, and the feasibility requirement on the other. While the two extreme cases are reasonably clear—the secured bondholder on the one hand and the common stockholder on the other—there are many shades of gray in between.

Considerations of fairness may require that the claim of one class be subordinated to others, that interest be fixed rather than contingent, or that a security of a superior grade and quality than that proposed be issued. To be feasible, the plan should, among other things, result in a reorganized company which can reasonably be expected to meet obligations imposed by the proposed capitalization.

(c) Role of the SEC

Under the Bankruptcy Code the SEC does not have authority to initiate, hold hearings, or determine issues in bankruptcy proceedings. However, at the request of the judge, the Commission may participate in such proceedings in order to provide independent expert assistance to the court and investors on matters arising in the proceedings. Where the commission considers it appropriate, it may also file advisory reports on reorganization plans. Thus, the facilities of the Commission's technical staff and its disinterested recommendations are placed at the service of the judge and the parties, affording them experts in this specialized area of corporate law and finance. The Commission pays special attention to the interest of public security holders, who may not otherwise be effectively represented. Where the Commission files a report, copies or summaries of it must be sent to all security holders and creditors when they are asked to vote on the plan. The SEC has no authority to veto or require the adoption of a plan of reorganization and is not obligated to file a formal advisory report on a plan.

The Commission's advisory reports on plans of reorganizations are usually widely distributed and serve an important function. However, they represent only one aspect of the Commission's activities in cases in which it participates. As a party to a bankruptcy proceeding, the SEC is actively interested in the solution of every major issue arising therefrom and the adequate performance of its duties requires that it undertake, in most cases, intensive financial and legal studies. It has endeavored to assist the courts in achieving equitable, financially sound, expeditious, and economical readjustments of the affairs of corporations in financial distress.

The SEC has not considered it necessary or appropriate to participate in every bankruptcy case. Apart from the fact that participating in every one of the cases instituted during the fiscal year would be a great burden on a limited staff, many of the cases involve only trade or bank creditors and a few stockholders. The Commission has sought to participate principally in proceedings in which a substantial public interest is involved. This is not the only criterion, however, and in some cases involving only limited public investor interest the Commission has participated because it thought it had evidence to suggest that an unfair plan had been or was about to be proposed, the public security holders were not adequately represented, or the reorganization proceedings were being conducted in violation of important provisions of the law.

One of the prime duties of the court and the trustee is to make a thorough study of the debtor to assure the discovery and collection of all assets, including claims against directors, officers, or controlling persons who may have mismanaged the company's affairs, diverted its funds to their own use or benefit, or been guilty of other misconduct. The staff of the Commission participates in the court's and the trustee's investigations so that it may be fully informed of all details of the financial history and business practice of the debtor.

[3] BANKRUPTCY AND LIQUIDATION[21]

When it appears that there is no hope for success even after drastic financial surgery, or if prospects are so uninviting as to make further expenditure of funds, time, and talent unattractive, then the only remaining course may be liquidation. If debts exceed assets, final liquidation may take one of two forms:

- assignment; or
- bankruptcy.

(a) Assignment

An assignment is a formal private method for the orderly settlement of debts. In some states it is a common law procedure, in others a statutory matter. Assets are assigned to a trustee, usually selected by creditors, to be liquidated by him for the settlement of all claims against the liquidating company. All creditors must agree to the proposed settlement, since any one dissenting creditor can throw the liquidating company into bankruptcy because assignment constitutes one of the acts of bankruptcy. To ensure the faith of creditors in the proposed liquidation, it is customary to appoint as assignee or trustee the Adjustment Bureau of the local Credit Men's Association. Assets are sold and the proceeds distributed pro rata to creditors in full and final settlement of the debts. Since the assignment is a good faith undertaking all around, it is customary for the creditors to release the debtor from further liability. The assignment is usually a faster, less costly method of liquidation than the more formal bankruptcy procedure.

(b) Bankruptcy

Until 1933, the Bankruptcy Act, in its first seven chapters, provided only for what is still commonly regarded as the essential function of a bankruptcy procedure, the orderly liquidation of an insolvent debtor under court supervision. This involved, of course, the equitable distribution of the proceeds of the liquidation among the creditors of the bankrupt and released the insolvent firm or individual from further liability for the debts.

A firm may become involved in a bankruptcy proceeding either voluntarily or involuntarily. In a voluntary action, a petition is filed by the insolvent firm; involuntary bankruptcy results from the action of creditors.

Six acts of bankruptcy are set forth in the Bankruptcy code. These occur when,

- the alleged bankrupt has concealed, removed, or permitted to be concealed or removed any part of its property with the intent to hinder, delay, or defraud his creditors;
- the alleged bankrupt, while insolvent, and within four months of the petition, has transferred any portion of his property to a creditor, so as to give one or more creditors a preference over others;
- the alleged bankrupt, while insolvent, has permitted any creditor to obtain a lien upon any of its properties through legal proceedings;
- the alleged bankrupt makes a general assignment for the benefit of creditors;
- the alleged bankrupt, while insolvent or unable to pay debts as they mature, arranges for or permits the appointment of a receiver or trustee to take charge of its property; or
- the alleged bankrupt admits in writing its inability to pay debts and its willingness to be adjudged a bankrupt.

Whether the petition is voluntary or involuntary, once the firm is adjudged a bankrupt, there is no difference in procedure, which is handled through a referee. The referee will arrange the meeting of creditors, claims will be proven, and the creditors will be given an opportunity to select a trustee in bankruptcy. If this cannot be done promptly, a temporary receiver in bankruptcy may be appointed to conserve assets and manage the bankrupt's affairs until the trustee can be selected and take over. The referee acts for the court administratively. The receiver or trustee is actually in charge of the bankrupt's affairs and property. The bankrupt is required to file schedules listing his assets and his debts as well as a "statement of affairs." To the trustee falls the task of liquidating the assets of the bankrupt, making the final accounting, and paying the liquidating dividends, all subject to the supervision and approval of the referee. Finally, the petition for discharge of the bankrupt is granted thereby releasing him from any further obligation with respect to the debts. The bankrupt may not be discharged from subsequent debts through another bankruptcy proceeding for six years. The distribution of the proceeds from the liquidation of the bankrupt must follow priorities stipulated in the Bankruptcy Code. Certain unpaid wages and taxes take highest priority with secured claims coming next and general or unsecured claims following.

21.6 CHAPTER SUMMARY

In this chapter we discussed the wide variety of changes that the firm's financial structure may undergo. In addition to the repurchasing and refunding of outstanding securities, these changes also encompass total financial reorganization including the radical forms of bankruptcy and liquidation. These changes emphasize the dynamic nature of the firm's financial structure and point out the need for active participation on the part of the financial manager.

FOOTNOTES

1. A more extensive treatment of this subject appears in Charles Ellis and Allan Young, *The Repurchase of Common Stock*, New York, Ronald Press, 1971.
2. "Greenmail" is the term now commonly applied to such a transaction.
3. For a more detailed analysis of this motive for repurchasing see, Ellis and Young, *Ibid.*, Chapter 4; Wayne Marshall and Allan Young, "Controlling Shareholder Servicing Costs", *Harvard Business Review*, January-February 1971, pp. 71-78; and Wayne Marshall and Allan Young, "A Mathematical Model for Re-Acquisition of Small Shareholdings," *Journal of Financial and Quantitative Analysis*, December 1968, pp. 463-469.
4. Another type of repurchase program is intended to prevent the creation of new common shares. Such a defensive measure occurs in the repurchase of warrants or convertible securities that might lead to subsequent dilution through the creation of new shares.
5. Allan Young, "The Financial, Operating and Security Market Parameters of Repurchasing: A Behavioral Approach," *Financial Analysts Journal*, July-August 1969; Ellis and Young, *op. cit.*, Chapter 6; Joseph Finnerty, "Corporate Stock Issue and Repurchase," *Financial Management*, Autumn 1975, pp. 62-65; Richard and Corine Norgaard, "A Critical Examination of Share Repurchase," *Financial Management*, Spring 1974; and Edward Dyl, Richard White, and

Richard and Corine Norgaard, "A Critical Examination of Share Repurchase: Dyl and White vs. Norgaard and Norgaard," *Financial Management,* Autumn 1974, pp. 68-73.

6. Much of this discussion is drawn from Bertrand Horwitz and Allan Young, "The Case for Asset Disclosure of Treasury Stock," *C.P.A. Journal,* March 1975; Allan Young, "Accounting for Treasury Stock," *Journal of Accounting, Auditing and Finance,* Spring 1978, pp. 217-230; and B. Melcher, "Stockholders' Equity," *Accounting Research Study No. 15,* New York, AICPA, 1973.

7. For some of the evidence bearing on this issue see, Allan Young, *Journal of Accounting, Auditing and Finance, op. cit.,* pp. 226-230.

8. For a considerable time the British legal tradition on this subject was influenced by a continuing reaction to the infamous South Sea Bubble which was a financial collapse made harsher by the South Sea Company's absurd attempt to support an unsustainably inflated price by repurchasing its own shares in the open market. The English restriction began with the 1887 decision in Trevor vs. Whitworth which gave the following view:

> No doubt if certain shareholders are disposed to hamper the proceedings of the company, and are willing to sell their shares, they may be bought out; but this may be done by persons, existing shareholders, or others, who can be induced to purchase the shares, and not out of the funds of the company.

(Robert A. Kessler, "Share Repurchases Under Modern Corporation Laws," *Fordham Law Review,* Vol. 28 (1959-1960), p. 644. In recent years, however, the British prohibition of repurchases has been relaxed somewhat by the Companies Act of 1980.

9. Elvin B. Latty, "Some Miscellaneous Novelties in the New Corporation Statutes," 23 *Law and Contemporary Problems* 363, at 378, 1958. See also Ralph J. Baker and William L. Cary, *Cases and Materials on Corporations,* 4th ed., Mineola, Foundation Press, 1969.

10. On the other hand, some studies have come to generally differing results, but these are in the minority. For example, see Samuel S. Stuart, Jr., "Should a Corporation Repurchase Its Own Stock?" *Journal of Finance,* June 1976, pp. 911-921.

11. Ellis and Young, *op. cit.,* Chapt. 10; Marvin Rosenberg and Allan Young, "The Performance of Common Stocks Subsequent to Repurchase by Recent Tender Offers," *The Quarterly Review of Economics and Business,* Spring 1976, pp. 109-113; Robert Coates and Albert J. Fredman, "Price Behavior Associated with Tender Offers to Repurchase Common Stock," *Financial Executive,* April 1976; and Kenneth R. Marx, "The Stock Price Performance of Firms Repurchasing Their Own Shares," *The Bulletin,* New York University, 1976.

12. For the development of the optimal call strategy on a convertible and callable bond see, M.J. Breenan and E.S. Schwartz, "Convertible Bonds: Valuation and Optimal Strategies for Call and Conversion," *The Journal of Finance,* December 1977, pp. 1699-1715.

13. Railroads and utilities especially, because of their earlier heavy incurrence of debt, have in recent years faced vast refunding problems.

14. For a further analysis of the problem of determining the overlapping interest cost in a bond refunding see, Douglas, R. Emery, "Overlapping Interest in Bond Refunding: A Reconsideration," *Financial Management,* Summer 1978, pp. 19-20.

15. A portion of the duplicate interest is offset by the proceeds derived from the temporary investment of the new issue. No underwriting costs are shown because the fee of the underwriter ordinarily is represented by his markup, and from the

point of view of the company, the cost rate of the new money is the significant consideration.

16. Alternatively, the call expenses (call premium, legal and other fees) can be *immediately deducted* for income tax purposes rather than written-off over the life of the bonds as in the above illustration. If this tax treatment is used and we assume a tax rate of 50%, the return from refunding is increased to about 24%. This very high post-tax return from refunding shows that the main question is often not *whether* to call (rather than use funds for other activities), but rather *when* to call (at this time versus at a later date when refunding rates may be even lower). Thus, the primary cost of refunding may not be the out-of-pocket call expenses, but rather the "expenditure" or extinction of the *call option itself.*

17. Techniques for handling risk differentials between alternate investment opportunities were discussed in Chapters 2 and 18.

18. Business failures, as defined by Dun & Bradstreet, "include businesses which have ceased operations following assignments or bankruptcy; ceased with loss to creditors after such actions as execution, foreclosure, or attachment; voluntarily withdrew, leaving unpaid obligations; were involved in court actions such as receivership, reorganization, or arrangement; or voluntarily compromised with creditors." (*The Business Failure Record,* Dun & Bradstreet, Inc., 1982, p. 15).

19. In June 1978, the Supreme Court ruled some sections of the Bankruptcy Code unconstitutional and as of this writing Congress is currently revising this statute.

20. Chapter XI gave the management of a bankrupt firm far more power and was thus much more desired by them.

21. A February, 1984 Supreme Court ruling has given management the power to file for bankruptcy when burdensome financial commitments, such as large litigation claims or union contracts, present themselves. ("Labor's Pain: Unionists are Alarmed by High Court Bankruptcy Filing," *The Wall Street Journal,* February 24, 1984, pp. 1 and 13.)

SUGGESTED READINGS

Aharony, Joseph, "Analysis of Risk and Return Characteristics of Corporate Bankruptcy Using Capital Market Data," *Journal of Finance,* September 1980.

Asofsky, Paul H. and William Tatlock, "Reorganization, Procedures and Corporate Taxes Greatly Affected by Bankruptcy Tax Act," *Journal of Taxation,* March 1981.

Batterson, L., "Strategies for Avoiding Company Liquidation," *ABA Banking Journal,* April 1982.

Broderick, P., "Reorganizations From A to G: Which One is Right for You?" *Mergers and Acquisitions,* Winter 1982.

Carmichael, K., "Comments, Please, On Own-Share Buying," *Accountant,* November 12, 1981.

Carpenter, David A., "Analysis of Alternative Courses of Action for a Debtor's Troubled Business," *Journal of Commercial Bank Lending,* September 1981.

Fraser, Donald R. et. al., "Share Repurchase: Your Best Investment?" *Financial Executive,* November 1980.

Harris, Edwin C. and George F. Lengvari, "Using Life Insurance To Repurchase Corporate Shares," *CA Magazine,* July 1980.

Harris, Robert S., "The Refunding of Discounted Debt: An Adjusted Present Value Analysis," *Financial Management,* Winter 1980.

Kaye, Michael, "Preferences Under the New Bankruptcy Code," *The American Bankruptcy Law Journal,* Summer 1980.

Klee, Kenneth N., "Legislative History of the New Bankruptcy Code," *The American Bankruptcy Law Journal,* Summer 1980.

Levine, Richard L., and H. David Sherman, "Trade-Offs in the New Bankruptcy Law," *Harvard Business Review,* March-April 1980.

Mann, Curtis L., "The New Bankruptcy Code—Some Early Problems and Suggested Solutions," *Commercial Law Journal,* January 1980.

Palmon, Dan, and Uzi Yaaru, "Stock Repurchase as a Tax-saving Distribution," *The Journal of Financial Research,* Spring 1981.

Rosenberg, R.J., "New Chapter 11: The Creditors' Side of the Equation," *Credit and Financial Management,* February 1980.

Schlenger, Jaques T. et. al., "Recapitalizing a Closely Held Business," *Practical Accountant,* April/May 1980.

Weedenbaum, Murray, "Business Bankruptcies Soar," *Dun's Business Month,* April 1982.

Wittebort, Suzanne, "The New Boom in Stock Repurchases," *Institutional Investor,* August 1980.

Yawitz, J.B., and J.A. Anderson, "The Effect of Bond Refunding on Shareholder Wealth," *Journal of Finance,* December 1977.

Young, Allan, "Accounting for Treasury Stock," *Journal of Accounting, Auditing and Finance,* Spring 1978.

APPENDIX A:
MAJOR TELEPHONE COMPANY METHOD OF ANALYZING REFUNDING OPPORTUNITIES

The after-tax method which a major telephone company uses to analyze refunding opportunities is shown in Figure 21.2, 21.3 and 21.4. The procedure normally assumes that the face amount of the new issue is large enough to finance the refunding. The refunding face amount, therefore, equals the sume of the refunded issue face amount plus the total refunding costs. Total refunding costs include the call premium, expenses of calling the old issue, the 30 day carrying cost of the new issue (the overlap period between issuance of the new issue and calling the old issue is assumed to be 30 days), tax savings on expenses, discount or premium on the new issue, and the tax effect of the unamortized discount or premium on the old issue.

Once the required face amount of the new issue is determined, the interest savings (the difference between the cash flow *without* refunding the old issue and the cash flow *with* refunding the old issue) is calculated on a semi-annual basis. The refunding is considered to be profitable when the present value of the semi-annual after-tax cash flow savings, discounted at the after-tax new issue cost, is greater than the additional amount that must be paid back at maturity. Before making a decision to refund, however, certain qualitative factors must be considered. For example, the savings must be weighed against the probability that interest rates will fall further in the future, thereby producing a greater saving. (Bear in mind that a new issue normally cannot be called for 5-10 years, depending on the call provisions.)

Figure 21.2 presents a set of assumptions used to summarize the refunding method described in Figure 21.3. In order to further clarify the method, Figure 22.4 shows sample calculations which ascertain the estimated total savings from refunding a $100 million issue, with a 10 percent coupon, due in 40 years and callable at the end of the 5th year at an 8.57 percent call premium.

FIGURE 21.2 *Assumptions and symbols used by in refunding by a major telephone company*

			Example Figures*
F_O	=	face amount of the refunded (old) issue	$100,000,000
I_O	=	coupon rate on the refunded issue (%)	10%
N_O	=	number of years from issue to maturity of the refunded issue	40 Years
N_C	=	number of years from issue to call of the refunded issue	5 Years
C	=	call premium (%)	8.57%
P_O	=	net proceeds to company from the sale of old issue	99%
E	=	expenses of calling the refunded issue	$200,000
F	=	face amount of the refunding (new) issue	to be calculated
I	=	coupon rate of the refunding issue	8%
N	=	number of years from issue to maturity of the refunding issue (We assume $N = N_O - N_C$ in analyses)	35 Years
I_S	=	short-term interest rate	9%
P	=	net proceeds to company from the sale of new issue	99%
t	=	marginal corporate tax rate	46%
NCF_O	=	tax-adjusted semi-annual net cash flow on old issue	
NCF	=	tax-adjusted semi-annual net cash flow on new issue	
S	=	semi-annual cash flow savings ($S = NCF_O - NCF$)	
M	=	difference between the old and new issue face amount ($M = F - F_O$)	
PV_k	=	present value discounted at a rate of k	

*Figures will be used in the example, Figure 22.4.

Note: Percent figures should be converted to decimal numerals when calculating.

FIGURE 21.3 *A method used by a major telephone company for refunding analyses*

Step I:	Determination of New Issue Face Amount

Component: Description	Equation or Symbols
1. **Face amount of old issue:** Amount of outstanding debt to be refunded	F_O
2. **Call Premium**	$F_O C$
3. **Expenses of calling old issue:** Legal & Trustee, Advertising, Postage and Printing Expenses	E
4. **30-day carrying cost of new issue:** The profit from the 30-day short-term investment less the 30-day interest expense on new issue. The proceeds of the refunding issue are assumed to be invested at the short-term rate during the 30-day overlap period.	$\dfrac{F}{12}(I - PI_s)$
5. **Tax effect on expenses:** Tax effect on the call premium, calling expenses and the 30-day carrying costs which are written-off immediately for tax purposes.	$t[F_O C + E + \dfrac{F}{12}(I - PI_s)$

6. **Discount or premium of new issue** $F(1 - P)$

7. **Tax effect on unamortized discount or premium on old issue;** Since only N_c of the N_o years in the life of old issue have elapsed, an amount $F_o(1 - P_o) N/N_o$ remains to be written-off. $tF_o (1 - P_o) N/N_o$

8. **Face amount of refunding issue:** This is the sum of 1, 2, 3, 4, 5, 6 and 7 above. F

9. **Difference in face amounts of old and new issues:** F is normally assumed to be larger than F_o, since F is the sum of F_o and the total refunding expenses. $F - F_o$

Calculation of F:

$F = F_o + F_oC + E + F/12 (I - PI_s) - t[F_oC + E + F/12 (I - PI_s)] + F(1 - P) - tF_o (1-P_o) N/N_o$

Solving for F, we get

$$F = \frac{F_o + (F_oC + E) (1 - t) - F_ot (1 - P_o) N/N_o}{P - (I - PI_s) (1 - t/12)}$$ [1]

Step II: Estimation of Semi-Annual Cash Flow Savings

Component (Semi-Annual Basis)	Equation or Symbols
1. Interest on old issue	$1/2F_oI_o$
2. Amortization of discount or premium of old issue	$F_o/2N_o (1 - P_o)$
3. Tax effect on old issue $[t(1 + 2)]$	$1/2F_ot [I_o + 1/N_o (1 - P_o)]$
4. Net cash flow (NCF_o) on old issue (1-3)	$1/2F_oI_o - 1/2F_ot [I_o + 1/N_o (1 - P_o)]$
5. Interest on new issue	$1/2FI$
6. Amortization of discount or premium of new issue	$F/2N (1 - P)$
7. Tax effect on new issue $[t(5+6)]$	$1/2Ft[I + 1/N (1 - P)]$
8. Net cash flow (NCF) on new issue (5-7)	$1/2FI - 1/2Ft [I + 1/N (1 - P)]$
9. Cash Flow savings (S) (4-8)	$NCF_o - NCF$

Calculations of S:

$S = (1 - t/2) (F_oI_o - FI) + Ft/2N (1 - P) - F_ot/2N_o (1 - P_o)$ [2]

Step III: Estimation of Present Value of Savings from Refunding

$$PV_k = \sum_{i=1}^{2N} \frac{S}{(1+K)^i} - \frac{M}{(1+K)^{2N}}$$ [3]

Notes: If the present value as estimated is positive, the refunding is profitable. By testing different values of I, it is possible to determine the point at which the present value equals zero. This is the "break-even point" for refunding the given issue.

FIGURE 21.4 *Sample calculations of a method used by a major telephone company for refunding analyses*

Step I: Determination of New Issue Face Amount	
1. Face amount of old issue	$100,000,000
2. Call premium	8,570,000
3. Expenses of calling old issue	200,000
4. 30-day carrying cost of new issue (Note: F is to be calculated)	-.0008F
5. Tax effect on expenses	-4,034,200 + .0004F
6. Discount of new issue	.01F
7. Tax effect on unamortized discount on old issue	- 402,500
8. Face amount of new issue (solving for F with sum of 1 through 7)	$F = \dfrac{104,333,300}{.9904}$ = 105,344,608
9. Difference in face values (M) (8-1)	M = 5,344,608

Step II: Estimation of Semi-Annual Cash Flow Savings	
1. Interest on old issue	$5,000,000
2. Amortization of discount of old issue	12,500
3. Tax effect on old issue [t(1+2)]	2,305,750
4. Net cash flow on old issue (1-3)	2,694,250
5. Interest on new issue	4,213,784
6. Amortization of discount of new issue	15,049
7. Tax effect on new issue [t(5+6)]	1,945,263
8. Net cash flow on new issue (5-7)	2,268,521
9. Cash flow savings (4-8)	S = 425,729

Step III: Estimation of Present Value of Savings from Refunding

$$PV_k = \sum_{i=1}^{70} \frac{425,729}{(1+.0218)^i} - \frac{5,344,608}{(1+.0218)^{70}} = 14,031,886$$

Where k = semi-annual after-tax new issue cost (.0808/2 (1-.46) = .0218)

Note: When k = 2.56%, the (Savings) equals zero.
The break-even rate, therefore, is 9.48%.

It should be noted that the direct substitution of all the variables in equations 1, 2 and 3 would provide the same answers.

LEASING

22.1 INTRODUCTION

Leasing is really a form of intermediate term financing, but it has become sufficiently important in its own right to warrant a separate chapter. There are records that leasing began over three thousand years ago with Phoenician ship charters. While the leasing industry grew rather slowly at the start of this century, in the last three decades this form of financing has expanded at unprecedented proportions. The annual growth rate of leasing was approximately 30 percent during the decade of the 1950's, 15 to 30 percent during the decade of the 1960's and about 15 to 20 percent during the decade of the 1970's and early 1980's. Leasing is one of the most important of the basic corporate changes occuring over the last 40 years.

While real estate (land and buildings) at one time constituted virtually the sole form of asset under lease contract, today it is possible to lease a variety of fixed assets such as automobiles, trucks, airplanes, railroad cars, ships, specialized equipment for industry, and computers. In effect, anything that can be bought by business can also be leased. As a result, a large and expanding leasing industry has developed.

22.2 MAJOR PARTICIPANTS
IN THE LEASING INDUSTRY

Leasing is one of the primary businesses for a number of companies, such as U.S. Leasing Company, Firstmark Leasing Corporation, and Equilease Corporation. There are also direct leasing giant manufacturing corporations, such as IBM and Xerox, as well as consumer finance companies, such as C.I.T. Financial that have diversified into leasing. Specialized leasing firms, such as subsidiaries of banks[1] and insurance companies, (for example, Chase

Manhattan Leasing Corporation, and Equico Lessors—a subsidiary of the Equitable Life Assurance Society) operate in this field by buying assets usually only after a leasee has been found. Finance subsidiaries of major manufacturers (often referred to as "captive leasing companies") such as General Electric Credit Corporation, Ingersoll Rand Financing Corporation, Ford Motor Credit Corporation, and International Paper Corporation are also major leasing companies.

The growing competition with banks forced many independent lessors to function as brokers between banks and other lessors and lessees. These firms compete against huge securities houses, such as Morgan Stanley & Co., as well as large banks, which arrange lease deals for themselves and their correspondent banks. Itel Corp., for example, is the largest independent lease underwriting firm in this country. In effect, the company operates as a specialized investment banker, locating potential leasing transactions, structuring financing, and locating sources to fund the transaction. Not to be overlooked as a major type of lessor are the partnerships composed largely of wealthy individuals who enter the field primarily to receive various tax advantages discussed below.

The remainder of this chapter centers on the following important aspects of leasing: (1) the basic nature of leasing; (2) its advantages and disadvantages; (3) the tax implications of leasing; (4) accounting for leases; and (5) the lease versus buy decision.

22.3 BASIC NATURE OF LEASING

A lease is a contract in which the owner (lessor) of a particular asset agrees with another party (the lessee) to pay a fixed sum to use the asset for a specified period of time. Thus, the obligation to make lease payments exposes the lessee, like the borrower in a loan, to the risk of bankruptcy, in the event payment is not made as required.

The lessee may have the option of renewing the lease or purchasing the property at the termination of the initial contract period. However, as will be discussed below, the parties to the lease contract need to be careful in structuring this, as well as other aspects of the lease arrangements, if it is to qualify for the generally more favorable tax treatment of a lease (as opposed to a sale).

In this section, we discuss the four basic types of leases, the residual value, and the implicit lease rate.

[1] TYPES OF LEASES

The four basic types of leases include: (1) operating or service leases; (2) capital leases; (3) sale and lease back; and (4) leveraged leases. These are discussed below.

(a) Operating or Service Leases

Leases of this type normally provide for maintenance and service expenses to be borne by the lessor. In addition, such leases can usually be cancelled at the option of the lessee prior to the expiration of the original lease period.

This option may be quite valuable should the leased property become obsolete or for any other reason not suitable to the needs of the lessee. The lessee, of course, will have to pay for this privilege which may be regarded as a form of insurance against obsolescence.[2] (The lease payments on operating leases are further increased as a result of the lessor assuming maintenance and service expenses.) The basic analytic decision for the lessee, therefore, is to gauge the burden of this increased cost against the value of the reduced risk.

Because of their increased risk, lessors tend to restrict operating leases to rather brief periods. In addition to computers and other office equipment such as copiers, operating leases are also popular for automobiles, airplanes, and trucks. IBM, for example, has long been one of the primary operatives in the area of service leasing.[3]

The present value of operating lease payments often is less than the lessor's original cost. Nevertheless, the returns to lessors may be quite handsome. Such leases are normally written for periods considerably less than the expected life of the leased equipment and, therefore, the lessor expects his returns to be increased as the result of subsequent renewal lease payments and/or through disposal of the leased equipment.

(b) Capital Leases

Much of the recent boom in leasing has been in the area of capital leases. These leases are generally noncancellable, so they do not contain the insurance feature that operating leases possess. In addition, capital leases normally do not call for the lessor to be responsible for maintenance and service expenses and generally provide for the lessee paying property taxes and insurance on the leased property. Thus, the lessee's payments under financial leases generally are less costly than those under operating leases. On the other hand, capital leases are usually suitable when the user needs an asset for only a short period of time.

A firm seeking to lease property or equipment (rather than buy) through a capital lease normally first selects the items it would like to use. In the case of equipment, price and delivery terms are negotiated initially with the manufacturer just as if a purchase were contemplated. However, instead of paying for the item directly or arranging credit with the manufacturer, the lessee at this point gets in touch with a lessor, which could be a bank, leasing company or other financial institution. The lessor then buys the equipment from the manufacturer and executes a lease agreement with the lessee, who generally is given the right of renewal (perhaps at a reduced rental) at the expiration date of the original lease. The lessee, however, usually cannot cancel the lease prior to the time it is fully amortized or the lessor is paid. This is the major difference between capital and service leases.

In effect, a capital lease is more akin to a term loan. The lessee receives the use of an asset for a period roughly approximating its useful life and in turn agrees to make payments which have a discounted value roughly equal to its face value. The discounting process generates the return to the lessor on the lease agreement.

(c) Sale and Leaseback

One variant of the basic financial lease is the sale and leaseback arrangement. In some instances, this amounts to the lessee buying an item, selling it to the lessor, and then leasing it back. In other cases, the lessee builds something to his own specifications for use, and then sells the item to the lessor, while at the same time agreeing to lease it back.

Lessor participants in sale and leaseback arrangements are often life insurance companies in the case of real estate and commercial banks, specialized leasing companies, or again life insurance companies if the leased property is machinery and equipment.

(d) Leveraged Leases

A particularly sophisticated type of lease financing is the leveraged lease,[4] which is typically a full-payout (or fully amortizable) non-cancellable lease involving three parties:

- *A lessee,* who is contractually bound to fulfill his obligations under the lease.
- *A long-term creditor* (lender), who furnishes the major portion of the purchase price of the leased asset (80 percent or less). The loan is non-recourse to the owner/lessor and is usually secured by a mortgage on the leased asset and an assignment of the lease and lease payments.
- *A lessor* (equity investor), who acquires the asset in connection with a specific lease arrangement and who provides the remainder of the purchase price (20 percent or more). The lessor's security position in the asset, the lease and the lease payments, are subordinate to obligations of the long-term lender. The lessor must repay his debt in full.

Many variations of leveraged leases occur in practice but the three parties mentioned above are always present. Figure 22.1 illustrates the basic leveraged lease. Figures 22.2 and 22.3 illustrate variations of the leveraged lease. In Figure 22.2 another party enters the picture, the trustee lessor, who is a trustee of a trust created to hold legal title to the leased asset. For tax purposes, the benefits of the lease transaction will flow through to the owner lessor. In Figure 22.3 still another party is involved, the indenture trustee, who is a trustee of a trust which holds the security interest in the lease and the leased asset for the benefit of the lender.

FIGURE 22.1 *The basic leveraged lease*

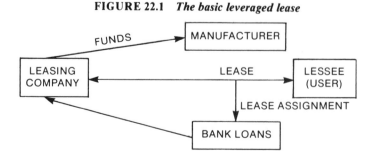

FIGURE 22.2 *Variation of a leveraged lease*

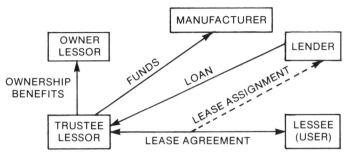

FIGURE 22.3 *Another variation of a leveraged lease*

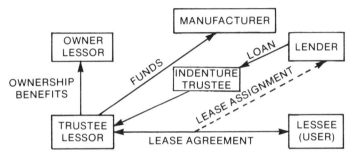

In a leveraged lease the savings to the lessee can be considerable. The savings result when the lessor, who puts up only a fraction of the money, claims all the tax benefits on the entire cost of the equipment. Thus, the lessor can reduce the lease rate he charges with corresponding savings to the lessee. However, other than the lower lease payments, which often result from leveraged leases, the lessee is indifferent to whether the arrangement is a straight financial lease or a leveraged lease. From the lessee's point of view, the lease vs. buy decision is not directly affected by whether the lessor borrows a portion of the funds needed to buy the equipment. Finally, wealthy individuals who are seeking tax shelters often act as lessors in leveraged leases because of the tax breaks offered.[5]

[2] RESIDUAL VALUES

In most leases, the owner/lessor retains the rights to the residual value of the asset at the end of the lease term. These values, discounted back to the present time, help determine the leasing arrangements at the beginning of the lease term. The discounted amount varies with the interest rate on the debt in the lease and the lease term.

The formal definition of residual value is the worth of the leased asset at the end of the lease term. One might at first think that buying would be the more favorable alternative where residual values are expected to be substantial.

That way the buyer could obtain ownership of the residual value at the end of the lease term. However, given the risks of business today, and the rapidity with which technological advances can create obsolescence, it is relatively uncommon to expect high residual values. The uncertainty in estimating residual values underlies the practice of discounting them, in the lease versus buy decision, at a higher rate than that attached to the other pertinent cash flows (see section 22.9 for a discussion of the lease versus buy decision).

An exception to the notion of low expected residual values is land or some other appreciating asset.[6] But even in this case, competitive market conditions can normally be relied upon to cause leasing companies to adjust their leasing rates and payment schedules accordingly. Thus, while residual values need to be considered in the lease versus buy decision, it is not likely that they will tip the scale and result in materially lower costs of owning. In general, when the lessor is more optimistic than the lessee about expected residual values, both may be satisfied to engage in the lease contract. If the lessee is more optimistic, however, a deal may not be struck.

Since residual values typically revert to the lessor at the expiration of the lease, they may be thought of as equivalent to a down payment on a secured loan made by the lessor to the lessee. Perhaps, for this reason, lessors may be willing to provide lessees with 100 percent of the financing needed to obtain use rights to an asset. Creditors, however, are generally reluctant to extend all of the funds needed to purchase a given major asset. From the lessee's point of view, a consideration in favor of leasing an asset would result if the present value of the expected residual value exceeds the down payment that would be required on a secured loan to buy the asset. In effect when the present worth of the residual value exceeds the difference between the funds needed to purchase an asset and the amount creditors would provide.

Capital leases may offer the lessee the right to purchase the leased asset at the expiration of the lease term. In order for a lease contract to qualify as a lease for tax purposes, however, the purchase price must approximate the fair market value of the asset at the termination of the lease term. Otherwise, there may be a tax ruling that the lease contract is in reality a conditional sale, thus eliminating much of the tax benefits of leasing. Such a ruling would be contrary to the interest of both the lessor and the lessee. Accordingly, in most cases contracts are structured so that the residual values will be considered as belonging to the lessor notwithstanding the existence of purchase options held by the lessee.

[3] IMPLICIT LEASE RATE

The implicit lease rate is the rate required on a capital lease to amortize the purchase price of the leased asset to the lessor and thus to provide him with the return on investment he is seeking. It is therefore the lessor's net rate of return after allowing for all his cash inflows and outflows. This rate will vary with the lessee's credit worthiness. A lessee who would have to pay 16 percent on a secured term loan would normally receive an implicit lease rate of about 16 percent.

22.4 ADVANTAGES OF LEASING

An interesting aspect of leasing is that the advantages accruing directly to either the lessor or lessee may usually be passed on to the other party. Thus, the advantages discussed below normally redound to the benefit of each and work toward an increased volume of leasing. In some cases, however, claimed advantages may not be actual.

[1] PROFITABILITY

Leasing is often a very profitable business to a lessor. This benefits both the lessor and lessee because competition often leads the lessor to share a portion of this high return with the lessee.

[2] SOURCE OF CREDIT TO SMALL FIRMS

High interest rates have aggravated the difficulty for small companies obtaining the credit necessary for expansion. Long-term loans, even if available, could be expensive and leasing may be the only plausible alternative. Money sources often view leasing companies as better credit risks than most small firms and, consequently, leasing companies have stronger lines of credit which they, in turn, can offer to their customers.

[3] FLEXIBILITY

Unlike conventional finance tools, the leasing term is restricted only by the useful life of the equipment. Leasing companies can write long-term leases (in some cases up to twenty years) as compared to standard commercial loans of three to five years. Leasing companies can also offer flexible payment methods tailored to meet the specific needs of the lessee, such as purchase options, payments that conform to the lessee's seasonal cash flow patterns, and a three to six month grace period when no payments are required. Further, although there is some evidence that they may be getting more strict, lease agreements generally contain fewer restrictions on future operations and the future indebtedness of a lessee than does an equivalent amount of financing in the form of a secured loan.

[4] LESSENS THE IMPACT OF INFLATION

As is the case with any debt arrangement, inflation continually decreases the net cost of lease payments. Assume, for example, that when the annual rate of inflation is 10 percent, a company enters into a six year lease with rental payments of $1,000 per year. The first payment will cost the full $1,000, but assuming a 10 percent annual rate of inflation, the second rental payment will be reduced to an effective net cost of $909. By the end of the sixth year, the final rental payment will have an inflation adjusted real cost of approximately $564.

In effect, inflation is a major reason why purchasing equipment for cash may be undesirable. Financing the acquisition may be more appropriate in a highly inflationary environment. Borrowing today's dollars at today's prices and paying them back with tomorrow's deflated dollars is an excellent hedge against inflation. Thus, any dollar spent on purchasing a long-life asset is the most expensive dollar.

[5] PROVIDES 100 PERCENT OF FINANCING

An advantage sometimes claimed for leasing is that it provides 100 percent of the financing required to obtain use of an asset, compared with the secured credit where the lender is likely to advance only a portion of the purchase price. However, as we have already seen, the residual value usually reverts to the lessor at the expiration of the lease term and is, in effect, the equivalent of a down payment. Ordinarily, therefore, leasing does not really provide the full financing of an asset.

[6] INCREASES CREDIT AVAILABILITY

Firms have sometimes contended that leasing permits the retention of credit availability from other sources. Lease payments, however, are contractual debts which if not made can place a firm into bankruptcy. Accordingly, potential creditors are not likely to ignore them when assessing the firm's credit worthiness. Financial analysts have traditionally capitalized lease payments so that the presumed debts of the lessee are correspondingly increased. The accounting standards relevant to leasing, discussed later in this chapter, (section 22.7) make it even less likely that leases will be ignored in determining the debt bearing capacity of a lessee.

[7] REDUCES THE RISK OF OWNERSHIP

If the lessor is larger than the lessee, he can spread the risks of ownership over more assets. In addition, the lessor may be able to lease to another party an asset no longer useful to its original user. As a result, a lessor with a large and effective sales and distribution organization may be willing to pass on some of these benefits to the lessee by writing favorable lease terms. When this condition does not exist a lessee may still be able to shift the risks of ownership (principally that of obsolescence) to the lessor by obtaining a cancellable lease.

[8] SIMPLIFIES THE ADMINISTRATIVE PROCESS

Leasing obviates the maintenance of ownership records, schedules and some nuisance expenditures such as legal fees, commitment fees, and compensating balances. Leasing also avoids the need to issue new securities as well as the cost of underwriting and the public disclosure required by such offerings. It is also easier for a lessee as opposed to the owner to predict the relevant cash flows.

[9] SPREADS OUT INSTALLATION COSTS

The total cost of acquiring a fixed asset, which includes such items as sales taxes, delivery, and installation charges, are usually included in the lease payments and amortized over the lease term along with the costs of the item. If the asset is purchased, these front-end costs, which in some cases are considerable, can result in a heavy initial cash drain before the asset begins to be productive.

[10] AVOIDS REFINANCING PROBLEMS

Many debts have balloon repayment features which require that the bulk of the principal be repaid or refinanced at the termination of the loan. Two of the risks associated with such refinancing are the possibility of the borrower's credit rating deteriorating or the possibility of a change in interest rates. Leases avoid these risks as well as short and intermediate term financing and refinancing.

[11] PROVIDES LESSOR SUPERIOR LEGAL STANDING

In bankruptcy, the lessor may be in a better position than a secured creditor because he retains legal title to the leased asset. Accordingly, if a lessee is unable or unwilling to meet his lease payments, the lessor has a superior legal right to take back the leased asset. On the other hand, a creditor, even if his loan is collateralized by a specific asset, normally runs into considerable costs and delays in attempting to recover losses incurred by default of the borrower. When risky firms seek financing, therefore, suppliers of capital may be more inclined to offer lease arrangements than secured loans. In some cases, however, such as highly specialized and potentially outmoded equipment, the superior position of the lessor may be illusory.

[12] PROVIDES SPECIALIZED SERVICING

Some lessors, particularly integrated companies which manufacture technical equipment, are able to provide highly efficient servicing that the lessee could not obtain elsewhere. Moreover, as the legal owner of the asset, the lessor may be expected to service it with greater care than an outside servicing firm hired by the lessee. The ability to obtain such high quality servicing is considered a primary reason for the recent growth in leasing.

[13] ORGANIZATIONAL INCENTIVES

Organizational necessities may lead to a lease rather than a buy decision even when not necessarily justified by the costs. Middle management personnel (as shown in Chapter 16) often have limits on their discretionary spending authority. Such an executive may, therefore, be able to lease items which he cannot buy without receiving higher level authorization, a step which is often time consuming. A leasing company may be able to take advantage of this condition by structuring the lease payments to fit within the budget constraints of middle management.

[14] LESSOR MAY HAVE A LOWER COST OF CAPITAL THAN THE LESSEE

There may be cases (particularly as the result of size) in which the lessor has a relatively low cost of capital and passes this benefit on to the lessee. This can make leasing more attractive than buying. In theory this disequilibrium should be eliminated by changes in the number of lessors and lessees. Despite the logic of this rearrangement, there are many intervening factors at play and advantages flowing from a low cost lessor.

[15] PROVIDES A VEHICLE FOR USING PROPERTY WHICH MAY NOT BE FOR SALE

Some property, not available for sale (e.g., space in shopping centers or nuclear reactor cores), may be leased. In these circumstances, contrary to accounting for leases generally, one authority maintains that "...it would appear to be substantially incorrect to reflect in financial statements as owned assets leases of property which typically are not, or cannot be, owned."[7] Governmental authorities often require elaborate approvals or even voter concurrence before certain assets can be acquired. These restrictions may lead to leasing rather than buying decisions.

[16] TAX ADVANTAGES

As will be discussed in the section on the tax consequences of leasing [section 22.6] there are a number of important tax benefits to leasing as opposed to buying.

22.5   DISADVANTAGES OF LEASING

Even in the face of the foregoing advantages, leasing may involve disadvantages, which have to be taken into account in the lease-buy decision.

[1] LEASING MAY BE MORE COSTLY

Perhaps the most obvious and significant disadvantage of leasing as opposed to buying is that it may be more costly. This is particularly true for operating leases where, as noted above, the lessee, in effect, is buying an insurance policy against the risk of obsolescence of the leased assets. This insurance policy needs to be paid for.

[2] RESIDUAL VALUES REVERT TO THE LESSOR

Since the leased property usually reverts to the lessor, the lessee loses the benefit of high residual values. However, three factors work to lessen the effect of this disadvantage. First, the lessee may be given the option of purchasing the asset at the termination of the lease term. Second, residual values are difficult to predict at the inception of the lease term and, therefore, are often discounted at rather high rates in determining present values. Finally, as noted above, where residual values may be expected to be substantial, as in the case of land, competitive pressures on lessors normally result in an adjustment in the lease payments in favor of the lessee.

[3] LESSEE MAY HAVE TO RENEW THE LEASE AT ITS TERMINATION

In the case of a lease without a purchase option at its termination there is the risk to the lessee that a renewal may have to be sought and a new lease signed at a less favorable rate than that provided in the old lease. As a result, after the second lease expires, the overall leasing alternative may prove more costly than an initial purchased decision.

22.6 TAX IMPLICATIONS OF LEASING[8]

If the government accepts the lease contract as genuine and not a conditional sales contract or an installment loan, lease payments are fully tax deductible. The Internal Revenue Service does not recognize sham arrangements in which a company writes-off the depreciation on an asset over a more rapid period than its useful life. This might occur if a firm "sets up a lease" with substantial payments in the early years and only nominal payments in the later years, or if the lease provides for a purchase option at a nominal price after very high lease payments over a brief period. For firms that buy rather than lease, user-owners can directly deduct, for tax purposes, depreciation and interest expenses as well as directly take the investment tax credit; alternatively, lessees can deduct their lease payments.

A key tax aspect of leasing is that it enables a lessor to pass on a portion of the tax benefits of ownership (the investment tax credit and interest and depreciation deductions), through reduced lease payments, to the user-lessee who might not otherwise be able to obtain them because of low earnings.

Leveraged leases increase the mutual tax benefits of leasing even further. For a modest equity investment the lessor gets all the tax benefits of ownership and can pass even greater savings on to the lessee. Moreover, the lessee's tax deductible lease payments may reflect the use of land whereas he could not deduct depreciation if the land were owned. On the other hand, lease payments may be correspondingly higher because the owner-lessor cannot take depreciation deductions on land.

22.7 ACCOUNTING FOR LEASES

There are few accounting issues which have evoked as much debate as the question of whether or not to capitalize leases and place them directly on the books of the lessee and, if so, how this procedure should be accomplished. Over the last two decades this issue has been subject to such differing authoritative opinions that prior to the formation of the Financial Accounting Standards Board (FASB) in 1973, the Accounting Principle Board (APB) had issued four opinions dealing with leasing.[9] In response to its first exposure draft in the leasing area the FASB received 250 comments from parties affected by, or interested in, the impending pronouncement—the largest number of responses to that time received by the FASB concerning any exposure draft. Moreover, subsequent to the issuance by the FASB of its supposedly definitive statement on leasing,[10] FASB Statement No. 13, "Accounting for Leases" in November, 1976, the FASB issued seven amendments and another six interpretations of its Statement No. 13.[11] Following further exposure drafts of amendments to FASB Statement No. 13, a statement was issued in May 1980 that integrated all these modifications.[12]

Fundamental to the accounting treatment of a lease is the question of whether it is classified as a capital or an operating lease. Capital leases are accounted for directly on the financial statements by the lessee as the acquisition of an asset and the incurrence of an obligation. To the lessor, they are accounted for as a sale or financing. Operating leases, however, do not transfer the benefits and risks of ownership and are not shown directly on the balance sheet of the lessee, nor need a sale or financing be recorded by the lessor.

[1] CLASSIFICATION FOR THE LESSEE

A lessee must classify a lease as a capital lease if it meets one of four basic criteria illustrated in Figure 22.4. Each of these standards is intended to test whether or not a transfer of the benefits and risks of ownership has effectively taken place.

[2] CLASSIFICATION FOR THE LESSOR

The concept of the transfer of the risks and benefits of ownership goes one step further from the standpoint of the lessor. In this case, the payments he will receive must be clearly specified. This notion is indicated by an additional requirement imposed for a lessor to classify a lease as a sales type or direct financing.

A lessor classifies a lease as a sales type or a direct financing lease, whichever is appropriate, if, at inception, it meets any one of the four preceding criteria (the lessor uses the interest rate implicit in the lease for discount purposes), and, in addition, both of the following criteria:

- collectibility of the minimum lease payments is reasonably predictable; and
- there are no important uncertainties about the amount of unreimbursable costs yet to be incurred by the lessor under the lease, such as an unusual guaranty of the leased property's performance.

The last distinction set forth is between a sales type and a direct financing lease. In a sales type lease, the fair value of the leased property at the inception of the lease is greater or less than its cost or carrying amount, if different. Such a lease normally occurs when manufacturers or dealers market their products through leasing and incur a profit or loss. Any lessor, however, whether or not a dealer, may execute a lease type transaction if it meets the requisite criteria.

A direct financing lease does not give rise to a manufacturer's or dealer's profit (or loss) to the lessor. In such a lease, therefore, the cost or carrying amount, if different, and the fair value of the leased property are the same at the inception of the lease. This classification[13] is summarized in Figure 22.5.

[3] ACCOUNTING BY THE LESSEE

The lessee records a capital lease as an asset and an obligation equal to the present value at the inception of the lease of the minimum lease payments during the lease term (excluding the unguaranteed residual value accruing to the lessor and that portion of the payments representing executory costs to be paid by the lessor).[14] As described previously, the lessee uses as the discount rate his incremental borrowing rate unless he can learn the lessor's implicit rate and it is less than the incremental borrowing rate.

FIGURE 22.4 *Criteria for classification as a capital lease by a lessee*

CRITERION	IMPLICATION
1. The lease transfers ownership of the property to the lessee by the end of the lease term.	1. A transfer of ownership actually occurs.
2. The lease contains a bargain purchase option (a provision allowing the lessee, if he so desires, to buy the property on a specified date, at a price sufficiently below its expected fair price at that time to indicate the likelihood of purchase).	2. A transfer of ownership probably will occur because on the termination of the lease it will be advantageous for the lessee to exercise his option of buying the property.
3. The lease term is equal to 75 percent or more of the estimated economic life of the lease property.*	3. If the length of the lease term is close to that of the property's economic life, the lessee will receive most of the benefits and risks of ownership.
4. The present value at the beginning of the lease term of the minimum lease payments (excluding executory costs such as insurance, maintenance, and taxes to be paid by the lessor, including any profit)[a] equals or exceeds 90 percent of the fair value of the leased property to the lessor at the inception of the lease over any related investment tax credit expected to be realized by the lessor. In making this determination, the lessee uses, as the discount factor, his incremental borrowing rate unless it is practicable for him to learn the lessor's rate implicit in the lease, and it is less than his incremental borrowing rate.[b] If both of these conditions are met, the lessor uses the implicit rate.*	4. The present value of the lease payments approximates the price for which the property could be sold in an arm's length transaction between unrelated parties. When the remaining value of the property on the termination date of the lease (its unguaranteed residual value) is high, the test probably will involve using the lessee's incremental borrowing rate as the discount factor in determining the present value of the lease payments.[c]

[a]The lessee's obligation to pay executory costs is excluded from the minimum lease payments but presumably counted by him as operating expenses. If the lessor pays executory costs that are included in the lease payments, an estimate of this amount (including any profit) is shown separately in footnotes; this amount is deducted by the lessee from minimum lease payments and by the lessor from minimum lease payments to be received.

[b]The lessor's rate implicit in the lease is that rate, which when applied to: (a) the minimum lease payments (excluding the portion representing executory costs to be paid by the lessor, together with any residual profit) and (b) the unguaranteed residual value accruing to the benefit of the lessor, causes the aggregate present value at the beginning of the inception of the lease term to be equal to the fair value of the leased property at the inception of the lease, minus any investment tax credit expected to be realized by him.

600

cBasically, the test for determining the present value of a capital lease (pvc) and the lessor's implicit rate in the lease (lir) differs as follows:

$$\text{pvc: 90 percent fair value of property} \quad \leqq \quad \sum_{t=1}^{n} \text{ minimum lease payments } (l+r)^{-t}$$

$$\text{lir: fair value of property} = \sum_{t=1}^{n} \text{ minimum lease payments}$$

$(l+r)^{-t}$ unguaranteed residual value $(l+r)^{-n}$

Thus in the case of the lir, if the unguaranteed residual value is high, the discount rate required to provide for both the minimum lease payments and the residual value equaling the fair value of the property would be high. In these circumstances, this rate probably would bring the minimum lease payments alone to an amount below 90 percent of the fair value of the property, as required in the pvc test. The rate, however, is also likely to be above the lessee's incremental borrowing rate, which the lessee then would use, if this were the case. The arrangement would then be classified as a capital lease, if application of the lessee's lower incremental borrowing rate resulted in bringing the minimum lease payments to an amount equal or above 90 percent of the fair value of the property.

*Tests 3 and 4 are not applicable when the beginning of the lease term falls within the last 25 percent of the total estimated economic life of the leased property.

For purposes of classifying a capital lease, the lessee uses the relationship between the fair value of the property to the lessor and the minimum lease payments. Accordingly, if the lessor's implicit rate is below the lessee's incremental borrowing rate even though the unguaranteed residual value for the lessor is substantial, the resulting high rate applied only to the minimum lease payments probably could bring them below 90 percent of the fair value of the property to the lessor.

In general, the leased assets are depreciated in accordance with the lessee's normal depreciation policy except that, in certain cases, the period of amortization is the lease term. These leased assets and the accumulated amortization must be separately identified in the lessee's balance sheet or in footnotes.

Each minimum lease payment is allocated between a reduction of the obligation and interest expenses so as to produce a constant periodic rate of interest on the remaining balance of the obligation (called the "interest" method).[15] Accordingly, under this procedure, interest charges applicable to capital leases are separately identified and presumably included in the interest payments reported by the lessee. At any given time, the amount of the obligation represents this unamortized balance, or the total future minimum lease payments still to be made (excluding executory costs including profits thereon) less the total imputed interest payments still to be made. The obligation is separately identified in the balance sheet, appropriately classified into current and noncurrent liabilities. A typical presentation is shown in Figure 22.6.

On operating leases, the lessee charges rentals as they become payable to expense over the lease term. Disclosure requirements are satisfied by footnotes and include a general description of the leasing arrangement as well as a breakdown of rental expense for each period, with separate amounts for minimum rentals, contingent rentals, and sublease rentals. For operating leases with initial or remaining noncancellable terms over one year, future minimum rental payments must be shown by year for five years and in the aggregate thereafter. The lessee classifies and accounts for leveraged leases in the same manner as non-leveraged leases.

[4] ACCOUNTING BY THE LESSOR

A sales type or direct financing lease implies that a transfer of the benefits and risks of ownership has occurred from the lessor to the lessee. The lessor,

FIGURE 22.5   *Classification of leases*

Basic Tests For The Lessor	Lessor Transfers Benefits and Risks of Ownership to Lessee	Basic Tests For The Lessee
	Lease Classified As:	
Meets test of a capital lease plus both of the following:	**Sales**—Fair value of property differs from cost or carrying amount.	**Capital**—Meets any one of the following:
1. Collectibility of lease payments reasonably assured.	**Financing**—Fair value of property and cost or carrying amount are the same.	1. Transfers ownership of property to lessee by end of lease term.
2. No important uncertainties about the amount of unreimburse-able costs yet to be incurred by lessor.	**Leveraged**—Involves at least a lessee, long-term creditor, and lessor (commonly called the equity participant); meets tests of direct financing leases; the amount of the financing provided by the long-term creditor is sufficient to afford the lessor with substantial "leverage" and is non-recourse as to the general credit of the lessor; meets certain net investment requirements.	2. Contains bargain purchase option.
		3. Term equals 75% or more of estimated economic life of leased property.
		4. Present value of minimum lease payments equals or exceeds 90% of fair value of leased property over related investment tax credit.
All other.	**Operating**	**Operating**—All other

FIGURE 22.6 *Accounting and reporting requirements by lessee for capital leases*

Balance Sheet

Assets

Leased property (Present value of minimum lease payments)	XXX	
less		
Accumulated depreciation	(XXX)	
Net Leased property	XXX	

Liabilities

Obligations (Present value of minimum lease payments)		XXX
less		
Accumulated principal allocation		(XXX)
Net obligations		XXX
Current	XXX	
Noncurrent	XXX	

Footnotes to Balance Sheet

Future Minimum Lease Payments

Year ending:	
19___	XXX
19___	XXX
19___	XXX
19___	XXX
19___	XXX
19___ in aggregate thereafter	XXX
Total minimum lease payments	XXX
less	
Executory costs, including profits	(XXX)
Net minimum lease payments	XXX
less	
Amount representing interest (Reduces net minimum lease payments to present value)	(XXX)
Present value of net minimum lease payments	XXX

Balance sheet changes in each period as follows:

Assets
—Depreciation
—Cash (Lease payments)

Liabilities
—Obligation (Principal allocation)
—Retained earnings
   —Interest allocation
   —Depreciation

therefore, does not record the property underlying such a lease in his balance sheet. He does, however, show an amount that is labelled net investment in direct financing and sales type leases, appropriately classified between current and non-current assets.

Footnotes explain the balance sheet amounts of net investment in direct financing and sales type leases. Shown are the minimum lease payments still to be received, which after subtracting the lessor's executory costs plus profits included in the lease, represent the minimum lease payments receivable.[16] This amount is further reduced by an allowance for uncollectibles to obtain the net minimum lease payments receivable. Adding the unguaranteed estimated residual value of leased property and the reduction of unearned income produces the net investment in direct financing and sales type leases, as reported in the balance sheet.[17] Figure 22.7 portrays these requirements.

As shown in Figure 22.7, the net investment in direct financing and sales type leases is the present value of the minimum lease payments plus the present value of the unguaranteed residual value, discounted at the rate implicit in the lease. For both sales type and direct financing leases, this figure is the fair value of the property. In a sales type lease, however, the fair value of the property is different from its cost; for direct financing leases, it is the same as its cost.[18]

For both sales type and direct financing leases, the lessor gradually writes-off his net investment in the lease over the lease term. He receives a regular amount from the lessee, some of which is applied to reduce the unearned income and some to reduce his net investment.[19] Thus, at any given time, the net investment in direct financing and sales type leases shown in the balance sheet is the unamortized amount of the original net investment. Another way to say this is that the net investment is the total future minimum lease payments still to be made (excluding executory costs but including profits) plus the unadjusted residual value accruing to the lessor less the total unearned income still remaining.

Since the lessor retains the benefits and risks of ownership in operating leases, he reports the property underlying such leases (as well as property held for lease) under non-current assets with or near plant and equipment. This property under operating leases is depreciated following the lessor's normal policy, with the accumulated depreciation deducted from the investment in the leased property. Footnotes provide a breakdown of the major classes of property on operating leases and held for lease as well as a schedule showing minimum future rentals on nonsalable leases by years for the ensuing five years and in the aggregate thereafter. Rental income is reported over the lease term as it becomes due. Initial direct costs are deferred and allocated over the lease term in proportion to the recognition of rental income.

The lessor records his investment in a leveraged lease net of the nonrecourse debt. He calculates a rate of return on the net investment for the periods (ordinarily years) in which the return is positive, based upon the original investment and the projected cash receipts and disbursements over the term of the lease. The rate is the one which, when applied to the net investment in the years in which it is positive, distributes the net income to those years. The lessor's net cash flow equals the gross lease rentals he receives less the repayment of the loan, interest, and tax charges. The net difference is the same as the amount allocated to income.

FIGURE 22.7 Accounting and reporting requirements by lessor

Balance Sheet

Assets

Current:

Net investment in direct financing and sales-type leases*	XXX

Noncurrent:

Net investment in direct financing and sales-type leases*	XXX
Property on operating leases and held for leases	XXX
less	
Accumulated depreciation	(XXX)
Net property on operating leases and held for leases	XXX

Footnotes to Balance Sheet

Total minimum lease payments to be received	XXX
less	
Executory costs, including profits	(XXX)
Minimum lease payments receivable**	XXX
less	
Allowance for uncollectibles	(XXX)
Net minimum lease payments receivable	XXX
Estimated residual value of leased property (unguaranteed)***	XXX
less	
Unearned income	(XXX)
Net investment in direct financing and sales-type leases	XXX

Balance Sheet Changes for Sales-Type Leases

Assets

+ Property	Purchase of property for cash
− Cash	
+ Net investment in sales-type lease	Sale of property at markup #
− Property	
+ Cash	Lease payment
− Net investment in sales-type lease (allocated portion)	
+ Property	
− Cash	
+ Cash	
− Net investment in direct financing lease (allocated portion)	

Liabilities

Retained earnings	
+ Markup on sale of leased property	
+ Amortization of unearned income	

Balance Sheet Changes for Direct Financing Leases

Purchase of property for cash		Retained earnings	
Lease payment		+ Amortization of unearned income	

*The present value of the minimum lease payments to be received plus the present value of the unguaranteed residual value.

**The present value of this figure equals sales under the sales-type leases.

***The total minimum lease payments to be received less executory costs plus the estimated unguaranteed residual value accruing to the benefit of the lessor equals the gross investment in the lease.

#The present value of the unguaranteed residual value is deducted from the net investment to determine the sales price and the same figure is deducted from the cost of the property to obtain the markup.

22.8 EFFECTS OF ACCOUNTING REGULATION IN THE LEASING AREA

It was predicted that the issuance of FASB Statements No. 13 would solve the problem of the accounting disparity between firms which leased their assets through transactions which were essentially purchases financed by debt and firms which bought their assets by financing through traditional debt instruments. (Prior to FASB Statement No. 13 only the latter firms disclosed the asset and the debt obligation on their balance sheets.) It was also expected that this similarity in accounting procedure would bring about considerable changes in the financial statements, costs of capital, share prices, and borrowing capacities of major lessees.[20] And while considerable changes involving leases have in fact come about in the financial statements, most of the expectations of FASB Statements No. 13 have yet to be realized.

The multiplicity of additional FASB amendments, interpretations, and proposals in leasing following FASB Statement No. 13 attests to the lack of definitiveness of this ruling. Moreover, while greater comparability between lessees and buyers of assets was expected, it is by no means certain that this has come about. Nor is it even clear that one can compare the financial statements of two lessees which are similar in other respects.

One of the primary problems with FASB Statement No. 13, which the multitude of further pronouncements to date in the area have failed to fully ameliorate, is the wide range of estimates which are necessary in order to implement this ruling. Despite the efforts at standardizing definitions, there is still considerable room for judgments and latitude on the part of both the lessee and the lessor. Terms such as the lessee's incremental borrowing rate, the lessor's implicit interest rate, the bargain purchase option, the bargain renewal option, the estimated economic life, residual value, executory costs, and fair value can differ substantially between companies and are open to considerable estimating differences.[21] Thus, while in some cases FASB Statement No. 13 has narrowed the accounting gap between lessees and buyers of assets, in other instances the judgments that are necessary may have created even greater differences (especially between lessees using different estimating techniques). Moreover, while substantial changes were expected in lessee's costs of capital, share prices and borrowing capacities, no evidence has as yet been uncovered that any of these conditions have taken place.[22] And since FASB Statement No. 13 only requires a change in the form of presentation of information which was already available in footnotes (in effect largely only redirecting the locus of disclosure) we really should not be too surprised that the reaction of the capital markets to this ruling has not been very substantial.[23]

22.9 THE LEASE VERSUS BUY DECISION

Once a firm has decided to acquire a particular asset (through a capital budgeting framework similar to that developed in Chapters 16, 17, and 18), the next major question is the form of financing.[24] One alternative is to use working capital. However, as explained in Chapters 7 through 11, if the asset is long-lived, a current form of financing may not be suitable. If long-term sources of financing are to be used, the alternatives we have considered thus far in this book are debt, preferred stock, common stock and retained earnings. In this chapter we consider using another long-term source for obtaining the required financing—leasing the asset. But, from a financial point of view, undertaking a leasing arrangement is tantamount to financing with long-term debt. Thus, in the analysis which follows we compare acquiring an asset using long-term debt with the undertaking of a lease arrangement.

In the next two sections, we use a hypothetical example to demonstrate the important considerations in the lease versus buy decision from the perspectives of the lessee and the lessor.

FIGURE 22.8 *The Adams Company, basic facts and assumptions for lease vs. borrow and buy analysis*

Common Conditions	Lease Conditions	Borrow and Buy Conditions
1. Cost of equipment including installation and delivery charges = $1,100,000.	1. Adams can lease the equipment for 5 years paying annual lease payments of $300,000 at the end of each year.	1. An investment tax credit of $100,000 applies. This is approximately 9%.
2. The effective tax rate of the company is 50%.	2. The lease is non-cancellable and non-renewable, but Adams can purchase the equipment at the end of 5 years for its estimated residual value of $100,000.	2. $1,000,000 in net financing is needed if Adams borrows and buys.
	3. The lessor will maintain the equipment.	3. Adams can borrow $1,000,000 on a 15% term-loan for 5 years. The loan is to be amortized over this period by equal yearly payments sufficient to extinguish the balance at maturity. These payments are computed as follows:

$$\frac{\$1,000,000}{\text{Present Value Annuity Interest Factor (15\%, 5 years)}}$$

$$= \frac{\$1,000,000}{3.3522} = \$298,311.55.$$

4. The equipment will certainly be used for 5 years, at which time its expected residual value is $100,000. The equipment can be sold at its estimated residual value, but Adams will only do this if the operation in which it is used proves unprofitable.

5. Sum of the years-digits depreciation is to be used.

6. Maintenance expenses are expected to be $60,000 per year and to be contracted for by paying a service firm this amount at the end of each year.

[1] FROM THE LESSEE'S PERSPECTIVE

In our hypothetical example, the Adams Company believes it can lease or borrow and purchase a piece of equipment according to the facts and assumptions presented in Figure 22.8. Before we begin the analysis, an explanation of some of the key concepts and their mode of computation is presented as follows:[25]

- *Depreciation*—The tax effects of depreciation are an advantage of ownership not present in leasing. In our example, the cash flow benefits of the sum of the years-digits depreciation are computed as follows to the nearest dollar for an asset with a depreciable cost of $1,000,000:

Year	Depreciation Factor	Depreciation Deduction	Tax Benefits
1	5/15	$333,333	$166,666
2	4/15	266,667	133,334
3	3/15	200,000	100,000
4	2/15	133,333	66,667
5	1/15	66,667	33,333
Totals	15/15	$1,000,000	$500,000

- *Maintenance Expenses*—These expenses are a cost of ownership; however, the item is tax deductible. Its yearly cash flow cost is $30,000 [60,000 x (1-50%)].
- *Interest Expenses*—This item also represents a tax deductible cost of ownership and is computed as follows:

Year	Total Payment on Debt	Amortization of Principal	Remaining Balance	Interest	After-tax Cost of Interest
1	$ 298,312	$148,312	$851,688	$150,000	$ 75,000
2	298,312	170,559	681,129	127,753	63,877
3	298,312	196,143	484,986	102,169	51,085
4	298,312	225,564	259,422[a]	72,748	36,374
5	298,312	259,402[a]	—0—	38,910	19,455
Totals	$1,491,560	$999,980[a]		$491,580	$245,791[a]

[a] Difference here due to rounding.

- *Lease Payments*—Because the lease payments are tax-deductible in full in the year incurred, their after-tax cost in each of the five years is $150,000 [$300,000 x (1-50%)].
- *Salvage or Residual Value*—This is an advantage of ownership lost under leasing. For purposes of our analysis we will include it as a cost of leasing. Our assumption is that the lessee will want to continue the operation at the end of the 5-year period and thus will have to purchase the equipment for $100,000 at that time.[26]

- *Discount Rate*—This is perhaps one of the most controversial aspects of the lease vs. buy decision. Choice of a high or low discount rate will often swing the decision one way or the other. Leasing decisions, as with other capital budgeting decisions, are made on the basis of present values which are initially determined by the discount rate used. In our analysis, the cash flows under both the lease and the borrow and buy alternatives are relatively certain and hence should be discounted at a relatively low rate.[27] In our example, the after-tax cost of the company's debt seems the most appropriate discount rate to use since all cash flows are on an after-tax basis.[28] (This would amount to 7½%—15% x 0.5—so for ease of computation we will use 8%).

In comparing the net present values of the two financing alternatives, the revenues associated with the equipment under consideration are assumed to be equal. This allows us to delete them from the analysis as all financial decisions are on an incremental basis. Our objective here is to choose the least cost present value alternative (or, in effect, the alternative with the least cost present value of cash outflows) whether it be leasing or borrowing and then buying. This analysis is presented in Figure 22.9.

All cash flows relevant to each alternative are placed on an after-tax basis and then summed. The net differences in after-tax cash outflows in each of the relevant years between leasing and borrowing and buying is then computed. Finally, these net differences are placed on a present value basis and the numbers summed once again in order to see if the ultimate net advantage lies with leasing or with borrowing and buying.

We have made no explicit adjustment for risk—in effect, assuming that the average risk of the leasing cash flows is equal to the average risk of the borrowing and buying cash flows. In most cases this assumption will be reasonably accurate as most of the cash flows are fairly certain. For example, the payments for interest and amortization of principal are set by contract. Further, contractual agreements fix the lease payments and a maintenance contract is also entered into. Depreciation deduction methods may be changed by agreement with the tax authorities. However, such a procedure is not normally undertaken. The only real uncertainties relate to the tax rate and the salvage value. Should the effective tax rate change, the decision may be altered. However, as there is no way of determining the likelihood of this, the possibility is not considered in our analysis. The most uncertain element is the residual value. While in our case we assume that the lessee will have to purchase the equipment at its residual value at the end of five years, an adjustment can be made to the analysis in the form of a higher discount rate should it be felt that a greater degree of uncertainty is attached to the residual value than to the other fund flows. Thus, for the illustration shown here, it is reasonable to assume that the average risk of the leasing cash flows is approximately equal to the average risk of the borrowing and buying cash flows and that both are relatively low.

In our illustration, leasing produces the lower net present value cash outflows by $19,000 and is therefore preferable if the expected facts are realized.[29]

FIGURE 22.9   *The Adams Company: lease vs. borrow and buy analysis*

(Numbers in Thousands)

Year	The After-Tax Cash Outflow From Borrowing and Buying					The After-Tax Cash Outflow From Leasing		
	Depreciation (1)	Maintenance (2)	Interest (3)	Amortization of Principal (4)	Total (2) + (3) + (4) - (1) (5)	Lease Payments (6)	Residual Value (7)	Total (6) + (7) (8)
1	$(167)	$30	$75	$148	$86	$150		$150
2	$(133)	$30	$64	$171	$132	$150		$150
3	$(100)	$30	$51	$196	$177	$150		$150
4	$(67)	$30	$36	$226	$225	$150		$150
5	$(33)	$30	$19	$259	$275	$150	$100	$250

Comparative Cash Outflows

Net Advantage to Leasing or (Borrowing and Buying) (5) - (8) (9)	Present Value Lump Sum Factor (8%) (10)	Present Value of Net Advantage to Leasing or (Borrowing and Buying) (9) x (10) (11)
($64)	.9259	($59)
($18)	.8573	($16)
$27	.7938	$21
$75	.7350	$56
$25	.6806	$17

Net Advantage to Leasing $19

[2] FROM THE LESSOR'S PERSPECTIVE

We now turn our analysis around and look at the position of the lessor. In essence, a potential lessor often has to decide whether to lease or sell an asset he owns. Let's analyze his decision using a framework similar to that employed for the lessee. We can use the earlier illustration in this case if we include a few additional facts and assumptions, outlined in Figure 22.10, for the Baker Company, a potential lessor.

In order to determine whether to lease or to sell we first have to compute the net cash outlay in each case. For the leasing alternative this is $1,000,000 (the initial cost—$1,100,000 less the investment tax credit—$100,000.) If the asset is sold, the net cash outlay is $1,000,000[30] (the initial cost—$1,100,000 less the after-tax gain on the sale—[$1,300,000 - $1,100,000] x .5). If the asset is leased the annual after-tax cash inflows are determined as in Figure 22.11 which shows the present value of the after-tax cash inflows.

FIGURE 22.10 *The Baker Company: additional facts and assumptions for lease vs. sell analysis*

Common Conditions	Lease Conditions	Sell Conditions
1. Cost of equipment including installation and delivery charges = $1,100,000.	1. Same as in Figure 23.8 relative to lease payments, investment tax credit, depreciation and residual value. The same assumptions used by the Adams Company are now used by the Baker Company. However, as the result of specialization, maintenance will only cost $10,000 per year at the end of each of the next 5 years.	1. Baker can sell the equipment for $1,300,000, but will lose the investment tax credit and have to pay income taxes on the transaction.
2. The effective tax rate of the company is 50%.		
3. Conditions surrounding the financing of the acquisition are irrelevant since they are the same whether the asset is leased or sold.		2. Funds from the after-tax proceeds of the sale can be invested in assets of approximately equal risk as the contemplated lease. The after-tax rate of return on such an investment will be 4%.

We could also calculate the rate of return on the lease investment according to the methods outlined in Chapter 17:

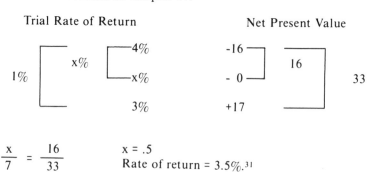

Trial Rate of Return   Net Present Value

$$\frac{x}{7} = \frac{16}{33} \qquad x = .5$$

Rate of return = 3.5%.[31]

FIGURE 22.11 *The Baker Company: lease vs. sell analysis*
(Numbers in Thousands)

			After-Tax Cash Inflows of Leasing		
Year	Lease Payment (Lease Payment x .5) (1)	Residual Value (2)	Depreciation Benefit (Depreciation Deduction x .5) (3)	Maintenance Expense (Maintenance Expense x .5) (4)	Net Cash Inflow from Leasing (1) + (2) + (3) - (4) (5)
1	$150	—	$167	$5	$312
2	$150	—	$133	$5	$278
3	$150	—	$100	$5	$245
4	$150	—	$ 67	$5	$212
5	$150	$100	$ 33	$5	$278

Comparative Net Present Value to Selling

Present Value Lump Sum Factor (4%) (6)	Present Value of After-Tax Cash Inflows from Leasing (4) x (5) (7)
.9615	$300
.9246	$257
.8890	$218
.8548	$181
.8219	$228

Total $1,184
Net Present Cash Inflow from Sale (1,200)
[Proceeds—Tax Payment (Gain X .5)]
[$1,300,000 - ($1,300,000 - $1,100,000 x .5)]
Net Present Value of Lease Investment $ (16)

Thus, the after-tax rate of return to the lessor on this prospective lease is approximately 3.5 percent. This is below the after-tax opportunity rate of return of 4 percent. Similarly, the net present value is—$16,000. Hence, according to either the net present value or rate of return method, the lease investment should not be made under present circumstances.

Although we found earlier that the lease commitment on these terms was worthwhile to the lessee—the Adams Company—it is not similarly advantageous to the prospective lessor—the Baker Company—and the transaction will not be complete without further negotiation. However, as the net advantage to leasing for the Adams Company, as shown in Figure 22.9 is approximately equal to the negative net present value of the lease investment, perhaps the lessor and the lessee can reach an agreement to increase the lease payments slightly and thus make the deal profitable for both parties.[32] [33]

22.10   CHAPTER SUMMARY

Although complex in its accounting and tax considerations, leasing is an area of considerable financial importance to the financial manager. It is also an area undergoing a marked rate of growth.

In this chapter, we looked at the major participants in the leasing industry, the nature of leasing, its advantages, disadvantages and some of its tax implications. We also outlined the current accounting procedures of lessees and lessors and developed a decision-making framework for the lease vs. buy and lease vs. sell problems.

FOOTNOTES

1. In 1963 the Comptroller of the Currency ruled that federally chartered banks could lease personal property. In the following decade over 500 banks entered leasing; and this constituted much of the surge in leasing noted above. Operating in the same direction was a Federal Reserve Board decision permitting bank holding companies to participate in equipment leasing. Since that time, most large banks have set up leasing subsidiaries which have become major lessors.
2. A large lessor firm may not have as great a risk of obsolescence as a small lessee. By spreading the risk of obsolescence among many customers, the large lessor, in effect, obtains a form of self-insurance. Also a large lessor may be able to lease to a second lessee customer equipment that is obsolete to the original lessee.
3. Banks and bank affiliates are excluded from participating in operating leases under Regulation "Y" of the Federal Reserve Board. New York State law does not consider operating leases to be equivalent to an extension of credit.
4. Most multimillion dollar leases are now leveraged leases.
5. For special procedures used to evaluate leveraged leases see, Peter W. Bacon and Peter J. Athanasopoulos, "Analyzing Leveraged Leases—Another Alternative," *Bankers' Magazine*, July-August 1979, pp. 92-95 and Wayne F. Perg, "Leveraged Leasing: The Problem of Changing Leverage," *Financial Management*, Autumn 1978, pp. 47-51.
6. This will not be the case if changing population or use patterns are expected to result in a deterioration in the value of the land.

7. G. Richard Baker, "Leasing and the Setting of Accounting Standards: Mapping the Labyrinth," *Journal of Accounting, Auditing and Finance,* Spring 1980, pp. 197-206.
8. The tax rules governing lease transactions are highly complex and have been substantially altered by the Economic Recovery Tax Act of 1981 and the Tax Equity and Fiscal Responsibility Act of 1982. For a more detailed analysis of the tax aspects of leasing, see Chapter 24.
9. APB Opinion No. 5 "Reporting of Leases in Financial Statements of Lessees" (September 1964): APB Opinion No. 7 "Accounting for Leases in Financial Statements of Lessors" (May 1966): APB Opinion No. 27 "Accounting for Lease Transactions by Manufacturer or Dealer Lessors" (November 1972): APB Opinion No. 31 "Disclosure of Lease Commitments by Lessees" (June 1973).
10. William L. Ferrara, "The Case for Symmetry in Lease Reporting," *Management Accounting,* April 1978, p. 24.
11. FASB Statement No. 17 "Accounting for Leases—Initial Direct Costs" (November 1977); FASB Statement No. 22 "Changes in the Provisions of Lease Arrangements Resulting from Refundings of Tax-Exempt Debt" (June 1978): FASB Statement No. 23 "Inception of the Lease" (August 1978); FASB Statement No. 26 "Profit Recognition on Sales-Type Leases of Real Estate" (April 1978); FASB Statement No. 27 "Classification of Renewals or Extensions of Existing Sales-Type or Direct Financing Leases" (May 1979); FASB Statement No. 28 "Accounting for Sales with Leasebacks" (May 1979); FASB Statement No. 29 "Determining Contingent Rentals" (June 1979); FASB Interpretation No. 19 "Lessee Guarantee of the Residual Value of Lease Property" (October 1977); FASB Interpretation No. 21 "Accounting for Leases in a Business Combination" (April 1978); FASB Interpretation No. 23 "Leases of Certain Property Owned by a Governmental Unit or Authority" (August 1978); FASB Interpretation No. 24 "Leases Involving Only Part of a Building" (September 1978); FASB Interpretation No. 26 "Accounting for a Purchase of a Leased Asset by the Lessee During the Term of the Lease" (September 1978); FASB Interpretation No. 27 "Accounting for a Loss on a Sublease" (November 1978). In addition to the above, the FASB has also issued nine technical bulletins in this area. Not to be outdone, the Securities and Exchange Commission has issued three releases on leasing.
12. Financial Accounting Standards Board, *Accounting for Leases,* FASB Statement No. 13 as amended and interpreted through May 1980 (May 1980).
13. The general sale-leaseback transactions fall within this classification. These transactions involve the sale of property by the owner and a lease of the property back to the seller. The seller-lessee accounts for the lease as a capital lease if it meets one of the criteria for a capital lease; otherwise it is treated as an operating lease. Any profit or loss on the sale is deferred and amortized proportionately with the amortization of the leased property, if it is a capital lease, or proportionately with rental payments charged to expense over the lease term, if an operating lease. The buyer-lessor records the transaction as a purchase and a direct financing if it meets the tests of a capital lease and the two tests specified for a sales type or direct financing lease; otherwise, he records the transaction as a purchase and operating lease.
14. The amount recorded as the asset and obligation is the fair value, if that figure is below the present value of the minimum lease payments. Executory costs, including profits, are estimated if they cannot be determined from the provisions of the lease.
15. A familiar illustration of the constant rate of return is the mortgage that an individual has on his home. He pays a constant rate of interest on the outstanding amount borrowed which is amortized over time so that initially a greater portion of the regular payments go to interest and a lesser portion to principal. This is

eventually reversed. His total payments are greater than the amount borrowed because they involve interest along with principal.

16. The present value of the minimum lease payments receivable is equivalent to the sales price used to determine the profit recognized in the current period in sales type leases.

17. The unguaranteed residual value is added because, along with minimum lease payments receivable, it represents a component of the lessor's gross investment in the lease. The reduction of unearned income brings the gross investment in the lease to its present value, which is the net investment in direct financing and sales type leases, as shown in the balance sheet. This is the counterpart to those footnotes to the lessee's balance sheet, where the reduction of interest payments to be made brings the net minimum lease payments to their present value.

18. Gross Investment (GI) is the sum of the minimum lease payments less executory costs including profits (LP) plus the unguaranteed residual value accruing to the benefit of the lessor (R). Net investment in the lease (NI) is the gross investment less the unearned income (UI) or NI = GI - UI. For sales-type leases, unearned income is the difference between the gross investment and the present value of its two components or UI = GI - (PVLP + PVR); for direct financing leases, it is the difference between gross investment and the cost or carrying amount, if different, of the lease property (C), or UI = GI - C. Accordingly, for sales-type leases, the net investment equals the present value of the minimum lease payments plus the present value of the unguaranteed residual value accruing to the benefit of the lessor, or GI - (GI - (PVLP + PVR)); for direct financing leases, net investment equals the cost of the property or GI - (GI - C).

19. The rate of earnings is the lessor's implicit rate in the lease. This rate applied to the outstanding net investment produces a declining amount of income that is earned over the life of the lease. The amount applied to reducing the net investment, on the other hand, gradually rises (the same "interest" method used by the lessee).

20. Bernard Shakin, "Letting it All Hang Out: New Accounting Rule on Leases May Have Wide-Ranging Effects," *Barrons,* November 11, 1977. Increased symmetry between lessor and lessee accounting was also expected.

21. Dan Palmon and Michael Kwatinetz, "The Interpretation Process Involved in the Implementation of FASB Statement No. 13., *Journal of Accounting, Auditing and Finance,* Winter 1980, and James D. Blum, "Accounting and Reporting for Leases by Lessees: The Interest Rate Problem," *Management Accounting,* April 1978, pp. 25-28.

22. Prior to the issuance of FASB Statement No. 13 most of the information needed for its implementation was already presented in footnotes to the financial statements.

23. John D. Martin, Paul F. Anderson and Arthur J. Keown, "Lease Capitalization and Stock Price Stability, Implications for Accounting," *Journal of Accounting, Auditing and Finance,* Winter 1979, pp. 151-163.

24. There may, however, be cases in which a proposal to acquire an asset through debt will be rejected, whereas the same proposal to acquire the same asset by leasing will be accepted. This can transpire if the effective cost of the lease is substantially lower than the cost of debt. In this case the cost of capital used in capital budgeting would have to be reevaluated in the light of new financing through leasing which is to be used as a form of debt. This might result in a finding that projects formerly found to be unacceptable are now determined to be acceptable.

25. In what follows we employ a rather straightforward form of the lease vs. buy analysis. However, while additional complexities might be added, the basic form of the analysis remains the same and is adequate for most such decisions. Those

who are interested in some of the more complex decision models which have been developed should consult the suggested readings at the end of this chapter. A treatment of the use of linear and integer programming and sensitivity analysis in choosing among various lease proposals can be found in Jane O. Burns and Kathleen Bindon, "Evaluating Leases with LP," *Management Accounting,* February 1980, pp. 48-53.

26. An alternate treatment would be to consider the residual value as a benefit of ownership rather than as a cost of leasing. In this case the estimated residual value would be discounted back to the present time and subtracted from the costs of ownership. However, as residual values are rather uncertain, a high discount rate, as mentioned previously, is often normally used to reflect this condition.

27. The essence of the controversy over which discount rate to use usually boils down to a debate between the proponents of the firm's weighted average cost of capital and those who favor the after-tax cost of debt. For many firms these rates will be somewhat similar and the decision will usually be unaltered by the choice between them.

28. In our illustration we discount all cash flows at the same discount rate. When there are appreciable differences in the degree of risk among the various cash flows (such as the risk of making lease payments of a given amount—which are relatively certain—vs. the risk of the residual value being equal to the anticipated figure—which is often highly uncertain) different discount rates can be applied to each of the cash flows to reflect these differences in risk.

29. Had we rounded the discount rate used down to 7% rather than up to 8% as above, our decision would be the same as the net advantage to leasing increases a little to $21,000. This is because, as noted in Chapter 17, lower discount rates penalize longer lived cash flows relatively less than do higher discount rates and the advantage of leasing is in the later years. Borrowing and buying is better in the early years of the equipment's use.

30. This is used as a simplifying assumption, but our analysis is not materially altered if the net cash outlay for the sale alternative is different. Also, in view of the rapidity with which interest rates have been changing in recent years, we have used rates that are simply illustrative and reflective of current conditions.

31. There is a slight error in this method of interpolating by taking equal differences on an exponential (compound interest rate) function. But the procedure is reasonably accurate for our purposes. The net cash inflows discounted at 4 percent provide a present value of $1,184,000, and discounted at 3 percent, a present value of $1,217,000. Thus, to obtain a present value figure equal to $1,200,000 the net proceeds from the sale would require a rate of return of about 3.5 percent.

32. We would readily convert this lease vs. sell analysis to a leveraged lease vs. sell analysis by adding a set of columns for the loan amortization schedule on the loan involved. The interest payments on this schedule would represent tax deductible cash outflows, while the loan repayments would be non-tax deductible cash outflows. Of course, the initial cost would be reduced by the amount of the loan. For the analysis of more complex leveraged lease problems, see the references mentioned in footnote 5 to this chapter.

33. We are aware of no study of the costs of leasing vs. the costs of buying over a large number of potential lease contracts, but a number of researchers have uncovered rather substantial rates of return to lessors on lease contracts. For example see, Vincent J. McGugan and Richard E. Laves, "Integration and Competition in the Equipment Leasing Industry," *The Journal of Business,* July 1974, pp. 382-396 and Ivar W. Sorenson and Ramon E. Johnson, "Equipment Financial Leasing Practices and Costs: An Empirical Study," *Financial Management,* Spring 1977, pp. 33-40.

SUGGESTED READINGS

Bacon, Peter W., and Peter J. Athanasopoulos, "Analyzing Leveraged Leases—Another Alternative," *Banker's Magazine*, July-August 1979.

Baker, G. Richard, "Leasing and the Setting of Accounting Standards: Mapping Labyrinth," *Journal of Accounting, Auditing and Finance*, Spring 1980.

Blum, James, D., "Accounting and Reporting for Leases by Lessees: The Interest Rate Problems," *Management Accounting*, April 1978.

Brealy, R.A. and C.M. Young, "Debt, Taxes and Leasing—A Note," *Journal of Finance*, December 1980.

Brief, Richard P., and Joel Owen, "Accounting for Leveraged Leases: A Comment," *Journal of Accounting Research*, Autumn 1978.

Clark, John J., Thomas J. Hindelang, and Robert E. Pritchard, *Capital Budgeting*, Englewood Cliffs: Prentice-Hall, Inc., 1979.

Ferrara, William L., "The Case for Symmetry in Lease Reporting," *Management Accounting*, April 1978.

Ferrara, William L., et. al., "The Lease-Purchase Decision," *Management Accounting*, May 1980.

Finnerty, Joseph E., et. al., "Lease Capitalization and Systematic Risk," *Accounting Review*, October 1980.

Hagedorn, Robert E., "How to Make a Lease-vs-Buy Decision," *The Practical Accountant*, September 1980.

Harmon, Robert R., and Kenneth A. Coney, "Persuasive Effects of Source Credibility in Buy and Lease Situations," *Journal of Marketing Research*, May 1982.

Hawkins, Robert, "Leasing as a Financial Service," *The Banker*, April 1982.

Hershman, Arlene, "The Leasing Business Revolution," *Dun's Business Monthly*, October 1981.

————— , "New Game in Off Balance Sheet Financing," *Dun's Business Monthly*, February 1982.

Laros, Michael A., "Leveraged Leasing: Optimizing the Lessee's Decision-Making Process," *Financial Executive*, December 1981.

Martin, John D., Paul F. Anderson, and Arthur J. Keown, "Lease Capitalization and Stock Price Stability: Implications for Accounting," *Journal of Accounting, Auditing and Finance*, Winter 1979.

Melnick, Richard J., "How New Law Allows Lenders to Buy Tax Benefits by Leasing," *ABA Banking Journal*, November 1981.

Nakayama, Mie, et. al., "Due Process and FASB No. 13," *Management Accounting*, April 1981.

Palmon, Dan, and Michael Kwatinetz, "The Interpretation Process Involved in the Implementation of FASB No. 13," *Journal of Accounting, Auditing, and Finance*, Winter 1980.

Peller, Philip R., et. al., "1981 Tax Act: Accounting for Leases," *Financial Executive*, March 1982.

Reilly, Robert F., "Cost of Funds Employed Method in Lease vs. Buy Analysis," *Financial Executive*, October 1980.

Schiffman, Alan T., "Accounting for Leases: How to Work with the Complex Rules of FASB 13," *The Practical Accountant*, July 1980.

Seidler, Lee J., and Patricia McConnell, "Tax Credit Sales: The Hows and Whys," *Journal of Accountancy*, March 1982.

Shapiro, Harvey D., and Ann Monroe, "How Big a Bonanza are Tax Swaps?" *Institutional Investor*, February 1982.

Smith, Bruce D., "How to Evaluate Leasing Profitability," *Journal of Commercial Bank Lending*, May 1981.

Weiss, Jerold M., and Israel Blumenfrucht, "New Rules for Leveraged Leases," *Management Accounting*, December 1981.

23

FINANCIAL ASPECTS OF MULTINATIONAL OPERATION

23.1 INTRODUCTION

Having covered some of the basic principles of modern finance, we turn now to a new environment—the world of international finance. International finance is complicated by a panopoly of problems that the domestic financial manager rarely, if ever, encounters. Decisions here are tempered by such factors as international tax codes and accounting standards, foreign government restrictions on capital flows, fluctuations between exchange rates, and changes in relative purchasing power between currencies. On the other side, the multinational enterprise's network of overseas subsidiaries which, for a very large firm, may be located in over 100 different countries, makes possible the exploitation of profit, cost, and price differentials by shifting funds to desirable locations through the subsidiary networks.

To cope with these problems and take advantage of potential benefits, a decision-making framework must be developed which is especially suited to the execution of world wide responsibilities. Certain aspects of international finance, such as capital budgeting, can be dealt with through a tempered extrapolation of various domestic financial decision theories. However, other areas such as international cash management, multinational organizational strategies, and the management of foreign exchange risks, are outside the realm of domestic considerations.

We begin with an introduction to some of the widely employed theories of international finance. The reader will then be given an orientation to the primary participants in the foreign exchange markets, the international financial institutions. We next look at some of the salient macro and microeconomic problems faced in the international arena. Having reviewed these problems, we discuss various techniques and innovations currently being employed in the field. Specifically covered are: ways of dealing with fluctuating exchange rates, determining exposure risks, and the unique problems of accounting, cash management, and capital budgeting when placed in an international setting. Appendices A and B deal with additional accounting and historical issues from an international perspective.

23.2 THE FUNDAMENTAL THEORIES OF INTERNATIONAL FINANCE

For a look at inflationary effects and other basic factors affecting exchange rates, it is useful to examine three fundamental theories of international finance:

- The Purchasing Power Parity Theorem (PPPT);
- The Interest Rate Parity Theorem (IRPT); and
- The Fisher Effect.

[1] THE PURCHASING POWER PARITY THEOREM

The PPPT has been summarized as follows: "Given a normal freedom of trade between two countries, A and B, a rate of exchange will establish itself between them and this rate, smaller fluctuations apart, will remain unaltered as long as no alteration in the purchasing power of either currency is made and no special hinderances are imposed upon the trade. But as soon as inflation takes place in the money of A, and the purchasing power of this money is therefore diminished, the value of the A money in B must necessarily be reduced in the same proportion... When two currencies have been inflated, the new normal rate of exchange will be equal to the old rate multiplied by the quotient between the degrees of inflation of both countries."[1]

Stated simply, the theorem merely assumes that changes in exchange rates reflect changes in relative prices between two currencies. These relationships may be expressed as follows:

$$(CX) = \frac{X_1}{X_0} = \frac{P^1_f / P^0_f}{P^1_d / P^0_d} = RPC;$$

where:

$$\frac{X_1}{X_0} = \frac{Y_0}{Y_1} ;$$

X_0 = LCs per \$ now;

X_1 = LCs per \$ one period later;

$(CX) = X_1 / X_0$ = change in exchange rate;

$Y_0 = 1 / X_0$ = \$'s per LC now;

$Y_1 = 1 / X_1$ = \$'s per LC one period later;

RPC = relative price change;

P^0_f = initial price level in foreign country;

P^1_f = subsequent price level in foreign country;

P^0_d = initial domestic price level;

P^1_d = domestic price level one period later; and

LC = local currency.

[2] THE INTEREST RATE PARITY THEOREM

This theorem states that the discount or premium between two currencies in the forward market will tend to equal the nominal interest rate differential between the two countries. (The forward market refers to the market for a "forward contract" which is a contract to buy a prearranged amount of a certain currency at a future date for a pre-arranged price.) The country with the higher interest rate has its currency at a discount when trading with a country that has a lower interest rate; conversely, the country with a lower interest rate has its currency at a premium when trading with a country that has a higher interest rate.

The relationship may be expressed as follows: the ratio of the forward and spot exchange rates will equal the ratio of foreign and domestic gross interest relationships. Or the discount or premium between two currencies in the forward market will tend to equal the nominal interest differential between the two currencies. In effect:

$$\frac{X_1}{X_0} = \frac{1 + R^0_f}{1 + R^0_d} = \frac{Y_0}{Y_1}$$

where:

X_1 = current forward exchange rate \$1.00 = no. of LC units;

Y_1 = current forward exchange rate 1 LC = U.S.\$;

X_0 = current spot exchange rate \$1.00 = no. of LC units;

Y_0 = current spot exchange rate 1 LC = U.S.\$;

R^0_f = current foreign interest rate 1 LC = U.S.\$; and

R^0_d = current domestic interest rate.

[3] THE FISHER EFFECT[2]

Very simply, the Fisher Effect proposes that nominal interest rates will rise to reflect anticipated levels of inflation. The relationship may be expressed as follows:

P_0 = initial price level;

P_1 = subsequent price level;

therefore, P_1/P_0 = rate of inflation;

P_0/P_1 = the relative purchasing power of currency;

r = the real rate of interest; and

R_n = the nominal rate of interest.

Therefore,

$$\frac{P_0}{P_1} = \frac{1 + r}{1 + R^n} \; ;$$

$$1 + r = (1 + R_n)\frac{P_0}{P_1} \; ;$$

$$r = [(1 + R_n)\frac{P_0}{P_1}] - 1; \text{ and}$$

$$R_n = [(1 + r)\frac{P_1}{P_0})] - 1.$$

[4] INTEGRATING THE THEORIES

How do these three theories come together to explain rate changes? Let us begin with the Fisher Effect. Nominal interest rates rise to reflect anticipated levels of inflation. Rising interest rates in turn cause rising prices. According to PPPT, changes in exchange rates reflect relative price differentials between two countries. So, as prices rise in country A relative to country B, the exchange rate between country A and B also changes, leading to the reduction of the value of A's currency relative to B's. Finally, as the interest rate differential between A and B increases, so does the discount for A's currency on the forward market (IRPT). Thus, the Fisher Effect, PPPT, and IRPT are interrelated, reflecting the fundamental economic factors (inflation, interest rates, and prices) leading to changes in exchange rates.

Other studies have also shown an extremely tight, proportional relationship between relative money supplies between nations and their exchange rates. All other things being equal, an increase of X percent in the quantity of money in nation A relative to nation B will result in an X percent depreciation in the exchange rate of A's currency, vis-a-vis B's currency.

23.3 FOREIGN EXCHANGE MARKETS AND INSTITUTIONS

Exchange rate forecasts and trading strategies are the forte of international financial institutions, such as large commercial banks. We turn now to an introduction to the foreign exchange markets themselves, along with their primary participants, the international financial institutions.

In a narrow sense, a foreign exchange market is a vehicle for transferring currencies among nations. However, there are also close connections between a nation's foreign exchange market and the country's other financial markets. For example, a foreign exchange market may provide a means of arranging credit and financing for different varieties of international transactions in co-operation with the nation's other financial markets.

Foreign exchange markets are most commonly found in national financial centers (i.e., New York, London, Paris, and Zurich). These markets are all closely related, and form a single market despite differentials in distance and time. Most market transactions are handled informally by telephone or telex. Although transactions are seldom written out in legal form, the unwritten code of the market is strict. Any participant who reneges on a transaction usually finds that reprisals are swift and thorough.

In a sense foreign exchange markets have existed as long as there has been international trading which necessitated the conversion of the currency of one country into that of another. As advances in transportation and communication facilities expanded the volume and stretched the boundaries of international transactions, sophisticated techniques were developed to deal with the conversion process. Today, these advanced markets handle enormous amounts of transactions swiftly and efficiently.

In a sense, foreign exchange markets are counterparts of their respective domestic money markets, since a substantial amount of the funds used to finance foreign transactions are borrowed from the domestic money supplies. It is this access to the domestic money market that makes a foreign exchange market so important to its internal economy. In essence, a foreign exchange market links the external world economy with the domestic economy. Thus, foreign economic transactions may have a direct impact on the volume of money in circulation domestically. Conversely, change in the volume of money in circulation domestically may affect foreign exchange through the same money market mechanism.

In general, there are two types of foreign exchange markets—the futures market and the forward market and a major group of participants which affects the operations of each—the central banks.

[1] THE FUTURES MARKET

The International Monetary Market was established in May 1972, as the first centralized market to trade futures in currency. It was patterned after futures trading in agricultural commodities. The London International Financial Futures Exchange and the MidAmerica Commodity Exchange began trading currency futures soon after.

It was only a question of time until the options market was wedded to the futures market. The Philadelphia Exchange initiated trading in various foreign exchange options, while the Chicago Board Options Exchange added a new wrinkle by offering options with European expiration, which may be exercised only on the last trading day before expiration. Several other exchanges also instituted trading in options on currency futures.

The futures market followed in the path of the forward market and both markets may be used for the same purposes. Trading in the futures market is done on an auction basis, where bids and offers on currency futures are made by open outcry. In the ordinary course of events, a firm desiring to execute a transaction would give its order to a so-called futures commission merchant who is a member of a commodity exchange. Big orders are apt to be attracted to the futures market because of its emphasis on liquidity. Also, ordinarily, delivery is not wanted by either buyer or seller in the futures market, and, therefore, there is a tendency to use it primarily for hedging purposes rather than for the purchase of currencies. On the other hand, the forward market provides greater room for flexibility since a firm can work out specific arrangements with the institution with which it is doing business rather than being tied to the specific contract terms of the futures market.

[2] THE FORWARD MARKET

The mechanism of the forward market functions primarily through commercial banks and foreign exchange brokers.

(a) Commercial Banks

Although corporations account for the bulk of the supply and demand for currencies in the foreign exchange markets, they do not participate directly in the forward market. Instead, they use their commercial banks. Governments also use commercial banks primarily because they can be assured that their transactions will be carried out in secrecy. Thus, commercial banks acting as both agents for their customers and participants for their own accounts, are one of the primary participants in the forward market.

These institutions generally maintain working balances abroad with correspondent banks to accommodate trading requirements. Banks may vary with respect to their emphasis on customer service. Some place less stress on customer service, and instead may trade primarily for their own account. This difference in emphasis is due mainly to the bank's internal management policies tempered by considerations of shareholder preferences as well as more formal legal and banking restrictions.

It is desirable for the corporate financial manager to familiarize himself with the policies of various banks regarding the banks' positions with respect to exchange risk and exposure. Generally speaking, a bank with more liberal risk and exposure limits, larger forward dealings, and larger position commitments is more likely to give more flexible service to its major corporate customers.

(b) Foreign Exchange Brokers

Foreign exchange brokers are usually small individual firms located in local exchange markets. The broker acts as both an agent and a middleman, supplementing the system of a physical meeting place for many types of foreign exchange transactions. The broker does not, however, carry a position for his own account.

Brokers fill the transaction gap between the commercial banks and their customers. For example, few banks have the time to seek out transaction partners every minute of every trading day. This would demand continuous calling and searching, which is impractical from the banks' point of view for reasons of competition and efficiency. The broker provides this service, and in the course of a normal exchange day, he may make several hundred phone calls, matching exchange buyers and sellers in complete secrecy. This is particularly important to the commercial banks. If they chose to alter substantial currency positions, they would not necessarily want their competitors to know their strategies. The brokers' role is usually confined to local market deals. They are seldom used for international transactions, where commercial banks generally choose to deal directly with one another.

[3] CENTRAL BANKS

These institutions are primarily responsible for maintaining efficient monetary systems (i.e., encouraging domestic growth without inflation). Central banks intervene actively in the international money markets to attain their domestic economic goals. Essentially, these banks deal in foreign exchange to make orderly markets for their respective currencies, thus promoting a favorable climate for their country's international trade and investment. A variety of factors dictate the actions pursued by central banks including their own country's balance of payment (deficit or surplus), domestic and international interest rate differentials, and current market psychology. For example, in mid-1985, because of concern about the continued high level of the dollar, the central banks of Western Europe and North America operated closely with one another to affect a decline. At times, they have taken other joint action to achieve other objectives.

This concludes our orientation to international finance. The next section of this chapter deals with some of the salient problems encountered by the corporate financial manager in the world of international finance.

23.4   THE UNIQUE PROBLEMS OF INTERNATIONAL FINANCIAL MANAGEMENT

International finance poses a unique array of problems for the financial manager of a multinational corporation (MNC). Responsible for a network of subsidiaries that may straddle the globe, he must continually cope with the vagaries of world wide inflation which affect international prices and currency exchange rates. His difficulties are aggravated at present because he operates within a framework of floating exchange rates and international interdependencies which makes one economy sensitive to changes in others.

Exchange rate fluctuation is the direct cause of an MNC's exposure to exchange risk. Exchange risk management, in turn, requires an understanding of international accounting standards (FASB Nos, 8, 52, 70 and their various revisions) and international cash management.

Taxation, a consideration that underlies financial decisions, has special implications for the multinational corporation.[3] Additionally, the international financial manager will often find it necessary to modify conventional (i.e. domestic) capital budgeting techniques to incorporate factors peculiar to international finance.

The purpose of this section is to set forth these problems. We begin at square 1 with exchange risk management.

[1] PROBLEM 1: CHOOSE THE BEST POLICY FOR FINANCIAL MANAGEMENT UNDER FLUCTUATING EXCHANGE RATES

The crucial factor in establishing a policy for exchange risk management is management's attitude toward risk. Although managerial caution is prudent, extreme caution may not produce optimal results in the world of international finance.

There are perhaps three basic options available to the financial manager when choosing an exchange risk management policy.[4] We will begin with the most conservative of these options.

(a) Option 1: The Pessimistic Criterion—Choose the Best of the Worst

This option typifies a conservative attitude towards exchange risk. The financial manager estimates a future value for the exchange rate and bases all decisions on this assumption. Since his attitude toward risk is conservative, the worst case is assumed for forecasted exchange rates during the planning period. In order to minimize the corporation's losses, therefore, the financial manager would only undertake projects which appear profitable under these adverse conditions. In other words, he develops a quasi-hedge by simply choosing the best of the worst.

The management of such an organization may sleep well at night; secure in the knowledge that the corporation is not likely to lose much because of unfavorable rate fluctuations. However, such a policy also implicitly condemns many foreign currency transactions as nonfeasible or unattractive, because of their unacceptable risk. The opportunity cost of these potentially profitable but foregone projects may be quite high in the long-run. Thus, such a policy may be undesirable for many corporations.

(b) Option 2: The Optimistic Criterion—Hedge Nothing

In option 1 conservative management attempts to hedge everything by taking only those projects with negligible exchange risk. Option 2 is the antithesis of the conservative pessimistic policy. Managers who employ this optimistic criterion choose to ignore exchange rate fluctuations. Any losses incurred due to changes in exchange rates are considered to be the normal cost of conducting business. This policy which reduces opportunity costs (i.e., fewer projects foregone due to exchange risk) and hedging costs (i.e., cash spent on hedging), may be attractive under the following considerations:

- normal foreign currency cash flows are modest relative to other cash flows;
- anticipated fluctuations in the exchange rate are expected to be small during the planning period; and
- the company has no intermediate or long-term foreign commitments.

Proponents of this "optimistic" hedging policy argue that it is best to ignore exchange rates since hedging does not maximize the value of the firm. They feel that the cost of hedging will offset any related gains, on the assumption that present foreign exchange and capital markets are efficient. Hence, gains and losses due to exchange rate fluctuations are equally possible.

According to the IRPT, for example, the forward premium or discount for a currency depends on interest yield differentials between two countries. Thus, one can examine yield spreads between countries to predict the direction of foreign exchange rates, along with forward premiums or discounts. So, the MNC will gain nothing by hedging via the forward market or any other mechanism, since yields in local capital markets represent the opportunity costs of investments needed to hedge against exchange risks.

Then again, an assumption underlying the optimistic policy is that there is a good correlation between exchange rate changes and prices paid or received by the corporation in its ordinary business. This is not necessarily true and may lead to unanticipated earnings changes if the nominal monetary value of some of its assets and liabilities do not change in tandem with changes in exchange rates. These unanticipated changes in earnings affect the value of the corporation. At least hedging provides a cushion which makes earnings changes more predictable. Indeed, prudent hedging may increase the value of the MNC (vis-a-vis its earnings stream) by smoothing these earnings variations. Thus, an extremely optimistic hedging policy may also lead to suboptimal results.

(c) Option 3: Hedge Selectively

This policy is a compromise between the two extreme options and, in the long run, may be the most prudent. It involves a selective hedging policy, which weighs several factors comparatively for each exposure. In this way, the financial manager can determine which exposures are potentially the most hazardous to the firm. Generally, this policy should be capable of accommodating the following factors in the hedging decision practices:

- the timing of the procedure (the cost of covering an exposure often depends on the direction of the hedge);
- the relevant set of host country rules and regulations (capital and funds flow restrictions may vary from country to country);
- the accurate forecast of exchange rates (the firm should develop some procedure for estimating foreign currency fluctuations);
- the projection of future corporate transactions by both amount and duration (this will be important in selecting the timing and magnitude of hedges for respective projects); and
- the after-tax cost benefit analysis (this will determine whether exposure reduction is actually worth the cost).

Thus, a selective hedging policy which incorporates these factors may be useful to financial managers who find the other "extreme" policies impractical. There is no perfect decision model, however, and each manager must decide for himself which policy is best suited to his needs.

We will now consider the problem of accurately defining and recognizing exposure in the multinational enterprise.

[2] PROBLEM 2: DETERMINING THE CORPORATION'S EXPOSURE RISK

Essentially, an exchange risk management program involves three primary objectives:

- Mitigating the adverse influences of currency fluctuations on the overall earnings stream or equity so that investor expectations (resulting from changes in risk perception) will not be impaired (translation or remeasurement exposure);
- Minimizing the effects of currency fluctuations on current income (transaction exposure); and
- Lessening the outcomes of both of these fluctuations on the net present value of the firm's future cash flows (economic exposure).

To accomplish these objectives, it is important that the financial manager recognize the firm's financial risk exposure. This arises whenever a company has activities in different countries that involve the use of various currencies. In these circumstances, the company incurs an operating currency exposure whenever its cash payments in a particular currency are not matched by cash receipts in that currency; gains or losses will occur whenever fluctuations in exchange rates take place. Additionally, the company has a balance sheet exposure related to the amount of local currency assets and liabilities that have to be converted to the parent's reporting currency and the applicable accounting rules for affecting such conversions.

In the jargon of foreign exchange the balance sheet exposure under current rules may be called a "translation" or "remeasurement" exposure and the operational exposure is known as a "transaction exposure." A third type that is more difficult to identify is the "economic" exposure.

(a) Translation or Remeasurement Exposure

Translation or remeasurement exposure arises from the necessity of expressing the balance sheets of foreign subsidiaries in the reporting currency of a parent company during periods of rate fluctuations. Such exposure is dependent upon two factors. One is the procedure required to express a foreign subsidiary's local currency financial statement in the reporting currency of the parent. This aspect of the exposure is determined by the rules of the governing accounting body and is therefore outside the direct control of the company. The other factor is the relationship between the assets and liabilities that are exposed, as defined by the rules, in the balance sheet of the subsidiary; this relationship is controlled by the company.

As explained subseqently in Appendix A, FASB Statement No. 52 sets forth the presently applicable rules for expressing the local currency financial statements of a U.S. foreign subsidiary in the reporting currency of the parent. These rules call for two methods to make the conversion. One, in effect, provides for translating, at the current rate, the local currency net investment in the foreign subsidiary's balance sheet into the reporting currency, usually dollars, of the parent; the resulting gain or loss depends on the size of the subsidiary's net investment and is directed to the parent's equity. The second method provides for remeasuring the various local currency items in the foreign subsidiary's balance sheet, at prescribed rates, to the parent's reporting currency; in this case, the resulting gain or loss depends on the composition of the subsidiary's balance sheet items and flows through to the parent's net income.

A corporation with centralized control of its outside activities may analyze the exposed balance sheet positions of its foreign subsidiaries to isolate areas where transaction or remeasurement gains or losses are likely, and could be severe. If there is a net liability position during a period of fluctuating exchange rates, a financial manager can anticipate that an appreciation in the local currency (vis-a-vis the parent's reporting currency) will result in a translation or remeasurement loss, if this net liability position remains unchanged. Conversely, a translation or remeasurement gain will occur if the net liability position does not change, and the local currency depreciates against the dollar.

Analyses of this sort allow management to determine whether relationships between exposed balance sheet positions and cash flows are significant during the reporting period. For example, management may want to separate the effects of operating transactions (i.e., sales revenues, cost of goods sold, operating expenses) from financial transactions (i.e., dividends and purchases of fixed assets, or any financing-related cash outflows). Since management generally has greater control over the timing of financial transactions it may be able to mitigate the effects of translation or remeasurement losses due to cash flows in this area. For example, if the local currency is depreciating, management may want to accelerate dividend payments to the parent to avoid accumulating cash.

(b) Transaction Exposure

Transaction exposure is defined as follows:

the net intercurrency transfers for each subsidiary with respect to each foreign currency during each planning period that are not covered by forward exchange or other offsetting transactions and are, thus, subject to exchange losses. Transaction exposure arises because of projected transactions in currencies other than the local currency of the subsidary involved. For example, if the exchange rates of the local currency drops, foreign currency payables will cost more in terms of the local currency, and if the local currency increases in value, foreign currency receivables will result in fewer local currency units.[5]

Consider an example. A U.S. multinational has a payable denominated in pounds owed to a U.K. manufacturer worth, at prevailing rates, $1,000. If the dollar drops 20 percent against the British pound, the cost of that payable will increase to $1,200. On the other hand, if the dollar is revalued upward by 20 percent, the cost of the payable would decrease to $800. The percentage increase in the amount of the payable constitutes the transaction exposure in this example.

Generally, projections of transaction exposures are based on estimated cash flows and budgets for a given time period. The exposed loss is actually "realized" if the U.S. multinational must exchange dollars for pounds at the lower rate to effect payment. Conversely, if the exchange occurs at the higher rate, the firm realizes a profit which is taxable since it results from normal operations during the period.

(c) Economic Exposure

Exchange rate fluctuations can lead to economic exposure if a firm's long-term earning power is susceptible to declines, due to long-term changes in the exchange rate. These declines in earning power will lead investors to capitalize the firm's earnings at a higher discount rate.

Generally, economic exposure results when a firm's cost disbursements (i.e., operating expenses, materials and wages) are not matched by its revenue receipts for goods and services during periods of exchange rate fluctuations. The effect of this input-output imbalance can be mitigated if the firm has the ability to change prices to maintain profit margins. This procedure may not be available, however, because of competitive pricing considerations and government regulations.

The opposite side of this phenomenon is that the firm's long-term earning power may increase due to changes in economic factors. For example, after a local currency devaluation, local currency revenues from the firm's export sales should improve. The devaluation, in effect, results in lower export prices which should give the firm a competitive price advantage in foreign markets. Therefore, the firm can increase its local currency receipts by the devaluation amount simply by maintaining its prices in relation to foreign currencies. Generally, the immediate effects of a local currency devaluation will only be felt on the firms exposed assets and normal operational transactions.

One skill that is essential to applying any type of exposure analysis is the ability to understand the underlying accounting rules. Exposure determination and many other types of financial analyses must be considered within the context of international accounting rules, if their practical applications are to be correctly executed. So, we will turn now to a discussion of the accounting standards which currently dictate reporting procedures for all U.S. based multinationals.

[3] PROBLEM 3: UNDERSTANDING THE INTRICACIES OF INTERNATIONAL ACCOUNTING

A big U.S. multinational firm may have several hundred reporting entities operating in a number of different national environments. Even though their statements are expressed in local currencies, the entities could have varying degrees of financial independence. Accordingly, the decision as to whether the results of their operations are more realistically measured in their local currency or in that of their parent, may depend upon the degree of control they exercise over their own operation.

Establishment of accounting rules to provide guidelines in researching these decisions, is a thorny problem. In order to provide an understanding of the underlying issues and how they may be resolved, it is desirable to be familiar with the changes that have occurred as the rules evolved.

(a) Background

Although the difficulty has been recognized for some time and different countries had sought to cope with it in different ways, the first basic effort at developing uniform procedures in the United States was in FASB Statement No. 8, "Accounting for the Translation of Foreign Currency Transactions and Foreign Currency Financial Statements," which was issued in October 1975. Before this Statement, the most authoritative method in the U.S., proposed by the American Institute of Certified Public Accountants, was the current/non-current system, which provided for translating current items in the balance sheet at current rates and long-term items at historical rates of exchange. FASB Statement No. 8 adopted the so called temporal method which provided reporting guidelines that did not differ materially from the former monetary/nonmonetary technique, whereby financial assets are translated at current rates and physical assets at historical rates. (This method had been favored by the National Association of Accountants).

The Statement also required that the exchange gains and losses be fully reflected in the earnings of the period in which the change in rate between the dollar and the foreign currency occurred. Such exchange gains or losses could be a consequence of translating assets and liabilities at different rates of exchange. They could also result from actual changes in cash flows as a result of the settlement of a contractual requirement denominated in foreign currency at a rate different from that at which it was recorded.

(b) The Problems of FASB Statement No. 8

From its inception, FASB Statement No. 8 was subject to a deluge of criticism from many sources including corporations, practicing accountants and academicians. Skepticism was levelled at its objective of expressing in dollars, in conformity with U.S. generally accepted accounting principles, the elements of foreign currency statements. It was contended that it was unrealistic to use a single unit of measurement, such as the dollar, to remeasure foreign currency transactions. This approach distorted the fact that different entities operated in different economic environments and were not simple extensions of the parent.

In FASB Statement No. 8, inventories and fixed assets flowed, at historic rates, from balance sheet to income statement, while revenue and other costs generally were translated at average rates. In addition, the effect of currency fluctuations on monetary items was recognized immediately. The results of this differing handling of exchange rate changes, which were reflected in current income, created violent earnings swings that dismayed management.

In order to provide a degree of stability, some managements adopted hedging tactics. Much of the change, however, was the outcome of accounting methodology that had little resemblance to economic fact. As a result, the hedging efforts often were expanded to protect illusory economic exposures.

On top of these difficulties, the use of historic costs created a false anchor in economies that were experiencing rapid inflation. Many of the subsidiaries of U.S. multinational companies operated in countries where prices were rising rapidly. To use historic costs under these circumstances appeared misleading to many users of financial statements.

The extent of the negative reaction, led the FASB to establish, in January 1979, a project to reconsider FASB Statement No. 8. An exposure draft was released in August 1980, revised in June 1981, and finalized as FASB Statement No. 52 in December 1981.

(c) The Theme of FASB Statement No. 52

In discussing the objective that underlies this Statement, the FASB refers to an enterprise within which there are a number of separate entities that operate in different economic and currency environments. In order to consolidate the financial statements of these separate entities into the single statement of the enterprise, the elements denominated in foreign currencies are translated into the enterprise's reporting currency. Since the overall performance of the enterprise depends upon the results of the constituent entities, the translation must be accomplished in a manner that reflects the expected economic effects of the rate changes on the enterprise's cash flows and equity.

To achieve this objective, the financial results and relationships of the individual entities are measured in the currency of the primary economic environment in which they operate. This currency is identified as the entity's functional currency. Only by retaining the functional currency relationships of each operating entity, the Board concluded, can the aggregate performance in different operating environments be measured for purposes of consolidation.

Encompassed in this approach is employment of the current rate of exchange for translating the functional currency to the reporting currency of the enterprise. If all of a foreign entity's assets and liabilities are measured in its functional currency and translated at the current exchange rate, a change in this rate affects the entity's net assets. The theory is that the net investment rather than specific assets or liabilities is exposed to the risk of a rate change.

Under this method, all elements of financial statements are translated using the exchange rate in effect as of the dates the elements are reported. For assets and liabilities, the exchange rate at the balance sheet date is used; for income statement items, a weighted average exchange rate for the period may be used. Figure 23.1 shows in some detail the translation bases employed for balance sheet items by the major methods that have been used.

An important distinction is drawn in FASB Statement No. 52 between gains or losses that result from the translation process alone and those resulting from cash flows because of changes in exchange rates: (a) the former are described as "translation adjustments" and are not included in net income, but are reported as a separate element of equity; (b) the latter, called "transaction gain or loss," are flowed through income when the rate changes rather than when the transaction is settled.

The FASB requires that the translation adjustments should eventually be absorbed into income when the related investment is substantially liquidated. Also certain transaction gains or losses are treated differently. Thus, those attributable to economic hedges and intercompany foreign currency transactions are excluded from net income and treated as translation adjustments.

FIGURE 23.1 *Comparison of four basic translation methods**

Balance Sheet Item	**Temporal Method	**Monetary/Nonmonetary Method	**Current-Noncurrent Method	Current Method
ASSETS				
Cash	C	C	C	C
Marketable securities:				
Carried at cost	H	C	C	C
Carried at current market price	C	C	C	C
Accounts and notes receivable	C	C	C	C
Inventories:				
Carried at cost	H	H	C	C
Carried at current replacement or selling prices	C	H	C	C
Carried at net realizable value	C	H	C	C
Carried at contract price	C	H	C	C
Prepaid expenses	H	H	C	C
Fixed assets	H	H	H	C
LIABILITIES				
Accounts and notes payable	C	C	C	C
Accrued expenses payable	C	C	C	C
Other current liabilities	C	C	C	C
Deferred income	H	H	C	C
Long-term debt	C	C	H	C

C = indicates the current rate in effect at the balance sheet date.

H = indicates the historical rate or the rate in effect when the asset or liability was originally acquired or recorded on the books.

*First three columns based on FASB Statement No. 8 and R. Aggerwal, "The Translation Problem in International Accounting: Insight for Financial Management," *Management International Review* 2-3 (1975), pp. 67-79.

**These represent the translation methods that have been used. The temporal method was required by FASB Statement No. 8; the monetary/nonmonetary and the current-noncurrent methods were practiced prior to FASB Statement No. 8; the current method is now required by FASB Statement No. 52.

(d) The Resulting Mixture

A primary thrust of the new procedures is to shift remeasuring foreign currency transactions from the "single unit of measurement" approach of FASB Statement No. 8 to the "net investment" approach of FASB Statement No. 52. Typically, this requires measuring all elements of the financial statements in the functional currency and using the current rate of exchange for translation from the functional currency to the reporting currency, if they are different (Subsidiary A in Figure 23.2). A complete changeover, however, was not effected. In certain circumstances, the former approach is still called for.

In a highly inflationary environment, a currency loses its utility as a store of value and therefore becomes an inadequate measuring unit. In this case, the FASB decided that the reporting currency should be employed as the functional currency, in effect requiring the continued use of the FASB Statement No. 8 methodology (Subsidiary D in Figure 23.2).

If an entity's books of record are not maintained in its functional currency, remeasurement into the functional currency is required. Thus, the French subsidiary of a U.S. multinational firm, whose functional currency is the franc might have, in turn, a dependent German subsidiary operating under its direction. The functional currency of the German subsidiary, therefore, would be the franc. Accordingly, its records, if maintained in marks, would have to be converted into francs. This process represents remeasuring into functional currency and the resulting gain or loss would be reflected in the net income of the French subsidiary, along the lines of FASB Statement No. 8. Eventually these gains or losses would flow through to the net income of the U.S. parent (Subsidiary B in Figure 23.2).

If a foreign entity's functional currency is the reporting currency, remeasurement into the reporting currency obviates translation. Thus, the U.S. parent might have a dependent foreign subsidiary operating under its direction. In this case, the functional currency of the subsidiary would be the dollar. If the subsidiary kept its records in its own currency, remeasurement into dollars would follow the procedures of FASB Statement No. 8 (subsidiary C in Figure 23.2).

These differences are summarized in Figure 23.2. The confusion created by this strict interpretation of the functional theory approach may be avoided through reorganizing foreign entities so as to provide for each of them employing its own functional currency. Additionally, management is given some latitude in making functional currency decisions. Thus, the FASB states, "Management's judgement will be required to determine the functional currency in which financial results and relationships are measured with the greatest degree of relevance and reliability."

FIGURE 23.2 *Variations in currency remeasurement relationships*

U.S. Parent
(The reporting enterprise,
on a consolidated basis,
whose reporting currency
is the dollar)

Subsidiary A

a. Manufactures and sells products in Country A.

b. Its functional currency is local currency A.

  1. Balance sheet translated on basis of current method.

  2. No gains or losses flow to parent net income.

  3. Translation gains or losses absorbed directly in parent's balance sheet equity account.

Subsidiary B

a. Sales entity of A, distributing A's products at A's direction in Country B, but keeps records in local currency B.

b. Its functional currency is local currency A.

  1. Balance sheet items are remeasured into A's currency on basis of the temporal method.

  2. Gains or losses flow to A's net income and eventually to that of the reporting enterprise.

Subsidiary C

a. Sales subsidiary of parent; distributes parent's products in Country C and keeps records in local currency C.

b. Its functional currency is the dollar.

  1. Balance sheet items are remeasured into dollars on basis of the temporal method.

  2. Remeasurement gains or losses flow to parent's net income.

Subsidiary D

a. Self-contained entity operating in a highly inflationary environment.

b. Its functional currency is defined as the reporting currency of the enterprise, in this case, the dollar.

  1. Balance sheet items are remeasured into dollars on basis of the temporal method.

  2. Remeasurement gains or losses flow to parent's net income.

Note: All items not expressed in the functional currency are *remeasured* into the functional currency on the basis of the temporal method and the resulting gains or losses flow into net income. All items expressed in a functional currency are translated into the reporting currency on the basis of the current method and are reflected in the parent's equity account.

Application of the procedures of FASB Statement No. 52, which involve primarily the current-functional-currency method, but also may make use of the temporal method of FASB Statement No. 8, is illustrated in Appendix A to this chapter. Appendix A also shows the application of the procedures for presenting supplementary information about changing prices in the international area.

[4] PROBLEM 4: THE COMPLEXITIES OF INTERNATIONAL CASH MANAGEMENT

Any firm that has or intends to develop an overseas operation inevitably must deal with the problem of international cash flows. Cash management is a well accepted principle now for domestic activity, but its application to the international area is still relatively new.

To a large extent, the goals of an international cash management system are similar to those of any domestic cash management system. During periods of currency fluctuations, however, the international cash management system, in addition to managing the firm's sources, positions, and movements of funds, takes on the added responsibility of minimizing exposure risks.

The financial manager attempting to implement an international cash management system may find a number of obstacles in his path. These complications are mainly due to regulations in the host country where the foreign operation is located. For example, one of the primary functions of the cash management system may be to manage inter-country fund flows between subsidiaries and their customers or suppliers when fund transfers abroad may be curtailed by foreign government restrictions on cross border cash movement. Similarly, the cash manager may be responsible for dividend payments by the subsidiary to the parent company in the U.S. However, dividends remitted to the parent company from the foreign subsidiary may be subject to foreign taxation. Cash managers responsible for credit or billing transactions may find that credit standards and acceptable techniques for the collection of receivables may be substantially different abroad. Finally, foreign commercial banks may be lacking in their ability to transfer and process funds from the foreign subsidiary.

Another complexity of international cash management involves the financing of foreign operations via foreign sources. Here, the financial manager may have to make a variety of complex decisions concerning leverage ratios, repayment currencies, debt instruments, and foreign financial markets. An effective system for international cash management should be able to reconcile these funds flow problems through a profit maximizing network.

[5] PROBLEM 5: THE ISSUES UNDERLYING INTERNATIONAL CAPITAL BUDGETING

In essence, the goals of the MNC normally are similar to those of any solely domestic firm. Thus, in attaining its objectives the MNC tends to apply the same basic capital budgeting principles to its foreign operations as it uses for its domestic projects. The analysis of an overseas subsidiary, however, must be tempered by the special issues encountered abroad. Along these lines there are worldwide opportunities to evaluate; the local human resources and political environment to take into account; and the special risks of war, inflation, and expropriation to consider.

An international company must also anticipate additional investments beyond its original commitment. Some of these investments may be involuntary. For example, if a project is initiated in a country that provides tariff protections for new, marginal industries, it may be necessary for the parent company to expand its operations after the tariff barriers are terminated. In this way, the project may be able to establish the economies of scale essential to compete in foreign markets. Moreover, additional reinvestment in the host country of the foreign operation may be necessary, if governmental restrictions there disallow total repatriation of cash flows.

Another issue peculiar to international capital budgeting is the treatment of exchange risk. An international firm can obtain its funds from a variety of sources in locations worldwide. It is necessary, therefore, to interrelate exchange risks and the cost of borrowing in foreign currencies.

Implicit in the MNC situation is the roles played by the subsidiary in the international network. If the subsidiary is regarded primarily as a financial conduit to help in the guidance of fund flows throughout the system, conventional rate of return analyses may not be appropriate. In this case, reliance may have to be placed on subjective judgement.

When rate of return analysis is used, the financial manager must still make up his mind whether to assume a parent company or subsidiary perspective. This calculation, in turn, is dependent upon the determination of its cost of capital and net cash inflows.

With respect to the cost of capital, whether to use that of the parent or the subsidiary may depend upon the degree of assistance provided by the parent. While the bias is towards using the parent's cost of capital, there may be justification to employing that of the subsidiary if it is encouraged to operate on its own initiative.

With respect to cash flows, should the subsidiary be evaluated only on the basis of those remitted to the parent, or should all cash flows generated overseas be included in the analysis? The answer is not clear since certain cash flows created by overseas projects may have to be retained in their host countries due to foreign government restrictions.

23.5 THE TECHNIQUES OF INTERNATIONAL FINANCIAL MANAGEMENT

Having discussed the salient problems of international financial management, we will now consider some of the techniques that corporations currently employ to deal with these complexities. The techniques for handling problems shown in this section of the chapter correspond both in number and kind to the problems developed in the prior section.

[1] TECHNIQUE 1: INTEGRATING THE COMPONENTS OF A POLICY TO DEAL WITH FLUCTUATING EXCHANGE RATES

In the preceding section, we described a selective hedging policy as the most prudent for coping with fluctuating exchange rates. It is desirable that such a policy incorporate the components listed below in order to assure its effectiveness. Otherwise, the firm runs the risk of incurring substantial earnings variations which may be detrimental to its valuation by investors.

- A system for forecasting exchange rates: this system should provide the necessary information as to the probability, timing and magnitude of exchange rate variations during a given planning period;
- Developing hedging procedures: selecting the appropriate hedging option to meet the various exposure risks of the firm to exchange losses; and
- An organization capable of implementing exchange risk management policies: the international financial department must carry out the necessary policies and arbitrate any conflicts which may arise.

We now suggest how to facilitate the development of these components.

(a) Component 1: Developing a System for Forecasting Exchange Rates

Exchange rates represent prices of currencies relative to currencies of other nations. These intercurrency prices are linked to various economic factors common to each nation, which primarily determine the supply and demand for a particular currency on the foreign exchange markets.

Demand for the U.S. dollar is also an outgrowth of the demand for U.S. goods and services worldwide. (Since foreign countries must pay for U.S. goods and services in dollars, the more goods they purchase from the U.S., the greater their demand for U.S. dollars). Of course, the converse of this situation is that the U.S. also purchases vast quantities of foreign goods. This in turn produces an increase in the supply of dollars on the foreign exchange markets.

Additionally, social, political and psychological factors play an important role in determining the supply and demand for a given currency. Thus, worldwide confidence in the ability of America's administration to control inflation and maintain government stability is reflected in the market's demand for the U.S. dollar. These factors are intangible, however, and therefore difficult to quantify in any foreign exchange rate calculation.

Exchange rates respond to the sales or purchases of currencies by the world's central banks, but these transactions represent delicate operations. (Central banks may attempt to strengthen their national currencies by purchasing their own currencies in the marketplace. This may produce an increase in demand which may prevent the depreciation of that currency's price on the market). For this reason, one should be cognizant of indicated central bank intervention in order to predict exchange rates.

The techniques used to forecast foreign exchange rates may vary for different time horizons. Short-term exchange rates (i.e., less than three months in the future) tend to move randomly on a daily basis and thus are extremely difficult to predict. Intermediate exchange rates (i.e., three months to two years) are more predictable. Generally, the use of the PPPT and the IRPT are helpful in these forecasts. It will be remembered that according to the PPPT the differences between foreign and domestic inflation rates equal changes in the spot exchange rate during the same period. IRPT carries this idea one step further, defining the effects of inflation rates on interest rates, which represent the price of money in each currency. According to IRPT, the difference between current forward and spot exchange rates will equal the difference between foreign and domestic rates of inflation over the same period. Thus, some additional criteria for the financial manager may be short-term and intermediate predictions of relative inflation rates and interest rates between nations. These factors will directly affect relative currency prices over the same period.

Useful techniques for forecasting long-term exchange rates have been based on derivatives of the PPPT. Generally, one bases future exchange rate forecasts on predictions of future inflation rates, which determine relative price differentials and hence the relative purchasing power between two currencies. (One assumes that exchange rates and inflation rates are subject to similar effects).

Recently, mathematical models have also been developed which incorporate numerous economic factors in the exchange rate forecasts (i.e., money supply growth, balance of payments comparisons, etc.) These models produce forecasts based on the relationships of these variables to current spot and forward exchange rates. (Many large commercial banks actively trading in the foreign exchange markets currently utilize these techniques.)

Due to the complexity and diversity of all factors involved in exchange rate forecasting, no one of these methods previously discussed will yield consistently accurate forecasts if used in isolation. When applied currently with the informed judgements and intuitive estimates of an expert, the techniques can be quite effective in producing reasonable estimates. Foreign exchange forecasts based on these techniques are available at most of the nation's major money center commercial banks, or through their affiliated correspondent bank overseas.

(b) Component 2: Developing Hedging Procedures

The financial manager will have a number of hedging options which may differ considerably in several areas. Cost flexibility, availability and suitability for tax purposes in a given country are some factors which may change, depending on the hedging technique employed. For this reason, it may be useful to delineate hedging techniques according to their suitability for reducing each kind of exposure to exchange losses.

A major technique for hedging *transaction exposure* is through use of the forward exchange or futures markets. Once a contract has been created, the established exchange rate is fixed for the specified period. Regardless of the fluctuations in the value of the currency which occur thereafter, the original contract rate will be honored. Utilizing these markets, a firm that obtains for its product the dollar equivalent of foreign currency with, say, 90 day payment terms can sell that foreign currency for delivery in 90 days. Thus, the firm can create an effective hedge to cover its 90 day receivable. For example, consider a firm that sells its products for payment in 90 days. The firm has just acquired an exposed asset—the accounts receivable amount to be received in three months. This puts the firm in a "long" asset position. To hedge this transaction, the firm would want to go "short" the same currency, i.e., create an offsetting liability in the same currency for the same amount. Then, no matter which way the currency fluctuates, the residual differences between the firm's exposed asset and liability positions will "wash out".

Conversely, a firm that must make a foreign currency payment in 90 days for the purchase of a product has an exposed liability on its books. The hedge in this case involves the foreign currency at the contract rate for delivery in 90 days when the payment falls due.

There are "real" and "opportunity" cost components in a contract. The real costs arise from the differences that may exist between the current ("spot") and contract rates. When these two rates are the same, the contract rate is described as "flat". But the contract rate may also be at a discount from or at a premium above the spot rate.

As an illustration of the real cost, take the case of an exporter who sells to a buyer in the U.K. and prices his product at $175. Based on an assumed current rate of exchange of $1.75 equals one pound, the exporter would receive 100 pounds from the buyer. Since payment is made in 90 days, however, the exporter is uncertain of the amount of dollars he would actually obtain. He therefore sells a 90-day forward contract when pounds are trading at a discount in the forward market; the rate at that time for 90 day delivery is $1.72. Accordingly, the exporter receives proceeds of $172, thereby incurring a real cost of $3.00 or about 1.75 percent of the transaction to eliminate exchange uncertainty. On the other hand, had the pound been selling at a premium, the forward sale would have resulted in a profit.

Let us assume that the 90 day forward rate at the time of the transaction was flat at $1.75; at the delivery date 90 days later, the spot rate of the pound rises to $1.78. In these circumstances, had the exporter not entered into a forward contract at $175 he could have sold the 100 pounds he received for $178. As a result, the exporter would have foregone a profit of $3.00 which represents the opportunity cost of his contract.

Most multinationals limit their use of exchange contracts to covering one or more items, like foreign currency loans obtained by foreign subsidiaries, or hedging payables against imports. Generally, the contracts are only used to hedge against assets that are intended for transferral.

These contracts have a few limitations which should be illuminated. For example, gains made on foreign currency contracts are fully taxable as ordinary income in the U.S. Also, the cost of cover rises rapidly as the strength of the currency increases. This is because the contract rate generally reflects at least all the information that is readily available to a corporate treasurer.

An alternative to the forward or futures markets is hedging through a group of strategies that change the balance sheet of a foreign subsidiary. These strategies are known as "leading" or "lagging" procedures. "Leading" is the acceleration of payments prior to their due dates when receipts are denominated in a weakening currency, or payments are denominated in a strengthening currency. "Lagging" is the delaying of payments after their specified due date when payments are denominated in a weakening currency, or receipts are denominated in a strengthening currency.

In either case, the objective of this technique is to take advantage of anticipated changes in exchange rates, so as to maximize exchange gains and minimize losses. As an illustration, assume the following conditions:

- A U.S. parent company has a payment of $1 million due to a U.K. subsidiary in the current month: according to its terms, the payment may be delayed up to six months.
- The spot rate $/£ rate is $1.7120. ($1.7120 equals £1 or £0.5841 equals $1.00)
- The forecasted six months $/£ rate is $1.640.

If undertaken now, therefore, this $1 million payable would yield the subsidiary £584,112 ($1,000,000/1.7120 = £.584,112). However, if paid in six months, the subsidiary would obtain £609,756 ($1,000,000/1.64), permitting it an exchange gain of £25,644 (£609,756 - £584,112), while the cost to the parent remains unchanged, since it pays $1,000,000 in either event.

Some companies have conducted lead/lag analyses considering the relevant borrowing, investing and tax rates in each country. Although this approach can fine tune a conventional analysis like the above example, its profitability depends on the accuracy of the exchange rate forecasts.

When cash inflows and outflows are denominated in currencies other than that of the local country, the firm can try to reduce the risk of a currency "squeeze." This condition occurs when the currency in which the inflows are denominated decreases relative to the currency in which the outflows are denominated. To avoid a "squeeze", an effort should be made to obtain imports from countries whose currencies are likely to be weaker than the currencies of countries to which exports are directed. If effecting such relationships is not possible, the company can hedge by building price flexibility into its strategy. The inclusion of price escalation clauses indexed to the value of the parent company's reporting currency is helpful. Another approach is to use multi-currency units for pricing or financing purposes. A variant on this multi-currency approach is the Special Drawing Rights (SDR) or Eurocurrency Unit (ECU).

Since both weak and strong currencies are in the SDR and ECU baskets, their attraction as hedges stems from the likelihood that at any given time, some of these currencies will be rising while others are falling. Illustrative of this condition, in the summer of 1980, the Chemical Bank ventured into new territory by issuing CDs indexed to the SDR. Presumably, the bank expected to attract funds from central banks, institutional investors and companies which wanted to reduce their foreign-currency risk. Similarly, in October, 1982, Citicorp issued 15 million ECU Eurobonds in 1,000 ECU denominations designed to attract small investors concerned about unsettled European currency conditions.

As a guideline to the financial manager we summarize as follows some of the popular hedging techniques:

In case of devaluations;
1) sell local currency forward—
   the cost is the discount paid plus the risk that the currency will move in the opposite direction;
2) reduce levels of local currency cash and marketable securities—
   the cost is in operational and tax problems;
3) tighten credit (reduce local receivables)—
   the cost is a possible loss of business if credit terms are standard;
4) delay collection of hard currency receivables—
   the cost is funding the delay;
5) increase imports of hard currency goods—
   the cost is financing the imports;
6) delay payments of accounts payable—
   the cost is the impairment of the credit reputation that may result;

7) accelerate dividend fee remittances to parent and other subsidiaries—
   the cost is in financing the remittances if funds are not available;
8) speed up payment of inter-subsidiary accounts receivable—
   the cost is in lost interest;
9) delay collection of inter-subsidiary accounts receivable—
   the cost is in lost interest; and
10) invoice exports in foreign currency and imports in local currency—
   the cost is in sales lost plus a possible premium on import payments.

In case of revaluation, take the opposite action in each of the ten techniques above.

(c) Component 3: Organizing the Firm for Exchange Risk Management

The scope, importance and location of a company's international financial function will depend upon such factors as:

- the size of the company's international organization;
- the location of available talent within the company;
- historic precedent; and
- top management's attitude toward the importance of international financial considerations.

In the light of these factors, we outline four major alternatives that the financial manager might consider in organizing his firm's international finance activities.

[i] Alternative 1: Centralize at Headquarters

A firm may centralize all international policy making and financial services within the corporate financial unit at the corporate headquarters. Such "internalization" of the finance function implies that the financial manager is well versed in both international and domestic finance. This arrangement may not be practical especially when a firm has large numbers of financial personnel. A possible compromise in this case is to retain several 'experts' in international finance at the firm's headquarters under the managerial supervision of the firm's chief financial officer.

[ii] Alternative 2: Centralize Internationally

The company may opt to centralize international policy and financial services at the international headquarters. Usually, three kinds of companies conduct their international financial functions in this manner:

1) Companies that manage their business outside the U.S. through a legally, operationally independent foreign subsidiary. The chief international executive in these companies is likely to have a fully staffed financial department concerned with every aspect of international finance. Conversely, the corporate financial unit probably will not have a separate international financial executive;
2) Companies in capital intensive industries, whose international divisions have historically operated independently and have their own financial functions; and

3) Merchandising companies, where the international financial function has been traditionally limited to basic services (i.e., accounting, taxes, and some budgeting in technical areas). Some of these companies, however, have been modifying this approach by:

    a) relieving the financial staff of its large accounting function thereby enabling financial managers to concentrate on financial planning, capital procurement, and working capital controls;

    b) giving the corporate financial staff a more active role in the development of international financial policies; and

    c) delegating more responsibility and a greater voice in management decision to international financial managers.

[iii] Alternative 3: Split Between Headquarters and International Staff

Companies may prefer to split the responsibility for international financial services between the corporate and international staffs. Although this approach is probably the prevalent form of organization, there has been a tendency toward centralizing at the corporate level. This centralization trend is an effort to avoid the main problems of the dual international financial function: conflicting decisions and the confusion of overlapping responsibilities.

[iv] Alternative 4: International Finance Function Carried On Within the Operation Itself

Some firms regard their foreign operations as independent profit centers and therefore establish the international financial function within the operation, itself, rather than locating it at international or corporate headquarters. If this route is taken, the MNC relinquishes much of the centralized control of fund movements that permitted it to take advantage of differences in interest rates, taxes, and profit margins. In these circumstances, it may still, however, provide guidance in buying and selling forward contracts, timing remittances, and long-term financing.

The final choice as to the best form of organization for its international financial function will ultimately depend on two principal factors:

1) the firm's particular strategic and market considerations; and
2) management's attitude toward operational autonomy.

[2] TECHNIQUE 2: DEVELOPING A PROCEDURE FOR DETERMINING THE FIRM'S NET EXPOSURE TO EXCHANGE RISKS

In our earlier discussions, we identified three important types of exposures to exchange risks;

1) translation or remeasurement exposure;
2) transaction exposure; and
3) economic exposure.

It is desirable to evaluate the firm's net exposure in each particular area. The reason for analyzing transaction, translation or remeasurement and economic exposures separately stems mainly from their differing effects on cash flows. Translation or remeasurement exposure arises from the application of accounting principles and therefore these gains and losses do not involve cash and are not subject to taxation. Transaction gains and losses, on the other hand, are the direct result of intercurrency operations. As such, they represent real cash gains or losses and are therefore subject to taxes.

One way of reconciling the effects of translation or remeasurement vs. transaction exposure is to calculate the firms economic exposure. Here, the firm's net balance sheet exposure is combined with an assessment of its future cash flows to determine its net overall exposure positions. Relatively few firms currently employ any method of economic exposure analysis, although it is useful in determining the real economic value of the firm in an exposed environment.

(a) Translation or Remeasurement Exposure

The French and United Kingdom (UK) subsidiaries of an MNC are summarized in Figure 23.3 to illustrate the calculation of exposures. Defining translation or remeasurement exposure in terms of the local currency items on the subsidiaries' books, we net out the items denominated in non-local currency. The French subsidiary, for example, has 850,000 French Francs (FFr) receivables but, of this amount 500,000 FFr are denominated in Swiss francs (SFr). Similarly, the subsidiary has 200,000 FFr payables, of which 150,000 FFr are denominated in pounds sterling (£).

Let us first consider that the FFr is the subsidiary's functional currency. The MNC's net translation exposure applicable to the French subsidiary, under present FASB requirements when all balance sheet items are translated on a current basis, would then be determined in the following manner:

FIGURE 23.3 *The subsidiary balance sheet of a U.S. parent company*

French Subsidiary
(all amounts denominated in French Franc equivalents)

Assets		Liabilities	
Cash	100,000	Payables	200,000
Receivables	850,000	£150,000	
SFr 500,000		Debt	400,000
Inventory (at cost)	500,000	Capital	1,350,000
Plant & Equipment	500,000		

United Kingdom (U.K.) Subsidiary
(all amounts denominated in Pound Sterling equivalents)

Assets		Liabilities	
Cash	50,000	Payables	300,000
Receivables	500,000	FFr 20,000	
Inventory	400,000	Debt	750,000
Plant & Equipment	900,000	Capital	800,000

Local Exposed Assets

Cash	100,000
Receivables	350,000*
Inventory	500,000
Plant & Equipment	500,000
Total Exposed Local Assets	1,450,000

Local Exposed Liabilities

Debt	400,000 FFr
Payables	50,000**
Total Exposed Local Liabilities	450,000

*850,000 FFr less 500,000 FFr non-local receivables.
**200,000 FFr less 150,000 FFr non-local payables.

Net Translation Exposure

1,450,000 FFr local exposed assets - 450,000 FFr local exposed liabilities = 1,000,000 FFr net local translation exposure.

Thus, the French subsidiary has a 1,000,000 FFr long translation exposure, after all non-local items are netted out of its exposed assets and liabilities. The gains and losses from this translation exposure are not included in income. Accordingly, investors may tend to give less attention to their effects.

Now, let us assume that the reporting currency of the parent, the dollar, is also the functional currency of the French subsidiary. In this case, the MNC's net remeasurement exposure applicable to the French subsidiary, when the various balance sheet items are remeasured into dollars on the basis of the temporal method, would be determined as follows:

Local Exposed Assets

Cash	100,000 FFr
Receivables	350,000*
Total Exposed Local Assets	450,000

Local Exposed Liabilities

Debt	400,000
Payables	50,000**
Total Exposed Local Liabilities	450,000

*850,000 FFr less 500,000 FFr non-local receivables
**200,000 FFr less 150,000 FFr non-local payables

Net Remeasurement Exposure

450,000 FFr local exposed assets - 450,000 FFr local exposed liabilities = FFr net local remeasurement exposure.

Since the functional currency of the French subsidiary is the U.S. dollar, the balance sheet items are remeasured into dollars by means of the temporal method. On this basis, the exposed assets and liabilities balance each other out. Had there been a remeasurement exposure, the resulting gains or losses would be included in income.

Reducing translation or remeasurement exposure involves altering a subsidiary's balance sheet relationships. In general, an effort is made to:

• Curtail exposed assets or increase exposed local currency liabilities in a foreign country when the local currency is weakening; and
• Increase exposed assets and decrease liabilities in a foreign country when the local currency is strengthening.

(b) Transaction Exposure

This exposure may be calculated on a current basis by first determining all non-local currency items carried on the books of each subsidiary. Remember, transaction exposure is a cash exposure arising from operations. Generally, transaction exposure occurs when a subsidiary has payables or receivables on its books denominated in a currency other than its local currency. Since the MNC in our example has several subsidiaries incurring transaction exposures in several currencies, it is best to calculate the entire firm's transaction exposure on a currency by currency basis. This will enable the parent corporation to devise an optimal hedging strategy to cover its full exposure in a given currency.

Let us begin by calculating the MNC's French franc currency exposure, with reference to the balance sheet data in Figure 23.3. The FFr currency exposure is calculated by adding together all FFr denominated items on non-French books. This amounts to 20,000 Pounds worth of FFr payables on the books of the U.K. subsidiary. The pre-tax calculation for this transaction exposure simply involves multiplying the exposed local currency amount (£20,000) by the appropriate local currency/FFr exchange rate. (In this case, 8.0F Fr for each pound sterling as shown in Figure 23.4). Similarly, the MNC's exposure in pound sterling is £150,000 worth of FFr payables on the books of the French subsidiary. On the other hand, there is also a SFr transaction exposure of 500,000 SFr receivables on the books of the French subsidiary. The conversion from the amount expressed in the local currency of the subsidiary, as carried on its books, to the amount of the non-local currency, in which payment is to be made or received, is shown in Figure 23.4.

In summary, the transaction exposure of the English subsidiary is 160,000 FFr payables, while that of the French subsidiary is 18,750 pounds sterling, offset by 250,000 SFr receivables.

[i] After-Tax Transaction Exposure

Thus far, the transaction exposure has been calculated on a before-tax basis. Since local tax authorities absorb a portion of any adjustment due to

FIGURE 23.4 *Calculating the transaction exposure of an MNC*

Location of Subsidiary	Asset or Liability Item	Currency In Which Item Is Stated	Amount of Item	Rate of Exchange Between Currency of Subsidiary and That of Denominated Item	Amount in Denominated Currency (plus for asset: minus for liability)
England	Payable	French franc	20,000 pounds	8.0FFr	160,000 French francs
France	Payable	Pound sterling	150,000 French francs	.125£/FFr	18,750 Pounds sterling
France	Receivable	Swiss franc	500,000 French francs	2SFr/FFr	250,000 Swiss francs

exchange rate fluctuations, it is desirable to determine the after-tax exposure as well. This may be done by multiplying the pre-tax exposure by 1 minus the local (host country's) effective tax rate. Thus, assuming this rate is 52 percent, the pre-tax 160,000 FFr exposure of the English subsidiary is reduced to 76,800 FFr on an after-tax basis (160,000 FFr x 1-.52).

[ii] The Local Tax Exposure

The 52 percent tax absorption, however, does not disappear but becomes the firm's local tax liability. This local tax exposure occurs because of the necessity of accruing taxes/credits for exchange adjustments arising from non-local items on local books. In other words, this represents a tax on the subsidiary's transactions in currencies other than its local currency. Since these nonlocal currencies are already recorded in local currency units, the local tax exposure is calculated by merely multiplying the local currency amount by the applicable tax rate. In the case of the British subsidiary, the local tax exposure is £20,000 multiplied by 52 percent or 10,400.

[iii] Using the Parent's Currency as the Base

The foregoing analysis indicates that the before-tax transaction exposure of a non-local currency may be divided into a reduced after-tax transaction exposure and an increased local tax exposure. In the prior illustration, the before-tax transaction exposure of the French franc was about 160,000 FFr. The reduced after-tax transaction exposure was 76,800 FFr and the increased local tax exposure was 10,400 pounds sterling.

When the before-tax transaction exposure of the non-local currency is converted to the currency of the multinational parent, the amount will equal the sum of the reduced after-tax transaction exposure, expressed in the currency of the parent, and the increased local tax exposure also expressed in the parent's currency. Thus, according to Figure 23.5, five FFr equal one dollar and £.625 equals one dollar. Accordingly, the before-tax transaction exposure of the French franc in dollars is $32,000 (160,000 FFr ÷ 52). The after-tax exposure is $15,360 (76,800 FFr ÷ 5) and the local tax exposure is $16,640 (10,400 pounds ÷ .625).

The sum of the $15,360 after-tax transaction exposure of the FFr and the $16,640 local-tax exposure of the pound sterling equals the $32,000 before-tax transaction exposure of the FFr.

FIGURE 23.5   *Tax and exchange rates*

TAX RATES

United States (Parent firm)	48%*
France (subsidiary)	50%
United Kingdom (subsidiary)	52%

EXCHANGE RATES**

	$	£	SFr	FFr
$	—	$1.60	$.40	$.20
£	$.625	—	.25	.125
SFr	2.5	4.0	—	.50
FFr	5.0	8.0	2.0	—

* Assumed
**These rates are illustrative only, actual rates change daily.

(c) Economic Exposure

Another approach to exposure analysis is the economic approach. When used concurrently with methods like those just discussed, this economic analysis provides the financial manager with a more complete picture of the total effects of currency fluctuations on the firm's performance.

In the economic procedure the following factors are examined:

- completed transactions in foreign currencies (i.e., balance sheet exposures); and
- future transactions in foreign currencies (i.e., order backlogs and expenses related to this backlog).

Once these factors have been determined, a simple formula may be applied:

Net Balance Sheet Exposure	+	Committed Future Cash Flows	=	Net Total Exposure. (After-Tax)

In the above formula, committed future cash flows include the following:

- customer backlogs;
- firm order quotations;
- costs to complete the backlog inventory; and
- operating expenses incurred to deliver the backlog.

The economic procedure provides a picture of the real economic effect that fluctuating exchange rates have on operations.

[3] TECHNIQUE 3: EVALUATING THE PERFORMANCE OF FOREIGN OPERATIONS

Specific formuli are useful in gauging the merits of individual projects. If management desires to evaluate the performance of a foreign subsidiary, various other considerations may be involved.[6] In these circumstances, a key tool for measuring MNC foreign operations might be the budget system containing a set of goals tailored for each subsidiary. The multinationals have strategic motivations for going abroad which do not necessarily get expressed in return on investment calculations. For example, a firm may willingly forego economies of scale in production to achieve greater security of supply by having multiple or redundant production facilities. In addition, operating in several nations may give a firm greater bargaining leverage in dealing with local governments or labor unions. Being an MNC may also lower the firm's risk profile by reducing its dependence on the state of only one nation's economy. The firm may employ various types of secondary criteria, as well, in their overseas evaluation process. In other words, the individual elements of each subsidiary's budget used in the evaluation process should be selected on the basis of the strategic role of the subsidiary within the enterprise.

If the subsidiary serves the home market of the host country (many subsidiaries have this as a primary function), both the revenue and cost aspects over which local management has control should be included. Thus, while a subsidiary manager might be evaluated on a primary goal of annual profit or rate of return based on the parent's cost of capital, he should also be judged on meeting such secondary criteria as market share, introduction of new products, and strength of brand franchise. More particularly, if the role of the subsidiary is to produce goods for export to other divisions of the MNC, then the evaluation should focus on items associated with the manufacturing functions, such as man-hours per unit of production, product quality, and overhead costs. Items which may be controlled by a central planning group (such as accounts receivable) would not be under the control of the subsidiary and thus should not enter into its evaluation.

There is not likely to be any quantitative or qualitative measure which is sufficient to evaluate the performance of foreign operations. Accordingly, an optimal system should encourage a free flow of ideas and information worldwide. It is desirable for local managers to have the opportunity to explain their operating results and seek help for their problems. The considerable range of variation under which subsidiaries scattered over the globe operate, emphasizes the importance of headquarters management in their evaluations of overseas subsidiaries, leavening quantitative results with substantial doses of personal judgement.

[4] TECHNIQUE 4: ESTABLISHING A SYSTEM FOR INTERNATIONAL CASH MANAGEMENT

Exposure management is implicit in the optimal performance of any international cash management system. The proper acquisition and use of funds, as well as the timing and cost of fund transfers are also crucial factors. In this section, we suggest several techniques to assist the financial manager in accomplishing these tasks.

(a) Pooling Funds

In a pooling strategy, each affiliate has access to a central reservoir of funds to cover its disbursements. In return, the affiliate surrenders control over excess funds. This approach is helpful to an optimal funding strategy since corporate objectives take precedence over subsidiary objectives. As a result, the MNC can take advantage of its global perspective, making surplus funds from the cash rich subsidiaries available to cash poor subsidiaries.

Fund pools, set up on a single or multiple currency basis, may take the form of:

- a centrally accessible point bank account for all corporate operations;
- separate accounts for each corporate member; and
- a corporate holding company which collects and disseminates funds through a centrally accessible account.

Regardless of the method used to pool the firm's funds, it is important to make arrangements for the investment of surplus funds. In this way, the firm will assure itself of earning a return on all its available resources.

(b) Minimizing the Costs of International Funds Flows

Transferring funds internationally involves the costs of actually executing foreign exchange transactions and the opportunity costs arising from the time that payments are in transit. Foreign exchange transaction costs may be curtailed in various ways, such as:

- reducing the number of payments made by corporate entities through offsetting intra-company payments and receivables (i.e., a corporate netting system) and by invoicing in the currency needed for transaction purposes (i.e., a reinvoicing center);
- increasing the average size of foreign exchange transfers thereby obtaining a better foreign exchange rate from the banks;
- shopping for the best competitive rates among banks in different exchange markets; and
- negotiating with banks for a waiver of telex costs on certain payments.

Of these methods, the establishment of netting and reinvoicing systems ordinarily are the most effective.

[i] Establishing a Netting System

In Figure 23.6, a simple pattern of intra-company relationships is shown for a multinational system consisting of a parent and two subsidiaries. In this case, there are six movements of these funds among the entities, totaling $52.5 million. The details of these relationships, denominated in the currency of the seller and converted to the currency of the parent (dollars) are spelled out in Figure 23.7 to show the movements of funds to the seller and rearranged in Figure 23.8 to show the movement from the buyer. These gross movements may be simplified through either bi-lateral or multi-lateral netting agreements.

FIGURE 23.6 *Intra-company payment relationships*

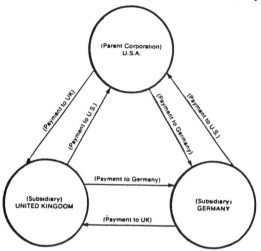

Total Volume of Payments Transactions in Dollar Equivalents: $52,500,000

Total Number of Intracompany Transfers: 6

FIGURE 23.7 *Description of all intra-company payments flowing to the seller**

Intra-company payments denominated in the currency of the seller (column 2) and converted to the currency of the parent (column 3).

1 Seller		2 Purchaser	3 $ Equivalent
U.S.A.	Germany U.K.	$10,000,000 5,000,000	$10,000,000 5,000,000
Germany	U.K. U.S.A.	DM10,000,000 5,000,000	$ 5,000,000 2,500,000
U.K.	Germany U.S.A.	£10,000,000 5,000,000	$20,000,000 10,000,000
			$52,500,000

*Assume the following conditions: Exchange rates:
1 English £ = 2 US$
2 German DM = 1 US$

FIGURE 23.8 *Description of all intracompany payments flowing from the buyer*

Payments are expressed in dollars, the currency of the parent.

Payment Made By:	Payment Made To:	Amount
U.K. subsidiary	U.S. Parent	$5.0 million
German subsidiary	U.S. Parent	10.0
U.S. parent	U.K. subsidiary	10.0
German subsidiary	U.K. subsidiary	20.0
U.S. parent	German subsidiary	2.5
U.K. subsidiary	German subsidiary	5.0
	Total	$52.5 million

FIGURE 23.9 *The basis of netting*

	U.S.	U.K.	Germany	Total
U.S.				
Payments received by US for sales	—	$5,000,000	$10,000,000	$15,000,000
Payments owed by US for purchases	—	10,000,000	2,500,000	12,500,000
Net Amount: $2,500,000		(5,000,000)	7,500,000	$2,500,000
U.K.				
Payments received by UK for sales	10,000,000	—	20,000,000	$30,000,000
Payments owed by UK for purchases	5,000,000	—	5,000,000	10,000,000
Net Amount: $20,000,000	5,000,000		15,000,000	$20,000,000
GERMANY				
Payments received by Germany for sales	2,500,000	5,000,000	—	$ 7,500,000
Payments owed by Germany for purchases	10,000,000	20,000,000	—	30,000,000
Net Amount: ($22,500,000)	($7,500,000)	(15,000,000)		($22,500,000)

Under a bilateral netting system, each entity pays the other only the balances involved after subtracting receivables from payables. Thus, as indicated in Figure 23.9, the U.S. parent has sold $10 million of goods to its German subsidiary, but has also bought $2.5 million of goods from the subsidiary. On balance, therefore, the German subsidiary can settle these offsetting transactions by forwarding $7.5 million to the parent. Similarly, the parent has sold $5.0 million of goods to the U.K. subsidiary but has bought $10.0 million of goods from it. In this case, therefore, settlement may be effected by the parent paying $5.0 million to the U.K. subsidiary. Finally, the U.K. subsidiary has sold the equivalent of $20.0 million of goods to and purchased $5.0 million of goods from the German subsidiary, resulting in a net balance due from the the German subsidiary of $15.0 million. This bi-lateral netting operation results, as indicated in Figure 23.10, in only three separate movements of funds.

Under a multi-lateral arrangement, the firm establishes a clearing center through which the system is administered. Through use of this center, the net amount due to or from each entity is determined by striking a difference between the total amounts owed it from all the other participants and the total amount it owes the other participants. In effect, the center is on one side of a transaction and an entity on the other. Thus, the U.S. parent is owed $15.0 million from the U.K. and German subsidiaries, but must pay these subsidiaries $12.5 million; on balance, therefore, the center forwards this $2.5 million to the parent. Similarly, the U.K. subsidiary is owed $30.0 million, must pay $10.0 million, and therefore is the net recipient of $20.0 million. On the other hand, the German subsidiary is owed $7.5 million by the other entities but must pay them $30.0 million. Accordingly, on balance, it contributes $22.5 million to the center. This multi-lateral netting operation also results, as indicated in Figure 23.11 in three separate movements of funds.

Both the bi-lateral and multi-lateral arrangements cut fund movement from six to three. Under both arrangements, also, the final amount received or paid by each entity, on balance, is the same. Thus, in the bi-lateral arrangement, the U.S. parent receives $7.5 million from the German subsidiary and pays $5.0 million to the U.K. subsidiary, resulting in the same $2.5 million amount that it received from the clearing center in a multi-lateral system. In the bi-lateral arrangement, the U.K. subsidiary receives $5.0 million from the U.S. parent and $15 million from the German subsidiary totaling the $20 million it receives from the clearing center in the multi-lateral arrangement. Under both arrangements, the German subsidiary pays $22.5 million, but in the bi-lateral case, it forwards $15.0 million to the U.K. subsidiary and $7.5 million to the U.S. parent, while in the multi-lateral case, it contributes $22.5 million to the clearing center. The primary difference between the two systems is that the total volume of payments in the bilateral case is $27.5 million compared with $22.5 million in the multi-lateral case.

FIGURE 23.10 *Intracompany payments with bi-lateral netting*

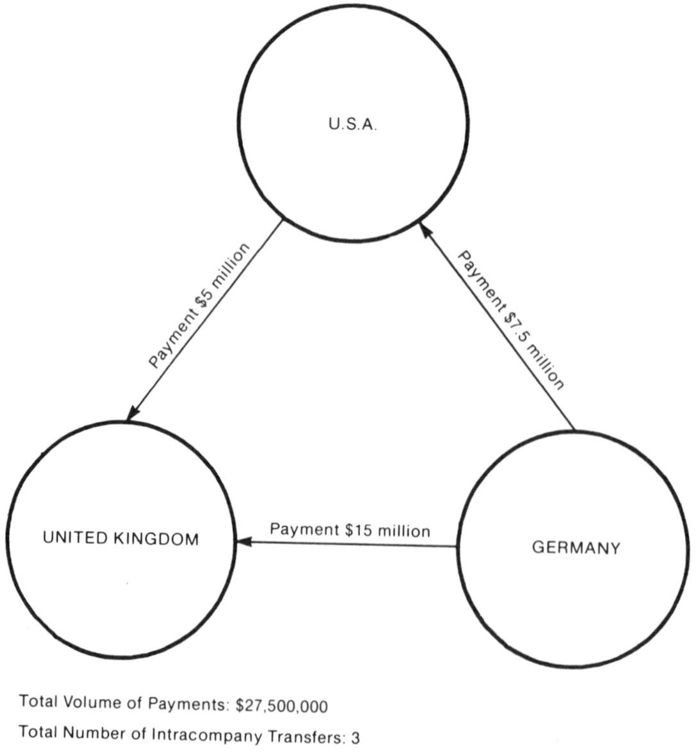

Total Volume of Payments: $27,500,000

Total Number of Intracompany Transfers: 3

FIGURE 23.11   *Intracompany payments with multi-lateral netting*

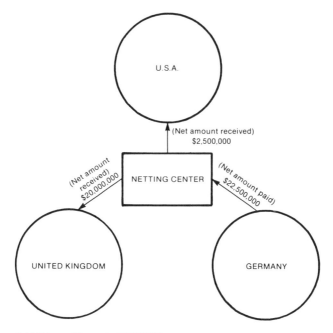

Total Volume of Payments: $22,500,000
Total Number of Funds Transfers: 3

Multi-lateral netting systems are primarily used by large companies with sizeable, say at least $45-50 million, cross-border funds transfers emanating from many different sources. Both trade and non-trade items would be common to such a company's payment patterns (i.e., dividend remittances, service fees, as well as management and royalty fees).

When implementing the multi-lateral netting system, the multinational firm first establishes a clearing center through which the system is administered, as illustrated in Figure 23.11. It is desirable to locate the center in a major European financial city, where exchange control restrictions are minimal. Various non-resident foreign currency accounts, determined by the number of currencies to be handled, are opened in the name of the clearing vehicle, with the local branch of the firm's lead bank (or another major bank with the ability to provide this service). Management of the system is usually assumed by the firm itself, or by members of the bank's international cash management staff.

The operating mechanism of a multilateral system is straight-forward. Each participant contacts the netting center (usually by telex) and informs it of how much the participant owes the other participants during that month. The center matches payables and receivables (usually using dollar equivalents when a U.S. parent is involved; these amounts are then re-converted into local currencies). Participants are told which of them will be net payers or net receivers, and by how much (in terms of their local currencies). Thereafter, usually two days prior to the settlement date, the center will purchase and distribute the exact amounts needed for these foreign exchange transactions, broken down by subsidiary. The participants, conversely, pay the center by depositing their respective amounts in a central bank account on the payment date.

Use of the clearing center creates operating differences between the multilateral and bi-lateral netting systems. In principle, however, both are the same and afford similar benefits, as summarized below:

- Netting reduces the volume of intracompany foreign currency conversions, thereby reducing the costs associated with these conversions (i.e., administrative, bank costs);
- Netting reduces the total amount of funds transferred. This can lower a firm's total currency exchange costs associated with these currency transfers. It may also alter the company's lead-lag and hedging strategies by providing better current account information;
- A practice of monthly netting may increase funds availability and lower flotation costs; and
- Netting imposes a discipline on the company's international operations by standardizing intercompany procedures. This eases the path toward effective, centralized management decision-making.

[ii] Reinvoicing Systems

Such a system involves the routing of cross-border intercompany sales from an exporting entity to a specially formed reinvoicing center which, in turn, resells to an importing entity. A major function of this reinvoicing center is to centralize all transaction exposures on its books. It accomplishes this by making payment to the exporting locations in their own local currencies, while receiving payment in the currency of the importing locations. No participant incurs any transaction exposure because they are all payers and receivers in their own local currencies.

The reinvoicing company takes title to the goods involved. However, the actual physical movement of the goods remains unchanged. They go from the manufacturer directly to the purchaser.

Figure 23.12 depicts the different transaction exposures incurred by each participating entity in a multinational system, consisting of a parent and two subsidiaries, when a reinvoicing center is not available. In each case, a transaction exposure arises because the entity must make payment in a currency other than its own. By substituting a reinvoicing center, as illustrated in Figure 23.13, these exposures are eliminated. Reinvoicing centers may be established with the aid of any one of several large commercial banks providing international cash management services.

(c) Maximizing the Usefulness of Cash

Cash at rest produces no return. Therefore, an important element of cash management is directed towards converting cash as rapidly as possible into income producing uses. As on the domestic scene, the starting point for this activity is the cash budget. Recognition of its importance results in multinational parents giving increasing attention to the development of effective cash budgets by their overseas units. In some areas of the world where the multinational enterprise operates, budgeting sophistication is low and therefore the multinational parent may have to provide substantial guidance in introducing such a system and in establishing programs for training personnel to operate the system.

Within the framework of need established by the cash budget, it is important to accelerate the movement of cash. The netting program discussed above contributes toward this end for movements within the multinational system. To accelerate the flow of cash from customers to a unit of the system, methods such as those employed within the United States are used, but their application to the international area is complicated by such factors as the variety of currencies involved, timing differences, and the lack of adequate banking networks in some areas.

When available, multinational enterprises make use of the lockbox techniques that we have described previously (Chapter 8). When such facilities are not available, other devices may be employed to speed the availability of cash. For example, accounts may be opened at the same banks used by customers thereby facilitating the clearing of checks.

Available cash must, of course, be put to use promptly. If it is not immediately necessary for operating purposes, the cash must be invested in sources that provide adequate liquidity, safety and a return commensurate with these requirements. The guidelines that the multinational parent establishes for this purpose will depend upon its own sophistication in the area of international investment, the local investment scene, regulatory limitations, and the timing needs indicated by the cash budget.

(d) Special Financing Arrangements

Financing in the international area both creates unique risks and affords opportunities. The unique risks arise from the exposures implicit in transactions involving different currencies. While there are various methods available to protect against exchange risk, it is desirable for relatively small or unsophisticated companies to concentrate their borrowing in funds denominated in the same currency as that of the assets and revenues of the operation to be financed. In this way, the company is automatically protected against exchange risk with a minimum involvement of management effort. Even large companies may find this method useful because floating exchange rates make hedging a difficult job. In effect, hedging is a form of insurance, an approach a company may or may not prefer.

Opportunities in the area of international financing occur because of the differences in interest rates that characteristically exist. Qualified international management can take advantage of these differences by borrowing in low interest financial markets and shifting the funds raised to units within the multinational system that require them. Such shifts can be arranged through the variety of links that financially join the units of the system such as transfer payments, dividends, interest, management fees, accelerating or slowing payment of receivables, and the granting of loans.

"Back-to-back" transactions that get around currency problems are also available in the international area. They involve parallel loans representing the simultaneous exchange of funds between firms located in different

FIGURE 23.12 *Transactions exposures without reinvoicing*

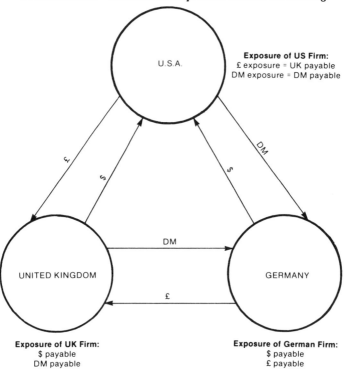

Exposure of US Firm:
£ exposure = UK payable
DM exposure = DM payable

U.S.A.

UNITED KINGDOM

GERMANY

Exposure of UK Firm:
$ payable
DM payable

Exposure of German Firm:
$ payable
£ payable

FIGURE 23.13 *Transaction exposures with reinvoicing*

Each country pays and receives payment in its own currency

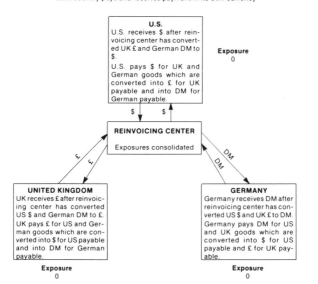

U.S.
U.S. receives $ after reinvoicing center has converted UK £ and German DM to $.
U.S. pays $ for UK and German goods which are converted into £ for UK payable and into DM for German payable.

Exposure
0

REINVOICING CENTER
Exposures consolidated

UNITED KINGDOM
UK receives £ after reinvoicing center has converted US $ and German DM to £.
UK pays £ for US and German goods which are converted into $ for US payable and into DM for German payable.

Exposure
0

GERMANY
Germany receives DM after reinvoicing center has converted US $ and UK £ to DM.
Germany pays DM for US and UK goods which are converted into $ for US payable and £ for UK payable.

Exposure
0

countries. For example, one loan may be made by a non-U.S. firm in the currency of the country where it is located, to a U.S. firm's affiliated unit in the same country. The other would be in dollars from the U.S. firm to an affiliated unit of the non-U.S. firm that gave the loan to the U.S. affiliate. This arrangement, of course, may only be done when each firm has an affiliated unit in the other country which requires funds. The method is particularly useful when exchange controls limit the import and export of funds.[7]

Another form of protection against exchange risk is a so-called "swap", which is typically used in countries with limited forward markets. In a foreign currency swap, an enterprise purchases a certain amount of local currency, usually at the spot rate, and simultaneously agrees to sell this amount of local currency at an agreed upon designated future date. The sale is made to a company in another country that has to make payment in that currency. The swap occurs when the two companies make reverse arrangements. In a credit swap, an enterprise provides an interest free, hard currency loan to a bank outside a host country. A branch of that bank in the host country, in turn, lends local currency to a subsidiary in the host country at an agreed interest rate. When the specified time period is over, both loans are repaid in the currency in which they were denominated. As a result, neither party is subject to exchange risk.[8]

Special arrangements such as parallel loans and swaps not only afford some protection against exchange risks but also make unique methods of financing available. These methods may be utilized to avoid regulations limiting the movement of funds, obtain funds when local financing is difficult, reduce currency conversion costs, and lower interest charges.

[5] TECHNIQUE 5: CAPITAL BUDGETING FOR THE MULTINATIONAL CORPORATION[9]

As we have indicated, essentially the capital budgeting principles developed for the domestic firm apply as well to the MNC. To the extent differences are incorporated, they reflect the distinctions arising from the MNC's international operations. When a foreign subsidiary operates largely on an independent basis and deals primarily within its own country, there is some logic to ignoring these distinctions inasmuch as the effort to incorporate them may not justify the refinements obtained. As decision-making is reserved to the parent, which adopts a worldwide point of view and the subsidiary's activities enter into the international stream, the recognition of these distinctions becomes increasingly important.

To illustrate the type of distinctions that may occur, let us assume that a MNC employs in its capital budgeting analysis the traditional net present value approach (17.5[3]). Two of the essential ingredients of this procedure are the determination of the firm's cost of capital and net cash flows.

(a) Determining the Cost of Capital

Under the assumption that the MNC is integrated worldwide, with funds obtained where interest rates are lowest and directed to their most profitable outlets, an appropriate cost of capital is the sum of the costs (expressed as a percentage) of each financing source, weighted by the proportion of that financing source in the firm's capital structure. Although MNC's employ varying bases for determining the discount rate in their capital budgeting analyses, a survey conducted several years ago indicates that the most widely used rate is the global weighted average cost of capital.[10] (See Chapter 18 for a discussion of the cost of capital and the weighted average cost of capital.)

However when the cost of capital refers to new investment decisions, the values of debt and equity may be determined by the marginal cost of funds (i.e., the change in the global weighted average cost of capital) rather than the cost of existing debt and equity. If a new investment makes the firm's earnings stream riskier, therefore, the overall cost of capital will rise and the project will not be undertaken unless its return justifies this higher rate caused by the greater risk. The marginal cost may still be the same as the existing cost of funds, however, if the new investment is of an "ongoing" nature, i.e., no change in the overall risk of the firm occurs due to the project.

In the equity component of the overall cost of capital it seems appropriate to net out intracompany holdings and those held by joint venture partners. What is left, therefore, is the amount attributable to third parties which primarily will be the equity held in the parent company. The cost of equity for the parent then is determined by the same basic approach developed in the domestic case. As discussed previously, the cost of retained earnings, in principle, may be considered the same as that of common stock. Since the cost of common stock is based on dividend payments, however, in the case of the retained earnings of a foreign subsidiary, an allowance may have to be made for the additional taxes and other costs that may be involved if these earnings are repatriated.

In the debt component of the overall cost of capital to the parent, the additional considerations are the taxes and exchange gains or losses involved in repaying principal and interest on debt denominated in foreign currency. Thus, assume that the parent borrows in foreign currency for one year at a nominal rate of 12 percent, the foreign currency appreciates against the domestic currency by 5 percent, and the tax rate is 50 percent. The exchange adjusted interest cost is 12.6 percent (12% x 1.05); the after-tax cost is 6.30 percent [12.6% x (1 - .5)]; the repayment of principal on an after-tax basis costs 2.5 percent [5% x (1 - .5)]; and the net after-tax cost of the loan is 8.8 percent (6.3% + 2.5%). Further adjustments in this rate may be made if the loan is hedged to take into account the differences between spot and forward exchange rates as well as those of the tax effects involved. Essentially, the same procedure is followed if the borrowing is done by a subsidiary. In this case, it seems reasonable to net out all intersubsidiary and parent subsidiary obligations, leaving only the debt owing to third parties. In this case, too, a double layer of taxes is involved—that paid to the country of the subsidiary and of the parent.

In summary, when a subsidiary is considering a capital budgeting decision of its own, there is some logic, as we have previously mentioned, to determine an independent cost of capital if the subsidiary finances itself locally. On the other hand, based on the concept that a multinational enterprise is an integrated grouping of parent and subsidiaries, a strong case may be made for taking into account the system point of view. In these circumstances, the parent's overall rate may still be used according to this principle; a foreign subsidiary has no independent capital structure because its liabilities are part of those of the global firm and should not be viewed in isolation. On this basis, the proper required rate of return for evaluating the performance of a proposed investment of a foreign subsidiary is the international firm's global weighted average marginal cost of capital.

(b) Determining the Cash Flows

The cash flows emanating from an overseas investment are subject to various risks, such as exchange adjustments, political uncertainties, and expropriation, that are not encountered by the domestic firm. These considerations may be incorporated into the capital budgeting framework by employing a risk adjusted discount rate for the project. In lieu of this generalized approach, an alternative technique is to modify the cash flows to reflect the specific risks of a particular project.

In employing the cash flow adjustment approach, the point of view is still maintained that the corporation views itself as truly multinational. In these circumstances only cash flows which are remitted to the parent are relevant. Accordingly, projected flows must be reduced to take into account the additional taxes that the parent may have to pay after allowing for applicable foreign tax credits.

The after-tax funds that are expected to be remitted to the parent can then be further adjusted for any of the additional uncertainties that may arise from foreign operations. For example, the possibility of expropriation may be taken into account along with an estimate of the value of the net compensation to be received. In making this estimate, consideration should be given to the direct payments that the firm might receive from the local government, compensation for political insurance, tax adjustments, and any other direct or indirect elements that may be involved.

Similar adjustments could be made so that the expected cash flow stream would reflect any of the other uncertainties stemming from the firm's international operations that management might want to consider. For this purpose, the different sources of a project's cash flows may have to be broken out and analyzed separately. For example, in determining the impact of an exchange rate change on project revenues, the percent of sales that are local as opposed to exports would have to be ascertained.

Making separate adjustments in funds that the parent would receive, as described above, has the advantage of focusing on the various uncertainties involved. As a result, management may gain a better insight into their implications and the type of surveillance that may be desirable. In reaching a decision as to the capital budgeting approach to adopt, however, management must determine to what extent the benefits from these calculating refinements are justified by the additional efforts involved.

23.6   CHAPTER SUMMARY

This chapter dealt with the financial aspects of multinational operation. The major theories of international finance and foreign exchange were presented. This was followed by an analysis of the predominant foreign exchange markets and institutions. Finally, the unique problems of international financial management, and techniques for their solution were developed.

FOOTNOTES

1. J. Holmes, "The Purchasing Power Parity Theory: In Defense of Gustav Cassel as a Modern Theorist" *Journal of Political Economy*, October 1967, p. 686.
2. It should be noted that the Fisher Effect not only relates to international financial management, but also contains an important theoretical interpretation of interest rates in general.
3. Issues dealing with international taxation are developed in Chapter 24.
4. These options are developed by Frederick Militello, "Financial Management Under Fluctuating Exchange Rates: Options and Strategies for a Multinational Company", unpublished paper, pp. 3-17.
5. *Ibid.* p. 18.
6. Sidney Robbins and Robert Stobaugh, "The Bent Measuring Stick for Foreign Subsidiaries," *Harvard Business Review*, September-October, 1973, pp. 80-88.
7. Sidney M. Robbins and Robert B. Stobaugh, "How to Use International Capital Markets: A Guide to Europe and the Middle East," *Financial Executives Research Foundation*, New York 1976.
8. Sidney M. Robbins and Robert B. Stobaugh, *Money in the Multinational Enterprise*, Basic Books, New York, 1973, pp. 128-131.
9. For a report of the results of a 1979 survey of capital budgeting procedures used by 58 U.S. based multinational companies see David J. Oblak and Roy J. Helm, Jr., "Survey and Analysis of Capital Budgeting Methods Used by Multinationals," *Financial Management*, Winter 1980, pp. 37-41.
10. Vinod, Bavishi, "Survey on Capital Budgeting Practices for the Multinational Corporation," Unpublished paper.

SUGGESTED READINGS

Ashby, David F.V., "Eurocurrency Mismatching Does Matter—Up to a Point," *Banker*, January 1982.

Bhagwat, Avinash, "The Quest for Successful Adjustment in the World Economy: A Report on the Fund's Annual Meeting," *Finance & Development*, December 1981.

Brau, Edward, "The Consultation Process of the Fund," *Finance & Development*, December 1981.

Callier, Philippe, "One Way Arbitrage: Foreign Exchange and Securities Markets," *Journal of Finance*, December 1981.

Camps, Miriam, *Collective Management: The Reform of Global Economic Organizations*, New York: McGraw-Hill Book Co., 1981.

Colley, G.M., "The Tax Planning Implications of Foreign Exchange," *CA Magazine*, April 1981.

Cornell, Bradford and Marc R. Reinganum, "Forward and Futures Prices: Evidence from the Foreign Exchange Markets," *Journal of Finance*, December 1981.

Crockett, A., "Issues in the Use of Fund Resources," *Finance & Development*, June 1982.

Donovan, Donald J., "Real Responses Associated with Exchange Rate Action in Selected Upper Credit Tranche Stabilization Programs," *International Monetary Fund Staff Papers*, December 1981.

"EMS: After the Snake," *Banker*, May 1982.

Feder, Gershon and Knud Ross, "Risk Assessment and Risk Premiums in the Eurodollar Market," *Journal of Finance*, June 1982.

"FASB Finally Issues New Rules for Foreign Currency Translation," *Practical Accountant*, March 1982.

"Financial Futures: A Hedge for Euroloans," *Banker*, January 1982.

Furstenberg, George M., "Incentives for International Currency Diversification by U.S. Financial Investors," *International Monetary Fund Staff Papers*, September 1981.

Garcha, Balwant S., "Channeling Limited Resources for the Greatest Impact," *Finance & Development*, December 1981.

Geannotti, J.B., "FASB Statement No. 52 Gives Treasurers the Scope FASB Statement No. 8 Denied Them," *Euromoney*, April 1982.

Guitan, Manuel, "Fund Conditionality and the International Adjustment Process: A Look Into the 1980's," *Finance & Development*, June 1981.

Jacobs, Rodney L., "The Effect of Errors in Variables on Tests for a Risk Premium in Forward Exchange Rates," *Journal of Finance*, June 1982.

Kaul, P.N., "Technical Assistance from the Fund: Central Banking Department," *Finance & Development*, June 1981.

Kemp, O.S., "Managing International Cash Flows? Consider These Risks!" *American Import/Export Management*, June 1982.

Mendelsohn, M.S., "How Central Banks Manage Their Reserves," *Banker*, April 1982.

Nayes, P., "Exposure Management: A Look at How Foreign Exchange Transactions Affect Earnings for the Overseas Trader," *American Import/Export Management*, May 1982.

"New FASB Rules for Foreign Currency Translation," *Financial Executive*, February 1982.

Oblak, David and Roy J. Helm, Jr., "Survey and Analysis of Capital Budgeting Methods Used by Multinationals," *Financial Management*, Winter 1980.

Robbins, Sidney and Robert Stobaugh, "The Bent Measuring Stick for Foreign Subsidiaries," *Harvard Business Review*, September-October 1973.

_____ and _____, "How to Use International Capital Markets: A Guide to Europe and the Middle East," *Financial Executive Research Foundation*, New York, 1976.

_____ and _____, *Money in the Multinational Enterprise*, Basic Books, New York, 1973.

Roof, B.M., "FASB Statement No. 8—Did it Help or Hinder Multinational Reporting?" *Financial Executive*, March 1982.

Seidler, Lee J. and P.A. McConnel, "FASB Statement No. 52 on Foreign Currency Translation: A First Look," *Financial Analysts Journal*, January/February 1982.

"SDR Issues: New IMF Borrowing?" *Banker*, March 1982.

"Statement of Financial Accounting Standards No. 52—Foreign Currency Translation," *Journal of Accountancy*, February 1982.

Steinherr, Alfred, "Effectiveness of Exchange Rate Policy for Trade Account Adjustment," *International Monetary Fund Staff Papers*, March 1981.

Wood, Geoffrey E., "Do Exchange Rates Overshoot?" *Banker*, May 1981.

Wood, W.D., "Surveillance Over Exchange Rates," *Finance & Development*, March 1982.

APPENDIX A: APPLICATION OF THE PROCEDURES OF FASB STATEMENT NO. 52

THE BASIC APPROACH

Translation of the records of most subsidiaries of U.S. MNC's will be done by the current-functional currency method, as prescribed in FASB Statement No. 52, with translation gains or losses accumulated and reported in a separate component of equity, while gains or losses from foreign currency transactions are reported currently in income. In some cases, however, as indicated previously, the procedures of FASB Statement No. 8 still will be used. Remeasurement will be done in a manner similar to the temporal method and all exchange gains or losses will be included in determining net income for the period in which the rate changes occur. Accordingly, Figure 23.14 provides an illustration of the application of both methods.

For purposes of the illustration, it is assumed that a foreign subsidiary of a U.S. MNC has the starting balance sheet, income statement for the year, and ending balance sheet, all expressed in local currency (LC), as shown in the Figure. The subsidiary has a long-term debt denominated in dollars owed to a non-affiliate. At the beginning of the year, the exchange rate between the local currency and the dollar is LC1 = $1. The LC declines during the year and at year end the rate is LC2 = $1. As a result the subsidiary's long-term debt is now $50 and it incurs a conversion loss of $25. At the beginning of the year, the operating income is offset by the conversion loss of $16.67 ($25/1.5), which is not reported separately but is included in the foreign exchange loss. As a result, the operating income is changed to a loss of $1.67 ($15.00 - $16.67). The ending local-currency balance sheet is translated at varying rates into dollars according to the temporal method provided in FASB No. 8. Consequently, the asset section is not in line with the liability plus capital section. In order to bring about an equality between the two sections, a net loss of $10.00 is required in the retained earnings account. Retained earnings at the beginning of the year is zero dollars and at the end of the period a negative $10.00, producing an actual loss of $10.00. Since the combined operating income and conversion loss was a negative $1.67, a translation loss of $8.33 is incurred. This figure is included with the conversion loss of $16.67 and shown as a foreign exchange loss of $25 in the income statement.

In Part B, illustrating the application of the current-functional currency method, all the elements of the income statement are translated at the average rate for the year, in accordance with the current-functional currency method provided in FASB No. 52, producing net income of $26.66; the translated loss from conversion is shown separately as a transaction loss for the year. The $26.66 of net income flows into the retained earnings of the ending balance sheet. An account, labelled "equity adjustment from foreign currency translation" is provided in the ending balance sheet to bring about equality between the asset section and the liability plus capital section.

Under the temporal method, the company reports a net loss of $10 after a foreign exchange loss of $25. Under the current-functional currency method, the company shows net income of $26.66 after the conversion (transaction) loss of $16.67. The variance between these figures reflects the different exchange rates used and the exclusion of translation losses from the income statement in the current-functional currency method. In the balance sheet under the latter method, however, there is a substantial equity adjustment arising from the use of the low current exchange rate in the balance sheet, when a large net monetary balance exists.

It is apparent that substantial variances often result between the temporal method of FASB Statement No. 8 and the current-rate method of FASB Statement No. 52. When the local currency is the functional currency, the risk exposure of the foreign entity, viewed in terms of its net investment and translation adjustments, are excluded from income. Reported results will generally be both more realistic and reduce the violent swings in earnings from exchange fluctuations, as occurred in the temporal method of FASB Statement No. 8.

ADJUSTING FOR INFLATION

As described in Chapter, 3, FASB Statement No. 33 provides for presenting supplementary information about changing prices. With respect to the international area, it originally called for remeasuring into U.S. dollars amounts that were previously measured in a foreign currency and then restating the translated results into constant dollars. In contrast, FASB Statement No. 52 requires that the financial statement of an enterprise should retain the functional currency relationships of the economic environment in which the foreign entity conducts its operations.

In recognition of the change in objectives of foreign currency translation, the FASB undertook an extensive review. Eventually, it reached the following conclusions in FASB Statement No. 70, issued December 1982.

1. Enterprises for which the U.S. dollar is the functional currency for all significant operations should continue to report supplementary information about changing prices as previously.
2. Enterprises that measure a significant part of their operations in functional currencies other than the U.S. dollar, are exempted from presenting historical cost information measured in units of constant purchasing power.
3. Enterprises that have disclosed historical cost information in units of constant purchasing power as a substitute for current cost information may continue to do so. Included are enterprises without significant amounts of inventory and property, plant and equipment and those engaged in certain industries, as specified previously.
4. Enterprises that use functional currencies other than the U.S. dollar should initially measure current cost amounts and increases or decreases therein in the functional currency. Previously, the measures of current cost amounts and their changes were done in translated dollars rather than in the functional currency as now required. This change reflects the current emphasis on reporting the effects of transactions in the functional currency environment.
5. Current cost amounts in nominal units of the functional currency may be: (a) translated into dollar equivalents and changes in those amounts restated to reflect the effect of U.S. inflation (translate-restate); or (b) first adjusted to reflect the effect of local inflation and those restated amounts then translated to dollar equivalents (restate-translate). Under

FIGURE 23.14   Illustrating the Application of FASB Statement No. 8 and FASB Statement No. 52

STARTING BALANCE SHEET

	Local Currency Statement	A. FASB Statement No. 8 (The temporal method) Exchange Rate	A. Dollar Currency Statement	B. FASB Statement No. 52 (The current-functional currency method) Exchange Rate	B. Dollar Currency Statement
Cash	LC 100	1 -1	$100	1 -1	$100
Inventory	100	1 -1	$100	1 -1	100
Fixed Assets	100*	1 -1	$100	1 -1	100
Total	LC 300		$300		$300
L.T. Debt	LC 50	1 -1	$ 50	1 -1	$ 50
L.T. Debt**	25	1 -1	25	1 -1	25
S.T. Debt	50	1 -1	50	1 -1	50
Capital	175	1 -1	175	1 -1	175
Ret. Earn.	0	1 -1	0	1 -1	0
Total	LC 300		$300		$300

INCOME STATEMENT

	Local Currency Statement	A. Exchange Rate	A. Dollar Currency Statement	B. Exchange Rate	B. Dollar Currency Statement
Sales	LC 150	1.5-1	$100	1.5-1	$100
C. of G.S. (Inventory)	75	1 -1***	75	1.5-1	50
Depreciation	10	1 -1***	10	1.5-1	6.67
Operating income	65		15		43.33
Conversion Loss	(25)	1.5-1+	25.00++	1.5-1	
For. Exc. Loss					(16.67)
Transac. Loss					
Net Income	LC 40		$(10)		$ 26.66

ENDING BALANCE SHEET

	LC				
Cash	LC 250	2 -1	$125	2 -1	$125.00
Inventory	25	1 -1	25	2 -1	12.50
Fixed Assets	90	1 -1	90	2 -1	45.00
	LC 365		$240		$182.50
L.T. Debt	LC 50	2 -1	$ 25	2 -1	$ 25.00
L.T. Debt**	50	2 -1	25	2 -1	25.00
S.T. Debt	50	2 -1	25	2 -1	25.00
Capital	175	1 -1	175	1 -1	175.00
Ret. Earn.	40		(10)		26.66
Equity adjustment from foreign currency translation	—				(94.16)
Total	LC 365		$240		$182.50

*Depreciation on a straight line basis over ten years.
**Denominated in dollars owed to a non-affiliated company.
***Historical rates for cost of goods sold and depreciation of fixed assets since the exchange rate at which the elements are recognized is known.
+Taken at the average rate for the period; the conversion loss of $16.67 is included in the foreign exchange loss.
++Includes conversion loss of $16.67 and translation loss of $8.33.

the latter approach, a parity adjustment that reflects the difference between U.S. and local inflation is required to adjust the total change in the parent's net income to a U.S. perspective.

6. Adjustments to current cost information for the effects of general inflation may be based on either the U.S. Department of Labor, Bureau of Labor Statistics CPI—or functional currency general price level indexes.

Both the translate-restate and restate-translate approaches show the same information in total. The differences lie in the application of inflation adjustments to individual components of the current cost information on the basis of U.S. or local inflation and in the exchange rate used. The FASB provides a simple example to illustrate these differences.

The only assets of a foreign entity that has no liabilities in two successive years are as follows:

	Year 1	**Year 2**
Cash	LC 100	LC 100
Inventory	200	400
Total	300	500

The exchange rates in the local currency (a functional currency) and the dollar are:

Beginning of the year	LC1 = $1.00
Average for the year	LC1 = $0.90
End of the year	LC1 = $0.80

Local inflation for the year is assumed to be 20 percent and U.S. inflation is 10 percent.

After the appropriate exchange and inflation adjustments are applied, the two approaches permitted by FASB Statements No. 70 produce the results shown in Figure 23.15.

FIGURE 23.15 *Results of applying translate-restate and restate-translate adjustments*

		A Translate-Restate	B Restate-Translate
(a)	Beginning of year net investment in end of year dollars $300 x 110/100	$330	$330
(b)	Purchasing power loss	(10)	(18)
(c)	Increase in specific prices	180	180
(d)	Effect of increase in general price level	(20)	(36)
(e)	Excess of increase in specific prices over increase in general price level	160	144
(f)	Translation adjustment	(80)	(56)
(g)	Increase in the net investment in terms of U.S. purchasing power	$ 70	$ 70
(h)	End of year net investment	$400	$400

(a) **Beginning of year net investment in end of year dollars** *(A)*—The beginning of year net investment of LC300 is converted into dollars at the beginning of year rate of $1.00 and expressed in end of year dollars by adjusting for the U.S. inflation rate of 10 percent. The result is $330 (LC300 x $1.00 x 100).

(c) **Increase in specific prices**—The only change in assets that occurs during the period is the increase in the current cost of inventory of LC200. Translated into dollar equivalents at the average rate of $0.90 produces an increase of $180 (LC200 x $0.90).

(h) **End of year net investment**—In terms of local currency, the end of year net investment is LC500. The end of year exchange rate is $0.80. In terms of dollars, therefore, the end of year net investment is $400 (LC500 x $0.80).

We now consider the items where different results are shown under the two methods. These differences arise because of the translation adjustments and the method of showing the effects of inflation on the purchasing power gain or loss on net monetary items and on the current cost of inventory.

Under the translate-restate approach, shown in part A of Figure 23.15 the differentiated items are determined as follows:

(b) **Purchasing power loss** *(A)*—The net monetary position is represented by the LC100 at the beginning of the year. Translated at the beginning of year of $1.00 yields $100 on which a purchasing power loss of $10 is incurred because of the U.S. inflation rate of 10 percent (LC100 x $1.00 x 0.10).

(d) **Effect of increase in general price level** *(A)*—The beginning year inventory of LC200, translated at the beginning of year exchange rate of $1.00, multiplied by the U.S. inflation rate of 10 percent, results in $20. This amount is needed to maintain the U.S. purchasing power of the inventory (LC200 x $1.00 x 0.10).

(e) **Excess of increase in specific prices over increase in general price level** *(A)*—This item represents the inflation adjusted increase in the current cost of inventory. It is computed as the dollar equivalent of the nominal functional currency increase, which equals $180 less the U.S. inflation component of $20 or $160.

(f) **Translation adjustment**—This is stated in nominal U.S. dollars and represents the effect of rate changes during the holding period of the assets. It consists of two parts: The first is the product of the beginning of year, functional currency, current cost of assets, amounting to LC300, and the $0.20 shrinkage in the exchange rate during the period, which produces a decline of $60; the second is the product of the LC200 increase in current cost of the assets and the difference between the average and ending exchange rates of $0.10, representing a reduction of $20. The total translation adjustment, therefore, is a decline of $80 [(LC300 x -$0.20) + (LC200 x -$0.10)].

Under the restate-translate approach, shown in Part B of Figure 23.15, the differentiated items are determined as follows:

(b) **Purchasing power loss** *(B)*—Measured in terms of the local inflation rate of 20 percent, the LC100 cash produces a purchasing power loss of LC20. This amount is translated at the average exchange rate for the year of $0.90 to yield a purchasing power loss of $18 (LC100 x 0.20 x $0.90).

(d) **Effect of the increase in general price level**—The beginning of the year inventory of LC200, multiplied by the local inflation rate of 20 percent, is

LC40, which is the amount needed to maintain the purchasing power of the inventory in local terms. Translated at the average exchange rate for the year of $0.90, produces a requirement of $36 (LC200 x 0.20 x $0.90).

(e) **Excess of increase in specific prices over increase in general price level**—This item represents the dollar equivalent of the nominal functional currency increase of inventory, which equals $180, less the inflation component to maintain the purchasing power of the inventory in local terms, as stated in (d) above ($180 - $36).

(f) **Translation adjustment (includes parity adjustment)** *(A)*—As stated previously, in the restate-translate method, current cost amounts in nominal units of the functional currency are first adjusted to reflect the effect of local inflation and those restated amounts are then translated into dollar equivalents. Accordingly, a parity adjustment is required to take into account the difference between the local and U.S. inflation rates. In theory, if the differential rates of U.S., and local inflation were accurately reflected in the exchange rates, the parity adjustment and the translation adjustment on beginning of year net assets would offset each other. Any difference resulting from combining these two elements, therefore, represents the effect of an exchange rate change greater or less, as the case may be, than that needed to maintain purchasing power parity between the functional currency and the U.S. dollar.

Although both the translation adjustment and the parity adjustment are required to adjust the end of year net investment and the change in the net investment to U.S. dollar measures, FASB Statement No. 70 calls for reporting a single, combined figure. We explain below, however, both elements of the calculation.

We start with the translation adjustment. The beginning of year functional currency amount of the net investment, LC300, is multiplied by 120/100 to take into account the effect of local inflation, yielding LC360. The product of this figure and the 20% shrinkage in the exchange rate during the period results in a decline of $72. The difference between the end of year functional currency amount of the net investment, LC500, and the beginning of year constant functional currency amount of LC360, is 140 in constant functional currencies. Multiplied by the -$0.10 difference between the average exchange rate of $0.90 and the ending exchange rate of $0.80, results in a decline of $14. The sum of both these changes, $72 and $14, produces the translation adjustment of -$86.

We now turn to the parity adjustment. For this purpose, we calculate the dollar increase in the net investment adjusted first for the effects of local inflation and then for the effects of U.S. inflation. As indicated above, the beginning of year net investment, adjusted for local inflation, is LC360 and translated at the beginning of year exchange rate of $1.00, it is $360. The end of year net investment of LC500, translated at the end of year exchange rate of $0.80, is $400. Therefore, the increase in the dollar equivalent of the net investment, adjusted for local inflation, is $40 [(LC500 x $0.80) - (LC360 x $1.00)].

To provide a U.S. perspective, the beginning of year functional currency amount of the net investment, LC300, translated into U.S. dollars at the beginning of year exchange rate of $1.00, is multiplied by the 10 percent rate of U.S. inflation: the result is $330. The end of year dollar net investment, as stated above, is $400. Accordingly, the increase in dollar equivalent of the net investment, adjusted for U.S. inflation, is $70 [$400 - (LC300 x $1.00 x 1.10)].

The parity adjustment represents the amount that adjusts the effects of local inflation on the translated net investment to reflect the change in net investment during the year in terms of U.S. purchasing power. Accordingly, it is the difference between the change in the net investment, expressed in terms of U.S. and local purchasing power, or $30 ($70 - $40).

In the example given by the FASB, the end of year exchange rate under conditions of parity would be $0.9167 (FC1 = $1 x 110/120) rather than $0.80. In these circumstances, the parity adjustment of $30 would be exactly offset by a translation adjustment of the same amount. The translation adjustment would be calculated by multiplying the beginning of year equity, adjusted for local inflation, LC360, by $0.833 ($1.00 - $0.9167), which equals $30. As stated above, the FASB provides for combining the translation and parity adjustments for display purposes. Accordingly in this case, the reported amount is $56 ($86 - $30).

While both the translate-restate and the restate-translate approaches reveal the same $70 increase in the net investment in terms of U.S. purchasing power, the restate-translate approach also shows the effect of the higher rate of local inflation. Thus the reported purchasing power loss is greater in the restate-translate approach, because of the higher rate of local than of U.S. inflation. Similarly, specific prices increase more moderately when measured against the higher local increase in the general price level.

APPENDIX B:
THE FOREIGN EXCHANGE SYSTEM:
THE HISTORICAL SETTING

Traditionally, a pivotal problem in international finance has been foreign exchange rate fluctuation: the relative values between the currencies of different nations are not always constant over time. The ramifications of this problem transcend virtually every area of international business, from the balance of payments deficits of large nations to the daily transactions of small businesses. Excessive exchange rate fluctuations can produce destabilizing if not cataclysmic effects on the economic performance of any multinational corporation.

One of the most controversial issues in international trade and finance has been that of the relative desirability of fixed versus floating exchange rates. Fixed exchange rates are exchange rates maintained within certain predetermined parameters. They are set by governments and are allowed to fluctuate only within certain restraining bands (referred to as intervention limits). Conversely, floating exchange rates adjust automatically to changes within their domestic economies and the external trading environment. In the purest sense, floating rates are not restrained by government parameters. The relative pros and cons of these two exchange rate methodologies are discussed below in this Appendix.

A reexamination of modern foreign exchange systems (since WWII) points to the rather nebulous conclusion that neither fixed nor floating exchange rates have been sufficient, when used to the mutual exclusion of each other, in providing stability to the foreign exchange markets or in mitigating the problems of trade deficits.

THE BRETTON WOODS SYSTEM

The early post WWII foreign exchange system resulted from the Bretton Woods agreement, so-called for its meeting place in Bretton Woods, New Hampshire, in 1947. The Bretton Woods System was based on the gold standard and utilized fixed exchange rates. The events leading to the establishment of this system make it easier to understand, even though neither the gold standard nor fixed exchange rates exist today.

With the exception of the United States, the nations of the western world were faced with the dire economic realities of industrial devastation after WWII. These nations desperately needed money to finance industrial expansion. American dollars represented the world's most powerful and stable currency and was the only one which was acceptable worldwide. Of course, the major problem, in this world of scarce supply and ravenous demand was the danger of worldwide inflation, and soaring prices. Paper currencies backed by war-ravaged economies were of questionable value. As a result, the United States—the country that at that time held 2/3 of the world's existing gold supply—pushed adamantly toward the gold standard eventually adopted at Bretton Woods.

The essential features of this gold standard were threefold:

- payments made to settle international trade imbalances were made only in gold;
- a country's domestic money supply was tied directly to the amount of gold it possessed; and
- each currency was fully convertible into gold, and exchange rates which were determined by the amount of gold in each currency unit were fixed.

As part of the Bretton Woods System, foreign currencies were converted into gold at the fixed price of $35.00 per troy ounce, thus ensuring that some stability would be maintained in the value of those currencies vis-a-vis the U.S. dollar.

Exchange rates were determined by taking the ratio of the gold content between the U.S. dollar and the foreign currency. Consider the following example:

31.1035 gms. of gold per ounce;
.8886 gms. of gold per dollar; therefore price of gold = $35.00 per ounce.
Gold content of German mark (DM) = .222168 gms; and

$$\frac{.888671}{.222168} = 4 \text{ DM} = \$1.00.$$

Therefore, the exchange rate between the dollar and the DM became 4 DM per dollar, or $.25 per DM.

However, exchange rate stability was only one of the problems that Bretton Woods sought to alleviate. Another major problem was trade deficits. The gold standard and fixed rates were also thought to be the solution here. In the case of payments deficits, a gold outflow would take place to finance the payment, resulting in the following succession of events: a contraction in the domestic money supply leading to higher interest rates and decreased investment, followed by decreases in disposable income. This sequence would eventually produce a decrease in domestic prices. Capital would then flow into the country in response to the higher interest rates; imports would decrease due to the reduction of domestic disposable income coupled with the relative increase in foreign prices. The ultimate outcome would be an increase in exports—due to the increase in foreign purchasing power and a decrease in the price of domestic goods being exported—equalizing the balance of trade deficit. The opposite forces would occur in a surplus trade country.

THE INTERNATIONAL MONETARY FUND

In addition to fixed exchange rates and the gold standard, the Bretton Woods System also established the International Monetary Fund (IMF). The IMF drew its resources from the reserves of its member nations. Each nation had a set "quota" to contribute to the IMF, 25 percent payable in gold, the rest in its domestic currency. Member nations were then permitted to draw on these IMF resources to finance short-term trade deficits. Countries could borrow unconditionally from the IMF up to the amount of their respective gold contributions. This became known as the country's "gold tranche position", which was counted in its currency reserves. Above this amount, a country could draw on a "credit tranche," subject to IMF approval and in accordance with certain restrictions governing its use.

IMF rules also governed the fixed exchange rates under Bretton Woods. Exchange rates for each currency were initially fixed at a "par value" against the U.S. dollar, and allowed to fluctuate only by a narrow deviation of 2 percent (± 1 percent above or below par). For example, in the case of the German DM, where the declared par value was 4.00 DM equals $1.00, the upper intervention band was 3.96 and the lower band 4.04.

Under this system, when the DM depreciated (i.e., devalued) against the dollar by reaching its lower intervention (-1%), the German Central bank (Germany's equivalent of the American Federal Reserve) would have to sell its dollar (or gold) reserves and buy DM on the foreign exchange markets. This would increase the demand for DM's, until the value of the DM rose from 4.04 DM per dollar to 4.00 DM per dollar, or the par value for the DM. Where the DM appreciated (revalued) by reaching its upper intervention (+1%), the German central bank would sell DM's, until the value of the DM fell back to par.

Several factors may require clarification at this point. First, it may be somewhat confusing to those studying foreign exchange for the first time that when the DM depreciates against the dollar its value changes from 4 DM per $ to 4.04 DM per $. It is easier to conceptualize this seemingly anomalous change in value if one remembers that prior to this depreciation, it took only 4 DM to buy 1 dollar (par value). However, after devaluation, one must pay 4.04 DM (lower intervention) to buy 1 dollar, a depreciation of one percent in the value of the DM.

Secondly, one might also ask how it was possible, under a system of fixed exchange rates, for the value of the DM or any currency to change relative to the dollar, without the usual forces of supply and demand in foreign exchange trading coming into play. The dollar value of a currency could change if a foreign country increased the gold value of its currency in relation to the dollar. In 1968, for example, the gold content of the DM was .222168 gms. of gold per DM, as shown in the original example:

$$\frac{\text{gms. gold per \$}}{\text{gms. gold per DM}} = \frac{.888671}{.222168} = 4 \text{ DM} = \$1.00.$$

In 1969, however, Germany revalued its currency by increasing its gold content to .242806 gms. per DM. The dollar value of the DM therefore, increased as follows:

$$\frac{.888671}{.242806} = 3.66 \text{ DM} = \$1.00.$$

As world trade expanded and a corresponding need for enlarged international reserves grew, the IMF, in 1969 created a new type of asset which could be included in such reserves. Termed Special Drawing Rights (SDR's), they became known as "paper gold" and were intended primarily for use in transactions involving governments or the IMF. Although SDR allocations have been made to IMF members at times, they constitute only a small portion of international reserves and other uses have been relatively minor, such as the issuance of Eurobonds denominated in SDRs.

THE COLLAPSE OF THE BRETTON WOODS SYSTEM

Eventually, it became apparent that a basic flaw existed in the Bretton Woods System. The dominant role played by the U.S. and secondarily, Great Britain, meant that these countries were the principal providers of world reserves. For this purpose, they had to run balance of payments deficits to enable other countries to accumulate dollar and pound reserves. These deficits, however, created doubt about the ability of the U.S. and British central banks to convert their currencies into gold at the agreed price. Sparked by France, a run on gold took place leading to a two-tier gold pricing system, whereby the U.S. maintained the official price of gold at $35 an ounce, while the private market was allowed to find its own level. Repeated financial crises occurred, including a devaluation of the pound. To help provide liquidity, an allocation of SDR's was made by the IMF to its member countries on the basis of their quotes. There was, however, no serious follow-through in this direction.

In August 1971, President Richard Nixon ordered the end of the long standing U.S. pledge to exchange dollars for gold. This was, for all practical purposes, the termination of the Bretton Woods System, since it marked the end of the gold convertibility of the U.S. dollar.

The intransigent exchange regulations of the Bretton Woods System did not allow participants to adjust their currencies for internal inflationary effects, and therefore had a tendency to produce recessions and uncontrolled expansions. Moreover, the continuing strength of the U.S. dollar as a world currency, on which the system was based, gradually faded. Finally, the system did not anticipate the rapid economic growth of other economies after World War II, coupled with inflation and the chronic balance of trade deficit in America. Still, the world clung to the precept that fixed exchange rates could stabilize foreign exchange markets and eventually improve imbalances in international trade.

THE SMITHSONIAN AGREEMENT

Following the U.S. unilateral suspension of official purchases or sales of gold, currency exchange rates were permitted to float for a short period. The world's leading trading nations (called the "Group of Ten") bargained over an appropriate course of action, leading to the adoption of a compromise.

The Smithsonian Agreement, as it is called, replaced the gold standard and fixed exchange rates of Bretton Woods. The Smithsonian Agreement attempted to establish a new durable structure of fixed exchange rates. Its objectives were twofold: first, to restore confidence and orderly conditions in the exchange markets, and second, to bring about an adjustment in the basic payments imbalances between the deficits of the U.S. and the excessive current account surpluses of some other countries.

The Agreement established new par values for all participating currencies. It provided for a devaluation of the dollar (the U.S. raised the price of gold to $38 per ounce) and for a revaluation of other major currencies. The Agreement also widened the intervention bands—previously set at 2 percent under Bretton Woods—to 4½ percent ($\pm 2.25\%$ above or below par). However, this realignment did not restore confidence, either in the dollar or in this system of fixed exchange rates. The dollar continued to weaken throughout 1971 and into the early part of 1972, with no apparent improvement in U.S. trade accounts.

In April of 1972, the nations of the European Common Market responded by establishing the "Snake in the Tunnel". The "Snake" simply set intervention bands among the currencies of its members at 2.25 percent ($\pm 1.125\%$ above or below par values). However, currencies of the group as a whole could fluctuate against other currencies within the larger band (i.e., "the tunnel" set by the Smithsonian Agreement (4½%).

THE COLLAPSE OF THE SMITHSONIAN AGREEMENT

Devaluation of the dollar, as well as the other measures taken, did not restore stability to the international financial system. Currency speculation continued. By 1973, the dollar came under heavy selling pressure and in February the price of gold was raised from $38.00 to $42.22 per ounce. These developments shook investor confidence in the ability of authorities to maintain a pegged rate system.

Finally, March of 1973 saw the end of the Smithsonian Agreement. A pegged rate system can work only in an atmosphere of international trust. Repeated financial crises plus spreading political differences eroded this trust. It had been believed when the Agreement was established, that the U.S. deficit could be corrected by the devaluation of the U.S. dollar. This was supposed to have made U.S. goods cheaper internationally, resulting in a competitive shift in trade to the U.S. However, the expected result did not materialize. To the dismay of international economists, the U.S. trade deficit did not fall below its then rather formidable 1972 total of $10 billion. Meanwhile, the influx of funds to the U.S. which had been hoped for, as a result of relatively higher American interest rates, did not develop.

TOWARDS THE PRESENT SYSTEM OF MANAGED FLOAT

The advent of floating rates provided the international currency background to the period of successive oil crises that started in the fall of 1973. Since the members of the Organization of Petroleum Exporting Countries (OPEC) generally took payment in dollars or eurodollars (dollar denominated deposits held abroad, mainly in London) there came into play an arrangement, popularly known as "recycling petrodollars." Dollars or eurodollars flowed from the oil buying countries to the members of OPEC, then to the major trading countries which embarked on a policy of lending dollars to the buying entities to permit continued oil purchases. This policy led to granting loans of questionable soundness and contributed to the precarious state of international banking relations that existed in the first part of the 1980's.

Flexible rates, with central bank intervention to prevent undue volatility, became the accepted practice. Gold was officially demonetized. Continued interest was manifested in the SDR's, which were expanded on several occasions and experienced several changes in the basis of valuation. Since January 1, 1981, the SDR has been valued in terms of five currencies (the U.S. dollar, German mark, U.K. pound, Japanese yen, and French franc). The composition of the currencies and their relative weights is revised every five years in accordance with the relative importance of each country in international trade.

The end of the Smithsonian Agreement heralded the beginning of the present foreign exchange system of "managed float". In essence, the major European countries, in March 1973, simply eliminated the "tunnel" binding the "snake".

The currencies participating in the margins of the European monetary union continue to maintain the narrow 2.25 percent fluctuation band among each other (except the lira, which is allowed six percent). All may allow their currencies, to float freely against the U.S. dollar, according to market forces. European monetary authorities intervene in the markets to maintain this floating range within certain specified limits.

In March of 1979, these arrangements were introduced to the long awaited European Monetary System, which includes West Germany, France, Italy, Belgium, Netherlands, Luxembourg, Ireland, and Denmark. This System establishes the Eurocurrency Unit (ECU) as a benchmark for currency measurement. The ECU is a weighted average of all the currencies in the European Monetary System. Use of the ECU provides a built-in hedge against intracurrency rate fluctuations for all participating countries.

There is sustained interest in the use of a basket of currencies to provide some stability to chaotic currency relations. The SDR has not gained the support that it was expected to attract. It remains to be seen, as a deeper investment market develops in Europe, whether or not the ECU will attract borrower and investor attention.

Persistent financial problems have strained the relations among the nations of the European Monetary System. Disagreements have come about concerning the relative worth of the currencies of the countries involved. The constituent nations tend to view these relations in the light of their own economic needs, making it difficult to bring about economic cohesion. However, while the base is shaky, thus far a breakup has been avoided. Thus, in March 1983, after intense negotiations, a realignment of the currencies was adopted; the centerpiece of the agreement was a 5½ percent upward revaluation of the West German mark and a 2½ percent devaluation of the French franc.

Constant arguments swirl about the most effective system for handling international currency relations. There is a consensus on the need for greater exchange rate stability to avoid the deviations from purchasing power parity for the world's major currencies. Such a condition has distorted competitive relations and led to protectionist measures in the past. The issue has repeatedly come about at the economic summit meetings that the major industrial countries of the world have been holding each year since 1975. They have not been able to reach an agreement, however, on the most effective system for achieving currency stability.

PROS AND CONS OF FIXED VS. FLOATING EXCHANGE RATES

Proponents of fixed and floating rates, each vigorously defend their espoused points of view. Fixed rate advocates contend that exchange rate changes under a system of floating rates will be largely the result of speculation rather than the result of changes in fundamental economic factors. This speculation is presumed to be destabilizing. In other words, instead of dampening fluctuations in exchange rates, speculation will make exchange rates unnecessarily erratic. Furthermore, they argue that speculatively generated exchange rate changes will be so large and unpredictable as to disrupt international trade and investment.

Floating rate advocates claim that while exchange rates do vary under a floating system, they do so primarily in response to fundamental economic factors. They recognize that speculation will undoubtedly occur under this system, but they argue that it will not, on balance, be destabilizing. Speculation will merely have the effect of dampening fluctuations in exchange rates as they respond to fundamental economic factors.

Neither floating nor fixed proponents advocate the present system of managed float. As indicated above, fixed rate advocates fear the speculative forces inherent in its floating tendencies, while floating advocates view the rate changes as reflecting ongoing economic developments. However, they claim that the present system is so highly managed that its performance is not a fair measure of how a purely free floating system could operate if fully adopted.

One might wonder about the outcome of these two arguments. Are fixed rate advocates correct when they claim that destabilizing speculation will have catastrophic effects on a system of floating rates? Or will exchange rates actually respond to fundamental economic factors, as the floating rate advocates would have us believe?

A study published by the Federal Reserve Bank of St. Louis in 1976 examined the hypothesis that speculation had been destabilizing to the foreign exchange markets (i.e., caused excessive swings in exchange rates) during the period between 1970 and 1976. The results permitted the conditional rejection of this hypothesis.

It would seem that there is a preponderance of theory on the side of the floating rate advocates. That is, the predominant factor determining exchange rate changes in the long-run is the degree of inflationary pressure in one country relative to inflationary pressure in another country, a fundamental economic factor.

At the ninth economic summit conference of the leading industrial nations in 1983, President Francois Mitterand of France was a particularly strong advocate of government intervention to stabilize currency values. His call for a "new Bretton Woods" could only generate agreement on the part of the conferees to study the issue further. Two years later, in the fall of 1985, as the finance ministers of the United States, Britain, France, West Germany and Japan (the Big Five) signed an agreement providing for mutual co-operation in solving the problem of a soaring dollar, the U.S., in its turn, in a major break from prior policy, indicated it might consider an international conference to review the twelve-year-old system of floating exchange rates.

CORPORATE TAX PLANNING AND MANAGEMENT*

24.1   INTRODUCTION

So complex and involved have business and corporate tax matters become that most larger companies have established corporate tax departments to administer and control the tax functions.[1] Companies seem to be increasingly aware that positive tax management is more than merely filing tax returns and maintaining relevant tax records. That it involves major advisory aid for top management in policy guidance is now recognized in most alert companies. Most firms now have tax managers and tax counsel, and there is more frequent reference to outside consultants when special tax problems arise in connection with mergers and acquisitions, recapitalizations, new financing, pension plans, and so forth. The development of staff experts on recurrent tax problems is now a widespread practice.

Company tax managers and tax counsel may perform all or some of the following functions in the larger companies:

- Advise on the tax implications of proposed company actions or policy decisions;
- Advise top management of tax developments and liabilities;
- Advise operating departments and executive officers on special tax problems;
- Establish tax accounts and tax accounting procedures;
- Coordinate policy and procedures on tax matters;
- Secure the cooperation of division and plant accounting departments in developing data for tax purposes;
- Work with other departments, such as the legal department on technical matters, engineering on depreciation and payroll on wages and salary data;

* This chapter was updated and revised by Mr. Robert Willens, M.B.A., C.P.A., Partner, Peat, Marwick, Mitchell & Co., and Mr. Arnold J. Fries, J.D., C.P.A., Manager, Tax Research and Planning, Continental Grain Co.

- Prepare and file company tax returns, and pay or authorize payment to tax authorities;
- Review assessments and tax bills for accuracy and company liability;
- Confer with tax authorities on assessments, extensions, allowances, rulings, interpretations, refunds, and penalties;
- Receive internal revenue agents assigned to company audits;
- Prepare and participate in administrative appeals, negotiation of settlements of contested claims, and tax litigation; and
- Maintain receipts, records, and files related to tax matters.

The burden of corporate taxes has risen significantly in recent years. Beginning with the rate of 1 percent in 1909, the rate rose to 12 percent during World War I, then receded to 10 percent in the 1920s, and rose to about 17 percent in the 1930s. During World War II, with the excess profits tax, top corporate rates reached 80 percent. In the 1950s, the corporate tax rate was 30 to 52 percent, in the 1960s and until late in the 1970s it was 22 to 48 percent, and in 1983 it was 15 to 46 percent.

Thus, in meeting the burden of federal income taxes, tax planning and management have become very important factors. There are many requirements to be observed in the application of tax law. The methods employed in handling a transaction will have a marked effect on the ultimate results of a corporation's operations.

24.2   THE TAX EFFECTS OF DEPRECIATION

The Internal Revenue Code of 1954 liberalized the deduction of depreciation by concentrating the deduction in the early years. In explaining its reasons for the liberalization of depreciation, Congress states that this would be "more in accord with the actual pattern of loss of economic usefulness." Congress, however, does not guarantee a taxpayer that the cost of the property will be recovered. Depreciation merely represents another deduction in the computation of taxable income.

A taxpayer must take the proper depreciation deduction each year. The failure to take an allowance in any year will not give the taxpayer the right to increase the depreciation deduction in later years. The Supreme Court in Virginian Hotel Corp. of Lynchburg v. Helvering stated the requirements very clearly when it noted: "Wear and tear do not wait on net income. Nor can depreciation be accumulated and held for use in that year in which it will bring the taxpayer the most benefit. Congress has elected to make the year the unit of taxation."[2] The rule is that the basis of property must be reduced by depreciation allowed or allowable. Allowed means that which results in a reduction of income taxes. Allowable means that which should have been deducted.

The Commissioner of Internal Revenue has recognized various methods of computing depreciation as long as they are reasonable and consistent. The requirement of consistency means that the method must be consistent with respect to a specific item. In other words, once a method is chosen for any particular property, it must be used consistently for that property. However, the taxpayer may use a different depreciation method for similar property acquired at any time, provided the new property is set up in a separate account. It is not necessary to use the same method for all assets.

Taxpayers have a choice of a number of methods:[3]

1. The straight line method;
2. The declining balance method, at a rate,
   a. twice that allowable under the straight line method; or
   b. one and one-half times that allowable under the straight line method, or
   c. one and one-quarter times that allowable under the straight line
3. The sum of the years-digits method; or
4. Any other consistent method, provided the total depreciation accumulated during the first two-thirds of the life of the property does not exceed that accumulated under method 2a.

In order to be able to use method 2 or 3 above without acquiring express permission, it is necessary that the asset have a useful life of at least three years. In addition, to use the double declining balance method and the sum of the years-digits method, it is essential that the property's original use commence with the taxpayer. In the case of 2b, the Commissioner's regulations provide that it may be applied to used property. For real property, methods 2a and 3 may not be used for other than new residential rental property. In addition, for used realty no method other than straight line may be used except for residential rental property with a useful life of at least twenty years (125% declining balance may be used in that case.) A change from method 2 to the straight line method may be made without receiving the permission of the Commissioner.

Another problem that must be resolved is the fixing of the depreciation rate. The rate, irrespective of the method, involves a determination of the useful life. A corporation may determine the useful life of an asset by the facts and circumstances for each asset. The Economic Recovery Tax Act (ERTA), however, replaced traditional depreciation methods with the Accelerated Cost Recovery System (ACRS) for most tangible depreciable property placed into service after 1980. This provides a quicker recovery of costs by applying a statutory set rate or period for the property. For properties placed in service before 1981, however, prior depreciation methods continue to be used.

ACRS abandons concepts such as "useful life," "salvage," "new-versus-used," and "depreciation," in favor of terms such as "class," "class life," and "cost recovery." Tangible depreciable property is placed into one of five recovery period classes based upon its mid-point life as of January 1, 1981. This is shown in Figure 24.1.

After determining the recovery class, a taxpayer may choose to use either the accelerated statutory rates or a straight line rate using one of three elective recovery periods. The rate is then applied against the adjusted basis of the property. Adjustments to the basis would include, for example, reductions for one half of the investment tax credit allowed and elected capitalization of interest and taxes during construction (under section 266 of the IRC).

The proscribed accelerated rates of recovery under ACRS for all but the 15 year real property class approximate a 150 percent declining balance rate for

FIGURE 24.1 *The accelerated cost recovery system*

Property With Mid-point Live Of	ACRS Period	Examples
4 years or less	3-year	Autos, research equipment
4 to 18 years	5-year	Computers, furniture & equipment
18-25 years for public utilities and 12.5 years or less for real property	10-year	Some utility structures and railroad tank cars
More than 25 years for public utilities	15-year	Water utility property
More than 12.5 years for real property	15-year	Buildings

plants placed in service after 1981. Rates for the 15 year real property class use a 175 percent declining balance method.

Therefore, the Treasury has yielded to business persuasion in two significant aspects of depreciation policy. It has permitted accelerated depreciation and has reduced its acceptable estimates of useful life. Business has yet to gain its third objective, however—depreciation based on replacement value rather than on original cost. As prices rise, the mere ability to recover original cost does not permit replacement of the assets which have worn out. Additional sums are required and these must come either out of retained earnings or from new capital. Thus, part of reported profits must be used to allow the company simply to maintain itself, and the corporate income tax, therefore, with inadequate depreciation allowances, cannibalizes corporate capital.

24.3 DEALING IN TREASURY STOCK[4]

Treasury stock has been defined as fully paid capital stock reacquired by the issuing company through gift, purchase, or otherwise, and available for resale or cancellation.[5]

The acquisition of treasury stock by donation does not result in income to the acquiring corporation. The IRC provides that gross income does not include any contribution to the capital of the corporation.

As a corollary to this rule, the donor cannot take a tax deduction as either a loss or an expense for the contribution. In effect, the contribution constitutes an additional cost of the donor's retained interest in the corporation. Under certain circumstances, a donation to a corporation of shares of its own stock may also be construed for tax purposes as an indirect gift by the donor to the other stockholders of the corporation, particularly where the corporation is family owned and a donative intent can be proven. In such an event, although no income tax is involved, the donor may be subjected to a gift tax.[6]

The purchase of treasury stock for cash generally does not create any income tax liability on the part of the purchasing corporation. But if the corporation receives its own stock as consideration for the sale of property by it, or in satisfaction of indebtedness to it, the fact that the debtor or purchaser is a stockholder will not prevent the transaction from giving rise to gain or loss to the selling corporation.[7]

It is now well settled that the reissuance by a corporation of treasury stock for money or other property results in no gain or loss to the corporation.[8] A corporation may issue treasury or unissued stock to its employees as compensation for services rendered. The corporation will be permitted to claim an expense deduction to the extent of the fair market value of the stock.

A distribution of treasury stock as a stock dividend is generally non-taxable to the recipient. It is immaterial whether the stock dividend is paid from treasury stock or unissued stock. The tax is, in effect, deferred until the stock is sold, and then is usually applied at capital gain rates.

24.4   THE ACCUMULATED EARNINGS TAX[9]

The financial manager will wish to see that there is a clear business purpose to his accumulation of surplus and retention of earnings. Otherwise his company may be charged with improperly accumulating earnings and be subjected to the accumulated earnings tax. This is a penalty tax imposed on companies which retain earnings for the purpose of enabling their stockholders to avoid the payment of the personal income tax on the increased dividends which would flow to them were the earnings not retained. Where there is a business justification for the accumulation of earnings, for instance to finance growth or to meet the reasonable needs of the business, no penalty need be feared. The key is the word reasonable. The company must be able to justify the reasonableness of its accumulation, though technically the burden of proof in a Tax Court litigation may, under certain circumstances, be transferred to the government. Every company is allowed up to $150,000 of surplus without need for justifying the accumulation. It is the excess which must be explained.

Evidence of unreasonable accumulation may be found where there is investment in property or securities unrelated to the business of the corporation, or if loans are made to shareholders or others having no reasonable relation to the conduct of the business. If the charge of unreasonable accumulated earnings is made and sustained, a penalty tax on "accumulated taxable income" is imposed, amounting to $27\frac{1}{2}$ percent on the first $100,000 of unreasonably accumulated income and $38\frac{1}{2}$ percent on any amount over $100,000. The tax is not imposed on all surplus: it is imposed upon a very technically defined "accumulated taxable income." The penalty tax is not imposed on any corporation that does not accumulate earnings over $150,000.

24.5   PERSONAL HOLDING COMPANIES

Family-dominated closely held corporations face a greater risk of being classed as "personal holding companies" as a result of the Revenue Act of 1964. Previously, a corporation was held to be a personal holding company when 80 percent or more of its gross income was from kinds of income designated as personal holding company income. Under the 1964 Act, the percentage was reduced to 60 percent and the base for this computation was changed to adjusted ordinary gross income.[10] A corporation will be classed as a personal holding company if (1) more than 50 percent of its stock is owned by five or less stockholders, and (2) 60 percent or more of its adjusted ordinary gross income is from personal holding company income sources.

A corporation may inadvertently fall into this category though it was not created for tax avoidance purposes. If it meets the two criteria, it must file a personal holding company tax return.

If a company is classified as a personal holding company, a penalty tax is levied in addition to the 46 percent corporate income tax. The penalty is 70 percent of the "undistributed personal holding company income." The purpose of the penalty tax is to discourage the creation of "incorporated pocketbooks." It is aimed at a corporation whose income is derived chiefly from investments and which is owned by a small group of individuals. It seeks to close a loophole that would permit individuals in high tax brackets to transfer income producing property to a corporation and have the income taxed at lower corporate rates in lieu of the higher individual income tax rates.

For example, Jones, who is in the 50 percent bracket, forms a corporation and transfers his income producing property to it in return for stock. The latter transaction constitutes a tax-free exchange. The income from the properties is now taxed to the corporation at no more than 46 percent. After accumulating income for several years, the corporation is liquidated and Jones receives the accumulated income, subject to a 60 percent capital gain deduction, at the maximum capital gains rate of 20 percent. Or if he dies before liquidating the corporation, the accumulation would be distributed to his heirs and would entirely escape the individual income tax.

The personal holding company tax is aimed at such situations. It seeks to penalize the use of a corporation as a shelter to avoid high bracket individual income tax rates. To prevent this, the 70 percent penalty surtax is levied on undistributed personal holding company income. In general, personal holding company income consists of rents, royalties, amounts received under certain personal service contracts, taxable income from estates and trusts, dividends, interest, and income from annuities.

For the purpose of calculating undistributed personal holding company income, certain adjustments are permitted to be made to the corporate net income, primarily to reflect its dividend paying capacity. Near the close of its taxable year, a corporation may avoid a presonal holding company designation by paying out sufficient dividends to escape the label. Over a longer term it may be able to effect changes in the sources of income or stock ownership to avoid the payment of the penalty tax.

24.6 MULTIPLE ENTITIES

Tax planning has usually involved a review of the possible advantages of doing business in a multicorporate form. Through the use of multiple corporations, greater flexibility in business operations may be gained. An enterprise can divide its operations to make some qualify for more favorable tax treatment such as that accorded to a Domestic International Sales Corporation (now called Foreign Sales Corporations) or a "tax option" corporation.[11] Also, liquidation of a portion of an enterprise's business is easier. A single corporation often cannot qualify its stockholders for the partial liquidation requirements which will ensure them of capital gains treatment. Nor can the single corporation often qualify for the tax-free spinoff provisions, because in each case the corporation is required to have engaged in at least two distinct businesses for a period of five years. If instead of one corporation, two or more had originally been organized, one could be liquidated completely with stockholders qualifying for capital gains treatment, while the other could continue the other portions of the business.

There are, however, disadvantages to multiple entities. If one or more members of the multiple corporate group operate at a loss, the loss cannot be offset against the profits of the successful ones. This could be accomplished if the multiple corporations qualify as an affiliated group and elect to file a consolidated return. While there is no additional tax for the privilege of filing consolidated returns, there may be added expenses of duplication of offices, books, and records. Should the IRS decide that the individual corporations have no separate tax existence, it could attempt to tax the group of companies as if they were one. This would evidently have the same effect as if the group filed a consolidated return. The IRS may also reallocate items of the income and expenses of a controlled group in a manner detrimental to the combined picture.

24.7 DIVIDEND RECEIVED DEDUCTION

Normally, intercorporate dividends are taxable to the recipient only to the extent of 15 percent; 85 percent is tax free. However, where the dividend is paid by one corporation to another in the same affiliated group, under certain conditions, it may be 100 percent tax-free. An affiliated group is one entitled to file consolidated returns (a parent and its 80 percent owned subsidiaries.) An affiliated group filing consolidated returns is not taxable on intercorporate dividends. An affiliated group filing separate returns may elect the 100 percent dividend exclusion. Such a group is limited to only one $150,000 minimum accumulated earnings credit for the tax on unreasonably accumulated earnings (see 24.4) and to one $10,000 exemption in determining liability for minimum taxes. The latter must be allocated to the members in proportion to each member's regular tax deduction.

24.8 STOCK OPTIONS

Stock options have long been a favorite corporate device for enhancing the total compensation of key executives at advantageous tax rates. Qualified stock options and restricted stock options were once popular executive compensation devices carrying favorable tax treatment. They are now no longer in use, however, and have been supplanted by incentive stock options.

Incentive stock options (ISO) were added to the IRC by ERTA. They may be received by an employee and exercised without being taxed. If the stock is held for the requisite holding period, it will be taxed at capital gains rates. No deduction is available to the employer from this option.

In order to be a capital gain, the employee must hold the stock for at least two years after the option is granted, and one year after the option is exercised. He must also remain with the issuing company until three months before the option is exercised.

For options to qualify as ISOs, they must meet various requirements including: (1) the term of the option may not exceed ten years; (2) the option price must be no less than the fair market value of the stock on the date of issuance (if the employee owns more than 10% of the company, the option must be at least 110% of the market value at the time the option is granted, and the term of the option may not exceed five years); (3) the option must be transferable only by inheritance; (4) the option must not be exercisable while previously issued ISOs are outstanding; (5) the annual option cannot exceed $100,000 plus any unused carryover from a previous year; and (6) the option cannot be exercised while there is outstanding any ISO which was granted to the employee at any earlier time.

Since the tax treatment of ISOs is somewhat less favorable than that previously accorded qualified and restricted stock options, the stock option medium of executive compensation has been relieved of some of its prior attractiveness, and emphasis has shifted to more generous bonuses and deferred compensation plans (see 24.14) and prerequisites as techniques for executive rewards.

24.9   LEASE VERSUS PURCHASE OF PROPERTY[12]

Leasing has become increasingly popular in recent years, and much attention is now devoted to the analysis of the financial advantages of leasing versus buying and borrowing. The tax treatment of leasing arrangements enters importantly into such calculations.

There are two basic tax advantages of leasing as compared with purchasing property. These are (1) a faster write-off of the cost of using property in the form of rent, and (2) a current rent deduction which could not otherwise be obtained, for example, for the cost of land, which is not depreciable. Under certain circumstances even the benefit of an investment tax credit on new property may be claimed by the lessee at the owner's election.

The deductibility of rental payments for the use of property is clearly permitted. However, this expenditure will only be recognized where the taxpayer is not acquiring an equity interest in the property. The problem, therefore, is to determine when such equity is acquired. This is not an easy matter to resolve. Each situation must be examined on its own merits. There are, however, certain guideposts which may help to resolve the tax consequences of such a situation.

Where equipment is leased at current rental rates for such equipment, without any purchase agreement, and where it is clear that the property reverts to the lessor at the end of the rental period, no problem should arise.

In order to retain the tax advantages of the lease arrangement and not lose title to the property at the expiration of the lease, many taxpayers have entered into transactions which provide for an option to purchase the property at the end of the lease period or which permit the taxpayer the right to use property for its estimated life.

In instances where the purchase price in the option is only a small part of the total rental payments, the transaction will probably be considered a conditional sale. Also, if the periodic rental payments are high compared to the total value of the property, the contract will be considered a conditional sale. The IRS illustrated the problem in Revenue Ruling 55-540.[13] The example used was that of a lease agreement that covered a period of 13 years, including renewal periods. The useful life of the asset was estimated to be from 10 to 15 years. No provision was included for the transfer of legal title to the property. However, during the first three years of the contract, 92 percent of the cost of the property would be paid in the form of rent. The IRS considered this arrangement a conditional sales contract. The amounts paid under the contract would thus have to be capitalized, and depreciation would be allowable to the "lessee" over the estimated life of the property.

Even though the lease may not contain any reference to transfer of title, it may nevertheless be construed as, in effect, being a sale of an equitable interest. This may occur where total rents over a short period approximate the fair market value of the property, and where the lessee may continue to use the property over its remaining useful life at very modest or token payments. It may also occur where periodic payments materially exceed the current fair rental values.

Another method employed for leasing property is the sale and leaseback arrangement. This covers a situation where a business sells its property and immediately obtains a long-term lease from the purchaser for the use of the property. The property involved is usually land and buildings, as distinguished from machinery and equipment. There are a number of business and tax reasons for a sale and leaseback. The chief advantage claimed for the seller of the business property who takes back a lease on it is that as lessee he may deduct full annual rental payments for corporate income tax purposes, as contrasted with the smaller allowances for current depreciation on the property and interest payments on a loan for a similar amount. The difference between these two charges and the rental income is in effect subsidized by the high federal corporate tax rate. A second relative advantage is that the land value of owned property cannot be depreciated whereas the rental payment for it under a lease can be deducted as a business expense. A third advantage is that the sale and leaseback offers greater financial flexibility. The cash received improves both the working capital position and the current ratio of the company. Or the funds may be used for other essential corporate purposes. If, in contrast to leasing, the corporation were to borrow funds, the note contract or bond indenture would probably contain restrictions on future borrowings and possibly on dividend payments until the debt had been substantially reduced. Furthermore, the sale and leaseback may improve the credit standing of the company because the fixed asset and its related indebtedness disappear from the company's balance sheet. There is an increasing movement today to disclose the impact of lease obligations on a corporation's financial statements.[14]

An additional important consideration is the tax saving that may result from the sale of the property at a loss. However, there has been a good deal of litigation over the deductability of such a loss, questioning whether it is real or apparent.

In one case where the selling price of the property was higher than its appraised value, the rent was considered reasonable, and the leaseback was for 20 years, the Court allowed the deduction.[15]

In another case, however, the loss was disallowed.[16] Here the court held that there was no sale but an exchange of property for other property of like kind. The exchange of like kind properties does not result in any recognition of gain or loss.[17] The leasehold, in this case, was for a period of not less than 25 years or more than 95 years, at the option of lessee. The Internal Revenue Regulations, in Section 1.1031(a)1-c, consider as a nontaxable exchange the exchange of real estate for a leasehold of 30 years or more. The court therefore followed this example.

In Standard Envelope Mfg. Co., where the lease period was for 24 years, the sale and leaseback was considered a sale and the loss was deductible.[18]

In Jordan Marsh a claimed loss deduction was allowed. The Court found that the sales price, though more than $2 million below the adjusted cost basis, was equal to the market value and that the rental called for in the leaseback was fair and normal. The lease was for a term of 30 years and 3 days with an option to renew for another 30 years.[19]

In City Investing Co. the taxpayer sold certain real property for its full value and immediately leased it back at the fair rental value of the property. The lease was for an initial term of 21 years, with renewal provisions extending to an aggregate of 204 years. The Commissioner asserted that the loss deduction claimed by the seller-lessee should be disallowed on the ground that the sale was a like kind exchange under Section 1031. The Court allowed the loss deduction on the ground that the seller-lessee was in the process of liquidating all its investments.[20]

The IRS takes the position that a transfer of business or investment property with a leaseback for a term of 30 years or more is a like kind exchange and that no recognition will be accorded to any resulting alleged loss.

It would appear, therefore, that where the sale and leaseback provides for a lease of less than 30 years, the selling price is at arm's length, and the rental is reasonable, the loss may be allowed.

Where the property is sold for a sum in excess of its adjusted basis, gain will result. This gain may be treated as a long-term capital gain. However, a transfer of property that has appreciated in value with a leaseback for a term of 30 years or more will also result in nonrecognition of the gain.

In the typical case, the sale and leaseback of business property (if it does not involve a like kind exchange) will generally produce capital gain or ordinary loss on the sale, and the seller-lessee's subsequent rental payments will be fully deductible from ordinary income. The rental payments will be fully tax deductible to the purchaser-lessor, and he will be entitled to deduct depreciation on the property, using its purchase-price as the basis therefore. For the seller-lessee, the former depreciation deductions are replaced by rental deductions. It is because of this condition that a sale and leaseback may be particularly attractive if the seller-lessee's basis for depreciable property is low in relation to its market value, or if the property includes raw land or other nondepreciable assets. By entering into a sale and leaseback, the seller-lessee may acquire rental deductions which have a greater tax benefit to him than the depreciation deductions, if any, to which he was previously entitled.

24.10 CORPORATE DISTRIBUTIONS[21]

There has been a good deal of controversy in the literature regarding the impact of taxes on corporate financial policy, particularly with respect to the effect of capital structure, financing decisions, and dividend policy. If there were a concensus, it would be logical to present it at this point. Unfortunately, the subject is clouded by controversy and contention. We lean toward the view that financial managers have favored internal finance over external and debt over equity, and that the preference has in part been tax-induced. Also, there is the position that dividend policy tendencies from 1920 to the present may be explained largely by factors, such as high individual tax rates and increasing corporate depreciation allowances under the tax laws. Rather than deal with these theoretical issues here we limit our discussion to technical tax aspects of corporate distributions.

For income tax purposes, corporate distributions may be divided into three categories:

- Dividends;
- Redemptions and purchases of stock; and
- Liquidations;
  a. Complete, and
  b. Partial.

Any distribution in excess of available earnings and profits will be treated as a return of capital. To the extent the distribution does not exceed the shareholder's basis for his stock, it will be applied to reduce such basis. To the extent it exceeds the basis the excess is taxed as a capital gain.

A distribution is taxable as a dividend to the recipient, whether made in cash or in other property, to the extent that it is made out of either the previously accumulated earnings of $10,000 and current year's earnings of $20,000. If it pays a single annual dividend of $40,000, the distribution would be a taxable dividend to shareholders to the extent of $30,000. Even though a corporation has a deficit at the beginning and at the end of its taxable year, if current year earnings are in excess of dividends paid during that year, the distribution will be taxable to the recipient. For example, a corporation has a deficit at the beginning of the taxable year of $10,000. It earns $25,000 during the taxable year and pays a dividend of $20,000. Thus, it has a deficit at the end of the year of $5,000. The dividends of $20,000 are taxable as income to the stockholders.

Where the stockholder is not a corporation, the amount of the dividend received will be considered as the amount of money received plus the fair market value of any other property at the date of distribution. In the case of a stockholder corporation, the value of the other property is considered as the lower of its fair market value or the adjusted basis[22] in the hands of the distributing corporation. The latter figure must be increased by any gain recognized to the distributing corporation in the case of a distribution of LIFO inventories or of property which is encumbered by a liability in excess of the adjusted basis of the property, or of property to which the so-called "recapture" rules apply. This property includes depreciable real or personal property. The Tax Reform Act of 1984 provides, almost universally, for corporate level gain recognition on a distribution of appreciated property. Thus, in practical effect, the amount of a distribution to a corporate recipient will be equivalent to the amount distributed to its non-corporate counterpart.

Where a corporation uses the LIFO method, gain is recognized to the extent of the difference between the inventory value under a method other than LIFO and the value pursuant to LIFO. If the property is encumbered by a liability or the stockholder assumes a liability of the corporation in connection with the distribution, and the liability exceeds the adjusted basis of the property in the hands of the corporation, gain will be recognized to the corporation equal to the amount of the liability less the adjusted basis of the distributed property. If, however, a liability is not assumed but is merely taken, "subject to", the corporation's gain cannot exceed the excess of the value of the property over its adjusted basis.

In instances where a corporation acquires the assets of another corporation in a tax-free reorganization[23] or tax-free liquidation, the earnings and profits of the acquired corporation become part of the retained earnings of the acquiring corporation. Any distribution of a dividend out of these earnings by the acquiring corporation will be taxable to the stockholder. Where one party has a deficit, however, such a deficit cannot be used to offset the other party's prior accumulations.

Earnings and profits are not necessarily the same as net income for income tax purposes. Earnings and profits as used to determine the taxability of dividends, include both taxable and exempt income and are reduced by corporate deductions even though nondeductible for tax purposes. The Internal Revenue Regulations provide that in determining the amount of earnings and profits, due consideration must be given to the facts; and while mere bookkeeping entries increasing or decreasing surplus will not be conclusive, the amount of the earnings and profits will be dependent upon the method of accounting employed in computing taxable income.[24]

More specifically, for the purpose of determining the taxability of dividends, fully tax-exempt interest must be added to the corporation's taxable income for the year. Also to be added are life insurance proceeds, the excess of percentage depletion over cost depletion, the corporate dividends received deduction,[25] and net operating losses from prior taxable years if used to reduce the current year's taxable income. In addition, the corporation must increase taxable income by the excess of depreciation deductions actually allowed over the amount available under the straight line method. Additions to taxable income added in the Tax Reform Act of 1984 include the deferred gain on installment sales and the excess of percentage of completion method income over completed contract income.

Deductions may be made for Federal income tax paid or accrued, life insurance premiums on the life of an officer, net capital losses, and charitable contributions in excess of the limitation. However, gains or losses on the sale or other disposition of property (such as the exchange of like kind property used in a trade or business) which are not recognized for tax purposes are not considered part of the earnings and profits for the purpose of determining the taxability of dividends.

Earnings and profits are reduced by the amount of any cash dividend. Where property is distributed, the amount of the decrease is the adjusted basis of the property. Earnings and profits must be increased when appreciated inventory assets are distributed.

No reduction of accumulated earnings and profits may be made in the case of nontaxable stock dividends or where a redemption or partial liquidation is accomplished and the distribution is chargeable to the capital account. A redemption or partial liquidation provides the corporation with the opportunity to reduce earnings and profits by disproportionately large amounts so that subsequent distributions are more likely to constitute returns of capital. This is so because in a redemption the charge to earnings is not limited to the redeemed shares' ratable portion thereof. Instead, the portion of the distribution that is attributable to unrealized appreciation in the corporation's assets is applied to reduce earnings. This rule, however, was altered in 1984. For distributions occurring after September 30, 1984, the reduction in taxable income is limited to the redeemed shares' ratable portion of taxable income.

The Code distinguishes between distributions in redemption of stock, which are to be treated as in payment for the stock exchanged (capital gain to the stockholder) and dividends (ordinary income). The general rule is that a distribution will be treated as a sale or exchange only if the redemption is not essentially equivalent to a dividend. In other words, on the shareholders' level, has there been a significant change of proprietary interest?

Three objective tests are enumerated in the Code which ensure that a redemption qualifies as an exchange for stock. Failure to meet these tests generally means that the redemption is considered a dividend unless the stockholder can prove that it is not the equivalent of a dividend. The three objective tests are:

- a substantially disproportionate redemption;
- a complete termination of the shareholder's interest; and
- a redemption of railroad stock pursuant to Section 77 of the Bankruptcy Act.

In determining whether a shareholder's interest has been reduced to the extent necessary to qualify for sale or exchange treatment, the Code provides for comprehensive "constructive" ownership rules. Thus, a shareholder will be treated as owning stock owned by members of his family and by entities of which he is a member.

A special provision exists where stock is redeemed to pay death taxes and estate expenses. If these redemptions meet the requirements of the Code, they will not be considered the equivalent of a dividend, even though they fail to qualify under the three objective tests.

Usually, amounts distributed in a liquidation of a corporation are considered as payments in exchange for stock. Liquidations may be considered complete or partial. (The Tax Equity and Fiscal Responsibility Act of 1982 (TEFRA) has narrowed the availability of the partial liquidation. Exchange treatment is only available to a non-corporate distributee: corporate shareholders are subject to the general rules governing redemptions discussed above.) A distribution is considered a partial liquidation if it is one of a series in redemption of all the stock of a corporation under a plan. A partial liquidation also covers a distribution not essentially equivalent to a dividend which is in redemption of a part of the stock under a plan of partial liquidation and which occurs within the taxable year in which the plan is adopted or the succeeding taxable year. Generally only a genuine contraction of a business will qualify as a partial liquidation, such as the discontinuance of a branch or a disposition of part of the business assets.

In a situation where a parent corporation completely liquidates a subsidiary, no gain or loss will be recognized to the parent upon receipt of the subsidiary's property. In order to be considered a tax-free liquidation, it must meet the following requirements:

- The parent, at the time of the adoption of the plan of liquidation and up to receipt of the property, must own at least 80 percent of the voting stock and at least 80 percent of all other stock (except nonvoting stock which is limited and preferred as to dividends); and
- The distribution must be in complete cancellation of all stock of the subsidiary, and the transfer of the property must take place within the taxable year; or
- The distribution must be one of a series of distributions in complete redemption of all the stock pursuant to a plan of liquidation to be completed within three years from the close of the taxable year in which the first distribution is made.

If at the time of the adoption of the plan the subsidiary was indebted to the parent, no gain or loss will be recognized to the subsidiary from the transfer of the property in satisfaction of the indebtedness. If, however, the subsidiary is "insolvent," that is, its indebtedness exceeds the fair value of the assets, the transaction will not qualify as a liquidation. Instead, the parent will be entitled to both a bad debt and worthless stock deduction. As a general rule, the property acquired in a complete liquidation of a subsidiary assumes the transferor's basis in the hands of the transferee. In the past an important exception to this rule provided that the parent's basis for the property may be determined by reference to its basis in the stock surrendered. This was the case under Sec. 334(b)(2) where the subsidiary's stock was obtained by "purchase" and where the liquidation plan is adopted within two years thereafter. For purchases occurring after August 31, 1982 Sec. 334(b)(2) is replaced by new Sec. 338 under which liquidation is no longer required and "step-up" treatment is available if an election is filed within eight and one-half months of the purchase. Under the election a target firm is deemed to have sold its assets to a new corporation for an amount equal to the value of such assets.

In the case of a close corporation, business transactions with shareholders will be carefully scrutinized by the IRS to see if they involve a disguised dividend. Thus, the corporation will be denied a deduction for excessive royalties paid to stockholder-licensors, excessive compensation paid to stockholder-officers, and excessive rent paid to stockholder-lessors. Also, alleged capital transactions may be deemed dividends and taxed as such to the recipient stockholders if they involve loans to stockholders where repayment is questionable; sales of securities or other corporate property to stockholders for less than fair market value; corporate purchases of property from stockholders for more than fair market value; or forgiveness by the corporation of a stockholder debt due to the corporation.

24.11 CORPORATE REORGANIZATIONS[26]

Gains and losses arising out of corporate reorganizations are treated under special provisions of the IRC designed to minimize tax barriers to normal business adjustments which involve transactions that do not basically alter the continuity of a business interest. As used in the IRC, the term corporate reorganization generally involves changes in capital structure of one or more corporations. It does not necessarily involve or mean bankruptcy.

Under the IRC, corporate reorganizations include "recapitalizations." A corporation may, without any immediate tax consequences, readjust its financial structure through a recapitalization. Typical tax-free recapitalizations include the exchange of existing preferred stock for new common stock, one class of common for another class of common, and existing bonds for new bonds. It is essential that a business purpose appropriate to the conduct of the firm serve as the basis for the transaction. If no business purpose other than tax minimization underlies the transaction and it, in fact, constitutes a device by which a disguised dividend is distributed, it will be treated in accordance with its real nature. For example, the exchange of existing common stock for new common stock and bonds will be treated, to the extent of the fair market value of the bonds, as the distribution of a corporate dividend, since the stockholders may now bail out corporate earnings by converting part of their equity to debt. Similarly, the distribution of a preferred stock dividend or the emergence of preferred stock in a recapitalization together with a sale of such preferred or its redemption—that is, the so called preferred stock bailout—is taxed as if the corporation had declared a dividend to its shareholders.

Under the IRC, the term corporate reorganization also covers mergers and acquisitions. The law allows shareholders of one corporation, as part of a merger or acquisition, to exchange, without tax consequences, their shares for shares of the corporation which has acquired the assets or stock of the corporation of which they were shareholders. Also, two corporations may consolidate by pooling their assets and issuing stock in a new corporation to the shareholders of both of the old corporations.

For these transactions to be treated as tax-free exchanges, besides meeting the statutory tests, two additional requirements imposed by the courts must be met. First, the transaction must have a real and not just an apparent business purpose. Second, the shareholders of the corporation or corporations which disappear must have a continuity of interest in the surviving or new corporation. The purpose of the so-called continuity of interest test is to insure that a purchase and sale of corporate assets or stock will not be disguised in the form of a corporate reorganization. For example, if all the shareholders of a corporation exchange their stock solely for bonds of the acquiring company, the continuity of interest requirement will not be met, for, in effect, they will have sold their equity interest to the new company. Under such circumstances, they are taxed at the time of the exchange. Further, a merger or acquisition, to constitute a reorganization, must also exhibit continuity of business enterprises. The IRS has adopted specific rules to define this concept. Under these rules continuity of business will not exist unless the acquiring party continues the acquired party's historic business or uses in a business a significant portion of the acquired's historic business assets. Thus, if the acquired party is engaged in manufacturing widgets, the acquiring party must continue this business. If it sells off the widget assets and uses them to further or commence a different business, continuity will be flunked. In a statutory merger (a reorganization) the continuity of proprietary interest test is met where at last 50% of the consideration received by the shareholders of the acquired entity consists of stock of the acquiring entity. In a 'B' reorganization, however, (acquisition of stock) or a 'C' reorganization (acquisition of assets) the test is more stringent; here, continuity is not met unless the consideration received by the shareholders consists solely of voting stock of the acquiring corporation.

Corporate separations are also included under the tax concept of corporate reorganizations. Under certain conditions, a corporation may be divided into two or more of its functioning business components without any immediate tax effects. For example, a corporation engaged in two separate businesses may spin-off one, distributing the stock in the new corporation to its shareholders. Or, where it holds the stock of a separately incorporated subsidiary, it may distribute these shares to its stockholders. In order to accomplish a tax-free corporate separation, a variety of complex statutory requirements must be met, involving the nature of the business, the previous record of activity and internal structure, the manner of stock distribution, and other matters. The tax law permits the division of existing corporations through the divestiture of phases of their business or of their subsidiaries for bona fide corporate reasons. Such transactions may result in the removal of corporate earnings or assets at capital gains rates through a tax-free spin-off and a sale at some later date of the distributed stock.[27]

Corporate liquidations as indicated earlier, are also covered under special provisions of the IRC. Unlike the corporate organization and reorganization provisions, these rules generally provide for taxation to the shareholder at the time of liquidation. Thus, when the stockholder surrenders his shares for cancellation or retirement and receives corporate assets in exchange, taxes are payable at capital gains rates, generally on the difference between the value of the assets received by the shareholder and the cost to him of the stock surrendered. Other special rules, however, as mentioned previously, permit the simplification of the corporate structure by allowing the tax-free liquidation of a subsidiary into its parent. The special rules also permit certain closely held corporations with appreciated assets, and not having large retained earnings, to liquidate with a minimal gain to the stockholders.[28]

24.12   GOING PUBLIC[29]

Sole proprietorships and partnerships desirous of obtaining additional capital in order to expand their business may have to incorporate. In addition, existing closely held or family owned corporations may have to make certain changes in their capital structure in order to induce the public to invest. These changes may create tax problems.

The general rule regarding the tax effect of a sale or exchange of property is that gain or loss resulting from the transaction will be recognized. However, there are a number of exceptions to this rule. In the case of certain exchanges, gain or loss may be postponed. These depend upon a statutory reorganization of a corporation or a condition which indicates that the new property is substantially a continuation of the old investment. It cannot be emphasized too strongly that gain is merely postponed. It does not mean that the gain is tax exempt.

When a sole proprietorship or partnership transfers property to a corporation solely in exchange for stock or securities of that corporation and the former owners are in control of the corporation immediately after the exchange, no gain or loss will be recognized on the exchange. The word control means the ownership, immediately after the exchange, of at least 80 percent of the total voting stock of all classes combined and at least 80 percent of the total outstanding shares of each class of nonvoting stock of the corporation. However, stock and securities issued for services performed for the controlled corporation or for debt of the transferee that is not evidenced by a security are not considered as issued in return for property so as to make the transfer nontaxable. The rendering of service will not be considered the equivalent of property. The recipient will be taxed on the fair market value of the securities received. When the transfer of property is by two or more individuals, it is not necessary that the parties receive back stock in proportion to their respective interest in the property prior to the exchange in order to make the transaction nontaxable between the individuals and the corporation. However, in appropriate cases such "disproportionate exchanges" may give rise to a gift or compensation constructively paid to the party who has received more stock and securities than he would otherwise have been entitled.

Where the taxpayer transfers property to a controlled corporation which assumes liabilities in excess of the total adjusted basis of the transferred property, the excess is considered taxable gain. For this purpose, the term liabilities will not include accounts payable of a cash basis transferor.

It is essential that the transferor and the corporation file information concerning the exchange with their respective income tax returns in the year in which the exchange was consummated. Where an incorporation precedes a secondary offering of stock to the public in amounts in excess of 20% of the new company's stock, the original transferors may be treated as having lost "control" and their incorporating transfers may be taxable. If, however, the public offering is effected expeditiously, the IRS has ruled that the public may be treated along with the initial incorporators as members of the same transferor group. In such a case the incorporating exchange will retain its tax-free status. Similarly, where the transferors sell stock that they have received in the exchange and where the sale was contemplated at that time, the control requirements may also be violated.

It may not always be advisable to transfer property to a corporation in a nontaxable exchange. Where property has increased in value, and it is transferred in a nontaxable exchange, the basis of the property in the hands of the corporation will be the old basis in the hands of the transferor. However, where the gain is recognized, the basis of the property to the corporation will be its current fair market value.

If a public issue entails only the sale of stock by a corporation, no taxable transaction results. The disposition by a corporation of shares of its own stock (including treasury stock) does not result in taxable gain or deductible loss to the corporation. The costs of issuing the stock are not deductible as an expense. They reduce the proceeds of the stock sale.

An existing corporation may have to make certain changes in its capital structure to induce public participation. Preferred stock, for example, may have to be redeemed. Whether the gain on redemption is to be treated as a capital gain or as dividend income becomes important. Problems involved in such a redemption were covered previously under the subject of corporate distributions (24.10). However, it must be remembered, that the purpose of these provisions is to prevent tax avoidance by disguising dividends as redemptions.

Another way to eliminate the preferred stock is to recapitalize the corporation. This would entail a corporate reorganization. The effect of a corporate reorganization is to render the exchange nontaxable in the same manner as a tax-free exchange. "The recognized purpose and scheme of the reorganization provisions is to omit from tax a change in form and to postpone the tax until there is a change in substance or a realization in money."[30]

The tax treatment of reorganizations is very technical. The taxpayer has the burden of proving that his transaction meets the technical reorganization provisions of the IRC in order to obtain the desired favorable tax treatment.

In order for a transaction to be treated as a reorganization, a business purpose must also be indicated as well as a continuity of interest. In Bazely v. Commissioner, the Supreme Court stated that the exchange of old shares prorata for new shares and callable 10-year debenture bonds did not constitute a reorganization. The court noted:

> What is controlling is that a new arrangement intrinsically partake of the elements of reorganization which underlie the Congressional exemption and not merely give the appearance of it to accomplish a distribution of earnings. In the case of a corporation which has undistributed earnings, the creation of new corporate obligations which are transferred to stockholders in relation to their former holdings, so as to produce, for all practical purposes, the same result as a distribution of cash earnings of equivalent value, cannot obtain tax immunity because cast in the form of a recapitalization-reorganization.[31]

The need to meet the demands of an underwriter for the retirement of preferred stock would appear to be a sufficient business purpose to satisfy any court requirement. The exchange of preferred for common would indicate a continuity of interest.

However, where the stockholder receives not only stock or securities permitted to be received without recognition of gain or loss, but also money and other property, that is, "boot",[32] gain is recognized, but not in excess of the "boot" received. In a reorganization, "boot" is taxed as ordinary income if the exchange has the effect of a dividend distribution. In situations where "boot" is prorata, that is where "boot" is distributed in proportion to stock ownership, the IRS will contend that the exchange has the effect of a dividend. However, certain Courts have disagreed and have found a capital gain even in cases where the "boot" was issued prorata. Loss is not recognized. Securities may be treated as "boot". They are limited to the fair market value of the excess of the principal amount received over the principal amount of the securities surrendered. If no securities are surrendered, the excess is the entire principal amount of the securities received.

In going public, the nonrecognition of gain to the corporation or its stockholders is one of the most important tax considerations. No gain or loss will be recognized to the corporation on the receipt of money or other property in exchange for its stock. If all that is involved is the sale of stock by the corporation to the public, no gain will be recognized. If any stock is subsequently sold by the stockholders, gain or loss on the sale will be recognized. The problem of going public, however, is seldom simple. Existing corporations may have to make certain changes in their capital structures. In order for these recapitalization transactions to be nontaxable, the taxpayer must meet the technical requirements of the IRC.

24.13   TAXATION OF INCOME FROM ABROAD[33]

In principle, the income of a U.S. corporation, wherever earned, is subject to the U.S. corporate income tax. Until 1962, however, foreign corporations, even though U.S.-controlled, were not subject to the U.S. corporate income tax until the income was paid out to the U.S. stockholder. Thus, tax deferral was possible. Furthermore, through the organization of "tax haven" corporations in certain strategic foreign locations, income could be accumulated in the foreign entity which either escaped taxation or could be brought home and taxed at capital gains rates.[34]

The situation resulted in a marked difference in the tax treatment accorded foreign branches in contrast with foreign subsidiaries of U.S. corporations. The income of the foreign branch was taxed currently, while the tax on the income of the foreign subsidiary was deferred until such income was actually repatriated. This situation and the concern over the effects on tax equity of the use of foreign "tax havens" led to the adoption in 1962 of rules for the attribution of the "subpart F" income of controlled foreign corporations (CFC).

The income which is attributed to the U.S. owners of the CFC includes "foreign-base company income." This consists of income derived by such corporations from certain types of passive investments, that is, dividends, interest, and certain types of rents and royalties. It also includes income from selling goods purchased from or performing services for related persons or corporations, when these goods or services are sold to or performed for persons or corporations outside the country in which the foreign corporation is incorporated. This provision is intended to forestall tax avoidance, which might occur if, for example, a U.S. company doing business in country X channeled the income earned in X to a subsidiary organized in country Y to take advantage of low tax rates in Y. In addition, a U.S. shareholder will be taxed on his share of the CFC's increase in earnings on the theory that such an investment constitutes a constructive repatriation, for the shareholder's benefit, of the CFC's accumulated earnings.

Prior to the passage of the Revenue Act of 1962, the accumulated income of foreign corporations could often be converted from ordinary income to capital gains at the time of repatriation through the redemption or sale of the stock of the corporation producing the foreign income. As a result of the 1962 Act, however, gains realized by a shareholder owning 10 percent or more of a foreign corporation, regardless of the transactions of the foreign corporation, are viewed as dividends, to the extent of the post 1962 earnings and profits attributable to the stock during the period the stock was owned while the foreign corporation was a CFC. This Act also provides that the gain on the sale or exchange of a patent, copyright, secret formula, or similar item sold by a parent corporation to a more than 50 percent controlled subsidiary be taxed as ordinary income.[35] The Tax Reform Act of 1976 extended this dividend treatment to encompass not only the sale, but also the distribution of the stock of a CFC by a corporate shareholder to its shareholders in a dividend or liquidating distribution.

In determining U.S. corporate tax liability, U.S. taxpayers may either (1) deduct from their gross income the amount of foreign taxes paid or (2) credit against their U.S. tax liability income taxes paid to foreign countries. The allowable foreign tax credit is limited. A U.S. corporation is allowed to credit against U.S. income tax the amount of income tax which is paid to foreign countries. The credit is allowed in full only if the effective total foreign tax rate is less than the U.S. tax rate applied to the same income. Thus, in general, the United States collects income tax to the extent of the difference between the lower worldwide foreign tax rate imposed on the U.S. taxpayers' foreign source income and the higher U.S. tax rate on this same income.

Since 1976 the overall limit on the foreign tax credit has been the only method available. This limit is the percentage of the total U.S. tax equal to the proportion which the income from all foreign countries bears to the total income of the taxpayer.

The law provides a proportional credit to an American corporation for the income taxes paid by a foreign corporation from which it receives dividends if the American corporation owns 10 percent or more of the foreign company's voting stock. A credit may also be obtained for taxes paid by a foreign subsidiary of such a foreign corporation if the latter holds at least 10 percent of the voting stock of the former. In fact, the American corporation may claim a credit even for taxes paid by a third tier foreign subsidiary as long as the 10 percent test is met at each level and the domestic parent owns indirectly 5 percent of the voting power of each. Foreign taxes denied as credits under the limitation detailed above may be carried back to the two preceding taxable years and forward to the five succeeding taxable years.

When a domestic corporation receives dividends from a foreign subsidiary and elects to take the foreign tax credit, it must "gross up" its tax base by including not only the dividends received but also the income tax paid by the foreign corporation on the earnings from which the dividends were paid. For example, a domestic corporation which receives $100 of dividends from a foreign subsidiary where the tax rate on net income is 20 percent, includes $125 in its gross income and claims a tax credit for foreign taxes paid of $25. "Gross up" has been described as an attempt to put a foreign subsidiary operation in the same position as a branch of a U.S. corporation for purposes of the foreign tax credit.

The special complexities of the taxation of operations abroad have been recognized by the IRS in creating a separate office to deal with such problems, and staffing it with specialists who spend all their time on the taxation of international business. The financial manager of a corporation engaged in overseas operations can do no less. At least one high level specialist in the tax department should spend full time on the analysis of the peculiarly intricate problems associated with the taxation of income from foreign sources. These complexities are illustrated by the special rules in Sec. 367 that apply to organizations, liquidations, and reorganizations involving foreign corporations.

24.14 TAX TREATMENT OF RETIREMENT PLANS[36] AND DEFERRED COMPENSATION

Financial managers have had a growing responsibility in the selection and conduct of retirement and deferred compensation plans which, while maximizing benefits to employees, minimize the cost to the company. The tax treatment of the various types of arrangements can enter importantly in cost considerations.

Generally speaking the tax treatment of various types of retirement plans does not vary greatly. Where a trust has been formed as part of an employer's pension, profit-sharing, or stock bonus plan for the exclusive benefit of his employees or their beneficiaries, the income from the trust is not taxable if the plan meets the following conditions:

- the plan is permanent;
- distributions of benefits under the plan are on the basis of some predetermined formula;
- the principal or income from the fund is not used for any purpose other than distribution to employees until all commitments to employees and their beneficiaries have been met;
- the plan benefits either:
  a. 70 percent of all the employees, or 80 percent of all eligible employees, provided not less than 70 percent of all employees are eligible, or
  b. all employees within a classification which does not discriminate in favor of certain highly paid employees, and
- the contributions and benefits under the plan do not discriminate in favor of highly paid employees.[37]

A plan which meets these "nondiscrimination" tests and other tests as to funding, participation and vesting is referred to as a qualified plan. Although advance rulings by the IRS on the qualifications of plans are not required, if such a ruling is requested it will be issued by the local district director.

The tax treatment of the employer's contribution to a retirement plan depends first on whether such a plan qualifies under the provisions of Section 401 of the IRC and, second, on the nature of the plan. If the retirement plan qualifies under Section 401, the extent of the employer's deduction for contributions depends on whether it is a pension, profit-sharing, or stock bonus plan. Deductions for contributions to qualified pension plans, whether trusteed or not, may not exceed 5 percent of covered payrolls, except where a larger amount is necessary to provide the unfunded cost of past and current service credits, distributed as a level amount or as a level percentage of compensation for the future service of each employee. As an alternative, the employer may deduct the amount actuarially necessary to pay the normal cost of the plan for the current year (on the assumption that it has been in effect since the beginning of the covered service of each employee), plus 10 percent of total past and supplementary service costs as of the date they are included in the plan.[38] The employer's contributions to qualified profit-sharing and stock bonus plans are deductible up to 15 percent of the compensation of covered employees.[39] Where qualified pension, profit-sharing, or stock bonus plans have been established in combination, the employer's deductible contributions are limited to 25 percent of the compensation of covered employees.[40]

Employees participating in a qualified retirement plan do not include in their current taxable income amounts representing their employer's contribution to such plans. Tax liability results only when benefits are distributed.[41] Employees may not deduct their own contributions to the plan.

Deferred compensation contracts differ from pension and similar retirement programs in that they do not constitute a formal plan providing retirement benefits for employees generally (or for a particular group of employees, where the nondiscriminatory requirements of Section 401 are observed), and they are therefore usually not funded. Under such contracts, the employee agrees to forego a specified portion of current compensation which will be paid to him over a specified and limited period of time in the future, often after retirement.

The employer is permitted to deduct amounts paid as deferred compensation to employees only in the year when paid, regardless of the fact that the employee is no longer rendering service in the employer's behalf, as long as the total compensation is reasonable when measured by the years of active employment. As far as the employer is concerned, therefore, salary payments under deferred compensation contracts may not be deducted until actually distributed to the employee, even though accruing in a year preceding distribution.

TEFRA changed the overall limits on contributions and benefits available under pension plans. For defined benefit plans, the maximum *dollar* limit on benefits is lowered to $90,000 from the previous $136,425 (the dollar percentage of annual compensation is not changed). The maximum sum that can be contributed to defined contribution plans (e.g., profit-sharing and savings plans) is reduced to $30,000 from $45,475. These new limits, first effective in 1983, were increased in 1986, at which point they were adjusted for post 1984 cost of living increases as measured by the social security benefit index used at that time. The percentages of compensation limits (25 percent for defined contribution plans and 100 percent for defined benefit plans) are not changed, except that for most disabled, contributions may now be based on their compensation prior to disability.

The new $90,000 defined benefit limit for highly compensated individuals is actuarially increased for benefits commencing after age 65. If benefits are payable prior to age 62, the $90,000 limit is actuarially reduced, using an interest rate of at least 5 percent, but not below $75,000 at age 55. If retirement occurs before age 55, the $75,000 floor is reduced.

The aggregate limit on benefits for a participant covered by both a defined contribution and a defined benefit plan maintained by the same employer is reduced from 140 percent to 125 percent of the otherwise applicable separate *dollar* limits. This means the aggregate benefits in the two plans cannot exceed by more than 25 percent the maximum benefits allowed in any one plan. The 140 percent aggregate limit continues to apply where the limits on the benefits applicable to the separate plans are determined by a percentage of compensation rather than dollar amounts. Because this situation applies only to participants subject to the dollar limitations it generally has only affected highly paid employees.

The major impact of TEFRA on pension contributions relates to senior management. The Act forces more pension benefits to be paid outside qualified plans through unfunded, nonqualified excess benefits plans. Current charges against earnings for such nonqualified plans are not tax deductible until paid to the employee.

24.15   CHAPTER SUMMARY

From this cursory examination of some of the complex and intricate aspects of the taxation of domestic and foreign corporate income, the need for expert tax managemen and planning in even a fair-sized company must be apparent. Reporting directly to the Vice President-Finance should be a Tax Manager who is both a certified public accountant and a lawyer. Not only should his department be charged with routine tax management duties, such as the preparation and filing of hundreds of tax returns and their supporting schedules as well as the gathering of the internal data necessary for effective tax reporting, but, more importantly, it should be engaged in continuous tax planning.

Nearly every major and many minor corporate decisions involve tax consequences. Often the tax consequences of alternative courses of action will help shape the decision. The tax manager needs to be involved in advance in the planning of any major corporate move. For this to occur, there needs to be an awareness on the part of top corporate management of the savings which can result from effective tax planning. It takes quite a while in most cases to generate such an awareness and its resultant action—the involvement of the tax manager in both short- and long-run planning and in major corporate policy decisions.

The tax manager must receive advance notification of proposed corporate moves, such as the acquisition or disposition of a plant, or a function, or of costly assets; changes in existing capital structure, or, method of doing business; the reshuffling of corporate structures, involving affiliates, subsidiaries, mergers, consolidations, negotiation of contracts, licenses, sales agreements, leasebacks, exchanges, and other commitments. The tax consequence of all such actions, if contemplated, should be explored in advance, and top management should be informed of the results of the tax evaluations and surveys.

Management should be warned of proposed courses of action which appear to be vulnerable to tax challenges by the IRS. For example, an advance to a thinly capitalized corporation will be regarded as an equity investment rather than as a loan, regardless of what is alleged, and related payments by the recipient corporation will not be allowed as interest expense or treated as a return of capital, but will be treated as nondeductible dividends. Or if the terms of a so-called rental agreement are such as to give the lessee an equity in the rented property, the agreement will be treated as a purchase and the "rental" payments will be regarded as capital expenditures. Or in an acquisition, the net operating loss of an acquired corporation may not be utilizable because of the extent of changes both in the ownership and in the conduct of the business. Or the organization (or reorganization) of a foreign based corporation may not qualify as tax-free because the requisite IRS approval was not obtained in advance of the action.

An alert tax manager who functions in a planning role, in addition to his other operating duties, will warn management of the tax consequences of its proposed moves and analyze alternative courses of action in terms of relative tax costs, as well as make proposals for corporate moves designed to alleviate the tax burden. In the course of any calendar year, the financial savings which flow from his tax advice can more than compensate for the cost of his services. Effective financial management requires highly competent tax planning, not just routine performance of tax department duties.

FOOTNOTES

1. Our purpose in this chapter is only to present an introduction to corporate tax management. So vast and complex is the field that a mere chapter can do little more than provide an initial orientation.
2. 319 U.S. 523 (1943).
3. See Chapter 14 for a discussion of depreciation methods.
4. For an extended analysis of the financial aspects of treasury stock, see Chapter 21.
5. IRC Section 118(a).
6. Gifts are taxable to the donor, not to the donee.
7. IRC Regulations, Section 1.311-1(e)(1), Rev. Rul. 83-38, I.R.B. 1983-10, 10.
8. IRC Section 1032.
9. For an extended analysis of the financial aspects of corporate dividend policy, see Chapter 14.
10. Adjusted ordinary gross income means gross income less capital gains, less certain deductions attributable to rents and royalty income and less certain items of interest income.
11. A tax option corporation, also referred to as a "Subchapter S" corporation, cannot be a member of an affiliated group except in the situation where it solely owns inactive subsidiaries.
12. For an extended analysis of the financial aspects of leasing in general and the lease versus purchase decision in particular, see Chapter 22.
13. Revenue Ruling 55-540, "Guide to Be Used in Determining the Treatment for Federal Income Tax Purposes of Leases of Equipment Used in the Trade or Business of the Lessee," *Internal Revenue Bulletin 35,* August 29, 1955. Also see *Frank Lyon Co. v. U.S.,* 435 U.S. 578 (1977).
14. See Chapter 22.
15. May Department Stores Co., 16 TC 547 (1950).
16. Century Electric Company v. Commissioner, 15 TC 581 (1950), 192 F. 2d 155 20 Cir (1951), cerc. den. 342 U.S. 954 (1952).
17. IRC Section 1031.
18. 15 TC 41 (1950).
19. Jordan Marsh v. Commissioner, 269 F. 2d 453 (CA 2. 1959).
20. 33 TC 1 (1962).
21. For an extended analysis of the financial aspects of corporate dividend policy, see Chapter 14.
22. By adjusted basis of property we usually mean the cost of the property plus any additional capital expenditures made on it and less any depreciation taken and any dispositions (sales).
23. A tax free reorganization is strictly defined in the Code and is discussed later in the chapter. Even if the transactions meet the strict statutory rules, they will not be considered as tax-free unless there is also a good business purpose for the transactions and a continuity of proprietary interest. Thus, the introduction of new capital and new stockholders in what would otherwise be a tax-free reorganization

may make the transaction taxable. In such an event, the prereorganization earnings of the predecessor will be considered in determining the taxability of future distributions.

24. IRC Regulations, Section 1.312-6(a).
25. This deduction is taken in arriving at taxable income and amounts to 85 percent of the dividends received from other domestic corporations. The percentage is increased to 100 percent in the case of certain affiliated corporations. See Dividend-Received Deduction section in this chapter (24.7).
26. For an extended analysis of the financial aspects of corporate reorganizations, see Chapter 21.
27. See Robert Willens, "Section 355—The Minefield of Subchapter C," *The CPA Journal,* April 1980.
28. Under the provisions of Section 333, the liquidation must be effectuated within one calendar month.
29. For an extended analysis of the financial aspects of initial public stock issuance, see Chapter 13.
30. Morey Cypress Trust, et. al., 3 TC 84 (1944).
31. 331 U.S. 737 (1947).
32. "Boot" is considered as something in addition, specifically cash or nonlike property received in reorganizations or other exchanges. It is the consideration received in addition to that which may be exchanged tax-free. Where "boot" is given, the taxpayer giving the "boot" has no tax consequences. "Boot", however, is generally taxed to the recipient.
33. For an extended analysis of the financial aspects of multinational operation, see Chapter 23.
34. A foreign corporation is considered controlled if more than 50 percent of its voting stock is controlled by U.S. persons or companies, all of whom own at least 10 percent of the voting stock.
35. IRC, Section 1242.
36. For an extended analysis of the financial aspects of retirement plans, see Chapter 25.
37. IRC, Section 401.
38. Amounts contributed in excess of the deductible portion under these limitations may be deducted in succeeding taxable years to the extent of the difference between the amount contributed and the amount deductible under the limitations in each succeeding year.
39. Contributions in excess of 15 percent of covered compensation may be carried over and deducted in succeeding taxable years within the preceding limitation. On the other hand, in years in which the contribution is less than 15 percent of covered compensation, a credit carryover arises which is available in succeeding years to absorb contributions exceeding the 15 percent limit.
40. IRC Section 404. Contributions in excess of this amount may be deducted in succeeding taxable years, provided the total deduction does not exceed 30 percent of the compensation of covered employees.
41. IRC, Section 402.

SUGGESTED READINGS

Asofsky, Paul H., and William Tatlock, "Reorganization, Procedures and Corporate Taxes Greatly Affected by Bankruptcy Tax Act," *Journal of Taxation,* March 1981.
Bandy, Dale, "How to Minimize the Threat of the Accumulated Earnings Tax," *Practical Accountant,* February 1981.

700

Bittker, Boris I. and James S. Eustice. *Federal Income Taxation of Corporations and Shareholders*, New York, Warren, Gorham and Lamont, 1979.

Cavitch, Zolman, *Tax Planning for Corporations and Shareholders*, New York, Mathew Bender, 1980.

Clestal, Jack, et. al., "Working with Consolidated Returns: Why, When and How," *Practical Accountant*, July 1981.

Dichman, H. T., "Business Approach to Subchapter S," *Journal of Small Business Management*, January 1981.

"FASB Proposes Standard Regarding Sale or Purchase of Tax Benefits Under ERTA," *Journal of Accountancy*, December 1981.

Fuller, James P., "Rules Governing Income Earned Abroad and Employer Allowances Simplified by ERTA," *Journal of Taxation*, January 1982.

Hoffman, William H., *Corporations, Partnerships, Estates, and Trusts*, West Publishing Co., 1979.

Homer, A. and R. Burrows, "Taxation of Overseas Earnings," *Accountancy*, May 1981.

Ivy, Madie and Robert Willens, "Proposed Sec. 385 Regulations Bring Order Out of Chaos," *N.Y. State C.P.A. Journal*, October 1980.

Johnson, G., "Tax Law Boosts ESOPs, Backers Say," *Industry Week*, October 5, 1981.

Kapleau, Paul H., "Acquisitive Reorganizations: A Look at the Tax and Accounting Rules," *Practical Accountant*, May 1981.

Kelliher, William B. and Murray B. Schwartzberg, "How the New Tax Law Affects Businesses," *Practical Accountant*, December 1981.

Kreiser, Larry and Richard Kender, "How to Select the Optimum Depreciable Life of Business," *Journal of Taxation*, March 1981.

Lenrow, G. I. and H. J. Cuddy, "Analysis of the Economic Recovery Tax Act of 1981." *Best's Review*, October 1981.

Lowenthal, Franklin, "Decision Model for the Alternative Tax on Capital Gains," *Accounting Review*, April 1981.

Ludwig, Ronald L. and John E. Curtis, Jr., "ESOPs Made Substantially More Attractive as a Result of Economic Recovery Tax Act," *Journal of Taxation*, October 1981.

Murray, S. H., "Lease in Name Only," *Nations Business*, November 1981.

1984 Federal Tax Course, Englewood Cliffs, N.J., Prentice Hall, 1983.

Perkins, T. R., "Family Partnerships: One Possible Means of Saving Income and Estate Tax Dollars," *Trusts and Estates*, August 1980.

Schneider, Leslie J., *Federal Income Taxation of Inventories*, New York, Mathew Bender, 1980.

Tarr, Herbert, "Basic Tax Guide to Acquisitions," *Practical Accountant*, August 1981.

Weinman, Herbert M., "Conformity of Tax and Financial Accounting," *Taxes*, July 1981.

Weiss, J. M. and I. Blumenfrucht, "ERTA's Incentives for R&D," *Management Accounting*, February 1982.

Willens, Robert, "Section 355—The Minefield of Subchapter C," *The CPA Journal*, April 1980.

APPENDIX A:
SELECTING THE FORM OF ORGANIZATION

In the choice of the form in which to conduct business activities, careful consideration must be given to the various methods available. If certain corporate attributes are desired, such as limited liability and uninterrupted business existence, the tax consequences of this form of business organization must be weighed against those of a partnership or sole proprietorship. The failure to consider these points may create problems at a future date.

Each year numerous corporations are either created or dissolved primarily for the purpose of effecting tax minimization. There are tax disadvantages as well as advantages to operating as a corporation. Although all ordinary income is subject to a graduated tax, capital gains of a corporation on the sale of assets held over one year are taxed at a maximum rate of 28 percent. There is a minimum tax of 15% on certain tax preferences in excess of the greater of regular income taxes paid or $10,000. This tax is in addition to the normal income tax. Most states also tax corporations on their income or capital allocable to that state. Furthermore, there is double taxation of corporate income as the corporation does not get a deduction for dividends paid to stockholders who are also required to pay a tax on the receipt of the dividend. There are also a number of penalty taxes, like that on improperly accumulated earnings (24.4) and the tax on personal holding companies (24.5).

For federal income tax purposes a partnership is not subject to tax as such. The partnership is considered as a conduit, the individual member of the partnership being taxed on his distributive share of partnership income. A sole proprietorship is taxed directly.

In the case of a partnership or sole proprietorship, the income of the business retains its basic nature, in the hands of the owners. Usually, in the case of a corporation, the character of a distribution is changed. For example, short- and long-term capital gains and losses and contributions of the partnership or sole proprietorship are treated as such by the partner or proprietor on his individual return. In the case of a current distribution by a corporation from capital gains, the distribution will be treated by the stockholder as ordinary dividend income.

To insure a minimum overall tax cost, the owners of a corporation will attempt to offset the corporate earnings by withdrawing reasonable salaries for themselves. Salaries to the corporate owners are free from the corporate income tax. Among other points to consider are corporate dividend policy (24.7) outside sources of income of the owners of the business, unreasonable accumulation of surplus (24.4), personal holding company tax (24.5), and multiple entities (24.6).

There are obvious tax advantages to the corporate form of organization. It is easier to split income among the members of a family by incorporating a business and making a gift of stock, than through the use of a family partnership. In the case of dissolution, the corporate form produces a tax benefit to the shareholders in that liquidation may be achieved at capital gain rates. In addition, certain fringe benefits, such as stock options (24.8), deferred payment plans (24.14), and group term insurance, are available to the corporate stockholder-officer because he is considered an employee. Certain closely held corporations have the right to elect to be taxed similar to partnerships and yet assure their stockholder-officers the employee benefits of a corporate form of organization. If such an election is made, some tax deficiencies of the corporate form, like the loss of the right to pass the capital gain income through to the stockholders, the double tax on corporate income, and the penalty tax on improper accumulation of surplus (24.4) may be eliminated.

APPENDIX B:
FILING AND PAYMENT OF CORPORATE TAX

The corporate federal income tax return must be filed in the Internal Revenue district where the corporation has its principal place of business or principal office or agency. The return on Form 1120 is due on or before the fifteenth day of the third month after the close of the corporation's year, subject to two three month extensions, the first being automatic upon request by the due date. A corporation must pay its estimated tax installments, if its income tax is expected to exceed $40. The first installment is generally due by the fifteenth day of the fourth month of the taxable year. Any underpayment of estimated corporate taxes, with certain exceptions, is currently subject to a penalty charge of 16 percent per annum on the amount of the underpayment for the period of underpayment. However, no penalty for under-payment will be assessed if the corporation takes the last year's tax, and uses this as an estimated tax, or if the corporation uses the information on the prior year's return to compute a tax at this year's rates, or pays an amount equal to 90 percent of the tax on the current income. (For corporations with taxable income of $1,000,000 or more in any of the three immediately preceding years, only the latter exception is applicable.

A corporation is subject to tax rates based upon different brackets on ordinary taxable income up to $100,000, and 46% for ordinary income above $100,000. In determining taxable income, the problems involved in computing gross income and deductions are the same as for an individual engaged in a trade or business. To be deductible, an expense must be ordinary and necessary, paid or incurred during the taxable year, and specifically authorized by the Internal Revenue Code (IRC). There are some provisions regarding deductions, however, peculiar to corporations. A corporation may deduct:

- Eighty-five percent of dividends received from taxable domestic corporations and certain foreign corporations;
- Amortization of organizational expenditures for a period not less than sixty months;
- Partially tax-exempt interest on U.S. Savings and Treasury bonds issued prior to March 1941;
- Dividends paid on certain preferred stock of a public utility; and
- Dividends received from certain preferred stock of a public utility.

Certain closely held "small business" or "Subchapter S Corporations" may elect to have the corporate income taxed directly to the stockholders rather than to the corporate entity. To be eligible for this "tax option", the corporation must meet certain requirements. It must be a domestic corporation, and have no more than 35 shareholders. It cannot be a member of an affiliated group, although it may own stock in a subsidiary corporation that has not begun business and has no taxable income. All shareholders must be individuals, estates, or certain types of trusts. No resident alien may be a stockholder, and the corporation may not have more than one class of stock outstanding. (Differences in voting rights, however, are permitted.) In addition, to the extent the corporation has passive income (income from rents, interest, dividends, royalties, annuities or gains from sales or exchanges of securities) in excess of 25 percent of gross receipts in any year, the increment above 25 percent will be taxed at the maximum corporate rate. There is no limit on the permissable net worth or volume of business.

The shareholder of such an electing corporation is taxed on his prorata share of corporate income, whether distributed or not. He thus avoids the double taxation involved when an ordinary corporation pays one tax on the corporate earnings and the stockholder pays a second tax on the distribution of the earnings in the form of dividends.

Rules similar to those for partnerships apply to pension plans of a Subchapter S Corporation and to employee fringe benefits. For this purpose any person owning 2 percent or more of the corporate stock is treated as a partner. The fringe benefits barred to such shareholders include:

- Group term life insurance;
- Death benefit exclusion; and
- Exclusion for amounts paid from an accident or health plan.

Corporate capital gains, and corporate ordinary income generally may be passed through to the year and shareholders, who pick up these items on their individual tax returns. Corporate net operating losses from tax option corporations as passed through to shareholders based on the number of days they held the stock during the year. An election for this tax option, once made, remains effective for all future years until terminated. Should a revocation or termination occur, a five year period is generally required before reinstating the election.

APPENDIX C:
ACCOUNTING METHODS

The IRC does not prescribe any specific method of accounting. Taxable income must be computed by that method regularly used by the taxpayer. But the method employed must reflect income clearly. In addition, the method used must be consistent from year to year unless permission is received from the Commissioner of Internal Revenue to change.

There are two methods available for reporting income and expenses. These are: (1) the cash basis, and (2) the accrual basis. However, variations are permitted or required in certain instances. As a general rule, a request for a change in accounting method must be made within 180 days after the beginning of the tax year in which the taxpayer wants to make the change. The Commissioner's consent is not needed where a subsidiary corporation must change its method to conform to that of an affiliated group in order to file a consolidated return.

Corporate net income reported for tax purposes will usually differ from net income reflected on the books of the company. Certain income items recorded on the books, such as proceeds of key man life insurance or interest earned on state and municipal bonds, are not included in income for tax purposes, while some book deductions, such as life insurance premiums on the life of a corporate officer (where the corporation is the beneficiary) and interest paid on a loan to purchase tax-exempt bonds, are not deductible for tax purposes. The basic corporate tax form, 1120, has a schedule the purpose of which is to show the reconciliation between the income shown on the books and the income reported for tax purposes, as well as an analysis of all changes in the corporate surplus account not affecting income.

Special methods of accounting are allowed or required by the Code. There are special rules, for example, for reporting installment sales, income from long-term contracts, the valuation of inventory, deductions for depreciation, bad debts, depletion, and other items.

In its first return, a taxpayer may elect that method of valuing inventory which is in conformity with practices in the trade and which clearly reflects income. Whichever method is chosen, it should be consistently applied from year to year. The Commissioner places greater emphasis on consistency than on choice of method as long as the method employed conforms to the code requirements.

In manufacturing and retail operations, the most significant item in determining the cost of goods sold is inventory. The choice of method in the valuation, therefore, can have a material effect on the business net income and hence on the taxpayer's income tax liability.

The principal methods employed in such evaluation are (1) cost, and (2) cost or market whichever is lower. Cost may be determined by specific identification, or on a first in, first out (FIFO), a last in, first out (LIFO) or an average cost basis. Market means the bid price existing at the inventory date. (See Chapter 10).

The elements of cost to be considered in the case of merchandise or raw materials purchased are the invoice price of goods, less trade and other discounts plus freight duty or other transportation charges incurred in acquiring possession of the goods and indirect production costs incident to and necessary for items of production. Cash discounts approximating a fair interest rate may or may not be deducted at the option of the taxpayer, provided a consistent course is followed.

The inventory on hand also may include merchandise produced by the taxpayer. The cost of this merchandise is determined on the basis of the cost of raw materials and supplies consumed, expenditures for direct labor, and expenditures for manufacturing overhead.

The election to use LIFO is optional with the taxpayer and is made by filing form 970 with the tax return for the first taxable year for which the method is adopted. The election, once made, must be continued until permission to change is secured from the IRS. If LIFO is adopted for tax purposes, it must be used in annual reports to stockholders and for credit purposes. LIFO may, however, be used for only a portion of the inventory, while the remainder may be computed by any other method.[1]

The use of LIFO gives the company greater control over variations in its profitability due to price level changes. If prices are rising and the firm wants to reduce its reported profits over what they would otherwise be, it can increase its acquisition of inventory toward the end of the year. On the other hand, if profits are falling (though prices are increasing), it can increase its stated profitability by failing to replace inventory, letting it run down, thereby charging into the cost of sales for the current year inventory carried at costs based on lower prices in prior years. If prices are falling, it can reverse the techniques in the two instances. However, if decreases in inventory in a period of rising costs are not replaced by year end, LIFO may cause a greater tax than FIFO.

---

1 Under LIFO a taxpayer may still use FIFO, and average cost computation, or any other proper method in the view of the Internal Revenue Service, for determining the cost of any increase in units over the opening inventory.

APPENDIX D:
ACCOUNTING PERIODS

Net income for federal income tax purposes, must be reported on an annual accounting basis. With certain limitations, the taxpayer has the right to choose an accounting period or to change accounting periods.

A new corporate taxpayer, where it maintains a set of books, may choose any year end. This period must be consistent in future years unless, under certain conditions, the permission of the Commissioner is received. The choice is restricted to a calendar year or fiscal year. The term calendar year means a 12-month period ending on December 31. A fiscal year is one that covers a 12-month period and normally ends on the last day of the month other than the month of December. The term fiscal year may include a 52-53 week year. This method has an annual period that varies from 52 to 53 weeks with each week ending on the same day of the week. For example, in the retail field, each week ends on a Saturday and each "month" consists of four such weeks, the fiscal year consisting of 13 "months". Because of the 52-53 week concept, the fiscal year may thus not always end on the last day of a particular month.

What facts should be considered in selecting a year end? If a business is seasonal, a "natural" year is preferred. This is usually the time of year when inventories and accounts receivable are at their lowest, and when the business shows the best cash position. In the retail field, for example, January 31 is considered a "natural" year end.

Where seasonal factors are minor any year end may be considered. However, in the case of a small closely held corporation, the accounting load of the taxpayer's tax advisor should be considered, as well as the requirements of preparing financial statements. In addition, it must be remembered that the accounting period of an affiliated company which is involved in a consolidated return must generally be the same as the taxable year of the parent corporation.

The tax year for a corporation begins at the time of incorporation. Its first taxable year may be selected for any period not exceeding 12 months from incorporation, and must be adopted on or before the time for filing the return for such taxable year. The time for filing a corporate return is 2½ months after the close of the taxable year.

For example, a company is incorporated on April 9. The corporation has the right to end its first year at any time up to and including March 31 of the following year. If it elects to close its first "year" on January 31, the tax period will run from April 9 to January 31 of the following year. Its tax return will be due on or before April 15 of the calendar year in which its tax year ends. The next tax period will consist of the months from February 1 to January 31 of the following year.

If a taxpayer desires to change its accounting period it must first obtain permission from the Commissioner by filing an application on Form 1128. A corporate taxpayer does not have to obtain permission where:

- It has not changed its annual accounting period at any time within the 10 prior calendar years;
- The short tax year required to effect the change (a period less than 12 months) is not a taxable year in which there was a net operating loss; and
- The taxable income for the short tax year when placed on an annual basis is 80 percent or more of the taxable income for the taxable year immediately preceding the short period.

Where a return is filed for a short tax year because of a change in accounting period, that is, the period from the end of the old tax year to the beginning of the new, the net income for the short period must be "annualized". After the tax is computed on the annualized income, it is prorated for the number of months in the short period. The annualizing of income is accomplished by multiplying the income for the short tax year by a fraction whose numerator is 12 and whose denominator is the number of months in the short period.

For example, assume a corporate taxpayer has been reporting income on a calendar years basis. It decides to change to a fiscal year ending October 31. Its taxable income for the 10 months, the short tax year, amounted to $25,000. The tax on an annual basis would be $4,650 ($25,000 at 15 percent and $5,000 at 18 percent). The tax for the 10-month period, however, would be $3,875 ($4,650 x 10/12). The proration of the annualized tax is completed by reversing the fraction.

In selecting the short tax year, it is preferable to avoid a peak period. Thus, if the corporation in the above illustration were in the retail field, with a peak period in December, its annualized income for the 10 months would be less than regular income for the period January 1 through December 31. This is due to the fact that the most profitable months, November and December, have not been included in the annualizing calculation.

APPENDIX E:
CORPORATE MINUTES

The effect of corporate minutes on federal taxation cannot be minimized. In 1935 the Board of Tax Appeals, in a case dealing with an unreasonable accumulation of surplus, emphasized the importance of proper minute writing when it stated:

> The testimony concerning the purpose for which the corporation was formed and the purpose for which its surplus was accumulated is corroborated by the minutes of the meeting of the directors of the company—the contemporaneous record reflecting the company's activities and the reasons therefore. We are not ready to disregard this testimony or say that the recorded thoughts of the

company's guiding heads, the writing of which was begun more than a decade ago, was artfully drawn for self-service against the future day of a trial. Those denials of wrongful intent, those declarations of a purpose other than the avoidance of taxes in the building of a surplus, we believe, as against the evidence of circumstances from which might be drawn inferences to the opposite effect.[1]

Many tax cases are won and lost at the time of the writing of minutes. Tax management and planning must include the preparation of proper minutes.

What are some of the tax problems that may be avoided by writing correct minutes? While these are numerous and varied, only a cursory examination of specific problems can be undertaken here.

Numerous instances arise where a stockholder lends money to a corporation and the IRS attempts to treat the advance as an additional contribution to capital. As part of the supporting evidence that the advance was intended as a loan and not as a capital contribution, the recording of this fact, together with all the terms of the loan, in the minutes, would be helpful proof of the nature of the transaction. It is in the corporation's interest that advances be accepted as loans as any interest paid on loans is a deductible expense, whereas a dividend payment on equity is not deductible. Proposed regulations issued by the IRS in this area increase the need for documentation because of the presumptions contained in these regulations.

Care should be exercised to show in the minutes that where variations take place from year to year in executive compensation, the reasons for the variations are differences in performance. Otherwise the IRS may contend that the fluctuating payments to officer-stockholders constitute disguised dividends.

Contributions to charitable organizations are deductible when paid. However, in the case of an accrual basis corporation, where a payment is made on or before the fifteenth day of the third month following the close of the corporation's taxable year, at the election of the corporation the contribution may be considered as paid in the taxable year. The contribution, to be deductible, must be authorized by the Board of Directors during the taxable year. If such an election is made, an authenticated copy of the minutes adopted during the taxable year authorizing the contribution must be attached to the corporation's tax return.

In instances where a corporation may want to make a death benefit payment to the widow of a deceased officer and permit her to exclude the payment from her income as a "gift", it is important that the minutes show a donative intent. The wording of the minutes granting the "gift" becomes very important. Generally, where the minutes state that the payment was made to the widow in recognition of the faithful services rendered to the corporation by the deceased, the payment will be treated as compensation. Gift status is generally difficult to establish for payments to families of former employees.

1 Cecil B. DeMille Productions, Inc., 31 BTA 1161 (1935).

FINANCIAL ASPECTS OF EMPLOYEE PENSION PROGRAMS AND OTHER FORMS OF EXTRA COMPENSATION

25.1 INTRODUCTION—THE FINANCIAL MANAGER'S ROLE IN ADMINISTERING PENSION PROGRAMS AND OTHER FORMS OF EXTRA COMPENSATION*

The financial manager does not normally have direct responsibility for the determination, administration and supervision of the employee pension program and other forms of extra compensation of a large firm. These increasingly important aspects of corporate life, however, have significant financial implications and, to this extent, represent an important input into the overall financial planning of the firm. Moreover, in smaller firms, the financial manager may play a more direct role in the development and administration of the pension program and the company's other forms of extra employee compensation. Thus, all financial managers need to be keenly aware of relevant developments in the pension field as well as in the related area of employee compensation generally, and extra forms of employee compensation in particular. The great bulk of medium-sized and big companies now have pension plans that cover most of their employees. To fill in the gap represented by small companies without plans, a move has been made toward multi-employer programs; the cost savings achieved by pooling measures enable the companies to sponsor a plan they could not otherwise afford.

The financial manager plays an important part in formulating overall policies for the management of pension plans. Except in small companies, the policy-making responsibility usually rests with a pension committee, of which a financial officer is usually a member. When the top role is assumed by an

---

* Much of the material in this chapter is drawn from Dan McGill, *Fundamentals of Private Pensions*, 4th ed., Richard D. Irwin, Homewood, Illinois, 1979.

individual executive, he is likely to be either the personnel director or a financial officer, probably the treasurer.

The continuing evaluation of the financial aspects of a pension program is the direct responsibility of the financial officer. With respect to insured programs, this means reviewing the costs, earnings, and terms of the whole range of insurance contracts. He must evaluate the implications of changes in laws, the economic environment, the working population, costs and earnings with an eye toward possibly modifying contractual arrangements or shifting from one type of program to another.

The review of trusted plans also entails an appraisal of management's performance in handling the investments. During the early years of pension fund management, not much attention was given to this phase, but in recent years increasing interest has been focused on the results of handling the pension investments. There are various reasons to account for this. For one thing, funds have grown so enormous that in many instances they represent huge amounts of assets, and therefore sheer prudence requires that the effectiveness of their investment management be reviewed. Then again, an increased investment return may provide an offset to wage costs and thus represent a contribution to corporate profits. Finally, although most pension plans are drafted to limit pension liabilities, there is some opinion that they have characteristics of a general liability of the corporation and at least impose a fiduciary responsibility on the employer. Should management want to gauge the quality of investment performance, consideration would have to be given not only to the rate of return but also to the liquidity needs and risk aspects of the funds. The level of return must be related to objectives, and these may vary from fund to fund.

In the everyday administration of pension plans, the influence of the financial officer is less marked. In most cases, the personnel department assumes this responsibility. When the function is given to a specific executive outside the department, the financial officer is likely to be designated. The only major area of pension activity in which a representative of the financial department usually has little voice is in the conduct of actual negotiations with unions, but even here his role is in assessing the cost aspects of a plan cannot be ignored. While management has the major responsibility for administering pension plans, policy is sometimes decided by joint union-management representation, and the union may even be given charge of handling the funds.

Not only are the pension and other forms of extra compensation fields currently evolving at a rapid pace, and growing in importance in the overall corporate setting, but they represent a rather broad spectrum of relevant subareas which need to be understood if one is to grasp the real significance of these areas. For example, aside from the obvious financial implications of the pension and extra compensation fields, these areas also have significant accounting, actuarial, legal and tax aspects in which important current developments are occurring. Thus this chapter will deal with the financial aspects of employee pension programs from the following perspectives:[1]

- Accounting considerations;
- Various types of pension plans;

- The Employee Retirement Income Security Act (ERISA) and other legal constraints; and
- Funding concerns.

In addition, in terms of the above considerations, the following forms of extra compensation will also be discussed:

- General Stock Purchase Plans for Employees;
- Employee Stock Savings Plans;
- Profit Sharing Plans; and
- Other Forms of Employee Non-Salary Benefits.

25.2 ACCOUNTING CONSIDERATIONS

[1] PENSIONS

In recent years employee compensation has characteristically included various extra benefits, including pensions and stock options. Considerable controversy has arisen about the magnitude, method of computation, and most appropriate recipients of these benefits. In addition, the methods of accounting for them are complex and have varying influences on reported profits.

An important decision in the accounting for pensions is how past service costs should be handled. They have been charged to surplus, charged to income in the period of the plan's inauguration, and amortized over current and future periods. While the last method is required by both the Internal Revenue Service (IRS) and the Financial Accounting Standards Board (FASB),[2] there is nevertheless considerable latitude in the periodic charges that may be incurred.

In addition to the problem of funding past service costs, companies have encountered the need to change the basis underlying their pension programs. By reason of this, they have been able to alter and even postpone the payments required by these plans. Moreover, in some instances, there is sufficient flexibility to permit adjustments in the payments made in different periods.

Changes in this area have occurred as the result of established minimum standards for participation, vesting and funding for employee benefit plans of private enterprises. ERISA also established requirements for annual reporting, fiduciary responsibility and administration. In light of this legislation, the FASB undertook to promulgate specific financial accounting and reporting standards for pension plans. They issued FASB Interpretation No. 3 (December, 1974) on the effect of ERISA on financial accounting and reporting standards for pension plans. This interpretation discusses the financial reporting requirements to comply with ERISA. Further, in March, 1980, by issuing Statement No. 35, "Accounting and Reporting by Defined Benefit Pension Plans," the FASB began to deal with pension reporting generally, by specifying accounting and reporting standards for defined benefit pension plans. (Such plans are defined in 25.3). The purpose of FASB Statement No. 35 was to eliminate the broad diversity of ways in which pension plans until then had provided financial information that might be used in assessing their present and future ability to pay employees' benefits when due. FASB

Statement No. 35 is concerned with financial reporting by pension plans themselves, rather than reporting in employers' financial statements as to the cost of the plan they sponsor.

This accounting standard called for information on the net assets available for benefits and the actuarial present value (both vested and nonvested) of participants' accumulated plan benefits. Pension plan investments (other than contracts with insurance companies) are to be presented at their fair market value or an appropriate surrogate. Data on changes in a plan's assets and participants' benefits is also to be disclosed.

Pension plan assets and liabilities are to be recorded on the accrual basis. Contributions receivable are to include amounts due from employers, from the participants or from other funding sources, whether the result of formal or legal action.

The statement of actuarial present value of accumulated plan benefits is to represent the discounted present value of all anticipated future payments to plan members based on the employees' service up to the benefit information date. Events that change the assumptions behind the calculation of the actuarial present value include information about plan amendments, changes in the nature of rates, mortality data and employee turnover. Information as to the methods and assumptions used to determine the value of plan investments, assumed rates of return, inflation rates and retirement ages are also to be disclosed.

In May, 1980, the FASB issued its Statement No. 36, "Disclosure of Pension Information," which extended to employers the same disclosure requirements which FASB Statement No. 35 mandated for the pension plans themselves. These disclosures, however, will not affect employers' income statements or balance sheets; they will only appear in footnotes to the financial statements.

FASB Statement No. 36 requires certain minimum disclosures for all pension plans, with additional disclosures required from defined benefit plans. (Such plans are defined in 25.3).

The minimum disclosures that apply to all pension plans include:

- Identification of the plan and the employees covered;
- Statement of accounting and funding policies;
- Statement of current provision for pension costs; and
- Identification, including nature and effect, of any material item(s) that would prevent interperiod comparability of the information presented. These items might include, but are not limited to, accounting changes, changes in actuarial assumptions or adoption or amendment of a plan.

In addition to these minimum disclosures, an employer company must disclose the following information for its defined benefit pension plans:

- Vested accumulated plan benefits, computed on a present value basis using actuarial assumptions;
- Nonvested accumulated plan benefits, computed on a present value basis using actuarial assumptions;
- Net assets of the pension plan available for the payment of benefits;
- Rate of return assumed in computing both vested and nonvested accumulated plan benefits; and
- The benefit information date (when the information was determined).

[2] STOCK OPTIONS

The treatment of stock options creates additional problems. If a corporation elects to compensate its executive personnel by means of salary and a cash bonus, the full amount is chargeable to earnings for the year. In the event the corporation elects to adopt a stock option plan for its officers, the amount charged to earnings is questionable. While disagreement exists, the prevailing accounting rule has been that the cost of the stock option is measured on the date the option is granted; the cost is represented by the difference between the fair value of the shares and the option price.

Thus, corporations are able to provide compensation to their executives without charging earnings for the full cost of the compensation, since an option that extends over a period of time could be worth a substantial sum at the time of grant. Should the market price of the optioned stock advance markedly, the recipients could exercise their options and receive these gains as salary supplements that the issuing corporation would not have to record.

25.3 VARIOUS TYPES OF PENSION PLANS

Pension plans can be divided into two distinct broad categories and each of these categories can be further subdivided into a number of subcategories. The two primary types of pension plans are defined benefit plans and defined contribution plans.

[1] DEFINED BENEFIT PLANS VS. DEFINED CONTRIBUTION PLANS

A *defined benefit pension plan* is one which promises a specific result. This type of pension plan promises its beneficiaries that upon attainment of a specific age and / or the culmination of a designated period of service with the firm or participation in the pension plan, they will be eligible to receive a fixed and determinable benefit. This benefit is determinable from the provisions of the pension plan.

On the other hand, a *defined contribution pension plan* is one which promises no specified result. In essence, for such a plan, all the employer agrees to do is to put aside money from time to time, (often pursuant to a proscribed formula) so that the employee will be entitled to receive an undetermined benefit at some later date. This benefit is based upon the funds contributed by the employer (in some cases this is added to funds contributed by the employee), and the investment performance of these funds during the period of contribution and withdrawal. Fundamentally, defined benefit plans "guarantee" a specified result, whereas defined contribution plans designate a given input of funds. The benefit which results is a function of that input.

Most of the largest pension plans are multi-employer collectively bargained plans and tend to be of the defined benefit variety. However, since the passage of ERISA in 1974 (see 25.4[4] for a discussion of ERISA), the number of defined benefit plans has decreased considerably. Most newly established plans are defined contribution, although the rate of inauguration of such plans has also declined since the passage of ERISA. Defined contribution plans are generally easier to understand and operate and often involve a lower financial commitment and administrative costs.

For all defined benefit pension plans, the amount that is to be contributed by the employer during the years of service of each employee must be determined actuarially. (See Appendix A for a discussion of actuarial factors in pension programs.)

[2] TYPES OF DEFINED BENEFIT PLANS

The types of defined benefit plans may be subdivided by the manner in which benefits are calculated. They can be divided into four basic categories of pension plans as follows:

- Flat benefits;
- Fixed benefits;
- Unit benefits; and
- Variable benefits.

Some plans have compound benefit calculation formulas and therefore carry the characteristics of a number of the above types of defined benefit plans.

(a) Flat Benefit Pension Plans

Under such a plan, benefits depend on neither the participants' compensation history nor the duration of their service to the firm. For such plans, however, there are minimum service requirements for participation. The benefit is the same for every employee who meets the plan's minimum service requirement. Thus, for flat benefit pension plans the percentage of benefits to compensation is greater for lower paid employees than for higher paid employees.

(b) Fixed Benefit Pension Plans

Such a plan provides a retirement benefit based upon compensation and, in most cases, is stated in terms of a percentage of compensation. Normally, all employees retiring with at least the minimum number of years of service for plan qualification will receive the same percentage of their compensation (as defined in the plan) as their retirement benefit.

(c) Unit Benefit Pension Plans

This type of plan produces a benefit in terms of time. The time can be years of employee service or participation in the plan. For unit benefit plans based upon time alone, all employees who retire with the same number of years of service would receive the same benefit regardless of their respective rates of compensation.

(d) Variable Benefit Pension Plans

A variable benefit pension plan adds an adjustment factor to a basic pension formula found by one of three methods described above. This plan first determines the basic pension benefit and then multiplies it by a factor that is a function of some variable external indicator, such as the Consumer Price Index, one of the popular security price indicies, or even the investment performance of the pension plan's own trust fund.

[3] TYPES OF DEFINED CONTRIBUTION PLANS

Such plans promise no specific benefit in dollar terms and are characterized by a benefit which is based upon the contributions made toward the account of each beneficiary and the investment performance of the fund between the dates of the contributions and the dates upon which benefits are paid. Such plans may be subdivided, on the basis of the factors upon which employer contributions are made, into four basic subcategories as follows:

- Profit sharing;
- Money purchase;
- Thrift or savings; and
- Stock bonus.

(a) Profit Sharing Pension Plans

(Profit sharing plans are discussed in greater detail in 25.6[2]. They are considered here briefly in relation to other types of defined contribution plans.) Such plans are the most common variety of defined contribution plans and are based upon employer contributions as a function of company profits. In the case of *discretionary profit sharing plans*, the employer decides after each period how much (if anything) to contribute. Even though the employer is not obliged to contribute to the pension plan, even in profitable years, these contributions must have a substantial and recurrent relationship to profits over a reasonable period. On the other hand, *formula profit sharing plans* obligate the employer to make specified contributions each year in relation to profits. However, if there are no corporate earnings, as defined by the plan, no employee contributions are required.

(b) Money Purchase Pension Plans

Such plans require employers to make annual contributions pursuant to some formula (normally related to compensation), regardless of whether or not profits were earned during the year. The contributions are allocated among the accounts of individual plan participants. Failure of an employer to make the contributions called for in the plan, results in a funding deficiency which can be punishable by federal assessment of excise taxes.

(c) Thrift or Savings Pension Plans

Under such plans the employee must contribute along with the employer. At least to some extent the amount of the employer's contribution allocated to each employee depends upon the amount of the employee's contribution. A thrift plan can be either of the profit sharing or money purchase variety. In the latter case, employer contributions are required (as long as employees make theirs) regardless of company profitability. Thrift profit sharing plans may require employer contributions according to some proscribed formula in relation to profits (thrift profit sharing formula plan) or make them optional to the employer in relation to profits (thrift profit sharing discretionary plans). But, in either case, company contributions to the plan are allocated among individual participants according to their respective contributions relative to the contributions of other participants.

(d) Stock Bonus Pension Plans

As in the case of discretionary profit sharing plans, stock bonus plans make the employer contribution discretionary. However, unlike discretionary profit sharing plans, stock bonus plans do not require corporate profits in order for the employer to make a contribution. Employer contributions to stock bonus plans can take the form of cash, stock of the company sponsoring the plan, or stock of a parent or subsidiary firm. Cash contributions are used to make purchases of the employer's stock in the open market. Payments to participants in stock bonus pension plans are made in the form of stock (except for fractional shares, which are paid in cash). Only firms whose shares are publicly traded can have stock bonus plans.

[4] TARGET OR ASSUMED BENEFIT PENSION PLANS

A hybrid type of pension plan which has some of the characteristics of both defined benefit plans and defined contribution plans is the target or assumed benefit pension plan. As in the case of defined benefit plans, the target plan contains a benefit formula. Employer contributions are intended such that if the entire array of actuarial assumptions (see Appendix A for a discussion of actuarial pension assumptions) worked out to be absolutely precise, these employer contributions would yield exactly the targeted, or assumed benefit. Thus in terms of funding, target plans resemble defined benefit plans. However, since each participant in the plan has his own separate individual account in terms of money already in the plan, target plans have important characteristics of defined contribution plans. Employer contributions are made individually for each employee in terms of actuarial calculations relevant to each individual. The benefit to each individual participant is in terms of his or her account balance at retirement. Thus, the target plan does not guarantee a given benefit and is similar in this sense to fixed contribution plans generally. In fact, it is highly unlikely that the targeted benefit and the actual benefit will ultimately coincide.

[5] INSURED PENSION PLANS

Aside from whether a pension plan is of the defined benefit or defined contribution variety, another important issue is who should administer the pension plan. Broadly speaking, there are two possibilities. There are so-called insured pension plans, administered by a life insurance company and there are programs sometimes referred to as non-insured pension plans, administered by a company appointed trustee. We shall discuss the first type here and the second in the following subsection.

Life insurance companies which administer pension plans operate under a funding instrument and receive employer contributions under the plan. The use of a funding agency, rather than the employing firm, is required by the Internal Revenue Code (IRC) in order for the employer to obtain current income tax deductions for contributions made in one tax period relative to benefits paid in a later period. The funding agency is normally either a life insurance company (insured pension plans) or an independent trustee (non-insured plans).

Employee contributions to insured pension plans may be currently allocated to purchase insurance or annuities for the individual participants. Some or all of the contributions may be accumulated in an unallocated fund and used to satisfy benefit payments as they arise. They may also be used to acquire annuities for participants at retirement or when a vested right occurs. Allocated funding instruments are those which require the current allocation of funds to purchase insurance or annuities for individual plan participants. Wherein allocation is deferred, the plan is said to use an unallocated funding instrument.

[6] NON-INSURED PENSION PLANS (TRUST AGREEMENTS)

Trust agreements represent a type of unallocated funding instrument which can be administered by a life insurance company. But they can also represent a vehicle through which non-insured pension plans can be set up. The trust agreement is the most popular instrument for funding pension benefits as measured either by the number of participants covered or the volume of assets held. Of all funding instruments, the trust agreement is the most flexible, as it can permit unlimited use of all types of investment vehicles. Large pension plans often find the trust agreement particularly useful.

Under a trust arrangement plan, contributions are deposited with a trustee (often a bank, but occasionally a natural person or groups of persons can be used). The trustee invests the contributions, accumulates the earnings, and pays the plan benefits. The trustee is also responsible for providing a periodic accounting of plan activities. The basic mandates of trust law guide the activities of the trustee.

Trust funds, in essence, represent a kind of self-insurance, with the trustee acting as investment counsellor and providing whatever administrative functions are called for in the trust agreement. Trust fund plans call for no specified contractual guarantee in terms of fixed investment returns.

[7] COMBINATION PLAN (LIFE INSURANCE AND AUXILIARY FUND)

A hybrid variety of pension plan, combining some of the features of insured plans and some of those of non-insured pension funds is the so-called combination plan. Such plans can combine any variety of instruments, but their use of life insurance supplemented by an auxiliary fund is common. In this combination, such plans provide life insurance protection to the date of retirement. The policy accumulates cash values that become a part of the principal sum needed to provide retirement benefits. The primary benefit of the combination plan is that it combines the rate guarantees of life insurance contracts with the funding and investment flexibility of the auxiliary fund. A combination plan can be set up with any type of life insurance which provides protection to the date of retirement, accumulates a cash value, and is contractually convertible into an annuity.

[8] THE RELATIONSHIP BETWEEN THE BENEFITS IN PRIVATE AND PUBLIC PENSION PLANS

The major government program that may affect the terms of private pension plans is the U.S. Government's Old Age, Survivors', and Disability Insurance. The Social Security Act of 1935 created this program and intended to provide some retirement protection in old age for all gainfully employed persons except those specifically excluded. The plan is financed by means of contributions by employers, their employees, and the self-employed. Since its enactment, the trend has been toward extending the coverage, liberalizing the benefits, and hiking the tax to the extent that the viability of the fund has at times come into question.

In order to create a balanced pension program, most companies provide benefits that are payable separate from, and are additions to, Social Security payments. If adjustments are made for Social Security, the IRS requires that this not be done in a manner that leads to discrimination in favor of the better paid employees. Various tests have been prescribed to determine whether the required integration exists with Social Security benefits.

Some tie-in may also exist with state unemployment compensation and workmen's compensation programs, although ordinarily these do not affect private pension plans. A small percentage of companies reduce company pension payments by any unemployment compensation benefits a retired worker may receive. Some states have also established restrictions on the collection of dual benefits. The chances of this problem arising are not great because of the reluctance of firms to employ aged persons. Most companies permit employees receiving workmen's compensation as a result of industrial accidents to be eligible for disability pensions; in some cases, however, restrictions are imposed on the maximum level of these combined payments.

25.4 ERISA AND OTHER LEGAL CONSTRAINTS ON PENSION PLANNING

[1] THE REGULATORY CLIMATE PRIOR TO THE PASSAGE OF ERISA

ERISA was signed into law in 1974. Prior to that time, pension plans were subject to no more than peripheral governmental regulation which was predominantly an indirect undertaking through the IRC. Corporate pension plans sought to comply with the federal taxing authorities in order to achieve a current income tax deduction for employer contributions to pension plans which disbursed benefit payments at a later time. (The tax treatment of pension plans is discussed in Chapter 24.) In addition, state laws governing general insurance, trusts, and fiduciary responsibility had provisions that affected the operations of pension plans.

[2] THE PROTECTION OF EMPLOYEE BENEFIT RIGHTS

The passage of ERISA fundamentally altered the regulatory environment in the pension area by providing legislation which encompassed most of the components of this field. ERISA deals with the protection of employee benefit rights. The primary areas of concern are as follows:

- vesting;
- participation;
- reporting and disclosure;
- fiduciary responsibility; and
- funding.

These provisions apply to all pension plans established or maintained by employers engaged in interstate commerce or by employee organizations representing employees engaged in interstate commerce, except primarily governmentally sponsored plans and church sponsored plans. All state laws applicable in these areas are superseded by these provisions except state laws that regulate insurance, banking and securities.

(a) Vesting

Prior to ERISA, employers, except under special circumstances, were under no legal obligation to provide vesting rights prior to retirement for employer financed pension plans.[3] However, even before 1974, most employer financed plans voluntarily provided for some sort of pre-retirement vesting. Still, Congress believed that more liberal and more general pre-retirement vesting privileges were in the public interest. Thus, three standards of vesting are included in the Act and an employer, with the consent of the collective bargaining agent, is required to choose one of these standards.

The first standard, which requires that no vesting privileges be granted prior to ten years of service, calls for full vesting of all accrued benefits after a plan participant has accumulated ten years of recognized service, irrespective of his age at the time.

The second standard does not require full vesting until a plan participant has attained 15 years of recognized service, regardless of age; however, it employs a progressive or graded vesting concept. Under this standard, a plan must vest a minimum of 25% of a participant's accrued benefits upon his attainment of five years of recognized service. Another 5% must be granted each year over each of the next five years and a further 10% each year during the following five years.

The so-called Rule of 45 is used in the third standard. Under this rule, an employee with five or more years of service must be at least 50% vested in the accrued benefits from the employer's contributions if the sum of his age and years of service total 45. The employee's vesting percentage increases for each year thereafter as shown in Figure 25.1.

FIGURE 25.1   *The rule of 45*

If Years of Service Equal Or Exceed	And the Sum Of Age and Service Equals or Exceeds	Then the Vested Percentage Is
5	45	50
6	47	60
7	49	70
8	51	80
9	53	90
10	55	100

Source: Corporate Controller's Manual, Ed., Paul Wendell, Warren, Gorham & Lamont, Boston, Mass., 1981, Ch. 27, by James Ratliff, p. 27-11.

According to this standard, the minimum vested benefit upon an employee's attaining ten years of service must be at least 50%; another 10% is to vest for each additional year of service.

In general, all years of service, including those rendered prior to an employee's entrance into the plan and before enactment of ERISA, are included as years of recognized service. The overall cost impact on a plan of each of the three vesting standards is quite similar, given a representative group of participants.

The IRS can require more rapid vesting if one of the following two abuses occurs:

- there has been a pattern of abuse, i.e., the dismissal of employees just prior to the time that their accrued benefits are to vest; or
- forfeitures of accrued benefits under the plan are occurring which discriminate against a given group of participants.

Once vested, employee benefits are non-forfeitable except if the plan participant dies before retirement (and in the absence of a plan provision calling for joint and survivor annuities.) However, the following exceptions also apply to the non-forfeiture of vested benefits: A) If a participant in a contributory plan withdraws his own required contributions prior to the at least 50% vesting of his employer financed benefits, the latter can be cancelled if the plan generally calls for this; and B) Retirement benefits during a period of employment can be suspended if a plan participant retires and then returns to work for the same employer. Misconduct by a vested participant or acceptance of employment with a competitor are not adequate grounds for forfeiture of benefits.

Records must be kept by employers as to each participant's years of service and the degree to which accrued benefits have vested. A statement of accrued benefits and their vested status must be provided to each participant when they leave the plan.

(b) Participation

Prior to ERISA, there was no limit under the IRC as to age or years of service which required participation in a pension plan. ERISA, however, specifies requirements regarding both age and years of service. Broadly, speaking, the service requirement cannot exceed one year,[4] unless the pension plan grants full and immediate vesting rights, in which event up to three years of service may be required for plan participation.

Under most circumstances, the minimum age requirement for plan participation cannot be higher than 25. That is, generally, an employee cannot be denied plan membership due to his age or service once he reaches 25 years of age and has accumulated a minimum of one year of service. However, both of these conditions must be fulfilled i.e., he must be at least 25 years of age *and* have acquired at least one year of service. For example, an employee hired at age 20 may have to perform five years of service before he is eligible for plan membership. Should this employee be hired at age 24 or later, however, the maximum service requirement can be no more than one year. These age and service requirements relate strictly to the accrual of plan benefits and are irrelevant for vesting. (Vesting rights were discussed immediately above in 25.4[2](a). ERISA does not demand retroactive recognition of service for purposes of determining plan participation and benefit accruals. However, a retroactive recognition of service to determine vesting status is required.

ERISA generally prohibits setting maximum age limits for plan participation. However, in order not to discourage employers from hiring older workers, defined benefit pension plans and target benefit plans can exclude from participation any employee who is first hired within five years of his normal retirement age.

Breaks in service are handled in a specific way according to ERISA for purposes of participation, benefit accruals, and vesting. In general all service with an employer (both pre-break and post-break) is to be included in totaling an employee's service for the participation requirement. A one year or longer break in service, however, will allow the employer to require a one year waiting period before re-entry. At that time, both the participant's pre-break and post-break service are to be added and, in addition, he is to be given full credit for the waiting period. However, plans which can employ a three-year service requirement may require those employees who incur a one year or longer break in service prior to meeting the three year service requirement to begin service anew to satisfy their service requirement.

(c) Reporting and Disclosure

All pension plans subject to ERISA must annually file certain reports as well as other reports covering certain specified events.

Within seven months after the end of the plan year, the pension plan must file an annual report with the IRS. This report must include the following:

- identifying information;
- statistics on participants;
- a balance sheet;
- an income statement; and
- other information about the operation of the plan.

An independent qualified public accountant must examine the financial statements of the annual report.

Pension plans subject to the funding requirements of ERISA (see 25.4[2](e)) must retain an enrolled actuary on behalf of all of the plan participants. The actuary is to prepare an annual actuarial statement which gives his opinion as to whether or not the ERISA funding requirements have been met. The actuary is also to provide a statement of the actuarial assumptions and methods used, and information from the most recent actuarial valuation.

When a pension plan is terminated, normally the sponsor will submit a form to the IRS to ask for a determination as to the qualification of the plan at that time. The Pension Benefit Guarantee Corp. (PBGC) (see 25.4[3]) is also to receive a termination report. Alternatively, the termination report is to be submitted to a trustee appointed to administer the affairs of the terminated plan. Further, the administrator of the plan is to report the following:

- the amount of benefits payable to each plan participant;
- the proportion of these benefits insured by the PBGC;
- the fair market value of the plan assets at termination;
- the actuarial present value of accrued plan benefits at the termination date; and
- the actuarial assumptions employed in determining the actuarial liability.

The establishment or amendment of a pension plan will normally result in the plan sponsor requesting an IRS determination of the plan's qualified status. The major difference between qualified and nonqualified plans is the timing of the corporate tax deduction. In the former, the deduction is taken at the time corporate contributions are made to the plan, and, in the latter case, at the time the benefits are paid to the plan participants. The request for qualified status is accomplished by the submission of appropriate forms and information and by the administrator of the plan submitting a plan description.

In addition to reports filed with the Federal Government, the plan is required to make certain information, including a summary annual report and plan description, available to plan participants.

(d) Fiduciary Responsibility

According to ERISA fiduciary responsibility is placed upon any person who exercises any discretionary authority or control with respect to the management of a pension plan. Fiduciary responsibility is also relevant to those who exercise any discretionary authority over the management or disposition of plan assets; have authority in the administration of the pension plan; or provide paid investment advice to the plan. Thus, according to ERISA, officers of the plan's sponsor, its directors, members of a pension plan's investment committee, and those who are responsible for choosing these individuals are fiduciaries. The plan document must list one or more named fiduciaries who jointly or severally have authority to administer the plan.

Plan fiduciaries cannot divert any plan income or assets to any use other than the payment of benefits to plan participants and their beneficiaries, and the coverage of the reasonable expenses of administering the plan. This injunction is fundamental to the goal that plan assets should be used for the exclusive benefit of plan participants and their beneficiaries.

Plan fiduciaries are to see to it that employer contributions remain with a plan and are not returned to the employer. There are, however, a few exceptions to this general rule which allow employers to recover a part or all of their contributions. These follow:

A. If a contribution is made to a newly-established or amended plan with the condition that the plan receive a favorable IRS ruling as a tax-qualified plan, and if an adverse ruling results, the employer may recover his contributions if the plan specifically so provides.

B. A contribution based upon a mistake of fact, such as a mathematical error in the determination of the amount required to be paid by the plan, can also be recovered to the extent of the error.

C. A plan which has terminated in an acceptable manner and which has fully discharged all obligations and benefits may result in the employer recovering a portion of his contributions if a plan surplus remains. Such a recovery can occur only to the extent that the surplus came about as a result of an erroneous actuarial computation which resulted in the actual costs being less than expected on the basis of the actuarial assumptions employed.

Also, with respect to plan fiduciaries, ERISA requires conduct designed to prevent diversion of plan assets as the result of unwise or improper investment policies. In general, the following is required in this respect:

A. A rate of return on plan assets in accordance with current rates and market conditions must be sought;

B. An adequate level of liquidity must be maintained in terms of the reasonably expected cash flow requirements of the plan;

C. The price paid for acquired assets must not exceed their fair market value at the time of acquisition; and

D. All other general conduct that would serve as a guide to the actions of a prudent investor must be maintained, i.e., the so called "Prudent Man Rule."

(e) Funding

This subsection deals with the funding requirements of ERISA. (See 25.5 for a discussion of the general financial considerations of pension plan funding.)

Prior to ERISA, the IRS promulgated rules which were believed to set a minimum standard of funding on employers in order to retain qualification of their pension plans under the tax laws. Under this approach, employers were required to make aggregate contributions to their pension plans which were equal to the cumulative normal cost of the plan plus interest on the initial actuarial liability. However, the initial actuarial liability or any other layer of supplemental liability did not have to be amortized.

ERISA changed the entire concept of minimum contributions. The fundamental funding change was that the plan's supplemental liability was to be amortized over a specified period of time and, in addition, the normal costs of the plan had to be funded. The period of amortization depends upon whether the plan was in existence on the effective date of ERISA and whether it is a single employer or a multi-employer plan (see 25.4[4]) for a discussion of multi-employer pension plans). A separate amortization schedule is used for experience gains and losses and for liabilities produced by plan amendments or changes in actuarial assumptions. Only defined benefit plans need amortize the supplemental liability.

For pension plans which do not have an accumulated funding deficiency from previous years, the minimum funding standards of ERISA will be satisfied if the annual employer contribution to the plan does *all* of the following:

A. Is sufficient to amortize, over a period not to exceed 30 years, any net loss from any changes in actuarial assumptions;

B. For multi-employer plans, 20 years and for single employer plans, 15 years are the minimum periods to amortize any net experience gain or loss incurred by the plan;

C. Is sufficient to amortize any waived funding deficiency over a period of 15 years on an equal installment basis;

D. Pays the normal cost for the plan year for services incurred;

E. Is sufficient to amortize (over a minimum of 40 years for multi-employer plans and 30 years for single employer plans) the net increase in unfunded past-service liabilities from plan amendments; and

F. Is sufficient to amortize (over a minimum period of 40 years for multi-employer plans or any single employer plan in existence on January 1, 1974, and 30 years for single employer plans starting after January 1, 1974) past service costs, both principal and interest on a level payment basis.

Every pension plan which is subject to the ERISA minimum funding standards must set up a funding standard account. This account is to provide a cumulative comparison between the actual employer contributions and the contributions required according to the minimum funding standard discussed immediately above. The main function of this account is to offer flexibility in funding by allowing contributions which are greater than the required minimum, with accumulated interest, to decrease the required minimum contributions in future years.

Each year the following items affect the funding standard account:

A. It is charged with: 1) the normal cost for the year, 2) the share of the supplemental liabilities, and 3) the share of experience losses which must be amortized annually; and

B. It is credited with: 1) employer contributions to the plan, and 2) the portion of any experience gains resulting from changes in actuarial assumptions that are to be assigned to that year under the amortization rules.

When the contributions to the plan, adjusted for actuarial gains and losses, meet the minimum funding standards, a zero balance will result in the funding standard account. If the minimum contribution level is not met, a deficiency, called an "accumulated funding deficiency," will appear in the funding standard account. This deficiency will accrue interest at the valuation rate and is subject to a federal excise tax of five percent. If the accumulated funding deficiency is not corrected or paid off within 90 days of the mailing by the Secretary of the Treasury of a notice of deficiency to the employer, a 100 percent federal excise tax is imposed. Civil court action may also result from an employer's failure to meet the minimum funding standard.

[3] THE PENSION BENEFIT GUARANTEE CORPORATION

As part of ERISA, the Pension Benefit Guarantee Corporation (PBGC) (located in the Department of Labor) was established. The purpose of the PBGC is to administer a program of pension plan termination insurance to ensure the ultimate fulfillment of the vested rights of plan participants. In doing this, the PBGC is empowered, in certain circumstances, to impose a lien on corporate assets for certain unfunded pension liabilities of pension plans. The PBGC applies to all qualified defined benefit pension plans, with specified exceptions, or all plans that have met all the requirements for qualification for the preceeding five years.

[4] MULTIPLE EMPLOYER PLANS

Pension plans can be classified as multiple employer or single employer plans. When firms which are not financially related have their employees covered by the same pension plan, the plan is called a multiple employer pension plan. In this case, employer contributions are usually paid at a constant rate into one common fund. In addition, benefits are normally paid on a uniform scale from the pooled assets of the fund. We would *not,* for example, have a multiple employer pension fund if two or more employers pooled their contributions solely for investment purposes with a separate account kept for each employer.

A special variety of multiple employer plan is given singular treatment by ERISA and is called a "multiemployer plan" in the Act. Such a plan is a multiple employer plan maintained pursuant to a collective bargaining agreement to which more than one employer is required to contribute. However, no one employer may take as much as 50% of the initial contributions nor 75% of the subsequent contributions. Typical of multiemployer plans are industries with many small firms, intense competition, a high rate of business failure and numerous skilled craftsmen as employees. These characteristics make a single employer plan unlikely and so the multiple employer form offers retirement benefits to workers who might not otherwise have available this form of financial security. The advantages of a multiemployer plan are that it stabilizes the experience of the pension fund, provides economies of large-scale operations, provides for the transfer of pension credits among the participating firms, and standardizes pension costs among these competing firms.

25.5 FINANCIAL ASPECTS OF FUNDING CONTRIBUTIONS TO PENSION PLANS

[1] CONTRIBUTORY VS. NON-CONTRIBUTORY PLANS

Pension plans to which only employers contribute are called non-contributory; those to which participants are required to contribute as a condition for plan membership are referred to as contributory pension plans. Participation in a contributory pension plan is normally voluntary, especially when such plans commence operation. However, it is sometimes a condition of employment that employees hired after a plan is already established contribute to the plan.

While at one time, most pension plans were of the contributory variety, at the present time, noncontributory plans predominate. To employers, contributory plans have the advantage of reducing the costs of their own contributions and, of course, make possible the payment of larger benefits to participants.

To the extent that retirement benefits can be viewed as deferred wages, however, it is logical that employers should bear the total burden of contributions. Additionally, from a practical standpoint, employee contributions considerably complicate plan record keeping and administration. Further, contributory plans can result in employee demands to borrow from the plan with the pledge of their accounts as collateral. Should such requests be granted, the plan begins to operate as a banker with additional attendant complications. ERISA provides some further complexities for contributory plans by requiring that accrued benefits be separated into an employer derived segment and an employee derived portion. It further requires rather complex buy back provisions for employees who quit and later return. Non-contributory plans avoid all these problems.

While contributions that employers make toward qualified pension plans are tax deductible as an ordinary business expense (and thus a considerable portion of the cost is shifted to the government), employee contributions are not tax deductible to the employee. Dollar for dollar, therefore, the non-contributory approach is the more efficient financing device when the overall after-tax profits of the employer and the after-tax income of employees are considered. And, in fact, in the case of an employer who is considering an across the board wage increase vs. an assumption of a portion of his employees' pension plan contribution, a greater increase in employees take home pay will result from the latter alternative.

[2] MEETING THE OBLIGATIONS OF EMPLOYER CONTRIBUTIONS

Since the passage of ERISA, with relatively few exceptions, employers engaged in interstate commerce can no longer follow the current disbursement approach to financing employer pension plan contributions. Under this method, retirement benefits are paid when due, but no prior or anticipatory funding is undertaken.

The current predominant method for the financing of pension plans by employers (and employees, in the case of contributory plans) is for funds to be set aside for the payment of benefits with an insurance company or trustee prior to the date on which such benefits become payable. The sums so set aside in any period are in direct relationship to the participant benefits assumed to have accrued during that period. Also of considerable relevance in determining the amount of funds to set aside each year for the payment of future benefits is the earnings rate on these funds which is anticipated from the time the employer sets the funds aside until they are eventually disbursed in the form of participant benefits.[5]

The type of funding whereby funds are set aside for the future benefit of plan participants in an amount sufficient to meet the retirement benefits of participants as they come due is often referred to as advance funding. There are a number of advantages of such a funding arrangement such as the following:

(a) Security of Benefits

Advance funding enhances the security of the benefit rights of plan participants. Without advance funding, plan participants are virtually totally dependent for their retirement benefits on the future willingness and ability of the employer to meet his obligations. However, by advance funding a segregated fund is set up which is irrevocably committed to the payment of participant benefits. This fund is administered by an independent third party who is a fiduciary to plan participants. The greater the ratio of assets controlled by the fund to its actuarial liabilities, the more secure the claims of plan participants.

(b) Protection of Plan Termination Insurance Program

Advance funding also protects the program of plan termination insurance against abuse. As noted in 25.4[3], the PBGC insures the vested benefits of participants in defined benefit pension plans. To the extent that plans are advance funded, the resources of the PBGC need not be employed to help satisfy participant claims.

(c) Enforcement of Fiscal Responsibility

Advance funding also ensures a measure of fiscal responsibility by those who design and administer pension plans. In effect, it forces employers to face up to the cost of their pension plans.

(d) Reduction of Employer Outlay

A significant advantage of advance funding for the employer is that it is less costly than the current disbursements approach. Under the current disbursements method, no interest is earned on the employer's contributions. Thus, the total cost of the pension plan is the sum of the individual payments the employer makes. With advance funding, however, every employer contribution is credited with interest from the date of payment until the time it is disbursed as a retirement benefit.

(e) Aid in Financial Planning

Advance funding also permits a more accurate estimate of costs for pricing, budgeting, and financial planning in general. However, advance funding does have some drawbacks. The managers of the pension fund may earn a lower rate of return on fund assets than the employer could have achieved by retaining the funds and employing them in his own business. The fund earning rate may even be less than the rate of interest the employer pays on borrowed funds. Income taxes limit the above two possibilities, still, they represent disadvantages of advance funding when prevalent. Advance funding can also result in the accumulation of larger asset pools in the hands of the funding agency. This may produce an appearance of affluence which may result in claims by plan participants for greater benefits than called for by the plan.

[3] PORTFOLIO POLICIES OF PENSION PLANS

Since the larger the plan rate of return on existing assets, the lower the required present and future employer contributions, plan rates of return are an important element of the financial aspects of plan funding. Rates of return are a function of portfolio policies and investment practices. Thus, a few brief comments as to pension plan investment practices are in order here.[6]

The ERISA "Prudent Man Rule" serves as both a guide and a constraint on the operations of the investment portfolio of a pension plan. (See 25.4[2](d) for a discussion of the effect of ERISA on the portfolio managers of pension plans and a discussion of the "Prudent Man Rule.")

A growing number of corporations are reevaluating their pension fund management arrangements and more than one-fourth of the Fortune "500" industrials manage some portion of their funds in-house. This trend will probably accelerate in the future.

In externally managed pension funds, a recent development has been a trend toward devoting a small but growing portion of their portfolios to nontraditional investments generally referred to as "collectibles" or "intangibles." This category includes gold, silver, other precious metals, art, coins and stamps. Such investments do not appear to be inconsistent with the "Prudent Man ERISA Rule."

The actuarial ability of portfolio managers of pension plans to time plan disbursements for benefits allows them to gear plan investments to scheduled plan benefit payments. This represents a constraint on the required plan liquidity. For example, maturities for fixed income securities which coincide with the anticipated benefits schedule may have to be sought. However, to the extent that employer contributions are sufficient to meet anticipated benefit payments, an expected future positive cash flow will result, with little plan liquidity then required. In this case, the highest yields can be sought commensurate with the maintenance of an appropriate portfolio risk level.

25.6 OTHER FORMS OF EMPLOYEE EXTRA COMPENSATION

We now look at some other forms of employee extra compensation. In this category we will consider employee stock purchase plans, profit sharing plans, and other forms of employee nonsalary benefits.

[1] EMPLOYEE STOCK PURCHASE PLANS

Some of the benefits of employee stock purchase plans are that they create greater interest on the part of the worker in his company and job, confirm public belief in the capitalistic system, provide a convenient means of additional financing, and encourage thrift among employees. Other than stock options dealt with in Chapter 24, we can identify two kinds of employee stock purchase plans; general stock purchase plans for employees and stock savings plans for employees.

(a) General Stock Purchase Plans for Employees

The general stock purchase plan enables employees to buy stock furnished by the company in accordance with a definite program. If a new issue is used, it may be specifically intended for employee purchase, or it may be the unsubscribed portion of an original offering to stockholders. To prevent employees from overextending market commitments made through the company, a ceiling is ordinarily placed on the maximum number of shares that may be acquired by this means; moreover, because the supply of stock is limited, offers are usually open only for a specified period of time.

Employers rarely contribute to these plans; the employee pays for the stock through payroll deductions, direct cash outlays, or some combination of these methods. Sometimes a down payment is required. A number of companies offer their shares at a discount price, which may be a designated percentage of the market value or a specified number of points below the market. The market price in turn may be the level prevailing on the date the plan is offered, the subscription made, or the purchase completed, or the lower of the initiating or completion dates. The price may also be an average over a period of time.

An important decision confronting the financial manager is the amount of discount, if any, that should be provided. In some companies the employee stock purchase plan may actually be a significant source of new capital. Under these circumstances, there will be some pressure on the financial manager to restrict the size of the discount since it cuts down on the cash intake. In the other direction, a discount encourages sales; it also provides a buffer against employee losses, thereby modifying the danger that a market decline will generate complaints.

The discount is the principal direct inducement for participation; in addition, when stock is bought in the open market, the company often absorbs brokerage and related fees. Some firms charge the employee interest on unpaid balances, while others pay him interest on contributions made prior to the actual purchase of the stock. Dividends may be disbursed in cash, used to reduce the employee's contributions, or applied to the purchase of additional shares; the employee usually does not receive the benefits of these distributions until his stock is fully paid.

(b) Stock Savings Plans for Employees

In stock savings programs, the employee is encouraged to save by means of paralleling contributions of some sort by the employer, and arrangements are usually made to invest at least a portion of the funds in common stock. These programs afford the benefits of a general stock purchase plan with less risk that a severe market decline will generate employee ill will, and also provide for supplementary retirement features that protect against inflation.

Through payroll deductions, the employee gives up to some maximum limit. The employer, in turn, usually contributes a fixed portion of the employee's savings, although the basis may vary with profits or length of service. The employer's contribution may be as low as 10 percent of the employee's share, for short periods of service in plans of this sort, or it may be on a matching basis, with 50 percent representing a common figure. In some cases, the company may even extend guarantees beyond its own commitment; for example, that at termination it will give the employee at least his own contribution plus interest even though the value of the securities in his account from both his and the company's contributions is less than this amount. The funds accumulated are generally deposited in an irrevocable trust, administered by a bank or trust company, for investment in the company's own shares. Often the employer's portion is placed in these shares, while the employee's contributions are restricted to U.S. Government securities, perhaps only saving bonds, or to government bonds and company stock. On occasion, the participant employee may have some latitude in selecting the type of investment he desires, usually with respect to his own contributions.

The major cost to the company, of course, is its matching contribution. Other costs include trustees' fees and expenses connected with the operations of the plan and trust fund. Some companies also pay the brokers' fees that may be involved, while others include these charges in the price of the securities as they are allocated. Purchases may be made in the open market, privately, or from the employer, but at no more than the market price. Moreover, these purchases may be placed regularly each month, which affords the advantages of dollar averaging.[7]

To determine when the employee gets his securities, three general approaches have been developed. One provides for immediate delivery of the securities bought with the employee's funds; the stock bonus given by the company may be distributed annually or periodically after the acquisition of a certain amount of securities with the employee's funds. In so-called cycle plans, starting each year both the employee's and employer's funds are accumulated for a designated period, say, three years, after which the securities and available cash are distributed to the employee. In contrast to these early distribution plans, under another method, sometimes called the terminal distribution plan, the employee's and the employer's deposits are invested according to some prearranged method, in securities which are accumulated until the employee's set retirement, death, or termination of employment.

As defined by the IRC a type of employee stock savings or thrift plan is a stock bonus plan. Such a plan is one which is "established and maintained by an employer to provide benefits similar to a profit sharing plan, except that the contributions by the employer are not necessarily dependent upon profits and the benefits are distributed in stock of the employer company."[8] (See 25.6[2] for a discussion of profit sharing plans and 25.3[3](c) and (d) for a discussion of employee savings or thrift plans and stock bonus plans respectively.) In some cases, the contribution formula of a qualified stock bonus plan promises a fixed or minimum annual contribution, regardless of company profits.

A type of employee benefits plan that has become significant recently, partly because of Congressional tax inducements, is known as an employee stock ownership plan (ESOP). Generally, an ESOP is any type of qualified employee benefit plan that invests some or all of its assets in employer securities. ERISA, however, defines an ESOP far more narrowly. ERISA defines ESOPs as qualified stock bonus plans or combination qualified stock bonus plans and defined benefit plans, which are designed to invest largely in the securities of the employer. Thus, such plans can be leveraged by means of financing secured by the stock and the guarantee of the company and other commitments.

The participation and vesting provisions of an ESOP must meet the ERISA requirements in these areas (see 25.4[2](a) and (b) for ERISA participation and vesting requirements.) Although an ESOP can have a contribution formula based on employer profits, it is more normally a flat percentage of covered compensation so as to provide an assured cash flow to purchase employer securities or to service loans undertaken to acquire securities of the employer. The IRC provisions which determine the deductibility of employer contributions are also relevant for ESOPs.

If distributions of an ESOP are in the stock of the employer and otherwise conform to the conditions of the IRC, they will receive the favorable tax treatment of deferral of tax on market value appreciation. Employer contributions may be in either cash or employer securities.

ESOPs provide a number of advantages to employers. They can be a fruitful device for transforming a publically owned firm into a company which is owned solely by the trust and a few major stockholders. Also, corporate divisions can be sold off to a company ESOP. ESOPs can give major stockholders liquidity for their holdings by buying them. In addition, newly issued shares can be sold to ESOPs with less expense and normally far less complexity than through a public offering of securities. Finally, by owning the stock of their employers, participants in ESOPs gain a proprietory interest in the affairs of the firm. Balanced against this, ESOPs appear to have no disadvantages to employers except their cost.

ESOP participants enjoy the advantages of employer contributions regardless of employer profitability. They also receive the full benefits of ownership of shares. However, for individuals who owe their livelihood to a given employer, participation in an ESOP may represent tying their financial security too closely to the success of that employer. A base pension may be an appropriate supplement in this case.

A special form of ESOP which provides employers with an additional benefit, in the form of an additional investment tax credit, is known as a TRASOP (Tax Reduction Act Stock Ownership Plan). For such plans, an employer can claim the additional tax credit (in addition to the investment tax credit) if it contributes to a qualified plan an amount of stock or cash which has a value equal to the additional credit. Thus, due to the fact that a tax credit reduces an employer's tax liability dollar for dollar, the employer can provide his employees with a benefit which is cost free. To be qualified, such plans must, among other things, provide for full vesting and no distributions for seven years, except if service is terminated.

The TRASOP tax credit is oriented toward payroll costs. It is currently at .75 percent of covered employees compensation, but is scheduled to terminate on December 31, 1987.

Amounts contributed by an employer to a leverage ESOP, and applied by the plan to pay the principal on a loan incurred to purchase employer securities, are subject to a deduction limit equal to 25 percent of the participants' compensation. An unlimited deduction is permitted for amounts applied to interest on the loan.

[2] PROFIT SHARING PLANS

(a) The Meaning of Profit Sharing

Companies distribute profits to employees in different forms—bonuses, commissions, or salary adjustments—and any one of these may be called a kind of profit sharing. However, such a general application of the notion is inadequate in that the essential characteristic of profit sharing is that company contributions fluctuate with current profit levels. Also, incentive is inherent in the concept. For our purposes, profit sharing may be described as any formal plan which distributes to employees, in addition to their established wages, a share in the profits.

Some of the reasons for establishing such a program may be summarized as follows:

- A desire to have the workers feel that they are partners in the organization, thereby stimulating them to do everything in their power to make the business more profitable;
- An interest in obtaining improved morale among employees, leading to greater cooperation among workers and better management of them;
- An intention to establish a flexible wage structure under which supplemental payments rise as the business becomes more prosperous and decrease as profits recede; and
- A wish to hold desirable employees, principally through deferred plans which may require a minimum service period to obtain vesting.

(b) Kinds of Profit Sharing Plans

Profit sharing may be divided into two major categories: immediate payment (cash) and deferred distribution (trust) plans. There are also combination plans in which part of the profit is paid out currently and part is deferred. The first type embraces plans that provide for distributions promptly or soon after allocations have been determined. Under a deferred plan, the employer makes current contributions based on the company's profits and allocated to the accounts of individual employees. These funds are invested and eventually distributed to the employees after a specified period or upon retirement, death, or disability. The principal value of this arrangement is that it provides for employee retirements or other benefits without binding the company to prescribed payments.

While current payment plans are visualized as providing a supplement to the basic wage, deferred payments are directed toward furnishing the employee with financial security when his need is greatest, much like a pension plan. Plans may also combine cash and deferred payments. In these cases, the company immediately pays part of the employees' share in profits and places the remainder in a trust fund to be distributed at a later time.

(c) Considerations in Formulating Profit Sharing Plans

The typical operating questions that arise in connection with establishing profit sharing plans concern eligibility, the percentage of profits to be distributed, the definition of profits, their allocation, vesting, and the frequency of distribution.

Financial issues, like the nature of the company's business, the stability of its operations, the size of its investment return, and its capitalization, influence decisions on the percentage of profits to be distributed. Various methods may be established for determining the size of the profit base to be carved and distributed among eligible participants. It may be calculated before or after taxes, attainment of a minimum profit level may be a prerequisite for any distribution, or certain funds may be withheld for internal business use. Companies may even decide to relate distributions to dividends rather than to profits. Similarly, different techniques are employed to allocate profits to participating members. Each employee may receive a percentage based on the relation of his earnings to the total compensation paid by the company; each employee may be given a designated percentage of his income; the distribution system may integrate salaries or wages and years of service; or some other combination may be worked out that suits the company's needs.

(d) The Flexibility of Profit Sharing Plans

The creed of modern business is that the firm must assume part of the social obligation of providing for the long-term economic welfare of its employees. Management has met this responsibility by:

- introducing pension plans;
- encouraging workers to follow habits of thrift and personal budgeting to prevent financial exigencies from interfering with their efficiency; and
- developing positive incentives through extra means of compensation.

Grappling with these problems emphasizes the importance of seeking compensation methods that contribute to the desired objectives without adding the pressure of inflexible costs. Deferred profit sharing is an outgrowth of such investigations.

These plans may be molded to varying aims. By providing for employee contributions, the funds may be augmented more rapidly and habits of thrift cultivated.[9] In order to give employees a stronger sense of participation in the company's affairs, the money accumulated may be directed to the purchase of the company's stock, although ordinarily only the company's contribution is used for this purpose. Funds may also be invested in annuity contracts. These furnish employees with an assured life income or with lump sum distributions in the event of death. The latter method may create an estate of some importance and thus provide extra insurance protection.

By granting loans to members and permitting pre-severance withdrawals, deferred plans help employees meet special financial needs. Lending enables employees to meet unexpected emergencies like sickness, accident, or death, to buy homes, or to take care of any worthy need or personal problem that is approved by the administrative body established for this purpose.[10] In addition, partial and sometimes complete withdrawals may be allowed under specified conditions. If one of these conditions is a layoff, the plan may be seen as augmenting supplementary unemployment benefits. (See 25.6[3](a) for a discussion of Supplementary Unemployment Benefits.)

A common practice has been to add nonintegrated profit sharing to an integrated pension plan.[11] Some companies, however, have established integrated profit sharing plans with retirement benefits. In such a plan, the participating employees may contribute a fixed percentage of their compensation above a certain amount, while the employer's contribution is related to earnings within the limits imposed by the employee contributions and rules of integration. Gearing the employer's contributions to earnings creates a flexibility that financial management may find desirable.

A common management objection to profit sharing is that it might encourage unions to demand a voice in management decision such as pricing; some labor leaders, in turn, have claimed that it is antagonistic to the union principle of "equal pay for equal work" and might be used by firms with negligible profits to sidestep other benefits.

(e) Profit Sharing vs. Pension Plans

Profit sharing plans and pension plans differ significantly. In profit sharing plans, the rules for participation, vesting,[12] service, the basic need considerations and the types of settlement options to use, represent design problems similar to those encountered in pension plans. ERISA, however, has relatively little effect on profit sharing plans vis-a-vis its considerable effect on pension plans. Nevertheless, fiduciary standards, reporting, disclosure and executive limitations need to be considered. Profit sharing plans also have greater flexibility in employee contributions than do pension plans. However, in order for a profit sharing plan to meet the IRS rules on current deductibility of employer contributions, merely making a single or occasional contribution out of profits will not do. Such contributions out of profits must be recurring and substantial.

One of the interesting features of profit sharing plans is that they can sometimes employ individual accounts for plan participants and offer participants the choice of various types of investment vehicles for their accounts. For example, a plan participant may be given the choice of having his account balance invested in bonds, common stocks, balanced or venture funds, or some combination of these.

A profit sharing plan may also make benefits available to participants after a relatively brief deferral period (as little as two years). Easing access to cash can reduce inflationary pressures and may increase incentives by shortening the distance between contributions to the plan and their actual enjoyment. Profit sharing plans can also pay benefits in the form of stock of the employing firm.

[3] OTHER FORMS OF EMPLOYEE NONSALARY BENEFITS

There are a number of lesser forms of nonsalary benefits worth mentioning briefly. The forms of employee benefits discussed in this subsection are generally of lesser value than those analyzed earlier in this chapter, nevertheless, each of them can be of some consequence in a given firm and are thus worthy of consideration by the financial manager.

(a) Supplementary Unemployment Benefits

Income security is a major goal of labor leaders. To achieve this end, they have bargained for severance pay, more liberal state unemployment compensation, and deferred profit sharing plans with withdrawal privileges. Another effort along the same lines is the supplementary unemployment benefit or SUB plan. In the SUB plan benefits, which may or may not be related to unemployment insurance, are paid to employees from an employer financed fund. A major consideration from the employer's viewpoint in establishing a SUB plan is financial—the costs involved. In general, these should be specifically ascertainable, with a maximum limitation to prevent the possibility of their exerting unforeseen pressures on the company. Even though the funds provided may not prove sufficient at any one time to meet required benefits, no increases should take place unless they are renegotiated. To guard further against drains which would prematurely exhaust the fund, it is desirable to establish strict rules on the buildup of eligibility and on the payment of contributions.

As originally conceived, the SUB plan was a move in the direction of the guaranteed annual wage. It established the notion that the employer would assume the responsibility, in the event of unemployment, of providing the employee with a portion of his pay up to a designated limit. In extending the amount and duration of payments, successive contracts have made progress in this direction. A further step suggested by the unions is to place various separately financed and administered security programs, including supplemental unemployment benefits, pensions, and medical and other related insurance, in a single, centrally funded and administered program.

(b) Financial Counselling

This usually represents a package of financial advisory planning services performed by a group of professionals in this field. An employer might engage a financial counseling firm to provide such services to specified executives at a fee per executive, which is paid by the employer or, more rarely, paid partly by the employer and the executive.

The typical services provided to executives are:

- estate planning;
- tax counselling and preparation of executives' tax returns;
- evaluation of executives' financial affairs;
- investment counselling; and
- advice on the compensation package.

While such a benefit is taxable as compensation to the executive, a corresponding offset can usually be taken if the service would otherwise have given rise to a tax deductible expense had he paid for it himself.

(c) Interest Free and Low Cost Loans to Executives

This has become a widespread and very beneficial fringe benefit to high level executives particularly in periods of high interest rates. Examples of such loans are for mortgages and to exercise stock options. Generally, an employee who borrows from his employer on a low cost basis is not taxable on the amount of interest that the company does not charge. Further, in most cases, the company is not considered to have received interest income with respect to interest not charged to its executives on such loans. However, the transaction must represent a true loan and cannot be a disguised salary or bonus. Thus, the loan must be made in a businesslike way, with all the formality normally attendant to such transactions.

(d) Paying the Executives' Charitable Donations

Some firms contribute to charities selected by the executives up to a given dollar amount. In other cases, the firm will match the executives' charitable contributions dollar for dollar up to a specified limit. Such donated amounts are not taxable to the executive, however, they get no deduction for amounts so contributed. All deductions are taken by the employer and are subject to the employer's own deduction limit on charitable contributions.

(e) Company Payments of Business or Professional Dues

Such payments are deductible by the company, yet tax exempt to the executive. Company payment for subscriptions to journals of a business or professional character would get the same treatment.

(f) Covering Executives' Moving Expenses

A company can cover most moving costs with full deductibility for its outlay and full tax exemption for the executive. Thus, the actual cost of moving is only about half of the pre-tax amount.

(g) Child Care Expenses

A corporate tax credit is now provided for employers who pay for the care of employees' children or other dependents. As a result, more companies are offering employees the choice of this benefit.

25.7 CHAPTER SUMMARY: TOWARD A UNIFIED PROGRAM OF EMPLOYEE BENEFITS

In general, the financial manager seeks the maximum in employee benefits at the least cost to the employer, given the tax affects on each of the benefit payments. However, the topsylike growth of extra compensation benefits over the past several decades has created the danger that because of competition or bargaining pressures, companies will be pushed into introducing specific plans piecemeal, which will result in a patchwork arrangement rather than a unified program. Accordingly, it is important for the financial manager to step back from the hurly-burly of direct negotiations and operations in order to view these benefits as part of a calculated company pattern. In this way, it may be possible to develop particular plans that contribute to desired objectives at the least cost.

The compensation program of a company is intended to attract employees, hold them to the company, provide adequate incentive for superior performance, and reduce the likelihood that personal financial pressures will create emotional problems that interfere with operating efficiency. To achieve such a program, financial management must recognize the varying needs experienced by those on different rungs of the managerial ladder; the implications of the tax code, which may change from time to time; and the problems created by outside competition. At the same time, the financial burden of the program on the company must be held down.

An increasing number of companies have attempted to tailor their non-salary benefits to the individual needs and desires of each of their employees. "Supermarket" and "cafeteria" are names that personnel officers have given to this approach. Instead of giving an executive a cash amount in salary and bonus, plus an array of predetermined non-cash benefits, this approach allows the executive himself to choose what he will take, within a designated total dollar limit, from a broad spectrum of benefits. Each executive thus chooses that mix of cash and benefits which he feels best suits his own financial needs. The tax position of the executive is a factor which is of considerable relevance in this choice. Also some items can be purchased for the executive by the employer at a lower cost than the executive would have to pay if he purchased these items himself. For example, an employer usually can provide group term life insurance and accident and health insurance at costs below what an executive would have to pay. Companies which are adopting or contemplating a "cafeteria" plan should therefore explain the various options to their executives.

FOOTNOTES

1. Tax aspects of pension plans as well as employee stock options and deferred compensation are dealt with in Chapter 24 and actuarial factors are developed in Appendix A.
2. See, APB Opinion No. 8, "Accounting for the Cost of Pensions," New York, AICPA, 1966. See also FASB Interpretation No. 28, and FASB News Release, January 1, 1979, and "Restatement and Revision of Accounting Research Bulletins," in *Accounting Research and Terminology Bulletin,* New York, AICPA, 1961, pp. 117-118. Accounting in this area is currently in transition and changes may be forthcoming in the near future.

3. Vested benefits represent rights to receive moneys regardless of whether or not the employee continues in the service of the employer firm. The benefits resulting from an employee's own contributions are non-forfeitable. Thus, this subsection relates excusively to the vesting of benefits resulting from employer contributions.
4. In general, ERISA defines a year of service as one thousand hours of work during a twelve month period.
5. A sort of compromise between the current disbursement approach and the type of funding required by ERISA is called the terminal funding method. Under this approach, no funds are set aside for active participants, but, as each participant reaches retirement, his benefits are paid in full. The terminal funding method is not allowed for tax qualified pension plans and other pension plans which are subject to the funding provisions of ERISA.
6. A more extended discussion of the portfolio policies of pension plans is clearly beyond the scope of this chapter. However, the interested reader can pursue the relevant references in the suggested readings section at the end of this chapter.
7. In dollar averaging, the investor sets aside the same amount of funds regularly for the purchase of securities, regardless of the fluctuations of the market. As a result, he obtains more shares at the subsequent lower prices to which the shares may fall than at the higher prices to which they may rise. This means that the investor is assured of obtaining a lower average cost per share than the average of the market prices paid.
8. Internal Revenue Service Regulations 1.401-1(b)(i)(iii).
9. Among the objections cited against employee contributions are the difficulty of convincing employees of the advantages of deferrment, the tendency for participating employees to want a greater voice in management, and the possibility that under certain circumstances a voluntary contributory plan may have to be registered with the SEC.
10. The maximum an employee can borrow from a qualified pension or profit sharing plan is $50,000 or half of his vested interest, whichever is less. Up to $10,000 can be borrowed, however, even if that is more than half the amount vested. A loan must be repaid within five years unless it is used to buy a principal residence.
11. Integration refers to the correlation of a retirement plan with Social Security benefits.
12. ERISA applies the same vesting rules to profit sharing as to pension plans.

SUGGESTED READINGS

"Accounting for the Conversion of Stock Options as a Result of the Economic Recovery Tax Act of 1981," *FASB Technical Bulletin Number 82-2,* March 2, 1982.

Black, Fischer., "The Tax Consequences of Long-Run Pension Policy," *Financial Analysts Journal,* July-August, 1980.

Bond, Michael J., "The Use of Interest-Free or Low-Interest Loans by Publicly Held Corporations to Reward Executives," *Taxes,* August, 1980

Brannon, Gerard M., "Some Aspects of the Public/Private Dichotomy in Pension Plans," *National Tax Journal,* September, 1980.

Crowell, Richard A. and Robert E. Mainerm, "Pension Fund Management: External or Internal?" *Harvard Business Review,* November-December, 1980.

Cummings, J. David, et. al., "Effects of ERISA on the Investment Policies of Private Pension Plans: Survey Evidence," *The Journal of Risk and Insurance,* September, 1980.

Curtis, John E., Jr., "ESOP, TRASOP Rules Clarified and Changed by the Technical Corrections Act of 1979," *The Journal of Taxation,* October, 1980.

Danker, Harold, et. al., "Employer Accounting for Pension Costs and Other Post-Retirement Benefits," *Financial Executive,* April, 1981.

Ezra, D. Don., "How Actuaries Determine the Unfunded Pension Liability," *Financial Analysts Journal,* July-August, 1980.

Foster, Kenneth E., "A Different Perspective on Executive Compensation," *Compensation Review,* Third Quarter, 1980.

"GAO Study Reveals ESOPs May Adversely Affect Participants," *The Journal of Taxation,* October, 1980.

Garro, James F., "Book Value Executive Compensation—Is It For You?" *Financial Executive,* January, 1980.

Gibson, Keath P., "Accounting For the Cost of Defined Benefit Pension Plans," *Financial Executive,* March, 1981.

Givner, Bruce., "Using the Non-Discriminatory Classification Test in Designing Qualified Plans," *Taxes,* November, 1980.

Golden, Howard J., "Fiduciary Responsibility and Prohibited Transactions Under ERISA," *Risk Management,* June, 1980.

Graham, David S. and Charles M. Tarver, "A Pension Fund Alternative: Investing in Timberland," *Pension World,* June 1981.

Gulotta, Michael J., "Pension Insurance: Controlling Tomorrow's Premiums Today," *Financial Executive,* May, 1981.

Haneberg, Ron., "Cash-Deferred Profit Sharing Plans," *Financial Executive,* July, 1980.

Hirsh, Leonard S., "Qualified Cash or Deferred Arrangements Offer Unusual Tax Benefits and Flexibility," *The Journal of Taxation,* March, 1982.

Koch, Donald G., "A Plan for Distributing Deferred Compensation to High-Bracket Executives," *Management Accounting,* April 1980.

Lanoff, Ian D., "Is Social Investment or Private Pension Plan Assets Lawful Under ERISA?" *Risk Management,* November, 1980.

LeRoux, Margaret., "ERISA Advisors Criticize Limited Role," *Business Insurance,* September 15, 1980.

McMillan, John D., "Evaluating Executive Benefits," *Financial Executive,* March 1980.

Randolf, James W., "Terminating an ERISA/PBGC Guaranteed Pension Plan," *Best's Review,* February, 1981.

Sarvin, Rakesh K. and Robert L. Winkler, "Performance-Based Incentive Plans," *Management Science,* November, 1980.

Schotland, Roy A., "Divergent Investing for Pension Funds," *Financial Analysts Journal,* September-October, 1980.

Stein, Bruno., *Social Security and Pensions in Transition—Understanding the American Retirement System.* New York: Free Press, 1980.

Tepper, Irwin., "Taxation and Corporation Pension Policy," *The Journal of Finance,* March, 1981.

Wendell, Paul, ed., *Corporate Controller's Manual.* Boston: Warren, Gorham, and Lamont, 1981, Chs. 27, 28 and 29.

Zeikel, Arthur and Robert L. Peck, Jr., "Portfolio Management: Dedicated Portfolios," *Journal of Accounting, Auditing and Finance,* Fall, 1982.

APPENDIX A:
ACTUARIAL FACTORS IN EMPLOYEE PENSION PROGRAMS

As noted in 25.3[1], employee pension programs are either of the defined benefit or the defined contribution variety. In the latter case, the employer meets his obligations fully and completely under the pension program by the payment of the sum of money defined in the pension plan. However, in the case of defined benefit plans, a current obligation of an actuarially determinable amount is created upon the crediting of future benefits to plan participants. And, if the pension plan is to operate on a sound financial basis, these future benefits must be met by employer contributions which, over a reasonable period of time, are sufficient, with cumulative investment earnings and other relevant actuarial assumptions, to discharge these benefits as they arise. Thus, in the case of defined benefit plans, an actuarial estimate of future participant benefits must be made. In addition, an actuarial estimate is required for the earnings on employer contributions to the plan from the time these funds are received by the plan until they are disbursed in the form of participant benefits.

The determination of the actuarial present value of future plan benefits and of the plan assets needed to meet these benefits is a function of the actuarial estimates of:

- the probability of occurrence of each of the events requiring the payment of plan benefits;
- the various factors which will influence the amount of plan benefits (such as future compensation levels, years of service, marital status, age at retirement, etc., of plan participants); and
- the earnings rate on plan assets.

An individual determination of the actuarial value of future plan benefits is made for each plan participant and then aggregated to form the actuarial value of future plan benefits as a whole.

Therefore, actuarial assumptions are needed in the following areas: [1] Plan decrements (the possibility that some kind of event will occur to prevent plan participants from collecting their full plan benefits); [2] Salary or the factors affecting the determination of plan benefits (where applicable); and [3] The rate of return on plan assets.

Each of these factors and their sub-components is discussed below.[1]

Decrement Assumptions

The primary decrement assumptions are as follows:

- mortality;
- disability;
- withdrawal or termination; and
- retirement.

(a) Mortality

The receipt of a pension benefit by active employees is affected by the risk of their death prior to their retirement. Additionally, the mortality of retired plan participants acts to terminate the payment of their pension benefits. However, although the death of a plan participant (whether active or inactive) acts to terminate his retirement benefits, it often results in the creation of a death benefit obligation of the pension plan toward his beneficiaries.

(b) Disability

Qualification for a retirement benefit may be affected by the disability of an active employee and thus lower the cost to the pension plan. However, should the plan provide for a disability benefit, the cost reduction resulting from disability would be offset to some extent.

(c) Withdrawal or Termination

If an employee withdraws from active service or is terminated, he may be prevented from receiving benefits under the pension plan. However, if an employee has succeeded in attaining some of his vested rights, withdrawal from active service will not result in a total loss of his retirement benefits.

(d) Retirement

Retirement benefits paid to employees who take early retirement are generally less than the benefits paid to employees who attain the normal retirement age before retiring.

With the increase in the mandatory retirement age from 65 to 70, which Congress passed in 1978, many workers are now choosing to work beyond their 65th birthday. However, only about half of the private pension plans currently in operation are giving additional credit toward retirement benefits for such work.

SALARY ASSUMPTIONS

In cases where employee salary is a factor in the determination of pension benefits, an actuarial estimation of future employee salary increases is necessary. This estimation includes the following components:

- merit;
- productivity; and
- inflation.

(a) Merit Component

Theoretically, at least, merit increases result from an employee progressing through his career and performing at a more competent and responsible level as he acquires more experience. Yet, in many cases, the proportion of total pay increases which are attributable to this source seems to decline as the employee gets older.

(b) Productivity Component

Labor's share of productivity gains also result in salary increases, but this factor varies from industry to industry and seems to have diminished over the years. Normally, an actuarial estimation of productivity increases is set with careful consideration being given to historical data.

(c) Inflation Component

In recent years, the most significant component of future salaries has been inflation. While, as stated above, the merit component of future salaries generally increases at a decreasing rate, the inflation component of future salaries is most likely to increase at a constant compound rate.

RATE OF RETURN ASSUMPTIONS

The expected rate of return on pension plan assets has a very significant affect on the employer contributions deemed to be necessary to meet the needs of a defined benefit pension plan. This is the case because these contributions are compounded over many years and small variations in the assumed earnings rate will be magnified many times. While at times, the assumed rate of return is allowed to vary over time, the more common practice is to employ a constant compound rate. The relevant components of the rate of return assumptions are:

- the pure rate of return (or the pure interest rate);
- the investment risk; and
- the inflation component of the rate of return.

(a) The Pure Rate of Return (or the Pure Interest Rate)

The pure rate of return is the return required by security holders who anticipate neither inflation nor risk of loss of principal or income. Stated differently, it is the return the market allocates to investors holding securities bearing no chance of loss of principal or income after removing the effects of anticipated inflation. The pure rate of interest has historically been about 3%.

(b) The Investment Risk

As noted in Chapter 2, the securities markets provide investors with an increased or a premium rate of return according to the amount of relative risk in the securities they hold. In general, securities which are relatively risky, vis-a-vis the total available population of securities, will earn higher returns than securities which are relatively less risky. However, these returns will be more volatile for such higher risk securities.

(c) The Inflation Component of the Rate of Return

A premium for the rate of anticipated inflation is generally applied. The assumed rate of future inflation is one of the most subjective among the array of assumptions the actuary is called upon to make since historical rates of inflation are generally not very good predictors of future rates of inflation.

1   The remainder of this appendix is drawn considerably from Howard E. Winklevoss, *Pension Mathematics: With Numerical Illustrations*, Richard D. Irwin Inc., Homewood, Illinois, 1977.

INDEX